X-mas '95

THE COLLECTED WORKS OF MAX HAINES

THE COLLECTED WORKS OF MAX HAINES

by Max Haines

The Toronto Sun Publishing Corporation Limited

Other works by Max Haines

Bothersome Bodies (1977)
Calendar of Criminal Capers (1977)
Crime Flashback #1 (1980)
Crime Flashback #2 (1981)
Crime Flashback #3 (1982)
The Murderous Kind (1983)
Murder and Mayhem (1984)
The Collected Works of Max Haines, Vol. I (1985)
That's Life! (1986)
True Crime Stories (1987)
True Crime Stories, Book II (1988)
True Crime Stories, Book III (1989)
True Crime Stories, Book IV (1990)
The Collected Works of Max Haines, Vol. II (1991)
True Crime Stories, Book V (1992)
Doctors Who Kill (1993)

First Printing: September 1985
Second Printing: March 1986
Third Printing: October 1986
Fourth Printing: November 1986
Fifth Printing: September 1987
Sixth Printing: February 1988
Seventh Printing: August 1989
Eighth Printing: October 1990
Ninth Printing: September 1991
Tenth Printing: October 1994

Canadian Cataloguing in Publication Data
Haines, Max
The Collected Works of Max Haines, Vol. I

ISBN 0-919233-18-X
1. Murder II. Title
HV6515.H345 1985 364.1 '523 C85-099354-4

Published by
The Toronto Sun Publishing Corporation Ltd.
333 King Street East
Toronto, Ontario   M5A 3X5

To the memories of
Alex Haines and Julius Roll

ACKNOWLEDGEMENTS

In gathering the material contained in this collection, I have travelled over a six year period to the United States, England, France, Holland, Jamaica, and throughout Canada.

Police forces at all levels have been extremely co-operative in providing me with documentation and, in many cases, first hand information of the crimes contained in this book. Fellow journalists, particularly those connected with newspapers, have given freely of their time and knowledge. Librarians have never ceased to amaze me with their patience in locating little used material to provide me with obscure information about a particular case.

I am indebted to certain members of the Toronto Sun Publishing Corp. Ltd. for their assistance. These include Linda Fox, Julie Kirsh and her staff, Vince Desai, Glenn-Stewart Garnett, John Landry and Joe Marino, without whose hard work this undertaking would have been impossible.

A woman named Marilyn helped too.

— M.H.

CONTENTS

Foreword

Part 1
CONS AND SCAMS

Part 2
THE POISONERS

Part 3
CANADIANA

Part 4
THE DOCTORS

Part 5
NASTY LADIES

Part 6
ALL IN THE FAMILY

Part 7
FAMOUS NAMES

Part 8
MONSTERS

Part 9
AMERICANA

Part 10
AROUND THE WORLD

Part 11
QUESTIONABLE CASES

Part 12
MERRIE ENGLAND

FOREWORD

Truth is stranger than fiction and Max Haines has spent most of his adult years proving it. This mild mannered, soft spoken father of three daughters has researched more than 1,000 cases of crime, most of them murder, from the single passion killing to premeditated multiple homicides, many with the twist of the bizarre.

His research technique, honed as a student at Dalhousie University, has been put to use in most places on the globe, interviewing witnesses, police and digging in libraries.

A murder trial in Halifax, N.S. when he was only 18 really sparked his interest in this most capital of crimes. Despite 12 witnesses who saw an accused drag a woman down a street shortly before her death, the man was acquitted.

That started Max on a hobby that became a full-time job shortly after starting to write the cases in a column for the Toronto *Sun*. He was happy to give up his part ownership in a textile factory in Montreal to concentrate on mayhem.

His fascination with crime and his ability to tell a story made his Crime Flashback newspaper column famous. Since then, he has been labelled Master of the Macabre and Mister Murder, but his interest is almost scientific.

He wants to know what makes a killer, and has come to the chilling realization that any one of us is close to being a potential murderer. He backs this up by saying that not all killers are the monsters we make them out to be.

He has talked to many of them and gets letters from others he has written about. But he adds a caveat . . . all murders are disgusting, there are no glamorous corpses.

He has proven another point . . . crime does pay, but not for those who commit it.

Ed Monteith
Editorial Director
Toronto Sun Publishing Corp.

He Fooled the Gestapo

- Part 1-

CONS AND SCAMS

THE GOAT GLAND CAPER

Now that Toronto has the C.N. Tower, the tallest free standing building in the world, we citizens must be wary that some rascal doesn't sell it. In the world of swindlers and con men such a proposition is not altogether ridiculous. Over the years con men have sold the Brooklyn Bridge, Eiffel Tower, and once even rented out most of the State of Arizona.

Who was the most ridiculous con man of all time? Here is my nominee for champ: John Romulus Brinkley. You see, John didn't sell buildings or bridges. He sold something that man has been searching for through all recorded history — youth. For a price our hero would return the virility of youth. To use his own words, "You'll be back a kickin' and a scratchin' in no time."

In 1885 John first saw the light of day in Beta, a North Carolina hamlet of 200 dirt poor farmers. When John was six his mother died of tuberculosis. Four years later he lost his father to the same disease.

By the time John was 16 he had outgrown Beta. The grass looked so much greener in Baltimore that he decided to try his luck in the big city. Being smarter than most former citizens of Beta, John decided to start at the top. He applied for admission to Johns Hopkins Medical School. The dean of the school informed him that there were a few formalities which had to be complied with before he could be admitted to the famous university. There was the minor matter of a grade school education, not to mention a high school diploma.

John felt these prerequisites were totally unfair and unwarranted. He sought out a school where, for a price and a minimum of study, he could obtain a medical degree of sorts. Quick as a bunny, he managed to acquire one of these watered down degrees from the Eclectic Medical University of Kansas City. While he was at it he managed to woo and win Sally Wilkie, a fair damsel from his home state of North Carolina.

Armed with a degree in one hand and winsome Sally in the other, John set up his practice in Fulton, Kansas. Soon he and Sally were blessed with a baby daughter. After the birth of the child Sally found that she really wasn't crazy about John after all. In fact, when she thought about their relationship she discovered he was too despicable to live with. She asked him for a divorce, but John refused to give in to her demand.

Apparently Sally's affection for her husband could be turned on in fits and starts. In the next few years they had two more daughters, and again Sally approached John for a divorce. This time he said good riddance and granted the lady her freedom.

John's practice had never really flourished. In fact, it consisted mainly of selling patent medicines. In the summer of 1910, while visiting in Memphis, John met and married one Minnie Jones. Now that he again had female companionship, he looked around for a town where he could make a buck. He and Minnie picked Milford, Kansas, which had neither a doctor nor a hospital.

History is a little vague as to where John got the bright idea that the glands of a goat could be transplanted to male humans and rejuvenate their sexual drive and performance. The story goes that a farmer who had not been, shall we say, active for 16 long years, asked for the operation. John complied, and the following year the farmer's wife gave birth to a bouncing baby boy.

Say what you will about John Romulus Brinkley, he recognized a good thing when he saw it. He tried the operation on a few willing relatives, and soon word got around Kansas that there was a doctor named Brinkley who could restore love to your heart and put that old gleam back in your eye. John's practice mushroomed, so that the scallywag actually built a 50-room hospital to accommodate his patients. Naturally, it was called the John Brinkley Hospital.

The patient entered John's hospital on Monday, had his goat gland operation, and was released on Friday, apparently full of vim, vigor and whatever. The one thing he didn't have on Friday was $750, because that was the exact amount John charged for his and the goat's services.

This was just great for the would-be Kansas studs, but it didn't do a thing for the billy goats. In fact John was going through goats faster than Midas goes through mufflers. Soon the billy goat population of Kansas was drastically depleted. Undaunted

John's agents spread out through Arkansas in their quest for billy goats. In their wake they left an overabundance of widowed nanny goats, but then someone has to suffer in the interest of medical science.

Business became so lucrative that Doc Brinkley raised his price to $1,500 per operation. To give you an idea of the loot involved, Doc and his assistants were now performing 50 transplants per week.

There were a few practical problems. The railway had to build a new spur to Milford in order to take care of the goat supply being shipped into the town. Doc built a wing onto the hospital to house his staff of assistants and nurses.

Milford even had its own baseball team. They were aptly called the Brinkley Goats.

By 1922 radio was coming into its own, and John immediately realized that the newfangled instrument held tremendous possibilities. Not one to do things half way, he built his own station, KFKB in Milford. He started to advertise his gland operation and as a result had to double his hospital's capacity to accommodate 100 suckers per week.

John then stumbled on the idea of diagnosis by radio. The listener could write into KFKB and John would tell the sufferer what his or her trouble was and prescribe a remedy over the air. The idea was a hit. John produced the cures himself. Most of them consisted of different strength Aspirin and Castor oil. The diagnosis-from-a-distance business became so popular that John designated a different number for the different strengths of his phony prescriptions. "Yes, Ma'am, Number 9 and Number 14 should fix you up in no time," his resonant voice would reassure the listeners of KFKB.

His program was called "Brinkley's Medical Question Box", and it became so popular that only the most interesting cases were answered on the air. An incredible 50,000 letters per day were arriving at KFKB by 1923. No kidding, they actually had to build a new post office in town to handle the flow of cash pouring in.

John accumulated a few trinkets along the way. He now had a Cadillac, a Lincoln, his own airplane, two yachts, and diamond rings more numerous than fingers. He had come a long way from Beta, North Carolina.

In the background there were some faint rumblings. The American Medical Association took a dim view of the goat business, but that association was nowhere near the powerful body it is today and didn't do that much to slow John down. A man from New Jersey died of tetanus after being rejuvenated, but John bought his way out of that particular scrape.

One day while vacationing in Florida, John told his startled wife Minnie that he needed a diversion. He thought he would try politics. "By gosh," John said. "I'll run for the governorship of Kansas." The final candidacy filing date had passed, so John had to run as a write-in candidate. To vote for him, one actually had to write his name on the ballot. John campaigned with his airplane and his radio stations. To give you an idea of his power and popularity, out of 617,369 votes cast for the three candidates, John came in third with 183,278 votes. The winner of the election won by a miniscule 251 votes over the second place finisher. John had really thrown a scare into the political machines of the state, and he had accomplished it all, virtually alone.

John went back to selling his medicine with a vengeance. He built a strong radio station in Mexico, and for years raked in a fortune selling his medical miracles. Annoying pressures were brought to bear on him by the medical profession in the U.S., and he was finally forced to shift his headquarters to Del Rio, Mexico. In order to avoid any minor discomforts, John built himself a $200,000 home complete with pool.

Still, the handwriting was on the wall. Throughout the late 1930s the public was becoming more informed, and the governing medical and radio authorities were gaining more control in policing their professions. Despite the tremendous revenue he was generating, the Mexican government forced him to close down the radio station.

The American Medical Association publicly branded him a quack. An indignant John sued them for libel. The jury found the Medical Association innocent, and in fact thought the word quack properly described the particular brand of medicine John was dispensing.

Several men who weren't all that rejuvenated by their goat transplants brought judgments against John. He had to pay damages to satisfy these judgments and little by little he was divested of the trappings of wealth. First the plane went, then the yachts and cars, and finally his home.

In February, 1941 Brinkley declared himself bankrupt. It is estimated that over 200,000 gullible people were bilked out of $10 million by John's various schemes. This figure does not take into account the thousands of nanny goats who became widows due to his machinations.

John never fully recovered from the disgrace of bankruptcy. In May, 1942, at the age of 56, he dropped dead of a heart attack.

THE CAPTAIN OF KOPENICK

The Captain of Kopenick was quite a guy.

Wilhelm Voigt was already in his late 50s in 1906. He had spent many years in jails throughout Germany for petty crimes such as stealing food and clothing. As his record grew longer, his sentences increased correspondingly in length.

Now working long hard hours at his trade, that of a cobbler, the little man with the moustache constantly tried to think of a better way of life. Willie had tried to leave the country, but with his record it was impossible to obtain a passport. In fact, his last two jail sentences had been for trying to steal one from the immigration authorities. Life was one long drag.

Willie lived in Berlin with his sister and, with each passing day, his moustache grew grayer and his back became more stooped. All around him Prussian pomp and ceremony was being flaunted by strong young men in fancy officer's uniforms. They clicked their heels and snapped salutes, and had the respect of the whole populace.

One day old Willie passed a store window, and from that day on his life was never the same. There, displayed in the window, was a Prussian officer's uniform complete with gold braid. Willie made discreet inquiries. Yes, it was possible. Why not? Then and there Willie decided to transform himself from a weary little shoemaker into a Prussian officer in the Kaiser's army.

He didn't just dash in and purchase the uniform. First there was training to be completed. Willie observed how real officers walked and saluted. He rehearsed before a mirror for hours. He listened to the officers bark out orders to their men. He emulated their actions and their voices. Only when he felt he was absolutely prepared, did he enter the store and purchase the shiny uniform. It didn't quite fit, but it served the purpose.

A little, old cobbler had entered the shop; an officer in the Kaiser's army emerged. Soldiers snapped salutes at Willie. He brought up his right hand in that bored gesture he had worked so hard to perfect. All of a sudden Willie had something which had escaped him all his life — respect.

Willie practised being an officer for many weeks. He had a plan. Returning to his legitimate occupation of cobbler, he travelled a few miles out of Berlin to the town of Kopenick. Willie was particularly interested in the town square and the town hall. He poked around until he was familiar with the location of the various offices.

Willie was ready to put his plan into action. He left his sister's flat as a cobbler carrying a box under his arm. Proceeding directly to the railway station, he locked himself in a restroom. Out popped Wilhelm Voigt, Captain of the Guards.

He then had a short slug of schnapps at a cafe, and thus fortified, stopped the first five soldiers he met. Actually Willie didn't stop them, he barked, "Halt!" and they damn well snapped to attention. Willie (or maybe we should call him Capt. Voigt) made the corporal in charge identify himself and the other four men. He then informed them that they were now under his command. While Capt. Voigt was thus engaged another five soldiers happened to be passing. Willie barked his command once again, and so it came to pass that the instant captain had his own private army of 10 men.

Capt. Voigt ordered his men to the railroad station, and the whole kit and kaboodle headed for Kopenick. Capt. Voigt led his men on the march to the town hall.

The good burghers of Kopenick didn't get to see that many military men, and the sight of the elderly captain leading his unit of 10 caused some heads to turn in the small community. Once at the town hall, Capt. Voigt barked out orders. He seemed to know the lay of the land by instinct. The Captain placed guards at all entrances to the building.

Capt. Voigt marched straight into the office of the burgomaster, Dr. Langerhans. Poor Langerhans almost keeled over. Nothing like this had ever happened to him before. Capt. Voigt informed the burgomaster that he was under arrest on the command of His Majesty. When asked for some document or warrant, Capt. Voigt contemptuously informed Langerhans that his soldiers were his warrant.

Once the Captain had this situation well in hand, he proceeded to the office of the Inspector of Police. Voigt explained his mission to the inspector, and at the same time, with his authoritative air, ordered him to attend to the crowd which was now gathering in the town square. The inspector scampered out into the square to keep the peace. Next Capt. Voigt visited the Treasurer's office, confiscated his books and placed him under arrest.

To give you an idea of Voigt's complete command of the situation, the burgomaster actually asked him for permission to meet with his wife. Willie, I mean the Captain, said he could even bring her along, because he was transferring the burgomaster and the treasurer under heavy guard to Berlin. The available cash on hand was to be transferred as well. About 4,000 marks were gathered up, which the Captain nonchalantly placed in a bag. He would take care of the cash personally.

By now rumors had spread throughout the town. Millions of marks had been embezzled by the treasurer and the burgomaster. Hundreds of citizens had gathered to see the fun.

A police officer from the neighboring district of Teltow appeared in front of Capt. Voigt and demanded to know what was going on. Undaunted Capt. Voigt explained the facts to the officer. Taking in the situation at a glance, one of Germany's finest volunteered to assist in any way possible. As a matter of fact, it just so happened that Capt. Voigt needed a man of his calibre to accompany the burgomaster, his wife and the treasurer back to Berlin. He had ordered two closed carriages for this very purpose. A few moments later the carriages arrived and the Teltow officer and his prisoners galloped off to Berlin with instructions from the Captain to report to the proper authorities.

In the meantime Capt. Voigt dismissed his army of 10 men. He hopped the train for Berlin, picked up the box containing his clothing from the checkroom, entered the restroom, and emerged as the cobbler Willie Voigt. Willie hid the money in a deserted shed and went back to his sister's home. The whole operation had taken 12 hours.

The Teltow officer found it difficult to understand why no one was expecting either him or his prisoners. He kept being passed from office to office, until finally he found himself telling his story to the Chief of Police of Berlin and the Adjutant-General, Count Moltke.

The Chief looked at the Adjutant-General and the Adjutant-General looked at the Chief. A light went on. Some little man had duped an entire town. Too many people knew the circumstances to keep it quiet, so it was decided to make the story public and try to apprehend the fugitive. A reward of 2,500 marks was offered for information leading to the capture of the Captain. Even the Kaiser showed an interest and asked to be kept informed of developments.

Despite the German reputation for seriousness, it seems no one could talk or write about the Captain of Kopenick without a chuckle in their hearts and a smile on their lips. Everyone had a good belly laugh. The story spread from Germany throughout the rest of Europe and even to North America.

It took 10 days before the authorities got onto Willie's trail. They traced him through a sabre he had to leave in the restroom. It was too long to fit into the box he had brought for his officer's uniform.

If Willie had caused the world to laugh before, now that he was identified it was even more of a howl. A little jailbird cobbler had been the culprit who had police, soldiers, and municipal officials jumping to his command. Willie explained that it really wasn't the money he was after. He had hoped to find a passport in those offices in Kopenick. Besides, it sure was a lot of fun having everyone marching and saluting.

Well, as it turned out, everyone liked Willie. He was a harmless little man. Even during his trial everyone liked him. When the judge sentenced him to four years in jail, he recommended that the accused receive light duties while confined.

In jail everyone sought out Willie's company. He was something of a celebrity. Good behavior earned him his release in 20 months. In August, 1908 he walked out of jail a free man, some say on direct orders of the Kaiser himself.

Such was the affection the German people felt for their self-made instant hero that a committee was formed to provide for Willie. In fact one Berlin family endowed him with 100 marks a month for life. Willie even managed to have quite a show business career. He was in great demand in music halls throughout Europe and appeared on the New York stage. He performed one role only, the one he made famous in real life; that of a German officer shouting out commands. A book was written under his byline entitled "How I Became the Captain of Kopenick". Willie was finally given that which he cherished above all else — a passport. He moved to Luxembourg where he quietly went into retirement.

Willie died in 1922 at the age of 72. He was buried in the cemetery of Our Lady in Luxembourg. When Willie's body was being carried through the gates of the cemetery, as chance would have it, a company of soldiers was marching past. In keeping with a time honored military custom whereby soldiers honor the dead, they saluted the hearse. The Captain of Kopenick had received his last salute.

THE GENTLE FORGER

Whenever I think of counterfeiters, I think of well organized gangs who produce and distribute millions of dollars. The greatest counterfeiter the United States has ever known was not a master criminal. No, he was an old man who lived with his dog in a flat on the top floor of a tenement building near Broadway and 96th St., in New York City.

Edward Mueller had for years been a superintendent of apartment buildings until the death of his wife in 1937. With his children grown up and married, he found it difficult at the age of 63 to continue to look after the large buildings. Instead he and his mongrel terrier took a sunny flat of their own, and Mueller decided to become a junk dealer.

He purchased a cart and went about the streets trying to find and buy junk. After a year at this precarious occupation he discovered that he wasn't making enough money to take care of the rather humble needs of himself and his faithful companion. He decided to become a counterfeiter.

Mueller, who was known to all his acquaintances as a sweet tempered, good-natured little guy, went about his task with typical nonchalance. His married daughter happened to have an old studio camera. One day on a visit to her home, he photographed a one dollar bill. Then he made some zinc plates, which he touched up by hand. The finished job looked pretty satisfactory to old Mueller. Later the Secret Service said it was the most amateurish counterfeiting job they had ever come across. In touching up the bogus plates, Mueller had somehow transposed one of the letters in the word WASHINGTON. All his finished bills spelled the word WAHSINGTON. This rather glaring error was never noticed by Mueller or any of his victims.

In November, 1938 Edward Mueller turned out his first phony bill on his hand driven printing press. He hung the bill up to dry on a clothesline in his flat. The very first bill was used to purchase some junk. Mueller noticed that no one ever took a second look at a one dollar bill.

It was not long before the bills came to the attention of the Secret Service. Not a rash of bills, mind you, more like a trickle. You see, Mueller lacked one quality most counterfeiters have in great abundance. He was not greedy. He printed only enough dollars to take care of the needs of himself and his dog, with one exception. On Sundays he loved to buy enough candy to treat the neighborhood kids.

As the months rolled into years, the mysterious counterfeiter who manufactured only ones, and then only in limited quantities, completely baffled the Secret Service. The case had become the longest unsolved counterfeit operation in U.S. history. Who could be turning out 40 or 50 one dollar bills a month and distributing them all over New York City? And such lousy reproductions. Even the paper the money was printed on was of such poor quality that it could be purchased at any corner stationery store. Believe it or not, one of Washington's eyes was an inkblot.

In the first year 585 phony bills were successfully put into circulation. At the end of five years the total had risen to 2,840, or less than two a day. What kind of strange personality was content to turn out such a small quantity of bills? No one seemed to know. Agents swarmed over the area where most of the bills surfaced, but while they uncovered more phony bills all the carriers were victims rather than the culprit they were seeking. From time to time the Secret Service were engaged in other far more important cases, but they always returned to the strange unsolved case of the phony ones.

For 10 years Mueller churned out his incredible product, and was only found out by accident. A fire took place on the top floor of his tenement building. Mueller was not in his flat at the time of the fire, but his pet terrier was suffocated by smoke. The firemen had thrown most of the contents of Mueller's flat into a vacant lot. Mueller went to live with his daughter in the suburbs until his flat could be repaired.

Nine young boys ranging in age from 10 to 15 used the vacant lot as a playground. One of the boys found what he considered to be play money. Adults had been accepting the same quality money as the real thing for 10 years. It seems strange that a 10-year-old immediately recognized it as phony. Another youngster carted home the old printing press. His father saw the boys playing with the money and became suspicious enough to inform the police. One look at the word WAHSINGTON, and the Secret Service knew they were on the trail of their old nemesis. The boys led the police to where they had found the money. It was an easy matter to find out that the press and money had been tossed out of the burned flat.

And who was the tenant of the flat? None other than dear old Edward Mueller. When questioned about his activities, Mueller readily confessed to printing the bills. He explained that in all the years he had been producing the money, he never gave more than one dollar to any one person, and he never made more than he absolutely needed to sustain himself and his dog.

Although Mueller and his phony ones had cost the Secret Service more time and trouble than any other individual counterfeiter, everyone liked the old man. After he was out on bail he became accustomed to dropping in on the authorities to pass the time of day. All five foot three of him would saunter up to the Secret Service offices. To a man, everyone was happy to see him.

When he came to trial, 73-year-old Mueller loved every minute of it. He had been indicted on three counts — possessing plates, passing counterfeit bills, and manufacturing the bills. Mueller was found guilty, and received the light sentence of one year and a day. A fine is mandatory with such a sentence, and a chuckle went through the courtroom when the judge announced the amount of the fine — one dollar.

Edward was released after serving four months, and went to live with his daughter in the suburbs. He loved to relate to friends and neighbors how he had hoodwinked the Secret Service for 10 years. Later a movie was made of Edward's counterfeiting career. Famed character actor Edmund Gwynn played the part of Mueller. Edward attended the movie, and thought it was just great.

THE MONEY MACHINE

Ralph Wilby was born in Weston, Ont., to a hardworking honest family. After leaving high school, he got a job as a bookkeeper. Ralph put some debits where some credits should have been, and before you could say contingent liability, he was caught and received a year in jail. Released from the inconvenience of this enforced vacation, Ralph next popped up in Norfolk, Va. He sought and obtained gainful employment as a bookkeeper, but it wasn't long before Ralph had his hand in the till again. This time he was deported to Canada.

By this time no legitimate outfit would hire Ralph. It was really too bad because he had decided to turn over a new leaf and go straight. First, though, he had to come up with some scheme to get a job. Leave it to Ralph. He remembered a legitimate accountant named Alexander Douglas Hume, who had worked in both Canada and New York. Mr. Hume had joined the Canadian Army and had been shipped overseas. Ralph decided to take his name. Under the name A.D. Hume, Ralph got a position with the William T. Knopp Management Co. Now in high gear, our hero met Helen Redwin. Helen was the possessor of an hourglass figure and a well turned ankle. Knowing nothing of Ralph's past indiscretions, she became Mrs. A.D. Hume within two weeks.

The happy couple set up housekeeping in a three-room apartment in Jackson Heights, a suburb of New York. The Knott Co.'s main function in life was to manage a total of 15 huge department stores. Ralph was by this time a mature 35. He stood 5 ft. 6 ins., had an engaging smile, and was considered a find by the Knott brass. They put

Ralph on the audit team checking on the stores. It wasn't long before he gained a reputation for detecting any shortages or outright thefts by employees. Of course we know that Ralph, operating as A.D. Hume, knew the ropes pretty well.

Time passed, and the U.S. entered the war. U.S. citizens were being called into the service, and this caused a hardship to Ralph's company, with many of their top employees being drafted. They took him off the audit team, and with a terrific recommendation from his boss, Mr. Casey, Ralph became assistant auditor stationed at the head office in New York City. While others were being called away to war, Ralph escaped the draft. Canadian military records showed that he was overseas, and American records had him exempt from the draft because he was married. He rose rapidly in the company. He loved his job, his apartment in the suburbs, and his lovely wife Helen.

Then one fine day Mr. Casey took Ralph into a private room and introduced him to an IBM machine. Mr. Casey explained that when manufacturers and wholesalers sold merchandise to any of the 15 Knott department stores, they sent the invoices to this room. The stores checked to see that they received all the merchandise in good order and then they sent along the packing slip. The invoice and packing slip were matched, and then this beautiful IBM machine would spit out the cheque to the supplier. Another machine sitting beside the IBM job signed the cheques with Mr. Casey's signature.

Ralph idly inquired about how many cheques the machine handled. Casey replied that the IBM Machine produced around seven or eight hundred cheques a day, amounting to over $700,000 per week.

Ralph immediately had a frog in his throat. He took out his handkerchief and gently coughed into it.

Mr. Casey put his hand on Ralph's shoulder and told him that from now on he was making him responsible for the cheque-producing IBM machine.

Ralph had an absolute coughing fit.

It was too much for the new leaf that Ralph had turned over. The set-up was ripe for plucking. Ralph decided right then and there to have a go. For starters he sent an invoice to himself from a non-existent firm he called Frederick B. Hecht Co. of St. Louis in the amount of $4,800. Then he sent along the corresponding packing slip, already checked, supposedly from one of the Knott stores. Ralph matched them, gave instructions to his staff, and walked away with a cheque for $4,800. He took a train to St. Louis and showed up at a bank, claimed to be Frederick B. Hecht. He wanted to open an account and was greeted with open arms. There was one thing though; he really should have some sort of references. No problem. Ralph told the manager to dash off a letter to the William T. Knott Co. of New York, Attention Mr. A.D. Hume, and he should receive a reference by return mail. Ralph left the 48 bills for deposit as soon as the manager received the reference letter.

Ralph scampered back to New York and waited for the bank manager's letter to himself. Sure enough, it arrived and Ralph answered that the Frederick B. Hecht firm was above reproach. The manager was delighted to deposit the cheque.

To balance the books, Ralph made up minute charges and spread the $4,800 over the 15 stores. It was peanuts to an outfit doing $40 million a year. Ralph repeated this basic scheme over and over until he had deposits in every city close to New York. The take amounted to over $100,000.

Was Ralph happy? Well, no, he wasn't. For one thing, he was doing extremely well at his legitimate occupation, and liked his job and his pretty wife in the suburbs. For another thing, he was working like a dog, making trips out of town depositing cheques and the paperwork involved was getting too much for him. He started to look peaked. All in all, Ralph figured it wasn't worth it and decided to give back all the money. He thought and thought, but it was no use. That IBM machine giveth but it just wasn't equipped to taketh away: Ralph couldn't give back the money without exposing himself.

Then the little con man had another turn of mind. Why be small potatoes? Ralph accelerated his fraud, and within three months had deposits of over $400,000. Then, out of the blue, a man called Davidson, who worked for an organization called the F.B.I., called on Ralph. He wanted to know if he knew a Frederick B. Hecht. Ralph almost passed out. He had made up the name. What could the F.B.I. want with Hecht? Ralph figured the feds were onto his scheme and were playing cat and mouse with him. He was wrong. All they were inquiring about was a routine check of German sounding names, who had recently changed domiciles. One way to accomplish this was by checking bank accounts that suddenly were transferred or closed.

Ralph put Davidson off for a week, and withdrew cash from all his accounts. He ended up with $400,000 in a cardboard box. Then he told Mr. Casey he was taking his long overdue vacation. Ralph and the wife left that very day, and didn't stop until they hit Victoria, B.C.

Ralph never did return from his vacation. Davidson of the F.B.I. contacted Mr. Casey and told him of trying to trace a Mr. Hecht through Ralph.

Whenever a fellow disappears who has control over an IBM cheque writing machine, his superiors tend to have headaches. Mr. Casey had a throbbing migraine.

It took a lot of digging, but they finally uncovered Ralph's fictitious companies. The authorities then went into Mr. A.D. Hume's background and found he was really overseas with the Canadian Army. They ended up with our friend Ralph Wilby of

Weston and his rather illuminating police record.

Well, the ledgers hit the fan. Police started tracing Ralph and Helen, finally catching up with them in the nice little house they had bought in Victoria. He had left New York as A.D. Hume, and was brought back as Ralph Wilby, con artist extraordinaire. He was of particular interest to an insurance company that stood to lose a bundle unless he came up with the $400,000. Finally he made a deal. Ralph figured he had spent $10,000 of his own money on expenses travelling around the country perpetrating his con. He said he would give back everything he had left if they gave him $10,000 for his trouble. The insurance company jumped at the proposition. Ralph directed the R.C.M.P. to some tin cans he had buried in his back yard in Victoria, where almost all the money was recovered.

Ralph got seven years in Sing Sing. Helen, who never knew a thing about Ralph's illegal activities, got a divorce. Ralph served his seven years in Sing Sing, and upon his release received his $10,000 and was deported back to Canada.

I don't know where Ralph Wilby is now. Perhaps that unobtrusive little guy in your accounts payable department . . . nah, it couldn't be!

ELIJAH THE RESTORER

It is hard to say just when John Alexander Dowie, better known as Elijah the Restorer, decided that money and sex were the most important things in life. It is even more difficult to pinpoint the exact moment when the Restorer decided to embrace religion.

John Dowie was born in 1847 in Edinburgh, Scotland. When he was 13 his family emigrated to Australia. John took to reading the Bible. He worked hard, saved his pennies, and returned to Scotland to study for the ministry. Four years later he came back to Australia where, at the age of 25, he was ordained a Congressionalist Minister. John settled down for a while, but soon tired of the ministry, and became an evangelist taking the good word to the Australian countryside.

Along the way John, who had the same normal urges as the rest of us mortals, met a rather angelic young lady with the unbelievable name of Jane Wrath. It wasn't long before Jane became Mrs. Dowie. Despite suffering from annoying headaches, she joined her husband in spreading the gospel.

One day, quite by accident, John mentioned to a group of the faithful who had gathered to be saved, that he had laid hands upon Jane's headache-racked head, and lo and behold, her headaches disappeared, vanished, caput, never to return. John was as surprised as anyone to find out that from this humble beginning people started to come to him to be healed. They even gave him freewill offerings for the promise of a cure.

John, not one to look a heavenly gift horse in the mouth, quickly formed the Divine Healing Association to handle the flow of hard cash. For six years he healed, and the suckers paid. Still, he thought, bigger and better things must lie in store for him in America. In 1888, with the faithful Jane by his side, he set sail for San Francisco, ostensibly to form another branch of his association. He wandered across the land, setting up several branch healing offices, but when he set foot in Chicago he knew he had really arrived. If ever a place needed saving and healing, it was Chicago.

John eyed the Chicago World's Fair being held in 1893 with the anticipation of a carny operator. He set up his tabernacle close by the main gates of the fair, and started preaching and healing. Business was so good he was at it 15 hours a day, seven days a week. He even managed to collect enough crutches and canes to form a respectable backdrop for his preaching platform. Money was pouring in from his branch offices. By 1895 he had become a money making machine and a confirmed enemy of legitimate doctors. While the established medical authorities agreed that emotion and psychology played some part in therapy, they claimed that John was causing all kinds of human misery by keeping his followers from seeking medical attention. Our hero fought the establishment at every opportunity, and kept on counting the cash.

John bought a seven-storey building on Michigan Ave. He and Jane occupied two luxurious floors. Each Sunday he preached to a packed audience in the Chicago auditorium. He was making so much money he formed his own bank, the Zion City Bank, to look after his investments. Quietly John, who had a definite flair for finance, picked up 6,500 acres between Chicago and Milwaukee. To put together the huge package John had shelled out $1,250,000.

Dowie then announced that he was forming the Christian Catholic Church in Zion, and that all his faith healing branches were henceforth to direct their incomes to this new religion. Once this little transaction was successfully completed, John took off for Europe to set up still more faith healing operations.

When he returned, he had another blockbuster to unload on the public. He intended to form his own city on the land which he controlled. It was to be called Zion. John stated that he was the reincarnation of the prophet Elijah, and those who followed him to his new city would, of course, have to consider him their new God. Not everyone accepted this garbage at face value. Legitimate religious organizations ridiculed Elijah the Restorer, as he was called, but enough of the faithful followed blindly to make the scheme a success.

Five-thousand souls started to build the City of Zion for their leader and themselves. Factories, a bank, and a college were all constructed and all, of course, belonged to Elijah. It is estimated that by 1901 John's little personal empire had assets worth over $5 million. There was no stopping our boy. He built a bakery and factories producing soap and candy. He alone appointed the mayor and all the officials of Zion. He even had his own army. Elijah called them the Zion Guard, and outfitted them in outlandish uniforms embroidered with doves of peace.

At age 55, and at the height of his career, Elijah took to spending more and more time at his summer home. On a warm summer evening he could be seen entering the luxurious $200,000 home away from home with a female member of his flock. It appears that Elijah still had those desires he always had as plain John Dowie.

Elijah made a fatal mistake. Now worth an estimated $23 million, he decided to tackle New York City. He sent thousands of advance men to set up accommodations for a crusade he planned for the month of October, 1903. He rented Madison Square Garden, and poured hundreds of thousands of dollars into the publicity campaign for his crusade.

Complete with choir and long flowing gowns, Elijah opened his crusade before a packed Madison Square Gardens audience of 12,000. Elijah had miscalculated the gullibility of his big city audience. As he tore into the sins of urban life, the crowd who had heard the same thing many times before, started to boo the great one. Thousands got up and left. The second night his audience had dwindled to 6,000. Each successive night was worse. The debacle had cost Elijah a fortune.

Worse still, because of the many months of massive effort which had gone into saving souls in New York, his own City of Zion had started to go under from neglect. Not wanting to face reality, Elijah took off for Mexico to open still more healing establishments. When he returned, it was too late. Zion was having trouble paying its bills. In the end the courts declared the city bankrupt and placed its affairs in the hands of a receiver.

It never rains but it pours. Some indiscreet lady picked this inopportune moment to tell all about Elijah's little capers in the summer house. It didn't help matters that she was a married woman. Soon other married ladies came forward and spilled the beans about Elijah and his dalliances.

Elijah's wife Jane announced that she was leaving the great one. This was the last straw. Depressed and heartbroken at his sudden and swift downfall, Elijah went to bed one evening in March 1907 and died in his sleep.

Unbelievably, a disciple of Elijah's, one Wilbur Voliva, started to raise money by preaching much the same line as his predecessor. Little by little he succeeded in raising enough money to satisfy creditors, until in the end he was able to bring Zion out of hock. He died in 1942.

Today, some of the children of the followers of Elijah and Voliva still live in Zion. Without a doubt it is a town with one of the strangest histories in America, founded by one of the greatest con artists the world has ever known.

THE DIAMOND MANUFACTURER

Not many con men get to tackle one of the most powerful companies in the world and take them to the cleaners.

Henri Lemoine did.

Henri was born in Paris to a very prominent family. He excelled in school and was getting straight A's in college right up until the time he sold the dormitory to his classmates. This necessitated a hasty exit and spelled the end of Henri's formal education. Various activities followed. Henri talked some fool into believing he was the heir of Louis XIV. It cost the poor sucker 1,000 pounds to be called king for a few days. Of course, in the off season Henri sold the Eiffel Tower to gullible Americans. Occasionally Henri was caught while perpetrating his cute little capers, which would result in his being hauled off to prison. Each time he was released he pulled a bigger and better con. Through it all Henri was married to a real doll who knew that hubby operated outside the law. Like Henri, she liked the money and loved the thrill of it all.

In January, 1905 Lemoine, hat in hand, called at the office of Henry Feldenheimer, one of Paris' most prominent diamond dealers. Henri reached across a desk and passed over six uncut diamonds to Feldenheimer. Adjusting his jeweller's glass, Feldenheimer said, "Remarkable. Absolutely remarkable. They're absolutely perfect."

You see, there was nothing remarkable about the stones themselves, just the fact that Henri claimed to have manufactured them by artificial means. Naturally, Henri was in that office to obtain financial assistance because his experiments had supposedly wiped him out. Now that he was ready to start production, he needed further cash for new facilities.

Feldenheimer said he needed a few days. Taking the stones, he set up a meeting with Sir Julius Wehner, one of the governors of De Beers Consolidated Mines Ltd., the great South African diamond company. The thought of artificial diamonds had almost the same effect on Sir Julius as the advent of the automobile must have had on horseshoe manufacturers. Sir Julius developed a little twitch in the corner of his mouth.

Not being a gullible man, Sir Julius wanted to see Henri actually produce diamonds. Feldenheimer said this could be arranged, but first he had to attend to a little detail. The detail was a quick legal document drawn up between himself and our Henri, giving Feldenheimer 10 per cent of anything that would ever be realized from the invention of artificial diamonds.

And so it came to pass, on a dark starless night in Paris, there was a meeting in an attic apartment. In attendance were Feldenheimer, Sir Julius, Francis Oaks, a director of De Beers; and Alfred Beit, a financier.

Henri shouted from behind a curtain for his distinguished guests to be seated. Once they were comfortable, the curtains parted and there stood Henri in front of his extensively equipped laboratory. With a backdrop of bubbling vessels, retorts, and test tubes, Henri faced some of the most powerful men in the world completely nude, wearing only shoes and socks. He eyes twinkled as he explained to his startled audience that he wanted to make it perfectly clear that he had nothing hidden on his person.

The focal point of Lemoine's lab was a small furnace. He explained that by heating carbon and his secret ingredient, and sending an electric current through the mass, he could produce diamonds. To demonstrate he held a round pottery jar filled with carbon and his supposedly secret substance.

All the sceptics examined the jar and, convinced that there were no diamonds hidden in the dark substance, they returned the jar to Henri, who placed it in the furnace. An hour later Henri, still naked as the day he was born, pulled the jar out of the furance and out popped 25 rough diamonds. The astonished audience asked for an instant replay. An hour later Henri produced another 30 diamonds.

Sir Julius offered Henri the equivalent of $50,000 right there and then for his secret formula. Henri, cool customer that he was, said he wanted it in writing so he could think it over. Then he made a counter offer. He would write out the formula with the stipulation that it not be revealed to anyone until after his death. In the meantime, he would stop making diamonds. Sir Julius went for it. A sealed envelope went into the safety deposit box, Henri got the 50 big ones, and the De Beers group figured they had saved their organization from financial ruin by keeping cheap diamonds from being dumped on the market.

Then Henri Lemoine went for broke. He suggested to the De Beers boys that they should manufacture diamonds for industrial purposes. Feldenheimer, who was getting 10 per cent of all the action, pushed the scheme with Sir Julius. Believe it or not, the De Beers group went to the well again. This time they fell hook, line and sinker. They appointed Henri to build a turbo electric plant in Angeliers to produce the industrial diamonds. They wired him a quick $100,000 for starters from Africa. Several months later Henri hired a photographer to take a picture of a real turbo electric plant. He sent it to his backers in Africa. They were so delighted with the progress they hurried off another $100,000. Incredible as it shounds, Henri kept sucking money out of his African partners for three years. Each time he appeared close to production, another unfortunate delay took place, requiring more money. Finally the fish down in the Dark Continent decided to take a little swim to France to see the plant. They found a municipal plant just like the pictures they had received over the years. The police were consulted, and of course Henri's past was revealed to his erstwhile associates. They also found that not only had Henri built a nonexistent plant, he was also an expert at slight of hand. The police suggested that Henri had probably palmed the diamonds, and slipped them into the container just before he placed the jar into the furnace.

Henri was picked up and placed in jail. Not exactly a dummy, Henri got a lawyer. His lawyer maintained that Henri did nothing wrong. He said that Henri's wife took all the African money, divorced Henri, and disappeared. His client had been forced to deceive his partners. They had shown up too soon. For another paltry $90,000 Henri would produce the diamonds under supervision.

Truth is stranger than fiction. Sir Julius advanced Henri another $90,000. Henri started construction, then the delays started again. Patience ran out and so did Henri. He skipped the night before the authorities were going to pick him up. A short time later he was spotted on the streets of Paris. He was arrested, and spent six years in prison. They opened the safety deposit box, and Henri's note read, "It is very difficult to make diamonds."

Don't shed too many tears for our hero. From that January day in 1905, when he walked into Feldenheimer's office and professed to be able to make diamonds, he had taken the De Beers organization for an estimated half million dollars.

No one recovered a penny.

Once released from prison, he completely disappeared, and has never been heard of since.

However, there are those who knew Henri who swear they have seen him since his release in the company of his wife.

No, it couldn't be — not after the divorce, not the six years in prison; or could this have been Henri's biggest con of all?

THE SPANISH CONNECTION

You might wonder why some gentlemen become small time con artists instead of big time con artists. The answer is obvious. You don't require that much brain power to become a small change artist. Ah, but to become a con artist where the stakes are counted in the millions of dollars is quite another ball of wax.

Take Don James Addison de Peralta-Reavis, for example. Don appeared on the scene in 1883 in Arizona. All he claimed to be was the owner of the entire state. He said that he came to claim his inheritance, Le Baronia de Arizonae, which was granted by King Ferdinand of Spain to a Don Miguel on Dec. 20, 1748. Naturally, our Don was the living descendant of Don Miguel and the rightful owner of most of the counties of Arizona, as well as the city of Phoenix.

At first Don was met with a certain amount of ridicule. The enormity of his claim was beyond belief. Of course, if by any remote possibility it was valid, then everyone who owned a lot of land within the Baronia was susceptible to being dispossessed. Not only that, but all the mines, property, and anything of value would revert into the hands of Don James Addison de Peralta-Reavis, as Don liked to be called.

He hired a battery of top notch lawyers to assert his claim. With Don acting as his own publicity agent, he went about holding public meetings, explaining how the whole thing happened.

Don was a real charmer. He stated that he had no intention of being cruel or cheating anyone. It just so happened that Arizona, which had at one time been a part of Mexico, had been granted to an antecedent of his. Don had all the legal documentation necessary to back his claim. In fact, he was darn fair about the whole thing. He only wanted a small rent from everyone living on his land. Of course, the large producing silver mines would be taxed at a somewhat more ambitious rate.

The state of Arizona formed a committee to investigate Don's claim. This thing was becoming serious. All the maps and documents were examined, and the committee became convinced that they were genuine. The legalities were checked in Washington, and eventually an emissary was sent to Spain. Old records were checked and rechecked. There seemed to be no doubt about it, everything appeared to be exactly as Don had said all along. The King of Spain had indeed granted the area that was presently Arizona to the heirs of Don Miguel. The committee in its wisdom did bring up the fact that our Don had to prove that he was a descendant of Don Miguel, and that he was the only living descendant.

Don didn't blink an eye. He brought forth genealogical tables showing that only two descendants of Don Miguel were alive. One, of course, was himself. The other was a female descendant, Sofia Loreta Micaela. Then Don really pulled the carpet out from under the committee. He introduced them to his wife, none other than Sofia Loreta Micaela de Peralta-Reavis.

It took almost a year to trace and verify the claims of the Baron and Baroness, but in the end their claim was accepted as legitimate. Thousands of hardworking homesteaders paid a small amount each month to their new landlords. More substantial concerns, like the Southern Pacific Railway, anted up $50,000 for the right to move their trains through Don's property. In a short time our hero became a multimillionaire, and one of the most influential men in the western United States. Don lived like a king. He had what amounted to palaces in St. Louis, Washington, Madrid and Mexico City.

Unbelievably, Don ruled over his domain for 10 long years. Now and then some agency or committee would be formed to try to find some fraudulent act or phony document in the Baron's string of documents. All attempts to discredit our hero failed. Then one day a private detective, working secretly for private concerned individuals, was poring over documents in the archives of Spain. While holding one of the documents dated 1759 up to the light, the detective noticed the watermark of a paper producing mill in Wisconsin. There surely was no one producing paper in Wisconsin in 1759.

A long series of revelations followed, whereby Don was proved to be a fake. Jimmy Reavis was really born in Missouri. He had discovered that he had an uncanny ability to copy signatures. While in the Confederate Army he had made quite a name for himself by selling his particular service to forge weekend passes for his buddies.

After the war he worked as a streetcar conductor in St. Louis, and then gravitated to real estate. It wasn't long before he obtained a job in the land office of the U.S. government. Because of treaties with Mexico, he found that part of his job was studying the validity of land claims. In this way he became knowledgeable about what constitutes a legitimate land claim.

His scheme took over two years in preparation. He studied the Spanish language and even acquired Spanish mannerisms. Then he travelled to Mexico City, Washington, and Madrid, where he spent days in the old churches and archives. Painstakingly he gradually substituted forged documents for the genuine articles.

Don found a servant girl he could trust. He groomed and molded her as his wife and partner. When the true facts about Don were revealed, he and his wife disappeared and never surfaced again.

If you want to discount the $28 the Indians were paid for Manhattan, Don had pulled off the largest and most successful land swindle in the history of American real estate.

A BETTER IDEA

David Morton Roll had the appearance of a prosperous, high level executive. He dressed immaculately in expensive tailor-made pinstripe suits, which were enhanced by solid gold tie clips and cufflinks. His lean body and honest face oozed confidence. As well they might — you see, Dave was one of the coolest confidence men who ever lived.

Like many a small time practitioner of the con, Dave lived for the big score. That's how he came to be chauffeur-driven in an over-sized limousine to the elegant Shoreham Hotel in Washington, D.C. When Dave checked in, he let it be known that he was in somewhat of a rush. An important appointment with the Secretary of the Interior, no less. He'd be back for dinner, and would the clerk kindly let him know when Henry Ford's telephone call came through.

Well, now, that's a pretty fair country entrance in anyone's book. In the Washington of 1931 it stamped David Morton Roll as a man of influence. The slick con man wasn't through yet. Not by a long shot.

Sure enough, during dinner a telephone call came through from Henry Ford for Dave Roll. The pageboy shouted the name loud and clear throughout the lobby. When Dave took the call on the lobby phone he talked loudly enough so that he almost registered on a seismograph in Hoboken. He let drop key words like Muscle Shoals and $88 million. That was enough.

In 1931 Muscle Shoals was a 38-mile strip of the Tennessee River where the water fell in a steep grade for 135 feet. The rapids had tremendous water power potential. The U.S. Department of the Interior was considering developing it or privately leasing out the area for 99 years. The well-informed in Washington knew that Henry Ford had already tried unsuccessfully to purchase Muscle Shoals on two different occasions. Dave Roll knew too.

The sting was in. The news spread like wildfire. Henry Ford's top advisor was in town with 88 big ones to purchase Muscle Shoals. Soon invitations arrived at the Shoreham. Dave was being invited on the party circuit as he knew he would. Outfitted with white tails, the 42-year-old con man made a dashing figure at Washington's elegant watering holes. One thing, though, Dave wouldn't accept a cigarette nor, heaven forbid, take a drink. Everyone knew that back home in Dearborn, Henry didn't approve of such vulgar habits.

Dave made a terrific impression. At one of these forays he met Robert Latham Owen, who had served as a senator from Oklahoma for 18 years. Owen, who knew everyone who was anyone, had stayed on in Washington to practise law. He heard that Roll was in Washington to negotiate the purchase of Muscle Shoals for Henry Ford. The senator came right out and asked Dave if he could be his legal representative for the upcoming deal. Cunning Dave said he would be considered.

The very next day, Owen visited Roll at the Shoreham. Things started to pop. Dave received two phone calls, supposedly from Henry Ford himself. Then he revealed the details of his association with the automobile magnate. He showed the now drooling Owen documents purportedly from Ford stating that Ford was willing to pay $88 million for Muscle Shoals. If Dave paid anything less than $88 million, he was to keep the difference. Should the deal not go through, Dave was to be paid a flat fee of $250,000 for his services.

Owen was gasping for air. The hook was well planted. If the deal went through for say 80 mil, Roll stood to make a cool $8 million. The legal fees would be worth a fortune to the firm picked to guide the deal through the government and the courts.

Dave looked Owen in the eye and said, "You are our legal representative on the Muscle Shoals project. The fee is $100,000 per year." It would, however, be necessary for Owen to accompany Dave to Dearborn, Mich., to meet Mr. Ford. Dear Henry insisted on meeting his senior people. Owen, smelling cash, would have hitchhiked to Dearborn that same night.

Within a few days Dave and Owen checked into the Book-Cadillac Hotel in Detroit. On the first morning, while Dave was out for a walk, the phone rang. The caller identified himself as Henry Ford. Once Ford found out that Dave wasn't in he spoke to

Owen. He said he was embarrassed as he would not be able to meet with the two men. He had to leave town immediately on other business. Would Senator Owen mind answering a few questions on the phone. You bet your bottom dollar the senator didn't mind. Well, old Henry took the senator over the coals for about 20 minutes, covering every aspect of Owen's life. He ended the conversation by telling Owen to have Dave draw up an employment contract. The senator was Henry's kind of man.

Owen was ecstatic at the pleasant turn of events. Dave seemed less than pleased. On the return train trip to Washington, Owen inquiried as to what was wrong. Dave reluctantly revealed that despite apparently wallowing in money, ready cash was a problem. He told Owen that he had just made a $2 million settlement on his wife in order to obtain a divorce. The divorce had not been amicable, and had resulted in legal fees of $200,000. Dave found himself short a paltry $57,000.

"Not to worry, Dave, my boy, let me advance you the fifty seven thou." It was to be the first of many annoying little sums that the senator was to pass on to Dave Roll.

Just as Senator Owen had been lured into the trap, scores of other lawyers tried to approach Dave. They found out it wasn't easy. Out of the woodwork emerged one J. Jones. Jones acted as a buffer. He let it be known that if you wanted to do business with Dave Roll, you had to go through J. Jones. The Jones boy also let it be known that his boss always took his recommendations. May the saints preserve us, J. Jones also let it be known that he was on the take. He could obtain legal work amounting to hundreds of thousands of dollars for little gratuities of $5,000 here and $10,000 there. Complete secrecy was to be maintained until the deal was official. Oh, yes, cash in advance, if you please.

It is estimated that Dave and Jones, whoever he was, picked up $150,000 on this little sideline. Later, many of the lawyers taken by this scheme didn't come forward. They were none too anxious to let it be known that they had offered bribes.

It is a tribute to David Roll's gall that he lived in the lap of luxury for approximately three years while fleecing Senator Owen. Owen never received one cent, but as Roll later said, he didn't do a scrap of work, either.

The Senator became concerned when Dave's loans reached $200,000. To alleviate his fears, Dave signed a document guaranteeing one half of his anticipated total income from the Muscle Shoals deal. Owen figured that he had just cut himself in for approximately $4 million.

Dave kept the sham going as long as he could. Roosevelt defeated Hoover, helping him stall a while longer. In one fell swoop, the cat came jumping out of the bag. Roosevelt announced that the government was creating the Tennessee Valley Authority, which encompassed the Muscle Shoals development.

Owen was beside himself. He dashed off to Detroit, and this time actually met with Henry Ford. His worst fears became reality. Henry Ford had never heard of Dave Roll. Owen practically ran back to Washington. This time he had a friendly little chat with J. Edgar Hoover of the F.B.I. Lo and behold, J. Edgar found out that Dave Roll had previously been detained as an unpaid guest at the Colorado State Penitentiary for five years. Upon his release Dave had rushed directly from the penal institution into Senator Owen's open arms in Washington.

How did he do it? Roll's suckers were not dummies. They were senators, lawyers, and even judges. Yet the ex con was able to fool them all. He had so much gall he had never even changed his name. It does well to understand that when you are dealing in millions, $50,000 is not a great deal of money. When you are dealing in contracts amounting to hundreds of thousands of dollars, $5,000 is not a large amount. Roll was astute enough to realize this. Like all other con men, he played on one human frailty — greed.

Dave was picked up while having a steak in the Shoreham's dining room. He was charged with obtaining money under false pretenses. While in jail awaiting trial, Dave lived high off the hog. He had food, booze, and women delivered to the jail. He became one of the most popular prisoners ever held in Washington.

On June 12, 1934, his bail was reduced to $7,500. Dave handed over the cash and left Washington. To pass the time, while awaiting trial, he took a luxury suite at the Ritz Carlton Hotel in Atlantic City. For almost a month the champagne flowed.

On July 4, Dave doubled over in pain. Rushed to the hospital, he died on the operating table. Everyone knew Dave Morton Roll had more than an adequate supply of gall, but no one knew he had gallstones.

ANYBODY WANT TO BUY THE EIFFEL TOWER?

The mayor of Hostinne was a happy man that day in 1890 when his son Victor popped into the world. The affairs of the small town situated along the River Elbe in a section of Czechoslovakia known as Bohemia came to an abrupt stop. Little Victor Lustig would have the best education that money could buy. He would attend a private school in Dresden, then on to university, then who knows — become a renowned scientist, perhaps an eminent doctor. If Poppa only knew. Would you believe one of the most innovative and slippery confidence men the world has ever known?

The first part of the mayor's dream for his son came true. In his formative years Victor was shipped off to a boarding school in Dresden. After graduation he thought he would try his luck in Paris. Naturally he told his ever-trusting father that he was attending the Sorbonne, thereby assuring himself of a monthly stipend to keep body and soul together.

Now a tall, slim debonaire young man, he taught himself the intricacies of poker until there were few who had a chance sitting at the same table with him. He called himself Count Lustig, and plied his trade on the luxury liners crossing the Atlantic. One of Victor's colleagues on the ocean liners was the well known American gambler, Nicky Arnstein. The two became great friends and often combined their talents to fleece the wealthy industrialists. To alleviate the tedium of the ocean voyage Victor wasn't adverse to bedding down with a businessman's wife when the occasion presented itself.

In 1914 the war came along, effectively putting an end to his Atlantic gambling days, but bigger and better things were in store for the Count.

Equipped with $25,000 in profits from his gambling operations, Count Lustig found a plum just waiting to be plucked. One day, during the war, an unwary banker named Green in a small Kansas town was visited by a slim European; obviously a man of substance. Count Lustig had cased his mark well in advance. He knew the banker had a derelict, almost worthless, farm which he was itching to unload. The Count explained to banker Green that he had been forced to leave his native Austria and he was looking for a place to retire on a piece of land which he could turn into an estate. Green's eyes lit up like lanterns. He showed Lustig the farm that same day.

Back in the bank office Lustig took out $50,000 in bonds and offered $25,000 in cash for the farm. Had Green been an honest man he would have told the Count that the farm was only worth $5,000, but he chose to keep quiet. The Count had figured his sucker's reaction perfectly. A deal was struck. Green offered to cash the bonds. Count Lustig would sign off the bonds and would receive the deed to the farm and his change of $25,000 in cash in return for the bonds that evening.

The two men sipped a Cointreau while they completed the deal. The Count walked off with the $25,000 in cash and Green received a neatly wrapped parcel of bonds. A few hours later Green opened up his packet of bonds only to find cut up newspapers. A badly perspiring banker frantically knocked on the Count's hotel room door. The Count was long gone.

Count Lustig travelled the world living in the lap of luxury. He wore the best clothing, dined in the best restaurants and courted the most attractive women. He worked hard at his trade.

Take the time he sold the Eiffel Tower for example. In 1925 there was a lot of publicity given to the fact that the Eiffel Tower required a great deal of money to keep it in proper repair. Some were in favor of tearing it down altogether, and it was this news which gave the Count his great idea.

Staying at the plush Hotel Crillon, the Count had some impressive, but phony, letterheads printed. On the stationery purportedly from the Deputy Director-General of the Ministere des Postes et Telegraphes, he invited Paris' leading scrap dealers to a meeting to discuss a government contract.

Posing as a senior government official he explained to the gathering, in confidence, that the Eiffel Tower was to be dismantled and the 7,000 tons of scrap iron was to be sold. Those present were the select few being invited to tender. The highest bidder would, of course, receive the contract.

All during the meeting the Count was studying the businessmen looking for his mark. He found him in the person of Monsieur Andre Poisson, a man a bit less cultured than his companions — a man looking for an edge.

That same night the Count called Monsieur Poisson to his suite. He explained that government officials didn't make a great deal of money. Poisson didn't need any more of a hint. He produced a wad of bills. He presented Poisson with an impressive looking contract, and a promise that he would inform the unsuccessful competitors in the morning.

The next day the Count had left France and was luxuriating with a lady friend in Germany. The caper never did get much publicity. M. Poisson thought that discretion was the better part of valor. He kept his mouth shut.

The Eiffel Tower scam was so successful that two years later the Count dug up some more scrap dealers and sold the Tower for the second time. This time the victim screamed, so the Count had to retire from the Tower selling business.

All his life Victor came up with novel schemes to part the greedy from their money. Once he even borrowed $50,000 from the notorious Al Capone, with a promise that he would double the money for the gangster in 60 days. When he showed up with the $50,000 and explained that his scheme had failed, old Scarface was so impressed that he gave Lustig $5,000 as a reward for being so honest. That old twinkle came to the Count's eye. He again had exactly figured out his score's reaction.

All things come to an end. The Count entered the unfamiliar field of counterfeiting, working as a distributor, and was caught by the F.B.I. In 1936 he was sentenced to 20 years in Alcatraz. The man who sold the Eiffel Tower twice, died in prison.

One wonders if he ever ran across his old pal Capone in Alcatraz. At the time, Al had a job there in the laundry.

STANLEY RULED THE WAVES

What makes some men want to be somebody else? Usually the answer is money or power. It's not often that an imposter arrives upon the scene with no thought of hard cash hidden in the far recesses of his mind.

Stanley Clifford Weyman was one of those men who loved being an imposter for only the action and fun. He had a sense of the ridiculous that has rarely been duplicated.

Born in 1890 in Brooklyn, New York, to poor immigrant parents, Stanley longed for an education. Because his parents could ill afford to send him to school, he was forced to go to work at an early age. The young boy grew up to be a shy little man. Stanley always envied those lucky people in our society who were able to command respect, those action people who made the world go around.

There was one way to become important, and Stanley took the one way. He would pretend. Stanley Weyman worked at some menial task for a year or two, but always he would leave his job suddenly and assume a role, not for money, but for the hell of it.

One fine day, while the First World War was being fought in the trenches of Europe, Stanley decided to become a Lieutenant Commander in, of all things, the Rumanian Army. While he was at it, he became a Rumanian Consul General in New York. Stanley got the notion that he wanted to inspect a battleship.

With about as much thought as you would give to crossing the street, Stanley called the U.S. Navy Department in Washington. After the usual amenities, he mentioned that the Queen of Rumania had assigned him the pleasant task of bringing greetings from his country to the U.S. The Queen had mentioned that the inspection of a warship might be a nice gesture.

That's how Stanley Weyman, the Brooklyn store clerk, was given every courtesy of the U.S. Navy as he was piped aboard the U.S.S. Wyoming. Stan looked just great in his powder blue uniform trimmed in gold. At the age of 24 he had managed to hoodwink the entire U.S. Navy. After the inspection, he rented a private dining room at the Astor Hotel, and had all the brass over for a sumptuous meal. The tab? Don't bother me with such details. Send it along to the Rumanian Consulate in Washington.

Later, the party was over in more ways than one for the bogus Rumanian. Stan was traced and apprehended. He cheerfully spent two years in jail.

In 1920 Stanley read an ad in the newspaper that seemed tailor made for him. A New York development company was looking for a doctor to travel to Lima, Peru, to inspect sanitation conditions in that city. It was duck soup for our boy to lay his hands on phony credentials. With a name change here and a name change there, Stanley became Dr. S. Weyman. He so impressed the legitimate doctor reviewing the applicants that he got the job. Dr. Weyman arrived in Lima and did what he usually did.
He threw a party.

Everyone liked the doctor, and the doctor liked parties, servants, and new cars. In the sanitation department Stan went along with anything that looked like a good suggestion. It was the best he could do. He had no idea what anyone was talking about.

Back home his company couldn't believe the fantastic expense accounts. They were just too much. Who was this Dr. Weyman anyway? A closer scrutiny of his credentials revealed his true identity. Quietly and without fuss, Dr. Weyman was brought home and relieved of his duty. Gee, it had been great fun.

Stanley had hardly shaken the dust of Peru off his boots when he noticed another startling announcement in the newspapers. Princess Fatima of Afghanistan was not receiving the usual welcome afforded royalty while visiting the U.S. Stanley decided to change all that. Before you could say Charlie Chaplin, a dapper little man in top hat and cane presented himself to the Princess at her hotel. Under Secretary Stanley Clifford Weyman of the U.S. State Department at your service. Fatima was delighted.

Stanley explained that his mission was to escort the Princess to Washington, where she was to meet the Secretary of State and the President. First, of course, it was quite normal for the Princess to place $10,000 in his hands so that he could purchase gifts for the personnel at the State Department and the White House, as was the custom. Fatima slipped Stan the ten big ones.

Stanley didn't have honest-to-goodness larceny in his heart. He used the money wisely. First he hired a private railway car for the Royal entourage. Upon arrival in Washington, he ensconced the whole kit and kaboodle in the Willard Hotel. Stan looked sharp in his Lieutenant Commander's whites as he advised the State Department that he was assigned to arrange a meeting between Princess Fatima and the Secretary of State, Charles Evans Hughes.

A reception was duly arranged and Fatima and Hughes got along just swell. Toward the end of the evening Lt. Comm. Weyman told Hughes that it was the Princess' fond wish to meet the President of the U.S. Hughes went to a phone. It was all fixed. Weyman, Fatima, Hughes, and a few bodyguards crossed the street to the White House. The clerk from Brooklyn spent a pleasant half hour swapping yarns with Warren G. Harding, the President of the United States.

The Navy brass did a routine check on Weyman that came up ex con. The very next day they swooped down on Weyman's hotel suite. The little commander was long gone. When the story broke in the newspapers, a wide smile crossed the face of a shy clerk in Brooklyn.

When Rudolph Valentino died in 1926, Pola Negri appeared in New York. She locked herself in a suite in the Ambassador hotel, supposedly heartbroken over the great lover's death. The word out of her hotel was that she had taken ill because of her great loss. Medical bulletins issued from her suite came from none other than Dr. Stanley Weyman. It was simple. Stan merely showed up at the hotel one day and told Pola that he had been Rudy's doctor. He knew that Rudy would want him to look after her. Stan moved right into the suite.

Later, the little imposter, who always used his own name, began receiving so much notoriety, that it was difficult for him to pull it off. Maybe his last great performance was his United Nations caper.

In 1948 Stanley actually got a legitimate job as a journalist with the Irwin News Service. He was assigned to the United Nations, which at that time assembled at Lake Success. Stanley was a good journalist, but soon he was overcome by that old urge to be bigger and better.

While covering the United Nations, he became great friends with many of the delegates, one of whom was Ambassador Wan Waithayakon of Thailand. Stan suggested that he could help the Ambassador and Thailand, if he could be appointed Special Public Relations Counsellor with diplomatic status. The ambassador thought it a great idea. While being cleared for diplomatic status, the F.B.I. uncovered the dapper con man. Stan had come within an ace of becoming an honest to goodness diplomat.

In August 1960, Stan was employed as the night clerk in a New York hotel. One night two armed men walked into the hotel and demanded the cash box he was about to put in the safe. He refused to hand it over. One of the men lunged for the box. Stanley could have let go and the men would have fled. We will never know what went through his mind during those few seconds. All the roles he had played, all the fun he had had — now, if there was ever to be meaning to his life, would he grasp the chance? This was no role, it was real.

Later, Stanley Weyman's body was found riddled with bullets on the floor of the hotel. The cash box lay intact beside him.

I AM GOD

There was nothing unusual about George Baker's early life to distinguish him from the scores of black preachers spreading the word throughout the southern United States. No one ever thought he would become God.

George attended other preachers' sermons and observed their audiences closely. He discovered that the less people understood, the more attentive and impressed they became. He started using gobbledegook in his own sermons, such as 'God is personified and materialized, not only that, He is repersonified and rematerialized. He even materialized and rematerialates.' The faithful would scream Amen.

George decided to take his act north, but the sledding wasn't easy. On many occasions, to keep the devil from his door-step, he had to work. George cut grass and trimmed hedges for a living. On Sundays, he would head for the closest church that would let him use their pulpit to spread the word.

By 1914 George, now using the name Father Divine, was wandering the country, meeting with limited success. He stumbled on some tough luck which proved to be a blessing in disguise. The good folks of Valdosta, Ga., had him arrested as a public menace for preaching his particular brand of religion.

When it came time to issue a writ, no one knew his real name. They asked Father Divine, and he knew all right. He promptly supplied the answer. "I am God," he said. The writ was made out John Doe, alias God. In the rather comical trial which followed, Father Divine was found to be of unsound mind, and ordered to leave the state. The publicity of being called God by the courts didn't do his cause any harm.

Father Divine headed north again, preaching as he went. By the time he hit New York, he had a half a dozen followers, who had left their homes and friends to join his congregation. Once in the Big Apple, he rented a four-room flat, where he and the faithful lived. Each night they had a prayer meeting. Father Divine inserted ads in the newspapers and found jobs for his flock.

Most of Father Divine's followers were better off than they had ever been before. They had plenty to eat, clothes to wear, and a place to stay. True enough, the $10 or $15 a week they each brought in went to Father Divine, but in return he took care of their every need.

Well, folks, the idea caught on. At first a trickle, then practically a deluge. Everyone wanted to join the religious group which actually had God as its head man. By 1919 George had to move out of New York City altogether in order to establish himself in larger premises. He set up in Sayville, Long Island, and began serving free Sunday dinners. Father Divine refused to take any money for these dinners, sometimes actually refusing cold hard cash with the refrain, "The Lord will provide."

Father Divine began to attract some wealthy black people to his fold, as well as a sprinkling of whites. In order to relieve these trusting souls of their worldly goods, Father Divine would first demonstrate how all his followers were in a perpetual state of happiness. Once the hook was in, the newcomers were told that those who divested themselves of all their material goods could be elevated to the rank of Angels.

These Angels had preferred status. They were in immediate contact with God and could even on occasion stand beside him when he gave his sermon. Lineups formed to become Angels.

By 1930, when the rest of the world was reeling in the depths of the great Depression, Father Divine was rolling in the cash. It is estimated that he was chalking up a profit of around $1,000 a week. So many people were attending his free Sunday dinners that traffic jams were a common sight in Sayville. Finally the non-believers of the town had him arrested for public mischief.

Father Divine was convicted, fined $500, and sentenced to one year in jail. Justice Louis J. Smith, a healthy robust man of 55, who had passed sentence on Father Divine, dropped dead of a heart attack. Modestly Father Divine stated that he hated to do it, but God simply couldn't be treated in that manner. Later when his conviction was reversed, it served to add more fuel to the myth of his invincibility.

By now over 400 followers were turning everything they had or were able to earn over to him. Father Divine had one residence in New York which he naturally called Heaven. Other houses sprang up in Baltimore, Newark, Jersey City, and Bridgeport. These were extension heavens.

Father Divine branched out into the business world. At the height of his power he had 25 small restaurants, six grocery stores, 10 barbershops, 10 drycleaning establishments, and scores of peddlers hustling the streets of New York. He always charged less for everything than his competitors. The holy man had a terrific advantage. He had no labor costs. All of his employees were members of his congregation. They would say, "Peace, it's wonderful," and then get back to work. It is estimated that by 1940, Father Divine had an income of $10,000 per week.

In 1942, considerable pressure was put on the good father in an attempt to uncover anything illegal about his operations. Nothing illegal ever was unearthed, but he moved his headquarters to Philadelphia.

In 1946, he married a blonde, 21-year-old white girl, Edna Rose Ritchings. There were a few rumblings about the marriage, but Father Divine passed it over by explaining that he, God, was married in name only. He called his bride Mother Divine, and that seemed to please the faithful.

For years, he lived more like a king than a preacher. A full time staff was on call 24 hours a day to take care of his every wish. His wardrobe was one of the most extensive in the world. Chauffeur driven, he had his choice of Cadillac or Rolls Royce.

In 1965, the 85-year-old preacher lay near death in his huge home in Philadelphia. His inner cabinet chanted and prayed around his bed. He assured them all that he was not dying, but merely 'dematerialating' and some year in the future he would be 'repersonified' into another body and come back to them. As of this writing, he has not managed to pull it off.

THE GREAT IMPOSTER

Count Victor Lustig, posing as a French government official, sold the Eiffel Tower twice. Mild, unassuming Hans van Meegeren revelled in painting magnificent pictures and selling them as genuine Vermeers. Both of these illustrious gentlemen rank high on the list of all time imposters, but they still fall in the shadow of the greatest of them all — Ferdinand Waldo Demara.

You see, folks, the quality which separated Demara from all other imposters was his complete immersion into an unfamiliar occupation. He didn't plan a caper and pull it off; he actually became another person and lived other men's lives.

Fred was born in Lawrence, Mass., a city of 67,000 souls snugly tucked on the border of Massachusetts and New Hampshire. The good inhabitants of Lawrence had no way of knowing that the rather large, lumbering teenager, who never graduated from Central Catholic High School, would become their most publicized citizen.

At the age of 16 Fred ran away from home. He joined the Cistercian monks at Valley Falls, Rhode Island. After a year at the monastery, the kindly old abbot suggested that Fred was wasting his time with meditation and farm work. He had him transferred to the Brothers of Charity where he would have the opportunity to lead the life of a teacher.

In 1941, Fred left the holy order to join the army, but realized he had made a mistake the moment some pushy sergeant pointed to floors and said scrub. He went A.W.O.L., and joined the U.S. Navy shortly after the Japanese attack on Pearl

Harbor. It was here that Fred received his first introduction into the medical profession. Well, not exactly. He took a first aid course. Navy life didn't agree with him either, so he just walked away.

Fred had by now decided on a couple of rules which he was to follow most of his life. Number one was that, generally speaking, it was preferable to be a giver of orders than a receiver. Why not be an officer rather than an ordinary foot soldier? Why not a doctor rather than a first aid attendant? Why not indeed?

There was one roadblock, and Fred knew what it was. A high school dropout just didn't become an officer or a doctor. Fred decided to acquire someone else's credentials and lead their prestigious and respected lives. He found it surprisingly easy to write to universities and receive bona fide credentials of real college graduates.

That's how he became Dr. Robert L. French. He lifted the name from a college catalogue where the real French served on the faculty. The Trappists at the Abbey of Our Lady of Gethsemane near Louisville, Kentucky, were delighted to welcome a man of Dr. French's stature willing to join their silent ranks. Equipped with a degree from the University of Michigan, a Ph.D. in psychology from Stanford, and a Sterling Research Fellowship from Yale, he was an immediate hit among the Trappists.

Fred still had itchy feet. Always drawn to the teaching profession, and still posing as Dr. French, he next joined the Clerics of St. Viator. They enrolled him at DePaul University, where Fred took national psychology, cosmology, metaphysics, epistemology, ethics, and natural theology. Fred made straight A's. Finally he had to face the fact that to stay on any longer with the Clerics of St. Viator would mean he would become a Viatorian priest. Fred thought about it and simply walked away.

In quick succession he gained employment as an orderly at a sanitorium run by the Brothers of St. John of God in Los Angeles, and then became an instructor of psychology at St. Martin's College in Olympia, Washington. Fred was later to say that the days spent at St. Martin's College were some of the happiest of his life. He was well liked by both colleagues and students.

One fine day Fred was called to the dean's office. Two austere F.B.I. agents greeted him. They picked him up as a deserter from the Navy. For the first and only time in his life he was sentenced to jail, and spent 18 months at the U.S. disciplinary barracks in San Pedro, Calif.

Fred went to Lawrence to contemplate his next role. He had no trouble acquiring the educational credentials and birth certificate of Dr. Cecil Hamann, who was a biologist on the faculty of Ashbury College in Wilmore, Kentucky. Equipped with a Master's degree as well as a Ph.D. from Purdue, he again found himself being welcomed with open arms by another religious order, the Brothers of Christian Instruction in Alfred, Maine.

As Brother John, our Fred became one of the most influential men in the order, and actually assisted the organization in its efforts to obtain a college charter. In their wisdom, the good brothers decided to send Fred, or Brother John, or Dr. Hamann, whichever you prefer, across the border to Grand Falls, New Brunswick. Here he could study theology under a well-known expert who lived in the town.

While in Grand Falls, Fred became an acquaintance of Dr. Joseph Cyr, a young general practitioner. There is a bit of a controversy as to how Fred managed to get all of the doctor's credentials. Some say he simply stole them. Fred was later to claim that the doctor wanted to practise medicine in Maine, and that he had offered to present Dr. Cyr's credentials to the Maine medical authorities when he returned to Alfred. However, he obtained the credentials and had them clutched in his chubby hands when he went back to Alfred.

Canadian Navy officials in Saint John, N.B. were pleasantly surprised when large, good natured, Dr. Joseph Cyr offered his services to king and country. Fred was smart enough to slyly hint that he was considering the Army. When the Navy brass heard these not too closely guarded insinuations, they gave him the red carpet treatment. Within days Fred was transformed into Surgeon Lieutenant Dr. Joseph Cyr. Not bad for a high school dropout.

Assigned to the sick bay of the Halifax Naval Hospital, Fred kept giving everyone in sight a shot of penicillin. Not once did anyone suspect that he was other than what he claimed to be — a patriotic Canadian doctor who was giving a few years of his life to his country.

In June of 1951, Fred became the sole individual responsible for the health and welfare of 280 enlisted men and 12 officers on the Cayuga, a tribal class destroyer headed for Korea. The Korean war was in full swing, and Fred, who had never cut into anything more rare than a sirloin, was petrified. His first emergency came from an unexpected source. The Captain of the ship, James Plomer, wanted a tooth pulled. Fred almost flipped. He scurried to his cabin and stayed up all night reading up on dentistry. In the morning, he gave the Captain a shot of Novocain and extracted the tooth without any difficulty. The Captain complimented him and Fred gave a sigh of relief.

In the ensuing days Fred attended to the run of the mill ailments. Temperatures were brought under control, aspirins were dispensed, and nothing unusual occurred.

Then it happened. Am emergency. The destroyer was being rocked by heavy waves, and had just finished firing on enemy shore installations when a junk carrying horribly wounded South Koreans came alongside. Three of the men required immediate surgery to save their lives. The most seriously injured man was rushed to the

Captain's cabin, where a makeshift operating table had been set up.

The destroyer heaved, lanterns swayed. A nervous sick bay attendant assisted. Fred looked down at the dying man as many of the whitefaced ship's complement looked on. The wounded man's clothing was ripped off and, for the first time Fred saw the gaping bullet wound in the soldier's chest. His assistant was too nervous to find a vein in which to inject sodium pentothal. Fred calmly administered the drug himself. He even surprised himself with the steadiness of his hands. No one who witnessed the scene suspected that they were watching anything but a competent doctor at work.

Fred took a scalpel and opened the chest with incisions above the heart and above the breastbone. He deftly bent back a splintered rib, revealing the bullet within a fraction of an inch of the heart. He was later to confess that he dreaded the thought of the man hemorrhaging when he removed the bullet. When he extracted it the wounded man didn't hemorrhage. Fred placed gelfoam, a coagulating agent, into the wound, which caused it to begin clotting almost immediately. He then replaced the rib, sewed the man up, and outfitted him with an immobile bandage. Next he administered penicillin as a precaution against infection.

Two further operations followed in quick succession. Again and again Fred acted without hesitation. In all he operated non stop for 13 hours. In the end he slumped over in exhaustion. Within 72 hours all three of Fred's patients walked off the Cayuga. The ship left the area for a week, but when it returned it was confirmed that the three men had made miraculous recoveries. One was found working in the fields with Fred's bandages still wrapped tightly around his chest.

Lieutenant R.A.V. Jenkins was a public information officer for the Canadian Navy in the Far East. He released the story of Dr. Cyr's skillful operations to the press and radio for distribution back in Canada and the U.S. We must remember that Fred's feats were considered extraordinary even if accomplished by a trained doctor in such trying conditions. When Fred received the publicity no one dreamed that he was not a genuine doctor.

Back in Canada, the real Dr. Cyr was deluged with calls inquiring if the Korean hero was any relation. Dr. Cyr couldn't believe that someone had his name and his exact educational qualifications. He contacted the Navy.

Commander Plomer read the radio message to Fred.

"We have information Joseph C. Cyr, surgeon lieutenant 0-17669 is an imposter. Remove from active duty immediately. Repeat Immediately. Conduct investigation and report facts to Chief of Naval Staff, Ottawa." Plomer told Fred that the whole thing must be a mistake, but Fred knew the jig was up. Within a few days he was returned to Canada.

In Victoria, the Navy realized that Fred had joined up under a false name. Other than that he had done no harm, and really quite a bit of good. The Navy decided not to press any charges. They issued him his final paycheque and strongly suggested that he leave the country. Fred sold his story to Life magazine for $2,500. Then he hopped a plane to Chicago and got drunk.

Ben W. Jones was one of the best liked prison officers in the huge Huntsville jail in Texas. One of the largest prisons in the southern U.S., Huntsville housed many mentally disturbed and dangerous men. Jones seemed to be able to communicate with these men, and it wasn't long before his insight and leadership were rewarded. He was promoted to one of the toughest jobs in the whole institution, that of Warden of the maximum security block.

One day an insane prisoner took other prisoners hostage. He held a knife to a hostage's throat and was babbling incoherently. Ben Jones walked unarmed into the cellblock. He talked the deranged prisoner into releasing the hostages and became himself a hostage in their place.

He stood eyeball to eyeball with the madman and his knife. Perhaps for an instant Jones' mind wandered to a gaping chest wound on a rocking ship when he had cut into human flesh to save a man's life. For Ben Jones was none other than Fred Demara in another role. This time he talked the prisoner into handing over the knife. Fred and the convict walked out of the cellblock together.

A short time later a prisoner saw Fred's picture in a back copy of Life magazine, and Fred was exposed once again. He left the prison with Warden O.B. Ellis' words ringing in his ears, "Jones or Demara, whatever his name is, is one of the best prospects ever to serve in the prison system."

As always Fred was praised for his work in his chosen occupation and, as always he was totally unqualified to hold the position.

Fred is presently connected with a religious institution in California. He is living under his own name.

LOUIE WAS A GAS

It is one thing to con little gray haired ladies out a few hundred dollars, and quite another to hoodwink some of the richest and most powerful men in the entire United States. I abhor the former, but I must admit to having a sneaking admiration for the latter.

In 1916, most of the world was engaged in one of its periodic shoot-outs that we've come to expect every so often. The news was war, war, war, with hardly a weather report slipping into the daily journals to break the monotony.

Louie Enright was a little over 70 years of age, stood six feet tall, and had a white flowing beard. If he hadn't been in the con business, he could have made a fortune selling southern fried chicken. In April, 1916, he called a press conference at his home in Farmingdale, Long Island, N.Y. He announced that he had invented a substance that, when mixed with water, turned into gasoline. To be exact, one ounce of Louie's green substance, plus one gallon of water, produced a gallon of gas. Louie said the cost worked out to be a penny a gallon. To prove his point he showed the assembled reporters a four-cylinder car. He told them to examine it any way they wanted. Then he gave them a couple of ounces of his green liquid. The reporters themselves mixed it with water and poured it in the tank. Much to their surprise, the engine turned over and they drove away. The skeptical New York reporters poked and picked at that car, but couldn't find anything wrong with it. They didn't even trust Louie's water. They got some of their own from another source. The car seemed to love the concoction, and chugged merrily along.

The next day the story was front page news in all the papers. The U.S. government, as well as the industrial giants of the country, sought audiences with the great man. In England, parliament claimed that if the invention was made available to the British, it would win the war for them. In the middle of all this favorable publicity, a chemistry professor at Columbia University named Thomas B. Fraes released the following statement — "There is absolutely no known chemical or combination of chemicals that can be added to water to make the water combustible."

Louie countered that jealousy would get Fraes nowhere.

Then, who should show up at Louie's house, in a Ford, of course, but dear Henry himself. Gracious host that he was, Louie served Henry some tea. Then he gave Ford the same demonstration as the reporters. Henry F. drooled. He stayed with Louie for four days. Skeptical and suspicious, Ford finally satisfied himself that the invention was on the level. He wrote Louie out a cheque for $10,000 as a good will gesture, with the understanding that details of a contract and the exact price would be worked out later.

Louie made sure the news of Ford's involvement leaked to the press. Once the magic of Ford's name was coupled to the invention there was no suppressing Louie or the public's interest. Investment money started to arrive at Louie's house with the daily mail delivery. Everyone wanted to get into the act. Louie said thanks, but no thanks. He was out for bigger game.

Hiram Maxim's daddy had invented the machine gun. He ran the huge Maxim Munitions Works in New Jersey. With a war raging in Europe, to say Hiram was rich would be the understatement of the century. He was loaded. Hiram went to see if he could make a deal with Louie. After seeing the demonstration and putt-putting around Farmingdale in Louie's car, he became a believer. Maxim wrote out a cheque for $100,000; and in addition provided funds to build a lab to produce the green liquid beside Louie's house. The cumbersome details were to be worked out later. One of the details was a further payment of $900,000 when the first commercial batch of the miracle substance was produced.

Louie sent the furious Ford his $10,000 back. He never even cashed the cheque.

Six months went by, and the laboratory was built. Maxim started to have misgivings. It seems Louie, who by now was well over 70, started to spend an appreciable amount of time at the racetrack. He also liked to dip into the sauce on occasion. Not terribly bad habits for the average joker, but rather cavalier for a guy who was to revolutionize the world.

It now was a year since the reporters first met in Farmingdale. The U.S. had entered the war, and Hiram Maxim had the large and profitable task of providing his country with the necessary weapons. He lost interest in Louie and called off the deal.

Benjamin Franklin Yoakum was the next wheel to approach Louie. In case you haven't heard of Yoakum, he wasn't L'il Abner's dad. He merely was the past president of the St. Louis and San Francisco Railroad. Benjamin took in the impressive demonstration and as fast as you could say "sucker", he became Louie's partner. He put up $100,000 in cold cash. The only thing that bothered Yoakum was Louie's age. He wanted assurance that should Louie go to that great refinery in the sky, the secret formula would be turned over to him. Louie issued a sealed envelope to Farmingdale's First National Bank to be placed in a safety deposit box. It took two keys to open the box, one held by Louie and the other by Yoakum. Should Louie die in the meantime, Yoakum was to have his key.

Benjamin was so enthused that he went to the president of the United States, Woodrow Wilson, and offered the secret to the U.S. government. Wilson sent some army brass to see Louie's demonstration, and like everyone who went before them, they too were extremely impressed. Everyone became so excited by the idea of gasoline for a penny a gallon that Louie had to start stalling the eager beavers.

Finally, because of the stalls, Yoakum became suspicious and had Louie investigated. It was discovered that our hero was seen in the company of Franz Von Papen, the German spy, who had been stationed in Washington before the U.S. entered the war. Yoakum claimed that Louie was a German spy. His influence was such that he got the Supreme Court to issue an order to open the safety deposit box. All that was found inside were a few Liberty Bonds. Yoakum wanted Louie charged with treason. He couldn't come up with enough evidence to have Louie indicted on the charge.

It was estimated that Louie took in almost half a million dollars in the four years he played the game. He was finally nailed on a grand larceny charge, and was sentenced to seven years in prison. Now a frail old man, he was released after serving a year. A short time after his release, he died of natural causes.

What in tarnation made that car run when Louie mixed an ounce of his green solution with a gallon of water?

In the end, it took a great one like Thomas Edison to solve the mystery. He experimented extensively and found that acetone and acetylene, when combined with a dash of Prussic acid to neutralize the offensive odor of the acetylene, could turn over an engine when mixed with water. The new product did have some basic drawbacks. For starters, it was more expensive than gasoline; and for finishers, it would corrode a motor.

Louis Enright was one smart cookie to have come up with the product, and secondly to have pulled one over on everyone, including the government of the United States. On the other hand, there is still a lingering doubt. There are those who believe that it is conceivable that Louie stumbled onto the real thing.

AN ENGINE THAT WOULD RUN ON WATER

Seldom has anyone pulled the wool over the eyes of the entire scientific community and managed to get away with it. There was one loveable, tall, skinny con artist who succeeded where others failed.

John Worrell Keely had a rather unique scientific background. He had been a musician, carpenter, and circus performer. In short John didn't know an atom from a hole in the ground. Perhaps it was his ignorance of anything scientific which enabled him, on Nov. 10, 1874, to hold a preposterous meeting. At this meeting, he had gathered together a gaggle of hard nosed businessmen and scientists. The conference was held in John's laboratory on North 20th St. in Philadelphia. Looking dignified in his laboratory smock, John informed his audience that he had invented a machine which had unlimited possibilities. He explained that in essence he had invented an engine which would run on water and sound. What's more, he intended to demonstrate his revolutionary invention before their very eyes.

True to his word John unveiled his strange apparatus. He poured a pint of water into one of the machine's cylinders. Then he tapped a sort of tuning fork which was attached to the transmitter. Miracle of miracles, the motor turned and the amazed audience strained their collective necks for a better look. Further demonstrations quickly followed. Adjusting attachments to his apparatus John showed how, with only a pint of water, his motor could bend metal bars and cut wooden logs.

A few of the more dubious scientific types looked for subterfuge. Was there a hidden source of power? None could be found.

The invention had the potential to revolutionize the entire world. Some spoilsports asked an embarrassing question. Just how did the machine work? Let's let John tell it:

> "Molecular vibration is involved. The atoms and molecules are oscillated by sympathetic equilibrium. All matter consists of atomic triplets, and when I apply harmonies there is etheric disintegration. It is that simple and that complex."

So there.

The very next day John's lawyer, Charles B. Collier, held a second meeting. This time the audience consisted solely of bankers, investors and wealthy merchants. Collier explained that another group had already invested $280,000 in the proposed new company he had in mind to manufacture and market the new invention. The opportunity to invest the balance of the funds required would be given to this very gathering. Within a week the financial wizards coughed up $100,000 in cash. The Keely Motor Co. was formed, with John as president and Collier as treasurer. Within a few months the company had sold a further cool million dollars worth of stock.

In keeping with his new found station in life John moved into a modern, luxurious home. Occasionally he would be asked to elaborate on the actual theory which made his motor work. He always used mumbo jumbo, but in essence he would explain that ether was an integral part of all matter. This ether held molecules and atoms of molecules together. The nuclei of atoms were kept in place by ether. John claimed that he had developed a way to separate the molecules so that ether was released in a violent manner. This violence had a cumulative effect which smashed atoms and in turn released their ether, producing a still more powerful reaction. The tuning fork apparatus supposedly started the whole process when it was struck, giving off sound waves.

There were a few dissenting voices, but no one listened to them. The truth is that everyone wanted the new invention to be legitimate. Sales of stock in the new company sold briskly, and the money poured in.

Months drifted by, with no more detailed description or demonstration of how the revolutionary new invention worked. After the months turned into a year, newspapers got on John's tail and began to hint that there might be a fly in the ointment. Another few years went by and John and his new engine slowly began to lose credibility.

In 1878, his investors held a meeting which would have tolled the death knell for a lesser man. John, incredibly, guaranteed his backers that he would have a production model ready in three months. The banker types poured in still more cash. Two years later another meeting was called. This time John explained that he had miscalculated the time necessary to properly develop his new engine. Just a little more time was required. His investors gave him a vote of confidence, but by now the scientific community was openly questioning the legitimacy of the machine which would change the world.

It is a tribute to John's guile that he held his investors in the palm of his hand. They urged him to share his secret with someone else, so that in case anything happened to him, someone would be able to carry on. When John heard this, he knew he had them hook, line and sinker.

In 1882, a lady entered our hero's life. Mrs. Clara Bloomfield Moore was a wealthy Philadelphian whose husband had died, leaving her a fortune. She became enthralled with John and his invention. She believed that she had stumbled upon a way to become instrumental in changing the world. She started right off passing over large chunks of money to John to contribute toward perfecting his motor.

The presence of Mrs. Moore made John's other investors nervous. They now insisted on appointing someone who would be entrusted with the secret. John was forced to agree. They appointed a not too bright mechanic named William Boekel. He spent five months with John in his laboratory. Then he emerged and stated that everything was 100% on the up and up, and that he understood the theories which were the basis for the invention. The statement kept the suckers at bay for months.

In the meantime John was a busy boy. He got in touch with the army and told them he had a revolutionary new gun which might be of interest. It wasn't long before John was demonstrating the new weapon before the army brass. For all the world it looked like a plain steel tube. John opened a stop cock, poured in what he said was ether, and shut it tight. Then he hit the steel tube. A cartridge exploded, with the bullet striking a target 500 yards away. Several more rounds were fired in front of the startled audience. The steel rod was examined and poked at by army personnel. John received a fantastic press and shares in his motor company again took off.

One reporter did mention that he thought the rod was filled with compressed air, with which anyone could make a gun fire. His dissenting criticism was lost in the crescendo of enthusiasm for the amazing new weapon.

Years passed. Through it all, John lived extremely well without working. Mrs. Moore, now his out and out patron, was constantly at his side with her open purse.

In 1894, Mrs. Moore couldn't stand to see her dear friend and companion being the object of suspicion. She decided, once and for all, to end the speculation. The well known scientist, Edward A. Scott, was hired by Mrs. Moore to investigate John's laboratory and report back to her. Scott claimed that a thin platinum tube which supposedly carried sound waves from the tuning device to the motor, was actually hollow. It was really a tube which carried compressed air to activate the motor. Scott gave John some credit. He confessed that he was unable to find the source of the compressed air, but was sure it was stored somewhere on the premises.

John vehemently denied Scott's accusations. Another scientist, who was hastily brought into the lab, claimed the whole operation was legitimate. This announcement served to keep the wolf away from the door for several more months.

By now, John was approaching 70. He suffered from diseased kidneys, and on Nov. 18, 1898, the old rascal died. Four months later he was followed to the grave by Mrs. Moore. Her son rented John's old lab, and with the aid of engineers practically took it apart piece by piece. Buried under the floor they found a huge cylinder of compressed air. A hollow platinum tube led from the cylinder to the room, entering through the hollow legs of the platform holding the tuning device. Compressed air was the hidden power with which John had managed to hoodwink the scientific community for 24 years.

Years later a chap named Albert Einstein published his theories of relativity, which eventually led to the harnessing of atomic energy. Albert did it all without resorting to the use of ether or compressed air.

THE ARTFUL DODGER

I was pushed along by the crowd as I walked up the steps of the Rijksmuseum in Amsterdam. I entered the building and was engulfed by the same emotion that I felt upon entering Westminster Abbey in London; but this building does not house the famous dead of a nation. It contains, instead, the beauty and splendor of a country's art.

I was transfixed by the intensity of the overpowering "Nightwatch" by Rembrandt. "Winterlandscape" by Hendrick Avercamp held me spellbound with its fascinating detail. Room after room of the old Dutch masters passed before my gaze, and then I saw the work of the artist I had travelled so far to see. It was this artist, Jan Vermeer, who inadvertently inspired the greatest forgery in history.

In 1927, at the age of 38, Hans van Meegeren was a struggling painter in The Hauge. His paintings, while technically superb, were not in demand, and as a result didn't warrant much of a price. By 1930, van Meegeren discovered that his natural style closely resembled that of the old master, Vermeer. By applying himself, he found that he could produce a painting in the exact style of Vermeer. His were not forgeries of existing paintings, but original works that could pass as those of Vermeer. He discovered that authentic Vermeers were not that common. Only about 40 are known to exist. Every so often one is discovered in an attic or old barn.

By 1932 van Meegeren was constantly studying Vermeer's methods and materials. He purchased old canvasses used during the 17th century when Vermeer actually painted and removed all the paint from the canvasses. In this way he obtained authentic blank canvasses. He hardened and aged the paint by baking it in an oven at a precise temperature for an exact length of time.

After four years of tedious study of techniques, methods, and materials, he produced what was to pass as a genuine Vermeer. Van Meegeren titled his painting "Christ at Emmaus" and set off for Amsterdam. He told an art dealer there that he found it in the attic of a wealthy family in France, claiming that they had disposed of a number of paintings to him and this one was thrown in with the lot. The art dealer, who was an expert, examined the painting and declared it was an authentic Vermeer.

Later it was exhibited so that art dealers and experts from all over Holland could view and examine this major new find. All agreed to its authenticity. They even attributed the painting to a certain period in the artist's life.

Van Meegeren had created an original Vermeer. While the same painting under his own name would bring $150, he sold this painting for $250,000. In 1940, Holland was occupied by the German army. Van Meegeren discovered that the conquering Germans were enthusiastic collectors of Dutch art. He obliged them by producing five more masterpieces between 1940 and 1945. Hermann Goering acquired one for a whopping $600,000. The invading Germans had made van Meegeren a bona fide millionaire. He lived in a huge home, owned several businesses, as well as a substantial amount of property.

When Allied troops defeated Germany, a commission was formed to return confiscated works of art to their rightful owners. It seems there was this one Vermeer in Goering's collection that could not be traced. After a lengthy investigation the trail led to van Meegeren. No one questioned the authenticity of the painting, but everyone thought he had traded with the enemy. The charge that could be brought against him was treason, which was punishable by death.

Van Meegeren spent one night in jail. The next day he knew that the only way to combat the treason charge was to tell the complete truth. He told the police that Goering's Vermeer had been painted by himself, and also confessed to painting his other Vermeers. The experts couldn't admit to being fooled. They had subjected the paintings to every scientific test without uncovering any peculiarities. Van Meegeren claimed that he had committed no crime. He had never said that the paintings were by Vermeer, nor had he put a price tag on them. By merely presenting them for sale, the experts had authenticated them and offered him the fabulous prices he received. The art world of Europe was embarrassed. The police delicately released van Meegeren. In fact, some considered him a hero for putting one over on Goering.

Newly developed testing techniques uncovered that the Vermeers were recently painted. At last, the experts agreed that van Meegeren was what he claimed to be. To further satisfy themselves the Dutch government got a panel of experts together to officially settle the dispute. They settled it all right. Every painting van Meegeren claimed to have done was exposed to have been painted by him and not Vermeer.

Public opinion was so strong in favor of van Meegeren the authorities did not know which way to turn. He had fooled the experts in a country renowned for its knowledge of art. He had even bluffed the hated Germans. The little artist was a national hero.

Still, some penalty had to be meted out. They decided to prosecute him for forging Vermeer's signature. The sympathetic court found him guilty and sentenced him to one year imprisonment. The strain of being exposed and his lengthy court appearances proved too much for van Meegeren. In January of 1947, three months after his trial and before he could officially start serving his sentence, he passed away.

Room 227 of the Rijksmuseum features the paintings of Jan Vermeer. I couldn't help but linger. "Young Woman Reading a Letter" is a thrill to see. Vermeer must have painstakingly toiled at the canvas over 300 years ago. That is. . . . unless . . . naw, it couldn't be. . . .

HE FOOLED THE GESTAPO

It is difficult to say why children are attracted to certain vocations. More than one proud parent has pointed to a son, now a doctor, and remarked that it seems like only yesterday that the little boy was playing with his toy doctor set.

Elfreid Schmidt's parents thought that young Elfreid spent far too much time down at the streetcar terminal. He was always poking into the machinery to see what made it tick. Still, there was no harm in letting the boy indulge himself. A young lad growing up in Vienna in the 1930s had little time for his own pleasure. The ominous German war machine was infringing on the everyday lives of the average citizen. While Elfreid's family realized that their son had outstanding mechanical ability, they unfortunately didn't have the funds to enable him to attend university. He would have made a fine engineer. Instead, he became an expert draftsman, an inventor, and an apprentice locksmith.

In 1938, at the age of 19, Elfreid's life seemed destined to unfold like that of millions of young people throughout the war-threatened world. First, there was the problem of survival and then, hopefully, a normal life. Elfreid had a girlfriend, Elsa, who felt the same way.

There were problems. The Nazis were suspicious of anyone who didn't conform to the party line. Priests were among these citizens who were suspect. Elfreid's uncle was a priest, and there was a real possibility that he and other members of the family, including Elfreid, could be hauled off to a concentration camp by the Gestapo.

It was this fear for his uncle's welfare which first put the thought in Elfreid's mind. Ridiculous, insane, maybe so, but Elfreid Schmidt decided to deceive the Gestapo. While thousands shivered at the mere mention of the word, Elfreid decided to walk headlong into the lion's den. He would make the great German war machine jump at his beck and call.

The very next day he put his plan into action. Elfreid had made a blueprint of a diesel railcar some months before. It was so impressive, his uncle, the priest, had hung it in his home. Elfreid took the blueprint down. Then he purchased several rubber stamps, and sat down to write some letters. Letter number one was from Elfreid asking the German State Railroad to consider the enclosed blueprint. Letter number two was from the German State Railroad informing Elfreid that his blueprint had been sent along to the Ministry of Transport in Berlin. Letter number three was from the State Railroad to Elfreid, praising the blueprint in the most complimentary way possible. Modesty was not one of Elfreid's most prominent traits. Finally, there was a letter to Elfreid from the State Railroad advising him that a factory had been chosen to produce his diesel railcar. Accompanying this letter was an application for employment at a salary in keeping with his outstanding engineering abilities.

A few years earlier, Elfreid had had some experience in corresponding with official government agencies. The letters he manufactured were perfect in every detail. He was cunning enough to keep the original blueprint. To anyone studying the blueprint, it appeared that it had gone through several government departments. Across its face were official rubber stamp markings with words like "Received" and "Approved". Obviously, copies had been made and the original returned. Elfreid hung the blueprint up on the wall. It was now a more impressive document than ever.

In the meantime, Elfreid heard rumors that the Gestapo was going to arrest his uncle. He had to act fast. Our hero sat down and created his *piece de resistance.* He had no trouble obtaining a copy of the University of Berlin's letterhead. He then wrote himself a letter from the University, stating that they took great pleasure in informing him that the Fuhrer, Adolph Hitler, had bestowed upon him the title of Honorary Engineer. On Aug. 25, at precisely 11 a.m., he was to be received by the Fuhrer at the Reich Chancellery.

Elfreid, who knew a thing or two about human nature, tried out the letter on some friends. They stumbled over themselves congratulating him. The word spread like wildfire. He became something of a celebrity, and no Gestapo agent would monkey around with the uncle of someone who was being honored by the Fuhrer.

Once the wheels of Elfreid's ruse were spinning, there was no turning back. On Aug. 24, the inventor of the revolutionary railcar left for Berlin. He stayed in the capitol city for three days, spending his time sightseeing. He found a postcard with a description of Hitler's office, and sent letters back home about his unusual experiences. Elfreid manufactured a phony diploma, complete with swastikas and eagles. Naturally, he presented it to himself.

By the time Elfreid returned home, his fame had spread far and wide. Top Nazi officials organized rounds of social functions for him. Elfreid gulped and took on an air of condescending aloofness. While not a polished public speaker, he managed to develop a pretty fair patter describing his private meeting with Hitler. Elfreid discovered that he could elicit a few ohs and ahs from his audience by letting them know that Hitler had given him his ultra secret telephone number. Elfreid loved to drop the line, "And then the Fuhrer said to me, 'If you ever need me, don't hesitate to give me a call.'"

Everyone fell hook, line and sinker for the locksmith's scam. No one raised the semblance of a doubt. Of course, Elfreid, once he had a taste of power and respect, did everything to hold on to his new station in life. He managed to get his hands on a German Army uniform. While he was at it, he picked a smart major's uniform, but Elfreid was no dummy. He dreaded the thought of ever getting caught impersonating an officer. He doctored up the uniform with some braid here and ornate cord there. When asked about his strange uniform, he made up fantastic lies about the different insignias. Everyone was impressed when he told them his silver cord was the rare silver honor cord of the Third Reich, and had been presented to him by Hitler himself. Elfreid loved to see those colonels come to attention and dash off a snappy salute.

It wasn't all fun and games. Elfreid put his new-found fame and power to practical use. He produced an ornate card for himself which stated that he was the recipient of the Silver Honor Cord from the Fuhrer. All members of the Armed Services and all government officials were to assist him in any way possible. He would produce the card without hestitation to keep an acquaintance out of jail or get medicine for a sick friend. The card never failed to achieve the desired results.

Elfreid stretched his luck about as far as it would go. When he heard that a friend of his mother's, Herr Huber, was shipped off to notorious Dachau, he took matters into his own hands. Mustering up every ounce of courage, he stormed into Vienna's tenth district headquarters and stared eyeball-to-eyeball with a top Nazi official. Pulling out all stops, Elfreid informed the Nazi that Herr Huber had been sent to the dreaded death camp because a personal enemy wanted to confiscate his business. Just last week the Fuhrer had told him that he frowned on such practices. Elfreid gave the official 48 hours to produce Herr Huber, or Hitler himself would hear of the entire matter. The official stuttered. Herr Huber was released and later made his way to Hungary and eventual safety. By using his influence, Elfreid saved scores of people from certain death.

On Nov. 2, 1938, Elfreid Schmidt was drafted into the Luftwaffe. You would think the jig would be up, but it was possible for Elfreid to take his training without his new buddies knowing they had a decorated honorary engineer in their midst.

When a Vienna newspaper did a feature article on the famous locksmith, Elfreid figured he was finished. Upon returning to his barracks, his captain was waiting. Instead of being shot, he was congratulated. Elfreid swiftly sized up the situation. He modestly informed the captain that he hadn't revealed his illustrious past because he wanted no favors. He just wanted to be treated like his buddies. The captain put his arm around Elfreid's trembling shoulders and almost wept with pride for his modest private.

While Elfreid didn't want favors, it was impossible for him to be treated like the other men. His captain insisted that he wear his phony Silver Honor Cord over his uniform. He was not allowed to work, and was told that he could come and go as he pleased. Later he was transferred and assigned to the office of Col.-Gen. Edward von Lohr, who insisted on putting his private Mercedes at Elfreid's disposal.

On Feb. 16, 1939, after seven months of subterfuge, it all came to an end. Elfreid was called into the General's office. A routine check had disclosed that he had never been decorated by Hitler. Accused of being a spy, he was tossed into a military jail. Elfreid, who had his head screwed on right, knew that he had to make up a plausible excuse for being a phony decorated engineer. He wrote his girlfriend, Elsa, telling her that everything he had done had been to impress her. Elfreid knew the letter would end up being studied by his keepers. He was right, and what's more, they believed every word.

On May 25, Elfreid Schmidt appeared before a Luftwaffe court. It was a strange trial. Even those straitlaced military types had wide smiles on their faces. Occasionally they broke into laughter. It was obvious that the court had received instructions to sweep the whole thing under the rug. Elfreid was an embarrassment, and as such was to be given no further publicity. He received a total of six months in prison for assorted offences. As he had already served three months awaiting trial, he was released in 90 days.

Elfreid served in the Luftwaffe until the war's end. Later he married and when last heard of was working as a conductor on a streetcar in Vienna.

DRUGS WERE HIS GAME

The story of Philip Musica could be held up as the typical American success story. Phil started with nothing and rose in the financial world until he controlled one of the oldest and most respected companies in the U.S. Phil had a secret. You see, he also was a thief, a confidence man and fraud.

Antonio and Maria Musica had scrimped and saved for years to raise the money for passage to America. At last, in 1890, they bundled up their only offspring, six-year-old Philip, for the crossing from Naples to New York. The voyage apparently agreed with Maria. As soon as she arrived in America, she started having more children. Louise, Grace, Arthur, George, and Robert were added to the Musica menagerie.

Once in the land of milk and honey, Antonio met with success of another kind. He opened a small grocery store and managed to make a moderate living. As the years went by, his first born, black haired, good looking Phil, helped him in his business. By the time Phil was 21, he felt he and his father were ready for bigger and better things. By gathering every cent they could lay their hands on, the two Musicas opened an importing business under the rather uninspired name of A. Musica and Son. The firm specialized in imported Italian foods.

Phil, cunning rascal that he was, had a scheme. It was simple enough. He had false bills of lading and false invoices made up for each shipment he received. He knew a customs inspector who was on the take. The customs inspector substituted the phony documents for the real thing. The bogus documents were made out for far less weight than what had actually been shipped. When Phil took delivery of his imported foodstuffs, he paid tax on the lower weight, thus paying taxes on only a fraction of what he imported. He sold his wares at substantially lower prices than his competitors.

A. Musica and Son prospered. Soon, sales topped the half million dollar mark. For nine years the firm grew. Phil and his parents moved from the lower East side slums to a luxurious home in Brooklyn.

Phil dressed immaculately, owned a fine team of horses, attended the opera, and even became a friend of the great Enrico Caruso. Unfortunately, in 1909 the scheme was exposed, and both father and son were indicted. Antonio beat the rap, but Phil was fined $5,000 and served five and a half months in Elmira Reformatory.

Upon his release Phil opened a human hair business, and quickly embezzled a total of $600,000 from 22 different banks. The scam was clumsy and below Phil's potential talents in such matters. He was exposed and incarcerated for three years.

A dapper, suave, more cautious middle-aged man emerged from jail. Phil changed his name to F. Donald Coster. He opened a small hair preparation factory in Mount Vernon, N.Y., under the name Girard & Co. This time he gathered his younger brothers into the business. They all took new names. Arthur became George Vernard, George became George Dietrich, and Robert became Robert Dietrich.

Prohibition was in effect, and Girard & Co. was allotted 5,000 gallons of alcohol a month to manufacture their hair preparations. Naturally, they had to account for the sale of every drop. Here is how they did it. Girard & Co.'s biggest customer for the product was W.W. Smith & Co. In reality, W.W. Smith & Co. consisted of a one-room office in Brooklyn manned by George Vernard. W.W. Smith & Co. would receive the allotment of alcohol and sell it to bootleggers for cash. George would then write a cheque to Girard & Co. When the feds checked the books, Girard & Co. could show orders for the sale of the alcohol, and cheques for payment. Nearly $8 million passed through W.W. Smith's bank account in the ensuing years.

In 1924, Coster got the bright idea to have an audit performed on Girard & Co. He hired Price, Waterhouse & Co., no less. That's when our boy discovered that all that time auditors didn't check stock. It seemed so simple. You could adjust profit by adjusting stock, if no one ever checked. Coster wanted to expand. His bankers introduced him to a Wall St. analyst, Julian Thompson. Coster supplied Thompson with a list of firms he did business with as references. One of the names on the list was W.W. Smith. Had Thompson checked, he would have found out about the one room in Brooklyn, but he never bothered to check the list.

Thompson introduced Coster to the Bridgeport City Trust Co. They loaned Girard & Co. $80,000 and bought a further $27,500 worth of Girard & Co. stock. The company moved to Bridgeport. In 1925, they had sales of $1 million, with profits of $250,000. Coster was astute enough to repay his bank loan.

The following year F. Donald Coster took dead aim at McKesson & Robbins, an old established respectable middle-sized firm which had been incorporated in 1833. Coster handed over a cheque for $1,100,000, and took over McKesson and Robbins.

As soon as they took over the company, Coster and his brother George began their swindle. They confined it to crude drugs. No matter what quantity of drugs were sold, phony paperwork always adjusted McKesson & Robbins inventory to produce huge profits. Non-existent warehouses were set up in Montreal and throughout the U.S. Twice a year, when Price Waterhouse sent a letter requesting verification of quantities in the warehouses, a secretary would send back the proper answers. This was the only function she performed during the entire year.

In 1928, Coster approached his old Wall St. friend, Julian Thompson. He wanted to take over the major drug jobbers in the U.S. With Thompson's help he managed to get the backing of two investment houses and pull off the merger. Forty-nine of the largest wholesale jobbers in the U.S. now came under the ownership of McKesson & Robbins and F. Donald Coster. Our boy now controlled $80 million in sales of distributed drugs and $5 million in manufactured items. Of course, he also controlled the phony crude division, which always made tremendous profits, no matter what the economic conditions.

In 1937, the directors of the company instructed the company to convert several million dollars of crude drug stock into cash. Julian Thompson had left Wall St. to become McKesson & Robbins controller. It was his job to see that the crude drugs were converted to cash. He took to bugging Coster to sell off the crude drugs. Naturally, Coster couldn't do it. The drugs didn't exist.

By chance, at this very crucial time in their affairs, Thompson noted that although there was $21 million worth of crude drugs on the books, not a dollar was being spent on insurance. When he questioned Coster, he was told that W.W. Smith carried the insurance. Thompson decided to look further into the affairs of W.W. Smith. A trip to Montreal uncovered a fictitious warehouse. An even shorter trip to Brooklyn revealed that one room office. Thompson, who had known nothing of the giant swindle, returned to Bridgeport and confronted Coster. For he first time in 15 years, he realized that he was associated with a master crook.

Coster accused Thompson of trying to ruin McKesson & Robbins. Thompson reported the company's true financial condition to the N.Y. Stock Exchange. That same day, trading in shares of the company was suspended. Within a week F. Donald Coster was exposed as the former convict, Philip Musica.

Straightening out the company's affairs took months. It is estimated that the fleecing had amounted to close to $8 million. The only restitution Coster-Musica ever made was the proceeds of his yacht and a piece of land totalling $51,000. The rest was never recovered.

On Dec. 15, 1938, Philip Musica went into the bathroom of his home in Fairfield, stood against the bathtub and placed a revolver to his head. The force of the shot dropped his body neatly into the tub.

After his suicide, it was found that only the crude drug division of the company was crooked. The rest of the organization was on a sound financial basis. The company gradually recovered, and today is one of the leading drug houses in the U.S. In 1977, the company's sales amounted to $306 million, or over a million dollars for every working day of the year.

RAGS TO RICHES
TO RAGS

Suave businessmen, sophisticated in the ways of finance, have conned respectable companies out of millions of dollars. Smooth as glass con men have perpetrated swindles that would make you wince. It is not often that just plain folks pull off the big con. Ernest and Margaret Medders were about as plain as vanilla ice cream on a Sunday afternoon.

After spending all of his 51 years in Memphis, Tenn., the best we can say of Ernie is that he was of average height, average weight, and average looks. Let's face it, Ernie didn't stand out in a crowd. In 1961 he was managing to keep bread on the table by the sweat of his brow as a mechanic's helper at Gulf Oil. His remuneration from Gulf was the munificent sum of $200 per month. Sometimes Ernie peddled vegetables to make ends meet.

Margaret didn't have a lazy bone in her body. Besides having her hands full looking after her 10 children, she worked as a practical nurse at St. Joseph's Hospital in Memphis. The Medders existed without the finer things in life in a low rental housing project.

Margaret and Ernie were honest hard working folks. You can be the judge as to whether they were cunning con artists or not.

One fine afternoon, while Ernie was slugging grease at the oil company, and Margaret was hustling bedpans down at the hospital, they were informed that they were to become the plaintiffs in a major lawsuit. A clever Southern lawyer was filing a suit on behalf of 3,000 plaintiffs who purportedly owned a large portion of one of those huge Texas oilfields. Margaret, Ernie, and all their relatives were among the 3,000 plaintiffs.

Are you sitting down for this one? They were seeking a cool $500 million.

To give the Medders the benefit of the doubt, it is important to understand the great effect the news of the lawsuit had on them. Ernie went from one illogical step to the next. He firmly believed the plaintiffs would win the case. It was only a hop, skip and jump for his mind to rationalize the facts, so that he became convinced he would be the sole plaintiff to collect. He had no trouble at all convincing Margaret that they practically had $500 million big ones in their greedy little paws.

Margaret couldn't contain herself. She told everyone down at St. Joseph's how very fortunate they had been and how very rich they were about to become.

It took no time at all for the good Roman Catholic nuns, who ran St. Joseph's, to hear of the blessing which had befallen a member of their flock. The nuns, whose order was officially, if inappropriately, named The Poor Sisters of St. Francis Seraph of the Perpetual Adoration, may have been just that at some distant time in the past, but in 1961 they were loaded. They just ached to find a way to help Margaret over the short period of time she had left to be poor. Besides, you never know how grateful dear Margaret and Ernie would be to the holy order after they collected the pot of gold at the end of the rainbow.

The Poor Sisters commenced to loan the Medders money. At first just a trickle of a few thousands, but once they got into the swing of things, the amounts rose to over $50,000 a month.

In keeping with their new position in life, the Medders moved to Muenster, Texas. Having had enough of low rental housing, they built a house, financed, of course, by the Poor Sisters back in Tennessee. Money is a strange commodity. It takes no time at all to get used to spending it, and even less time to become accustomed to the good things it will buy.

With the Poor Sisters sending cheques of between $30,000 and $55,000 each month, the Medders reasoned, "What the heck, let's have a little fun."

The Medders purchased a 185-acre farm and built a 15-room brick home smack dab in the middle. The pool, interior decorating, and landscaping set them back about a quarter of a million dollars.

Ernie discovered that he had a fancy for Black Angus cattle, and proceeded to build a respectable herd to go with his stable of Appaloosa horses. Margaret took to money like a fish takes to water. Most of her wardrobe consisted of European originals. Bits and pieces of jewelry used up about $2,000 a month of the Poor Sisters' cash.

Mrs. Medders had a natural flair for spending money. She built her own hairdressing salon in her home just for the fun of it. Margaret's daughters were attending an exclusive finishing school in Dallas. Margaret couldn't stand the thought of their living in a drafty dormitory. She bought the girls a $40,000 home beside the school.

Then there were the parties. Ernie and Margaret knew how to throw a party. Once they had a thousand guests down to the farm, which was now complete with a huge cattle auctioning arena. Buses transporting the party goers to the farm were equipped with well-stocked bars. Charter planes delivered others from distant points. Guy Lombardo and his Royal Canadians provided the musical entertainment.

Despite his limited knowledge of ranching, Ernie found that after a few years his cattle raising venture was turning a profit of over $100,000 a year. This was just a drop in the bucket compared to the fantastic amounts required to maintain the Medders' lifestyle. Most of the tab for all the fun and games was still being picked up by the Poor Sisters.

Perhaps the pinnacle of the Medders' fabulous plunge into the good life occurred in April, 1966. Ernie and Margaret now numbered among their friends the Governor of Texas, John Connally. Through contributing to Democratic causes and their personal relationship with Connally, they attended a ball in Houston honoring President Lyndon Johnson. Believe it or not, Margaret and Ernie were invited to attend a reception at the White House the following week.

On May 4, the practical nurse and the mechanic's helper flew to Washington to be the guests of the President of the United States. During the course of the evening, President Johnson discovered that the Medders were leaving town the following day. He volunteered that he was going to Texas, and would the Medders like a lift on the Presidential jet. Would they? Wild horses couldn't have kept them away. Next day the Medders flew home on Air Force One.

Just after this highlight in the Medders' lives, those spoilsports, the Poor Sisters, informed them that they had been cut off from the fountain of cash. The order of nuns had wakened up to the fact that they had been taken. The decision was made to keep the lid on the whole thing. The nuns did not plan to take any action against the Medders.

At this time, Ernie was making real money at his cattle operation. They could still come up covered with roses if only they could curtail their irresponsible extravagances. It was too late. They had become accustomed to wealth. The parties continued.

Ernie invited 1,200 kids to his ranch for a horse show. He also threw a huge party for Jeane Dixon, the Washington clairvoyant. Now that the Poor Sisters had cut them off, the Medders simply borrowed from banks, until they too refused to advance them another penny. Margaret still managed to decorate her person with a $70,000 necklace, a $60,000 ring, and a mink coat valued at $55,000.

Pressed for payments by everyone, they had to confess that they were broke. The old lawsuit, which had managed to stay in court for years, was finally thrown out. There would be no inheritance. The Medders were forced into bankruptcy. Their assets were stripped from them in order to make partial payments to their creditors. It is estimated the Poor Sisters are poorer by $2 million. Other sundry creditors totalled a further million.

When last heard from the Medders were back in Memphis, living on social security.

THAT OLD TIME RELIGION

The religion industry ranks right up there with the stock market for giving rise to more swindlers and charlatans than any other group of individuals toiling under the guise of legitimacy. Down through the years phony saviors have managed to line their pockets at the expense of the innocent, the insecure, and the ignorant.

One of the very first to stumble onto the religion business in the United States was Robert Matthews. Robert first saw the light of day in upper New York State at the turn of the 19th century. He took to religion as naturally as a duck takes to water.

He wasn't yet in his teens when he discovered that dark summer clouds were sometimes followed by thunder. Often Robert would scare the living daylights out of his friends by telling them that his relatives in heaven would soon be roaring at them. When a clap of thunder sounded across the skies, it seemed proof positive to the youngsters that cunning Robert did indeed have supernatural powers.

It was a revelation to Robert when one of the children offered him his candy if he could make the bad noise go away. As the song was later to proclaim, Robert knew that this could be the start of something big.

Robert took on a pious air, and by the time he was 16 everyone called him Jumping Jesus. A few years later his hair turned prematurely white. Never one to waste an opportunity, Robert let it grow down past his shoulders. His impressive white luxuriant beard flowed to below his belly button. Robert really looked like a cool cat.

He took to extolling the virtues of vegetarianism, and was downright adamant in his attitude toward liquor and tobacco. In 1820, he had succeeded in gathering a modest following, but the big bucks still eluded him. For six years he struggled at the religion business before he got his big break.

His first step was to call himself Prophet Matthias, which everyone agreed had a better ring to it than Robert Matthews. He travelled to what was then Batavia, and is now Buffalo. By accident he started to preach against all service clubs and secret orders. The poor, who couldn't afford to belong to such organizations, were quick to follow the Prophet.

This was all very good except for one thing, which the Prophet couldn't condone. All his followers were poor.

As the old bank robber, Willie Sutton, once said when he was asked why he robbed banks, "Because that's where the money is", Prophet Matthias took off for New York City, because that's where the money was.

Once in the Big Apple, phony Prophet Matthias preached that he was really God on earth. A well educated merchant, Sylvester Mills, fell for the Prophet's line. Within a month, what Sylvester had belonged to Prophet Matthias, and what Matthias had belonged to himself. The Prophet's physical appearance underwent an abrupt change. He now wore bracelets and necklaces of pure gold. He worse silk blouses and velvet caps adorned with half moons and stars.

The Prophet Matthias operated out of Mills' home, which had been turned into a temple. Some close relatives of Mills' thought his religious fervor had gone far enough. They swore they would have the gullible Sylvester committed unless he banished the Prophet from his home. Mills succumbed to his relatives' wishes. Before doing so, he introduced the holy one to another religious fanatic, Elijah Pierson. This latest believer had just retired from the retail business. Both he and his friend, Benjamin Folger, were loaded.

It took only a month for both men to sign over their worldly possessions to Matthews — whoops, sorry — Matthias. The Prophet, by this time, had a large, wealthy following. He had money and the respect of his people, and should have left well enough alone, but he couldn't. He wanted sex.

The Prophet Matthias came up with a terrific scheme. One fine day, when the juices were flowing, he proclaimed that he would populate the world with divine souls. Miracle of miracles, he picked Mrs. Folger, the wife of our friend Benjamin, to produce the first divine male child. Now get this, folks, Prophet Matthias would honor Mrs. Folger by providing the first seed himself. To keep old Benjamin occupied, he would be provided with a lady, and together they would produce the first female child.

Everything worked out famously. Before you could turn around, Mrs. Folger became pregnant, and the whole tribe waited for the birth of the male child. Matthias, scalliwag that he was, had accepted the fact that he was taking a fifty-fifty chance on the baby's being a boy. It wasn't. Mrs. Folger gave birth to a girl. The faithful lost their faith. It was too much. God should have been able to produce a boy.

Remember poor old Elijah Pierson? He wanted his money and property back. Elijah insisted until he became a pain in the neck. One day Matthias fed him a nice fresh batch of blackberries. Six days later, Elijah was dead. Considerate Prophet Matthias attributed the sudden death to pneumonia, and buried Elijah without notifying the civil authorities.

Then Ben Folger began to act up. He wanted his money, property, and wife back, in that order. The Prophet invited Ben to discuss it over tea. Ben took violently ill and immediately suspected that his good friend the Prophet had poisoned him. Ungrateful Ben called the police. He even went so far as to suggest that it might be a good idea to raise the dear departed Mr. Pierson, the better to find out if he had been rushed to an early grave by means of poison. Elijah's liver was found to be chock full of arsenic.

While all these annoying events were taking place, the good Prophet Matthias took off. The authorities caught up with him in Albany.

He was brought back to White Plains to stand trial for murder. Just before the trial began, the self-proclaimed God asked permission to address his now decimated flock of faithful followers. The court granted him the opportunity in the town graveyard. Still trying to pull it off, the Prophet pointed to a stone wall and declared, "I shall make this wall fall."

The faithful flock and assorted court officials almost flipped their biscuits when a portion of the wall slid away. Later, some boys let the cat out of the bag when they revealed that the Prophet had paid them to hide behind the wall and, at the proper signal, pull some loose stones away, allowing the wall to crumble.

In spite of the theatrics, Prophet Matthias' trial for the murder of Elijah Pierson went ahead as scheduled. The evidence against the Prophet was skimpy. There was no doubt about it, Elijah had been poisoned, but there was absolutely no proof that the Prophet had committed the foul deed. Reluctantly, the jury returned a verdict of not guilty.

Robert Matthews left the jurisdiction of the court, and was never heard of again.

DIAMONDS ARE FOREVER

In years gone by ladies and gentlemen of dubious character have revelled in the joy of leading the rich and famous down the gently winding garden path. Their motives have ranged from the mere fun of it all to cold, hard cash. This tasty tidbit of fraud and deception was instigated by the latter motive.

Phil Arnold entered this world in Hardin County, Kentucky in 1830. Following the prescribed well-worn path of conformity, he married, became a farmer, and commenced to raise a family. In the 1860s, the call of gold emanating from California swept the country, and Phil heeded that call.

Once in California, with a partner, John Slack, he developed a minor claim, which they sold for $50,000. Phil banked his share. He took a job as assistant bookkeeper with the Diamond Drill Co. of San Francisco, whose main function was to provide diamond tipped rock drills to producing mines. Phil became fascinated with all aspects of the diamond business. He learned all he could from his own company. Then he sent away for books and periodicals which contained further information on diamonds.

In 1871, Phil quit his job. He looked up his old partner, John Slack, and together they hatched a scheme. Phil took off for London, England, where he purchased $12,000 worth of uncut, imperfect diamonds. Slack waited for Phil in St. Louis, and the pair travelled to Arizona. They contacted Indians, who traded garnets for whiskey, and came away with a peck of the red stones. They then mixed some of the garnets with the diamonds and headed for San Francisco.

When George D. Roberts, a well-known mining promoter saw the loot, his mouth drooled and his eyes sparkled. The two men explained that they had been shown a diamond field by an Indian, whom they later killed. The field was in the midst of unfriendly Indian inhabited territory in Colorado. You couldn't just go there and dig the diamonds out of the ground. You needed an escort to ensure protection, and that took money, which Phil and Slack didn't have.

Roberts insisted that he be let in on the ground floor. He promised the prospectors that he would round up a few men with the money to take care of everything. The first man he contacted was William Ralston, a banker. Ralston was game enough, but insisted on having the diamonds examined by an expert. They were turned over to a local jeweller for appraisal. The appraisal came back with a value of $100,000. Phil had guessed correctly. He knew that no jeweller in San Francisco would know the difference between a poor uncut diamond and a good quality one. The jeweller wrongly assumed the diamonds were of top quality, and appraised them according to their size. Phil and Slack let it drop that it had only taken them a couple hours to dig up the stones. Everyone drooled.

To allay even the most suspicious minds, the two men agreed to take Ralston's representatives to the diamond field. Once there, he could dig diamonds himself. The prospectors had only one stipulation. Ralston's representative had to be blindfolded. Everyone agreed and the ridiculous party took off. Phil and Slack travelled in circles for four days, making it appear that they had travelled a great distance. Once his blindfold was removed, it didn't take the mark more than a few moments to unearth his first diamond. Within two days he had about 40 uncut diamonds in his breeches. Phil suggested they move on before Indians appeared on the scene.

Back in civilization Ralston was elated. He formed a group to finance the venture, and planned on travelling east with the two prospectors to try to entice Eastern money into the deal. The two bumpkins felt that around now some show of good faith was in order. Ralston's syndicate handed over $100,000 as good faith money.

The New Yorkers, who showed interest, were none other than bankers Henry Seligman and August Belmont. You may have heard of the illustrious August — the Belmont racetrack is named after him. These two gentlemen insisted that Charles Tiffany, of the well known jewelry firm, appraise the stones. Tiffany had never seen an uncut industrial diamond in his life. He did know, however, that back in the west the diamonds had been appraised at $100,000. He saw no reason to disagree with that appraisal.

The very evening Tiffany's appraisal was made public, Slack said he wasn't a businessman and was tired of the whole thing. He would sell out his share for $100,000, chargeable against the final purchase price. The syndicate raised the hundred big ones that very night. If you are keeping track, the two prospectors have now received $200,000.

The two men took off for England and Holland. They purchased about $50,000 worth of the lowest quality uncut diamonds they could find. Back they dashed to their diamond field, scattering diamonds with great abandon in cracks and crevices.

At this point in the scam, Slack got cold feet. He figured they had spent $10,000 in travel expenses and a further $50,000 on diamonds. He and Phil split the remaining $140,000. Slack rode into the sunset with his $70,000 safely tucked in his saddle bags, and was never heard of again.

Meanwhile, the smart moneyboys hired Henry Janin, a leading mining engineer, to accompany Phil to the diamond field. Some of the backers travelled with him. Once at the site, the men, working only with spades and knives, had great fun turning up $5,799 worth of diamonds and $2,226 worth of rubies. Janin figured the field would yield $5,000 to a ton of ore, or about five million dollars an acre. The whole operation looked to be worth billions. Janin, who was a bona fide diamond expert, had never actually visited a diamond field in his life. The diamonds were real, so who can blame him for being duped? His figures were in fact correct, except that the two prospectors had planted all the diamonds. Nature had never had a hand in any of it.

Back in San Francisco, the elated promoters formed the San Francisco and New York Mining and Commercial Co. When Phil heard how good everyone thought the mine was, he played his trump card. He told the boys he was being cheated. They told him a deal was a deal, and forced $450,000 into his chubby little hands. Grumbling, Phil reluctantly left town.

Phil went back to Kentucky and pretended to be really surprised when he heard that some surveyor had let the smart moneyboys in on the secret that no real mine existed. Phil bought himself 32 choice acres and a herd of prize-winning cattle. One day the syndicate's lawyers showed up and instituted a civil suit to collect $350,000. Finally, to get some peace and quiet, Phil settled with them for $150,000.

In all, Phil had collected $70,000, plus $450,000; adding up to a cool $520,000. His only expense was the settlement money of $150,000. Phil had pulled it off. He was rich.

Phil opened a store in Elizabethtown, Ky., as well as a bank. The bank proved to be a bad idea. He fought incessantly with the two other banks in town. One day Phil shot one of his competitors in the arm. His banking adversaries retaliated. They let Phil have it with a full charge of buckshot in the back. He was dead before he hit the ground.

Phil Arnold had taught the whole mining community a lesson. He was the last man to successfully salt a mine in the United States.

Vince Desai

Sweet Adelaide

– Part 2–

THE POISONERS

PEACHES, CREAM AND POISON

I have always maintained that poisoners, as a group, are the most cowardly of all murderers. They have at their disposal the ability to divorce themselves completely from their victim as the end draws near.

In France, back in the days of Louis XIV, poisoning was such a common occurrence that many potential victims let their pets have a generous helping of porridge before partaking themselves. There were more dead dogs in France, at that time, than there were snuffboxes.

It was quite in order for the common folk, like you and me, to administer poison to a rich parent or an unwanted lover, but heavens, that would never do for the aristocracy. No, nothing could be more uncouth. The killer managed to be twice removed from the victim. Here is how it worked.

The practice of poisoning became so fashionable that certain apothecaries, better known as pharmacists here in Canada, became well known for their ability to mix up a fatal powder in whatever strength the occasion called for. These dispensers of custom-made poisons only dealt with an elite group who administered poison. There were only about two dozen top notch poisoners in all of Europe. Like specialists in many fields today, their fees were atrocious, but the results were guaranteed.

A member of the aristocracy of France would turn over a large sum of money to the poisoner with explicit instructions as to how the deed was to be carried out, then sit back and wait for the funeral.

Now that we have established the ground rules, I would like you to meet Madame Marie de Brinvilliers, an aristocractic lady who was to become one of France's extraordinary poisoners, if not the all time champ.

Marie was born to many of the finer things of life. Her father was a wealthy government official, who saw to it that the apple of his eye attended the best private schools and generally led a life in keeping with her social standing. As if all this wasn't enough, Marie was a stunning looker, with a voluptuous figure.

Baron Antoine de Brinvilliers was the son of another highly placed government official. He was a handsome devil, who did credit to his French Army officer's uniform. The lovely Marie and the dashing Antoine became lovers and were married.

All was not peaches and cream. Heavens no. You see, both the Baron and Baroness had one thing in common. They both slept around whenever the opportunity presented itself. The records of the old case hint that right after the marriage ceremony Marie saw fit to dispense a sexual favor to one of the church officials in the vestry.

Everyone has their own moral standards. Who are we to judge? Both Marie and Antoine seemed to condone each other's promiscuous dalliances, but the situation was nevertheless a potentially explosive one. Antoine had received a large dowry from Marie's daddy, which he promptly blew on gambling and other ladies.

At just this susceptible moment, Antoine became friends with a man called Godin. It was a mistake. Godin was no sooner under Antoine's roof than he made himself comfortable under Marie's sheets. Godin and Marie became lovers, and it is certain that their affair was carried on so openly that Antoine knew that something was rotten in the State of Denmark.

Whereas Antoine didn't seem to mind the shenanigans going on in his house, Marie's aged father was furious. He arranged to have Godin arrested and thrown into the Bastille, which from early descriptions can only be compared to Toronto's Don Jail as a place where one would not care to stay for an extended period of time. While thus detained, Godin met another character, named Exile, an apothecary whose specialty it was to make nasty little white powders which killed. Wouldn't you know it, Godin and Exile became good friends while passing the time of day in the Bastille.

When both men were released, Godin provided Exile with a home in return for all the little secrets of the poisoner's trade. He passed along these juicy tidbits to his mistress, Marie. Why, you might ask, did Marie want such information? Because her ever loving daddy was becoming a nuisance, that's why. It was getting so that a girl couldn't hit the hay with whomever she desired. Besides, daddy had all that lovely cash, just when hubby Antoine was running short. Daddy had to go.

Immediately after the lovers made their momentous decision, Daddy came down with a rather mysterious malady. His loving daughter was at his bedside throughout, but it was no use. After a short but painful illness, Daddy died.

Marie went wild. She had money, a husband, a lover, or should we say lovers; for Marie, the passionate one, did not confine her horizontal activities exclusively to Godin.

The path of true love never runs smooth. Now, Marie's two brothers objected to her way of life. Impetuously, one day, she dashed off a note to Godin which said, in essence: Quick, get out the powders. Marie, in her haste for results, broke one of my hard and fast rules for murderers. Never, but never, commit anything to paper. Godin told Marie that it would take a great deal of money to hire a professional poisoner. Then he tucked away Marie's note for safekeeping.

The de Brinvilliers' social circle was shocked by the sudden demise of Marie's two brothers. She was really rolling now. Marie figured poisoning was the answer to any problem. Her husband was a bore, and she thought it might be a good idea for him to be removed permanently from the scene. A by-product of this not so original idea would be her marriage to Godin.

Now, our friend Godin was no fool. He knew that Marie was no longer his private domain. Besides, how would he ever be able to enjoy breakfast, never being sure whether there was a little white powder in his cafe au lait?

Without warning, Godin died. His death was not considered to be murder, so we will never know whether or not Marie slipped him a little something, out of anger. His belongings revealed incriminating letters from Marie, particularly the one describing how she wanted her brothers poisoned post haste.

Once the cat was out of the bag, it became necessary for Marie to leave Paris hurriedly. She entered a convent in Liege, using a ficticious name. For three years Marie was confined to the convent, which must have been comparable to cutting a mouse off from his cheese supply.

When her real identity was discovered, she was arrested. She was carrying a detailed confession of her crimes, which she had written while in the convent.

Marie didn't fare well. In her time, torture was prevalent in France, and she was beaten and burned in an effort to get her to reveal all the lurid details of her past life.

Marie de Brinvilliers was finally beheaded for her crimes.

LOVE AND LETHAL LUNCHES

If you ever plan on hastening a friend's or relative's demise by adding a touch of poison to their food, there are certain rules which even the most impulsive must observe. It's only basic common sense to place the poison in the proper food and, for goodness sake, be certain the right person consumes the laced goodies. Theresa Wasserleben and her mummie, Maria Godau, observed the former rule, but were decidedly negligent in complying with the latter.

Maria, still a fine cut of a woman in her early forties, had been thoroughly embarrassed when some question arose as to how her late husband had expired. It seemed simple enough to Maria. One fine day back in Cottage Hill, Alabama, Hubby Godau suffered severe tummy cramps. The stomach trouble became more severe until the poor gentleman curled up and died. Nothing could be more straightforward, thought Maria. It was ulcers, or bladder trouble, or something — take your pick.

Busybodies, such as police and medical authorities, disagreed. Those suspicious souls kept insisting that it was murder by poison. Finally, to clear up the entire matter, Maria went through the rather tiring experience of standing trial for murder. Her insistence that it was all a mistake was borne out. Marie was acquitted.

But that was all behind the closely knit mother and daughter team. Now, two years later, Maria thought it best for all concerned if her impetuous and extremely well stacked daughter Theresa entered the matrimonial sweepstakes. The card Theresa drew from the deck was a giant of a man, who answered to the tongue twister of Freidrich Wasserleben. He also came running if you shouted Freddie.

Freddie tipped the scales at 250 lbs. and stood 6 foot 3 inches in his hand-knit stockinged feet. The apple strudel of Theresa's eye hailed from Hamburg, Germany. He had hastened to leave there as a teenager in order to join the German Navy. After his discharge from the Navy in 1893, Freddie migrated to America and settled down in Mobile, Ala. Here, at a dance, the 44-year-old stevedore met 18-year-old Theresa. Freddie took one look at the long-legged, more than amply endowed Theresa and said, "That's for me." Theresa had very few objections and Maria, sitting on the sidelines, had absolutely none.

As they say in the story books, in due course the couple were wed, and went dashing away on their honeymoon. Now, folks, you have to keep an eye on those mothers-in-law. Freddie assumed that he and his brand new wife would be bedding down in his cozy apartment. He assumed wrong. While the lovebirds were away cooing, or whatever, Maria moved all their belongings into her home. An exhausted Freddie returned from his honeymoon to find out that he would be living under his mother-in-law's roof. At first he objected; but once it was pointed out how much more cheaply three could live than two, he consented to the surprise living arrangements.

The surprises were just beginning. Maria informed Freddie that she had bought him a waterfront saloon. Now that wasn't hard to take, thought Freddie. Anything was better than the stevedore business. Big Freddie, with all those muscles, loved dishing out the suds down at the saloon.

Meanwhile, Maria wasn't finished with the surprises. One frosty Friday, Freddie closed up the saloon and came directly home, as was his habit. Instead of Theresa rushing to the door to meet him, he was confronted by Maria, who informed him that Theresa had gone to Birmingham to visit a friend for a few days.

As Maria so subtly put it, "What the hell, let's make the most of it." She initiated the festivities by opening a bottle of schnapps, which put Freddie in the mood for bigger and better things. Folks, it embarrasses me to have to relate to you that Freddie and his mother-in-law made their way to the sleeping quarters. Oh, what's the use. They jumped into the sack and didn't come up for air for two days. From this brief interlude on, Freddie became lover to both his wife and his mother-in-law on a more or less permanent basis.

Other matters concerned the menage-a-trois. Let's face it, Freddie, while he may have been super in the stud business, left a lot to be desired when it came to dispensing suds. The saloon went broke.

Freddie, demonstrating his well known ability to bounce back, joined the Mobile police department. Maria was elated at the news. With her customary eye for the future, she took out a nice fat insurance policy on Freddie's life. As far as Maria was concerned, Freddie became a walking, talking $15,000 on the hoof. You couldn't be too careful. After all, police work could be dangerous.

Freddie turned out to be a darned good cop. He apprehended his share of drunks and thieves, but darn the luck, he never got as much as a scratch in the line of duty. Years went by. Everyone liked the big, good natured cop. In fact, when Freddie was on night duty, he got in the habit of checking up on ladies whose husbands he knew were out of town. Some of these ladies were so grateful, they invited Freddie into their homes for an hour or six to partake of horizontal fun and games. Freddie was always willing to serve and protect. What with the string of ladies on the night shift and Maria and Theresa at home, the now 50-year-old Freddie was almost always in a state of exhaustion.

There comes a point in every little tale of sex and mayhem when someone has to make a decision. Now was that time. Maria and Theresa decided to murder Freddie. Fifteen thousand fresh crisp dollar bills were more desirable than one exhausted Freddie.

The mother and daughter team were in the habit of packing a lunch for the breadwinner before he went on the night shift. How convenient, thought Maria, as she liberally laced the lunch with arsenic. The two little devils stayed up all night waiting for word on Freddie's death. Nothing happened. As the sun rose over Mobile, Freddie came whistling up the front walk, big as life and twice as cheerful. He didn't even have a suggestion of a tummy ache.

Something had gone wrong. Theresa said to Maria, "Don't worry, Mamma, if at first you don't succeed, try, try again. We will poison Freddie tomorrow." Well folks, there were many tomorrows, all of which were followed by that infuriating Freddie whistling up the front walk.

Now, Freddie had no idea he was being poisoned. For months the ladies he would visit always made him a nice light snack. He never ate the lunches Marie and Theresa prepared. In fact, he got in the habit of splitting his lunch with four or five of his fellow cops. Some took ill, but no-one ate his entire lunch, so that their intake of arsenic was never fatal. On some occasions Freddie would just toss the poisoned lunch into the garbage. He always noted what was in his lunch, as Maria and Theresa had developed the annoying habit of questioning him about it. He was always quick to compliment them, although he never ate a bite.

While all this was going on, the two ladies were becoming impatient. One night they decided to hurry things along. Freddie was asleep in the very bed which had seen so much action in the past. Marie took the nightstick and rained blows down on his head. Then, for good measure, she shot him three times in the head with his service revolver.

Mother and daughter managed to carry bulky Freddie downstairs and outside to a waiting wagon. They carted the dead man to a vacant lot and dumped his body into Hall's pond. Scampering back home, they tidied and cleaned up like little beavers, leaving no evidence of murder in the bedroom.

Next day, Freddie's body was found. The police had the distasteful duty of informing the widow and concerned mother-in-law of their loss. Well, folks, you should have been there. The tears flowed. Maria and Theresa wailed unto the heavens. It was quite a show.

At first the police picked up Freddie's known enemies. Like every policeman, he had a few. Speaking of policemen, the investigating officer stumbled across the fact that several of Freddie's buddies were sick. Three were in hospital, but what was even more unusual, they had all become ill after partaking of Freddie's lunch.

A search of Freddie's home uncovered a mattress in a hayloft. It had three slugs deeply imbedded in the soft material. They had been fired from Freddie's own service revolver. You didn't have to be Sherlock Holmes to figure out the rest. Soon the details of Maria's previous murder trial were brought to light. The jig was up.

In the summer of 1912, the two ladies were found guilty of murder and were sentenced to life imprisonment. During the trial Maria stated that Freddie was not a bad sort, but she would never forgive him for giving away her home-cooked meals.

A NASTY LITTLE
FELLOW

As I drove into the peaceful village of Bovingdon, it was early in the morning. The dew was lifting from the rolling English countryside. I couldn't help but think of Graham Young driving up to work over these very same roads, his mind contemplating how much antimony he would administer to his fellow employees. Would Diana Smart get enough to send her home for a few days? Would Peter Buck be back today? If so, it just might be his turn for a dose.

But the Graham Young story doesn't start in this quaint English village. It begins in Honeyport Lane Maternity Hospital, North London, on Sept 7, 1947; for that was the day Graham was born.

Molly Young didn't have an easy pregnancy. She had pleurisy while carrying Graham, and although her new son grew to be a healthy baby, it was discovered that Molly had contracted tuberculosis. She died two days before Christmas when Graham was three months old.

Fred Young, a machine setter by trade, was beside himself with grief at the loss of his wife. He decided to keep his little family as close to him as possible without the benefit of a mother. Fred had one other child, a daughter, Winnifred, who was 8-years-old at the time of her mother's death. Winnie and her father went to live with Fred's mother at Links Rd., while Graham moved in with an aunt and uncle at 768 North Circular Rd. in the Neasdon section of North London. The two addresses were not that far apart, and the little family managed to get together each weekend.

Three years later, Fred Young met another lady named Molly. At the age of 33, Fred calculated that he could still have a chance for a happy and contented life with a new wife and his two children. He married Molly, purchased the house at 768 North Circular Rd., and moved in with Winnie and 3-year-old Graham.

As Graham grew up it was noted that he wasn't a joiner, or what is known as a group person. He read incessantly. Other than playing with his sister and a cousin, he kept pretty much to himself. Throughout his early years in school he was considered to be well above average in his studies. His stepmother, Molly, doted on Graham, who appeared to return her love with genuine affection.

At the age of 9, Graham Young was experimenting with varnish and nail polish. He was not doing anything malicious with these substances, but experimenting with them to ascertain the qualities inherent in various products. For a 9-year-old child, many would think this advanced element of curiosity in Graham's makeup to be a very admirable trait.

When Molly found acid and ether in Graham's room, she rightly felt that her son's interest had become abnormal for a child his age. Upon being questioned, Graham told his mother that he had found the substances in garbage thrown out by the local drugstore. Later she found books on witchcraft and the Nazi party in Graham's room.

By the time Graham was 12, his teachers believed that he had an outstanding future in the field of chemistry. Unknown to them, he was poisoning rats and performing autopsies on their bodies. His family was continually amazed at his advanced knowledge of chemicals. They could show Graham a detergent or waxing agent and he would rhyme off the chemicals which made up the product and what interaction was involved to make the substances perform as advertised.

At the age of 13, Graham knew the exact quantities of various poisons which could prove to be fatal. He also knew the effects of administering small quantities of certain poisons over a prolonged period of time. In fact, Graham was now an expert on the subject of poison. While everyone thought him a quiet little boy, no one knew the extent of his weird obsession.

In April of 1961, Graham gave a cock-and-bull story to the chemist in his neighborhood, and managed to purchase 25 grams of antimony. He signed the poison book with the fictitious name M.E. Evans, and gave a phony address. Out of his allowance received from his father, and with money from odd jobs performed at a local cafe, Graham continued to purchase quantities of antimony.

His closest school chum, Chris Williams, remembers that Graham often showed him a vial of poison. Chris thought it was a great joke, somewhat akin to the country boy showing his pet frog to his buddies.

Once the boys had a falling out, as little boys often do. A few days later Chris had severe stomach pains. He had to leave school for the day. All through the spring and summer of 1961, Chris suffered from severe stomach pains which were often accompanied by vomiting. Later he realized that his discomfort always followed those occasions when he and Graham skipped school together. On those days Graham was in the habit of sharing his sandwiches with Chris.

Chris' stomach pains and headaches became so bad that he was forced to visit his family doctor, Dr. Lancelot Wills. The doctor couldn't find anything specifically wrong with Chris, but thought his headaches were migraines.

One day, while cleaning Graham's room, Molly found a bottle of antimony. She had no idea what it was, but clearly understood the skull and crossbones on the label. She told Fred of her discovery. They both faced Graham and forbade him to have such dangerous substances in the house. Molly then went around to the chemist shop named on the bottle and, in no uncertain terms, told the chemist never to sell Graham any dangerous materials. Unknown to his parents, Graham merely changed chemists.

It wasn't long after this incident that Molly Young began to have an upset stomach. She felt weak and lethargic. She often discussed her illness with Graham. It was his custom to have tea with his mother every day after school. Finally, Molly became so ill, she was taken to hospital, where she made a speedy recovery. Her illness was thought to be an ulcer. Poison was never suspected.

It is interesting to note that once antimony has passed through the body, no trace can be detected. Molly's recovery was to be temporary.

One day Winnie, now an attractive 22-year-old girl with a steady boyfriend, collapsed outside a cinema. She, too, was having periodic spells of abdominal pain accompanied by vomiting. This most recent attack set Winnie thinking. Why hadn't it occurred to her before? Her kid brother with his silly chemistry experiments. No doubt he had used some of the family dishes to perform the experiments. Some toxic substance might have adhered to a cup, causing Molly and her to become ill. She decided to speak to her father.

Fred Young didn't believe that Graham would bring poison into the house after being told to keep the terrible stuff away. Nevertheless, Fred gave Graham a real tongue lashing.

Soon Fred came down with a severe case of cramps. He never complained much, because at the same time his wife Molly became seriously ill. This time she had a complete new set of symptoms. She woke up on Easter Saturday, 1962, with a sensation of pins and needles in her hands and feet. Graham was concerned and solicitous towards his stepmother. It was decided to rush Molly to the hospital.

Once in the hospital Molly said to one of the doctors, "I hope you're not going to be long about this, because I've got my husband's dinner to get." Within minutes of making this frivolous remark, Molly Young, aged 38, was dead. For about a year, Graham had been feeding Molly antimony and observing the results. On the evening before Molly died, Graham had laced a trifle with twenty grains of thallium. It was this massive dose which caused her death. Graham probably didn't know it, but he had just become the first person in England ever to commit murder by the administration of deadly, tasteless, odorless thallium.

A post mortem failed to reveal the true cause of death. The following Thursday, Molly was cremated. Graham Young, at the age of 14, had committed the perfect murder. When mourners gathered at the family residence to pay their respects, Graham doctored a sandwich with a small quantity of antimony. One of his mother's relatives became violently ill. Graham was just having a little fun.

A few days after his wife's funeral, Fred Young suffered a series of stomach pains accompanied by violent bouts of vomiting. Finally his daughter Winnie forced him to see their family physician, Dr. Wills. The doctor could find no reason for the illness, but was startled when, at the conclusion of the examination, Fred collapsed on the office floor. He was rushed to Willisden General Hospital, where Molly had died less than two weeks before.

After spending two days in hospital, often comforted by his son who visited him constantly, Fred Young began to feel better. Graham seemed to enjoy himself around the hospital, amazing doctors by his knowledge of things medical. Fred was taken home, but in a few days his pains became so severe that Winnie rushed her father back to the hospital.

That same night doctors were surprised when extensive tests confirmed that Fred was suffering from antimony poisoning.

We must pause here to keep in mind that Graham was a quiet, studious youngster of 14. It was difficult for his family to accept the facts as we are able to do from the benefit of hindsight. Graham's father was the first to actually believe that his son had been administering poison to the entire family for more than a year. Doctors told him that one more dose of antimony would have proven fatal. Fred Young recovered, but has a permanently damaged liver as a result of his son's handiwork. He also lives today with the realization that Graham was responsible for his stepmother's death.

While Fred Young lingered in hospital with his dark suspicions, direct action came from another source. Graham's chemistry teacher, Mr. Hughes, heard of Mr. Young being rushed to hospital so soon after his wife's death. Lately, Mr. Hughes had wondered about Graham's lack of interest in his chemistry experiments. It appeared that the boy was obsessed with experiments using poisons, and recording data derived from his experiments in a notebook. Mr. Hughes decided to stay late at school and search Graham's desk. He found several bottles of poison.

Recalling Chris Williams' illness, Mr. Hughes felt the whole thing was just too much. He contacted the headmaster of the school and together they went to see Dr. Wills. The three men exchanged notes and, for the first time, the magnitude of Graham's poisonous endeavors came to light.

They arranged for a psychiatrist, posing as a child guidance counsellor, to consult with Graham. Graham loved to display his knowledge of pharmacology and had a learned discussion with the psychiatrist, who was amazed at the lad's knowledge. He went straight to the police with his suspicions.

Next day, Detective Inspector Edward Crabbe searched Graham's room. He found quantities of antimony, thallium, digitalis, ionine, atropine, and barium chloride. When Graham was searched, police found a vial of antimony, as well as two bottles of thallium, in his shirt. Later he referred to the vial of antimony as his little friend. Taken to jail the following morning, Graham revealed his entire career as a poisoner to the police.

Graham Young was unique. Obviously his age alone set him apart from most killers, but, above all, the fact that he lacked any motive made his crimes different. He did not dislike the people he poisoned. They were given poison specifically because they were close at hand and could be observed. Graham was experimenting, much as a scientist does with guinea pigs.

On July 5, 1962, Graham was tried in London's Old Bailey, one of the youngest ever to appear in the famous old court. He was charged with poisoning his father, his sister, and his schoolchum, Chris Williams. The charge of murdering his stepmother was not pressed. Her ashes had been scattered, and it was believed nothing could be gained by bringing further charges against such a young boy.

Dr. Christopher Fysh, a psychiatrist attached to the Ashford Remand Centre, where Graham had been housed awaiting his trial, told of his conclusions after having extensive conversations with Graham. He quoted Graham as telling him, "I am missing my antimony. I am missing the power it gives me." The doctor elaborated on Graham's knowledge of drugs, and stated that on several occasions Graham had corrected him in minor areas when the properties of various drugs were discussed. Dr. Fysh suggested that Graham was obsessed with the sense of power his poisons gave him. In the doctor's opinion, given the chance, Graham would continue to experiment on humans. Dr. Fysh thought Graham should be confined to a maximum security hospital. As a result, he was sentenced to Broadmoor for a period of 15 years.

In July, 1962, the gates of the ominous old brick structure closed behind 14-year-old Graham Young. He was one of the youngest patients ever to be admitted, but not the youngest. That distinction belonged to Bill Giles, who died there at the age of 87. He had been convicted of setting fire to a hayrick at the age of 10 in 1885. Giles had spent 77 years in Broadmoor, and coincidentally died three months before Graham was admitted.

About a month after Graham arrived at Broadmoor, an incident occurred which, all things considered, gives one room for thought.

John Berridge was a 23-year-old patient who had killed his parents. Quite suddenly one day he went into convulsions, collapsed and died. A post mortem revealed that his death was due to cyanide poisoning. The inquiry which followed established that no cyanide was kept at Broadmoor. However, the investigation also revealed that laurel bushes, from which an expert could extract cyanide, grew adjacent to the institution.

Several patients immediately confessed to poisoning Berridge. Among those confessing was Graham Young. He was the only one who could explain in detail the processes involved in extracting cyanide from laurel bushes. The authorities chose not to believe any of the confessions. They leaned towards the theory that somehow the poison was smuggled into the institution. The Berridge case remains unsolved to this day.

At first Graham Young, the lad from the respectable suburb of North London, had difficulty adjusting to the maximum security institution, but as the years went by he seemed to respond to psychiatric treatment. Dr. Edgar Udwin held high hopes for a complete recovery and early release for his young patient.

Meanwhile, Graham's family regarded his poisonous ways as a mental illness. His sister Winnie, cousins, aunts, and uncles all felt that Graham had been sick and was now on the road to recovery. His father Fred had a difficult time accepting this live and let live view. He could forgive Graham for almost everything, but he could never forget that his own son had studied and apparently enjoyed the death of his poor wife Molly.

After consulting with Graham's sister Winnie, it was decided by Dr. Udwin that Graham be released for one week in November, 1970. In the eight years of Graham's incarceration at Broadmoor, Winnie had married and was now the mother of a baby girl. She and her husband decided, in conjunction with Dr. Udwin, that no precautions against poison be taken during the week of Graham's visit.

Winnie now lived in a fashionable suburb of Hemel Hempstead, a city of 85,000, located about 30 miles north of London. Graham visited for the week, and the experiment was a huge success. With his doctor's consent and his family's urging, he visited at Christmastime for another week and was a delight to have in the house.

On Feb. 4, 1971, Graham, at the age of 23, was released from Broadmoor. He was sent directly to Slough, to the government resettlement centre for 13 weeks training as a stock keeper and shipper.

Nearing the completion of his course, on April 24, 1971, Graham performed two tasks which were to have far reaching effects. He applied for a job as storekeeper at John Hadland Photographic Instrumentation Ltd., Bovingdon, Hertsfordshire. Then he went to the centre of London, walked into a drugstore, and purchased 25 grams of antimony.

It was a stroke of luck when Graham's application for employment was accepted at Hadland's in Bovingdon, a quaint rural village only three miles from Hemel Hempstead.

Graham would have the steadying influence of a member of his family, but would still live and work in an independent environment. He took a room at 20 Maynards Rd. in Hemel Hempstead. His landlord, Mohammed Saddiq, a native of Pakistan, had no idea a murderer and former inmate of Broadmoor was his new roomer. At the time Mr. Saddiq didn't speak one word of English.

Seven years later, when I knocked on the door of 29 Maynards Rd., Mr. Saddiq well remembered his infamous tenant. He led me up the stairs to the room Graham had occupied. He pointed out the windowsill where Graham had stocked enough poison to kill scores of people. There, in a corner, was the bed under which Graham kept his diary of death. Mr. Saddiq assured me that his star roomer never ate at his home, nor had he ever entered his kitchen. Seven years before, Mr. Saddiq has considered himself fortunate to have such a quiet, well behaved roomer in his home.

I drove the three miles to the village of Bovingdon, and met with a director of Hadland's, Terry Johnson. Mr. Johnson explained how Graham Young became an employee of the firm. Young answered an advertisement and was granted an interview. He was highly recommended by the training school, having just completed a course in storekeeping, the exact position the firm was attempting to fill.

He accounted for the previous nine years by telling Mr. Foster of Hadland's that he'd had a nervous breakdown upon the death of his mother, but was now completely cured. Before hiring Graham, Mr. Foster checked out his story.

The government training centre got in touch with Dr. Udwin, the psychiatrist who was instrumental in securing Graham's release from Broadmoor. He obligingly sent along a letter confirming that Young was normal and competent in every way. At no time was Hadland's informed that Young had been a patient at Broadmoor, or had been convicted of being a poisoner.

On May 10, 1971, Graham went to work. He became assistant storekeeper at a salary of 24 pounds a week. The one hundred employees at Hadland's are a friendly, cheerful group. Mr. Johnson, who showed me the premises, was called Terry by everyone we met. Hadland's exports expensive industrial photographic equipment all over the world. The firm received some measure of satisfaction from its mention in Guinness Book of World Records. They have produced a camera which takes 600 million pictures a second.

The men in the storeroom welcomed Graham in his new position. Within days he had gained the reputation of being a bit quiet, but certainly a nice enough bloke. His boss, Bob Egle, was 59-years-old and looking forward to retirement. Bob had been married for 39 years. He found out that his new assistant Graham loved to hear of his wartime experiences, especially his evacuation from Dunkirk.

Fred Biggs was 60 and senior employee in the Works in Progress Department. The two older men liked Graham Young.

Jethro Batt worked side-by-side with Graham in the stores. Each day after work Jethro would give Graham a lift the three miles back to Hemel Hempstead.

Twice a day May Bartlett wheeled a tea wagon down the long hall to the stores area. Members of the staff would then fetch their tea from the wagon. That is, before Graham came to work at Hadland's. Soon it became customary for Graham to pick up the tea from the wagon and distribute it to his fellow employees in the stores.

About a month after Graham started working at Hadland's, his boss Bob Egle became ill. He took a few days off work, but the pains in his stomach persisted. On June 18, he and his wife took a week's vacation at Great Yarmouth. The time off seemed to work wonders. Bob appeared so much better when he returned.

Two days before Bob was due back, Graham had travelled to London and purchased 25 grams of thallium. Within 24 hours of stating that he was feeling just great again after his vacation, Bob Egle took terribly ill at work. He went home, complaining of numbness in his fingers. Later he began to stagger. By morning the weight of the sheets on his bed caused him excruiating pain.

On successive days Bob Egle was transferred from west Herts Hospital in Hemel Hempstead to the intensive care unit at St. Albans City Hospital. He lingered in great pain for eight days before dying.

Back at Hadland's, everyone was concerned about the well-liked boss of the stores passing away so suddenly. None seemed to take it any harder than the new man, Graham Young.

A post mortem was performed on Bob Egle. Death was attributed to broncho-pneumonia in conjunction with polyneuritis. The following Monday, several members of the staff indicated a desire to attend Egle's funeral. It was decided that the managing director, Mr. Geoffrey Foster would attend representing management, while Graham Young would represent the staff. The two men travelled together to the funeral. Foster remembers being surprised at Young's intimate knowledge of the medical diagnosis surrounding Egle's death.

Diana Smart, a fill-in employee in the stores section at Hadland's, didn't feel well all that summer. Nothing severe, but she was in enough discomfort to force her to go home several days during that July and August.

In September, Peter Buck, the import export manager, noticed that he always felt queasy after tea time. A few weeks later Diana Smart's attacks became more severe. Around this time Jethro Batt also became ill. One day he accepted a cup of tea from Graham and then gave him a lift to Hemel Hempstead. Next day Batt couldn't raise himself out of bed. Pains racked his stomach and chest. In the ensuing days his hair began to fall out in large tufts. He suffered hallucinations and became so distressed that he wanted to kill himself. Batt was admitted to hospital. Unknown to him or his doctors, the fact that he was removed from Graham Young and his poisonous ways saved his life. He gradually recovered.

In the meantime, David Tilson experienced violent stomach pains accompanied by vomiting. He was rushed to St. Albans Hospital, where he too started to lose his hair. After a short while, he began to recover and was discharged.

It seemed that everyone at Hadland's was taken ill. By now the death of Bob Egle had the entire staff on edge. Could the outbreak of the strange undiagnosed illness be the same thing that killed Bob?

On a weekend early in November, the stores department at Hadland's was sorely understaffed. Bob Egle was dead. Both Tilson and Batt were off sick. Fred Biggs and his wife came in on a weekend to help Graham Young catch up. Graham made tea that Saturday for Biggs. Next morning Fred could hardly move. He would never return to work. Twenty days later Fred Biggs was dead.

By now, as one can well imagine, rumors were running rampant through the Hadland plant. For some time previous to the current outbreak of sickness in the area, a virus had on occasion swept through Bovingdon, causing stomach complaints. These outbreaks were often blamed on the Bovingdon Bug.

To quell the rumors and suspicions of the employees, the management of Hadland's decided to call in Dr. Robert Hynd, Medical Officer of Health for the Hemel Hempstead area. Dr. Hynd inspected the plant and could find no cause for the wave of illness. Despite the doctor's statement that the cause of the illness didn't originate in the plant, rumors still persisted. They ranged from toxic chemicals being used in the manufacturing processes to medieval curses. After Fred Biggs died, some men even considered leaving Hadland's.

Management took another stab at coming up with the solution to the riddle. They called in the local general practictioner, Dr. Iain Anderson, to have an informal, morale boosting chat with the employees.

Everyone gathered in the cafeteria to hear Dr. Anderson. He explained that the authorities had ruled out radiation. They also checked out thallium, which was sometimes used in the manufacture of index lenses such as those manufactured at Hadland's. However, Hadland's did not keep thallium on the premises, so this agent had been dismissed as a possible cause of the sickness. The doctor leaned heavily toward a particularly strong strain of the Bovingdon Bug as being at the bottom of all the trouble. He assured the employees that the authorities were doing everything possible to isolate the cause of the dreadful sickness.

At the conclusion of his talk, the doctor inquired if there were any questions. Dr. Anderson was amazed when one employee, Graham Young, posed complicated questions regarding heavy metal poisoning and its effects. The doctor had a hard time getting the young man to sit down. The meeting was hastily brought to a close.

Dr. Anderson later made it a point to find Young and pursue the subject of poison. Again, he was dumbfounded at Young's detailed knowledge. Who was Graham Young, anyhow? Dr. Anderson and the chairman of the board, John Hadland, discussed the matter. Hadland called in the authorities, who checked Young's record at Scotland Yard. It revealed that he had been released just six months earlier from Broadmoor, where he had been sentenced for poisoning.

In Graham's room at 29 Maynards Rd., police uncovered his diary, detailing the dates and quantities of poison he had administered to Hadland employees. Graham Young had been playing God. He chose that some should die, while others should live. All were observed during their illness.

Young confessed to all his crimes, and to this day has never shown any remorse for the suffering he caused. All tests and examinations have indicated that he has above average intelligence, and is, in the legal sense, perfectly sane.

Young received several sentences of life imprisonment for his crimes. His victims, some of whom still live and work in the Hemel Hempstead area, want to forget Graham Young.

As I prepared to leave the Hadland plant with its airy, cheery atmosphere, I asked director Terry Johnson, who had lived through the terror which was Graham Young, how in a sentence he would describe what went on there.

He answered without hesitation, "It was unbelievable."

VENOM MARKED
POLICY PAID

There have been some strange and fascinating murder weapons employed by men and women intent on hastening their victims' demise. We have run the gauntlet from conventional baseball bats and bullets, to more bizarre rare poisons and simulated accidents. You may think that we have explored every method used to commit the dastardly act of murder, but — would you believe a rattlesnake?

Bob James was born in Alabama around 1921 to dirt poor cotton farmers. He finished a couple of years of formal education before his brother-in-law, who was a barber, sent him to a barber school in Birmingham. Young Bob learned a trade and, for a while, worked at a part-time job. For all intents and purposes he promised to become a law abiding, hardworking citizen.

Then one day, he just took off without telling a soul. For years he drifted across the U.S., working at odd jobs. Bob James was one of those men who was always trying to impress the ladies. He became pretty good at it. He perfected his natural Southern drawl to go with a practised line, and had no trouble finding female companionship.

Bob wasn't that bad to look at either. He had wavy red hair, delicate, even features, and was of average build and height. Altogether, not an unattractive man.

Bob's mother passed away, leaving her only boy a few hundred dollars insurance money. Son of a gun, Bob thought, what an easy way to get cash if the need ever arose. In the meantime, he gravitated to Los Angeles, California, where, in 1931, he opened a high class barbershop. The shop did well, at least well enough to provide Bob with the means to wine and dine his lady friends.

In 1932, he married Winona Wallace. Winsome Winona was no sooner Mrs. James than Bob suggested she take out a few insurance policies on her life. Naturally her ever-lovin' husband was the beneficiary. Within two months of her marriage Winona had a total of $14,000 insurance, payable to Bob should she meet her death accidentally.

A short while later Bob and Winona took a vacation, sort of a belated honeymoon. The vacation was interrupted near Pike's Peak, Colorado, when unfortunately, their car went over a cliff. Lady Luck had smiled upon Bob. He had been able to jump clear of the plunging car and run for help. When he brought some men back to the scene of the accident, he almost fainted when he discovered the car hadn't plunged all the way down the cliff. About 100 feet down the hill a huge boulder had stopped the vehicle. Miraculously, Winona was alive. Rushed to a hospital in Colorado Springs, she recovered, but could remember nothing of the details of the accident.

When Winona was released from the hospital, thoughtful Bob rented a lonely cabin near Manitou so that his wife would be able to rest quietly while she regained her health. Bob later mentioned to acquaintances that he was concerned about Winona. She seemed to be suffering from dizzy spells.

It wasn't long after voicing his concern that Bob, accompanied by a young boy helping him carry groceries, found Winona's body in the bathtub. There she was, lying on her back, with her feet dangling over the end of the tub. Death was obviously due to drowning. Winona was ultimately sent to her final resting place without any official inquiry ever being made into her death.

Bob collected the fourteen big ones without even a murmur of suspicion from the insurance companies. Now loaded with cash, he went on a buying spree, purchasing clothing, luggage, and a shiny new Pierce Arrow convertible.

To settle his nerves about his great loss, Bob took a trip back home to Birmingham. Remember his brother-in-law, the barber? Well, wouldn't you know it; he had a robust, healthy 18-year-old daughter, pretty as a picture and twice as willing. Bob fell hard for his niece, Lois.

When Bob left Birmingham Lois was there, cuddled up beside him in the convertible. Once back in L.A., he enrolled Lois in a school where she learned to become a manicurist. She also worked part time in his barbershop.

But Bob couldn't change the habits of a lifetime. Soon he was cavorting with several other ladies and, in a moment of weakness, married one. As soon as the nuptials were officially consummated, Bob couldn't stand the new wife. He immediately instituted proceedings to have the marriage annulled.

On the rebound, he became involved with another manicurist in his shop. Mary Busch couldn't wait to marry Bob. In fact, she insisted on having the marriage ceremony performed before Bob's previous marriage was officially annulled. Bob, cunning devil that he was, got a friend to pose as a minister and perform a phony ceremony. Mary thought she had really tied the knot. Bob, of course, was the beneficiary of the $10,000 worth of insurance policies taken out on Mary's life.

During the summer of 1935, Bob and Mary lived in apparent happiness in a small bungalow at the foot of the Sierra Madre mountains. It was a romantic but lonely spot, just perfect for what Bob had in mind.

In June, Jim Hope, a drifter, walked into Bob's barbershop looking for work. He was made to order for the scheme Bob was hatching. Bob told Hope that he would pay him $100 if he could get him a rattlesnake. Hope at first thought the proposition a bit strange, but $100 was big money back in 1935. He managed to purchase one from a snake dealer for $6. Bob placed a chicken in the rattler's cage. When he looked in the following morning, the chicken was dead. He knew then he had a murder weapon in his possession.

By informing Bob that she was pregnant, Mary gave him the opportunity he needed. He convinced her that she should have an abortion. In preparation for the abortion, gullible Mary followed Bob's instructions to the letter. On Aug. 4, 1935 Bob persuaded Mary to let herself be strapped to the kitchen table. She was then blindfolded and a strip of adhesive tape was placed over her mouth. Bob brought his cage containing the rattlesnake into the house. He opened the sliding glass side of the reptile's cage and placed Mary's foot inside. The snake struck. The box was taken away and later destroyed by Hope. He sold the snake that same day.

Later Mary's leg swelled and she began to suffer excruciating pain. That evening Bob and Hope drank whiskey waiting for Mary to die. Despite the pain, the stricken woman continued to live. In desperation Bob filled the bathtub with water and drowned his wife. The dead woman was then carried outside, where the upper portion of her body was placed in a fishpond in the yard.

A friend found Mary's body. She had apparently suffered a dizzy spell and fallen into the pond. The local coroner stated that the cause of death was due to an accident. The insurance companies balked, and Bob had to settle for $3,500 on his total claims of $10,000.

Bob had apparently succeeded again. Six months went by before a liquor store proprietor called on his lawyer with a strange story. He told how the previous summer a man named Hope had come into his store in an agitated state inquiring where he could buy a rattlesnake. He had mumbled something about planning to murder a woman. The liquor store owner had thought about it for some time. He decided that since a woman had died under suspicious circumstances he had better tell the story.

Soon the police were on the trail of the rattlesnake purchase, and the whole story started to fit together. Hope was apprehended. To save his skin, he confessed to the police. Bob then confessed, giving a slightly different version, in order to implicate Hope.

Now that Mary's death had turned into a murder case, the authorities decided to look into the circumstances surrounding Winona's death. They came up with a man who had visited the scene of the car accident at Pike's Point. Now that they asked, he had always wondered how a man could leap from a runaway car and not even get a wrinkle in his suit. The investigating officers knew they had a double killer on their hands.

Because of the weird rattlesnake angle, the murder trials of Jim Hope and Bob James received national coverage. Hope was found guilty of murder in the first degree and sentenced to life imprisonment. Bob James was also found guilty of murder in the first degree. After many appeals he was hanged. James was the last man to hang in California. The state introduced the gas chamber a short time later.

THIS TIME ANNA
LOST HER HEAD

It has been necessary to turn over many a yellowed document to reveal the diabolical life of Anna Zwanziger. But Anna is worth every cobweb, so let's start at the very beginning.

Herr Schonleben, a fat, jolly man, ran a successful saloon in Nuremberg, Germany. One day in 1760, a young lad burst into Herr Schonleben's watering hole and informed the jolly German that Frau Schonleben had just given birth to a lovely little girl. The lovely little girl was to later be remembered as a lovely little monster. Her name was Anna.

As the years passed, Herr Schonleben often reflected while down at the saloon serving his patrons, that his teenage daughter was not a raving beauty. She had rather thin lips and a decidedly too thin nose. Dark brown eyes stared out of sockets which appeared to be set much too far into her head. The overall mousey appearance was not enhanced by a somewhat sallow complexion. No, you definitely had to say Anna was not a looker.

Anna's daddy kept a sharp and alert eye out for unsuspecting potential husbands. That's how Herr Zwanziger got into the act. Hearing of the generous dowry which would accompany Anna en route to the altar, Herr Zwanziger, a struggling attorney, paid her a call. Anna, overcome by her newfound popularity, was thrilled by the dashing attorney. It wasn't long before Fraulein Schonleben became Frau Zwanziger.

After the nuptials it was only a matter of days before Anna found out that Zwanziger's main occupation was not the law, but a passion for good friends and alcoholic beverage. Year after year, Zwanziger drank his days and nights away until he had gone through Anna's money and his liver. Herr Zwanziger was laid to rest after the proper complimentary eulogies had been expressed by those who knew he was a good for nothing.

Zwanziger left our Anna with a host of bad memories and bad debts. She was now faced with the very real task of making a living. She tried many avenues to support herself, but was singularly unsuccessful at all of them. For a while she operated a confectionery business. It failed. She tried selling toys and cooking for a hospital. She even travelled with a circus, but hated the transient life.

The years swiftly flew by, as they have a habit of doing. Anna, now in her late 40s, was driven to perform her first dishonest act. She stole a ring from a neighbor's house and got away with it. When she sold the valuable ring, she received enough money to keep her going for several months. This crime business, thought Anna, is not half bad. Besides providing the necessities of life, it gave her a precarious thrill. Anna moved to the little town of Pegnitz to gather her wits.

At this time Anna became obsessed with the idea that she had no one to take care of her in her approaching old age. Someway, somehow, she must become affluent enough to take care of the problem herself.

As luck would have it, while these dire thoughts were dancing through her head, she learned of a judge named Glaser, who was separated from his wife. Glaser was looking for a housekeeper. Anna applied for the job, was interviewed, and was accepted for the position.

It is believed that Anna hatched her little scheme before she left Glaser's office. It was as simple as all get out. She would become Frau Glaser. Of course, there was the present Frau Glaser to be dealt with before this new thought of Anna's could become a reality.

Cunning Anna decided first things first. She had to somehow lure Frau Glaser back to her hubby's bed. She set about accomplishing her devious ends by sending little notes to the estranged wife pointing out how the judge longed for her company. Soon Frau Glaser was replying to the concerned and considerate housekeeper that she too longed to be reinstated in the judge's comfortable big home. Once given the opening, it didn't take Anna long to effect a reconciliation and, at the same time, ingratiate herself with both Frau and Herr Glaser.

One thing you had to say about Anna: she did things with a flourish. Frau Glaser's homecoming was accompanied by large bouquets of flowers strategically placed around the house. Anna even hired a local orchestra for the happy reunion. The whole thing went off smashingly. Frau Glaser walked into the front door of her home and into the arms of her husband.

Within days Frau Glaser was suffering from severe stomach pains. It was no wonder either. Anna had given her three massive doses of arsenic. The housekeeper was apparently beside herself at this tragic turn of events. Her grief was almost uncontrollable when Frau Glaser died in agony.

After the funeral, which was interrupted on several occasions by wails of sorrow from Anna, our heroine decided to get down to business. It was time to turn on the charm and become the new Frau Glaser.

Alas, the best laid plans of mice and men often go astray, especially in the murder business. Herr Glaser showed a decided tendency to be left alone during his period of mourning. In fact, he became something of a recluse. Within a matter of days after the funeral, Anna was shattered when she was informed that her services were no longer required.

It had all been for naught, but what the heck, now that she had perfected a murder method there had to be other fish ready for frying. Sure enough Anna came up with another judge.

Herr Grohmann was a middle aged, wealthy gentleman who lived in Sanspareil. He suffered from gout. Anna became his housekeeper, but the setup wasn't exactly perfect. Grohmann had a young, attractive girlfriend whom he planned to marry. We'll see about that, Anna thought to herself. She turned on the charm, but Grohmann wasn't susceptible to sex in an unattractive package when he was already sampling the real thing with his betrothed.

Anna didn't have a chance. All her anger was directed at Grohmann himself. She dipped into her rather ample packet of arsenic and gave Grohmann a suitable dose in his chicken soup. He was dead three hours later.

Anna once again found a post as housekeeper in the home of a member of the legal profession. Herr Gebbard was a prosperous, overweight magistrate. His wife was a nag, and very, very pregnant.

Now fun's fun, but her two previous murders had brought Anna no material gain. She figured three times lucky. Things would be different this time around. Anna set about feeding arsenic to Frau Gebhard. During her mistress' inevitable illness Anna nursed her night and day. She was so devoted she wouldn't allow anyone else to feed her patient. Despite the loving care, Frau Gebhard became weaker and weaker. Just before she was about to give up the ghost, clever Anna called in a doctor. The medic noted that his patient was beyond help. His diagnosis proved to be extremely accurate.

Frau Gebhard died two hours after he examined her.

Anna took care of the funeral arrangements. Everything was going along just swell. Soon Gebhard would grow tired of mourning for his dearly departed spouse, and lo and behold, he would discover sweet considerate Anna.

Darn the luck. Would you believe that one of the servant girls in the house was a gorgeous well endowed fraulein. Rightly or wrongly, it seemed to Anna that Gebhard was paying far too much attention to her. Anna slipped her just enough arsenic to take her out of contention for a few weeks.

Again the path seemed clear for Anna to take the romantic initiative. This time it was Gebhard himself who spoiled everything. To end his period of mourning, he decided to throw a huge dinner party. Anna hated the idea of young, good looking frauleins twittering about trying to get their tentacles into what was rightfully hers. Try as she might, she couldn't talk her master out of his party.

That's when she lost her cool. If Gebhard wanted to throw a dinner party, she would prepare one he would never forget. Anna laced all the food with arsenic. Everyone except Gebhard became frightfully sick right at the dinner table. The other servants in the house, many of whom knew Anna wanted Gebhard for herself, thought the whole thing so funny they made the mistake of laughing right in front of the housekeeper.

That same evening they too came down with severe cramps after partaking of supper. Neither guests nor servants died from Anna's little treats, but the servants suspected the truth. They went to Gebhard and insisted that the remainder of their meal be examined. A chemist informed him that the food had been laced with arsenic.

Anna was dismissed immediately. The next day Gebhard, figuring that he had been too lenient with his housekeeper, informed the police of his suspicions.

Anna was traced to her hometown of Nuremburg, where she was arrested and charged with murder. She maintained her innocence throughout her trial. When she was found guilty she collapsed in court. Later, awaiting her execution, she wrote a long confession in which she admitted her murderous ways.

Anna was executed by the sword, when she was decapitated in July, 1811.

WICKED DOCTOR CREAM

The 1920s have often been referred to as the golden age of sport. Babe Ruth was clouting home runs, while Jack Dempsey was clouting anyone who stood in his way.

In the murder business the period between 1880 and 1895 should be called the golden age of mayhem. It gave rise to so many unusual murders. A chap known as Jack the Ripper, who was never positively identified, but who lives on in infamy, was roaming the streets of London cutting up ladies of the night. On this side of the big pond, a God-fearing, church-going New England lady named Lizzie Borden was accused of chopping up her Mummie and Daddy with a hatchet.

With the murder stage being so crowded with nefarious players, it is no wonder that Dr. Neill Cream never gained the notoriety he so richly deserved.

Neill was born in Glasgow, Scotland in 1850. His family migrated to Canada when he was five. Nothing is known of his formative years other than that he applied himself diligently to his schoolwork and did exceedingly well throughout high school. He continued on to McGill University in Montreal, where he received his medical degree. He later took post graduate work in London and Edinburgh before returning to Canada.

For the next five years Neill Cream led an eventful, if somewhat jaded existence. He set up practice in various Canadian towns and cities, but was always forced to stay on the move. You see, Dr. Cream's medical standards were decidedly below the norm, particularly when he was examining female patients. In fact, it wasn't an uncommon sight to see a lady running out of Dr. Cream's office in a state of undress. Finally, he found the temperature so unbearly hot that he left Canada for Chicago, in order to have more freedom to practise his particular brand of medicine.

In 1881, Dr. Cream went too far. He gave a huge quantity of strychnine to a patient named Stott. It is believed that the motive was two fold. Stott had a pretty wife whom the doctor was examining all the time, although her neighbors later stated that this was very strange since she was never sick a day in her life. It is believed to this day that Mrs. Stott was involved with Cream in her husband's sudden demise. At the time of Stott's death, Cream was trying to place a large insurance policy on the unfortunate man's life, with himself as the beneficiary.

Stott's death at first was attributed to natural causes. Then Dr. Cream did an extraordinary thing, which he continued to do throughout his criminal career. He started writing letters. He wrote to both the coroner and the district attorney suggesting that Stott's body be exhumed. Finally, at the anonymous urging of Cream the body was disinterred. Upon examination, it was found to be chock full of strychnine.

Dr. Cream and Mrs. Stott took off, but were soon apprehended and indicted for murder. Mrs. Stott, cute that she was, testified for the state. Charges against her were dropped. Dr. Cream was found guilty of second degree murder and was sentenced to life imprisonment. In 1881, the prison gates of Joliet closed behind the strange doctor, but his career was far from over. In 1891, after Cream had spent just under 10 years in prison, Gov. Fifer of Illinois commuted his sentence, and Neill Cream walked out of prison, a free man. The governor had made a horrendous error.

While he had been serving time in prison, Cream's father died, leaving him an inheritance of $16,000, a veritable fortune before the turn of the century. Dr. Cream picked up the cash and headed for England, arriving in London on Oct. 1, 1891. Whether it was the London fog or whatever, Dr. Cream didn't waste any time pursuing his secondary occupation, that of poisoner.

A 19-year-old prostitute, Ellen Donworth, let herself be picked up by Cream. During the course of the evening her tall, austere looking friend, sporting a top hat, offered her a drink out of his flask. She took two long drags of the bottle and almost immediately began to suffer from convulsions. Her friend was nowhere to be found, but neighbors called a doctor, who rushed the girl to the hospital. She died en route. An autopsy revealed that Ellen had died of strychnine poisoning.

The police had no clues to the poisoner's identity, but never fear. Our Dr. Cream made sure that he received some of the recognition he craved. He wrote the coroner offering to reveal the killer's identity in return for 200,000 pounds. The letter was signed A. O'Brien. The coroner tried to set up a rendezvous, but O'Brien-Cream never showed up.

One week after the Donworth murder, another prostitute, Matilda Clover, was found in her room writhing in agony. Her client for the evening, a man who called himself Fred, had given her some pills. Before she died, she described Fred to a friend who lived in the same house. Fred was a tall, well-built man, who dressed in a cape and tall silk hat. For some reason, Matilda's death was thought to have been caused by alcoholism, but Cream would have none of it. He dashed off a note to a distinguished doctor, accusing him of poisoning Matilda with strychnine. The doctor took the letter to the police. Other distinguished people received letters accusing them of poisoning Matilda. Because of the veritable shower of letters, Matilda's body was exhumed. The cause of her death was attributed to strychnine. Scotland Yard now realized that a systematic killer was on the loose in London.

The winter months drifted by without any further murders at the hands of the mysterious poisoner, with an abnormal urge for revealing his crimes in letters. Later, when every move Cream made was reviewed, the reason he stopped poisoning prostitutes during the winter months became clear. He had taken a trip to Canada, where strangely enough, he had printed 500 circulars, a copy of which follows:

ELLEN DONWORTH'S DEATH

To the Guests of the Metropole Hotel. Ladies and Gentlemen:

I hereby notify you that the person who poisoned Ellen Donworth on the 13th last October is today in the employ of the Metropole Hotel and that your lives are in danger as long as you remain in this Hotel.
London April 1892.

Yours respectfully,
W.H. Murray

Dr. Cream never used the printed circulars, and no one knows to this day why he had them printed. They do serve to reveal Cream's perverted obsession with publicity of any kind.

With the coming of Spring, and with Cream back in England, things started to percolate once again.

Emma Shrivell, an 18-year-old prostitute and her friend, Alice March, lived in a furnished flat near Waterloo Road. In the middle of the night their screams woke the landlady. Both girls were in great pain and were convulsing violently. During brief periods when their agony subsided, they told of having a distinguished gentleman as a supper guest earlier that evening. The gentleman wore a tall tophat, called himself Fred, and claimed he was a doctor. The girls let him talk them into taking some pills. Alice March died before reaching the hospital, while Emma Shrivell lingered for five hours before she too died.

Quite by chance a bobby walking his beat had seen the two girls let their guest out into the night. He was able to provide a full description. The publicity surrounding these two deaths brought forth other ladies who had managed to escape the clutches of the mysterious Fred.

Lou Harvey told of pretending to take the pills, but unknown to Fred she had thrown them away. Violet Beverley refused a drink offered to her by the obliging Fred. Both of these ladies gave detailed descriptions of their weird acquaintance to the police.

Then Dr. Cream, still craving notoriety, did the ultimate. He complained to Scotland Yard. Using the name Dr. Neill, he told them that the police were following him and harrassing him with accusations that he was the killer of March and Shrivell. Neill told the Yard that he had nothing whatever to do with the crimes, claiming that a Dr. Harper was the real culprit.

It is difficult to understand exactly why Dr. Cream would furnish the police with information which would lead them to his doorstep. It wasn't long before the authorities discovered that Dr. Neill was really Dr. Cream. Several of the surviving ladies identified him as the elusive Fred. So did the bobby who had seen him leave March and Shrivell's flat the night they died.

Dr. Cream was 42-years-old when he was adjudged to be legally sane and placed on trial for murder. On Nov. 15, 1892 he was hanged for his crimes.

With death only seconds away Cream's sense of the dramatic was not to be denied. As the trap door sprung open he yelled, "I am Jack the R----." Reporters ran to their files, only to find out that Dr. Cream had been securely locked up in Joliet when Jack was operating in London.

Dr. Cream suffered his greatest indignity when more than 80 years after his execution, Madame Tussaud's wax museum in London announced they were removing his wax image from their Chamber of Horrors. It seems there was a decided lack of interest, and anyway he wasn't scary enough.

A SWEET CASE OF MURDER BY POISON

To perform murder in Victorian England and have the case still considered to be a classic is no mean feat. In those days young people often died due to maladies caused by unsanitary conditions, contaminated water, and tainted food. Those who didn't die of natural causes were often eased into oblivion with the help of some poison or other which was not readily detected. An innovative approach was required to stand out in such a crowd.

Dr. George Lamson was such a trail blazer. At the age of 20 he was studying medicine in Paris. In 1878, by the time he was 28, he was practising medicine in London, England, and had taken a wife.

Pretty Kate John was everything a Victorian wife should have been — pleasant, gracious, devoted, and loyal to her handsome, educated husband. Kate's younger brother, Hubert, died of natural causes a year after the couple's marriage. This tragedy did have a silver lining. Hubert left the Lamsons an amount of money which enabled the good doctor to purchase a medical practice in Bournemouth.

Kate had another brother, Percy. Sixteen-year-old Percy had curvature of the spine, which left him paralyzed from the waist down. Confined to a wheel chair, he was placed in a private school, Blenheim House in Wimbledon, where he seemed to fit in well with the other boys.

All went well for some time. Being a doctor, and husband to a woman who deeply cared for her afflicted brother, it was only natural that Dr. Lamson displayed a certain concern for Percy. On Dec. 3, 1881, he visited Blenheim House.

The principal of the school, William Bedbrook, fetched Percy when the doctor arrived. Dr. Lamson had brought some treats. From a black bag he produced some hard fruit candy and a fruitcake. The doctor cut the cake with a penknife, offering a slice to Percy and the principal, as well as taking a slice himself. All three almost finished the cake at the one sitting.

During the course of idle conversation, Dr. Lamson mentioned that he had recently returned from America and had brought back something new — gelatine capsules. The gelatine dissolved after the capsule was swallowed, effectively doing away with the disagreeable taste of some medicines. Both the principal and Percy tried one. The principal's was empty, but Percy's was filled with sugar from a sugar bowl sitting on a table nearby. He swallowed it without tasting the sugar at all.

The doctor terminated his visit and left the school, informing the principal that he had to catch a train later that night for Florence.

That evening Percy complained of heartburn and went to bed. Later he began to vomit and convulse violently. Two doctors were summoned, but they could do nothing for the boy. At 11:20 that same evening Percy died.

On Dec. 6 a post mortem was held, and it was the opinion of the doctors that Percy had been poisoned. Dr. Lamson was located in Paris. Once informed of the death in the family he immediately returned to London. By that time the story of his visit to the school was known to the authorities. He was arrested and charged with murder.

On March 8, 1882, Lamson's murder trial began in London's Old Bailey. The prosecution quickly established that Percy had been done in by aconite, one of the most lethal poisons known to man. Dr. Lamson had purchased aconite shortly before his visit to the school. He also was deeply in debt and stood to gain financially from Percy's death.

In all murder cases involving poison, the prosecution must establish that the victim was in fact poisoned, and that the accused administered the poison. It was this second point that proved to be a sticky wicket. Bedbrook, the principal, was present at all times during Lamson's visit. The hard candies weren't touched. All three ate the cake. The sugar, which went into the capsule consumed by Percy, came from the school's own sugar bowl.

Despite this little problem, and the doctor's insistence throughout that he was innocent, he was found guilty and sentenced to hang. The sentence was carried out on April 28, 1882. The day before he was hanged Dr. Lamson confessed in writing to the murder of his brother-in-law. He never did state how he had administered the poison, and the solution to the case has baffled criminologists down through the years.

Here is the diabolical method most accepted by those who have closely studied the case. The speculation is that the doctor injected aconite into a raisin, which he then placed back into the cake. He marked the part of the cake containing the fatal raisin, making sure he gave the piece to his victim.

THE PRIM AND
PROPER POISONER

If you lived in Victorian England you were either a have or a have-not. It was a period in history when the distinction between the two groups was never more distinct. To be of the genteel upper class one led a pampered life devoted to the conformity of the day.

The world stopped at tea time. You received your mail on a silver salver. Your maids brought you everything. To stoop or exert oneself was thought exceedingly rude. The vulgarity of actually handling money was avoided. One paid one's tradesman by having him leave his "book" every three months or so. The lady of the house would see that a cheque for the full amount was in the "book" which was picked up on the occasion of the next delivery.

This was not to say that Victorians didn't occasionally dispose of their wives, husbands or lovers. Heaven forbid, no era of history has been free from these rather routine crimes.

It may be said that, generally speaking, this class of English society did not lend itself to unique murderers. It is distressing to report in this day of women's liberation that the one unique and original murderer that did exist was a woman.

In 1871, Brighton, then as now, was an extremely popular seaside resort. The old homes, many of which are still standing, are now used as flats. Over 100 years ago many of them were occupied by one family.

Mrs. Edmunds and her little girl lived in one of them. Her little girl, Christiana, was a 43-year-old virgin, who was, as Noel Coward used to say "exceedingly on the shelf." You see, Christiana like the house, was neat, tidy and extremely boring. The only two men who ventured around were the vicar and the doctor. Now the very thought of anything as sexy as pounding surf would have given the old vicar a bad case of hives. Such was not the case with the doctor. Dr. Beard was in his early 40s, good looking, pleasant, sexy; but alas, he was married. Not only was he married, but it appears that he was happily married, which in some circles deserves distinction.

The doctor suspected that Christiana sought out his medical services when really she was looking for something quite different. Be that as it may, the doctor would have none of it and treated Christiana as he would any other patient. What the doctor didn't know was that Christiana was madly in love with him. She never spoke to her mother or anyone else of her love for the doctor. We only know of her turmoil in the light of later events.

From her desperate position, and in her distraught state, she reasoned that the doctor would really fall for her if he didn't have that cumbersome Mrs. Beard around his neck. Under the pretense of having to kill some bothersome cats, she purchased a supply of strychnine. The next time the good doctor and his wife came to tea she gave Mrs. Beard a chocolate laced with strychnine. Soon Mrs. Beard collapsed. The doctor seemed to realize what was happening. He immediately induced vomiting and saved his wife's life.

Dr. Beard was upset, as well may be expected, and refused to treat either mother or daughter again. He made the decision not to report the attempted poisoning to the authorities. The topic was never mentioned by any of the participants who had tea in the Edmunds' parlor that day.

At this point Christiana had gambled and lost. Had she dismissed the whole thing criminologists would not be studying her case for over 100 years. She made the decision that was to give her method a horror of originality and wantonness that is unsurpassed by any female criminal.

She sent four youngsters at different times, to buy chocolates at the local sweet shop. She gathered up the chocolates and injected them with poison. She then had the youngsters return with the candy saying they tasted bitter. In each case the boys returned with candy the shopkeeper had given them in exchange. In this way she succeeded in getting quite a large supply of poisoned candies in the shopkeeper's stock. Not satisfied with this, Christiana injected the good chocolates she now had, and dropped them in shops around Brighton, figuring that someone would pick them up and eat them.

The entire population became susceptible to the poison so readily available. Only one little boy, Sidney Barker, ate the chocolates in sufficient quantity and was dead within the hour. Many became violently ill. Christiana sent chocolates to herself and was a volunteer witness at the inquest into Sidney Barker's death. She testified that she too had become very sick after eating the chocolates. The jury said the little boy had died through misadventure.

Again Christiana was off the hook. She wasn't suspected of making half the town sick or of the boy's death. In her love-crazed mind she figured now that everyone was being poisoned, including herself, the doctor would realize he had been mistaken when he thought she had attempted to poison his wife. It is warped reasoning, but at the time Christiana was in such a mental state that she would do anything to get back in the good graces of the doctor.

Next she wrote to Sidney Barker's father beseeching him to sue the confectioner who had sold the poisoned candy. She tried to disguise her handwriting, but the police had no trouble tracing the writer. The authorities then found out about the four boys buying candy at the same shop and returning it.

Christiana Edmunds was arrested. Feeling against her was strong in Brighton. Every resident or visitor had been a potential victim. The site of the trial was moved to the Old Bailey in London.

The most distinguished doctors available appeared for the defense, arguing that as a middle aged spinster Christiana was insane at the time she committed her acts. The jury didn't agree. They only deliberated an hour and brought in a verdict of guilty. She was sentenced to death by hanging.

Her sentence was later commuted to life in the Broadmoor Lunatic Asylum. Many people who had visited this institution believe that for a woman of Miss Edmunds' background, the former sentence would have been more humane.

A strange and special consideration was given to Christiana while in Broadmoor. Every six months her mother would come and visit her. Christiana was allowed to discard her drab asylum dress and don the dress she wore at her trial. A maid was provided and tea was served in the governor's study. Mother and daughter would nibble on small cakes as they discussed the weather, old friends, and state of the Empire. No distasteful topic was ever uttered by the two women.

This ritual continued till the day Mrs. Edmunds received word that her daughter had died in the asylum.

THE MYSTERY LINGERS ON

Even today the name Marie Lafarge conjures up images of a dark chateau in France, a murdered husband, and a sensational trial. Over 100 years later criminologists are still uncertain as to the answer to the perplexing problem: Did Marie really do it?

Born in France, Marie was a ward of her uncle and aunt. Uncle was an executive of the Banque de France, and, to put it mildly, was loaded. Marie was brought up with the finer things of life. She was, however, not blessed with a pleasing countenance. While not exactly ugly, Marie had a long, rather thin nose which was almost constantly dripping. From the neck down Marie was just great. A large dowry awaited any man willing to overlook the perpetual drip.

In 1839, Marie's uncle and aunt had a heart to heart chat concerning the lack of men in their ward's life. Being of a practical nature Auntie decided to advertise, seeking a husband for her 23-year-old niece.

Charles Pouch Lafarge applied for the position and was accepted. It is only fair to point out that Charles was exactly twice Marie's age. A coarse, gruff man, who was an ironmonger by trade, he was many other things by inclination. Charles thought that overindulgence in eating, drinking, and sex was the only thing in life.

Gentle, protected Marie and rough tough Charles were married in August, 1839. The ceremony was barely concluded before Charles bundled up his new bride and carted her off to his chateau in Glandier. Marie was greeted at the chateau by Charles' mother and sister. The realization that they would be living with her was bad enough, but the appearance of the chateau was even worse. It was an old rat infested mansion in an advanced state of decay.

That very night Charles ingratiated himself with his new wife by eating like a pig, drinking like a camel, and snoring like a lion. Marie realized that she had made a terrible mistake. The more she thought of it the more she knew she would never let this coarse man have her body. The future looked bleak. Marie wanted out.

She decided to write Charles a letter. It is too long a missive to reproduce here, but the following excerpts will give you the general idea:

"Charles, on my knees I ask your forgiveness. I have deceived you terribly. I do not love you. I love another. He is handsome; he is noble. We were brought up together. We have loved each other since we were able to love anything.

Poor me! I thought a kiss on the forehead would be all you would expect. Habit and training have put an immense barrier between us. In place of gentle words of love and sweet nothings, there are these feelings which take voice in you and which revolt me."

When Charles opened the letter you could hear the screaming and cursing on the other side of the channel. His mother and sister had to restrain him. Of course, there was no other man in Marie's life, but in her own way she managed to achieve the concession she sought. From then on Marie and Charles spent their nights in separate bedrooms.

Charles, having demonstrated his anger at this celibate turn of events, gradually decided that in order to keep Marie and her considerable dowry he had better calm down. Marie, too, decided to make the best of an awkward situation. Like many couple before them they drifted into a life of quiet desperation. Charles shared his thoughts with Marie, who dutifully displayed a more than passing interest in her husband, his hobbies and his business. To the outside world they appeared to be a happy, devoted couple.

At about this time in their marriage, Charles' iron business began to sour. Having lived so long with a degree of security, it now preyed on his mind that he might lose everything. To make matters worse, Marie took ill. Nothing serious, but cause for some concern. Charles was really touched when he was informed that while ill, Marie had made out a will leaving everything she possessed to him. So touched was he that he made out his own will, leaving everything to his wife. Marie quickly recovered.

Unfortunately, unlike Marie's illness, Charles' business problems didn't go away. There was one ray of sunshine in an otherwise dark future. Charles purchased the rights to a patent concerning the manufacture of iron, which he felt was worth a fortune, if only he could interest financiers in the venture.

At this juncture in their marriage Marie and Charles were truly concerned with each other's welfare. Certainly Charles figured that once his patent was accepted and proven, he would be wealthy beyond his wildest dreams. He and Marie spent their evenings talking about luxurious trips, homes in Italy, and clothing fit for royalty.

Off Charles went to Paris for a prolonged business trip to see if he could interest the money boys in his patent. Since it was just before Christmas Marie baked a lovely cake for her husband. She placed it into a Christmas parcel, in which she also affectionately placed a new pair of socks, a pair of slippers, and most touching of all, a picture of herself.

Upon receipt of the parcel Charles knocked off most of the cake in one sitting. Within hours he was suffering from terrible stomach pains. In a few day the pains subsided.

After the turn of the year Charles became convinced that his mission to raise money had met with failure. He returned to Glandier.

A few days after his homecoming his stomach pains returned. A doctor was immediately summoned. He prescribed several different medicines, none of which seemed to do any good. Marie personally insisted on tending to her husband's every wish during his illness. She spoonfed the weakened man, but despite this gentle care every meal was followed by violent bouts of vomiting.

Charles' mother had comforted her daughter-in-law throughout the family crisis. Now she intuitively felt that something was rotten. What's more, she thought that something was Marie. It appeared to her that Marie was just too insistent on taking care of Charles. Once she thought she saw Marie drop some white powder into her son's broth. Marie purchased a packet of arsenic, ostensibly to reduce the rat population of the chateau.

Enough is enough. Charles' mother told her son of her suspicions. Charles, despite his weakened condition, was at first furious with his mother. When Mummie actually showed him the whitish sediment at the bottom of a cup at his bedside, he realized that her suspicions were well founded.

A doctor was called, and he quickly tested for the presence of arsenic. The sediment in the cup proved to be arsenic, but the discovery was too late to save Charles. He had been systematically poisoned for far too long. Next day he was dead.

Charles' mother contacted the police the moment her boy closed his eyes. The post mortem revealed that Charles' death was due to arsenic poisoning. Marie was arrested and later stood trial for the murder of her husband. In all the history of crime it remains as one of the most publicized murder trials ever held.

The case against Marie appeared to be airtight. Her gift of the Christmas cake, followed by her husband's illness, weighed heavily against her. Her purchase of arsenic, which she never fed to the chateau rats, was also difficult to explain. It was also proven at her trial that she alone prepared all of Charles' food during his illness. Marie was found guilty and received a sentence of life imprisonment.

From the moment of her confinement at Montpelier, Marie's lawyers began their struggle to free her. They were assisted by the work of a well-known chemist, who took an interest in the case. Monsieur Raspail purchased the same experiment equipment which the authorities had used to prove that Charles had died of arsenic poisoning. He was amazed to discover that some of the zinc gauze used in the experiment contained arsenic.

It is not easy to interfere with a French jury's decision. Year after year Marie's lawyers worked diligently to establish her innocence. In 1852, after 12 long years in confinement, Marie was given a full pardon.

Old friends took her to a resort to recover from the hardships of prison, but to no avail. Her will to live was gone. Marie Lafarge died a few months after her release.

MYSTERIOUS MURDER
OF WEALTHY LANDOWNER

In order to fully comprehend the singularly unsatisfactory Bravo case, it is necessary for us to dwell for a moment on the personalities involved in their relationship to one another.

Come back with me to Victorian England and meet my cast of characters. Florence Campbell was a good looking young girl of 19 when she met and married a Captain Ricardo. Florence and the handsome captain tied the knot in 1864, and almost immediately the anticipated connubial bliss started to fade. The captain preferred the bottle over Florence's considerable charms. Rather than go through a divorce, the couple decided on a separation. In conjunction with their separate living accommodations, Florence was to receive an allowance of £1200 per year. In 1871 the valiant captain died of natural causes. Being preoccupied with the consumption of alcoholic beverages as he was, Ricardo neglected to change his will before his demise. The will had been drawn up immediately following his wedding day. Florence hit the jackpot — she was left with an income of £4000 per year.

Florence moved into a large house, The Priory, on Bedford Hill Road in Balham. Into this house she brought her paid companion, a Jamaican lady, Mrs. Jane Cannon Cox, who was an interesting soul, to say the least. Florence had met Mrs. Cox by a roundabout route. It seems Mrs. Cox's husband had died in Jamaica years before, leaving her almost penniless. A Mr. Joseph Bravo, a wealthy landowner and businessman on the island, took an interest in the widow Cox. He was instrumental in sending her three children to school in England. She later followed the children, and hired out as a daily governess to provide herself with an income. She became acquainted with the children of friends of Mrs. Ricardo, and in this way entered Florence's life. The two widows took a liking to each other. It was quite natural for Florence to hire Mrs. Cox as a companion at a salary of £100 a year.

When Florence moved into the Priory with Mrs. Cox, one must realize that in a few short years Mrs. Cox's station in life had taken a turn for the better. From being stuck in Jamaica, without a husband or funds and with three small children, she now was a dear friend and companion of a wealthy woman in a huge house. She held court over a large staff of servants. The rolling grounds came complete with horses and carriages. Mrs. Cox never had it so good.

Whenever her benefactor, Mr. Bravo, was in England, Mrs. Cox would visit with the Bravo family. One day she brought Florence with her. On this particular summer day, Florence met Mr. and Mrs. Bravo and their son Charles. Whatever attracts people to one another was at work that day. Charles took to Florence like a duck takes to water. Florence took to Charles in much the same manner. We can only wonder if the fact that Charles had an endowment of £20,000 payable to him upon the death of his last surviving parent, had anything to do with the torrid romance which followed. About the only thing that marred the whole affair was Mrs. Bravo's distinct dislike of Florence. Such a minor obstacle was overlooked and within a few months Charles and Florence were married.

In January, 1876 we find Charles and Florence, accompanied by the ever faithful Mrs. Cox, comfortably ensconced in The Priory. On Tuesday, April 18 of that year, events were to take place in the house that were to place all our characters under minute examination. The English-speaking world was to follow their every utterance with meticulous care.

At 4 o'clock that afternoon, Charles decided to take one of his horses for a ride. At half past seven Mrs. Cox returned from shopping, and joined Charles and Florence for dinner. The evening meal had, as its main course, lamb with poached eggs on toast. All three participants ate a hearty meal. A butler decanted the wine, which we are told consisted of one bottle of Marsala, one bottle of Burgundy and two bottles of sherry. Not bad for three people. Those Victorians knew how to live.

At about a quarter to nine the ladies, somewhat drowsy after a good meal and the wine, retired for the night. They were soon followed by Charles who went to his own bedroom which joined that of his wife. The housemaid, Mary Ann Keeber, entered her mistress' dressing room, put away Florence's clothing and tidied up. Then she started to go down the stairs. She was standing in the hallway, when, all of a sudden, Charles' door flew open. He rushed into the hall shouting, "Florence! Florence! Hot water! Hot water!" Mary Ann, scared out of her wits, summoned Mrs. Cox. In the meantime, Charles had returned to his room and was violently vomiting out a window. Mrs. Cox sent Mary Ann for water and mustard. By the time she returned to the room, Charles had passed out on the floor and Mrs. Cox was massaging his chest. Busy Mrs. Cox then dispatched a coachman to fetch a Dr. Harrison.

Mary Ann woke up Florence, who said with an utter disregard for originality, "What is the matter?" After she came to her senses, she fetched a Dr. Moore who lived closer than Dr. Harrison. Dr. Moore was the first man of medicine to arrive on the scene. He examined Charles and could barely detect a pulse. Dr. Moore, who can be admired for his bluntness, if not his beside manner, stated, that in his opinion, the patient was suffering from the administration of poison and the family could expect the worst.

Then Dr. Harrison showed up. He was met by Mrs. Cox, who greeted him with the words, "I am sure he has taken chloroform." Because of this startling declaration, the two doctors searched the room and came up with three bottles; one containing chloroform, one laudanum, and one camphor liniment. The doctors then brought in two more colleagues who agreed that the patient had been poisoned.

At three in the morning Charles regained consciousness, and despite being in extreme pain, he was able to answer the doctor's questions. He admitted rubbing his gums with laudanum as a treatment for neuralgia. The doctors told him this couldn't possibly account for his condition. Charles said, "I have taken nothing else. If it was not laudanum, I don't know what it was."

At this point Mrs. Cox had a private consultation with one of the four doctors — Dr. Johnson. She said that Charles had told her, "I've taken some of that poison, but don't tell Florence." When approached with this information Charles repeated that he had only taken laudanum for his gums, and nothing else.

On Wednesday the dying man asked his family, which was now reinforced with the presence of his mother and father, to join him in the Lord's Prayer. Two days later, after 56 hours of suffering, Charles Bravo died. His last words were, "Be kind to my darling wife, mother; she has been the best of wives to me."

An inquiry into the death was held on April 25 at the Priory. Refreshments were served, and the matter was disposed of quietly and quickly. One disconcerting note was the wording of the jury's verdict: "That the deceased died from the effects of poison, but we have not sufficient evidence under what circumstances it came into his body."

When the facts surrounding the mysterious death became public, there was a great hue and cry for further investigation. The case became such a matter of conjecture that it ended up being argued in the House of Commons. Finally, the coroner was ordered to hold a new inquiry. On July 11, the second inquest was held at the Bedford Hotel in Balham. When called to testify, Mrs. Cox now stated that Charles had said to her, "Mrs. Cox, I have taken poison for Gully, don't tell Florence."

You might well ask — who in the world is Gully? In 1870, while Florence was still Mrs. Ricardo, she became attracted to Dr. James Manby Gully, a man old enough to be her father. Attraction led to deception, and deception led to you know what. The affair continued through the time of poor Captain Ricardo's death right up to her engagement to Charles Bravo. Before she married Charles, Florence told him of the intimate relationship which had existed between herself and the elderly doctor. She and the doctor returned gifts they had given to each other, and both agreed to end the affair. Florence stated that her husband promised never to let her past come between them, but almost immediately he started accusing her of still carrying on with Dr. Gully, which she swore was not the case. Mrs. Cox and Florence had thus provided a motive for suicide, and at the same time, one might argue, a motive for murder. Despite the two ladies' statements, everyone else connected with Charles Bravo depicted him as a jovial, hearty man who loved life and was a poor candidate for suicide.

Dr. Gully was dragged through the inquest and suspicion was cast in his direction, for he had a motive. He may very well have changed his mind and wanted to continue his dalliance with Florence. While he wasn't in the house on the fateful night, he could have coerced Florence or Mrs. Cox to administer the poison.

Did Mrs. Cox receive pressure from Charles to leave the house, as some claimed? Did she see the good life slipping away and decide to do something about it? Mrs. Cox did call Dr. Harrison to the scene, knowing full well that Dr. Moore lived closer to the Priory.

Even though almost everyone agrees that Charles did not commit suicide, it is always possible, taking into consideration that people act in strange ways. This theory begs a question. Why did he not admit it, when he was told that he was going to die anyway? Then, again, Charles' letters to his relatives were read at the inquest. In them, he praised his loving wife.

* * *

The inquest jury stated:
"We find that Mr. Charles Bravo did not commit suicide; that he did not meet by death by misadventure; that he was willfully murdered by the administration of poison; but there is not sufficient evidence to fix the guilt on any person or persons."

No one ever stood trial for the murder of Charles Bravo. Dr. Gully passed away shortly after the inquest. Florence Bravo disappeared from public view. There are those who say she died heartbroken within a year. Mrs. Cox returned to Jamaica and was never heard of again.

SWEET ADELAIDE

I don't know what chemistry was taking place in Victorian England that gave rise to murder with a difference. Jack the Ripper was swishing through the London fog slashing ladies' throats. Gentle Christiana Edmunds inserted poison into chocolates, and almost destroyed an entire village.

Adelaide Bartlett was an unlikely candidate to join these assorted killers and capture the headlines of a nation in 1886. She was born in Orleans, France, but was taken to England as a child. Her father was, as they used to say, a man of substance. When she married at the age of 19, her father is reputed to have bestowed a substantial dowry upon his daughter. Her husband Edwin, aided by this addition to his capital, prospered as a grocer. During the 10 years the couple were married he expanded his business until he owned six shops.

At 19, Adelaide had a slender figure, dark hair and complexion. While not a raving beauty, one would be uttering a falsehood if one said she wasn't pretty. Edwin, on the other hand, was 10 years older than his wife. Not only that, he had strange ideas. He held education in the highest esteem. In fact, he sent his wife to an English boarding school, then to a convent in France. She came home to Edwin on holidays. This arrangement no doubt served to improve Mrs. Bartlett's mind, although one wonders if it did anything for the natural urges that young married people sometimes impart to each other. Yet it appears the Bartletts always showed a certain affection for each other and rarely had disputes of any kind.

All went well with the Bartletts for several years. In 1884, they had occasion to move to Merton Abbey, near Wimbledon of tennis fame. Here they attended the Wesleyan chapel, and as a result met the Reverend George Dyson. George had a luxuriant moustache, stood erect and could be considered cute by the opposite sex. The Rev. George, like all good ministers, had occasion to call on the Bartletts, and soon the three became close friends.

Then a tendency came out in Edwin that was so strange and unnatural it bordered on the unbelievable. Edwin Bartlett not only tolerated, but encouraged, the Reverend and his wife to see each other at every opportunity. Edwin insisted on George becoming Adelaide's tutor to accumulate more of his beloved education. As time passed, George was seeing Adelaide up to five times a week. Sometimes her husband was not at home. George even wrote love letters to Adelaide. She read them to Edwin. Edwin wrote back thanking George for his signs of affection.

Finally Bartlett told Dyson of a most peculiar philosophy. He thought that a man should have two wives, one for intellectual companionship and one for servicing. We know for sure he was only getting companionship from Adelaide. It's true she gave birth to a dead child in 1883, so we know Adelaide wasn't a virgin when she first met the Reverend. Edwin also expressed the desire to have George marry his wife after his death. He made a will leaving everything to his wife, with Dyson the executor.

The Bartletts moved to 85 Claverton St. in Pimlico. With this kind of a set up, is it any wonder that something went wrong?

Edwin took ill. By mid-December, Adelaide called the closest medical assistance, one Dr. Leach. Dr. Leach took one look and diagnosed Edwin's trouble as mercurial poisoning. No doubt he ate something that he shouldn't have and was treated accordingly. Edwin improved and by Dec. 31 he was in such good spirits that he was planning his menu for New Year's Day.

Edwin Bartlett died either late on the night of Dec. 31 or early in the morning of Jan. 1. Only his wife was in attendance. She said she woke up and found him dead. She called Dr. Leach, who verified that Edwin was indeed very dead. He noticed a bottle of chloroform on the mantle. Mrs. Bartlett calmly passed it off as being used by Edwin to massage his gums. The good doctor called for a post mortem the next day. Various and sundry portions of Edwin were sent out for analysis. The report came back that the cause of death was poisoning by chloroform.

Mrs. Bartlett was held in custody and charged with murder, as was the Reverend Dyson. Then the Attorney General dropped the charges against Dyson. In one fell swoop, the Reverend George's status changed from that of accused to that of witness.

Mrs. Bartlett had engaged Sir Edward Clarke to defend her. He was considered then, and is considered still, to have been one of the very best. He spent 10 days in the British Museum studying up on the effects of chloroform before the trial.

As the trial proceeded Dyson revealed that he had purchased chloroform on Dec. 27 for Adelaide at four different chemists. He then poured the four different bottles into one large bottle, and gave it to her. She said she wanted it to administer to her husband to relieve some obscure pain. He gave her the one bottle on Dec. 29.

We all know what happened on the 31st.

Dr. Leach testified about the bottle of chloroform on the mantlepiece when he was called to the death scene. The post mortem doctors testified that when they opened poor Edwin's stomach they were amazed at the strong smell of chloroform. Rev. Dyson expressed his innocence of any wrong doing, and told of the weird relationship that existed between the three friends. It came out at the trial that Adelaide and Edwin had had intercourse only once during their entire marriage, and that brief encounter was to result in their stillborn child. No one asked the Reverend what his particular score was, but he maintained throughout that his relationship with Adelaide was close, but not intimate, whatever that means.

The Crown claimed Adelaide had administered enough chloroform to render her husband unconscious and then poured enough down his throat to kill him.

Things looked terrible for Adelaide, but Sir Edward Clarke had an ace up his sleeve. On the third day of the trial, Dr. Leach was cross-examined by Clarke. The doctor told a strange tale. On Dec. 26, when he visited his patient, Edwin told him of an unknown force that had control of him. His speech was erratic and incoherent. Indeed, the doctor thought he might be going mad. Upon further questioning Dr. Leach revealed that the administration of chloroform is a skilled operation. Vomiting usually follows shortly after a normal amount of chloroform is administered if food has been taken within four hours of the chloroform. Edwin had eaten mango chutney within the four hours. There was no evidence of vomiting. Dr. Leach further stated that he had never heard of anyone administering chloroform to a sleeping patient. Certainly the patient would wake up and cry out.

Now all Clarke had to do was to get the chloroform into Bartlett's stomach. First he called a Dr. Stephenson, who was an accredited expert on the subject of chloroform. Dr. Stephenson maintained that if a person was rendered unconscious by chloroform it would be possible to pour more down an open throat. However, to his knowledge, it had never been done intentionally before. Later he stated that it would be a delicate operation. If it did succeed there would be burn traces in the windpipe. There were none in Edwin's windpipe.

In summing up his case, Sir Edward Clarke theorized that despite his excellent disposition on the day he died, Edwin Bartlett was quite mad. Dr. Leach, the only professional man who attended him, insinuated as much. In a fit of depression, when his wife left the room for a moment to wash, he filled a wine glass with the chloroform from the bottle on the mantlepiece, drank it in one gulp, put the glass back on the mantle, and quickly put his head back on his pillow. The chloroform went down his throat without leaving a trace. Adelaide then returned to a husband deeply unconscious or even dead, and fell asleep herself. She woke up later to find her husband dead. Sir Edward spoke for five hours.

In two hours the jury returned and the foreman's voice rang through the hallowed chamber of the Old Bailey. "Not guilty".

Mrs. Bartlett stepped down from the dock, and into the fresh air to disappear forever into that oblivion that claims accused murderers. Sir Edward Clarke cried for the only time in a 50-year practice.

Later a distinguished surgeon passed a note to Clarke. It said, "Mrs. Bartlett was no doubt quite properly acquitted, but now it is hoped that in the interest of science she will tell us how she did it."

MEAN HENRY SEDDON

Misers collect and save money, not for what money will buy, but for the sheer joy of possession. They privately count and fondle their coin, and some say they even obtain sexual gratification from these rather mundane dalliances.

Eliza Mary Barrow was a nasty woman who lived in London, England, at the turn of the century.

She was ill tempered, dressed in rags, and was a born miser. A shilling had about as much chance of passing through Mary's hands as a camel would have getting through the eye of a needle. In fact, it was well nigh impossible, because Mary would literally starve rather than part with the coin of the realm. Because of her decidedly frugal bent she accumulated what passed as a small fortune.

Relatives back in 1902 were much the same as relatives today. They catered to those who managed to save more of the green than they themselves. Nasty Mary, wise in the ways of saving a pound, took every advantage of her kith and kin. From 1902 to 1908 she forced her dirty presence and nasty disposition on distant relatives named Grant. When both Mr. and Mrs. Grant went to their great reward, Mary adopted their two children, Hilda and Ernie. Mary tossed Hilda into an orphanage, but kept the seven-year-old Ernie as her ward. She tried to live with another set of relatives, but things just didn't work out. In a fit of rage, the nasty one spit in the face of this latest relative. Mary was asked, not that politely, to vacate the premises. Still lugging little Ernie with her she took an unfurnished flat at 63 Tollington Park.

Now I must point out that, because of the parsimonous life Mary had led during her 40-some nasty years, she was now more than somewhat comfortable. She had penny pinched her way to about £4000 and owned a public house with an adjoining barber shop. In 1910, you had to say Mary was loaded.

It was her misfortune to meet and become the tenant of Henry Seddon. You see, dear Henry was a miser himself and loved the feel of gold every bit as much as Mary. He lived in his own building, at 63 Tollington with his wife, four children, and a half-witted maid.

Henry and Mary became good friends. We suspect that Henry guessed early on in the game that Mary kept a few pounds in her room. Henry knew all about counting loose bills on a quiet summer's night. He liked doing it himself. It kind of boggles the imagination to picture two people in different rooms under the same roof, going into raptures counting money late at night. But then other characters who have graced these pages have done even stranger things late at night behind closed doors.

By the end of 1910, nasty Mary and tight Henry were very dear friends. Mary began to have a real fear of losing her fortune, and of course she shared her fear with Henry. Never one to be at a loss for ideas where money was concerned, Henry suggested an annuity. He would set up an annuity of £10 a month for life for Mary in exchange for her cash, stocks and property. Mary went for the deal, and received her first payment of £10 in gold in the first week of Jan., 1911.

For several months things proceeded smoothly at 63 Tollington. Then Mary started to complain of a tummy ache. It got so annoying that she visited a Dr. Paul three times in one month. The doctor did not consider her condition serious and treated her for an upset stomach.

On Sept. 1, Mary suffered from vomiting and diarrhea and became violently ill. One of Henry's daughters, Maggie, was sent to fetch Dr. Paul. He couldn't get away, but Dr. Sworn (so help me!) attended Mary. He treated her for diarrhea. Throughout September Mary's condition deteriorated rapidly until, on Sept. 14, she died. Dr. Sworn swore that the cause of death was diarrhea and unhesitatingly signed the death certificate.

That morning Henry, ever the stickler for detail, called on an undertaker. Henry dickered with the funeral director for the cheapest burial money could buy. He even asked for a receipt for a higher amount than he actually paid, so that when he charged Mary's estate with the cost of the funeral, there would be a little commission in it for himelf. No question about it, Henry was a prince.

Speaking of Mary's estate, there really wasn't that much left. Henry had almost all of her worldly possessions. Of course, her £10 a month income ceased upon her death.

Henry appeared to have it made, but not quite. Mary's relatives, expecting to pick up a quick inheritance, came out of the woodwork. They were amazed to find out that everything was tied up neatly by an unobtrusive little man named Henry.

They contacted the police with enough suspicious facts that, a month later, Mary's body was exhumed. It was found to contain more than enough arsenic to have caused her death. On Dec. 4, Henry was arrested. A month later Mrs. Seddon was arrested as well.

On March 4, 1912, the Seddons' trial for the murder of Mary Barrow took place in London's famous Old Bailey. Embarrassing little details came up at the trial. The day after Mary died, Henry had gone to a jeweller with a ring and a watch which had belonged to Mary. He had the ring adjusted to fit his finger, and Mary's name removed from the watch. Remember little Ernie? He was now 10 years old, and told how Mrs. Seddon had always given Mary her medicine. Then a chemist took the stand and swore that the Seddons' daughter, Maggie, had purchased arsenical flypapers just before Mary's death.

The jury returned a verdict of guilty in Henry's case, and not guilty in the case of Mrs. Seddon.

The trial had been a sensation, for the evidence against the Seddons was totally circumstantial. Before sentence was passed, Seddon himself said that because of his guilty actions before and after Mary's death, it didn't matter how she died, he would still have been blamed for her death. Tight Henry may have been right.

He was hanged on April 18, 1912. Mrs. Seddon remarried and moved with her family to the United States, where she lived out the rest of her life.

THE GREAT BILLIK

When Herman Billik hung out his shingle in Chicago, the residents of the Bohemian section of the Windy City sat up and took notice. The sign on West 19th St. proclaimed for all the world to see, "The Great Billik, Card Reader and Seer." To the superstitious Bohemians, the Great Billik was obviously a man whose powers were to be respected, and at the same time feared. Besides, Billik's services at 25¢ a sitting were reasonable enough, even for 1904.

Martin Vzral also lived on West 19th St. He had a loving wife and seven happy, healthy children. Martin had worked hard over the years and had built up a small, but prosperous milk business. Eventually Martin Vzral heard rumors that his neighbor, Billik, was truly a powerful wizard. Word of a cure here and a cure there was all that was needed to convince the superstitious Vzral that Billik was a man who possessed exceptional gifts.

Billik bided his time. Then he made his first overture to Martin. He walked into the milk depot and froze in front of Martin Vzral. As if in a trance, out of his mouth came words which could not be understood. Martin stood transfixed. Then, as suddenly as the trance had started, it appeared to be over. As if making a speech Billik pronounced, "You have an enemy. I see him. He is trying to destroy you."

Hearing such strong words coming from someone whom he felt was an honest to goodness wizard greatly distressed Martin. Actually he felt more than distressed. He felt lousy.

Billik, besides being a really cool wizard, was also a keen student of human nature. Without another word he walked out of the milk depot and left the frightened Martin standing there trembling. Days passed and no further pronouncements emanated from the wizard. Meanwhile Martin gravitated from a state of worry to terror and near panic.

From which direction would disaster strike? Would it be a mysterious illness which would sweep through his family? Would his milk business be gobbled up by his competitor, whose business was located just down the street? Would disaster strike from some as yet unknown source?

Billik figured correctly that the time was ripe to again visit Martin Vzral. The terrified Martin pleaded for help. He swore to Billik that his business competitor must be the culprit who was out to get him. Was there anything Billik, the powerful wizard, could do to save him and his family?

"Why certainly," replied the wizard. The cunning rascal had chosen and cultivated his victim perfectly. From secret bags and valises came strange and powerful powders and potions. Together they were brought to a boil and carried down the street in a bucket to Martin's competitor's front door. The whole mess was dumped on the doorstep. "There, now you can have nothing more to fear. My spell will cancel any curse or hold your enemy may have over you," Billik assured the grateful Martin and his family.

Beside himself with relief, Martin insisted that Billik accept some small token of his gratitude. Billik pretended to be above such worldly considerations. Finally, at Martin's insistence, Billik let a $20 bill be pressed into his hand.

Martin's business prospered, definite proof of Billik's spell over his competitor. Everyone seems to have overlooked the fact that he was doing just fine before Billik intervened with his magic potion.

It is difficult to comprehend the part played by witchcraft and superstitions in the lives of immigrants thrown together in large North American cities. Martin Vzral had implicit faith in the powers of Billik, the wizard. Billik preyed on his victim's beliefs.

During the ensuing months the entire Vzral family came under the power and influence of Billik. Billik seduced Vzral's wife. Martin's sons worked and turned over their pay to the wizard. Slowly but surely Martin was convinced that he and his entire family could be struck dead by Billik at any time. Martin withdrew his hard earned life savings from the bank and turned the whole amount over to Billik. The female members of the family served, and bowed to, the great one, who was by now almost a permanent guest in their home. Profits from the milk company were turned over to the wizard each month. Billik, in his wisdom, saw fit to send three of Martin's daughters out to work as domestics. More money flowed in to the magic man.

The dire circumstances under which Martin Vzral and his family were living became evident. They were now poor. Billik was rich. Billik dressed well, and purchased a carriage and team. In short, he was living the life of a retired gentleman.

Realizing that even the most successful wizards must prepare for a rainy day, Billik had Mrs. Vzral insure the lives of four of her daughters and her husband for amounts ranging from $105 to $2,000.

For a year the Vzrals lived in poverty, with the assurance that everything would somehow work out. Billik just kept dropping by for cash and to spin a few tales of horrible deaths to unbelievers. This kept the Vzrals trembling until he dropped around again.

Well, you can only push a man so far. One day, in the mildest manner possible, Martin hinted that he thought he should be allowed to keep a bit more of his company's profits. The wizard was fit to be tied. How dare the ungrateful Martin hold out on him? He, who had slaved over a hot cauldron day and night to keep evil spirits away from Martin's door. Such insolence had to be punished. So strong was Billik's hold over Mrs. Vzral that he was able to talk her into giving her husband a white powder in his food to bring him back to his subservient self. Mrs. Vzral complied, and Mr. Vzral died.

In April, 1905, an insurance company turned over $2,000 to the grieving widow. She in turn, passed it along to Billik. In an untypical act of generosity he allowed her to keep $100 for funeral expenses.

Once Billik got the hang of the arsenic business, he speeded up production. Mary brought in $800, Tillie $620, Rose $300, and Ella $105. And so a father and his four daughters were dead within a period of two years at the hands of a madman. It is amazing to relate that no one became suspicious over the rash of deaths.

Operating through the widow, Billik sold the milk business for $2,900. He then took a little vacation in Niagara Falls. While resting, it occurred to him that the widow was a threat. He decided to kill her. Back he travelled to Chicago, where he fed a huge stew laced with arsenic to Mrs. Vzral. She quietly passed away and was buried.

How could a family of nine be systematically murdered so that now only three members remained alive; yet no one asked questions? At the turn of the century it was altogether common for certain illnesses to sweep through a family, killing several members in a short period of time. The insurance payoffs were small, and did not arouse any suspicion. Then there was the wizard himelf. It is believed that many people may have known what was going on, but decided to remain silent, fearing retaliation from Billik.

Only after Mrs. Vzral's death did rumors spread throughout the community. Some say a resident of the area overheard a servant discussing the series of deaths in the Vzral family. The woman mentioned it to a cop on the beat, who in turn reported it to his precinct captain. It was as simple as that. The bodies were exhumed and found to be laced with arsenic.

The wizard was arrested and charged with murder. He was convicted and sentenced to death. Strange are the ways of mere mortals. A great hue and cry was put up to save Billik's life. Why such a despicable man should receive public sympathy I have been unable to uncover at this late date, but we do know that public prayer meetings to have his sentence commuted were held in 1908.

Unbelievably, one of those attending these prayer meetings to save Billik's life was Jerry Vzral, one of the surviving Vzral sons. Obviously the public meetings and prayers worked. In January, 1909 Billik's sentence was commuted to life imprisonment. After serving only eight years in prison, he was paroled in 1917. Presumably Billik retired from the wizard business — as he has never been heard of again.

THE WITCH OF
YORKSHIRE

For years after Mary Bateman practised her particular brand of sorcery in Northern England, many a child was disciplined with the threatening phrase, "Go to sleep now, or the Witch of Yorkshire will get you". Even today Mary's name appears on most lists of the ten most evil women who ever lived.

Born Mary Harker in 1768 at Ainsenby, close by Thirsk, to a hard-working, law abiding farming couple, she didn't waste any time letting her parents know that she was different. By the time Mary was six, she would lie at the least provocation, and would steal anything she could lay her hands on. The Harkers talked to the little girl, but their lectures only seemed to add fuel to the child's already smouldering hostility.

In 1780, the Harkers, now thoroughly convinced that their daughter was a bad seed, saw to it that she was placed as a servant in a good home in nearby Thirsk. For the next eight years Mary got into minor scrapes, but by continually moving from place to place, she managed to stay out of the grasp of the law.

When she went to Leeds, the largest city she had ever seen, she was unable to secure employment and almost starved to death. Strictly by chance Mary happened to meet a friend of her father's, who took an interest in her plight. This gentleman found employment for her and she seemed to settle down for three years.

At about this time Mary met John Bateman. The pair knew each other for only three weeks before marrying in 1792. We are unable to find out too much about John, as he remained on the scene for such a short period of time.

Mary had a penchant for stealing, cheating, and simply acquiring other people's property. In a matter of months John realized he had a tiger by the tail. The pair had to keep moving to stay a step ahead of the law. When Mary told him of her plans to become a fortune teller, John figured it was time to pull up stakes and bid adieu to his true love. He left Mary and joined the army.

Mary returned to Leeds and in 1799 we find her actively engaged as a fortune teller. To make ends meet she sold charms. It was a meagre living and not exactly what Mary had in mind. As a keen observer of human nature, and with a growing confidence in her own ability, Mary realized that, given the right victims, she could graduate to bigger and better things.

As if cast by Hollywood, a gullible, simple minded pair named Stead came upon the scene. Mrs. Stead approached Mary, convinced that another woman was stealing the affections of her man. Mary persuaded the not too swift Mrs. Stead to part with most of her worldly goods in return for a charm guaranteed to keep the man of the house out of direct contact ith the other woman. When Stead up and joined the army, effectively propelling himself into a training camp and out of the clutches of the scheming female, it was proof positive to his wife that the charm had worked.

Word spread about the supernatural powers of the Witch of Yorkshire. When a young girl, a relative of Mrs. Stead's, came to Leeds several months pregnant but without a husband, Mary said never fear, she would cast a spell on the impregnator of the young girl. The spell would bring him begging for the young lady's hand in marriage.

A small sum was, of course, required to take care of incidentals. Once this vulgar formality was taken care of, Mary cast her spell. Still the stubborn lover did not appear on bended knees. Instead, the young lady's condition grew more acute with each passing day. More spells were needed. Each required cash payments. Mary bled the poor girl dry, but nothing produced the desired results.

In desperation, Mary fed the simple girl some medicine and managed to induce an abortion. Ironically, the almost father showed up begging forgiveness and talking marriage. The now weak young girl did marry her sweetheart, but her ordeal had taken its toll. The poor girl died swearing that Mary Bateman was the cause of her downfall. No formal suspicion concerning her death was ever cast upon Mary.

Once the Witch of Yorkshire had tasted the fruits of the witchcraft business, she realized she had found her niche. We will never know how many frauds she perpetrated on the simple minded and weak spirited, but the score might very well exceed 100.

Three Quaker ladies, a mother and two daughters, were the next to fall under Mary's influence. The two sisters, the Misses Kitchen, owned a drapery shop in the heart of Leeds. Once Mary ingratiated herself with the sisters, she began demonstrating her various skills to them. Mary interpreted the stars, read their palms, and in general convinced the gullible ladies that she really possessed certain mysterious powers. As time went on they came to believe that she actually held the power of life and death over them.

In September, 1803, the younger sister took ill and was confined to bed. It seemed only natural for the elder sister to solicit Mary's help. Mary churned up a brew or two, but nothing seemed to work. The younger Miss Kitchen's condition deteriorated rapidly. A week after taking ill, she died in agony. When the end was inevitable, the girls' mother, Mrs. Kitchen, arrived from Wakefeld. She and her surviving daughter immediately took ill. Both died two days later.

With no other friends or relatives, it was left to Mary to attend to the Kitchens' affairs. The Witch of Yorkshire arranged a triple funeral, and then proceeded to sell off all the worldly goods of her three victims. She let it be known that the three ladies had gone to their great reward, having been stricken by the dreaded plague. The terrible disease was so feared that it was weeks before tradesmen dropped around to the Kitchens' place of residence to discreetly have their accounts settled. The place was empty.

While inquiries were made of Mary, she explained that she had sold the ladies' possessions to satisfy the most pressing debts. Those few more expensive pieces in her own home were, of course, gifts given to her by the deceased trio before their untimely demise.

By 1806, the Witch of Yorkshire had a reputation. Those who could afford to be fleeced were obliged by Mary. Her successes were remembered, while failures were attributed to stronger spells, usually cast by the devil himself.

Unfortunately for them, Mr. and Mrs. William Perigo of Bramley, picked this juncture in Mary's career to come within her sphere of influence. Mrs. Perigo got up one morning and felt a flutter in her chest. She consulted her physician, but he could find nothing wrong with her. Hearing of Mary's unusual powers, Mrs. Perigo contacted her in nearby Leeds. Mary welcomed the unfortunate woman with open arms. Here was a sucker just begging to be taken.

Mary explained that the nature of Mrs. Perigo's complaint necessitated her contacting a Miss Blythe, who would be able, through Mary of course, to cast out Mrs.

Perigo's ailment. Once this little idea was thrown out to Mrs. Perigo and was duly swallowed, Mary knew she had a live one on the hook.

There followed several letters from the elusive Miss Blythe, containing instructions on just how Mary should go about curing the ill Mrs. Perigo. Would you believe sewing guinea notes in the four corners of Mrs. Perigo's bed with strict instructions that they were to remain there for 18 months? The Perigos believed every word, and watched as Mary sewed. Week after week Miss Blythe sent letters, each one containing preposterous instructions, and each extracting money or food in order to make the spell work. The Perigos complied with every ridiculous request, and were slowly being drained of their life savings.

Mrs. Perigo's condition didn't change. As the 18 months were drawing to a close Mary realized that she had to kill the Perigos. It was unbelievably simple. She had the ever obliging Miss Blythe send a letter to the Perigos, instructing them to make a batch of pudding. Enclosed in the letter were six envelopes of white powder. Each day the hapless victims were told to place the powder into the pudding before consuming that day's portion. They were not to worry if they became ill. That was part of the spell. The trusting Perigos immediately became violently ill, but so great was their faith in Mary that they continued to eat the poisoned pudding. On the sixth and last day, the pudding tasted so bad Mr. Perigo couldn't force himself to eat it. Mrs. Perigo had trouble, but managed to consume all the pudding. She promptly died.

After Mrs. Perigo was laid to rest, Mary continued to fleece the bereaved husband. She hinted at the resurrection of Mrs. Perigo and, incredible as it appears to us now, Mr. Perigo continued to pay to keep the charm alive. At the expiration of the 18 months, Mr. Perigo thought there would be no harm in taking the guinea notes from the four corners of his wife's bed.

It was only when he discovered torn papers sewn into the bed that any doubts concerning Mary came into his mind. The more he thought about it, the more shattered he became. Unbelievably, the past 18 months of living hell had been orchestrated by the evil mind of Mary Bateman. It had taken a while, but Mr. Perigo was now awake. He told his story to the police.

The inquiry which followed revealed that furniture, food and money supposedly passed on to Miss Blythe did not exist other than in Mary's imagination. All the letters had been written by Mary. Some of the old uneaten pudding was produced. It was laced with corrosive sublimate of mercury.

At Mary's murder trial, the jury brought in a guilty verdict without ever leaving the courtroom. The Witch of Yorkshire maintained her innocence right up to the moment the trap door sprung open and she plunged to eternity.

HOW TO CURE
A HANGOVER

If there were 10 commandments compiled strictly for poisoners, certainly Number One would be Thou Shalt Cover Thy Tracks Whilst Procuring The Poison. Jean Pierre Vaquier didn't give two hoots for this little axiom and, as a result, ended up in dire straits. Along the way Vaquier managed to break another, more conventional commandment; something to do with coveting thy neighbor's wife. No doubt about it, Jean Pierre was a scalliwag.

In 1923, Alfred and Mabel Jones had been married for over 15 years when Mrs. Jones' catering business turned sour. When she obtained a contract to cater to a large racetrack, what appeared to be a boon turned out to be a bust. At about the same time hubby Alfred purchased The Blue Anchor Hotel at Byfleet, Surrey, which was barely breaking even. Mabel became despondent over her failure and had a nervous breakdown. Her doctor advised her to get away from it all. He suggested a long rest in sunny France.

As fast as British Rail could get her to the Channel, Mabel dashed off to the resort town of Biarritz, France, where she found accommodation at the Hotel Victoria. Actually she found a bit more than accommodation. She discovered the villain of our piece, Jean Pierre Vaquier.

Now J.P. was a well groomed, well dressed Frenchman who knew his way around a lady's heart as well as her boudoir. He also worked at the hotel, which helped.

J.P. couldn't speak a word of English, but the litle devil conveyed his dishonorable intentions to Mrs. Jones. That prim and proper English matron let it be known that she wasn't averse to intentions dishonorable. Within three days J.P. and Mabel were between the sheets doing whatever it is dishonorable Frenchmen do with prim and proper English ladies.

Everything was proceeding just hunky dory when Mr. Jones, spoilsport that he was, suggested that Mrs. Jones come on home. Mabel, reluctant though she was to terminate her rest in sunny France, decided to return to England. No need to rush things — she and J.P. headed for Paris and shacked up at the Hotel Palais d'Orsay. During one of her brief vertical interludes, she informed J.P. that, while parting was such sweet sorrow, it was nevertheless a necessity.

J.P. had more up his sleeve than his elbow. He informed Mabel that he was something of an amateur inventor and that he would shortly be travelling to England to market his revolutionary new sausage machine. He suggested that they take up where they left off when he arrived in London.

On Feb. 8, 1923, Mabel pulled into Victoria Station and into the waiting arms of her ever loving Alfred. Next day J.P. arrived in London and checked into the Hotel Russell. Within a few days he had contacted Mabel. They did not pass go. They did not collect $200. They went directly to bed.

Mr. Jones had become ill and was confined to his bed. Later he went to Margate to recuperate. J.P. was pretty well confined to bed for the month of February as well.

J.P. did extradite himself from the boudoir long enough to visit a chemist shop at 134 Southampton Rd. Fortunately, one of the partners in the firm, a Mr. Bland, spoke French and assisted J.P. in the purchase of enough strychnine to kill four people. Mr. Bland questioned the purchase and was told that it was for experiments to do with a new invention. J.P., of course, bought the strychnine under the fictitious name J. Wanker.

In the meantime, J.P. was running a bit low on funds. To alleviate this annoying inconvenience he took a room at — you guessed it — The Blue Anchor Hotel in Byfleet. Mr. Jones, who had recovered sufficiently to return to work, didn't know it at the time, but J.P. Vaquier planned to kill him at the first opportunity.

Vaquier watched and waited. He noticed that Alfred was in the habit of taking bromo salts, particularly after having a few too many the night before. He kept the bromo salts on a mantlepiece in the parlor. It would be no trick for J.P. to toss in some strychnine.

On March 28 a party was held at The Blue Anchor. Mr. Jones consumed more than his share of liquor. Next morning, Vaquier arose bright and early. While he usually had breakfast in the coffee room, this particular morning he dawdled over his coffee for almost two hours in the parlor. J.P. had laced the bromo salts with strychnine, but was compelled to sit close by the mantle to make sure no one other than his intended victim took any bromo salts.

Sure enough, Mr. Jones came downstairs well hung over and headed straight for the bromo salts. He took a generous portion and commented at how bitter the concoction tasted. By mid-day Jones was in agony. That afternoon he died.

Meanwhile J.P. had hurriedly emptied out the contents of the bromo salts jar, washed the jar, filled it with fresh bromo salts, and returned it to its place on the mantle.

Everything went wrong. When witnesses told the attending physician what had taken place, he had the suspicious bottle of bromo salts sent to a forensic lab. The bottle still contained traces of strychnine. So did the spoon and tumbler used by Mr. Jones. In fact, so did Mr. Jones.

All the guests at the hotel were photographed, including J.P. When his picture appeared in the press, who spotted it but Mr. Bland, the chemist. Bland immediately recognized his poison customer, Mr. Wanker. He called Scotland Yard.

J.P. was arrested and charged with murder. When he was found guilty, the debonair Frenchman had to be forcibly restrained, and was carried screaming from the court-room. He was hanged at Wandsworth Prison on Aug. 12, 1924.

A Christmas Tale

- Part 3 -

CANADIANA

WHO KILLED
MRS. HENNING?

Murder from a distance can be objective and academic. Vicious acts can be studied and appraised and, as an antique dealer looks at a rare vase judging its authenticity, the student of murder can turn over in his mind the many aspects of a sensational murder case. What was the real motive? Was it money? Was it sex? What made it sensational?

In actual fact, when a murder occurs, it is the most personal of all acts. Certainly to the killer, the victim, and the many people whose lives they touch, nothing could be more personal and tragic.

The police who hunt these killers get up in the morning and go to work. While many of us build houses, sell toothpaste, and provide all the necessary services that make this world go around, the police go to work to find someone who has taken that most precious of all possessions — life itself. Many other law enforcement officers protect, but not these men. They apprehend.

The Ontario Provincial Police have jurisdiction over 17 districts in Ontario. Whenever a major crime is committed, assistance is readily available from the Criminal Investigation Branch headquarters in Toronto. From headquarters, Ontario's top detectives are assigned to coordinate investigations into major crimes, wherever they may occur in the province.

The ringing of the telephone woke Detective Inspector Ron Kendrick from a deep sleep. He glanced at his watch; it was 4 a.m. While he didn't expect a call when he went to bed the previous night, he knew he could receive one at any time. Like a doctor, Inspector Kendrick was "on call". It was the early morning hours on Sept. 20, 1975. Someone in a village called Ayton had found a body in a service station. He had phoned in his grim discovery to No. 6 District Headquarters in Mt. Forest. The detective sergeant in Mt. Forest drove 10 miles to the scene, and after verifying that indeed a murder had taken place, he notified his superintendent. Now the superintendent was on the other end of the line to Kendrick.

Ron Kendrick is a strapping, 6 ft. 1 inch career policeman. He has had only one job in his life, and he is still at it. He joined the police force when he was 19-years-old, and now is a veteran with more than 20 years service on the force.

Inspector Kendrick drove west along Highway 401 to Highway 6, where he made a right turn and headed north. His headlights picked out small sleeping towns as he sped past Fergus, Arthur, Kenilworth, and finally Mt. Forest. Just a few miles past Mt. Forest, Grey County Sideroad No. 9 turns off Highway 6 to the left toward Ayton. It is 10 miles from Highway 6 along this road to Ayton. Daylight illuminated the rural landscape as Kendrick drove through the tiny town. The 400 souls who live there were hardly stirring as he pulled up among the several police cars already parked in front of Henning's BP Gas station and lunch counter. He looked at his watch; it was 7:30 a.m.

Lincoln Becker is 38-years-old. He receives a pension because of an industrial accident he once suffered. In Ayton you can usually find Lincoln helping out at the other BP station which is situated in the centre of town. From force of habit Lincoln usually ended his day with a cup of coffee out R.R. #1 at Mrs. Henning's lunch counter. On the night of Sept. 19 he joked and passed the time with Mrs. Henning. She was cheerful and good natured like always. Shortly after 1 o'clock, Lincoln left the lunch counter, said good night and walked out the door. Mrs. Henning locked up behind him.

Lincoln Becker was the last known person to see Aleitha Jane Henning alive.

Inspector Kendrick examined the body lying on the floor in the service station portion of the Henning establishment.

Mrs. Henning, a 58-year-old widow, had been severely beaten about the head. A great deal of blood emanated from head wounds. Later Dr. Ray Sawchuk, a pathologist, confirmed that a skull fracture was the cause of death. She had been stabbed several times in the chest. Mrs. Henning was fully dressed, wearing a blouse and slacks. She had not been sexually molested in any way. Her blouse was pulled up to just below the rib cage, exposing the area above the abdomen to the bottom of the rib cage. Here the killer started a slash from her side across the front of her body. At approximately the halfway point in this gaping wound the killer either extracted the knife and then continued on, or for some reason changed the direction of the knife cut slightly. Mrs. Henning was already dead from a fractured skull when she was stabbed and slashed.

On the lunch counter was the coffee cup used by Lincoln Becker the night before. Mrs. Henning had been killed before she had a chance to wash it.

For two months Ron Kendrick lived with the senseless Henning murder. He knew every minute detail of the victim's life. The Hennings had been in Ayton for approximately 20 years. Mr. Henning passed away six years previously and his wife carried on the family business. They had two children, a daughter, 22, married and living in Kitchener and a son, 27, married and living a few miles from Ayton. He had two children whom his mother adored. Mrs. Henning's family could shed no light on who would want to do this horrible thing to their mother. The victim was a church going, hard working individual. She didn't drink or take drugs. There were no men in her life. She was good natured and obliging.

The absence of a motive made the case difficult to solve. Nothing was touched in the garage or lunch counter. There was money in the cash register that was not disturbed.

Ron Kendrick says, "It's like someone walked in, killed her, and walked out."

The premises were locked and the one thing that everyone agrees on is that Mrs. Henning was security conscious. Once she locked up she wouldn't let anyone in unless she knew him. The assumption is that someone in the area is the killer.

With the help of six policemen working full time on the case, Inspector Kendrick managed to question an entire town. A reward was posted offering $5,000 for information leading to the arrest and conviction of the killer. The medical profile points to a schizophrenic.

Ron Kendrick feels that the out of the way location of Ayton, coupled with the act that the killer was probably known to the victim, made the entire case a complicated and different one.

As I drove through the small Ontario towns, I thought back to the early morning hours of the day when Inspector Kendrick had made the same trip. I swung off Highway 6 and drove west along No. 9. I realized why the police were so sure the killer is from the district. There simply is no reason to go to Ayton late at night. To travel north or south you don't go through the town. Travelling east or west you would simply take a more convenient and better road.

The signs have been taken down from Mrs. Henning's service station. For security reasons a lone perpetual light replaced the lighted gas pumps and lunch counter.

Directly across from the service station the new Normanby Central School stands out as the most modern building in town.

Who would kill and mutilate a woman who had never done any harm to anyone in her life?

The people of the small community are friendly enough, but they are guarded in the statements they make. Nothing of this magnitude had ever happened in the town before. There are very few people who live a few months or years in Ayton and move on, like in the big city. Most are citizens of long standing and everyone knows everyone else extremely well. They have been unnerved by questions from police and reporters. Above all, the thought of a vicious killer still among them is hard to accept.

I spoke to many of the townspeople and they were willing to talk to me only if I agreed not to have their pictures taken and not to use their names.

One lady remembered the last time tragedy had struck their town. Her father told her the story about two cattle drovers who had an argument. One hit the other over the head with a cane and killed him. That was in 1919. She told me that in that case, of course, the killer was known. No real violence had broken the peacefulness of the community for more than 56 years.

She continued, "You know, no one around here ever bothered to lock up their homes at night. There didn't seem to be any reason, but things have changed. We all do now."

A businessman in town told me, "In a small place like this we all knew Mrs. Henning very well. Everyone can remember the last time they saw her. It's strange how everyone remembers how pleasant and cheerful she was now that she is gone."

Another man said, "Everytime I talk to a stranger I get the feeling they think I killed Mrs. Henning. That's why everyone in town doesn't like being questioned."

A garage operator wasn't so amicable. "Why don't you guys drop it? Let it be. No one can undo this thing now. Let the police catch the guy and the town can go back to the way it was before."

Shock, anger, sorrow, and dismay register clearly with these people. This is not the impersonal non-involvement of a large city. A way of life was disrupted that is the backbone of rural Ontario.

The citizens of Ayton can't really comprehend why, late on the night of Sept. 19, or in the eary morning hours of Sept. 20, a madman descended on a tiny service station in their tiny town, and for no apparent reason viciously took the life of one of their own.

I can't either.

AUTHOR'S NOTE:
Three years after Mrs. Henning's murder an individual was apprehended and tried for the Henning murder. He was acquitted and the case remains unsolved.

THE TORSO ON THE MOUNTAIN

"We've found a dead man! Part of a dead man!" shouted Bob Weaver, age 10 and his brother Fred, 9, to their friends.

From the moment these words were spoken on March 16, 1946 no other crime ever perpetrated in Canada captured the imagination of the Canadian public as did what was to become known as the Evelyn Dick Case. From Antigonish, Nova Scotia to Port Alberni, British Columbia, everyone followed the exploits of a handful of characters who told unbelievable and horrible stories of what took place in the days and months before the youngsters' gruesome discovery on Hamilton Mountain.

The body was without arms, legs and head. Two days after it was found, Alexander Kammerer reported that a roomer of his, John Dick, was missing since March 6. Dick, who worked for the Hamilton Street Railway Co. as a conductor, had not shown up for work that day. The police located his wife, Evelyn, who lived at 32 Carrick Ave. She could throw no light on the disappearance, except to volunteer that she and her husband were living apart. They were married only five months. The next day, two brothers of John Dick positively identified the body as that of their missing brother. Mrs. Dick was now questioned more closely. She gave the first of her many statements.

Evelyn said she married John Dick using the name Evelyn White. She told him her husband was a navy man who had passed away, and that she had a retarded daughter Heather, age 4, who had been fathered by White. Evelyn admitted to having affairs with other men while married to Dick, but claimed that he saw other women as well. Then she told the most fantastic tale of all. She related how she had received a phone call instructing her to borrow a car. The caller told her he was a member of a hired gang who had been retained to kill her husband. The mysterious caller said the reason her husband must die was because he had been seeing another man's wife, and made an appointment to meet her on Claremont Dr. on March 6. She borrowed a Packard and when she arrived at the appointed spot the man was there with a heavy sack. After placing the sack in the back seat, he got into the Packard and the two drove away. The stranger volunteered that the sack contained a part of John Dick.

Finally they arrived at the mountain and the stranger dumped the contents of the sack on the ground. Evelyn said she became sick. The man tossed the body over the edge of a bank. She let her mysterious passenger off at the Royal Connaught Hotel and returned the Packard to its owner. To account for the blood in the vehicle, Evelyn wrote a note to the owner of the car saying that her little girl cut her finger. The police proceeded to check 32 Carrick Ave. Here they found pictures of handsome Bill Bohozuk. They also found bank books containing large balances and a bloodstained skirt of Evelyn's.

Evelyn was detained by the police. In the meantime, the authorities started to uncover the tumultuous life led by the main characters in our cast. First and foremost there was beautiful Evelyn, with long black hair and a natural flirtatious look that oozed charisma. She lived on Carrick Ave. with her mother, Mrs. Donald MacLean and her 4-year-old daughter, Heather. Her father lived at 214 Rosslyn Ave. He too, was living apart from his wife. When his home was searched police found a revolver and ammunition, as well as an axe, saws, and a butcher knife. The house also contained enough incriminating evidence to charge him with theft from his employer, the Hamilton Street Railway Co.

Bill Bohozuk, the handsome other man in Evelyn's life, was found to own a revolver as well.

The more the police poked around, the more suspect everyone became. The police even found a bloody necktie in the back seat of the Packard Evelyn had borrowed. Mrs. Dick now changed her story and claimed that she witnessed the shooting of her husband by one Anthony Romanelli. The story was still news when she gave out a statement that it too was false. A more thorough search of the now infamous house at 32 Carrick Ave. uncovered a bushel basket of ashes. Later these ashes were found to contain bits of bone and teeth. The missing parts of John Dick had been cremated in the furnace. It seems that every time a search was instituted at the house new evidence was uncovered.

On Friday, March 22, the whole affair blew wide open. The police found a ladies' beige travelling case in the house. When the lock was broken it was discovered that the case contained a cardboard carton filled with cement. Under the supervision of a pathologist, Dr. W.J. Deadman, the cement was chipped away to reveal the body of a newborn baby boy. There was a cord fastened around the infant's neck.

Evelyn was quick to give her third statement. This time she told of bad feelings between her husband and Bill Bohozuk. She was having sexual relations with Bohozuk, and her husband strongly suspected them. John Dick had kept telling everyone about the affair, but other than drive Bohozuk half crazy, he didn't do anything about it. She stated that Bohozuk told her he had killed her husband. She claimed he even brought some of the pieces of the body over to her home and put them in the little garage beside the house, to be later burned in the furnace.

While Evelyn continued to make statements, the investigation was grinding out more grisly facts. The baby in the cement was the child of Evelyn and Bill Bohozuk. She had given birth to a boy, in September of 1944, at the Mount Hamilton Hospital. The very day she was discharged from the hospital, she claimed Bill Bohozuk placed a cord around the baby's neck and strangled it. She made further statements incriminating her father, saying he and her husband argued bitterly.

In the end, Evelyn Dick stood trial for the murder of her husband. She was found guilty on Oct. 16, 1946, and was sentenced to hang. Her counsel immediately advised the court that there would be an appeal for a new trial. The following day, Oct. 17, Bill Bohozuk and Evelyn's father, Donald MacLean, stood trial for the same murder. One of the main witnesses to be called at their trial was none other than Evelyn. When this occurred, she refused to give evidence. It was felt she refused because she was appealing her case, and did not want to prejudice her chances. The judge was compelled to discharge the jury and delay the proceedings.

Evelyn's lawyer, J.J. Robinette, won the appeal for a new trial. It started on Feb. 24, 1947, and Robinette leaned heavily toward her father being the actual murderer. This time the jury brought in a verdict of not guilty. While everyone realized she had guilty knowledge of the crime, it was felt that there was a reasonable doubt as to whether she actually killed her husband.

Only four days later, she was back in court facing a new charge, that of murdering her own child. This time the prosecution proved that Evelyn left her home with a live baby and returned with a locked travelling case. The jury brought in a verdict of not guilty of murder, but guilty of manslaughter. She was sentenced to life imprisonment.

The next trial was that of Bill Bohozuk for the murder of the baby. He claimed he was not the father of the child, and had never killed the baby. Another field day for the press occurred when Mrs. Bill Bohozuk showed up. No one was aware that he was married. She had been living in the United States for months. Mrs. Bohozuk stated that she was with her husband all day on the date Evelyn claimed he had strangled the child. The jury obviously believed her. They took only ten minutes to find him not guilty.

Both Donald MacLean and Bill Bohozuk then stood trial for the murder of John Dick. When Mrs. Dick again refused to restify the judge instructed the jury to bring in a verdict of not guilty pertaining to Bohozuk. This they did without leaving the jury box. Donald MacLean heard all the same evidence one more time. He was finally acquitted of murder, but was convicted of being an accessory after the fact of murder. MacLean received a sentence of five years in prison.

No one was ever convicted of murdering John Dick and cutting off his arms, legs and head.

Epilogue

Whatever happened to all the characters in this tangled, fascinating case?

Mrs. Donald MacLean took little Heather and moved away from Hamilton.

Donald MacLean spent four years in Kingston Penitentiary and was released in 1951. He worked for some time as a parking lot attendant, and died in 1955.

Bill Bohozuk's whereabouts are unknown.

Evelyn Dick served 11 years in prison, and was paroled in 1958. She has disappeared from view.

MURDER IN THE BATHTUB

As teenagers Jane Whelpley and Terrence Milligan both attended school in Saint John, N.B. The youngsters never met in the Maritimes and had no way of knowing they would travel over a thousand miles to meet, marry, and encounter tragedy in Toronto.

Det. Donald Wright arrived at Terrence and Jane Milligan's apartment only half an hour after the police received a phone call from Terrence telling them that his wife was dead. It was 8 a.m. Sunday, June 11, 1967. Upon entering the apartment located at Eglinton Ave. E. and Birchmount in Toronto's east end, Wright found Jane Milligan dead in her bath. He immediately had an instinctive feeling that all was not as it should be. The bathtub had a barren look that was not typical. Wright's trained detective's eye noticed that there was no soap or facecloth near the tub. Jane Milligan's body was sitting in the tub with her back to the taps. While there is no rule that dictates how a person sits in a bathtub, Wright correctly deduced that the vast majority of people sit in a bathtub facing the taps. A mantle radio was lying in the tub in a foot of water beside the body.

The obvious conclusion was that death was due to electrocution. Wright scanned the scene and noticed that an extension cord had been used to plug the radio into an outlet in the livingroom. This allowed Jane to place the radio on the edge of the tub. Without using the extension cord she could have plugged the radio into an outlet in the bathroom, enabling her to place it in a safer location.

Would it be natural for Jane to go through the inconvenience of using an extension cord in order to place the radio on such an obviously dangerous perch?

Milligan told Wright that his blonde, 19-year-old wife had awakened him about 6 a.m. She asked him if he wanted breakfast. He declined and went back to sleep. When he awoke at 7:30 a.m., he called out to her but received no answer. He got up to look for his wife. He told Det. Wright that he found his wife dead in the bathtub. He said he pulled out the plug of the radio before touching her body. Within 10 minutes, under the inquisitive but still gentle questioning of the detective, Milligan changed his story. He now said he didn't even notice the radio, but touched his wife's body to see if there were any signs of life. When Wright suggested that he must have received a shock, Milligan volunteered that he was mistaken — no doubt he had unplugged the radio first.

Over and above Milligan's elaborate stories, Wright was amazed that the 22-year-old could be so composed after finding his wife dead only minutes before. The couple had been married less than a year. Milligan, who seemed to be a lucid, clean-cut young man, casually mentioned to Wright that he had a $15,000 double indemnity policy on his wife's life. He stood to collect $30,000 from the unfortunate accident.

After two and a half hours in Milligan's company, Wright came to the private conclusion that he had walked into a murder case. Within days Det. Wright had his vacation postponed. He was assigned to the Milligan investigation.

Wright checked the neighborhood to get a profile on Terry Milligan. The Milligans' immediate neighbor, Mrs. Marion Bakes, said she had often heard fighting from the young couple's apartment. She said that early in the morning of Jane's death, she had heard a rubbing noise, like the sound of flesh against porcelain, but had heard no loud noise or music from the adjacent apartment. Wright recalled that when the radio was recovered from the water the volume indicator was at the high position.

While Wright was becoming more convinced than ever that he had stumbled across murder, the pathologist's office released the cause of death — asphyxiation, probably due to electrocution. Wright couldn't believe it. He was sure the scene had been set up to give the impression of death by accidental electrocution. The detective was convinced that the cause of death was drowning.

Jane Milligan was buried, and that very same day Det. Wright received a call from the Toronto General Hospital. Terry was in the emergency ward suffering from exhaustion and alcohol. He had collapsed on a busy downtown Toronto street. Wright rushed to the hospital, thinking in the back of his mind that his suspect may have broken and was ready to confess. He did not find a repentant Milligan. Instead, the baby-faced suspect accused the police of trying to invent evidence to convict him of murder. Later it was discovered that Milligan had an IQ of 135, which placed him in the near genius class. This day the bereaved husband not very cleverly took Wright into his confidence and inquired where he could find a prostitute.

Wright checked into Jane Milligan's background, and found nothing unusual. She had finished Grade 12 and had been employed as a teller in a Scarborough bank.

While all the incriminating circumstantial evidence uncovered by Wright indicated foul play, the pathologist's report could not be denied. It stated emphatically that death was due to asphyxiation, probably caused by electrocution. There is something about an official report that seems to defy questioning. Despite this, Det. Wright decided to delve further into the pathologist's report. This may have been the single most important decision of the entire investigation. Wright found out that the pathologist had made only a cursory examination of the remains. He had been in a hurry to go to a medical convention in Montreal. A few scribbled notes were, in the main, what went to make up the report. Fortunately, Jane's vital organs had been retained after her body had been buried.

A second examination of the organs was conducted, and a quite different cause of death was discovered — death due to drowning, no evidence of electrocution. In addition, the new report included other information not previously mentioned. There were bruises to the body below the left eye, on the left elbow, and hip.

An inquest was called for July 27, 1967, and the police feverishly tracked down witnesses. Wright questioned employees at two electrical plants where Milligan worked. Both Sangamo Co. Ltd. in Leaside and Crouse-Hindes Co. of Canada Ltd. in Scarborough had large staffs. Wright located some workers who knew Milligan well and were willing to testify that he referred to his wife as "the old bitch". In fact, some specifically stated that Terry used to go out of his way to let them know that his wife was terribly careless about placing her radio on the edge of the bathtub.

On June 21, Milligan was served with a subpoena to appear at the inquest into his wife's death on July 27. When given the subpoena, he informed the authorities that he was leaving Toronto to live with his uncle on a farm in Prince Edward Island.

On July 27, Milligan returned to Toronto for the inquest. The jury determined that Mrs. Milligan's death was due to "homicide at the hands of her husband". Terrence Milligan was arrested and charged with non capital murder. Det. Wright's job was now over. He turned his thick file on the Milligan case over to Det. Sgt. Jim Crawford and Det. Sgt. Jack Evans, whose job it was to prove murder in a court of law.

The two detectives went over all the ground that Wright had already covered. They received the co-operation of Sangamo and Crouse-Hindes officials, and had offices made available to them in each plant. They stayed almost a week at each location, questioning employees. They found out that Milligan had implanted the idea of a radio in the bathtub to several of his co-workers. He insinuated that his wife was careless with the radio. Yet none of his neighbors in the east end of the city had ever heard him even mention this fact. Was he cunning enough to avoid bringing up this subject to his neighbors, perhaps fearful that they would mention it to his wife?

Crawford flew to Prince Edward Island with a search warrant to go through Milligan's belongings on his uncle's farm. One of his discoveries was a paperback book entitled "The Doomsters", by Ross MacDonald. Crawford's secretary later was to read the book and find out that two victims in the story met their deaths by having a radio thrown in the bathtub. Crawford, mindful that Milligan had spent the month before his arrest in Prince Edward Island, plodded across the countryside looking for friends of the accused. The islanders quickly identified the six foot, four inch Crawford as the big cop from the city. Soon he located friends of Milligan's who told him that Terry was not your typical bereaved husband. He had taken out girls and attended dances only days after his wife's funeral.

Evans and Crawford tried balancing Milligan's radio on the edge of the bathtub and found it very difficult. I know. I tried the same thing with the same radio on the same bathtub. Anyone with average intelligence would know that the slightest touch would either knock the radio to the floor or into the tub. Using any degree of common sense, you just wouldn't put a radio in such a precarious position.

Crawford and Evans had a plumber take the entire bathtub out of the apartment. The job was completed in eight hours, so as not to inconvenience the new tenants. They transported the tub to the basement at police headquarters. Policewoman Janet Ebert, clad only in a bathing suit, entered the bathtub. The water level was the same as the day Det. Wright walked into the Milligan apartment. Policewoman Ebert sat in the tub with her back to the taps, in the same position as Jane Milligan. She bent over and placed her head under the water. Later she verified that her head kept coming to the surface. She even tried to concentrate on keeping her head under water, but try as she might, there was a natural pressure for her head to bob to the surface.

Milligan's trial for non capital murder began on Monday, May 13, 1968. The prosecution succeeded in establishing that Jane met her death by drowning, not electrocution. The Crown paraded witness after witness to the stand, each one adding to the intertwined series of incidents that completely incriminated the accused.

David Keeler, who lived close by the Milligan apartment, testified how Terry had knocked on his door that fateful morning with the words, "My wife's drowning, let me call the police."

William Green, an electrical engineer, testified that anyone receiving an electrical shock while sitting in the bathtub, would certainly scream. Mrs. Bakes, the Milligan's immediate neighbor, who could hear the squeak of flesh on porcelain through the walls, testified that she heard no scream.

Eric Armstrong, a fellow employee of Milligan's at Sangamo, told of a strange conversation he had with Terry when he drove him home three weeks before his wife died. Armstrong said of the conversation, "He mentioned the fact that his wife was worth a lot of money, and he wouldn't mind doing away with her."

Even the manager of the cemetery where Milligan had picked out a plot for his wife, took the stand. He quoted Milligan as saying, "It is probably better than she deserves."

Crawford and Evans had done their job well. The jury took 10½ hours to find Millgan guilty of non capital murder. The judge congratulated them on their verdict, and Terrence Milligan received life imprisonment, where he is confined to this day.

Staff Sgt. Jim Crawford, now 28 years a cop, vividly remembers the case that took place over 15 years ago. The huge man whose dogged police work was most responsible for placing Terrence Milligan behind bars, says with a note of distinct satisfaction in his voice, "It was certainly one of my most interesting cases."

A MONUMENTAL
AFFAIR

Over 50 years ago, at a little after 6 p.m., on the night of March 5, 1930, someone activated firebox 566 at the corner of Dundas and McCaul Streets in Toronto. The person who sent in the alarm was never identified, and probably had no way of knowing that he was opening the curtain on one of Canada's most baffling murder cases.

Within minutes, fire companies from Adelaide, Queen, and College Streets were dispatched to Goldberg Bros. Monument Works at 153 St. Patrick St. Firemen burst into the premises and quickly extinguished the flames. Fireman James Ridout was groping in the darkness, trying to find his way back to the door when his hand fell on something peculiar. He directed the beam of his small flashlight to the object and quickly realized that he had come upon the body of a man slumped over a desk. The upper portion of the body had been terribly burned with the face charred beyond recognition.

In this manner, James Ridout found the body of Samuel Goldberg, 35, who was part owner of the monument firm. An autopsy performed on Goldberg revealed that a bullet had gone completely through his head. No weapon of any kind was found at the scene, but a small tin containing coal oil and a larger can of motor oil were found on the floor near the desk. Goldberg's clothing had been soaked in the oil.

The police, acting swiftly and efficiently, questioned friends and relatives of the deceased. Goldberg's wife, Sala, now a widow with two children; Norma, three; and Nathan, 21 months, could shed no light on the tragedy which had befallen her. Goldberg's partners in the monument business were his two brothers Harry and Abe, and his uncle, Abraham Steinberg. Harry and Abe were both absent from the company offices that day and were never suspected of having caused the tragedy.

Abe Steinberg said that he had left the company office at 5 p.m., and was considered by the police to be the last person to see Sam alive. Because of this the police questioned Steinberg extensively for three hours, and finally arrested him on a holding charge of vagrancy.

Bits and pieces of information were uncovered during the police's preliminary investigation. Goldberg, who neither smoked nor drank, was shot at close range. A quantity of charred paper was found on top of Goldberg's desk. The fire had been confined to the area surrounding the desk. No fingerprints were found anywhere near the body.

In the meantime, Abe Steinberg was released on bail of $5,000. Then, on March 7, two days after the murder, Det. Sgt. Arthur Levitt found a revolver while sifting through rubbish at the rear of Goldberg's office. The .38 calibre Colt had not been tossed away. It had been carefully placed under an old cement bag and pushed into the snow between a garage and a fence. The gun contained three fired and two live shells. Within days the police were able to trace the Canadian distributor of the U.S. manufactured weapon. The weapon had been sold on April 16, 1910, to the firm of Wood, Vallance & Co. in Hamilton. They in turn had sold it shortly after, but here the trail stopped. They could not trace the gun further.

The city of Toronto, and indeed most of Canada, was now humming with news of the mysterious murder of the mild mannered, respectable business man. Then, on March 25, Abraham Steinberg was charged with the murder of his nephew, a charge, which, if proven, carried an automatic death sentence.

The police revealed that a piece of lead had been found at the scene, and after the gun was located it was established that it had fired the fatal shot. An empty cartridge case from a .38 Colt revolver was found on a lot adjacent to the Goldberg property. Through the unglamorous task of sifting garbage and searching through snow, the detectives had uncovered the murder weapon, the lead slug and even the cartridge case.

The police were successful in finding young people who identified the murder weapon as belonging to Abe Steinberg. It seems that two years previously, Steinberg had owned a dry goods store in Chesley, Ont. Steinberg's son Phillip had shown his father's gun to several friends. They now came forward to identify the gun. One youngster remembered that the gun had a chip out of its handle and picked the murder weapon from a row of nine guns.

The police also discovered that some money had been short in Steinberg's accounts with the firm. When asked by the other partners about this matter, Steinberg had come up with the missing money. Since the incident took place, the Goldberg brothers said things were never the same, and tensions ran high at the monument firm. They particularly emphasized the bad feeling between Steinberg and their murdered brother.

On Oct. 6, 1930, Abraham Steinberg stood trial for the murder of his nephew. During the trial, it was revealed that when Steinberg's house was searched detectives had found overalls stained with human blood. Again the bad feeling between the accused and the murder victim was rehashed. In a sensational move, the Crown called one James Creighton who had spent time in the Don Jail with Steinberg. Creighton swore that Steinberg told him that he and Goldberg were always arguing. He also said Steinberg had told him that on the day of the murder he went to the monument works carrying a gun for protection. During a heated argument Steinberg had accidently killed Goldberg. Then he set the place on fire.

Rabbi Jacob Gordon told the strange story of a man who had knocked on his door at about 6 o'clock on the evening of the tragedy. The unknown man requested that the rabbi use his influence to prevent an autopsy being performed on Goldberg's body. The rabbi explained to the jury that religious custom prohibited a body from being cut. The visitor told the rabbi that there had been a fire at Goldberg Bros. and that Sam Goldberg had been burned to death. The rabbi had explained to the visitor that there was no way that he could prevent an autopsy if it was required and was the law of the land. The prosecution hinted strongly that Steinberg may have been the rabbi's visitor.

In Steinberg's defense, his wife took the stand and swore that the overalls found in their home did not belong to her husband. She said he had never worn nor owned a pair of overalls in his life. Defense attorneys admitted to the bad feeling between Steinberg and Goldberg, but put forth the rather plausible argument that disagreements between partners were a common occurrence and did not necessarily lead to murder. The defense also tried to discredit the Creighton story, and hinted of favors given in return for the co-operation of the witness. Lastly, Rabbi Gordon emphatically stated that due to being nearsighted he could not identify Steinberg as the man who had the strange visit with him.

On Oct. 10, 1930, after four hours of deliberation, the jury failed to agree on a verdict and was dismissed. Steinberg stood trial for murder a second time on Feb. 1, 1931.

This time, the defense came up with several witnesses who testified that Steinberg was in Max Rotenberg's store between 5:10 p.m. and 7 p.m. on the night of the killing and could not have been the murderer. Countering this evidence was that of youthful Max Milgram, who swore he saw Steinberg in the vicinity of the fire between 6:30 and 7:45 p.m.

Steinberg was found guilty and was later sentenced to be hanged on April 21, 1931. His lawyer lodged an appeal and was turned down. A second appeal to the Supreme Court of Canada was lodged. As a result of this move, a stay of execution was granted so that the appeal could be heard. The Supreme Court dismissed the appeal, and a new execution date of July 14, 1931 was set. Despite a petition containing 40,000 signatures pleading for Steinberg's life, the federal cabinet denied clemency, and in their official jargon stated that "there be no interference with the death penalty."

As the execution date approached, Steinberg maintained his innocence. His religious counsel, Rabbi Samuel Sachs, disclosed that Steinberg never veered from his claim of innocence.

On July 14, at exactly 8 a.m. Steinberg was hanged for the murder of his nephew. A clock in the Steinberg home which had not chimed for over a year, rang out the hour at precisely 8 a.m. on that fateful day.

All that day, Rabbi Sachs desperately tried to find a synagogue or fraternal organization to accept Steinberg's body. None would, and in the end Abraham Steinberg, draped in the prayer shawl which had been given to him as a boy in Poland, was laid to rest in a potter's field.

STRANGLER NELSON

The Boston strangler managed to kill and mutilate 13 innocent women, terrorizing the city of Boston for several years. Albert DeSalvo confessed to being the strangler, and was committed to an institution. He had terrorized an entire city to such an extent that women feared to walk the streets alone.

Way back in 1927, Earle Nelson operated in much the same manner as DeSalvo, except that he killed more frequently and moved from city to city. He cut a swath of rape and murder across the United States and into Canada.

Everyone who has researched the Nelson case agree on one thing — Earle Nelson was not normal. The best documented portion of his life began when he crossed the border from the U.S. into Canada.

William Patterson worked in a Winnipeg department store. He and his wife lived at 100 Riverton St. The couple planned to sell their home, so while Bill Patterson was at work his wife showed prospective buyers through the house. To attract potential purchasers, they had placed a "For Sale" sign prominently in a front window.

On a bright June day in 1927, Bill came home from work and was startled to find that his wife was not at home. His two children had spent the afternoon playing in a neighbor's back yard. Patterson couldn't believe that his wife would leave the children unattended. He phoned the police and reported his wife missing.

In the meantime, despite his concern, Patterson had the practical problem of caring for his two children. He prepared the youngsters for bed. Later, in his own bedroom, he noticed that someone had forced open a suitcase in which he and his wife kept their savings. When Patterson kneeled down to take a closer look, he caught sight of his wife's coat under the bed. When he extended his arm, reaching for the coat, his hand came to rest on the neck of his dead wife.

The distraught man raced to a neighbor's house, blurted out the story of his tragic find and collapsed. The police were at the scene in a matter of minutes. Near Mrs. Patterson's body they found an old blue jacket and a pair of cheap cotton pants which did not belong to Mr. Patterson.

One of Patterson's brown suits was missing, along with $70 from the suitcase. It was obvious that the killer had left his old clothing at the scene of the murder, having first changed into Mr. Patterson's suit.

In the pockets of the cotton pants the police found newspaper clippings of rooms to let in Winnipeg. An examination of Mrs. Patterson's body revealed that she had been raped and strangled. The police recognized the similarity between this crime and those being committed by a monster who was roaming through the U.S., raping and murdering as he went. The "For Sale" sign, the woman alone, the rape, strangulation and theft, all pointed to the same man.

Was it possible that the man known as "The Strangler", or "The Gorilla Man" was in Winnipeg? The answer soon became apparent. So sure were the police that they had one of the most notorious killers in history among them that they commenced to canvass every home in Winnipeg advertising a room for rent on the chance that they might come up with the killer.

On the day following the murder, the police found Mr. Patterson's brown suit in a pawnshop. In its pockets they found his cigarette lighter. The pawnshop proprietor distinctly remembered the man who had left the suit. He was an excellent customer. He had purchased an entire new outfit consisting of a light gray suit and overcoat. The customer had then asked the pawnshop owner for the location of a good barber. The merchant had accompanied the man to his own barber. The stranger had laughed and joked with the barber while in the shop. It is estimated that he had killed Mrs. Patterson only hours before.

A full description of the wanted man was sent to every law enforcement agency in the U.S. and Canada. By June 11, the stranger had managed to hitchhike to Regina, where he rented a room under the name Harry Harcourt. He was shocked to find his description all over the front pages of the Regina newspapers. In order to change his appearance, once more he bought old workclothes at a local pawnshop, and by June 13 left Regina on foot.

Back in Winnipeg, a second body was discovered. Lola Cowan, a 14-year-old schoolgirl, had been enticed to her killer's room on the promise that he would purchase some flowers the girl was selling. Lola was contributing to her family's income by selling flowers after school. When her body was found under a bed it was obvious that she had been sexually attacked and strangled. The strangler had slipped out of his room on June 9 without paying his rent.

With the news of the discovery of the second victim the entire west was in a state of fear. Citizens bolted their doors and peered suspiciously at strangers from behind closed drapes. A living fiend was in their midst.

Although a complete description of the killer was widely distributed, and he had left a hot trail, it wasn't until Wednesday, June 15 that he was spotted. Leslie Morgan owned and operated a general store in Wakopa, Man., a tiny community of six houses about 250 miles southeast of Regina and 16 miles southwest of Killarney. Morgan served a soft drink and some cookies to a stranger. He was sure he had just served the strangler, and informed the Manitoba Provincial Police in Killarney. The police caught up with the fugitive a few miles south of Wakopa. He was arrested without incident and taken to Killarney. At 10:40 p.m. he was placed in jail. It took him exactly 20 minutes to pick the locks on his cell door and escape.

Nelson made his way to the Killarney railway station, figuring that he might be able to hop a train. He remained hidden until 8:10 a.m. when he came out of hiding in order to board an incoming train. He had no way of knowing it was a special train loaded down with police arriving expressly to take part in the manhunt. Nelson was quickly apprehended, handcuffed, and escorted to Winnipeg under heavy guard.

Who was Earle Nelson and what terrible crimes had he committed which made him the most hunted man in two countries?

Earle Nelson was born in San Francisco on May 12, 1897. He attended school for a short time, but dropped out to become a transient laborer. By 1921 he had twice been confined to an insane asylum in California. After his second release Nelson married. His wife soon began to notice his childlike behavior. In fact, Nelson liked to play with children, and got along well with them. He would wander away from his wife and home for weeks at a time. When he returned he would behave as if he had been absent for only a few minutes. Finally, because of his erratic behavior, his wife had him confined for a third time. He escaped from the institution and was never recaptured.

When Nelson was safely behind bars in Winnipeg, police officials from a score of U.S. cities requested his fingerprints so they could be matched up with prints left at the scene of similar crimes in their cities. From these fingerprints and eyewitness reports, Nelson's path of terror was traced.

It is believed that he started killing on Feb. 20, 1926 in San Francisco. In succession, he went to San Jose, returned to San Francisco, then on to Santa Barbara and Oakland. In all, five women were killed between Feb. 20 and Aug. 16, a period of just under six months. Nelson then struck in Portland, Oregon, where he strangled three women in three days. He travelled back to San Francisco, on to Seattle, Wash., returning to Portland, Ore. Nelson travelled continually throughout the winter of 1926-27. He strangled a woman in Council Bluffs, Iowa, and killed two women and a baby in Kansas City, Missouri.

In 1927, killing as he went, Nelson struck in Philadelphia, Buffalo, twice in Detroit, and in Chicago. From Chicago he travelled to Winnipeg where Mrs. Patterson and Lola Cowan became victims number 21 and 22. It is difficult to pinpoint the exact number of the strangler's victims, as it is believed that he may have killed more women whose murders, for one reason or another, were not attributed to him.

Earle Nelson did not look or act like a gorilla. All through his trial, which was held in Winnipeg on Nov. 1, 1927, he was mild-mannered and polite to everyone who came in contact with him. His rather pleasant disposition had been used many times before to put unsuspecting women at ease. While posing as a prospective roomer he would always impress his potential victims with his polite chatter about church affairs. Many women who managed not to become victims came forward at the trial to testify how Earle Nelson had impressed them.

His trial was probably the most sensational ever held in Winnipeg. The courtroom was jammed, and thousands could not gain entrance to the courthouse. Nelson's wife and aunt were on hand to testify to Nelson's insanity in an attempt to save his life. Throughout it all Nelson remained composed and swore he never killed anyone. The evidence against him was overwhelming and he was found guilty.

On a chilly January morning at daybreak, Father J.A. Webb of St. Mary's Cathedral administered the last rites of the Catholic Church to Nelson. At precisely 7:41 a.m. his body plunged through the trap door of the gallows. Earle Nelson was 30-years-old. The date was Friday, Jan. 13, 1928.

THE DOCTOR WAS
A KILLER

Not that much exciting happens in Brighton, Ont. Located 100 miles east of Toronto, a superhighway now bypasses the town, and only a green sign marks the direction to the quiet peaceful little community. Before the highway was built you had to go through Brighton. Years ago, in horse and buggy days, it was a main stopover point to rest up before hitting the big city.

Murder most foul is committed every day in all parts of the world, but very few contain ingredients to intrigue an entire country. More than 100 years ago the tiny community of Brighton was the unlikely setting for such a murder.

Ah, but let's start at the beginning.

Billy King was born in 1833 on a farm just outside Brighton. He was a bright and ambitious lad who yearned for knowledge and didn't mind applying himself. By 1855, he had finished normal school in Toronto and returned home as a full fledged teacher.

Now Billy had other, quite different yearnings, and it was somewhat of a surprise to the locals when our handsome hero started to court Sarah Lawson. Sarah left quite a bit to be desired in the looks department. She wore a perpetual frown, which gave her a rather stern appearance. Her personality was diametrically opposite to what one would describe as warm. Not only that, Sarah was flat chested. The powers that be have a way of evening things out. Sarah's father was loaded.

I can imagine the ladies of Brighton gossiping in the yard goods store over a bolt of gingham — "That handsome King boy is after the Lawson money."

Sure enough, handsome Billy married ugly Sarah, and received a veritable fortune of $10,000 in cold, hard cash. The happy couple moved to Toronto, where a year later Sarah gave birth to a child. The baby died, and soon after this unfortunate occurrence the Kings started to bicker. Then they started to argue violently, until Sarah did what so many ladies have done before and since. She went home to mother.

Thus unburdened, Billy threw himself into a new career, that of medicine. He enrolled in a medical college in Philadelphia and graduated as a bona fide medical doctor in 1858. He returned to his home town of Brighton and put out his shingle. Soon the wife and Billy reached a reconciliation. Dr. King's practice prospered. Past differences were forgiven and forgotten. Everything was coming up roses until the fall of 1858. Actually it was exactly Sept. 23, when the bloom came off the roses and love flew out the window, for on that day Billy King first laid eyes on Melinda Vandervoort.

Well, folks, where Sarah was flat, Melinda was well-endowed. While Sarah's countenance was a perpetual frown, Melinda wore a smile. Dr. King was introduced to Melinda by his wife, which ended up being the biggest mistake she ever made. Melinda flirted with the smitten doctor at their very first meeting. The following day, she again showed up at the King residence, and this time the pair found themselves alone. According to future revelations, they embraced vigorously during this second meeting. It has even been suggested that Melinda told Mrs. King that she was mad about Billy and intended to have him for herself.

Sarah knew of Melinda's checkered past. Melinda had a reputation as a homewrecker and was rather notorious for stealing other women's men. Sarah warned Billy, who told her she was silly for thinking such a thing.

Within a month Billy and Melinda were together constantly. Sarah was totally neglected. It is difficult to ascertain just exactly when Billy decided to murder his wife. From letters written to Melinda, it is obvious that she would not consent to anything more intimate than a kiss from her lover. But she did offer much much more if only tiresome, flat-chested Sarah was out of the way, and they were free to marry.

Sarah became ill. She constantly complained of stomach cramps. She was nauseous and lethargic. Her husband, being a man of medicine, tended to her every need. When, of necessity, the good doctor had to make house calls, kindly Melinda cared for the stricken woman. Despite all this loving attention, Sarah's condition deteriorated. On Nov. 4, 1858, Sarah died.

Sarah's parents never did care for their son-in-law. Now that the worst had happened, they decided to find out once and for all if their suspicions were based on fact. While Dr. King was out of his house, Mrs. Lawson searched the premises. She came up with incriminating letters from Melinda written to Billy, insinuating how convenient it would be to have Sarah out of the way. The Lawsons demanded an inquest into their daughter's death.

You can imagine the speculation in old Brighton town during the fall and early winter of '58. The frost lay heavy on the pumpkin, the cold winter winds blew, but who cared — "Did you hear Dr. King may have done in his missus!"

Melinda thought it most prudent to visit relatives in Cleveland until things cooled off in once peaceful Brighton. Mrs. King's body was exhumed. It was found to contain arsenic. When the authorities went to arrest Dr. King, they found that he thought discretion the better part of valor. Billy had skipped to Cape Vincent, on the U.S. side of Lake Ontario. The love crazed doctor was trying to make his way to Melinda's side in Cleveland when he was finally apprehended.

Dr. King was brought back to Canada to stand trial for murder. His trial began on April 4, 1859 at Cobourg. Sarah's parents testified to having seen Dr. King administer a white powder to their daughter, which could have been arsenic.

Melinda caused a ripple through the courtroom when she denied ever having had designs on the medic. Fickle Melinda admitted that she had found a new flame in Cleveland, and was no longer interested in the hapless Billy. In fact, the voluptuous one went so far as to say that, if the doctor was guilty, he should be punished.

The jury agreed. They found Billy guilty and sentenced him to hang. After he was convicted, Dr. King confessed to murder. He claimed that he never administered arsenic to his wife, and had no idea how it had entered her body. He stated that he killed his wife with chloroform.

It matters little. On the morning of June 9, 1859, a huge crowd of over 7,000 gathered at Cobourg to witness Dr. King's hanging.

Whatever happened to Melinda? She never did marry her new beau from Cleveland. She gave him the same treatment she had given Dr. King. She then took up with another gentleman, who for a change, left her high and dry in Montreal. Melinda returned to Brighton, where she lived for many years, an object of scorn to many of the residents who knew her story. She took to drinking heavily, and died in the late 1890s, penniless and alone in an asylum in Toronto.

THE MAD TRAPPER OF RAT RIVER

"**T**here I was around the bend. I got down on one knee, took careful aim with my .303 and squeezed the trigger. The Mad Trapper was trying to scramble up the banks of the frozen creek. My first shot sent him tumbling down, but didn't penetrate his pack. A second shot had the same effect. Then he turned, and without taking real aim, fired his 30-30 Savage. The impact of the bullet send me sprawling."

I sat across the desk in Barrie, Ont. facing Earl Hersey, who was relating this tale of long ago, when he was involved in what may have been Canada's greatest manhunt ever. If you are over 60, the story may bring back memories of below zero temperatures, dog teams, and the Arctic Circle. For in 1931-32 the Mad Trapper of Rat River was the main running news story in North America.

It all began innocently enough. The Royal Canadian Mounted Police were the only real law in the Northwest Territories and the Yukon. A part of the Mounties normal routine was to periodically check up on trappers and prospectors, during weeks and even months of living in isolation. The world depression had drawn many an inexperienced man to the north country, ill-equipped to withstand the hardships of that cold, barren land. Many of these men owe their lives to the R.C.M.P.

Const. Spike Millen of the Mounties' Arctic Red River Detachment first met Albert Johnson by chance in a store at Fort McPherson. He cautioned him that trapping in the area required a license. Johnson headed north and built a cabin near Rat River for the winter trapping season. The location of Johnson's cabin was close by the trapping lines of three native men, William Vittrekwa, William Nerysoo, and Jacob Drymeat.

Everyone who came into contact with Johnson described him in the same way. Evidently he was a close-mouthed, rough man, who spoke with a slight Scandinavian accent. At the time of his appearance in the Arctic he was between 35- and 40-years-old, about 5 ft. 9 ins. tall, and of average build. It should be pointed out that, although living in isolation had its effect on many men, most were a gregarious lot who welcomed strangers. This was not the case with Johnson.

On Christmas Day, 1931, William Nerysoo entered the Mounties' quarters at the Arctic Red River Detachment. He told Const. Spike Millen that Johnson had sprung his traps and hung them on trees. It was decided that Const. Alfred "Buns" King and Special Const. Joe Bernard travel to Rat River to question Johnson.

Travelling by dog team through bitter cold, the men made the 25 mile trip in under two days. King approached Johnson's cabin. All seemed in order. Smoke was lazily drifting out of the chimney. King shouted, then pounded on the door of the cabin, but received no response, although he was certain that Albert Johnson was inside.

King decided that rather than force himself upon Johnson, he should report the strange incident to his superior, Inspector Eames, Commander of the Mounties' subdivision at Aklavik. He and Bernard covered the 80 miles to Aklavik in two days hard travelling. Together with Const. R.G. McDowell and Special Const. Lazarus Sittichinli, they headed back to Johnson's cabin. There was some urgency, as all the men wanted to celebrate New Year's Eve at Fort McPherson.

Again King approached the cabin. This time a shot pierced the still Arctic air. King was hit, but managed to crawl to safety. Johnson shot continuously from the cabin, while the Mounties returned his fire.

The three Mounties lashed the badly wounded King to a dogsled and set out on the 80 mile return trip. Their dogs had just made the trip to Johnson's cabin and were fatigued. The wind chill factor was equivalent to 90 degrees below zero. The terrain was rough and dangerous. The Mounties took only 20 hours to cover the 80 miles. The mad dash over the ice and snow certainly saved King's life. Johnson's bullet had gone clean through King's side. He recovered within a month.

Johnson's status had abruptly changed. He was no longer a reticent troublemaker. He had fired at and wounded a member of the R.C.M.P.

Insp. Eames headed a party of nine men to bring in Johnson. Among these men was Const. Millen, the only one who had actually met the wanted man. On Jan. 9, 1932, the posse approached Johnson's cabin. No one expected him to be there, but strangely enough, Johnson had not moved. Insp. Eames coaxed Johnson to give up, explaining that King was going to survive. Nothing worked. Johnson responded by opening fire on the Mounties. He had dug a pit within the cabin. It was virtually impossible to hit the fugitive with gunfire.

The Mounties were not in that good a position. Their adversary was warm inside the cabin. They were exposed to the elements, and the longer they stayed the more food their dogs consumed. Further delay would see the party short of dog food.

Eames had brought dynamite along for just such a contingency. Dynamite sticks were tossed at the cabin, but they proved to be ineffective. Finally, one landed on the roof and blew a portion away, but this did not bother Johnson, who continued firing. In desperation several sticks of dynamite were fastened together and tossed at the cabin. The walls caved in, but still Johnson returned the Mounties' fire. The battle had raged for almost a full 24 hours when Insp. Eames decided to return to Aklavik.

One man had held off a posse of nine well-equipped Mounties and trappers, all experienced men of the North. Word drifted down from the Northland. The Mad Trapper of Rat River was still at large. One man against the combined strength of the R.C.M.P. and the elements. Everything possible, including dynamite, had been used to bring him in, but all had failed. It was quite a story. The hunt was a welcome diversion from the depression which gripped the world. Radio sales throughout North American increased dramatically expressly to hear news of the Mad Trapper of Rat River.

From Jan. 16 to Jan. 29, a large posse under Insp. Eames hunted the wanted man. Often they would pick up his trail, but each time he would manage to elude his hunters. Even his pursuers began to admire his resourcefulness and stamina against impossible odds.

On the 29th of January a portion of the posse, four men in all, led by Spike Millen, found Johnson's camp. They waited until he was exposed beside a steep incline, but just as they were about to warn the surrounded man, Johnson spotted Millen. In an instant his 30-30 flashed into action. Millen and his companions returned the fire. During a lull in the shooting Millen shouted to the wanted man to surrender. The wind swirled in the still quiet that sometimes accompanies the bitter cold. The Mad Trapper, hunched behind a fallen log, remained silent.

Two hours passed. It was very possible Johnson was dead. Millen decided to take his man. Exposing himself, he walked forward a few paces. A shot whistled by Millen's ear as he lunged for cover. Johnson was alive. Millen returned his fire. The Mad Trapper shot once more. Millen sprang to his feet and collapsed in the snow. He was dead.

During the night Johnson scaled a cliff and escaped. Now Albert Johnson, the Mad Trapper of Rat River, was a murderer.

The Mounties brought their dead colleague back to Aklavik. Here Inspector Eames, who had great respect for the cunning of his adversary, regrouped his forces. For the first time in Canada, an airplane was employed in a manhunt. The plane's main function, other than to search for signs of the Mad Trapper, was to supply Eames' dogs with food. Previously, searches had to be terminated as dog food ran low.

On Feb. 5, famed bush pilot Wop May joined the hunt.

Inspector Eames and his party, being supplied by May and his Bellanca, could now extend their search area.

In 1930, Staff Sgt. Earl Hersey had been sent to Merschel Island to open and maintain a radio station. In the winter he made his quarters in Aklavik. Hersey was only 18-years-old. He and a colleague, Sgt. Riddell, had been loaned by the Army Signal Corps to the Mounties. Hersey knew more than radio. A crack shot, the young, tough sergeant was an expert with dogs and sled.

During the first week in February, Albert Johnson, now a rag-tag desperate man, who had lived off the barren land for over a month, made a break for freedom. During a raging blizzard he managed to cross the treacherous Richardson Mountains. He was spotted near Eagle River. On Feb. 13, thirteen men, trappers, Army personnel, and Mounties started off through the mountains via Rat Pass. Wop May in his Bellanca picked up Johnson's trail on Feb. 14, about 20 miles up the Eagle River.

Six dog teams followed Johnson's trail. The cunning Johnson was travelling in cariboo tracks in an attempt to evade detection. Young Sgt. Hersey, with his top notch team of dogs, led the hunt.

Years later, the 66-year-old Hersey describes the scene this way: "With six dog teams yelping and barking there was a lot of noise. We were travelling up the bed of a creek when I came to a hairpin turn. Later we all realized what happened. Johnson, out of sight around the bend, heard our noise and thought we were coming from the other direction. We spotted each other at approximately the same time. We were heading toward each other at a distance of about 300 yards. That's when the shooting started."

When the shot tore into Hersey's knee, elbow and side he dropped immediately into the soft snow. Hersey was paralyzed from the waist down, but had full use of his arms. He frantically burrowed as fast as he could in the snow. The Mad Trapper fired three more shots at Hersey, but all missed their target.

By this time the other dog teams appeared on the scene. Johnson ignored the Mounties' warning shout. A fusillade of bullets brought the wanted man down. His body had been hit by 17 bullets. The Mad Trapper of Rat River was dead.

Wop May, who was observing the shootout from the air, brought his Bellanca to rest beside the seriously wounded Hersey. In less than an hour, the wounded man was in a hospital in Aklavik. Throughout his ordeal he remained conscious and has total recall of the entire episode.

"My arm didn't hurt much, nor did the hole in my side, but my knee hurt like hell."

All Hersey's wounds were tended without the use of anesthetic. Later, Hersey noted a wrinkle on his bedsheet. He patted the wrinkle, but it wouldn't go away. A nurse mentioned the incident to a doctor, who examined the area. He found that a bullet had travelled clear through Hersey's side and had lodged about a quarter of an inch under his skin. The doctor cut the skin and presented Hersey with the bullet, which he has to this day.

Although there have been many theories about Johnson's life before he entered the Arctic, no one has succeeded in positively identifying him. He simply appeared in the North country as a quiet, gruff man with no past.

Sgt. Hersey continued in the Army until retiring in 1954 with the rank of Major. Today he devotes much time to Red Cross work. Almost all traces of the great manhunt have slowly disappeared. Hersey's mitts and parka are on display beside Johnson's homemade snowshoes in the R.C.M.P. Museum in Regina.

The Mad Trapper of Rat River has left one lasting memorial. Picking up a broom handle, Earl Hersey is quick to point out, "That bullet hole through the elbow has affected my golf swing to this day."

SLAUGHTER AT SHELL LAKE

Murder is the most reprehensible and horrendous crime that man can inflict on his fellow man. The motives which generate this most final of all acts can come from a variety of sources — greed, hate, lust, jealousy; the list is endless. But what of the murders which take place without motive, without reason and without explanation? Nothing can be more tragic. This is the story of one such murder.

Shell Lake, Saskatchewan is a tiny farming community of 250 people, situated about 90 miles north west of Saskatoon. The closest town of any size is Prince Albert. The huge farms often associated with western Canada are not evident in this area. The farms are small. Hardy men work long, hard hours in the fields to wrest a living from the ground. In addition to their crops, they raise horses, cattle, pigs and chickens.

Jim Peterson had a farm about four miles from Shell Lake. Jim's farm was about a mile square, and stood about 300 yards off Highway 3. A plain clapboard farm house was home to 47-year-old Jim, his 42-year-old wife, Evelyn, and their eight children, ranging in age from Larry, 1, to Jean, 17. An older daughter, Katherine, had recently married and was living in Chetwynd, B.C.

Wildrew Lang owned the farm adjoining the Peterson's. Lang and Peterson often worked together on each other's farms. During haying time they pooled their labor, first doing one farm and then the other.

At 8:30 on the morning of Aug. 15, 1967, Wildrew Lang started off in his truck for the Peterson farm. Because the men were always giving each other a helping hand, they rarely drove down their long driveways and along Highway 3 to the next farm. Instead they had worn a sort of path or crude road through a connecting field, in order to go directly from one farm to another.

On this perfect summer day, Lang and Peterson were going to clean out a granary, which was really an old house used for storage. It was located not too far from the Peterson house. Lang made his way across the field and started to load his truck alone. He idly thought that Jim should have joined him. They had discussed loading the grain the night before. Jim planned on hauling it to the elevator, so that he could give his 17-year-old daughter, Jean, a little extra money. Jean was a runner, and was soon to take part in a track and field meet in Dundurn, Sask. The whole Peterson family was excited about the prospect of Jean running.

What could be keeping Jim? Lang decided to go to the farmhouse and find out. As he approached the front door it dawned on him that it seemed to be so very quiet and still. It was close to 9 o'clock. Where was Jim? Eight active kids, and not a sound to be heard.

Lang opened the door and apprehensively called out, "Hello." He peered inside. There, on the kitchen floor, clad only in his shorts, lying face down, was the body of his friend, Jim Peterson. Lang didn't look any further. He drove the few miles to Shell Lake and made contact with the R.C.M.P. at Spiritwood.

Cpl. B.L. Richards arrived at the Peterson home, and while Lang waited in the car outside, Cpl. Richards entered the house. He instinctively knew that Jim Peterson was dead. In the living room, on a cot, he found the body of 11-year-old Dorothy. He continued on to the children's bedroom. In the first bed he discovered the bodies of Pearl, 9, and Jean, 17. In another double bed were three bodies — Mary, 13; William 5; and Colin 2. All had been shot in the head.

Cpl. Richards noticed a slight movement between the bodies of Pearl and Jean. He bent over and discovered tiny 4-year-old Phyllis, her face buried in the mattress. Richards lifted her from the bed and took her outside. The child didn't speak. Richards saw to it that she was taken to a farm across the highway.

Cpl. Richards then drove to Shell Lake for help. He returned accompanied by Dr. J.R. Michaud. As he approached the house for the second time he discovered the bodies of Mrs. Peterson and baby Larry, clad only in his diaper. The bodies were found outside the house. Mrs. Peterson had grabbed her infant son and jumped out a window in an attempt to escape. Both had been shot through the head.

Nine human beings had fallen that morning to some madman. Who could hate this

God-fearing, hard working family enough to kill them? Why the Petersons? Why was Phyllis spared?

The R.C.M.P. had no murder weapon and no motive, but they did have some clues. The killer had left an identifiable footprint on the Peterson's kitchen floor. It had been made by a runner boot, which had distinguishable markings. One of these markings were the words "Made in Taiwan". The bullets which had killed the Petersons came from a .22 calibre rifle.

Three days after the murder the R.C.M.P. received a call from a farmer. He gave them the name of someone whom he thought they should check out. The name was Victor Hoffman.

Victor was 21-years-old. He had been in and out of trouble for the past few years. From 1961 to 1964, he had been charged three times with breaking and entering. Each time it appeared that he was interested in stealing guns. He had received a two-year suspended sentence for these offences. More recently he had behaved strangely around his own home. When he started shooting his rifle in the air, explaining that he was shooting at the devil, his parents had him committed to the Saskatchewan Mental Hospital at North Battleford.

While being treated at the hospital he confessed to doctors that he had seen the devil many times. From as far back as he could remember, the devil had appeared to him. He described the apparition as being well over six feet tall with a face resembling a pig's. Doctors in the mental institution diagnosed Victor's illness as schizophrenia. They prescribed drugs to suppress his hallucinations, as well as electric shock treatments.

Victor received a series of 12 shock treatments, and seemed to improve. On July 26th he was released. While still introverted, he was capable of working on the farm and socializing with acquaintances. The doctors who released him felt that drugs would keep his illness under control.

The R.C.M.P. visited the Hoffman farm, and confiscated Victor's .22 calibre Browning rifle and his rubber boots. On Aug. 19, four days after the murders, and the day of the Petersons' funeral, the Crime Detection Laboratory in Regina informed the investigating officers that Victor Hoffman's rubber boots had made the track on the Petersons' kitchen floor, and his rifle had fired all the fatal bullets.

Victor Hoffman was taken into custody and questioned. He told the police that on Aug. 15 he got out of bed at 4 a.m. and worked on the family car. Then, without warning, Victor blurted out, "O.K., I killed them. I tried to change the rifling on it. I should have burned the house, then you would not have found those cartridges. I stopped at the gate. I don't know what made me do it. I collected 17 cartridges. I didn't want to shoot any more. The one I left didn't see me."

When Victor's rifle was examined, it showed signs of having been tampered with in order to make ballistic comparisons more difficult. Hoffman was obsessed with changing the characteristics of his rifle so that the fatal bullets could not be traced back to him. His statement also revealed why little Phyllis was spared. She had not looked up, and in his warped mind Hoffman ordained that she would live because she could not identify him.

Victor was studied extensively by psychiatrists. His story began to unfold. After working on the car on the day of the murder, the devil told him to go for a drive. The thought entered his mind that he should kill both his parents, but instead he put a box of shells in the glove compartment, and placed his loaded .22 on the front seat. Victor took off, and as he passed each house he had an urge to pull into the driveway and kill the occupants. As he drove past each farm the urge grew stronger, until at last he did pull into a driveway. It was the farm of Jim and Evelyn Peterson.

Victor opened the front door. Jim Peterson was sitting on the side of his bed in his shorts and was about to put on his shoes. Jim looked up, saw the rifle, and lunged at Hoffman. Victor emptied his rifle at Jim, whose forward motion brought him almost to Hoffman's feet.

The children screamed. Hoffman went out to his car, reloaded his rifle and systematically went through the house, killing all the children. He killed Mrs. Peterson and the baby in the yard. They had made their way out through a window.

Little Phyllis was purposely left alive. Hoffman says it was because she didn't see him. Psychiatrists feel that the reason she was spared was because his impulse to kill was exhausted. Hoffman had never met nor even seen any member of the Peterson family until the August morning he opened their front door.

Victor Hoffman stood trial for murder and was found not guilty due to insanity. He was confined to a mental institution.

FUNERAL PYRE ON
THE FARM

A Nazi concentration camp is an unlikely place for romance, but it was there in German-occupied Poland that Isaac Wertman met Rywa, his future wife. After they were liberated, Isaac and Rywa were married in Warsaw. It is ironic that the couple, who managed to escape Hitler's gas ovens, was destined to become linked forever with a young Canadian boy whose father had served as a soldier in the German army before emigrating to Canada.

Isaac and Rywa arrived in Canada in 1951 and settled in Toronto. The years drifted by, and two children were born to the two survivors. Yet their marriage was not a happy one. Rywa craved the attention of other men, while Isaac strived to make a living in the garment industry. The Wertmans bought a home on Warwick Ave. Their two children grew up and left their parents' home. Later they were to state that their mother and father constantly bickered. Isaac, a less aggressive individual than his wife, usually received the worst of these exchanges. It became obvious that he knew his wife was seeing other men.

Toward the end of 1972, Isaac left his wife and moved into an apartment. He initiated divorce proceedings. His lawyer advised him that half the value of the Wertman home was rightfully his. Rywa was informed that the settlement amount would be $25,000. She was beside herself with anguish at giving up half the value of her home.

Besides, Rywa had taken a lover. Max Goldstein was now firmly ensconced in the house on Warwick Ave. Posing as a roomer, it was a sort of open secret that Max was Rywa's lover and was footing some of the bills. In the meantime, Rywa took a job as a dancing teacher. It was in this way that she met 22-year-old Manfred Baron.

It wasn't long before Rywa was teaching Manfred dancing, and other things as well. He moved into the house on Warwick Ave. The young man, who was less than half the age of his lover, fell hard for the older woman. Manfred had been brought up on a farm near Acton and had never met anyone as worldly and sophisticated as Rywa. Later it was revealed that the purpose of his dancing lessons had been an attempt to gain confidence with the opposite sex.

The entangled lives of all the principals in our cast might have untangled eventually had it not been for Rywa's obsessive fear of losing half her home to her estranged husband.

Isaac Wertman worked on Spadina Ave. for a clothing firm owned by Harry Patinek. Isaac always opened up in the morning. Harry was surprised when he arrived at his establishment on the morning of May 8, 1974 and found his employees waiting outside for the doors to be opened.

As a concerned employer, Harry called Isaac's apartment several times. When he received no answer, he went to the apartment, but Isaac was nowhere to be found. Harry noticed that Wertman's car was in the parking lot. He decided to call the police. When the officer arrived, he and Harry took a look at Isaac's car. They found blood on the bumper and bloodstains on the asphalt surrounding the front of the vehicle.

An investigation into the disappearance of Isaac Wertman was conducted by the police. Almost immediately their inquiries turned up incriminating evidence. Neighbors stated that they had heard screams and scuffling emanating from the parking lot where Wertman's car was found.

Within 10 days the police had an idea of the involved lives being led by Rywa, Wertman and Manfred Baron. They approached Manfred at a construction site, and asked him about the missing Wertman. He surprised them by readily incriminating himself, revealing intimate facts about the case. He told the police officers that Isaac would never be found without his help. Then he took the total blame, saying that he had acted alone.

Manfred signed a detailed statement telling how he had waited for Isaac outside the latter's apartment building. He struck the older man over the head with a club, then shoved him into his car and drove to his father's farm near Acton. Isaac wasn't dead. When they arrived at the farm, Manfred hit his victim over the head again. Then he took Isaac out to the back field where there was a 45-gallon drum. He put the limp form in the drum and, using diesel fuel, managed in 15 hours to burn what had once been Isaac Wertman.

He later buried what remained of Isaac under some sod. When Manfred led the authorities to the drum, it had seven bullet holes in it which were never really explained. Manfred was placed in the Don Jail. He patiently waited for three weeks to receive help from his lover. When it didn't come he changed his story.

Now he involved his mistress. He claimed that he had only disposed of the body. He said Rywa had been there in the parking lot with him. She had killed her husband by shooting him with Manfred's .22 calibre revolver. Rywa had found out that very day that her husband definitely had a claim on her home, and talked Manfred into waiting for him in the parking lot.

The police then visited Rywa, who became almost incoherent when she heard that Manfred had changed his story. She accused her boyfriend of being the murderer. So we have the classic case which has been repeated so often, of lovers accusing each other of the actual act of murder.

A year later both Manfred and Rywa stood trial for conspiracy to commit murder. Conviction carried a sentence of 14 years imprisonment. Defended by separate lawyers, each accused the other of murder. It was indefinite whether Isaac had been clubbed to death or if he had been shot.

Dr. J.W.A. Duckworth gave the most hair raising evidence when he stated that Wertman's head had been cut off before it had been placed in the burning drum. He could not state with certainty if Wertman had been alive or dead when he was decapitated.

The defense pointed out that Rywa and Max Goldstein may have set up the naive Manfred to murder Isaac. In this way, Rywa would not have to pay her husband the $25,000 settlement, and would be free to marry Goldstein.

There was also evidence that as soon as Isaac was out of the way, Goldstein, who was then still living with Rywa, moved out of the Warwick Ave. home. Manfred, who occupied the basement of the home, moved back to Acton.

It had been close to the perfect murder, for had Harry Patinek not called the police, who discovered the blood in the parking lot and on Isaac's bumper, it is quite possible the murder would have gone undetected.

The jury deliberated six hours and reported back to the court that they were deadlocked. The next day, after two further hours of deliberation, they brought back a verdict of guilty in both cases.

Both Manfred and Rywa received sentences of 14 years in prison. Both appealed this conviction, and had their convictions overturned. At his new trial Baron pleaded guilty, and received an 11-year prison sentence. Tried separately, Rywa was again found guilty, and this time received an 8-year prison sentence.

ACCUSED PRIEST

Over the years, Montreal has been the scene of many notorious murders. In recent years mobsters have perpetrated horrendous mass killings, but none of them compare to the sensation caused by the Father Delorme murder. This particular crime has the dubious distinction of being Montreal's, and quite possibly Canada's, most sensational murder.

It happened long ago, but is still recalled by old timers, who remember the headlines and speculation which kept the good citizens of La Belle Province talking about little else for almost three years. You see, the principal character, and the man who eventually stood trial for murder, not once, but three times, was a Roman Catholic priest. To my knowledge Father Adelard Delorme is the only priest who has ever stood trial for murder in Canada.

Early on Saturday morning, Jan. 7, 1922, James Higginbotham and Elric Larin trudged through the crisp Montreal snow toward a shack on the corner of Colebrook and Snowdon Streets. Both men worked for the city, and the shack contained their tools. As they walked, they caught sight of the crumpled form of a man lying in the snow. There was no doubt that he was dead. The man's overcoat was saturated with blood, as was a quilt-like material wrapped about his head.

The two city employees summoned the police, who were at the scene in a matter of minutes. Investigating officers noted that the snow under the body had not melted, indicating that the victim probably was dead and cold before being placed where he had been found. Upon searching the body, the officers discovered letters addressed to Raoul Delorme, 190 St. Hubert St., Montreal.

The body was removed to the city morgue. The quilt-like material was unwrapped from the head, revealing six bullet wounds. The victim's hands were securely tied together with cord. There were no bullet holes in his overcoat.

When officers called at 190 St. Hubert St., they encountered a Roman Catholic priest, Father Adelard Delorme. Police accompanied him to the morgue to view the body. Father Delorme tearfully and regretfully identified the victim as his half-brother, Raoul.

Father Delorme explained that his half-brother was a commerce student at the University of Ottawa, and was at home on vacation. The priest became enraged when he was informed that someone had bound his brother's hands and poured six bullets into his head at close range. Then the murderer must have pinned the overcoat over the head and transported the body to the field where it was found. What coldblooded madman would do such a thing to a 24-year-old student?

On Monday, Jan. 9, a coroner's inquest was conducted into the death of Raoul Delorme. Father Delorme was the principal witness. He explained his family's history.

Adelard Delorme's father had been a wealthy contractor who died leaving an estate of over $160,000. The estate, consisting mainly of several properties located in Montreal's east end, was left to six relatives. The largest portion by far had been left to Raoul, who received an income in excess of $10,000 per year from the properties.

Father Delorme administered his late father's estate, and took care of Raoul's income as well. In fact, Raoul was attending the University of Ottawa solely to become equipped in the ways of finance in order to handle his own affairs upon graduation.

At the inquest, some curiosity was expressed as to why Father Delorme did not have a regular parish. He readily disclosed the details. Delorme was born in Ste. Anne des Plaines, Que. After attending the village school, he entered Ste. Therese College, and then studied theology at Montreal's Grand Seminary on Sherbrooke St.

At the time of the murder, he was 37-years-old, having been ordained for some years. Father Delorme had been appointed vicar of the Ste. Anne des Plaines Church in 1915, and later was transferred again as vicar, to the church at Tetreaultville, near Montreal. This latter move had been made at his own request, as his father's death and his position as sole executor of the estate made it imperative for him to be located near Montreal.

Father Delorme explained that after a year he found he could not properly attend to the affairs of the parish as well as his father's estate. He requested special dispensation to change positions once more. Permission was granted, and he became chaplain of

L'Assistance Publique. This enabled him to administer his father's estate.

On the evening of Jan. 6, Raoul phoned his brother from downtown Montreal. He informed Father Delorme that he was staying downtown for supper, and planned on visiting a theatre with friends. Raoul also mentioned that if he didn't return by 11:30 he would not be coming home that night. When, and if, he made that phone call, Raoul didn't realize that he only had hours to live.

Later that night Father Delorme stated that he had received several strange phone calls, with no one at the other end of the line. Once he thought he heard loud moaning. He claimed to have reported the incident to the phone company. Later, phone company officials stated that they had no record of his complaint.

Two days into the inquest, with detectives working around the clock checking out every possible clue, Father Delorme turned over a .25 calibre Bayard automatic revolver to them. He stated that he kept it in his car for protection. Normally he used his late father's old weapon but, by coincidence, a few days before the murder he had traded in his old weapon for his present one. Raoul had been shot with a .25 calibre weapon.

On Wednesday, Jan. 11 funeral services for Raoul Delorme were conducted at St. James Church in downtown Montreal. Father Delorme celebrated the requiem mass.

The Coroner's inquest was delayed several times in order to examine new evidence which was constantly being uncovered by the police. In the meantime, Father Delorme issued statements which were extremely newsworthy under the circumstances. Every word he uttered was conscientiously reported in the daily press.

A few days after the funeral Father Delorme announced that he was posting a $10,000 reward for the arrest and conviction of the murderer. He duly deposited this amount in the Bank of Hochelaga. Father Delorme was full of announcements. He also stated that once the murderer was convicted, he should be publicly executed at a local outdoor skating rink. Such proclamations were not becoming to a man of the cloth.

When it was learned that Father Delorme was the main beneficiary of Raoul's will, suspicion openly fell upon the priest. It seemed impossible, but as the days wore on, more and more circumstantial evidence pointed to Father Delorme as a murderer. It couldn't be. Nothing like this had ever happened in Montreal before. Saving souls, yes. Saving lives, yes. But a priest a murderer! There had to be some other explanation.

Father Delorme kept spewing quotable quotes. He likened himself to his Saviour, and compared the slanderous remarks made about him to those hurled at Jesus Christ during his last days on earth.

At precisely 7 p.m. on Feb. 14, 1922, Father Delorme was arrested and charged with the murder of his half-brother, Raoul Delorme.

The thought of a Roman Catholic priest standing trial for murder was so against the grain of the average Quebecker in 1922 that many thought it was all an English plot to undermine the church.

Those who remember the murder recall the unbelievable aspects of the case. The fact that the victim was bound and had been shot six times almost precluded the possibility that a priest could have been the perpetrator of such a horrendous act. Rumors of every kind spread throughout Montreal. Everyone had a pet theory. Newspaper circulation soared as the news spread through the province of Quebec and across the land. Word of a priest being tried for murder was reported in the press of Europe and even Asia.

Father Delorme's legal counsel pleaded that his client was insane, and therefore unfit to stand trial. For a while it appeared that this tactic would be successful, for on June 30 a special jury did find Father Delorme insane. He as committed to the Beauport Asylum. Almost a year later, in May, 1923, Father Delorme was released from the asylum on the grounds that he was now sane. The month following his release he was committed to trial for the murder of his brother. The trial began on June 20, 1923.

A tremendous amount of circumstantial evidence was presented in an effort to prove the priest guilty of murder. Motive was established when Monsignor Rheaume of Ottawa took the witness stand. He told of a day in February, 1921, when Raoul was to undergo a minor operation in Ottawa. On that occasion, Father Delorme and Raoul composed Raoul's will in longhand in the hospital. The Monsignor had signed it as a witness. Under the terms of the will Father Delorme was to receive the bulk of Raoul's estate upon his death.

To add fuel to the fire, it was established that only seven days before the murder a $25,000 insurance policy had been issued on Raoul's life. Father Delorme was the sole beneficiary and had paid the first premium.

Because there were no bullet holes in the victim's overcoat, it had been theorized that Raoul had been shot indoors. Dr. Derome, who performed the autopsy, lent credence to this theory, when he testified that the piece of quilt wrapped around the dead man's head corresponded to quilting found in Father Delorme's home. Dr. Derome, who achieved star status during the trial, also testified that he had found bloodstains in the priest's car. Father Delorme claimed these stains were the result of the scratches to his knuckles received when he had changed a flat tire.

A gunsmith, Cesar Haynes, testified that he had sold Father Delorme a .25 calibre revolver only 10 days before the murder. Upon comparing a bullet extracted from Raoul's head with one fired from the priest's gun, the gunsmith was willing to state that both bullets had most probably come from the same gun.

Raoul's rubbers and overshoes were found at home. The Crown felt that he had been killed in the cellar of Father Delorme's home. They claimed it was quite possible that Father Delorme had planned to kill his brother with one shot at close range. Upon testing, it was discovered that his revolver was constructed in such a way that the sight was off by one and three quarter inches. The initial bullet had travelled through the side of Raoul's face, rather than directly into his temple. They further claimed that once Father Delorme wounded his brother, he had no choice but to keep on shooting.

Every minute of the night of the murder came under close scrutiny. The house at 190 St. Hubert was home to Father Delorme, his three sisters, Lily, Rosa, and Florence, and, of course, Raoul, home from Ottawa on vacation.

All the occupants gave evidence that Raoul left the house after lunch, stating that he might not be back for supper. Lily and Florence had supper with Father Delorme. All three sisters left the house to attend the theatre about 8 o'clock that evening, and didn't return until 11:20 p.m.

At 8 o'clock Father Delorme went outdoors, where he was observed by several witnesses. He returned at 9:30. If Raoul was killed at home, Father Delorme was the only one there, and could have committed the crime between 9:30 and 11:30, when his sisters returned. Neighbors swore they heard Father Delorme's car at about 11 o'clock that night in the lane beside his garage. They heard the garage door open and close, but were unable to state if he was coming in or going out.

The victim's pocket watch had been torn from his body. A piece of watch chain was found hanging from his pocket. Strangely, the watch itself was anonymously sent by mail to Chief of Provincial Detectives Lorraine. The writing on the parcel containing the watch was carefully examined. Experts compared the handwriting on the parcel to that of Father Delorme. Three experts swore the writing matched that of Father Delorme, while a fourth refused to swear to it.

The Crown claimed that the priest had sent the watch as an erratic method of getting rid of it. The defense countered with the claim that someone had probably stumbled across the body and had stolen the watch. Later a guilty conscience may have forced them to mail the watch to the police.

Father Delorme stated simply that all the evidence against him was circumstantial. No one saw him kill his brother. He was in his cellar from about 10 o'clock that night until one in the morning repairing a furnace, until one of his sisters called out to him to come to bed.

The jury retired to reach a verdict. On July 21, they reported that they were hopelessly deadlocked. Sent back to continue their deliberations, they reported two days later that they stood at 10 for conviction and two for acquittal. They were dismissed.

The jury, made up of French and English citizens, were criticized for not bringing in a guilty verdict. It was believed that no one of the Catholic faith would find a priest guilty of murder. We must remember that a guilty verdict was tantamount to death on the gallows in 1923.

In February, 1924, Delorme's second trial for murder again resulted in a deadlocked jury. It all had to be done a third time.

Father Delorme's third and last murder trial began on Oct. 6, 1924, almost three years after his brother's body was found with six bullets in his head. On Oct. 31 the jury retired to reach a decision. Thousands stood outside the old courthouse awaiting the results of their deliberations. Three hours and forty five minutes later they returned with their verdict: Not Guilty.

Father Delorme made a brief statement: "I knew I would be freed," he stated, "because I am innocent. I hold no grudge against any person who worked against me in the case. I forgive all."

With that magnanimous statement he walked out of the courtroom a free man after spending more than two years and nine months in jail and asylums. The verdict was received outside the province of Quebec as a travesty of justice.

Father Delorme died of natural causes in 1942.

MURDER IN THE AIR

Three times a week, a Quebec Airways flight left Montreal for Seven Islands, with stops at Quebec City and Baie Comeau. It was so punctual and reliable that people along the route used to set their watches by the roar of the engines.

On Sept. 9, 1949, Patrick Simard was fishing for eels near his home at Sault-au-Cochon, Quebec. He glanced up, idly following the flight of the Douglas DC-3 as it approached Cap Tourmente. Then he heard a loud explosion, and as he watched in horror the plane veered crazily to the left and went into a power dive, heading straight for the peak of Cap Tourmente. Simard ran through thick bush towards the crash; it took him an hour to get to the scene. Scattered among the wreckage of the aircraft were the remains of the passengers and their luggage. Surprisingly, there was no fire, but the ominous smell of leaking gasoline hung over the entire area. The propellers had been turning when the plane smashed vertically into the ground. There was no swath of torn trees, only the aircraft with its wings ripped off and its horribly mangled nose sticking into the earth.

The plane had held four crew members and nineteen passengers. Simard checked to see if there were any survivors. Finding none, he started down the mountain for help. He met some men who were working on railway tracks nearby, and they took the news to St. Joachim, where it was relayed to Quebec City. Within hours Canadian Pacific Airlines, the parent company of Quebec Airways, had their investigating officials at the scene of the crash.

The left front luggage compartment showed signs of an explosion, and it was this explosion that had destroyed the control system of the aircraft, causing the disaster. They examined everything aboard the aircraft that could have caused an explosion. Items such as fire extinguishers and storage batteries were checked, but none of these was found to be the cause of the crash. The four crew members and nineteen passengers had been killed instantly upon impact, but the lack of fire made identifying the bodies relatively easy, and the next of kin were quickly notified. Because of the explosion in the baggage compartment, the authorities concluded that they were dealing with a criminal case and not an accident. On Sept. 12, the entire matter was turned over to the RCMP. The Mounties were to be assisted by the Quebec Provincial Police and the Quebec City Police Force.

The left front compartment had been loaded in Montreal with cargo destined for Quebec City. It was completely emptied in Quebec City and reloaded with cargo destined for Baie Comeau. This was routine practice, and was employed to reduce unnecessary delay during the flight's many stops. The authorities realized that the explosive material must have been put into the left front baggage compartment at Ancienne Lorette Airport in Quebec City.

The passenger list of the ill-fated craft was closely scrutinized, as was the list of insurance policies taken out on the passengers' lives. A cursory check turned up nothing unusual, and the police decided to place all relatives of victims who boarded the plane in Quebec City under observation and to conduct an investigation into their private lives.

Undertaking the investigation from another direction, the police started with the plane on the ground in Quebec City and the left front baggage compartment empty. They questioned Willie Lamonde, the freight clerk who had been on duty on Sept. 9, but he could recall nothing of significance except that several pieces of freight had been placed on the aircraft, in addition to the passengers' regular luggage. From company records the police were able to obtain the names of the senders and prospective receivers of all the air freight shipments, and they set about checking every name on the list. This approach bore fruit with the discovery of a 28 pound parcel sent by Delphis Bouchard of St. Simeon, Quebec, to Alfred Plouffe, 180 Laval St., Baie Comeau. Neither sender nor addressee existed, so it seemed reasonable to assume that someone had walked up to Willie Lamonde with a bomb and shipped it air freight to Baie Comeau.

The police begged Willie to try to remember who had given him the parcel. Willie's memory was now jarred by names and addresses he could relate to, and he came up with a mental picture of the person who had given him the bomb. He said it was a fat woman who had come to the airport by cab. He remembered this because the cabbie had carried the parcel to the scale for the fat lady. The cost of shipping the 28 pound parcel to Baie Comeau was $2.72, which she paid to Willie, who gave her a receipt. The police started the tedious task of questioning every cabbie in Quebec City, and almost immediately they found the right man.

Paul Pelletier, who worked for the Yellow Cab Co., had picked up the fat lady on Sept. 9 at the Palais Railroad Station. He described her as middle-aged and overweight, with dark hair and eyes. She didn't say one word to him on the trip to the airport, but because she was returning to the city with him, he had carried the parcel to the freight clerk. When they returned to the city she got out of his cab at the rear of the Chateau Frontenac Hotel, and Pelletier recalled seeing her walking toward Lower Town or the older section of the city.

Then, upon checking the relatives of victims, the police for the first time heard the name of Albert Guay, whose wife Rita had died in the crash. Albert had been fined $25 for causing a scene some months previously in a restaurant, where he had brandished a revolver at a waitress named Marie-Ange Robitaille. It was a small and relatively insignificant incident, but one that couldn't be overlooked by the authorities. The girl still worked at the restaurant and the police decided to question her about her relationship with Guay. The detectives confronted an attractive, shapely young girl who would have caused heads to turn anywhere.

Marie-Ange openly admitted knowing Albert Guay, and when asked if Guay had anything to do with a fat middle-aged woman, she immediately gave the police the name of Marguerite Pitre who lived at 49 Monseigneur Gauvreau St. The police stationed the cab driver outside Marguerite Pitre's house, so that when she came out he would be able to identify her. On Sept. 20 a taxi drove up and Pelletier had a good look at Marguerite as she got in. He positively identified her as the lady he had driven to the airport on Sept. 9. Marguerite had taken an overdose of sleeping pills, and the taxi had been summoned to rush her to Infant Jesus Hospital. The police decided to arrest her as soon as she was released.

Who was this strange woman? What circumstances tied her to the young waitress, Marie-Ange Robitaille? How was Albert Guay connected to the two women?

The tangled web started to unfold. Albert Guay was born in 1917 to a working-class family. As a child, he liked games in which he played the part of a ship's captain or commander of great armies, and always had illusions of power and wealth. By the time he was 22, he was working in a war plant and selling watches as a sideline. During the war he married the former Rita Morel, and when peace came he gravitated to the jewelry business as a full-time occupation, opening up a shop in Seven Islands,

Quebec. In 1948, he closed this store and opened a shop on St. Sauveur St., which he soon owned.

Guay was having a prolonged affair with Marie-Ange. It is almost certain that Rita Guay had knowledge of the affair, but being wise to the ways of men with wandering eyes, she figured Albert would have his fling, tire of the waitress, and return to her. Marie-Ange had lived in a room in Marguerite Pitre's house, and it was here that Albert Guay would come to make love to his mistress, with Marguerite's complicity. The heavy-set Marguerite, who always wore black, and as a result came to be known as The Raven, had met Guay during the war when the both worked in the same munitions plant. Another member of The Raven's family, her crippled brother Genereux Ruest, worked for Guay as a watch repairman in his jewelry shop. The Raven had come under Guay's influence when she started borrowing small amounts of money from him during the war. This led to more and more loans until finally she was compelled to comply to his every wish. When questioned, the Raven at first denied taking the bomb out to the airport, but when faced with the cab driver she confessed that she had delivered the explosives. Once started, the Raven continued to sing. She admitted getting in debt to Albert, until finally she owed him $600. He always demanded favors of her, and when Marie-Ange was only sixteen she had set the good-looking young girl up in her own apartment at his insistence. The Raven claimed that Guay promised he would forget the debt if she would get him some dynamite, knowing that her neighbor had acquaintances in the construction business who had access to explosives. The Raven told her neighbor that if she could get her hands on some dynamite it would be her chance to get out of Albert's clutches once and for all. Guay had told the Raven that he needed the dynamite for a friend who was removing tree stumps. In the end the Raven succeeded in obtaining ten pounds of dynamite and the nineteen blasting caps.

On Sept. 23, Albert Guay was arrested and taken into custody. He admitted everything except murder. Albert said he knew the Raven very well because she brought him leads for watch sales, and her crippled brother worked for him. He even admitted having the affiar with Marie-Ange, but claimed it was over before the plane crash. Through it all he swore he loved his wife dearly, and that the Raven was a barefaced liar.

The police descended on Genereux Ruest's workshop to search it for any evidence that a bomb had been manufactured there. They found an insignificant piece of corrugated cardboard coated with black deposits. It was the only thing in the shop that looked unusual in any way, and it was rushed to a Montreal laboratory for testing. In the lab, blasting caps were exploded using a piece of corrugated cardboard as a shield.

The explosions left black deposits on the cardboard matching the ones on the cardboard taken from Ruest's workshop. The same tell-tale black deposits appeared on the inside of the left front luggage compartment of the downed aircraft.

Armed with this incriminating evidence, the authorities faced Ruest. Finally he confessed that he had constructed a time mechanism, and that he and Albert had experimented with setting it off. He claimed Albert had brought him all the materials for the bomb, and that he had no idea that Guay planned to use it for anything other than clearing stumps. He said he was afraid to volunteer the information earlier because he thought the police would believe he knew of Guay's intentions.

Meanwhile, Marie-Ange Robitaille added her chapter to the increasingly well-documented life and loves of Albert Guay. She said she had met Guay at a dance in 1947, when she was sixteen years old. She thought he was a glamorous man-about-town in the jewelry business, and even though she knew he was married, it wasn't long before they were having sexual relations. Rita Guay had even complained to the girl's parents, but Marie-Ange moved out of her parents' home and moved into a spare room that the Raven provided. Several times she tried to break up with Guay, but each time he went after her and brought her back. There is little doubt that Marie-Ange was physicially attractive to Guay, but in the end she could see no future with a married man. She had only seen Guay once since the crash. On the occasion he had begged her to come back to him, pleading that since his wife was now dead, no obstacles stood in their way. She told him their affair was over, and she now told the police that she knew nothing about any bomb.

Despite the incriminating statements of the Raven and her brother, Albert steadfastly maintained his innocence. On Feb. 23, 1950, Albert Guay stood trial for murder. The jury took only seventeen minutes to find him guilty, and he was sentenced to death by hanging. Once in Bordeaux Jail awaiting death, he made a full confession, implicating the Raven and her brother as willing accomplices. Both had been motivated by money he had promised them from a small insurance policy he had taken out on his wife's life, and both had been well aware that he planned to blow up the aircraft.

Albert Guay was hanged on Jan. 12, 1951, and Genereux Ruest followed him to the gallows in 1952. The Raven was hanged in 1953.

WHERE'S HELEN?

Arthur Kendall, his wife Helen, and their five children, Jimmie, 12; Margaret, 10; Ann, eight; Jean, five; and Mary, one, lived on a farm in Elma Township in southern Ontario.

In the spring of 1952, Arthur and a neighbor put in a crop of flax. Arthur looked around for some way to supplement his farm income during the summer months while the flax grew to maturity. He went on a fishing trip to the Bruce Peninsula on the 24th of May, and met Ashford Pedwell, who owned a sawmill. The elderly Pedwell took a liking to the stocky, serious Kendall, and when Arthur volunteered that he was a carpenter as well as a farmer, Pedwell offered him a job running the sawmill. Kendall accepted the job with the proviso that he had to return to his farm in September to harvest his flax. This was agreeable to Pedwell, who told Kendall that he needed more hands for the mill, and asked Arthur to bring help with him when he came back.

The mill was located a few miles to the south of Tobermory on a side road, known as the Johnston Harbour Road, that led to Lake Huron. On May 26, Arthur started his new job; he had brought Jim Baillie, the son of a neighbor, with him, and the next week he hired two more boys, Gordon Neabel and George Hislop. The four men worked the mill and lived in a shack directly across the road. The shack came with the job, and was to be used as living quarters. It wasn't long before Baillie tired of the work and returned home.

Then Arthur asked his wife and children to join them. Not many women would feel that crowding into a shack measuring 12 by 14 feet with five children and three adult men was much of a vacation, but Helen Kendall didn't see it that way. They could all stand a change from the farm. The children were out of school, and there was a lake close by for swimming. All in all, the whole family liked the idea. Sleeping arrangements were a bit of a problem, but everyone seemed to fit comfortably enough into the shack. There were upper and lower bunks on each side of the single room. The two men slept in the upper bunk on the west side, while Arthur, Helen and eighteen-month-old Mary slept in the lower bunk on the east side. Jim and Jean had the top bunk on the east side, while Margaret and Ann shared the bottom bunk on the west side. They had a small stove and a table that could seat five.

Both the hired men were very impressed with Helen Kendall. Despite trying conditions, she managed to serve good meals and always kept the little shack clean and tidy. She was meticulous about her own appearance, and her children were always clean and neatly dressed.

Mrs. Kendall had no way of knowing that before she arrived on the scene, Arthur had met a waitress named Beatrice Hogue at the Olympia Restuarant in Wiarton. Beatrice was an attractive redhead who had a total of seven children, two of whom were from a previous marriage. When Arthur met her, six of the children were living with her at her home in Wiarton. Thomas Hogue, her husband, was a sailor on the Great Lakes and was away from home a great deal. Kendall saw a lot of Beatrice during the early summer, and it soon became obvious to friends and acquaintances that they were having an affair.

On July 26, Neabel and Hislop finished at the sawmill for the season. Helen served them dinner, after which Arthur gave them a lift down to Elma Township. He went by way of Wiarton and picked up Beatrice and her six children. Then he dropped the two men off and proceeded to his own farm, where he and the Hogue family stayed the night. Next morning he paid a visit to a neighbor, Martin Barker, and inquired if he would like to hire Beatrice to look after his house and children. Barker replied that she had too many children and let it go at that. Kendall then returned the Hogue family to Wiarton and went on to the little shack on Johnston Harbour Road.

The next we hear of Arthur and his family is when he and his children returned to their farm. They arrived back prematurely, as the flax wasn't ready to be harvested and it was still several weeks until school opened. Their appearance surprised the Kendall's immediate neighbor, James Broughton, and he went over to speak to his friend Art. Instead of greeting him warmly, Kendall was sullen and sharp. The children, who were normally great friends of Broughton, tried to avoid him. Helen was nowhere to be seen, but Beatrice Hogue and her children were very much in evidence. Broughton inquired about Helen. Art explained that his wife had left him, but Broughton found this hard to believe, being aware of Helen's deep affection for her children. Arthur said that he and his wife had had a fight in the shack. Angry words had been exchanged and Helen had thrown a cup of tea at him. He had then stormed out of the shack with the idea of driving his car off the wharf at Tobermory, but when he got there there had been too many cars and he couldn't get to the edge of the wharf. When he returned to Johnston Harbour it was early in the morning and young Jimmie had told him his mother had left right after he had driven away. Kendall claimed he never saw his wife again.

It was now Friday morning; he made breakfast for the children and went to work at the mill. On Saturday night, he dropped his children off at Mrs. Hogue's and went on to his farm. On Sunday night, he said, he slept with young Jimmie in his car outside Wiarton. He hung around Wiarton all day Monday, and on Monday night slept in the shack at Johnston Harbour with his son. On Tuesday, he loaded his car with some belongings and left Johnston Harbour.

Jim Broughton couldn't get Arthur's story or the children's strange behavior out of his mind. It was as if Arthur was talking about some other person, not Helen, the devoted wife and mother. Nothing seemed to fit. After a few days he decided to visit Arthur again. This time, accompanied by Lloyd Machon, another neighbor, he again inquired about Helen. Arthur was evasive, but gave the impression that she might be with her mother in Brantford. Later that day Broughton called Brantford and asked Helen's brother, Ross Cameron, if she was there. Her brother told him that she was not in Brantford, and the story of her disappearance so upset him that he decided to visit Arthur. That same night Ross Cameron went to the Kendall farm in Elma Township. Arthur came out of the house and met him in the yard. He avoided Ross' direct questions about Helen and didn't seem to want to talk about her. The children, who were usually underfoot making a fuss when their uncle visited, were nowhere to be seen. Finally Ross Cameron left the Kendall farm and went to the Sebringville Ontario Provincial Police Office, where he had previously arranged to meet Jim Broughton. The two men reported Helen Kendall as a missing person.

Arthur was questioned by the police but didn't give any new information. Helen's description was taken and her picture was distributed to police outlets across Canada and the United States. She had blue eyes, blonde hair, stood five feet seven inches tall, weighed 132 pounds, and was considered to be an attractive mature woman. The Kendall children were also questioned, but seemed reluctant to volunteer any information of a concrete nature. Mary was too young to interrogate, but Ann and Jean were questioned extensively, and each time they were gently pressed for an answer about their mother's disappearance, they burst into tears. Margaret, the eldest daughter, corroborated her father's story in every way, as did 12-year-old Jimmie. The police felt the children were not telling the complete truth and came to the conclusion that the Kendall children feared their father. The little shack and the family car were both examined, with no results. Everyone questioned knew of Kendall's relationship with Beatrice Hogue, but could offer no explanation as to what had happened to Helen.

On Sept. 3, approximately a month after Helen's disappearance, John Krugel was cutting bush on his property not far from the Kendall farm when he came upon a cardboard box containing women's undergarments. He notified the police, who later identified the contents of the box as belonging to Helen Kendall. Arthur Kendall appeared to be as mystified as anyone else at the weird discovery. During the month of September, the police were actively looking for Helen Kendall's body. The bush surrounding the shack at Johnston Harbour was thoroughly searched, and likely areas were also combed; but all to no avail.

Months passed, and the authorities began to receive complaints about the care of the eleven children living on the Kendall farm. On Jan. 7, 1953, they received a report from Dr. C.E. Connors of Listowel that Margaret had been attacked by her father with a whip. Evidently she had been warned not to stop off at the farm of Clarence Ronenburg on her way home from school, and when she did drop in on the farm, her father went over and gave her a horse-whipping. Kendall was arrested for this mistreatment of his daughter, but was later released when Margaret said that she had only received a slight punishment for disobeying her father.

The Children's Aid Society was successful in gaining custody of the Kendall children, and they were taken away from the Kendall farm for a full year. Arthur appealed this decision, and the children were eventually returned to him.

Kendall and his family moved several times to get away from the derogatory rumors that dogged them wherever they went. In 1954, Thomas E. Hogue was granted a divorce from his wife Beatrice, naming Arthur Kendall as co-respondent. The years sped by, and in 1959, Kendall's lawyer was successful in having Helen declared legally dead. Three months later Arthur married Beatrice Hogue.

It was now nine years since the happy Kendall family left their farm for what was to be a pleasant vacation in the bush. Margaret, the oldest girl, was married to a private in the Canadian Army, stationed in Winnipeg. Ann was living away from home, and Jimmie was now a strapping 21-year-old working for Canadian Canners in Exeter. The two children, still living with their father, Jean, now fourteen, and Mary, now ten, were of deep concern to Ann, who felt that they were being discriminated against, particularly now that they were the only Kendall children still at home.

The police received a telephone call from a friend of Ann's, advising them that Ann would now talk to them. They rushed to interview her. She now stated emphatically that she and her older brother and sister had seen her father kill her mother. In front of the officers she called her sister in Winnipeg and told her what she had done. The answer came back sharp and clear, "Ann, I've wanted to do it for years, but I never had the guts!"

Ann then told her story in detail. She said:

"After George Hislop and Gordon Neabel left, our sleeping arrangements were my mother and father in a lower bunk at the back of the cabin on the right as you walked in; my sister, Margaret, and I in the upper bunk above them. On the left of the cabin at the back, Mary and Jeannie slept in the lower bunk, with Jimmie in the bunk above. A curtain hung between the bunks.

"I don't remember details of going to bed the night before we left Johnston Harbour, but my mother always insisted that we go to bed as soon as it was dark. About dawn — daylight was coming through the one and only window in the cabin — I was awakened by a commotion under our bunk and I heard mother cry, 'No, Art, please don't.'

"I didn't hear my father say anything. I looked down over the bunk and I saw my father go from the lower bunk and lay a butcher knife on the table which was only one or two steps from the bunk. I saw blood on the knife. My dad was wearing only his work shirt; My mother her nightgown. When I awoke, Margaret was already awake and she put her hand over my mouth.

"I saw my father grab my mother around her shoulders; she was limp. He dragged her out the door. There was only a screen door on the cabin; I remember it slammed shut. I remember my mother's feet were dragging on the floor. I saw my father go past the window towards the bridge — east. I could see him dragging my mother on the road — walking in the direction of the mill.

"Dad was away about twenty minutes or half an hour. As soon as he came back he dressed, then he cleaned up the blood on the floor at the bunk. He took off the bedsheets and the pillow slips and he gathered my mother's clothes. He wiped the floor with my mother's clothes, then wrapped them up with the bedclothes and the butcher knife. He bundled them all up, put them in a shopping bag and went away. I saw him walk past the window. He was away a few minutes longer than the first time.

"As soon as he came back the second time he scrubbed the floor with a brush and rainwater from the tub filled from the cabin drainpipe. I had never seen him clean a floor before, either at the cabin or at home. While washing the floor he told us to get up and get dressed. It had always been a very strict rule in the house that we kids should never make a noise or get up until we were called. He then took Margaret away in the car to get drinking water from the spring. I remember he put the milk can we used for drinking water in the car."

Officers flew to Winnipeg, and Margaret's statement was in substance the same as Ann's. It concludes:

"Dad drove me to the fork in the road. As you go from the cabin towards the highway, you come to the mill gate, a culvert over the road where there is quicksand, a hill and a turn, then you reach the fork where my dad stopped.

"He told me to tell anyone who asked about mother that she left Thursday night when he was in Wiarton — the night he told us he took Mr. Pedwell for a shot in the arm. Dad told me to say that my mother and he had a quarrel, she threw a cup of hot tea at him, and after he left she walked out, taking her clothes in a shopping bag. I was to say that she told us she would never return.

"Dad told me not to make porridge; the old stove was in poor condition. I was to go to Charlton's store for corn flakes. Dad didn't actually threaten to kill me but when he told me to do or say anything, I knew better than to disobey him.

"Dad drove me back to the cabin. Before he went to work he told us kids to pick wild strawberries for dinner. I walked to the store for corn flakes and I had to knock to wake up the Charltons. We kids had breakfast. We didn't talk about mother, but I recall a general feeling that she had gone to hospital. It was only when we reached Mrs. Hogue's place that night that I realized mother wasn't sick in Wiarton.

"Dad came home for dinner at noon. Ann and I had picked strawberries and we had killed a rattlesnake. We laid it out on the ground for dad to see. I had made a stack of sandwiches and we had berries. There was no conversation about mother. Dad went to work and quit earlier than usual. He came to the cabin and told us to put on our good clothes, we would have supper where we were going.

"He drove us fast to Wiarton. On the way, he loaded some wood in the car and unloaded it in Mrs. Hogue's woodshed. I remember my father saying, 'Beatrice, this is my family.' Then he shaved. We had supper — spaghetti and margarine — I had never tasted either before. Dad and Mrs. Hogue appeared to have known each other before, and she also knew my brother, Jimmie."

Arthur Kendall was arrested on Jan. 27, 1961, nine years after his wife disappeared. A preliminary hearing was held on March 3, and Kendall was committed for trial. His trial began in Walkerton on Tuesday, Oct. 24, 1961.

Jimmie Kendall took the stand and told of the night his mother was murdered.

"The last night we were at Johnston Harbour Dad left the cabin in the car, saying he was taking Mr. Pedwell to the doctor. At dawn I woke up when I heard my mother cry, 'Don't, Art!' She said it three or four times. I was sleeping in the top bunk. I remember looking over the bunk. My mother looked kind of stunned. She was wearing a light colored nightgown. I saw my dad take my mother out of the cabin. He had his arms under her armpits and she was kind of limp. I believe my mother was still saying, 'Don't, Art,' as my dad took her down the road in the direction of the highway. I think she was still living when she passed the window. I haven't seen my mother since.

"I was frightened and I wondered if my dad was coming back to do the rest of us kids in. Dad came back alone within an hour. He was wearing hip rubber boots. He didn't speak. I noticed a butcher knife on the kitchen table with blood on it. Dad wiped the blood up off the floor with a rag. It took him about ten minutes. I was scared."

Arthur Kendall sat unmoved as his three children testified against him. The jury took only two hours to find him guilty of capital murder. He was sentenced to hang on Jan. 23, 1962. Seven days before he was to be executed, his sentence was commuted to life imprisonment.

Whatever happened to Helen Kendall's body? No one knows for sure, and it has never been found. The most popular theory is that Kendall disposed of his wife's body by placing it in Lake Scugog, which is located directly behind the Pedwell sawmill. The middle of the lake is blanketed with acres of green marsh grass, which lies about a foot underwater. The rooting of the grass is so tangled it can almost support the weight of a grown man. If Kendall parted this mass and lowered his wife's body under the tangled root system into five further feet of water, the body would never rise to the surface. Mr. Pedwell claimed that he lost many logs in this manner when he ran his sawmill.

Arthur Kendall has never once admitted killing his wife. Today he is confined to the Agassiz Correctional Camp at Agassiz, B.C. He claims his children lied at the trial in order to lay their hands on their mother's small estate, and asks thought-provoking questions. Why did his children wait nine years to change their stories? They were questioned by mature members of the OPP. Surely they would have told the truth to these professionals, if indeed it was the truth? Why, Kendall asks, would he kill his wife in front of his children when there were so many other places to commit murder, surrounded as they were by wild bush country?

Arthur Kendall is now 65 years old. He has been before the National Parole Board many times, but each time his parole has been turned down. He has been institutionalized for 15 years, and it is now 24 years since the fateful day when his wife disappeared from the little shack on the Bruce Peninsula.

His second wife, Beatrice Hogue, has remained devoted to him over the years. She has moved to Terrace, B.C., and visits Arthur at the correctional facility at every opportunity. Arthur now has permission to work on a farm two days a week, and he receives passes to visit Beatrice on special occasions such as Christmas.

* Author's note: Since this story was written, Arthur Kendall has been paroled. He lives quietly with his wife Beatrice in British Columbia.

A CHRISTMAS TALE

The day was muggy, bringing out tiny beads of perspiration on the foreheads of the two men as they laboriously scattered ashes across the lake. The last remains of Lucius A. Parmelee were thus brought home to rest near his birthplace of Waterloo, Quebec.

The wheel had turned for 85 years and in those 85 years "Christmas" Parmelee had been banker, chicken farmer, stock speculator, and what he was most proud of — bank swindler.

He roamed over two continents and while gangsters were shooting and kidnapping, "Christmas" was quietly relieving various banking institutions of their cash year after year for 15 long years.

It all really started in Cookstown, a few miles from Barrie, Ontario. Here at the age of 18, young Lucius accepted a position with the Union Bank of Canada. His starting salary was $200 a year. Now, allowing for inflation, this was not considered a princely sum even in 1907. However, the custom of the times accepted the fact that young men entering a career in banking would of necessity be subsidized by their parents. And so it was with Lucius.

The bank soon saw fit to transfer him to Warkworth, Ontario. Here his salary was raised to $350 a year, and he assumed the duties of a teller and ledger keeper.

Well, Parmelee was so good at this banking business that he finally ended up in Montreal. Here he learned the ins and outs of the various duties that are performed in the daily operation of a bank. Here too he formulated the opinion that something was rotten in the business, for while employees received starvation wages, it appeared the banks were the most successful institutions in the country. He felt so strongly about it he quit banking and headed West. He drifted from one job to another for several years before deciding to reenter banking with the idea of withdrawing more than he deposited.

Now in the early twenties, banking procedures were not as sophisticated as they are today. You took your withdrawal slip to the ledger keeper. He looked at your account, and if you had the slip covered with funds on deposit, he initialled the withdrawal slip and returned it to you. The slip was then presented to the teller, who in turn counted out your money.

Lucius would open a legitimate account and deposit a few dollars. Let's say he would present a slip to the ledger keeper for five dollars. Once initialled by the ledger keeper Lucius would merely write in the word hundred after the five, and as the slip already had the ledger keeper's initial on it, it was cashed without question.

Simple and crude, but effective enough to keep Lucius solvent. For a change of pace he would go to the United States and get rubber certification stamps made up. So as not to attract suspicion he would order a Royal Club of Canada stamp.

Later he would cut out the word 'club' and with a completely different stamp insert the word 'bank'. As everyone knows, certified cheques are rarely questioned.

In the fall of 1923, Parmelee arrived in Vancouver. He picked four banks; the Commerce, the Union, the Standard, and the Royal. In each he opened a savings account under the name of H.A. Stewart. He wrote each manager and asked them to transfer $500 into a current account. Each replied by letter thanking him for the business and enclosing a book of cheques. Next he made a practice of becoming known to the tellers and ledger keepers. Finally one day at each bank after months of being a customer, he asked each bank to change his current account to the Puget Sound Fish Co., with himself as manager and signing officer.

In this way Parmelee now had four current business accounts and not one embarrassing question had been asked.

His next step was to get some high quality cheques printed up suitably embossed with fish. He then got four small cheques certified in order to have an exact duplicate of the stamp at each bank. Once this was accomplished he made up four certified intialled cheques that were just itching to be cashed. It was just before Christmas, and the streets were crowded with shoppers. At exactly 10:30 the certified cheque was given to the teller at the Commerce who recognized Mr. Stewart at once and counted out the cash without question. Lucius tiptoed across to the Union and repeated his performance. Ditto the Standard Bank. Last on the list was the Royal on Granville Street. Here for some reason or other the teller left his cage to check with the ledger keeper. When his back was turned Lucius calmly walked out of the bank.

The day's receipts were $9,075.

From that December day on he was to be known as "Christmas" Parmelee. All through the 1920s, in Canada and the U.S., at Christmas the police and the banking associations would offer rewards, but never did he slip up. Things got so good that Christmas met up with a young lady and bought a chicken farm near San Francisco. He would have given up the banking business but disease wiped out his flock and he had to return to his old ways.

In 1930, during Christmas week in Toronto, he grabbed the Royal Bank at King and Yonge St., the Dominion on the corner across the street and the Bank of Montreal on Front and Yonge, for a total of $11,400, on one day within a half hour.

Later in New York, Christmas put the bite on the United States Bank on Upper Fiftieth Avenue. He cashed one cheque for $6,500, and then in his usual sense of the ridiculous, he got in another line, presented another cheque for $6,500 and left the bank with $13,000. By prearrangement he had booked passage on the *American Farmer* for that very hour, and upon leaving the bank he proceeded to the ship and in a few hours he was on his way to London, England.

His methods were always being improved. He took to dressing up as a clergyman. This, plus his patient build up of months before striking, saw him through the worst depression the world has ever known.

After 15 years of outwitting the authorities, Christmas was caught by one of those rare coincidences that defies belief. On a ferry outside of San Francisco, a bank teller, who was taking the same trip, spotted him. He had always dreaded this type of chance encounter, and as a result never took public transportation on weekends when the tellers may be out of their cages.

On this occasion he forgot — it was a bank holiday. "Christmas" Parmelee received one to fourteen years in San Quentin. He served three years before being deported to Canada. Once across the border, he was sentenced to six years in Kingston, and ended up serving five years. All in all he had been confined for eight long years.

Lucius got a job and really tried to go straight, but then as now the odds were stacked against honest work for an ex convict.

Just one more caper in Montreal, and he would quit for good. The old spark was gone, and Lucius was apprehended before he could get away. This time he was sentenced to 12 years and ended up serving seven.

On June 5th, 1955 Lucius A. "Christmas" Parmelee was released as a free man. He really quit the banking business for good. He made his living doing odd jobs, and was in some demand as a speaker and television guest. He even had a book of his exploits published. Always an avid reader, he used to haunt libraries and book stores in Montreal.

In 1967, he strolled into the International Book Shop on St. Catherine St. in Montreal. He became fast friends with the store's owner, Allan Goodman, and rarely missed a day visiting his friend and browsing through the store. Now an old man well into his eighties, he inconspicuously read the books Mr. Goodman picked out for him. He delighted in autographing his own book for customers. Living at the Salvation Army and reading — this was the old swindler's life.

One day he complained that his arm felt stiff. Realizing he was having a stroke, Goodman drove Lucius to the hospital. He died two days later.

Some friends who knew his past carried out the instructions found in his will, and scattered his ashes on top of the lake near Waterloo where it all began and ended for "Christmas" Parmelee.

THE BLACK DONNELLYS

People who say we Canadians don't have the flair or elan for intriguing crimes are wrong. Albert Guay and some friends in Quebec City once managed to place a bomb on an airplane. They blew up Albert's wife and 22 innocent people. Then there was Bill Coffin. One hunting season Bill shot three American hunters along the Gaspe coast. Albert and Bill were hung for their foul deeds.

But when you get right down to discussing Canadian crimes, the one that comes to mind is the grand-daddy of them all — the case of the Black Donnellys. What other case runs the gamut from a stolen cow to mass murder with assorted other crimes that covered a period of over 30 years?

Settle back now. We are going back almost 130 years to another way of life. We will travel from Tipperary, Ireland to Lucan, Ontario.

In 1846, James Donnelly, his wife Johannah and their two sons, James Jr., three; and William, an infant, left Tipperary and immigrated to Canada. For two years Jim worked without incident as a teamster in London, Ontario. Then, with Johannah again pregnant, they gravitated to the farm life they had known so well in Ireland. They moved 14 miles north to the village of Lucan. It was most natural for them to settle there. You see, Lucan was virtually 100 per cent Irish. You can name any typical Irish name, and chances are there was one in Lucan the day Jim Donnelly arrived.

The place was a pioneer village, and the villagers pushed back the wilderness with their own hands. They worked hard and they played hard. Sometimes the play took the form of hard drink, and who was to blame a man for "tossin' back a few" after 15 hours of backbreaking labor in the fields.

Like many of the inhabitants of the small town, Jim Donnelly hailed from County Tipperary. He could work, fight, and drink with the best of them. He had much in common with his neighbors and could have been friendly and lived in harmony with them, had he chosen. Jim didn't make that much of an effort. On his first day in the village he got into two fights, and won them both. The second day was spent settling down on 100 acres of good farmland situated about four miles from the village on a dirt road called the Roman Line. It didn't bother Jim that someone else owned the land. He started to build a cabin almost at once. Naturally enough, the legitimate owner heard of the stranger out on his land. He harnessed up a team and drove out. Jim and Johannah gave him hell, and drove him off what was, in effect, his own land. Word spread throughout the district that this Donnelly fellow was one tough cookie.

No one bothered the Donnelly clan for some time after that. Johannah helped Jim build the cabin from the ground up. She took a day off and gave birth to her third son, whom she named John. If you are keeping track, that's three boys in a row for Johannah. Jim and Johannah must have taken some further time off from working in the fields. She found herself in labor of another kind five more times in the succeeding years. The results of these endeavors were Patrick, Michael, Robert, Thomas, and at last a bouncing baby girl, Jennie.

Despite Johannah taking the day off here and there to give birth, the farm prospered. Jim made no friends. He was short with his neighbors, and when in his cups, he wasn't averse to taking on one or two in friendly fisticuffs at the bars in town. Still, nothing of a serious nature befell the family during the years the children came into the world.

Then a man named John Farrell came to Lucan. He heard he could buy the farm Donnelly was working from the legitimate owner real cheap. Farrell was warned of the tough Donnelly clan, but bought the land anyway. He drove out to his newly acquired farm with a friend. Now Farrell was a huge former blacksmith, who could and did lick most men he faced. He confronted Jim Donnelly, and gave him an hour to get off the farm. Jim looked at his bold adversary, took off his coat, and surrounded by his sons told Farrell he would have to beat him first. Standing in the doorway Johannah looked down the sights of a rifle at Farrell's friend. Donnelly and Farrell squared off. With the children cheering their father, he proceeded to give Farrell a terrible beating. The badly bleeding Farrell was helped on his horse by his friend, and the pair rode away.

Now I must point out that after probing the rather checkered history of the Donnelly family, the fight just described is the one incident where Donnelly seems to me to have a semblance of justification. It's true he laid claim to land that wasn't rightfully his, but still man and wife had worked the soil for eight long years. This, by frontier standards, had to give him some sort of squatter's title. Most men would have fought. This is the last justifiable violence that I can find in the Donnelly saga.

Unable to get his land by force, Farrell took Donnelly to court and was successful in gaining title to 50 acres.

Donnelly was forced to stand by and watch Farrell erect a house and barn on land he had worked.

The little inconveniences started to happen to Farrell. A cow of his was poisoned. One night his barn caught fire and burned to the ground. Farrell knew who was causing his wave of misfortune, but couldn't prove it. Hatred between the two men grew. Finally it exploded into personal violence.

In frontier days it was custom for everyone to donate labor to help a neighbor build a barn. And so it came to pass that Jim Donnelly and John Farrell found themselves in each other's company. Both had been into the sauce when Farrell started insulting Donnelly. Soon the two were at it with their fists. While lying on the ground during the fight, Donnelly's hand came in contact with an iron bar. He swung it viciously and it connected squarely with Farrell's head. He fell to the ground, and died three days later. Jim mounted his horse, and throwing curses to the crowd, galloped for home. He told his wife the news of the fight with Farrell, and together they decided that, rather than run, Jim would hide out in the woods that adjoined their farm.

It was June of 1857, and unbelievably Jim remained in hiding until the spring of 1859. Some say he used to dress in his wife's clothing and even managed to put in his seed and bring in the crops disguised in this manner. But this type of life was too hard even for tough Jim Donnelly. Finally he came out of the woods and gave himself up. He stood trial and received seven years in Kingston Penitentiary.

The years passed and the seven boys at home grew up. As they matured the boys took on their father's nature and mean disposition. Jim was away about three years when a wave of barn burning swept the Lucan area. Three barns in a row myseriously caught fire and burned to the ground. Someone thought it was quite a coincidence that the owners of the barns were the three main prosecution witnesses at Jim Donnelly's trial. The rumor spread until a constable was sent out to question the Donnelly family. Young Jim Jr. beat up the cop, and while the rest of the boys cheered the luckless constable dragged himself up on his horse and got the hell out of there.

Fires, poisoned cattle, and horses with their throats cut were the norm around Lucan after that. Then masked men started rolling drunks outside the bars. A regular local crime wave was taking place. While most residents of the district knew who was raging this private war, there was very little they could do about it. The hotel in the village bought meat from the Donnellys. When the owner became suspicious that the meat was stolen, he stopped buying from the Donnellys. The hotel mysteriously burned to the ground.

In 1866, the head of the "Black Donnellys" (for that is what everyone called them now) returned home from prison. Jim had served his seven years. The night Jim came back, a man who had testified against him seven years earlier lost his barn to fire. Year after year passed, and while there were periods of relative peace, they didn't last long. The Black Donnellys rode by night, robbing and burning as they roared on horseback down the Roman Line. Sometimes they were charged, and sometimes they even stood trial, but no one could be found to testify against them.

In the meantime, the entire district around London started to prosper. With this prosperity came better means of transportation. Two stage coach lines ran regularly between Exeter and London, passing through Lucan. James and William Donnelly worked for two years as drivers, and eventually in 1873 they bought a stage line. Their competitor, one John Flannigan, was favored by everyone and did a roaring business, due to the Donnelly's bad reputation. One fine morning Flannigan woke up to find his stages hacked to pieces, harnesses destroyed and all his horses mutilated. During the night someone had cut out their tongues. Flannigan put the animals out of their misery.

Now the villagers had a great fear of the Black Donnellys, but to mutilate a horse in frontier days was almost the equivalent of murder.

The Donnellys had gone too far.

Led by Flannigan, a mob of 17 marched down the Roman Line to the Donnellys' farm. They were met by Jim and his seven sons. The odds didn't bother them. They charged the mob and fought like wild animals. Years later, men who witnessed the battle told their sons of the bloodiest, toughest hand-to-hand fight they ever saw. The Donnellys beat the mob into a retreat. No matter what one thinks of the Donnelly clan, everyone agrees they could scrap.

Within a week the stubborn Flanningan had purchased new supplies and animals to start up his stage line again. The night before his first run was scheduled his barn burned to the ground.

Fires, animal mutilation and robbery continued. When the law interfered, the investigating constable was usually given a horrible beating. Mayhem replaced normal life, but certain inevitable events did take place. The one Donnelly daughter, Jennie, married and moved away. William Donnelly married Nora Kennedy, and during the wedding celebration managed to shoot at a constable. He received nine months in prison. The night he was sentenced, the constable was beaten up so badly by masked men that he lost his eyesight.

In 1877, James Jr. died of pneumonia. Robert got drunk one night and took some shots at a constable. He missed, but the constable wounded him. Robert received two years in prison, and in light of future events, this sentence probably saved his life. In 1878, Michael got into a fight with two hobos and was stabbed to death. Still, despite the loss of two sons and a further one in prison, the family continued to take vengeance on their enemies.

The beginning of the end came the day big James Carroll moved to Lucan from Exeter. He got himelf appointed special constable. Everyone knew his main duty was to get rid of the Donnellys. As fate would have it, Carroll was out of the village when a man named Thompson reported a stolen cow. As usual suspicion fell heavily on the Donnellys. A group of men, again led by John Flannigan, marched on the Donnelly's farm. This time they found old Jim and Johannah home alone. They questioned them, but grew impatient and wrecked their house instead. After this incident Donnellys' horses raced down the Roman Line night after night, leaving burned barns in their wake. It was almost war with the sides being the Donnellys against the world, with special emphasis on the men who had damaged the Donnelly house.

Records are unclear as to what specific incident was the straw that broke the camel's back. What is known is that many of the men, led by James Carroll, agreed among themselves that they would take the law into their own hands. Known as the Biddulph Vigilance Committee, they swore never to reveal the identity of a fellow member of the committee, no matter what the consequence. They met in the local schoolhouse.

In the early morning hours of Feb. 4, 1880, thirty one members of the committee advanced on the Donnelly farm. The occupants fought like cornered animals, but it was no use. The mob engulfed old Jim Donnelly, and finally culminated their attack by cutting his head off with an axe. Johannah was clubbed to death. Tom Donnelly was slashed and clubbed to death, and in the end he too was decapitated. Jim's niece, Bridget, had just come across from Ireland, and it was her bad luck to be a guest in the Donnelly house that night. She was clubbed to death. Eleven-year-old Johnny Connor was sleeping overnight at the Donnelly farm. He was the son of a rare friendly neighbor, and was there to look after the livestock the next day when the Donnellys were to appear in court. He hid under the bed and was overlooked by the mob. The vigilantes set fire to the house and left. Young Johnny managed to escape from the burning building.

The mob moved down the road to William Donnelly's farm. John who was sleeping at his brother's house, answered their knock. As the door opened two shotguns roared, and John fell dead. The blood crazed men left before William came to his brother's side. The killers thought they had shot the only male occupant of the house that night. The night's work done, the committee disbanded and straggled home individually.

Fourteen members of the vigilante committee were arrested and charged with murder. Eight of these were discharged, leaving six to go to trial for murder separately in London. These men were identified by young Johnny Connor, and were considered to be the ringleaders. They were James Carroll, John Kennedy, Martin McLaughlin, John Purtell, James Ryder and Thomas Ryder.

James Carroll went to trial first, and the jury could not agree. He was tried again, and this time the verdict was not guilty. The crown dropped the charges against the remaining five, as the evidence against them was the same as that against Carroll. All were set free.

The day the acquitted men returned to Lucan they were met by a band and greeted like heroes. There was a victory dance for them that night. For the rest of their lives they were considered bona fide heroes for ridding the district of the hated Donnellys.

The three surviving brothers, Robert, William and Patrick, never caused any trouble after the massacre. After he got out of prison, Robert ended up his days as a night clerk at a hotel in London. William ran the St. Nicholas Hotel at Appin. After dying of natural causes, his body was returned to Lucan for burial. Patrick ran a blacksmith shop in Thorold for many years. Legend has it that he attended the funerals of each of the six men who stood accused as the ringleaders of the mob that murdered his parents. It is said that he spit on each coffin and said, "There goes another of the bastards to hell." Patrick passed away in 1929.

RED RYAN REFORMED

With the possible exception of Alonzo Boyd and his gang, Canada has been relatively free of notorious bank robbers. There was one other desperado, who in his own way, had a greater influence on the Canadian parole system than any other single person who ever lived in this country.

Norman John (Red) Ryan was born in Toronto in 1895. From the time he could walk he was stealing other kids' toys. At first his family attributed this rather ominous trait to child's play. At the age of 12 he stole a bicycle and was actually convicted. The family knew they had a black sheep on their hands. Red graduated from petty theft to bank robbery and ended up receiving a 12-year sentence in Kingston Penitentiary.

In 1916, the First World War was raging. Red was released from prison on the condition that he enter the army. No sooner was he shipped overseas when he got into trouble in England. It seems Red went on a spree of robbing stores and ended up in a military jail. As soon as he was released he deserted, but because he joined the Merchant Navy the authorities went easy on him.

The war ended. Red was shipped home. It is believed that he committed many holdups from the very moment he arrived in Toronto. He was caught and stood trial for five robberies that were directly attributed to him. Red received a sentence of 25 years in Kingston Penitentiary.

Not being one to rest on his laurels he decided to do something about his confinement. On Sept. 10, 1923 Arthur Sullivan, Gordon Simpson, Edward McMullen, Thomas Bryan, and Ryan escaped from Kingston. They did it in spectacular fashion, by setting a barn on fire. In the confusion, they managed to go over the wall. McMullen was captured the same day, but the other four made clean getaways. Sullivan was shot and killed by police in 1923, Simpson was captured in New York in 1925, and Bryan managed to stay free until 1927 when he was apprehended in Chicago.

Ryan robbed a bank in Toronto of $3,000, twelve days after the escape. He then crossed the border to the U.S. In December, he got himself trapped in the Minneapolis, Minn. post office while in the midst of a robbery. Ryan, who was always willing to shoot it out with the police, was wounded. He was taken into custody and the American authorities deported him.

This time Ryan received life imprisonment, and this is really where the unusual saga of Red Ryan begins.

In Kingston, he came under the influence of a Roman Catholic priest, Rev. W.T. Kingsley. He seemed to become a changed man. At first he worked in the mail room and later served as an orderly in the prison hospital. In this latter position he distinguished himself by ministering selflessly to the very ill and going out of his way to be kind and considerate to the aged convicts. Red even became an altar boy.

Months drifted into years and stories began emanating from Kingston about the former hood who was now completely reformed. Reports concerning his activities were so complimentary that politicians started to make noises about rehabilitation instead of punishment. Finally the Prime Minister of Canada, R.B. Bennett, started to use his influence to get Red out of the pokey. Businessmen offered him jobs, if he could gain his freedom. On July 24, 1935, after serving only 11 years of his sentence, Red was released.

He didn't receive as big a welcome as General MacArthur got when Harry Truman fired him, but it was close. Red lived with his brother in Toronto and was in great demand as a speaker. Police in particular thought him a real model guest at their functions. Ten months passed, and indeed Red Ryan appeared to be the perfect bad guy turned good guy.

Ah, but it couldn't last.

On May 24, 1936, two masked men were cornered inside a liquor store in Sarnia during a holdup. A citizen who happened to be passing the store called the police. They reacted so fast the two men were still in the store when they arrived. The robbers elected to shoot it out. The first man to get hit was a police officer who was killed on the spot. Reinforcements arrived and the two robbers were shot dead. When they pulled the mask off one lifeless bandit they realized they were staring down at Red Ryan. His dead partner was a small time thief named Harry Checkley.

All the people who had clamored for Red's release now found themselves with egg all over their faces. The police started to look at a few unsolved robberies that had taken place while Red was playing Saint Ryan. Sure enough they found that he was responsible for several robberies that had taken place in Toronto.

Just as everyone had wanted Ryan's release, now everyone wanted parole regulations tightened. For several years after, every inmate who came up for parole knew that he had to live down the deception pulled off by Ryan. Statistics show that for years after the Ryan incident releases by parole diminished appreciably. Red Ryan was responsible for changing the lenient parole system of an entire country.

HE SPOTTED A FOOT

It has been said that the perfect murder is one where murder is not even suspected. The tragic accident that takes place so logically and unavoidably — the missing person who walks away from family and friends, never to be seen or heard of again — all these could very well be homicides. We cannot discuss these cases, for they have never been recognized as anything other than what they seemed to be on the surface.

But the near misses are intriguing.

Raymond Slemko was an electrician employed with the Baldwin Electric Co. in Toronto. On a cool September afternoon, in 1960, Slemko had to check some wiring in a trench beside an artificial rink in Dufferin Grove Park. Raymond thought he detected a slight odor, and asked Moses Spurrel, an employee of the A.J. Martin Excavation Co. to give him a hand. Both men started to dig. Raymond was later to tell the Supreme Court how he discovered the body of Eva Blumberger. "The electrical cord binding the blanket broke when I put my shovel under it, and I saw a foot."

Later that very day cement was to be poured into the trench and the body of Eva Blumberger would never have been discovered. She had been reported missing several days earlier by her family, and most probably would be missing forever had it not been for the curiosity of Raymond Slemko.

The cause of death was a fractured skull inflicted by vicious blows to the head. Eva had not been sexually molested in any way. The day after the body was uncovered, two private investigators, who had been employed by the dead girl's family to find her, turned their file on the case over to the police. The main information in the file contained the results of an interview with one Deszo (Dick) Bakonyi. The police picked up Bakonyi for questioning. After hours of interrogation, he was charged with murder.

Due to marriages between members of Eva's and Dick's families, their relationship to each other was rather complicated. Eva's father had died some years earlier, and her father's brother, who was Bakonyi's father, married her mother. This made Eva, Dick's stepsister, as well as cousin.

According to Bakonyi, on Sept. 12, Eva asked him if she could use his room for a meeting with her boyfriend. When Dick and Eva entered the room, Bakonyi claimed, a chloroform rag was placed over his mouth from behind. The next he knew upon regaining consciousness was that Eva was gone and there was blood on his bed. Dick said he had not seen Eva since the time of this attack.

The police came up with a somewhat different set of circumstances and events. Bakonyi's landlady, Mrs. Eugenia Rudski, identified the blanket which was wrapped around the body as belonging to her. It had been used on Bakonyi's bed. She described the evening of Sept. 12, when she thought she heard a dull thud emanate from Dick's room. She yelled through the door, inquiring what was going on, but didn't receive any reply. Next morning she washed some dark stains off Bakonyi's bedroom floor. Other bloodstains were found on the dresser, and on Bakonyi's trousers and shoes. All the bloodstains were the same type as Eva Blumberger's. The electric wire was the same type that Bakonyi used on his hi-fi equipment. Dick was a classical music fan, who owned extensive hi-fi equipment and over $1,000 worth of classical records.

Mrs. Ilene Fraser of St. Clarence Ave. happened to be in Dufferin Grove Park the day before the body was uncovered, and swore she saw Dick Bakonyi in the trench where Eva's body was later found. Mrs. Fraser thought nothing of it at the time, but the next day when the body was found, she came forward with her information. Later she identified Dick as the man in the trench from a lineup at police headquarters.

On Dec. 3, 1960, Bakonyi stood trial for the murder of his stepsister. The evidence against him was all circumstantial, but it spun a tight web of guilt. During the trial it was brought out that Eva thought she was pregnant. She feared exposure, and possibly tried to induce an abortion. An autopsy indicated that she was not pregnant. The day Eva vanished she left a note in Bakonyi's room, which read — "Dear Dan," (she sometimes called Bakonyi that) — "I was here. . . you were not here. Get the medicine or there will be troubles. I will call. Eva."

The prosecution brought out the fact that the motive for the killing could have been that Eva had accused Dick of being responsible for her imagined pregnancy. Even Bakonyi's story of being chloroformed came under ridicule. It was proved that Dick was with members of his family later on the night of Sept. 12, and didn't even mention the alleged incident to anyone. If you are forcefully chloroformed and have your stepsister abducted, it would seem quite natural that you would, at the very least, tell your family, if not report the incident to the police.

In Bakonyi's defence, his sister gave evidence that he was in her home at approximately the time Mrs. Rudski heard the dull thud from Dick's room.

After two hours of deliberation the jury found Bakonyi guilty of murder. When asked if he had anything to say before sentence was passed, the accused said, "I think I have, my lord. Eva Blumberger was my cousin. Before her death she was in trouble. I wanted to help her. That is the only reason I came to be entangled in this case. Probably because of this, I am going to lose my life. I am not afraid to die."

Bakonyi was sentenced to be hanged on May 23, 1961. On May 19, just four days before the execution was to be carried out, his sentence was commuted by the federal cabinet to life imprisonment in Kingston Penitentiary. Dick Bakonyi has since been released, and his present whereabouts are unknown.

WHO KILLED KAREN?

Criminal Investigation Branch File #621100540/73 is dog-eared. The thick file at the Ontario Provincial Police headquarters has been handled repeatedly. Stark black letters identify the documents inside: KAREN ANNE WOODCOCK — HOMICIDE.

Detective Inspector Lou Pelissero has been in charge of the case ever since the murder took place. Inspector Pelissero calls the case strange, unusual, and above all, frustrating. You see, the veteran policeman is almost sure he knows who committed the murder, but he can't do a thing about it.

Floyd and Karen Woodcock were married in Peterborough on May 15, 1958. By the summer of 1973, the couple lived in their own home in the village of Villiers in Otonabee Township, a few miles from Peterborough. They had seven children ranging in age from four to 15. Floyd was employed as a welder with the Outboard Marine Co. in Peterborough.

Karen had decided to go back to work. In the fall of 1972, she had enrolled in a commercial stenographic course at Sir Sandford Fleming Community College in Peterborough. Karen was a better than average student. She was active in the school paper and was well liked by both teachers and students. The 40 weeks flew by; June 29th was to be Karen's graduation. Certainly a happy day by anyone's standards, but particularly for a woman returning to school after raising seven children.

The Woodcocks' story seems to portray a contented, industrious couple forging their way ahead in the world. This may have been so, but their marriage did have one flaw.

Both were heavy drinkers, but not on a day-to-day basis. Every four months or so, Karen would go on a bout. Sometimes with her husband, and sometimes alone, she would stay drunk for three or four days.

Karen was well known in the beverage rooms of Peterborough. Regulars took her to their homes, where all-night drinking bouts would only be interrupted when someone passed out. Karen's drinking habits in no way were a reflection on her morals. No one has ever insinuated that she did anything but drink with her male companions. Usually these periodic bouts ended with Karen sleeping it off a her father's home. Floyd often picked her up at her father's house to take her home.

Floyd drove into Peterborough on June 29th to attend his wife's graduation. Quite by chance he ran into Daniel Robert Smith, a co-worker at Outboard Marine. Together they went to the McGillis Hotel. After only one beer they moved to the Grand Hotel. Floyd later excused himself to attend his wife's graduation. Still later, both he and Karen joined Smith at the McGillis. The three of them drank away the rest of the afternoon. At around 6:30 p.m. they left the beverage room to continue the party at Smith's residence. In the meantime, Karen Woodcock took a taxi to a liquor store where she picked up three bottles of gin and two bottles of wine. Smith paid for the two bottles of gin, and the Woodcocks paid the balance.

At around 8:30 p.m. Floyd suggested that it was time to call an end to the party. Karen would hear none of it. Floyd had often left his wife at parties before, and this was one of those times. He left and she remained, drinking with Smith until about 10:30 p.m. Then the pair went hotel hopping, visiting the King George Hotel and the Queen Hotel in Peterborough. At the Queen, Smith left Karen for a few moments to say hello to some friends. When he returned she was gone.

Karen left the hotel and contacted another friend, Daniel Johnson. She slept overnight at Johnson's residence on Reid St. The next day, Saturday, June 30, Karen and Johnson drank all day, consuming three bottles of wine. They had nothing to eat.

At 1:30 a.m., on Sunday, July 1, Mrs. Woodcock showed up at the home of her father, Edwin Mitchell, at 617 Ludgate St. in Peterborough. Mr. Mitchell, who was having a few drinks himself, can only remember that his daughter made a phone call and then left.

Percy Johnson is the father of Mrs. Woodcock's drinking buddy, Daniel Johnson. At 3:15 a.m. his phone rang. A female voice asked for his son. He quite naturally replied that his son was sleeping and hung up. It is believed that this is the call Karen made from her father's home.

Unable to reach Daniel Johnson, Karen left her father's house. At 3:30 a.m. Ronald Baldwin had just driven his babysitter home. He was returning to his own home when he spotted Karen. She wanted a lift. Ronald Baldwin drove her to the corner of Parkhill Rd. and Reid St. He was back in his own home at 4 a.m.

At 4:20 a.m., Harold Morton, an employee of Canadian Pittsburgh Glass was on his way to install a window at Minacola's Furniture Store. He noticed a woman hitch-hiking about 20 feet south of the Parkhill Rd. intersection. He thought she was drunk. It was Karen. Other than her killer, Harold Morton was the last known person to see Karen Woodcock alive.

At 7:20 a.m. Fred Simmond was driving to work. Beside the road, but plainly visible from his car, Fred spotted the nude body of Karen Woodcock. The exact spot was about two miles north of the Woodcock residence at Villiers, just south of Highway 7. Simmond never got out of his car. Instead he continued on to the home of Grant Elmhairst. The two men viewed the body together. They returned to the Elmhairst residence and called the O.P.P. detachment in Peterborough.

Beside the nude body, the police found an indentation in the soil where a rock had been dislodged. Karen had obviously been beaten about the head with the rock. An autopsy revealed that her death had been caused by a fractured skull. She had firmly held on to her purse strap with her left hand. The purse was open and the contents, which included $32.02, were intact. Karen had not been sexually interfered with in any way. None of her clothing was ever found.

Between the hours of 4:20 a.m. and 7:02 a.m. on the 1st day of July, someone picked up Karen Woodcock and rained blows to her head with a rock until she was dead. Who and why?

Every movement made by Karen Woodcock from the time she started partying after her graduation has been gone over moment by moment by Det. Insp. Pelissero. He thinks he knows the identity of her killer.

Many months before the murder, a drinking companion attempted to sexually attack Mrs. Woodcock while her husband was asleep upstairs in their home. No charges were ever brought against this man. Two days after the murder this same man came forward voluntarily to the O.P.P. in Peterborough. He had information which tended to support his claim that he was so drunk during the early morning hours of July 1st that he didn't know where he was. Upon investigating this man police believe he went out of his way to establish his movements as far away from the scene of the murder as possible.

Det. Insp. Pelissero succeeded in having this suspect submit to a polygraph test. Part way through the test the man changed his mind and refused to continue. From the amount of testing done, an expert in this field feels that this man had knowledge concerning the death of Karen Woodcock.

Despite this incriminating piece of information, there is no direct link between the murdered woman and the suspect. He is at large and refuses to even discuss the case with investigating officers.

MOTHER IN THE LAKE

Wayne Ford and his mother Minnie lived together in a red brick bungalow in the middle-class area of the Toronto suburb of Willowdale. Lorne Ford, his father, had died of natural causes when Wayne was fourteen. He left his wife and only child rather well-off financially; his estate amounted to over $100,000.

Minnie almost immediately had to cope with the arduous task of bringing up a strapping teenager without a man around the house. To neighbors and relatives, the short, pleasant widow seemed to be succeeding in raising her son, but they didn't know that all was not as it appeared to be at the Ford residence. Wayne was now a six-footer, weighing 180 pounds, struggling through his teenage years without the benefit of the steadying influence of a father. He felt that he was being smothered by his mother, who doled out money to him and sometimes even curtailed his freedom by denying him the use of the family Cadillac. Like many middle-aged widows left with one teenaged son, Minnie doted on her only boy. Or at least friends and neighbors called it doting; Wayne called it picking on him.

The reasons for Wayne's resentment of his mother are not as important as the fact that he started answering her back, until the pair were often shouting at each other. They seemed to argue incessantly about everything, including Wayne's friends, his long hair and his schoolwork.

By 1963, Wayne was a Grade 10 student at Earl Haig Collegiate, and his sporadic attendance was a cause of great concern to Minnie. She also worried when she gave him the Cadillac, watching anxiously as he and his friends roared out of the driveway. In the early spring of 1963 Wayne smashed up the car, incurring over $1,000 in damage, which was covered by insurance. Minnie was furious, not only because it deprived her of the car while it was being repaired, but because the accident confirmed that Wayne wasn't to be trusted with the vehicle.

The shouting and bickering erupted into a full-fledged battle the day Wayne came home from school and found the repaired car parked in the driveway. When Wayne asked for the car keys, Minnie refused. The pair started to argue violently. Wayne told his mother to go to hell; she retaliated by slapping his face. He returned the blow. Wayne later claimed that his mother then grabbed an ice pick, forcing him to retreat to his bedroom, where he picked up a small baseball bat. The argument moved out of the bedroom, down a hall, and into the kitchen. In the kitchen Wayne struck his mother several blows to the head with the bat, one blow in particular landing squarely on her left temple, causing Minnie to stagger and finally sink slowly to the floor.

Wayne sat down on a kitchen chair and stared at the body of his mother. He was later to state that he assumed she was dead. He thought of calling a hospital, except, he reasoned, there wasn't anything they could do. He even thought of calling the police, but he knew that if he did that he would be in a great deal of trouble. Finally he got up off the chair, placed a plastic bag over his mother's head and threw a sheet over her body. Then he jumped into the Cadillac and drove over to see his friend Ron Walli. A fellow student at Earl Haig Collegiate, Ron stood six feet tall, and like Wayne, was sixteen years old. Wayne confided to his friend that he had killed his mother.

From this point our narrative differs in detail and in insinuation, depending on whose version we wish to accept, Walli's or Ford's. We do know that Walli agreed to go back to the Ford house and help his friend. Walli claimed that he was influenced by a .38 calibre revolver which was lying at Ford's feet on the floor of his Cadillac. The facts do not change materially — we still have two sixteen-year-old boys from good homes matter-of-factly discussing the murder of the mother of one of them.

The two youngsters entered the brick bungalow and were confronted by the body. Wayne removed the gory sheet and noticed that there was now blood on the floor as well. Wayne grasped his mother's arms while Ron took hold of the legs, and the boys carried the 140-pound body down into the basement. The head clunked on each step as they made their way slowly down the stairs. Blood splattered the steps and walls, until finally they were all the way down. Then Wayne took hold of the arms and dragged his mother's body across the floor to the rear room of the basement. A ten-inch-wide smear of blood showed where the body had been dragged, so the two friends took a mop and pail and cleaned up the kitchen, stairs, and basement floor. Then they stuffed Minnie's body into a box about three feet square, tied up their package with a green plastic garden hose, and went upstairs to make plans to dispose of the body. Ron Walli went home and told his parents that he would be sleeping over at the Fords' the following night, so that Mrs. Ford, Wayne and himself could get away early on Saturday morning to go to their cottage at Lake Couchiching, where they would be spending the weekend. On Friday morning, the boys went to school, returning to Wayne's house at lunchtime. They didn't go back in the afternoon; instead, they sandpapered and repainted the stairs. They then had a few drinks and took in a movie at a drive-in. After the movie they returned to Ford's house, and with much huffing and puffing, they managed to lug the box containing Minnie Ford's body up the stairs and placed it in the trunk of the Cadillac. Then Wayne and Ron took off for the Ford cottage. A mile or so from their destination they tried to dig a grave with a shovel they had borrowed from a garage, but the ground was too hard and they gave up. After placing the box containing the body in a small garage beside the Ford cottage, they drove back to Toronto.

On Saturday morning they invited another boy, Larry Metcalfe, to join them for the weekend at Lake Couchiching. The three took in a Saturday afternoon movie, then headed for the lake. They started drinking on Saturday and continued to drink steadily until Sunday morning. They were tired and hung over until Sunday night, when Ford and Walli had a strange conversation. Ford confided to Walli that his mother hadn't died easily — she had continued to struggle even after she had received the blows with the baseball bat. It had been necessary to stick an ice pick in her head. Ford told Walli the handle had broken off and the spike was still in his mother's head. He asked his friend to get a pair of pliers and pull the spike out of his mother's skull. Walli flatly refused. Later Ford went out of the cottage, returning with a foot and a half of railway track. He asked Walli to take it out to the garage and knock his mother's teeth out with the heavy piece of metal. Walli agreed to this, but when he opened the box he became terrified and left, placing the piece of railway track in the garage. When Ford asked if the job was done, Walli lied and said it was.

That same Sunday evening Wayne and Ron decided to tell Metcalfe that Minnie Ford's body was in a box in the garage. Ford explained to Metcalfe that he had killed his mother, and Metcalfe claims that he was threatened into going along with disposing of the body. Ford's version is that Metcalfe was a willing partner, doing a friend a favor.

The three boys found a child's cart and wheeled the box containing the body down to the dock. They placed the box in an old rowboat and rowed about 300 yards into the lake. When they started to push the box overboard, the boat capsized, plunging the three boys into the water. Wayne pushed the box and it sank. Ron swam to shore, got another boat, rowed back to the overturned boat and picked up his two friends.

The boys dried their clothing, had a few drinks and decided to go to a dance in Orillia. On the way Wayne smashed the car into a telephone pole and ended up in the Orillia police station explaining the accident. They managed to give satisfactory answers, then walked to the dance where they got a lift back to the Ford cottage. Here they started to drink again, sleeping until Monday afternoon. On Tuesday they discussed the murder, agreeing that if they all kept their mouths shut no one would ever be the wiser. Ron hitchhiked to Toronto and he and his father returned to Lake Couchiching to pick up the other two boys.

By Thursday some of Minnie's friends started to wonder why they couldn't reach her. Becoming suspicious, they called the police, who made a routine inquiry at he Ford residence. Wayne showed the police into the house, explaining that he and two friends had gone to the family cottage on Saturday morning, expecting his mother to join them sometime during the weekend, but she hadn't arrived nor had he seen her since. Walli and Metcalfe were also interrogated, but stuck to their story of expecting Mrs. Ford to join them at the cottage. Wayne insisted that his mother just took off and left without any warning.

The days became weeks, then months. Wayne started to miss school, then quit altogether to try his hand at a series of odd jobs, but he stuck to none. At first his mother's disappearance was actively investigated as a missing persons case, but gradually the investigation wound down, and the police appeared only sporadically at the Ford home.

As the months passed, Wayne started to get into scrapes with the law. He was charged with carrying a concealed weapon, then was caught in possession of stolen goods. A year after his mother's disappearance, he was sentenced to a year in jail for possession of stolen goods and petty theft. When he got out he was charged with theft again, and drew two years in the reformatory. On May 17, 1966, three years after his mother's disappearance, he escaped from the reformatory but was quickly recaptured, receiving an additional six months in the Kingston Penitentiary for his escapade.

While he was serving his time in Kingston Pen, the box containing what was left of his mother's body bobbed to the surface of Lake Couchiching. On Nov. 23, 1966, two Toronto detective sergeants went to Kingston Penitentiary to formally charge Wayne with the murder of his mother. Later, during Ford's trial, the detective who had broken the news to Ford told of the conversation which had taken place between them on that day.

"At 10:50 a.m. I was at the Kingston Penitentiary and I was ushered into a small room adjacent to what is known as the board-reception room, and there for the first time I saw the male accused, Wayne Ford. He was standing alone in this room. I introduced myself and Sergeant Alexander to Ford, saying, 'I am Sergeant Crawford. This is Sergeant Alexander. We are from the Metropolitan homicide squad. We have a warrant for your arrest on a charge of murder. Do you wish to say anything in answer to the charge? You are not obliged to say anything unless you wish to do so, but whatever you say will be taken down in writing and may be given in evidence.' Now there was a pause of a few moments, and then I said, 'Do you want to talk to me now or in Toronto?' and the accused replied, 'I will talk to you in Toronto'."

In the days following his arrest, Wayne became very depressed. It was as if a great burden had been partially lifted from his shoulders. Now that his mother's body had been found, he was anxious to have the entire matter cleared up without delay. He wrote to the arresting officers. The letter is presented here in the same form as it was placed before the jury:

Dear Sirs:
This letter is to inform you that I intend to plead guilty to the charge of Capital Murder. I wish to wave (sic) all evidence in this matter in court also, and ask that this case be pushed through court as quickly as possible.
I am not receiving any visits or mail as of today. There is no need for anyone to visit me now.
I remain, Wayne L. Ford.

In the middle of May, 1967, four years after his mother disappeared, Wayne Ford stood trial for her murder. His two friends, Larry Metcalfe and Ron Walli, testified to helping him get rid of his mother's body. Their versions of the details differed from those stated by Wayne. They both claimed to have been forced and coerced by Wayne into disposing of the body.

Psychiatrist Dr. Robert Turner testified that Ford was a psychopathic personality. He was unable to cope with stress, had no sense of responsibility and was unable to control violent impulses. The jury brought in a verdict of non-capital murder. The now towering six-foot-three-inch Wayne Ford sat impassively as the judge said, "It is the sentence of this court that you be imprisoned for the balance of your natural life." Wayne Ford is still in prison serving his sentence.

TRANSATLANTIC
TREACHERY

It is now over 90 years since the murder took place. The railway station in Eastwood, Ont., where the two educated Englishmen disembarked for their walk with death has long since disappeared. Dark, foreboding Bleinheim swamp is still there, its floor oozing muck and strewn with decayed vegetation deposited over the centuries.

You can still enter Ross Anderson's General Store in the tiny hamlet of Princeton and, within two minutes, the genial owner will tell you that his grandfather arrived in Princeton in 1890, the very same year the crime was committed. He and everyone in the store are only too willing to direct you to the reminders of murder which remain after all these years.

The names Reginald Birchall and Frederick Benwell mean little to us now, but back in 1890 they were household words. The drama which unfolded in a Woodstock, Ont. courtroom was covered by reporters from England, Italy, France, Germany, Spain and the U.S. A direct line ran from the courtroom in Woodstock to London, England. The case is still considered by many to be Canada's most notorious murder.

Despite being the son of a respected English clergyman, Reginald Birchall was a ne'er do well. While still a young lad he developed expensive tastes which he could ill afford. As a result, he was always in trouble. Petty theft, rubber cheques, and never telling the truth kept young Birchall in one jam after another. The one constant in his life was the fact that he was always in debt. Even while attending Oxford University he insisted on maintaining a string of horses, which did nothing to alleviate his already precarious financial condition. This added burden, plus other sundry debts which accompany high living, necessitated Birchall terminating his education. He left Oxford.

Birchall was a fine looking man. With the air of aristocracy about him, coupled with his Oxford accent, he could charm the birds out of the trees. The bird he charmed was Londoner Florence Stevenson. Florence's father was not enthralled with his new son-in-law, and it is believed that Birchall was less than thrilled with the financial remuneration which resulted from his marriage.

In 1888, the Birchalls arrived in Canada and settled in Woodstock. Birchall did nothing to change his lifestyle. He and his wife passed themselves off as Lord and Lady Somerset. The self-styled lord soon was well known to southern Ontario social bigwigs and, of course, his creditors. With the wolf at the door, Birchall and his wife returned to England dead broke. They stayed with Florence's father. Reg's creditors traced him and gave him no peace. He became desperate for funds. There had to be some way for him to get his hands on some hard cash. That's when he got his great idea.

Birchall received a hot tip on a horse race, the Epsom Derby of 1890. A long shot, Sanefain, was a sure thing. As Birchall saw it, all he had to do was raise enough money to place a substantial bet — but how?

He hatched a diabolical, but extremely plausible scheme for the times. The colonies were thought to be the land of opportunity, where young Englishmen could seek fame and fortune. Realizing this, Birchall placed an ad in the *Daily Telegram:* Canada — University man — having farm — wishes to meet gentleman's son to live with him and learn the business with a view to partnership; must invest £500 to extend stock; board, lodging and 5% interest till partnership arranged."

Lieut. Col. Frederick Benwell of Cheltenham saw the ad, and thought it presented a great opportunity for his 25-year-old son, Frederick. In due time Col. Benwell, Frederick, and Birchall met. Col. Benwell was impressed. He signed an agreement to pay £500, but before any money changed hands, Fred was to visit the farm in Canada. Birchall seemed satisfied with this arrangement. Unknown to Fred Benwell or his father, another lad from a good family had answered Birchall's ad. Douglas Pelly, an Oxford graduate, also fell for the scheme, advancing Birchall £170, but he, too, wanted to see his investment.

On Feb. 5, 1890, when Reginald Birchall and his wife Florence boarded the *Britannic* at Liverpool, they were accompanied by two young, excited Englishmen just itching to set foot in the New World. They had no idea that Reg Birchall planned to kill them both.

Once aboard ship, Birchall went about poisoning the minds of his two companions. He set up a situation in which Pelly and Benwell became antagonistic towards one another.

They quarrelled openly in front of other passengers. Birchall wanted everyone to remember the bickering. Later, if both men disappeared, the natural assumption would be that one had killed the other, with the killer taking off. No suspicion would fall on Lord Somerset.

The *Britannic* landed in the U.S. The four principal players in the drama, which was soon to unfold, made their way to Buffalo. It was decided that Pelly and Mrs. Birchall would remain in Buffalo, while Birchall and Benwell went on ahead to Canada to inspect the farm. On Feb. 17, the two men set out by train for Birchall's non-existent farm. The men later were well remembered by fellow passengers on the train, and at the Eastwood Station near Woodstock, where they got off. They walked into Blenheim swamp.

Birchall assured his companion that the farm lay on the other side of the swamp. By walking over the frozen terrain Benwell would get the true feel of the area. Once in the swamp, Birchall pulled out a revolver and shot his companion twice in the head. He cut away all labels from Benwell's clothing and dragged the body further into the swamp. That same night he returned to Buffalo alone. He accounted for Benwell's absence with the not too convincing story that Benwell had become disenchanted with the entire adventure, pulled out of the agreement, and left.

The day after Birchall's murderous excursion to Canada, he and Pelly visited the Canadian side of Niagara Falls. Later Pelly was to relate that on two occasions while they were viewing the falls from precarious positions, Birchall almost seemed to be preparing to make a move, as if to shove him into the churning water. Both times strangers happened by, which apparently had the effect of changing Birchall's mind. In the light of future events, young Pelly owed his life to the chance passing of the strangers.

Back in England, Col. Benwell received a letter from Birchall stating that young Fred was doing well on the ranch. He added that he would appreciate the £500.

Meanwhile, on Feb. 21, two brothers, George and Joseph Eldridge, were cutting wood in Blenheim swamp. They found Benwell's body. The one in a million discovery, only four days after the murder, spelled doom for Birchall. News of the unidentified murder victim was in all the newspapers. Pelly read about the body found near Woodstock, the same location as Birchall's "farm". He immediately suspected that the body was that of Benwell. He confronted Birchall, who must have been stunned at the news of the body being found so soon. He decided to bluff it out.

Birchall told Doug Pelly that he was wrong, but to satisfy him, he and his wife would travel to Woodstock to view the body and identify it, if possible. This they did, and Birchall had the unnerving experience of gazing on the countenance of a man he had so recently killed and never dreamed of ever seeing again. He identified the dead man as Frederick Benwell, but made light of their relationship, saying that Benwell had been a chance shipboard acquaintance.

The police, headed by Canada's famed detective, John Wilson Murray, were satisfied with the identification. A cigar case initialled F.C.B. had been found near the body. However, Murray was far from satisfied with our friend Birchall. The detective let his suspect run free, but had the Niagara Falls Police follow his every move. In the meantime, he checked out his quarry. He found out about the letter written to Col. Benwell dated after the murder. Then he travelled to Niagara Falls and found Doug Pelly living with the Birchalls. After Pelly told his story, both Mr. and Mrs. Birchall were arrested and charged with murder. Mrs. Birchall was released after the inquest.

In September, Birchall's trial for the murder of Frederick Benwell opened in Woodstock's town hall. In that year of 1890, ballads were sung and poems were written about Reg Birchall and his scheme to become financially secure by means of murder. While there was never any doubt of his guilt, Birchall's trial caught the imagination of the world. Foreign reporters flocked to Woodstock to hear of Oxford educated men in the wilds of Canada, imaginary farms, hot tip horses, and murder.

It took the jury only 90 minutes to find Birchall guilty. On Nov. 14, 1890, his face white as a ghost, dressed in evening clothes at his insistence, he walked steadily up the gallows steps. He shook hands with the hangman and plunged to eternity. Reg Birchall was buried beside a wall of the Woodstock jail.

What happened to the rest of the cast in the Birchall drama?

Fred Benwell, the Colonel's son, who arrived in Canada with such high hopes, is buried in Princeton, Ont. The inscription on his stone reads: Frederick Cornwallis Benwell, Born 15th Sept. 1865, Murdered in the township of Blenheim Feb. 17, 1890.

Florence Birchall returned to England and later remarried.

Douglas Pelly, the boy who came so very close to being a victim, returned to England to a hero's welcome. A torchlight parade accompanied him to his home. Forever after he was known as the man who was almost murdered.

We mustn't forget Sanefain, the horse which gave Birchall the germ of the idea from which he hatched his diabolical plot. Ironically, in 1890, Sanefain did win the Epsom Derby.

WHATEVER HAPPENED TO MABEL?

Every large city has its share of missing persons. As every law enforcement officer knows, the vast majority are missing for less than 48 hours. The truth is, they're really not missing. A lover's quarrel or a teenager's spat with a parent tends to cool out within 48 hours.

Many others of a more serious nature are traced because of the elaborate plans they make before disappearing. There are, however, a handful of cases that do not follow these patterns.

Diametrically opposite to the well-planned disappearance is the one in which an adult is swallowed up during the course of his or her normal day. For no apparent reason, it seems as if an invisible hand has plucked a happy, healthy individual away to oblivion.

Do you remember the Mabel Crumback case?

It all started in May of 1950. Mabel was a 19-year-old beauty who lived at 661 Willard Ave., in Toronto. She had been going steady with Jimmy Bryan for several months. That Saturday, over 30 years ago, Jimmy and Mabel had finished playing tennis not far from her home. They came back to Mabel's house and spent the evening there. At 12:30 a.m. Jimmy left. As Mabel closed the door behind him, he promised to return for Sunday dinner.

From that moment to this, no known person has laid eyes upon Mabel Crumback.

On that particular weekend Mabel's parents were visiting friends in Detroit. Only Mabel and her eight-year-old brother, Gary, were at home. Gary woke up on Sunday morning and could not find his sister. The side door of the house, facing St. John Rd., was not locked. The front door, which was always kept locked, was also unlocked.

Later Mabel's bed came under close scrutiny. Authorities stated that there was evidence it had been slept in and had been made up. Gary swears that doors were closed in the house so that the family dog would spend the night in the kitchen. The dog was found asleep in an upstairs hall. Mabel's pyjama bottoms were found neatly folded under her pillow. Her pyjama top was never found. There was no sign of a struggle, and nothing was missing from the house other than the clothes she wore and her hair curlers. She had put her hair up in curlers earlier that night.

What kind of a girl was Mabel Crumback? At the time of her disappearance she worked in the office of Eastern Steel Co., and earned $28 per week. Everyone described her as a pretty, energetic, attractive young girl. She was religious, and attended St. John's Baptist Church, located diagonally across the street from her house. She sang in the choir and was active in the church's social activities. Mabel's doctor stated that she had had a physical checkup shortly before her disappearance. She was in good health and normal in every way.

During the extensive investigation that followed, a neighbor said that he and his wife were walking past the Crumback home shortly after 2 a.m. on that fateful Sunday morning. They lived on St. John Rd., but kept their car in a garage on Willard Ave. As they passed the Crumback home they heard loud noises. They noted that lights were still on in Mabel's room and in the kitchen. The side door of the house was open.

Young Gary was to state that he was awakened out of his sleep around this time. It seemed to him that he heard the dog barking. He thought he heard men's voices mixed with his sister's voice as well. Mabel's purse containing money was found in her room. That's it.

Nothing more of a concrete nature has ever been uncovered about Mabel Crumback.

Jimmy Bryan showed up the following day for his Sunday dinner. He was met by a horde of policemen asking every conceivable question. He could give them no helpful information.

Many baffling questions are left unanswered. The main one on everyone's mind at the time was whether Mabel left voluntarily or was forced. Did she go to bed between 12:30 and 2 a.m., only to be awakened by her abductor or abductors? If so, what was the reason for the bed being made up again? If she left voluntarily, why did she not take her money with her? If forced, why was there no evidence of a struggle? Why were her pyjama bottoms folded neatly under her pillow, but her top missing?

The neighborhood in which Mabel Crumback grew up is surprisingly the same as it was 32 years ago. On the corner of Willard Ave. and St. John Rd., the residence where the puzzle started still stands. St. John's Baptist Church still holds services much as it did when Mabel and her friends worshipped there. Newcomers to the neighborhood have no way of knowing that the house on Willard Ave. was once the most notorious address in Toronto.

If Mabel's abductors were between twenty and forty years of age in 1950, it is conceivable that they are alive and among us today. Without revealing their identity they could solve Toronto's most baffling missing person's case, and answer the question, whatever became of Mabel Crumback?

THE FARMER'S DAUGHTER

Everyone has heard one of those ribald stories about the farmer's daughter. Too few of us have been fortunate enough to know one in the flesh, so to speak. But a real honest-to-goodness "farmer's daughter" did exist right here in southern Ontario.

Her name was Emma Borland, and she lived about five miles south of Galt before the turn of the century. Mr. and Mrs. Borland knew they had a handful when Emma romanced her way through her teens. She was good looking, had a figure to match, and a yen for action. All those virile young males of Waterloo County provided the action, and Emma provided everything else.

Emma was only 21 when she married John Arnott, a wealthy merchant from Innerkip, who was quite a bit older than she. She turned over a new leaf and was a good and faithful wife to John for two years, when he passed on to his great reward. There were those around Galt who said she was too much for the poor soul in the bedroom. Be that as it may, Emma found herself at 23 completely free and a wealthy citizen to boot. Emma took up where she left off before she married John. She had a barrel of fun for three full years before she turned respectable again.

This time she married Tony Orr, who was a substantial farmer of the area. The entire Orr family was well known socially throughout Waterloo County. Despite Emma's past reputation, she fitted or was pushed gracefully into the social whirl of rural life. Again Emma settled down, and really was a good wife until she was about thirty-five. Then she simply ran away with the hired hand just like they do in the stories. A real handsome character named Tim Mulholland had been making love to Emma while Tony was tending the fields or whatever. Tony traced the couple to a hotel in Niagara Falls.

Tony really loved his wife. He took her back and this time hired an unattractive, pimply faced youngster named Jim Allison as his hired hand. Once bitten, twice shy, as they say. Anyway, they all lived happily for three more years, when all of a sudden Emma disappeared.

Tony and young Jim hitched the horses and drove into Galt to Sheriff Maynard Gould's office. Alex Allison, Jim's father, was a municipal official who worked in the same building as the sheriff. The youngster took the opportunity to go down the hall to see his father. Meantime Tony reported Emma as missing. He informed the sheriff that both he and Jim had hunted for her all morning. A neighbor had heard a gunshot go off earlier. Tony had looked for his own shotgun, and found that it was missing. The sheriff sympathized with Tony, but in the back of his mind he had the lingering suspicion that Emma was up to her old tricks again. Sheriff Gould agreed to go out to the farm with Tony. Young Jim was through visiting his father, and he joined the departing couple in the hall. While Tony attended to the horses, the sheriff asked Jim a pointed question. Did Emma have a boyfriend that Tony didn't know anything about? Jim informed him that there were at least two that he knew of, Weldon Trevelyan and Harry Blair.

The sheriff told Tony he would join him at the farm later. He went looking for Trevelyan and Blair. Trevelyan readily admitted meeting with Emma. In fact, he thought it was a damn shame she was missing. He claimed he would miss her too. Some stories just ring true. The sheriff believed Trevelyan. He continued on his way to question Blair. Upon being interrogated Blair admitted making love to Emma, but denied any knowledge of her disappearance. The sheriff shook his head. He believed Blair, too.

Gould proceeded to the farm. By the time he arrived, the men had already found the missing shotgun. It smelled of cordite, and had obviously been fired recently. At this point the Sheriff realized he had a possible murder on his hands. He wired John Murray, who was then head detective of the Ontario Police. Word came back that Detective Murray would arrive by train at nine the next morning. The sheriff accepted the invitation to spend the night on the farm. When he awoke at daybreak the next morning and looked out his window, he thought he saw a light go out in a grove of woods on the other side of a cornfield. Being half asleep, he dismissed it from his mind as probably being a firefly.

Tony, Jim and the sheriff drove to Galt and met Detective Murray at the train. After being briefed, the detective questioned the two main suspects, Trevelyan and Blair. He wasn't as convinced of their innocence as the sheriff was. In fact, the detective thought that possibly Tony had had enough of Emma and decided to do away with her.

Once at the farm, Detective Murray quickly discovered a patch of grass that was discolored. The discoloration, which was obviously caused by blood, led down to the cornfield. Detective Murray followed the bent foliage across the meadow to a grove of trees. There he and the sheriff found a shallow half dug grave with no body in it. Close by, under some leaves lay the body of poor Emma. She had been killed by a shotgun blast. Detective Murray figured that the murderer had come back after dark to dig the grave. The job wasn't finished. Then Gould remembered the light he had seen when he woke up. It must have been the murderer finishing his work for the night.

Would he complete the grave the following night?

In true Hitchcock fashion, the sheriff and the detective hid themselves in the bushes that night and waited for the murderer to show up. At around midnight a lantern came bobbing through the cornfield and up to the grove of trees. The officers grabbed the man with the lantern. To their utter amazement, it was Alex Allison, Jim's father.

Alex told a tragic story. His son Jim had killed Emma. He did not have the courage to conceal the body. He had confessed to his father when he and Tony had come to the municipal building to report the disappearance to the sheriff. Alex had dug all the previous night, but had to stop at daybreak.

They put handcuffs on Alex, and once his son saw him, he broke down and admitted killing Emma. Jim said he knew of the other men Emma was playing around with and thought he would try his luck. Emma laughed at him, and called him ugly. She said she would tell Tony to fire him. In a rage, Jim took the shotgun and killed her.

No charges were ever laid against Alex Allison, but his son Jim was hanged on Feb. 4th, 1898 in what was then called Berlin, now known as Kitchener.

THE BOYD GANG

During the rather checkered history of crime in the United States, there have been many famous gangs of bank robbers. Such names as Pretty Boy Floyd, Dillinger, and Bonnie and Clyde conjure up visions of daring raids, high speed chases and big money.

Here in Canada we have only had one bona fide gang of bank robbers — the Boyd Gang.

Edwin Alonzo Boyd was born in Toronto. His father was a retired police officer, but young Edwin had a natural inclination to wander. By the time he was 16 he had quit high school and travelled to western Canada. Although he was intelligent and had a good appearance, he could never get a good paying job. The menial tasks he was able to get bored him. In 1936, he was making his living by breaking and entering. He was caught and convicted on 21 individual charges, and received three years in prison.

For approximately ten years, which included a stint in the Army, it appears Boyd did nothing that brought him to the attention of the police.

Then, on Oct. 16, 1951, the Dominion Bank on the corner of Yonge St. and Lawrence Ave. was held up and robbed by two men. An alert employee spotted the two men and pressed the alarm button. The robbers completed their work, stuffing $12,234 into a shopping bag. Howard Gault was caught outside the bank with the money. The other robber got away from the scene in a stolen automobile which had been parked for the purpose of escape. Within hours, a small delivery truck driving on the outskirts of the city caught the attention of the police. They forced the truck to stop. They searched the vehicle and found a fully loaded 9 mm. Luger automatic pistol and a full makeup kit.

The Toronto police got their first introduction to the driver of the truck — Edwin Boyd. Subsequent investigation of Boyd's activities resulted in his being charged with several robberies. From Sept. 9, 1949 to Sept. 1, 1951 he was known to be connected with six bank robberies in the Toronto area.

While in jail awaiting trial on these charges, Boyd met Leonard Jackson and William R. Jackson. Both were awaiting their transfer to Kingston Penitentiary after having been convicted of armed robbery.

On Nov. 4, Boyd and the two Jacksons, who were not related, sawed their way through their cell doors and made a successful and dramatic escape from jail. Leonard Jackson took off for Montreal and Boyd and Willie Jackson hid out at the home of the parents of a friend, Valent J. Lesso, who was better known by his alias of Steve Suchan. Boyd and Willie stayed in hiding until Nov. 20, when they successfully held up the Boustead Ave. and Roncesvalles Ave. branch of the Bank of Toronto. They got $4,300. Ten days later, another bank was hit, the Royal in Leaside. It was relieved of $42,000.

Willie Jackson and Boyd took off for Montreal and moved in with Steve Suchan. Then Willie was picked up in a restaurant by the police. Once his identity was established, he was sent back to Toronto, and ended up in the Kingston Pen.

On Jan. 25, 1952, the Bank of Toronto on Kingston Rd. in Scarborough was robbed of $10,000. Then on March 4th, the Bank of Montreal on College St. had an unscheduled withdrawal of $24,496. Through witnesses it was established that Boyd was the leader of the gang.

On March 6, 1952, Sergeant of Detectives Edmund Tong and Detective Sgt. Roy Perry became suspicious of a 1951 Monarch occupied by two men. They drove alongside. Tong called out, "Pull over, boys."

The car stopped. Tong got out and walked over to the suspicious vehicle. As he did so, he was shot down. Perry tried to get to the left hand side of the car. He could hear the whine of bullets flying past. In an instinctive reaction, he thrust his arm up to protect his head. In so doing he took two slugs in the arm. Perry raised the alarm over the police radio. Tong was seriously wounded, but before he lost consciousness he told the first detective at the scene that the person who had shot him was Steve Suchan.

Suchan and Lenny Jackson got away, but police later discovered their hideout in Montreal. Suchan elected to shoot it out, and was wounded. The gun he was holding when captured was the gun that had been used to shoot Detective Tong. Lenny

Jackson was located in another apartment a couple of blocks away. He too fired at the police, and was wounded during the capture.

On March 23, Sergeant of Detectives Tong died of his wounds, and the two fugitives were returned to Toronto to face murder charges.

In the meantime, the police were trying to trace Boyd through his brother, Norman. They became convinced that Boyd was hiding out in a house on Heath St. Boyd was rushed in the middle of the night by the police. He was asleep in bed with his wife when taken by surprise.

Willie Jackson, who had missed some of the action because he was apprehended earlier, was now brought from Kingston to Toronto due to his previous involvement in other robberies.

Now that the police had the four main members of the Boyd gang under lock and key, they continued their investigation. It included implicating other gang members who may have been in on one or two of the robberies. Also investigated and charged were relatives and friends who helped the four bandits while they were free.

Then, on Sept. 8, 1952, with a flair for the dramatic, the four members of the Boyd gang, using a key they made themselves, opened their cell doors. They proceeded to saw their way through some bars on a window and dropped themselves onto a low roof below. For the next eight days these most wanted men in the country were sighted from Newfoundland to British Columbia. Newspapers daily featured every detail of their past lives. Across the country radio newscasts started with "The Boyd Gang is still at large."

On Sept. 16, the North York police department received a call that men were seen coming and going at an old barn north of Sheppard Ave., east of Yonge St. The four heavily armed men were taken by surprise. The Boyd gang was recaptured.

Leonard Jackson and Steve Suchan were tried, found guilty and hanged back to back for the murder of Sergeant of Detectives Tong.

Boyd and Willie Jackson were never directly involved in the murder. Boyd received a life sentence, while Jackson received 20 years imprisonment, in addition to the nine years he was already serving.

Whatever happened to the two surviving members of the Boyd gang?

Willie Jackson spent 14 years in Kingston Penitentiary. He was paroled in the mid 1960s and worked as the janitor of a Toronto church. Not many people knew of his past, and those who did considered him a completely reformed individual. When he talked of days gone by, it was as if he were talking about another person. Willie left Toronto several years ago to work in another church in Vancouver.

Boyd was paroled in 1962. He received a great deal of publicity and became hostile toward the close watch the parole authorities held over him. Four months after his release he was returned to prison as a parole violator. In 1966, Boyd was paroled for the second time. This time he made it.

Somewhere in a small town in Canada, a gray haired old man is employed as a social worker. He is a devoted member of a well known religious organization and spends most of his time assisting the physically handicapped. The parole authorities claim he is a living example of a reformed gangster. He was once Canada's most wanted fugitive — Edwin Alonzo Boyd.

MURDEROUS CHILD

Murder at any time is a repugnant act. When committed by an adult we look for deep rooted motives. What drove the murderer to the commission of the deed? Was it greed? Was it anger or passion? But when murder is committed by a child, we look elsewhere. What emotion or drive could compel a child to take another's life?

In 1849, in the township of Emily, near Peterborough, Ont., a murder took place which shocked the community and the nation. Eliza and Thomas Rowan were God-fearing, honest folks, who labored long and hard on their farm. When they heard that the widow O'Connor was having a difficult time making ends meet since the recent loss of her husband, Eliza and Thomas agreed to take in tiny, five-year-old Margaret O'Connor.

Soon the little girl was an integral member of the Rowan family. She loved to play with and feed the animals on the farm, and seemed to be always laughing and smiling. The Rowans loved the little girl as if she were their own. Previous to Margaret's joining the family the Rowans had adopted another youngster. For two years young George Green had been living with the family.

As an infant, George had been placed with Rev. Mr. Dick, a Presbyterian minister. In 1847, the Rowans had taken George to their farm. When the boy reached the age of nine, the Rowans realized he needed some formal education, but the district school was too far away for him to attend regularly. Every so often they would sit George down at the kitchen table and go over some reading and sums.

George seemed to take to his farm chores with vigor and good humor. He fed the chickens, milked some of the cows, and was a pretty helpful hand around the farm. When Margaret joined the Rowans, George and the little girl often performed chores together.

In the autumn of 1849, George was eleven, Margaret was five. Events were about to unfold which would effect both their lives forever.

Samuel Hannah lived about a mile down the road from the Rowans. One fine day Thomas hitched up his team. He was going to a plowing "bee" at Samuel's place. Eliza was planning on spending some time with a neighbor while Thomas was plowing. Her husband would drop her off on his way to the "bee".

Before the Rowans left their farm for the day, Thomas gave instructions to George to "raise ten or twelve rows of potatoes". This sort of casual instruction was over and above the normal chores the young lad was expected to do around the farm. Thomas shouted to George as the team galloped out of the yard, "When Margaret goes out to you, you may have her help you to pick the potatoes, and place them in the wheelbarrow."

George nodded and waved to the Rowans as they drove out of sight. The next time Thomas Rowan was to see George, the boy was running toward him on Samuel Hannah's farm shouting, "Margaret has been eaten by a bear!"

For some reason which he had difficulty explaining later, Thomas Rowan instinctively felt George was lying. He angrily turned upon the young lad, "You have killed the little girl. You have murdered Margaret." The words came fast and furious. They were unnatural words, directed against a protesting, sobbing 11-year-old child. The youngster swore he was telling the truth.

All the men rushed to the Rowan farm to hunt for some trace of the missing girl. George pointed out where the bear had come upon little Margaret. He illustrated how the unsuspecting child had held out her hand to the bear, an act she had performed many times when she gave young calves their milk bottles. The boy pointed to the place in the fence where the bear had jumped, carrying Margaret with him.

The men searched until darkness made it impossible to continue. They could find no evidence that a bear had dragged a child in the soft earth. They found no bear tracks or torn clothing. In fact, they could find no evidence that a bear had been anywhere near the Rowan farm.

With the search at a standstill, the men turned their attention back to George Green. They grilled him until finally he fell asleep, still insisting that a bear had carried the unfortunate Margaret away.

All the farmers in the area, as well as young George, were up bright and early the next morning to continue the search. Around noon they found the pathetic body of tiny Margaret O'Connor. She had been bludgeoned to death with a hoe which lay beside her body. Her attacker had struck her repeatedly in the head and all over her body until she was dead. The blade of the hoe which George had been using to "raise the potatoes" had blood and strands of the dead girl's hair adhering to it.

The men fixed their stares upon 11-year-old George Green. The savageness of the attack upon the helpless child was beyond their comprehension. Adamantly proclaiming his innocence, George was taken into custody and lodged in the Peterborough jail. On May 3, 1850, to my knowledge the youngest defendant ever to stand trial for murder in Canada faced his accusers.

The scene was strange. Solemn, educated men were to argue the merits of his case. A black robed, learned judge was to direct the proceedings, and, in the end, a jury was to pass judgment on his innocence or guilt. The object of all this attention was a small, trembling child.

Thomas Rowan explained the circumstances leading up to the finding of Margaret's body. Eliza Rowan then took up the story. She told the court that George confessed to the murder after he had been placed in jail. Margaret had come out to the field where George was digging the potatoes. George had never thought of killing Margaret before. It was only when she was with him in the field that he had "taken the notion of killing her." All of a sudden he struck her with the hoe again and again until she lay still.

The crowd in the courtroom looked down at the young lad in the prisoners' box. They stared in disbelief. The defense called no witnesses.

George was found guilty of murder and sentenced to hang on the 26th of June, 1850. On June 4, his sentence was commuted to life imprisonment in Kingston Penitentiary.

After a few weeks confinement, George became pale and weak. Several months later, two prisoners were relieved of their usual work detail. They slowly carried a tiny pine box which they placed in an unmarked grave. The little boy who had hacked Margaret O'Connor to death had arrived at his final resting place.

IN COLD STORAGE

D avid Wilfred Todd was born on May 3, 1934, in Hamilton, Ontario. From the outset he wasn't interested in school and only continued until he had completed Grade Six. Dave was something of a loner, a born watcher rather than a doer. After his brief academic career he started on a variety of laboring jobs not designed to tax his mental abilities nor make him a fortune, and by the time he was 25 he had held over 30 different menial jobs which he quit for one reason or another. Sometimes his reasons were not all that good — he loved to skip work and wander the streets of Hamilton, just bumming around looking in the shop windows.

Todd stood five feet, eight inches, with receding curly hair, a rather weak voice, and the limp handshake of the introvert. When you spoke to him he had the annoying habit of staring blankly back at you, and it was difficult to know what he was thinking about.

Grace Filmore was somewhat taller than Dave, but she didn't seem to mind, and dated him throughout the spring and summer of 1959. Though some of Grace's friends made no secret of the fact that they thought Dave wasn't good enough for her, she married him on Aug. 17, 1959.

After their marriage the young couple (Dave was 25 and Grace 20) lived in Hamilton, where Dave held a job as desk clerk at the Windsor Hotel for three years, which was something of a record for him. When the manager of the hotel left to open his own restaurant, Dave went to work for him. The new job didn't work out, because Grace objected to the long night hours, and after three months he left to join Hamilton Cotton Company, where he stayed one full year.

Like many young couples, the Todds felt that Toronto had more opportunities for them, and in 1965 they moved to Ontario's capital. They had just moved into 1 Deaville Lane when Dave got a steady job at Dunlop Rubber. He remained gainfully employed at Dunlop until the company closed its plant in 1970. Grace, who worked for the North American Life Insurance Company in Hamilton, managed to get a transfer to the Toronto office of the same company.

When Dunlop closed its plant, putting Dave out of work, the Todd marriage started to go steeply downhill. Instead of actively trying to find a job, Dave became paranoically suspicious of his wife's actions, and entirely without justification began to suspect Grace of being unfaithful to him. He kept phoning her office to make sure she was there. It got so bad that he made a point of picking her up at work so that she wouldn't have the opportunity to go with anyone else.

Occasionally Grace's company had a party and she and Dave would attend. Grace was charming and mixed easily with her fellow employees, but Dave would sulk in a corner, watching his wife. If any man put his arms around her or gave her a playful peck on the cheek, he seethed with silent rage. At home they started to argue incessantly, and Dave accused Grace of taking birth control pills to prevent her becoming pregnant by another man, though she explained that the pills were to relieve her pains when she menstruated.

Dave later claimed that at this time Grace would have nothing more to do with him in bed. She had never refused him before, but now she turned her back on him. He retaliated, truthfully or not, by bragging to her that he had slept with another woman. Grace, who knew her husband, probably didn't believe him, but the bickering went on. All their small differences, which hadn't seemed to matter earlier, came to the surface and festered, causing irreparable chasms in what had been a relatively happy marriage.

At the North American Life parties Grace loved to dance, while Dave sulked on the sidelines. Later his comment was, "I would be lucky to see her for about an hour without some other guy getting her on the floor." The scuttlebutt at the office affairs often revolved around salaries, while the unemployed Dave, hands deep in his pockets, became red-faced at what he considered the bragging conversation of the insurance people.

And so it went. Sometimes Dave would console himself by consuming 24 beers in one evening. After so much beer he occasionally fell asleep on the chesterfield, and finally he ended up sleeping there alone while Grace had the bed to herself. This became more or less the permanent arrangement. Throughout all the arguing Grace worked, earning the money on which they both lived. She took care of all the bills and even accompanied her husband when he bought a new pair of pants. Grace saw to it that Dave always had a few dollars in his pocket, but she often quarrelled with him for spending his allowance on liquor. When they went out in the evening for a few drinks at the nearby Mississippi Belle it was Grace who picked up the bar bills.

The few acquaintances they used to meet at the well-known club later remarked that even here Grace came off as being far more socially accomplished than her husband. He again took up the wallflower stance, and peered in from the perimeters of conversations. In fact, poor Dave Todd began to believe that now he was steadily unemployed, he was losing his wife's love and respect, yet he continued to do nothing about it. He became obsessed with hovering over her — keeping his eye on her, ever watchful to catch her in one of the unfaithful acts which were taking place only in his mind. Everyone who ever knew Grace stated that she was a respectable woman in every way.

Sometimes Dave, in his shy, introverted fashion, would try to initiate some activity he knew they both enjoyed. On Thursday night, July 29, 1971, he had talked Grace into going on a camping trip to one of Ontario's parks the next morning. She agreed, and things were looking bright for the Todds when they rose on Friday.

* * *

Just before Christmas 1971, Charles Cassidy, a twenty-one-year-old acquaitance of Todd's, told him that he could move in with his family at 4 Vendome Place. Cassidy's family included his sister Catherine, who was fifteen, and his mother. Todd had been having trouble getting up the rent at his previous residence at Deauville Lane, and was going around mumbling something about his wife leaving him. Cassidy knew that Todd had recently got a job as a truck driver, and felt that if given a break he would straighten out.

The whole Cassidy family thought it strange that Todd had brought along an electric freezer. Not only was it an unusual piece of furniture to have near the dining area, but it was locked, sealed and never used. It just sat there, humming away.

On the night of Jan. 12, 1972, Charles Cassidy, his sister Catherine, their mother and two friends, John Moore and Layne Jackson, were spending an evening at home watching television. The program they were viewing was a thriller, *One Step Beyond*. The young people joked about the story because of the weird plot which at one point revealed a body in a trunk. Right in their dining area they had a mysterious freezer humming away, while its owner slept peacefully in an upstairs bedroom. Well, they thought, it is quite one thing for a piece of fiction to have bodies in trunks, but in real life those things just don't happen. Still, the thought of something sinister in the freezer was too fascinating to resist. A screwdriver was produced; the screws holding down the hinges came out easily. Laughing and joking, the young people peered into the freezer. There, among the turkey pies and vegetables, was the tanned, solidly frozen body of Grace Todd.

* * *

Placid, timid David Todd readily confessed to killing his wife, but steadfastly maintained that he never meant any harm to come to her. He was charged with non-capital murder. A jury heard the psychiatric evidence in a report given by Dr. Peter Watts Rousell at the trial. The doctor had many interviews with Todd, and related in his own words what had taken place that Friday morning of July 30, 1971.

"She had taken a shower the next morning and they were having another verbal fight. She had made the quip about his being an old man and he quoted her, in addition to these remarks, as saying further 'You couldn't satisfy any of the whores around town. We are not man and wife. I tolerate you; I don't love you.' He quotes her as going on — he, of course, accusing her of walking out on him, which he went on to say was exactly what she was going to do after she had had an hour's sleep following her shower. She lay down on the chesterfield; she went on, 'By the time I am back to work, I will be under a new roof and when I get out today I am going to walk into the first man's bed I can get into.' He says, 'I took it that she had another man because she had been mixing all of a sudden this two years.' It was very evident as he described it, that this was in his mind because of his telephoning her so frequently, always asking her, as he described to me himself, who was in the office with her at any given time, and he says frankly 'I was at the point of watching everybody, even my brother-in-law and my brothers.' Concerning his brothers also, he disliked their putting their hands on her when talking to her or holding her arm. He said he was becoming rather depressed, wanting to avoid large crowds; just wanting to be with Grace where they would be alone; where he could have her all to himself. This was one of the chief reasons for camping as a vacation, to be alone with her; then he didn't have to worry about anybody else putting their hands on her. He indicated to me that they had planned to go to Simcoe. As this morning argument, Friday July 30th, occurring about 11:00 a.m. had built up and she had told him she was going to walk out, that she was going on no camping trip with him, he said 'I accused her of running out on me with another man and she laughed in my face.' She again referred to his being a watch-dog and she was referring, of course, to his picking her up at work and the constant telephone calls. He had not been sleeping during that year prior to the tragedy, staying on the chesterfield to satisfy his wife but occasionally putting away a case of 24 beer, almost, while he was on that chesterfield in one night. This would bring a further rebuke from his wife, that he was being a drunk and if he had not finished all the beer, to go back and finish what was left. His appetite was not so good. One year ago he says he weighed 200 pounds and, as one can observe Mr. Todd now, he gives his present weight at 150 pounds and is certainly no 200. Most of the weight has been lost since his wife's death. Apparently she criticized his weight, too, calling him 'hippo,' 'pear-shaped,' and telling him he was a disgrace to be seen in the street with being so fat. She told him to go on a diet. Apparently most of his weight had in fact gone on during the last two years prior to the tragedy.

"Meantime, returning to the fateful morning of July 30th with his wife's bitter statement, he said he was burning inside, wanting to scream, get something out of his system, a feeling going up into his chest and his head but somehow couldn't just let go. When she allegedly further taunted him that Friday, July morning that he was pussy-footing and screaming about women and he couldn't satisfy any of them anyway, at this point he had been telling her, while she lay not looking at him on the chesterfield, he being behind her, 'Won't you look at me while I am talking?' He indicated to me that he asked her three times and Grace had turned her back to him as she lay on the chesterfield. Having just said she was going to leave him after an hour's sleep, at this point he reached over and got the gun which was loaded, as he knew, and cocked. He says, 'I walked across and picked it up and I pointed it at her. Then she turned; I guess she was scared. She twisted and put her arm up and somehow I flipped it and it went off.'

"As he described this to me, he made this gesture. She — imitating her lying on the chesterfield, raising the right arm, head turning and as I understand it from his description, he was standing I think behind her, but this is the gesture that he imitated for me as he quoted those words; the turning to the right and looking back, bringing up the right arm. His wife, of course, fell back on the chesterfield. He said, 'I tried to walk up to her to say I was sorry and then I felt her pulse, her stomach and I got some towels to try and stop the bleeding.' He also indicated to me that he was crying at this point. He thought of an ambulance but just sat, scared, for an hour, wondering what to do. For the time being, he says, 'I put her in the freezer. I was going to call Bob Rowe who I respect; he is a man's man, to get his advice but I didn't. I was in the house for an hour. The car was full of things. I brought some of them up. I was talking to Larry Hough while I was unloading the car. I went to the bar but Bob was not at the bar and tomorrow never came when I would do something.'

"In June 1971, he indicated that he had told Larry Hough that when they returned from vacation, that is, he and Grace, that Larry could move in with them. Then it seems that Larry and friends came up and then of course with the freezer present, he had to start telling stories to 'cover up.' I was particularly struck by the cover-up stories so frequently alluding to Grace running off with another man, of course, it became his preoccupation all the way along. He himself slept on the chesterfield and regarding his state at that time, bearing in mind that the freezer with his wife's body was so close to him, he said, 'I felt my wife was with me. I dreamt good dreams, all the good times we had had together in the past. I was going to look at her twice, but somehow I couldn't. Someone was coming in.' At this point, when he was retreating into the happy and comfortable past, into what might be called his world of fantasy, of course the intrusion of the harsh reality of that freezer was always in front of him; the reality of keeping the secret of the body kept intruding on him.

"He invented more and more stories to cover her disappearance. The cash was running out. He was no manager of money. He admitted to feeling hopeless, as he has felt all the way along, drifting along, letting things happen. He has never thought of suicide during all this time. He felt very tired, he complains, after that. He lost a lot of weight, 50 pounds in all and is uptight. It is notable at this point of my examination he is giving a fairly straight, apparently, description of his actions and that is over this long period of time."

J. Crossland, QC acting for the Crown, wanted to know what caused mild-mannered David Todd to kill his wife. Dr. Rousell gave the opinion that after examining Todd, he felt that the accused didn't have the capacity at the time of the killing to form the intention. Crossland asked for the doctor's reasons for his opinion.

Dr. Rousell continued:

"This accused man, Mr. Todd, in my opinion first of all can be labelled under a true psychiatric diagnosis as an inadequate personality. Now although this is a true diagnosis, it does not imply that such a person is in any way insane within the legal meaning . . .

"The man himself, a wallflower, a quiet, always pleasant, easy-to-get-on-with individual, yet so inadequate in so many ways, could function and in fact, as his work record bears out, did function very well provided that he had that strong woman on whom he depended so much. She — it was in a sense very much like a mother-child relationship that really lay between them, so he is basically a clinging person, who when he has got somebody strong behind him, can function and function very adequately in a job so long as he doesn't have to take too much of the responsibilities. That is his basic personality diagnosis: inadequate personality."

The doctor then traced Todd's escalating possessiveness up to the morning of Friday July 30th, 1971:

". . . when there was the same set of accusations and recriminations as he described it, on both sides but with one difference and the difference was that this time she said, as he quoted, 'I am leaving you; I am not going camping with you. I will be under another roof when I come back from vacation,' so in the situation we have his description of his pointing the gun at her, trying to force her, in my opinion, as he expressed it to me, to make her stay and her subsequent actions as he described them which led to the gun going off and the subsequent tragedy that followed ... after all, his basic motive was to keep his wife. Following her death the only way he could, in his mind, keep her was to go into what is called a psychosis and this is a different matter because this does fall within the legal definition of insanity and a psychosis, by definition, is a disorder of thinking, feeling and behaviour accompanied by what is called a break with reality ... Following Grace's death, David Todd, in my opinion, became, so to speak, split into two different states of consciousness and behavior. First, the harsh reality of everyday living and having a roof over one's head, the presence of his wife's body in a freezer a few yards from him, knowing that money had to be obtained, knowing that he felt he had to conceal what he had done, this is the level of reality which is impossible to get away from. It was there. On the other hand, there is the seemingly incomprehensible behavior of this person who sleeps only a few yards — and makes a point of it — from the freezer containing the body of his loved one and his fantasy life, as he quotes from reality, dreams and indulges in all his happy memories, if you like, almost denying inside himself that she was dead, so in one way he keeps her alive through his happy memories and hangs onto the body and yet, in another way, he has to cover up and make up stories so he is forced into reality by the harsh things of life one moment and retreating from reality into his happy fantasies the next, and the mind in such chaos as a person — occurs in a person who is under extreme tension. He started to change his behavior. He went around with the young people far more and of course had to cover up with his stories about the refrigerator to them, and he lost 50 pounds in weight which, of course, is a leading symptom of ... a major nervous breakdown in the way I have defined it. An instance of his communication over the happiness aspect of it was his remark to, I think it was, Mr. Moore that she had come in one night and kissed him on the cheek. This is a fairly good example of the type of fantasy, wishful thinking, removed from the harsh reality of the situation which he appears to have been going through."

David Wilfred Todd changed his plea to guilty of manslaughter and was sentenced to 10 years in Kingston prison with the stipulation that he receive psychiatric treatment. He has since been released after serving his sentence.

Vince Desai

The Doctor and the Redhead

- Part 4-

THE DOCTORS

THE DOCTOR AND
THE REDHEAD

Dr. Bernard Finch had everything any man could ever want. He had a big home, lovely wife, two children, a Swedish maid, a Cadillac, and a thriving practice. He also had a mistress.

In August of 1956, an 18-year-old girl named Carole Tregoff was sent to the West Covina Medical Centre in West Covina, California to apply for a position as a receptionist. Carole was a tall, shapely redhead, in full bloom, so to speak.

Doctor Bernie took his time and it wasn't until the winter of 1957 that a cute little apartment was found and rented in the name of Mr. & Mrs. George Evans. Now, for well over a year Bernie and Carole "teamed up" pretty well every day at lunch, and sometimes before work in the morning. Carole had one embarrassing hurdle to get over. You see, she too was married. Her husband, Jimmy Pappa was not aware of his wife's affair. Their marriage was on the rocks and he and Carole were living together without sharing the connubial couch. It seems Jimmy was the only one who wasn't aware of the torrid romance.

Certainly Barbara Finch knew that something was wrong. She also knew that if she let her husband have a divorce, she would become, under California law, legally entitled to only 50 per cent of his assets. If she could prove adultery, she would get a much larger settlement. Not one to let sleeping dogs lie, Barbara called Jimmy Pappa and told him about his wife. When Carole came home from work that day, Jimmy did the manly thing. He punched her in the mouth. Carole packed up her belongings, left the house and filed for divorce all in the same day.

Meanwhile back at the Finch residence, conditions became intolerable. In May of 1959, the Finches were quarrelling and fighting on a regular basis. On May 16, Bernie beat up Barbara. On May 20, Barbara filed for a divorce. On May 21, she sought a restraining order that forbade her husband to harm her. At the same time the order prevented him from using or disposing of any funds or property, and as of June 11 the restraining order was signed into the record. At this time Bernie was worth three quarters of a million dollars. Not only could he not touch a penny without Barbara's consent, but every cent of income went into their joint account.

This was the tense state of affairs that existed on the night of July 18, 1959 when Barbara Finch drove up the driveway of her West Covina home. Barbara had taken to carrying a .38 calibre revolver for protection. As she started to get out of her car, she saw her husband and Carole Tregoff walking toward her out of the shadows. Instinctively she reached for her gun and pointed it at the advancing pair. Bernie grabbed the gun and took it away from his wife. He then proceeded to attack Barbara. Her screams were heard by their Swedish maid, Marie Anne Lidholm, who came running to Mrs. Finch's aid. Dr. Finch was in an uncontrollable rage. He grabbed the woman and threw her against the garage wall with such force that an impression of her head was implanted in the stucco wall. Bernie fired a wild shot into the air, and then ordered Marie Anne and his wife into the car. Barbara, fearing for her life, went in one side of the car and out the other, and kept on going. Bernie took off after her. Marie Anne saw her chance and ran to the house to call the police. Later she was to testify that she was dialling the police number when she heard a shot. Bernie admitted firing the gun. He claimed that he was flinging the gun away when his finger caught on the trigger, accidentally discharging the weapon. Firing so haphazardly he proved to be a fantastic shot. The .38 calibre slug made its way through Barbara's back and into her heart.

All this time Carole was hiding in the bushes just out of sight of the action. Only after the police came and finished their investigation did Carole finally get away. She didn't know that Bernie had left or that Barbara was dead. The only living person the police found at the scene was Marie Anne, who had called them in the first place.

Next day, Dr. Finch was arrested and charged with murder. Later Carole was charged as well. At the trial the prosecution brought out the fact that Bernie and Carole had hired an assassin to do away with Mrs. Finch. His name was John Patrick Coady, and he fingered the accused pair from the witness stand. In fact, he received a total of $1,200 for the job that he had no intention of doing. He told a convincing story.

Over and above Coady's damaging evidence, the police had come up with an attache case at the scene of the crime. The case did not contain what your average kindly old doctor would call the essentials. Instead it held two 10-foot-long ropes, an eight-inch butcher knife, a bottle of Seconal, a hammer, a flashlight and a box of .38 calibre cartridges. The attache case was quickly dubbed the "murder kit" by the press.

It took three trials to get a jury to agree, but finally on March 27, 1961, Dr. Bernard Finch and Carole Tregoff were convicted of murder in the second degree. Both were sentenced to life imprisonment.

In 1969 Carole was paroled, and is now employed under an assumed name as a medical records clerk in a hospital in California. Dr. Finch was eventually paroled, and is again practising medicine.

KILL NOT HEAL

Dr. Geza de Kaplany had interned at Milwaukee General Hospital in 1957. Later he specialized in anesthesiology at Harvard University, after which he taught at Yale University for a year. In 1961, he was chief medical resident at San Francisco's Franklin Hospital. Still later he accepted the post of staff anesthesiologist at Doctors' Hospital in San Jose, California.

At the age of 36 you might say Dr. de Kaplany was a high achiever. Even in the field of matrimony he hit the jackpot. In July of 1962 he married Hajna Piller, a model and former show-girl. She was gorgeous. Anyone who ever saw Hajna came away impressed by her beauty. Both had immigrated from Hungary to the U.S. while still single.

On the stifling hot night of Aug. 28, 1962, about five weeks after their marriage, Dr. de Kaplany killed his wife.

On the day of the crime, Mrs. de Kaplany visited her mother. She arrived home in the early evening and met her husband outside their apartment. They proceeded up to their apartment which was in a two-storey ranch style structure. The young couple commenced to make love on the bed. For no apparent reason Dr. de Kaplany jumped up from the bed. He had an entire torture kit with him. First he beat his wife with his fists. He then tied her hands behind her back with electric cord, and trussed up her feet in the same manner. To stifle her screams he placed tape over her mouth. Dr. de Kaplany slashed at Hajna's breast with a knife. He wasn't through. Calmly donning rubber gloves, he applied nitric acid all over her body.

Despite the fact that the doctor turned the hi-fi on full blast, Hajna's screams pierced the hot summer night, arousing the neighbors' interest. When the police and an ambulance arrived on the scene, they found the doctor pacing outside the apartment in a pair of Bermuda shorts and slippers. Hajna lay nude in agony on the bed, horribly burned over 60 per cent of her body. The officers and medical people had trouble breathing at the scene of the crime due to the nitric acid. Periodically they had to run out of the apartment to get a breath of fresh air.

Hajna lingered in agony for 33 days after the attack before she mercifully passed away on Sept. 30. During the time the doctors struggled to keep her alive she made many statements to the police, but in the end she really could not say just why her husband had done such a terrible thing to her.

On Monday, Jan. 7, 1963, Dr. de Kaplany stood trial for murder. During the trial he changed his plea from not guilty to guilty. Sanity meant the gas chamber, and insanity meant life imprisonment. The trial was a sensation and swayed back and forth on medical evidence attesting to Dr. de Kaplany's mental condition at the time of the murder.

The defence brought forward doctors who claimed he suffered from depression due to leaving an aged mother in Hungary. They said he suffered from paranoid schizophrenia. The prosecution countered with the actual torture paraphernalia which they lugged into court. It made an impressive display in front of the jury — surgical gloves, a quantity of surgical swabs, rolls of adhesive tape, electric cord, one pint of nitric acid, one pint of hydrochloric acid, one pint of sulphuric acid and two knives.

A sensation was caused at the trial when the defence put a young psychiatrist, Dr. A. Russell Lee on the stand. Dr. Lee claimed that de Kaplany suffered from multiple personality. He stated that de Kaplany had two people living in the same body. One was a kind and gentle doctor. The other was brutal and cruel. The brutal one went under the name of Pierre LaRoche. It seems de Kaplany heard some gossip about his wife being unfaithful to him. Instead of dealing with this rumor in a rational manner as de Kaplany would have done, he changed into the aggressive cruel Pierre, and tortured and killed his wife. De Kaplany would change his outward appearance and adopt the personality of Pierre LaRoche, for short periods of time.

Horrible pictures of poor Hajna were introduced as evidence, showing the agony in which she died. The jury could not believe that a man, sane in the legal sense, could perform such atrocities on his wife. They brought in a verdict of imprisonment for life.

When Dr. de Kaplany was taken away to San Quentin, a reporter asked him one final question as a guard assisted him into the prison van. "Have you any last statement, Doctor?"

"This is the end. I am dead," he replied.

DR. PRITCHARD
HANGED

Mothers-in-law have been the brunt of ridicule and snide remarks. It is one thing to ridicule one's mother-in-law, and quite another to remove her from the scene permanently.

One man accomplished this rather singular feat, and threw in his wife to boot.

Dr. Edward Pritchard married Miss Mary Jane Taylor in 1850 and, after accepting various medical posts, settled down to his own private practice in Glasgow, Scotland.

Now Dr. Pritchard was a tall, sensitive, attractive man, with a full flowing beard. He was extremely popular with his patients, but when it came to female patients, there were gossips who spread the word. It seems the good doctor performed extensive examinations on attractive ladies, when perhaps a more cursory examination would have sufficed. The doctor loved to spend money and loved to have a good time. He was a real charmer. However, this charm did not carry over to his professional colleagues. They frowned on the low standard of medicine he practised, and his private life.

All went well at home until May of 1863, when unaccountably a fire broke out in the servants' quarters of the Pritchard home. Mrs. Pritchard and another servant were out of town at the time. When firemen put out the blaze, the body of a young servant girl was found burned to death in her bed. She had made no attempt to leave the bed. It was one of those minor mysteries that occurs in every large city. While a few suspicious glances were tossed the doctor's way, nothing was ever done about it.

The experience was so distasteful the family moved to Clarence Place, and then things started to happen. The new home was four storeys high. The doctor and his wife lived in apparent harmony with four of their five children. The oldest lived with her grandparents in Edinburgh. The Pritchards had two servants, the cook, Catherine Lattimer, and Mary M'Leod, a maid who was hired to replace the poor unfortunate servant who was burned in her bed.

Mary herself got burned in bed, after a fashion. You see, she and the doctor had arrived at an understanding that was not exactly the normal master-servant relationship. Mary became pregnant. Edward hastily performed an operation on Mary which had the desired effect of producing a miscarriage. After a brief recovery period, Mary and Dr. Pritchard continued their illicit relationship.

In October of 1864, Mrs. Pritchard, who was always a robust healthy woman, started to suffer from headaches and stomach cramps. It got so bad, her husband confined her to bed. Her mother, Mrs. Taylor, wrote from Edinburgh that her daughter should visit with her to regain her health. At first the doctor wouldn't hear of being parted from his wife. Finally he yielded under pressure, and Mrs. Pritchard went to her mother's home. Here her health improved dramatically and rapidly.

On December 22nd, Mrs. Pritchard came home to be with her family for Christmas. Almost immediately, she became ill again. She was vomiting after every meal. She became so violently ill that late in January, Dr. Pritchard wrote his wife's cousin, one Dr. Cowan, in Edinburgh, to come and visit Mrs. Pritchard. One Feb. 7, Dr. Cowan arrived and applied a mustard poultice to his cousin. Upon his return to Edinburgh he urged Mrs. Taylor to go to Glasgow to attend her daughter. In the meantime, Mrs. Pritchard had her worst attack to date. Despite her husband, who stood at her bedside, she implored the cook to fetch Dr. Gairdner, who lived close by. When he arrived he was told by Dr. Pritchard that Dr. Cowan had given his wife stimulants. Dr. Gairdner suggested this be stopped immediately. He prescribed a simple diet, and next day he was advised that Mrs. Pritchard was much better. Despite this reassurance, Dr. Gairdner became apprehensive about the entire matter. He remembered that Mrs. Pritchard's brother was also a doctor. They had attended college together. He wrote Dr. Taylor, who in turn wrote to his brother-in-law, suggested that it might be best if his sister visited him. Dr. Pritchard wouldn't hear of being parted from his dear wife.

In the meantime Mrs. Taylor came to Glasgow to be with her daughter. She found her continuously vomiting and suffering from severe cramps. Within a week Mrs. Taylor started to feel ill. On the night of Feb. 16, she became so violently sick she was placed in bed with her daughter. Dr. Pritchard called another neighbor who was also a man of medicine, Dr. James Patterson.

If you are keeping score, this is the fourth doctor called in to treat one or the other of the two very sick ladies. Not counting Dr. Pritchard's ministrations, the total medical treatment up to this time was one mustard poultice, applied to Mrs. Pritchard. However, one must keep in mind that all the doctors were dealing with another doctor, who was the husband and son-in-law of the patients.

When Dr. Patterson entered the house, he was greeted by Dr. Pritchard and given the usual misleading symptoms. Upon examining Mrs. Taylor, Dr. Patterson gave the opinion that she was under the influence of dope, probably opium, and was dying of opiate poisoning. He said there was nothing he could do. At 11:30 p.m. he left the house. At 1 a.m. he got a call to return but refused, saying that death was inevitable. Mrs. Taylor passed away a few minutes after 1 a.m. Dr. Pritchard signed the death certificate "paralysis 12 hours. Apoplexy one hour."

Dr. Pritchard continued to supervise everything consumed by his wife who deteriorated rapidly. Finally on Friday, March 17, after four months of excruciating pain, attended by her husband and Dr. Patterson, Mrs. Pritchard passed away. During her final hours Patterson asked Pritchard to make up a simple sleeping draught, but Pritchard replied that he kept no drugs in the house.

Dr. Pritchard was again called upon to sign a death certificate. This time he wrote "gastric fever, two months."

On Monday, March 20, Mr. William Hart, who held a post roughly equivalent to that of our coroner, received an anonymous letter. In substance it told of the two deaths and suggested foul play may have been involved. When the doctor arrived back in Glasgow from his wife's funeral in Edinburgh, he was detained by the police. Routine investigation revealed his relationship with Mary M'Leod. To make matters worse it was revealed that poor Mrs. Pritchard had stumbled on her husband and Mary in sundry compromising positions. She had long before decided to sidestep a scandal, and put up with her promiscuous husband and maid. The bodies of Mrs. Pritchard and her mother were exhumed, and found to be full of poison.

Edward Pritchard was arrested and stood trial for murder on Monday, July 3, 1865. While his trial caused a sensation, it provided no duelling match between prosecution and defence attornies. There was really no defence. For a man who professed to have no drugs in his home, his two suppliers provided a list of drugs purchased by the physician during his victim's illness. They included enough poison to do away with half of dear old Glasgow.

Through it all the doctor remained a charming, polite scoundrel. He was found guilty and sentenced to hang. Before he was led to the scaffold in the presence of an Episcopalian minister, he confessed to both murders "in the way brought out in the evidence." Monster that he was, he kept his charming charade to the very end. Head erect, with a bold, almost marching step, he was hung before a huge crowd on July 28, 1865.

Handsome Edward had the distinction to be the last person to be publicly executed in Glasgow.

WAITE THOUGHT IT WAS A JOKE

It is seldom in the annals of crime that a man can first be suspected, then arrested and finally stand trial for murder without ever taking the entire matter seriously. One man went through the entire ordeal, laughing and joking to the end.

Dr. Arthur Warren Waite was born in Grand Rapids, Mich. in 1887. He took his Dental Surgeon's degree in Glasgow, Scotland, and practised in South Africa before returning to the United States at the age of 28. Dr. Waite married Clara Peck, the daughter of a Grand Rapids millionaire in September, 1915. Then he set up practice in New York City and at the same time did pure research at the Cornell Medical School. He played a good game of tennis, led an active social life, and all in all appeared to be a man who had everything.

There was one thing though; you see, the doctor decided to kill all his relatives.

Mrs. John E. Peck was Art's mother-in-law. Her daughter and the charming dentist were married for three months when she decided to visit the couple over the Christmas holidays. She arrived a healthy, robust woman. By Jan. 30, she was dead. A doctor certified that she had died of kidney disease.

Art informed Clara that her mother had confided in him during her brief illness that she wished to be cremated. Clara thought it strange that her mother had never mentioned this to her, but gave her consent to the request.

After his wife's funeral, Mr. Peck came to visit with his daughter and son-in-law. He was dead by March 12. Again, the doctor called it kidney disease and the body was to be cremated. Apparently Mr. Peck had confided this wish to Arthur and no one else. Dr. Art made all the arrangements. He had the body embalmed, and then it was to be shipped to Grand Rapids to allow the rest of the family to pay their last respects. Finally the remains were to be forwarded to Detroit for cremation.

Everything went according to plan, until the party accompanying the body met the rest of the family in Grand Rapids. Here, Clara's brother Percy, who never got along with Art, acted very hostile to the dentist. He had received an anonymous letter telling him not to allow his father's body to be cremated. Percy decided to take over all the details concerning his father's body. Arthur and Clara returned to New York.

Meanwhile, Percy gave the order to have an autopsy performed on his father. Then at his urging the authorities started to look more closely into Arthur's background. They found that as a student, Arthur had stolen money, and later in South Africa had tried to marry a wealthy lady whose father had him chased out of the country. Then the story broke that charming, considerate Art was having an affair with a married singer named Margaret Horton. We begrudgingly have to give him a certain amount of credit. It isn't easy to get married, kill your mother-in-law and father-in-law, and carry on with a mistress, all within a period of five months.

The floss that broke the dentist's drill was when five grains of arsenic were found in Mr. Peck's body. This was too much even for Art; he took some poison and when the police went to arrest him, they found him almost dead. He survived and stood trial for double murder.

It was during the trial that Dr. Waite distinguished himself. For starters, despite pleading not guilty, he never once denied killing his in-laws. In fact, he described the whole thing in detail. He even cracked jokes to the jury while he recounted the sordid affair.

In his own words, he said: "I started poisoning her from the very first meal after she arrived. I gave her six assorted tubes of pneumonia, diptheria and influenza germs in her food. When she finally became ill and took to her bed, I ground up 12 five-grain Veronal and gave her that, too, last thing at night."

Art woke up in the middle of the night, found his mother-in-law dead, and went back to sleep. He had ready access to the germs from his research work at the medical school.

Art went on to tell how Mr. Peck didn't die easy. He tried several types of poisons on him, but nothing seemed to work. He went through his supply of germs, then tried chloroform, and finally in desperation he held a pillow over his father-in-law's nose and mouth until he was dead.

The obliging dentist volunteered that he tried to kill his wife's aunt, Catherine Peck, by giving her ground glass in her food when she had visited at Christmas. He only spared her because he switched his attention to his mother-in-law, who seemed to be easier to finish.

In his jocular way the dentist explained that, if he had more time, he would have also poisoned his wife. Art thought this so humorous that he laughed out loud while giving his statement from the witness stand.

He wasn't all fun and games. It was learned that behind the scenes he had attempted to bribe two members of the jury. He also had paid an embalmer to put arsenic in an embalming fluid sampler, so that when the police tested it they would find arsenic, thereby explaining its presence in Mr. Peck's body.

The doctor said his motive for the double murder was to inherit his in-laws' fortune. He even joked that he had done his wife a favor by speeding up her inheritance. His mistress, Margaret Horton, testified that Arthur actually told her that he killed his wife's parents. He said he planned on going to an asylum for a short time as an imbecile.

Dr. Waite was found guilty. He carried off his charade to the bitter end, requesting that he be put to death at the earliest possible date. On May 24, 1917 he arose, ate a hearty breakfast and read a book of John Keats' poems. He then joked with his guards as he walked calmly into the execution chamber and was put to death in the electric chair.

THE DOCTOR
PRESCRIBED POISON

Poisoners as a group have always plied their dubious profession under an extreme disadvantage. They simply have to obtain their poison somewhere. Invariably a chemist or pharmacist ends up on the witness stand pointing a finger at the accused, exclaiming, "He said it was to get rid of rats", or some other innocuous expression designed to lend legitimacy to the purchase.

That is, unless the accused happens to be a doctor.

Dr. William Palmer was born on Oct. 21, 1824 in Rugeley, England and took his medical degree in London. During his student days he gained quite a reputation as a gambler with a particular affinity for the ponies. He returned to Rugeley and married a Colonel's daughter, Annie Brooks. Everything went along well with the doctor and his wife as he established a large and profitable practice. Dr. Palmer neither smoked nor drank, and who are we to criticize if he bet a bob or two on the horses now and then. The Palmers lived in a big house, and he appeared to have anything any man could want.

Then one day an annoying lady from Rugeley presented him with an illegitimate child. Being a man of medicine he thought it would be a good idea to give the newborn child a physical examination. The child died of convulsions shortly after the visit to the doctor's office.

Dr. Palmer and Annie proceeded to have five children during the course of their marriage, and all but one died of convulsions. The eldest, Willie, through the luck of the draw, outlived dear old Dad.

After the initial pleasures of married life had worn off, Dr. Palmer started to bet heavily on the horses. Then, as now, it was very difficult to beat the nags and he got deeper and deeper into debt. Finally his mother-in-law, Mrs. Thornton, was approached for a loan. She sent him 20 pounds, and in effect told him to get lost. William, never one to pass up a mark, invited Mrs. Thornton to come stay with him and Annie. She was dead within two weeks, and the Palmers inherited nine houses. The doctor was furious when he found out they were in need of repair.

Then Dr. Palmer invited an acquaintance of his, Mr. Bladon, to visit. He owed Bladon several hundred pounds, which he promised to pay back during his stay. Poor Bladon was hardly settled in the house before he passed away suddenly during the night, writhing with convulsions. Dr. Palmer was obviously distressed at losing his friend. He brought in a colleague, Dr. Bamford, during that last horrible night, and it was Dr. Bamford who signed the death certificate with the cause of death being English Cholera. In all fairness, we should point out that 80-year-old Dr. Bamford was a tottering, half-blind gentleman who looked up to Dr. Palmer and was flattered at being consulted. Kindly Dr. Palmer took care of his friend's funeral arrangements. He was even decent enough to tell Bladon's widow that while her husband owed him huge sums of money, under the circumstances, he would forget the debt.

Another gentleman named Bly was hounding Palmer for £800 when he was invited down to Rugeley for a visit. Exit Bly.

Around now, Mrs. Palmer was beginning to wonder. First her children, and now it seemed that everyone who walked into their front door was being carried out. She didn't have all that long to worry. Mrs. Palmer attended a concert in Liverpoool on the night of Sept. 18, 1854 and took a slight chill. Dr. Palmer prescribed bed rest. Their servant, Eliza Tharm, was preparing Mrs. Palmer's meals, but the considerate doctor insisted on carrying them upstairs and feeding his wife. The patient vomited continuously and grew weaker. Dr. Bamford was called in and was told by Dr. Palmer that his wife had English Cholera. She was dead in two weeks. Dr. Bamford duly signed the death certificate, and Palmer collected £13,000 in insurance money.

By now William had his own string of horses, and the added expense of trainers, stables and jockeys. His horses can best be described as slow. The doctor was spending money faster than he could kill people.

William, who never drank himself, had a brother who was an alcoholic. He convinced his brother that he would give him a loan which the brother would never have to pay back. William would take out insurance on his life, and when he died Dr. Palmer would get his money back. The brother, Walter, who was in a daze most of the time, went for it. Dr. Palmer sobered him up long enough to pass the physical exam required by the insurance company. You guessed it. Walter passed away, and Dr. Palmer again collected £13,000 insurance.

Still the flow of money coming in wasn't enough, and soon Dr. Palmer was borrowing from loan sharks and paying 60 per cent interest. The money lender, Mr. Pratt, demanded money on certain dates, and unlike previous lenders, he would not be put off.

One day at the race track, Dr. Palmer met John Parsons Cook. Now Cook was a friend cut from the same cloth as Palmer. He had his own stable and was a hard-drinking playboy. One day at the races Cook had a long shot come in by a nose. The men had a champagne supper and some further drinks to celebrate. During the celebration Palmer gave Cook some brandy, and he immediately took ill. When it came time to return to Rugeley, Palmer suggested that Cook return with him. There were comfortable lodgings at the Talbot Arms, right across the street from his own house. Cook thought the doctor most obliging, and the two men left together.

Once installed at the Talbot Arms, Cook's illness became worse. The more Dr. Palmer prescribed for him, the worse he became. Finally he died. After he passed away, Palmer produced cheques in his favor signed by Cook. The doctor was making his usual hasty funeral arrangements for his friend, when a spoilsport arrived on the scene. Cook's stepfather, a Mr. Stevens, advised Palmer that he would make all the arrangements. In fact, he thought the whole thing smelled to high heaven. Stevens was going to have a post mortem performed on Cook's body and an inquiry into his death.

On Friday, Dec. 14, the results of the post mortem were presented at the inquiry. No strychnine was found in the body, but the cause of death was given as tetanus which was the result of the administration of strychnine. A verdict of willful murder was returned against Dr. Palmer.

The whole of England talked of little else but the Dr. William Palmer case. There were many who couldn't believe that the gambler and mass murderer described by the newspapers was the same gentle doctor they knew. The bodies of his wife Annie and his brother Walter were exhumed. Annie's body was found to contain antimony. While no poison was evident in Walter's body, it was believed that he met his death by the administration of prussic acid. Traces of this acid would have evaporated since death.

Dr. Palmer's house and the Talbot Arms became so notorious that an enterprising photographer set up his equipment in front of the two establishments. For a small sum you could have your picture taken with the murder buildings in the background.

Dr. Palmer was speedily found guilty of murder. In 1855, there were still public executions in England. Before a howling crowd, shouting "Poisoner, poisoner," Dr. Palmer was hanged. He was 31 years old.

RUXTON'S NASTY TEMPER

Susan Johnson did what many people do when they stroll over a country bridge. She absently looked down at the meandering stream below. Could that be a human arm protruding from some newspapers on the river bank? Susan, who was vacationing in Moffat, Scotland, hurriedly returned to her hotel room where she told her brother of her suspicions. He travelled the two miles to the bridge and confirmed his sister's gruesome find. Then he called the police.

What confronted the authorities on that pleasant September afternoon in 1935 was not a pretty sight. The newspapers held the dismembered portions of not one, but two, bodies. There were four individual bundles containing small segments of both bodies. The victims were adult females.

Within the next two days additional parts of the same two bodies were found in the general area of the original four bundles. Complete sections of the two bodies had been cut away in an obvious attempt to hinder identification.

To add an element of mystery to the already strange discovery of two separate dismembered and mutilated bodies, police found a Cyclops eye in one of the newspaper bundles. This phenomenon, known as Cyclopia, is the fusing together of two eyes, which appear as a single eye in the middle of the forehead. This malformation is extremely rare in humans, but does occur more frequently in pigs. In the case of humans, it is usually accompanied by other deformities which result in death a few hours after birth. The name, of course, is derived from a mythical race of one-eyed giants whose chief occupation in Greek mythology was the manufacture of thunderbolts for Zeus. The human Cyclops eye was a strange and puzzling oddity to discover along a peaceful meandering river in Scotland.

A heavy rainfall had taken place on Sept. 19. It was ascertained that the bodies would have been washed away had they been deposited on the river bank before this date. Police began their investigation by checking out all women reported missing since Sept. 19.

In this routine manner, investigating officers found out that Mary Jane Rogerson, a nursemaid in the home of Dr. Buck Ruxton, had been reported missing some three weeks before Miss Johnson's gruesome discovery under the bridge. Police were also given to understand that Dr. Ruxton's wife had left him at approximately the same time. Mary Rogerson's mother identified several pieces of clothing found with the bodies as belonging to her daughter. She had sewn a patch into one of the garments herself.

Detectives were already well acquainted with Dr. Buck Ruxton. He had called on them several times in the previous three weeks to complain that his wife had left him, and that he wanted her found and returned. After the gruesome discovery he continued to call on the police, claiming that rumors were being spread connecting him with the bodies found under the bridge. Dr. Ruxton stated that the rumors were ruining his practice and must be stopped.

Police were not ready to act. Mrs. Ruxton had not been identified as a victim and, while Dr. Ruxton was strongly suspected of complicity in the murder, police found it prudent to wait until positive identification could be established. I must point out that visual examination of the bodies was ruled out as a method of identification. The mutilations to both bodies were so extensive that it was impossible to identify the bodies in this way.

Dr. Ruxton was born in Bombay, India. Thankfully he had his name changed from Bukhtyar Rustomji Ratanji Hakim to Buck Ruxton. He received his medical degree from the University of Bombay, and later specialized in surgery at the same university. He had maintained a comfortable home at 2 Dalton Square, Lancaster, since 1930, where he carried on a rather successful medical practice.

Mrs. Ruxton was the former Isabella Kerr. She had been married once before in 1919. After meeting Dr. Ruxton, she had her marriage dissolved, and married the doctor in 1928.

During the seven years of their marriage, Mrs. Ruxton and the doctor argued and fought incessantly. Dr. Ruxton was insanely jealous, and often unjustly accused her of having affairs with other men. Ruxton had a short temper and often struck his wife.

His diary reveals that they always kissed and made up. Theirs was an unhappy household.

The Ruxtons had three children, aged six, four, and two. Mary Rogerson, their nursemaid, was 20. Mary rarely left the Ruxton residence during the week. Usually she spent her day off with her parents. She had never been late for an appointment, nor had she ever stayed out overnight without informing her family. Neither Mrs. Ruxton nor Mary were seen by anyone after Sept. 14, 1935.

Three women, other than Mary, worked at the good doctor's home. Mrs. Agnes Oxley, a charwoman, worked at 2 Dalton Square every day of the week, except Saturday, starting at 7:10 a.m. Mrs. Elizabeth Curwen also showed up every day starting at 8:30 a.m. and staying until her work was completed. A third woman, Mrs. Mabel Smith, had only recently been hired on a part-time basis, working Monday through Thursday from 2 p.m. to 7 p.m. The work schedules of these women later proved to be of crucial importance.

On Friday, Sept. 13, Mrs. Curwen was told by Dr. Ruxton not to return until the following Monday. On Sunday, the 15th, Mrs. Oxley was surprised to find Dr. Ruxton at her doorstep at 6:30 a.m., advising her not to come to work. He told her that Mrs. Ruxton and Mary had gone on a holiday to Edinburgh. Mrs. Smith was not due at Dalton Square until Monday.

Dr. Ruxton had managed to dismiss his three employees, leaving him alone in his home on Friday night, Saturday and Sunday.

All that weekend Ruxton scurried about. To everyone who met him he appeared agitated and nervous. As his car was in for repairs, he hired a vehicle and placed his children with friends.

When the charwomen reported for work the following week they found two upstairs bedrooms locked. The house had undergone many changes over the weekend. The walls along the stairway appeared to be blood splattered. Rugs had been taken up and thrown into the back yard. These, too, had large brown stains. The doctor magnanimously gave the rugs to Mrs. Oxley and Mrs. Curwen. He explained that he had severely cut his hand while opening a tin of fruit, accounting for the bloodstains on the wall and rug. He also told them that he was preparing the house to be redecorated. The ladies worked hard all that week cleaning up.

To everyone, even those who didn't inquire, Dr. Ruxton gave conflicting stories about his wife's and Mary's sudden departure. To some he stated that Mary was pregnant, and that his wife had gone away with her to attempt to terminate the pregnancy. He told others that the two women were on vacation.

All week the charwomen cleaned and threw out rubbish. One of them later remembered a bloody piece of cotton wool which the doctor had her burn in the back yard, together with a bloody dress.

On Sept. 19, at 7:30 a.m., Ruxton brought his car around to the back door of his home. As Mrs. Oxley worked out of sight in the kitchen, he made several trips upstairs and back down to his car. After he left, Mrs. Oxley, who was now joined by Mrs. Curwen, noticed that the two upstairs rooms, which had been locked for five days, were now open. The two ladies entered the rooms and remarked on the vile smell emanating from them.

Next day Dr. Ruxton mentioned the smell to the two women. He suggested they buy a bottle of eau de cologne. Mrs. Curwen bought the cologne and gave it to the doctor. Later on the fragrance was much in evidence in the odoriferous rooms.

It must be noted that in the two weeks between Sept. 14 and the discovery of the bodies on Sept. 29, Dr. Ruxton was a busy little boy. He was scurrying around the countryside, trying to establish an alibi, ministering to his patients, placing his children, trying desperately to have his house decorated, and keeping three inquisitive women from finding out the truth while making up stories to account for the absence of his wife and nursemaid. All the while he was dissecting two bodies and disposing of the pieces. It was all enough to tire a man. No wonder everyone who saw him during this period remembers his desperate appearance.

After the bodies were discovered near Moffat, Dr. Ruxton became frantic. He contacted everyone he had seen in the previous two weeks asking them to support him in the story he would be telling the police.

Dr. Buck Ruxton was arrested and charged with the murder of Mary Rogerson on Oct. 15, 1935. Two months later he stood trial for murder at the Manchester Assizes.

Once the arrest was made, police swooped down on 2 Dalton Square and almost took the house apart. Floorboards and parts of the wall were removed to the Department of Forensic Medicine at Glasgow University. Stains appearing on both wall and floor were identified as human blood. Dr. Ruxton's hand was examined. It was established that a fruit tin could not have inflicted such a wound. The severe cut was self inflicted by a sharp knife. A local newspaper to which the doctor subscribed was found wrapped around a portion of Mary Rogerson's body. Also found with the body was a section of a sheet, which matched perfectly with the other section found in the doctor's house.

Although the doctor maintained his innocence, it is believed that during one of his frequent fits of temper he killed his wife. Mary Rogerson, the nursemaid, may have witnessed the crime and had to be silenced.

Dr. Ruxton was found guilty and sentenced to death. He was hanged at Strangeways Prison on May 12, 1936.

But what of the mysterious Cyclops eye found with the two bodies? Despite many far out theories put forward at Ruxton's trial, it is a mystery which hasn't been solved to this day.

DR. WILKINS WALKED THE DOG

Husbands who hasten the departure of their wives should exhibit some physical sign of anguish. Wailing at the moon, uncontrollable flailing, or even simple tears are recommended. Never, but never, nonchalantly decide to take the dog for a walk. Strangely enough, Dr. Walter Keene Wilkins of Long Beach, N.Y. did just that.

Dr. Wilkins was a kindly appearing gentleman, who sported a fine display of mutton-chop whiskers, as was the fashion in 1919. At 67 years of age, he was somewhat older than his dear wife Julia.

One chilly February evening the police of tiny Long Beach received a call from Max Mayer, a neighbor of the Wilkins'. Upon investigating the call, they found Dr. Wilkins bending over his wife's prostrate form in front of their home. He was washing blood from Julia's horribly battered face. The poor woman was rushed to the hospital by ambulance, where two hours later she died. It took some effort to notify the distraught husband. He was busy walking the two family dogs who, incidentally, answered to the rather prosaic names of Duke and Duchess. I might add, but only in passing, that the Wilkins owned a parrot and a monkey, whose names fortunately have been lost to posterity.

Dr. Wilkins had quite a story to tell. He and his wife arrived home from shopping. As they approached their house on Olive St., the doctor thought there was someone inside. He entered alone, advising his wife to stay outside. Suddenly, he was struck a vicious blow to the head. Luckily, he was wearing a derby hat at the time, which no doubt cushioned the blow. Nonetheless, he was jumped upon by at least three men, but managed somehow to scream a warning to his wife, who in turn yelled for help.

One of the doctor's attackers dashed past his fallen form and obviously hit Julia repeatedly over the head until she lay dying on the sidewalk. Slowly the doctor regained consciousness. He ran to his neighbor's home and raised the alarm. Then he returned to help his wife as best he could.

Robbery had obviously been the motive. The doctor had been robbed of his wallet and diamond stickpin. The house had been ransacked as well. It appeared that three assailants had taken part in the attack. Three glasses and a bottle of the doctor's good brandy were found on the kitchen table. It appeared as if three men were having a drink when the doctor entered the house.

Outside in the yard, the police found a half inch lead pipe wrapped in cloth. It was surmised that this was the weapon used on Dr. Wilkins. A broken machinist's hammer, held together with wire and wrapped in newspaper, was found beside the unfortunate Mrs. Wilkins.

Now, all of this business of hammers and pipes caused a tremendous amount of excitement around the tiny community of Long Beach. A great deal of pressure was put on the police to come up with the killer. Despite what appeared to be a galaxy of clues, the authorities were hard put to produce a bona fide suspect. In a kind of desperation born of frustration, they decided to look into the benevolent Dr. Wilkins' past. Well, folks, they found out a thing or two.

At the relatively tender age of 35, Wilkins had married one Miss Grace Mansfield. Now Grace wasn't a knockout, but she did have a father who indulged his new son-in-law to the extent of an allowance of $150 a month. When Wilkins failed to make any attempt to support Mrs. W., she divorced him and returned to being just plain Grace.

In 1893, Dr. Wilkins again entered the holy state of matrimony. This time he wed Suzanne Kirkland, a widow who owned a few rooming houses. The new Mrs. Wilkins fell downstairs one day. During her convalescence from this unfortunate accident she became depressed and nervous. The doctor prescribed ice cold baths. In fact, he filled the tub with ice. Suzanne stepped in and dropped dead. There was no question about it; Dr. Wilkins had a poor track record when it came to wives.

The most recent Mrs. Wilkins had managed to stay married and alive for a full 13 years, but disturbing facts were fast coming to light. Julia had also been married before and had about $100,000 in her name. Dr. Wilkins, it appears, had a fat zero in his name. So much for motive.

The string which had been used to tie newspaper around the murder weapon was traced to a butcher shop where the doctor had purchased the family meat for years. The wire used to repair the mechanic's hammer came from a roll of wire found in the Wilkins' home. It became downright embarrassing when Julia's false teeth were found in the house after the doctor had stated explicitly that his wife never entered the house on the evening she was killed. When it was discovered that the doctor had taken a blood stained suit to a dry cleaning establishment on the day after the murder, it was just too much. He was arrested and charged.

On June 5, Dr. Wilkins' murder trial began. It immediately became apparent that the evidence against him was overwhelming. When it was revealed that his diamond stickpin, supposedly taken during the course of the robbery, was found in his overcoat, his goose, so to speak, was cooked. The good doctor was found guilty.

The day after the verdict was delivered, Dr. Wilkins managed to hang himself with a piece of rope from a shower fixture. The doctor, who seemed to have a flair for the dramatic, didn't disappoint, even in death. He left three letters. One provided for Duke, Duchess, the parrot and the monkey. Another revealed that he preferred death to life in Sing Sing, and the third left his lawyer $50 to pay for his cremation.

THE DOCTOR AND
THE TRIANGLE

Gentlemen who monkey around with other gentlemen's wives sometimes find themselves in all sorts of hot water. Occasionally the hot water becomes positively scalding.

It takes two to tango, but it takes three to triangle. Let's follow the three corners of our love triangle to the day all hell broke loose.

Bob Rutledge Jr. was born and raised in Houston, Texas. He always found schoolwork relatively easy, and from the very early grades he was considered college material. He breezed through high school and entered university as a pre-med student. While still an undergraduate Bob had a strange but pleasant experience.

In 1943, Bob met a U.S.O. singer, whose group was entertaining soldiers at Fort Des Moines. He married the girl. Four hours later she left town with her group. I can find no record of what the young couple did during their short four-hour marriage, and maybe it is just as well. Bob and his blushing bride were divorced two years later without ever seeing each other again.

Bob went on to graduate as a full fledged medical doctor. He then joined the Navy and served 15 months at a Navy hospital in Boston. It was during his stint in the Navy that he met Sydney. I should explain — Sydney was a girl, and quite a girl at that. She had long blonde hair, and a very well proportioned figure spread over a height of six feet. At 23, Syd was a looker.

In 1946, Bob and Syd were married. A short time later Bob entered Children's Hospital in St. Louis to specialize in pediatrics, drawing down a cool $25 per week.

Syd, who was the daughter of a physician, was well aware of the long training period required to become a specialist. To pass the time and supplement their income, she obtained a job in Emerson Co. as a mathematician. Working directly across from her desk was the third member of our triangle, Byron Hattman. Byron glanced up from his drafting table and took in all six feet of the voluptuous Syd.

Byron was a graduate engineer, having received his diploma from the University of Pittsburgh. After a spell in the Marines, he had joined Emerson in St. Louis as an airplane instrument designer. Now 29 years old, Byron was a bachelor without a care in the world. He drove a big car, owned a sailboat, and loved to carry a substantial wad in his pocket.

Day after day Byron looked at the statuesque doctor's wife. In July the Emerson Co. had an outing, a cruise on the Mississippi River. As usual Dr. Rutledge was working at the hospital. Syd went on the cruise with a group of girls from work. For the first time, Hattman struck up a conversation. Soon the pair were enthusiastically discussing sailing. One thing led to another. Mattman invited Syd and some other girls to go sailing the following Saturday. Everyone accepted the invitation.

That weekend the girls had a great time on the boat. The next Saturday was another story. This time Hattman invited Syd to join him alone. Syd accepted and even told her husband of her innocent date. He approved.

The sailing session lasted until 6 p.m. During the trip Hattman impetuously told Syd that he didn't think it could be much fun being the neglected wife of a doctor. That afternoon Hattman made a date with Syd to have dinner. When Syd went home to change, she neglected to tell her husband about the dinner engagement.

We will never know for certain what took place that evening. It all depends on whom you choose to believe. Sydney was to forever state that she was viciously raped. Hattman always claimed she gave of herself willingly. Whatever happened that night, Syd did not mention a word of the evening's activities to her husband.

Poor Dr. Rutledge found out about his wife's having intercourse with another man in a most disturbing way. He overheard Hattman bragging about his conquest of Syd at another Emerson party — this time a day of golf at the Norwood Hills Country Club. Dr. Rutledge had the day off and decided to join his wife at the company function. Hattman didn't notice him changing his shoes when he was telling a group of employees of his romp in the hay with Syd.

This startling bit of information stuck in the doctor's craw for several weeks. Then he did something about it. He called Hattman on the phone, informing him that he knew what had happened. He issued a warning to Hattman to stay away from his wife. In passing, he also mentioned that it was quite possible Syd was pregnant. The doctor suggested that Hattman cough up $250 for the necessary abortion. Hattman replied tersely that he didn't much care if Syd was pregnant or not. He suggested that the doctor contact his lawyer for anything further. Some weeks later Hattman was advised that Syd wasn't pregnant after all. Nature had merely played one of her cruel little jokes.

Meanwhile Dr. Rutledge and his wife had a tete-a-tete concerning Hattman. It was then that Syd told him that Hattman had forced himelf upon her. He decided to stick by his wife.

During the month of October and the remainder of that fall, the Emerson Co. subcontracted a large job to Collins Radio Co. in Cedar Rapids. Hattman was directly involved in this job and had to split his time between St. Louis and Cedar Rapids. Each Monday he would travel the 300 miles to Cedar Rapids, and check into the Roosevelt Hotel, where he stayed for two or three days.

On Dec. 15, 1948 he never made the return trip. That morning a chambermaid, with the apt name of Carrie Chambers, found Byron Hattman dead on the floor of Room 729. Beside his head was a large bloodstain and an empty wallet. The room showed signs of a vicious struggle. Bloodstains covered all four walls. The victim had bruises about his face, broken ribs, and assorted cuts about the head. Later the coroner was to state that Hattman had been stabbed repeatedly in the chest. One of the thrusts had punctured his heart, causing death.

Hotel guest Eugene Pastock stated that he had heard a fight at about 5:45 p.m. the previous evening. He assumed it was a domestic squabble and never gave it another thought. Police, knowing nothing of the victim's private life, felt that Hattman had surprised a prowler.

Detectives called at the Collins factory where Hattman worked. Kenneth L. Ebershoff told them that Hattman had confided in him that he was having trouble with a Dr. Rutledge, because of the doctor's wife. Officials of the Emerson Co. also informed the police that Hattman didn't have an enemy in the world, except for a Dr. Rutledge, whose wife seemed to be having an affair with Hattman.

The police, now hearing the name Rutledge from two independent sources, decided to probe a little deeper into the activities of the good doctor. When they found out he had spent Monday night at the Montrose Hotel in Cedar Rapids, he became a prime suspect. Just as quickly Rutledge appeared to have an airtight alibi.

On the day of the murder, Tuesday, Dr. Rutledge had checked out of the Montrose early in the morning. The office manager of a garage, Mrs. Bee Nichols, stated that the doctor had brought his car into her garage that same morning to have a water pump repaired. He picked the car up before noon. Rutledge had been short of cash and told Mrs. Nichols he would send her the money through the mail. At 7:30 that evening Mrs. Nichols received a long distance call from Dr. Rutledge, apparently from St. Louis, confirming that he had just dropped her cheque in the mail. If this were so, he couldn't be the killer. It had been established that the murder had taken place in Cedar Rapids at 5:45 p.m. There was no way Dr. Rutledge could travel the 300 miles to St. Louis in one hour and forty five minutes.

Cedar Rapids detectives weren't taken in by the flimsy alibi. They filled the tank of their car with gas and took off for St. Louis. When the tank neared empty, about one hour and 45 minutes out of Cedar Rapids, they began canvassing gas stations. Sure enough, the police found the station where the doctor had not only purchased gas, but had made the long distance call to Mrs. Nichols, leading her to believe that he was calling from St. Louis.

When detectives went to pick up Dr. Rutledge, the ever faithful Sydney asked them to wait. The doctor was in the bathroom. During those few minutes Rutledge administered poison to himself and collapsed on the way to the police station. He survived, but while being washed in the hospital it was revealed that he had used large quantities of pancake makeup to hide the many superficial scratches he had obtained during his fierce struggle with Hattman.

The Rutledge murder trial was a sensation. The doctor and his wife held hands throughout the trial. Long cues formed each morning to catch the juicy details of the seduction of the doctor's wife. Much was made of the fact that Sydney could have left her job at Emerson at any time to escape Hattman's advances. She left the day his body was found in the hotel room.

Dr. Rutledge was found guilty and received a sentence of 70 years in prison. After serving only a year, he appealed and was released on $40,000 bail pending the results of his appeal. The Rutledges moved to Houston, Texas, where the doctor opened a clinic for the treatment of children.

On April 4, 1951, an Iowa court ruled that the doctor had received a fair trial. The next day Dr. Rutledge bought a long plastic hose. He drove his car to an isolated road about 15 miles from Houston where he attached the hose to his exhaust pipe and placed the other end inside the car. He then closed all the windows and turned on the gas. A drilling contractor found his body at 5:30 that evening.

In 1952, a court decision was made as to who would receive the proceeds of Dr. Rutledge's $10,000 insurance policy. While in the Navy he had named his first wife of four hours as the beneficiary, and had neglected to change it after his marriage to Sydney. A judge decided to divide the $10,000. Ironically, Rutledge's wife of four hours received the bulk of the money.

THIEVING MEDIC

Dr. Xavier Richier thought every day should be Christmas. He liked nothing better than to give presents, and it didn't bother the kindly doctor one little bit that the person he just loved to give presents to most was himself. The doctor didn't go for run of the mill department store gifts. He specialized in antiques, valuable paintings and rare objets d'art.

Dr. Richier was employed as medical officer for a mining company in Lievin, France, about 125 miles north of Paris. The balding, middle aged man of medicine did not have an impressive appearance. Staring out at the world from behind steel rimmed glasses, he had a hang dog look which belied the fact that he was a high class thief.

From 1960 to 1965, Dr. Richier had organized a highly skilled team of thieves, each member a specialist in the fine art of swiping fine art. The doctor himself acted as the brains of the outfit. One room in his unimpressive home at No. 6 Rue Thiers was devoted to research. Here the doctor spent hours each night poring over art journals and antique reference books. A row of filing cabinets contained information outlining the location and accessibility of most of the art treasures of France. The doctor knew what to steal.

Gang member Claude Mabilotte was an expert at gaining entrance to any building housing anything of value. His assistant, Andre Here, while still an apprentice, was learning his trade so well there were those who thought that, in a few short years, he would be as adept as the master at entering and stealing. Jean Richier, the doctor's brother, was a bona fide antique dealer turned thief. The fifth member of the gang, Marcel Bihn, was a professional restorer. Marcel could alter or modify a conspicuous item so that it could be peddled to a legitimate dealer.

The well organized gang had two unusual features. Dr. Richier booked orders for everything the gang stole long before they stole it. Certain rare and irreplaceable items were not sold. They were kept in a section of Dr. Richier's home for his own enjoyment and pleasure. This, of course, was a real stumbling block to the police. The most valuable treasures, normally the easiest to trace, never surfaced, for the simple reason that they never moved down the distribution pipeline. When he wasn't busy ministering to the miners' medical needs, the doctor liked to sit among his treasures and drool.

So conspicuous and well known were some of the stolen objects that the police correctly deduced that the brains of the gang must be an art expert who was keeping the most outstanding pieces for his own enjoyment. The 1510 Holy Martyr Tapestry, once a proud possession of the Le Mans Cathedral, now provided enjoyment for one person only — Dr. Xavier Richier. Beside it in the doctor's home stood the 16th century polychrome Virgin, liberated by the gang from the Church of St. Eloi at Thiennes.

The gang passed up many inferior, though still valuable, pieces. Sometimes their intimate knowledge of antiques amazed the art world as well as the police. Once in the dead of night, they entered the famous Chateau of Bussy-Rabutin and stole four antique chairs out of a set of 24. Next morning, after the theft was discovered, investigation revealed that the four missing chairs were the work of master craftsman Jean-Baptiste Boulard. The other 20 were reproductions. The gang knew that Boulard's signature was under the seat of the four genuine articles.

Nothing was too strange and cumbersome as long as it was beautiful and would bring the doctor enjoyment.

In 1963, one of the gang's best years, they stole the altarpiece of St. Denis Cathedral. Carved from solid silver during the middle ages, and considered one of the national treasures of France, the altarpiece had survived everything from the French Revolution to two World Wars. Despite its cumbersome measurements, 30 feet long and almost five feet deep, it didn't escape the master's touch.

One night, just as the caretaker of St. Denis was leaving, a stranger walked up the cathedral steps and explained that he had travelled hundreds of miles to see the famous altarpiece. The caretaker, anxious to get home to his hot supper, gave the key to the stranger, so that he could lock up after he had finished with his sightseeing. Next morning the key was returned to the caretaker. The altarpiece was long gone.

In five years the gang had swiped nearly $10 million worth of treasure. The police were baffled at the selectivity of the gang and the fact that some of the pieces never surfaced. The French police tried to ascertain the type of person who could be the brains behind the well organized gang. They came surprisingly close to the truth. The police correctly figured that the man was unmarried, living alone, and was probably a teacher or other professional who didn't worry much about his personal appearance.

The real threat to the gang's security came from within. Marcel, Andre, and Claude tired of taking orders from the doctor and decided to pull off an independent raid. They picked the Chateau de Neuville, located about 50 miles from Paris. At the time one wing of the chateau was being used to store antique furniture.

As a unit the gang was infallible. Without the doctor's brains they were common thieves. The raid, inadequately planned and poorly executed, was a disaster. They were caught red handed inside the chateau.

Although none of the three squealed on Dr. Richier, the police knew they had missed landing the big fish. They released Claude Mabilotte on condition that he attempt to recover some of the missing items. The ruse worked. He immediately contacted Dr. Richier by phone. It was tapped.

When the police finally picked up the doctor and raided his home in Lievin they were amazed. They had uncovered what amounted to a private museum.

When asked if he stole for profit, Dr. Richier became extremely agitated. "Never!" the rumpled little man roared. He said he stole because he took better care of the treasures than those in whose care they were entrusted.

All five members of the gang were charged with 76 different counts of theft. The gang didn't fare too badly. Marcel Bihn received seven years imprisonment, Claude Mabilotte six, Andre Here and Jean Richier, five each.

The man who had planned it all, Dr. Xavier Richier, didn't spend one day in jail. He received a five-year suspended sentence.

DR. BOUGRAT WAS A LOVER

When it comes to murders based on affairs of the heart, it seems there is no one quite like the French. Frenchmen display a certain style and elan toward their amours which is difficult to duplicate.

Take Dr. Pierre Bougrat as a classic example. At 32, Doc had a terrific practice in Aix, France, a gorgeous wife and a big home. To the casual observer it appeared that the young doctor had the world by the tail, but as you and I know, outward appearances are sometimes deceiving. In the doctor's case his wife left a lot to be desired in the love making department. Truth is she simply did not want to perform frequently enough to suit her husband.

Pierre looked elsewhere for his kicks. He discovered that in Marseilles, only about 30 kilometers from Aix, there was an abundance of houses which were not homes. The doctor found out that he could change out of his respectable clothing into the sloppy garb of the waterfront district, and have a barrel of fun every night.

Things went along famously for about a year, or until the frigid wife, suspecting that all was not kosher, put a private eye on Pierre. The detective reported back to Mrs. B. that her husband had a reputation as a real stud among the brothels of Marseilles. Now it so happened that Mrs. B. had an elderly father who thought the sun rose and set on his son-in-law.

In order to save her father from the disgrace of Pierre's philandering, Mrs. B. struck a bargain with her husband. They would continue to live under the same roof, but in the evening they would have separate bedrooms. Pierre never was so happy. That night he whistled while he, shall we say, worked down at the waterfront.

Another year went by. Then Mrs. B.'s father died and she no longer had any reason to stay under the same roof with Pierre. She pulled out bag and baggage, and presumably found another roof under which to stay. The doctor found himself the only occupant of his large home in Aix.

At this time in his career, the doctor met a prostitute named Andrea Audibert. It is not quite clear just what made Andrea different from all the other ladies of the night. Whatever, Andrea said try it, you'll like it; and for once in his life Pierre fell in love. He spent every evening with Andrea, partaking of her many charms. There was just one catch. Andrea was owned by a rough, tough, pimp named Marius. The doctor wanted Andrea to stop sharing her favors with utter strangers. He also found that studding around all night and doctoring all day was just too taxing on his constitution. He wanted to install Andrea as his housekeeper in his home in Aix. He decided to buy his true love's freedom from her pimp. The doctor was a bit shocked at the price of the merchandise. Marius wanted 9,000 francs, and Pierre had no choice; he promised Marius he would raise the money.

As luck would have it, one of the doctor's patients back in Aix was the paymaster of a local steel mill. Macques Rumebe visited the doctor each week for an injection. Over the years Rumebe and the doctor became familiar with each other's routine. It was an easy matter for the doctor to reschedule Rumebe's appointment to a day when the paymaster picked up the payroll from the bank and carried it to the mill. The doctor's office was situated between the bank and the mill. It was quite natural for Rumebe to pick up the payroll and drop into the doctor's office for his injection.

With a jaunty walk and a twinkle in his eye Rumebe entered Dr. Bougrat's office for his injection. He received a shot of arsenobenzol and was deader than a mackerel in a matter of minutes.

Rather unimaginatively, the doctor nailed Rumebe upright in a closet and sealed the door. Later he had some wallpaper hangers come in and paper over the hole thing.

Speedy Pierre scampered down to Marseilles, paid Marius 9,000 francs and returned to Aix with his new housekeeper, Andrea. In the meantime, Rumebe had been missed in a matter of hours. There were two schools of thought. He had either met with foul play, or had absconded with his company's payroll. Dr. Bougrat made sure which way the wind blew. He wrote to Rumebe's employer. In disguised handwriting he informed them that Rumebe had been leading a double life and had been carrying on a love affair with a prostitute in Marseilles.

In the routine investigation which followed, the police called on Dr. Bougrat to question him about his patient, Rumebe. The detective was shown into the house by Andrea. The officer couldn't get the nagging feeling out of his head that he had seen Andrea before. When he returned to the police station he spent several hours going through pictures of girls suspected of a variety of crimes. Sure enough, there she was, the Marseilles prostitute, Andrea Audibert.

With his curiosity now aroused, the detective started to track down the route by which a Marseilles prostitute became a doctor's housekeeper in Aix. It wasn't difficult to uncover that the doctor had paid the pimp Marius 9,000 francs on the day Rumebe disappeared. Had the doctor killed the paymaster in order to obtain the money to purchase Andrea's freedom? The detective was sure he was on the right track. Where could the doctor have disposed of the body so quickly before Rumebe was missed? The officer deduced that the body must be somewhere on the doctor's premises. He only had to find evidence of recent renovations and he was sure he would find the body. On his next visit to the doctor's house he was proved correct in every detail.

Dr. Bougrat was arrested and tried for murder. The cagey doctor admitted everything except murder. He claimed he had inadvertently given an overdose to his patient and that the entire affair had been a horrible accident. After he discovered his mistake he had panicked and nailed poor Rumebe up in the closet.

The intriguing story saved Pierre's neck from falling victim to Dr. Guillotine's diabolical machine. He was sentenced to life imprisonment on Devil's Island.

Pierre was sent to Devil's Island in 1929. He was soon recognized by both inmates and officials of the famous penal colony as an extremely capable physician. He became a trustee, and after serving almost six years, he was allowed a month's freedom in the town of St. Laurent du Maroni on the French Guinea mainland. Although he was still under a loose guard the situation was not escape proof.

The first thing Pierre did was to find a woman, and after six years who can blame him. Her name was Annette du Bois, and she turned out to be a real peach. After teaming up with Annette the doctor made up his mind never to return to Devil's Island. To make matters even better Annette had some loot of her own stashed away and she was willing to go anywhere with Pierre.

Annette and Pierre slipped aboard a Dutch freighter heading for Venezuela. The cagey medic had noted that Venezuela didn't have an extradition treaty with France. Sly fox that he was, he pulled it off. Once in Venezuela he found out that he could get a license to practise medicine in Caracas.

Believe it or not, Pierre married Annette, and set up housekeeping in Caracas. In time he built up a lucrative medical practice and became a respected doctor once again. For nine years Dr. Bougrat practised medicine by day and faithfully returned to his wife's side by night.

In 1944, Dr. Bougrat, a man who had crammed a lot of living into his 53 years, died of a fever epidemic which he was helping to fight.

THE LONG ARM
OF THE LAW

In England the years between 1875 and 1910 were a veritable Golden Age of murder. There were so many people stabbing, strangling and cutting up their fellow men that one hardly knows where to begin. But most of these gentlemen, while they are certainly noteworthy, left their victims where they fell. They didn't experience that blood-chilling confrontation with what has until recently been a fellow human being, and the utterly bothersome task of disposing of the body. So from this era of mass murderers we have plucked a mild, unassuming little man named Dr. Hawley Harvey Crippen . . .

Hawley was born in Clearwater, Michigan, in 1863, and from the very beginning of his academic career he was considered to be a good student. He was singleminded in his desire to become a doctor, and to this end he studied medicine in Cleveland and New York. After he qualified, he did post-graduate work, becoming an eye and ear specialist. Then he completed his education with further studies in London, England, before returning to the United States, where, between 1885 and 1893, he moved frequently, practising in Detroit, Salt Lake City, New York, St. Louis, Toronto, and Philadelphia.

In 1887, the doctor married one Charlotte Bell, who died, presumably of natural causes, in 1890. After his wife's death, Crippen returned to New York, where he again set up his practice. Dr. Crippen was now a mature 31-years-old. He was five feet, seven inches tall, with a decidedly receding hairline, protruding eyes that stared out from behind thick-lensed spectacles, and a small, well-kept moustache. While not altogether a ladies' man, Crippen was neat in appearance and a pleasant, intelligent conversationalist. When he was practising in New York he met a 17-year-old medical secretary called Kunigunde Mackamotzki, who had had the good sense to change her name to Cora Turner. The doctor took one look at Cora's substantial bust, slim waist and well-turned ankle and was smitten. The love-struck pair were married almost immediately.

By 1899, the Crippens were living in Philadelphia, and it was here that Cora let the mild Hawley in on a little secret — she wanted to be an opera star. Now, Crippen was no student of voice, but he had heard his wife sing and knew she had a pleasant soprano warble. On occasion, at parties, he would become rather proud when she rendered a tune or two, but an operatic career — that was something else. The little doctor looked quizzically at his wife. Yes, she said, she seriously wanted to study music. Hawley suggested that they relax in the bedroom and continue the discussion about singing another day. No, said Cora, there would be no sex in the Crippen household until she was promised that he would finance her singing lessons. She received a firm promise that very night.

Soon Crippen found that every cent he made was going for singing lessons for his wife. Cora was extremely serious when it came to her career, even to the point of taking the professional name of Belle Elmore. A few years passed, and Cora's singing lessons had practically bankrupted the distraught Crippen. Besides the financial difficulties her singing had brought him, deep down in his heart he didn't think she was all that good.

By 1900, the couple had been man and wife for eleven years. Like all of us, they had grown older; the doctor was now a worry-racked 42, and his once receding hairline was in full flight, while Cora, at 28, had begun to put on weight and was becoming slovenly in her appearance. More than that, as the months went by, she started to find fault with Hawley. Little by little she had become an overweight nag; and to make matters worse, she had failed to make a name for herself in the singing world. As she became more frustrated with her career, she more and more frequently denied Crippen that which every husband figures is his right. At the Crippen residence, conjugal bliss had given way to continual bickering.

Then the doctor decided to do something about his dilemma. He was offered, and accepted, the position of manager at Munyon's Patent Remedies in London, England. He figured the move would keep him one step ahead of his creditors, as well as providing him and Cora with a welcome change which might improve the climate of their marriage. Cora had other ideas; she felt that at last she would get an opportunity to appear on the stage of the British Music Hall.

The Crippens arrived in London and took furnished rooms in Bloomsbury. Even before they were comfortably settled, Cora started making the rounds of booking agents, trying to get a high-class singing position. She soon lowered her sights, and was satisfied to accept any singing job she could get. But she had one major drawback. While she made placid Hawley buy her expensive clothing to enhance her appearance when auditioning, she simply couldn't sing. She managed to obtain a few engagements in provincial halls, reaching the pinnacle of her career when she appeared on the same bill as George Formby, Sr., at the Dudley New Empire. A short time after this appearance, she was booed off the stage during another performance. Cora was finding out that the road to fame and fortune was a rocky one.

In 1905, the couple moved from Bloomsbury to 39 Hilldrop Crescent in the Holloway district. It was around this time that 22-year-old Ethel Le Neve became Dr. Crippen's private secretary. The doctor, now in his forties, fell hard for the winsome Ethel, and she for her part was not averse to the positive vibes coming her way from the little doctor. By 1907, Ethel and Hawley were lovers, and not only in the physical sense, for it is a fact that they sincerely loved and cared for each other. Crippen was charmed by the passive, unassuming Ethel, who gave so willingly of herself, in sharp contrast to the domineering, aggressive Cora. And that closed bedroom door in the Crippen residence had to be an additional factor.

Further aggravating an already explosive situation, Cora started to invite her theatrical acquaintances over to Hilldrop Crescent. Cora and her friends hardly missed a day whooping it up, while the mild-mannered doctor would shrug and pay the bills. One day after the gang had left the house, Hawley meekly mentioned to Cora that maybe she should cut down on the expensive food and drink she was serving her friends. Crippen received a blast, that could be heard as far away as Stonehenge on a clear day, for even suggesting such a thing. On occasion Cora would do more than party; some evenings she stayed out until the early morning hours, and Crippen knew full well she was having affairs with her broken-down Thespian buddies. On the other hand, Cora was aware that her meek husband was playing around, and if his infidelity managed to keep him out of her hair, so much the better. And so life went on at Hilldrop Crescent, both husband and wife leading separate lives, each tolerating the other's indiscretions.

On Jan. 17, 1910, Dr. Crippen strolled in to Lewis and Burrowes, Chemists, on Oxford Street. He purchased five grains of hyoscin hydrobromide, which, in small doses, is used as a sedative. The clerk had Crippen sign the poisons register — taken in large doses hyoscin hydrobromide is a deadly poison — and remembered the transaction because he could not recall ever having sold such a large amount of the drug before. It can be administered in tea or coffee, and is tasteless. Its effects in massive doses are loss of consciousness, paralysis, and death in a matter of hours.

Two weeks later, on the night of January 31, Cora and Hawley had another couple over for an intimate little dinner party followed by a game of cards. Clara and Paul Martinetti were retired entertainers, who were really friends of Cora's. They had a pleasant enough evening, and left at about one thirty in the morning. The Martinettis were the last people to see Cora alive.

The first sign that all was not normal at the Crippen household came when an organization Cora belonged to — the Music Hall Ladies' Guild — received a letter of resignation advising them that she had to rush to America to take care of a seriously ill relative. The letter was signed by Crippen using his wife's professional name, Belle Elmore, per H.H.C. By word of mouth the news spread that Cora was away in America. Some of her close friends remarked that it was strange that she didn't call someone with an explanation. Still, serious illnesses do strike suddenly and the entertainment set seemed satisfied for the time being.

Then Dr. Crippen commenced to make moves which were not designed to enhance our opinion of his intelligence. He pawned some of Cora's jewelry for £200. On Feb. 12, Ethel Le Neve moved into the house on Hilldrop Crescent, causing tongues to wag. As if that wasn't enough to raise an eyebrow or two, Hawley showed up at a Music Hall Ladies' Ball with Ethel. Only a blind man could have failed to notice that the brooch Ethel was sporting over her left breast was the property of Cora Crippen. Cora's friends didn't like the look of things, and started to ask the doctor embarrassing questions. They simply couldn't get over the idea of Cora leaving without so much as a goodbye. Crippen told the ladies that a relative of his who lived in San Francisco was seriously ill. He had been told that this relative had mentioned him in his will, and as the sum involved was substantial, Cora and he thought that one of them should go to California to protect their interests. He couldn't go due to his workload, so Cora had made the trip. That story pacified the ladies for a few more weeks.

Then the Music Hall Ladies' Guild received a telegram from Dr. Crippen advising them that dear Cora herself was seriously ill in California. An official of the Guild, a Miss Hawthorne, visited Hilldrop Crescent, and found the mild little doctor half crazy with worry. She left the house with tears in her eyes feeling guilty that suspicious thoughts about Crippen should ever have entered her mind.

A few days later Miss Hawthorne received another telegram from Crippen, this time advising her that the worst had happened — Cora had passed away from pneumonia. The ladies of the Guild inquired as to where the funeral would be held; they wanted to send flowers. Dr. Crippen told them that the body was to be cremated and the ashes would be sent back to London. He then inserted a memorial notice in *The Era*, a theatrical newspaper. Immediately after he placed the notice, he left for a short trip to Dieppe, France. When Cora's friends dropped around to his office, they noticed that Ethel wasn't at her desk. The ladies talked about Ethel's absence for a moment or two, but the consensus of opinion was that it was most natural for Crippen to have given his secretary some time off while he was away.

Ethel, however, had accompanied her lover to France, and was continually at his side, consoling and comforting him. She couldn't help but notice that the doctor carried a large leather hatbox with him when he boarded the boat for the English Channel crossing. When she inquired about the box while in Dieppe, the doctor replied that he had misplaced it during the crossing, and it never entered her mind again.

When the pair returned to London, Crippen found that the suspicions concerning his wife's disappearance had grown. It seems that Mr. Nash, a friend of Cora's, had just returned to London from New York. He had been there while Cora had supposedly passed through the city on her way to California. Nash knew Cora well, and knew how she felt about their mutual friends in New York. He found it incredible that she had never once contacted them. When he told Miss Hawthorne of his suspicions, they decided to contact Scotland Yard.

It was over four months since Cora had last been seen when Chief Inspector Walter Dew and Sergeant Arthur Miller knocked on the door of 39 Hilldrop Crescent. Dr. Crippen amicably invited the officers in for a cup of tea. In a somewhat hesitant manner Inspector Dew broached the reason for their visit. It seems some friends had become suspicious when they noticed Miss Le Neve wearing a piece of jewelry belonging to his wife. Dr. Crippen cleared his throat — there was something he had to explain to the officers — you see, his wife wasn't dead at all; she had run off with a music hall performer named Bruce Miller. She had been "carrying on" with him for some time, and had finally picked up and left without a word to any of her friends. He had been too ashamed and embarrassed to tell anyone the truth, so he had made up the story of his wife's death. In reality, he thought the two lovers had headed for Chicago.

"Now, doctor, about Miss Le Neve and the jewelry?" Crippen didn't bat an eyelash. He explained that his wife had left in such a hurry she had left her jewelry behind. With a knowing wink Crippen admitted that he had taken up with Ethel Le Neve after his wife ran away, and he was now her lover.

The Inspector looked at the Sergeant and the Sergeant looked at the Inspector. The whole story had a ring of truth to it. The two men conducted a cursory examination of the entire premises and found nothing suspicious. They advised Crippen to place an advertisement in a Chicago paper to assist in finding his wife and still the gossip once and for all. Crippen assured them that he would take their advice. The policemen apologized to Dr. Crippen for the disturbance and returned to the station satisfied that no crime had been committed.

On July 11, 1910, three days after the police visit to Crippen's house, Miss Hawthorne called Inspector Dew for a progress report on the Crippen affair. Dew told Miss Hawthorne that Cora had run away with another man, and that the whole matter was not of concern to the police. Miss Hawthorne informed Drew that something was wrong. Crippen and Le Neve had disappeared. Dew was forced to look into the case again. This time he found out that shortly after his meeting with Crippen on the previous Saturday, July 8, the doctor had written notes to his business associates resigning his position, cleaning out his office, and together with Ethel Le Neve had dropped from sight.

The doctor, who had appeared cool as a cucumber from the first day his wife was noticed to be missing, had finally panicked. Dew questioned Crippen's fellow employees and found a young man who had performed an unusual errand for him. The doctor had asked his colleague to purchase an entire outfit of clothing to fit a boy of sixteen. The young man gave a detailed description of the articles he had purchased for Crippen — brown tweed suit, boots, a hat and an overcoat. After some reflection, Dew came to the conclusion that the clothing had been purchased to disguise Ethel Le Neve in her flight with Crippen. On Tuesday, July 12, Scotland Yard decided to make a thorough search of 39 Hilldrop Crescent. For three days the police peered into and poked at the house while the garden was being dug up. On the third day some loose bricks were discovered under the coal bin in the cellar. The remainder of the floor had mortar between the bricks. The loose bricks were removed, and under a few inches of clay, the police found the remains of Mrs. Crippen — really just "a mass of flesh" wrapped in a pyjama jacket. The body had been dissected and the head was missing.

Inspector Dew checked back on Crippen's actions and found the chemist where he had purchased the hyoscin hydrobromide. Chemical analysis of Cora's remains confirmed that she had met her death as the result of the administration of this drug. On July 16 a warrant was issued for the arrest of Crippen and Le Neve for murder and mutilation. The story was a sensation, and became even more newsworthy because no one seemed to know where to look for the two fugitives. In England, during the time Crippen and Le Neve were at large, little else was discussed. Everyone had a theory about the missing pair, and they were constantly being spotted throughout England and the continent by both the police and the public.

In reality, Dew was on the right track. Crippen had dressed his lover as a boy, and the two of them had left the country, heading for Rotterdam, Holland. The doctor used the alias of John Philo Robinson, and Ethel took on the identity of his son George. They made their way to Antwerp, Belgium, where on July 20 they booked passage for Quebec City, Canada, on the SS *Montrose.*

It is quite possible that the fugitives would have made good their escape had it not been for the captain of the *Montrose.* Almost from the first hour the pair boarded his ship, the captain noticed the unnatural actions of the Robinsons. He watched the way they held hands, which seemed decidedly odd for a father and son. The second day out of Antwerp he noticed how feminine young Robinson's movements were when he caught a tennis ball on deck. By July 22, the captain was sure that he had Crippen and Le Neve on his ship. Captain Kendall radioed his suspicions to the managing director of the Canadian Pacific Shipping Co. in Liverpool, who passed the message along to Scotland Yard. Several messages went back and forth, and Scotland Yard became convinced that they had located the wanted pair. On July 23, Inspector Dew boarded the *Laurentic,* a much faster ship than the *Montrose,* at Liverpool. It was calculated that Dew would overtake his quarry just before the *Montrose* docked in Canada. The case now took on the aspect of a race. Each day the press carried the relative positions of both ships, vividly illustrating the relentless pursuit of the *Montrose* by the *Laurentic.* The distance between the two ships diminished steadily as the *Montrose* approached Canada.

It is well to remember that the passing of radio messages was relatively new to the public. Guglielmo Marconi had established wireless communication across the Atlantic in 1901. This added feature of the chase captured the imagination, not only of England, but of the entire world. At the time of Crippen's flight for freedom, only about one hundred ships were equipped with radios. Within six months over six hundred ships were so equipped and it is believed the Crippen case was instrumental in making radios a legal requirement for ocean-going vessels.

While all this was going on, Crippen and Le Neve thought they had succeeded in evading the authorities, and didn't even know that Cora's body had been discovered. Finally, on July 31 the *Laurentic* caught up with the *Montrose* off Father Point, Quebec. Dew boarded the ship and arranged with Captain Kendall to meet Crippen in the Captain's quarters.

"Good morning, Dr. Crippen, I am Chief Inspector Dew."

"Good morning, Mr. Dew," replied Crippen.

"You will be arrested for the murder and mutilation of your wife, Cora Crippen," stated Dew.

"I am not sorry, the anxiety has been too much."

The dramatic confrontation between detective and murderer was over. Extradition proceedings were dispensed with speedily, and the couple were returned to England to stand trial. Crippen's trial took place in October, 1910, and took four days to complete. Public interest in the Crippen trial was greater than in any other heard in London's famous Old Bailey. Huge crowds spilled out onto the street. People stood waiting for hours to catch a glimpse of the accused. The proceedings had all the right ingredients — a love triangle, promiscuous relations, poison, a mutilated body, a missing head, drama on the high seas, a beautiful young girl, and a man of medicine gone wrong.

When it was all over Dr. Crippen was found guilty of the murder of his wife. He was executed on the gallows at Pentonville on Nov. 23, 1910. His last request was that a photograph of Ethel be buried with him, and this request was granted and carried out. Crippen went to his death proclaiming Ethel's innocence.

Two weeks after Crippen's trial, Ethel Le Neve stood trial as an accessory after the fact at the Old Bailey. The evidence against her was flimsy, and it is doubtful if she ever realized that she was doing anything more than running away with her lover. Ethel steadfastly professed that she did not even know of Mrs. Crippen's death. She was acquitted, and left for Canada on the day Dr. Crippen was executed.

After five years she returned to England using an assumed name, Ethel Nelson. She married a clerk called Stanley Smith, and lived a quiet life in Croydon, South London. Only her husband and one other close friend ever knew her real identity. In 1967, 57 years after the Crippen-Le Neve trials, a gentle, grey-haired grandmother, lying close to death in Dulwich hospital, made a last request, that a locket containing a picture of Dr. Hawley Crippen be placed in her casket. So Ethel Le Neve passed from this earth.

Upstairs, Downstairs

– Part 5–

NASTY LADIES

LOUISE WASN'T A RESPECTABLE TENANT

Ladies with a criminal bent have always fascinated me. Down through the checkered history of the not so manly art of mayhem there have been many members of the distaff side who have stood out, even among murderers.

Louise Peete, at 37, give or take a year, was one of these exceptional women. She was smart, cunning, and above all, had a winning, pleasing personality. In May, 1920, she sauntered up to 675 South Catalina St. in the booming city of Los Angeles, Calif.

The occupant of the imposing English Tudor-style home was Jacob Denton, a wealthy mining man of 46. If Jacob could only have guessed at the nastiness Louise had in mind, he would most certainly have slammed the door shut. But such was not to be. Jacob was planning to take an extended business trip and wanted to lease his home.

Mr. Denton had twice been to the altar. Each time the union didn't last. His first marriage provided a daughter Frances and a divorce. His daughter lived with her mother in Arizona. Jacob's second wife had died of natural causes.

Jacob thought it a good idea to advertise his home for rent, and it was old silver-tongued Louise who answered the ad. Louise and Jacob struck a deal immediately, and Louise moved in the next day. Jacob was to retain his own room until he had to leave on his trip, in approximately one week's time.

On May 30, 1920, some of Jacob's friends threw a going away beach party for him. Louise was invited, and everyone had a great time. Jacob's friends were never to see him again.

On June 2, business acquaintances who had appointments with Jacob were somewhat miffed when he failed to show up. They called him at home. All the calls were fielded by Louise. A car salesman inquired why Mr. Denton never picked up his new car. Louise told him that Jacob had to rush away to take care of an important business matter. When pressed as to his location, she told her fantastic story for the first time.

In essence, she informed the car salesman that Mr. Denton had incurred a wound in his arm which had become infected. It necessitated his going away in order to conceal just how the wound was inflicted. She said the whole thing was a great embarrassment to Jacob. Later she called the salesman and told him that Mr. Denton had to have his arm amputated and would be staying in San Francisco for some time. She had received instructions to take delivery of the new car and turn in Mr. Denton's old one. Upon receipt of a cheque for the balance owing on the new car, the vehicle was turned over to Louise.

Our busy little lady scampered down to the Farmers' and Merchants' Bank. She told the bankers that because of Jacob's recent amputation she had to help him sign his name with his left hand. His signature would probably be quite different. The bankers were very understanding, and assured the obviously concerned Louise that they would honor all cheques with the altered signature. Mr. Denton certainly was a lucky man to have such a concerned friend.

Weeks went by and slowly Louise Peete acquired the assets of Jacob Denton. She was even cunning enough to see that Denton's daughter got her allowance cheques each month. Still a man doesn't drop completely out of sight, even if he is greatly affected by the loss of an arm. Friends began to enquire, and Louise continued to be a convincing liar.

In the middle of August, Denton's family retained a lawyer to look into his affairs with special emphasis on his present address. When Louise heard of the family's action, she rented the house on Catalina St. to a Mr. and Mrs. Thomas T. Miller. Then she went away for a short vacation in Denver.

While she was vacationing a group of Denton's friends visited his home. It was September when the self-appointed delegation explained to the Millers that their good friend Jacob Denton had disappeared. Would they mind if the house was searched? The Millers didn't mind at all.

Like homing pigeons, the group headed for the cellar first. Right off they noticed an alcove which had been boarded up. Once the boards were removed, they groped into a pile of earth. The first thing which came to light was a human foot. Then they uncovered the rest of Jacob Denton's body. He had been shot in the neck by a .32

calibre bullet. Upstairs, hidden in a closet, the police found the murder weapon.

Louise was located in Denver and charged with murder. She continued to lie, despite the overwhelming amount of evidence against her. She was found guilty, received a sentence of life imprisonment, and was shipped off to San Quentin.

Our story should end now with prison bars slamming closed behind Louise Peete, but it doesn't.

Every few years or so Louise would apply for parole, but was always turned down. She had two faithful friends, Mr. and Mrs. Arthur Logan, who had always believed in her innocence. They stood by her during her trial, and now that she was in prison they wrote to her, and visited her whenever they could.

After serving more than 20 years in prison, Louise received a parole. Now in her 60s, she was still a fine cut of a woman. Despite turning a bit gray, she retained her outstanding complexion, and looked 10 years younger than her age. The Logans, who were somewhat older than Louise, had not fared as well. Both were sickly, with Arthur, at 74, being extremely frail and quiet. The Logans hired Louise as a housekeeper and companion. It was Mrs. Logan who had to sign Louise's parole report every month.

For a while all went well at the Logan residence near Santa Monica. Only a month or so after Louise came to live with them, Mrs. Logan had Arthur committed to the Patton State Hospital as "mentally ill, dangerous, and insane." Arthur remained in the institution for 19 days before being released back into his wife's care. Louise, who had changed her name to Anna B. Lee for obvious reasons, helped Mrs. Logan to bring her husband home.

The next episode in a life just chock full of little twists and turns occurred when Mrs. Logan and Louise jointly placed a $2,000 deposit on a $50,000 home. Louise tried to borrow a quick thousand from the bank for her share. She was turned down. Mrs. Logan came up with the whole deposit. Louise borrowed a further $300 from Mrs. Logan just for fun.

Louise was not totally occupied with finance. No, siree. Affairs of the heart also played a prominent part in her life. In May, using her assumed name, she married Lee Judson. Lee was an elderly gentleman with an excellent reputation. He would have done better had he picked the first woman who passed him in the street. He couldn't have done worse.

As time went by Louise, in her cunning way, let it be known that Arthur Logan was becoming uncontrollable. Louise still was treated as a member of the Logan family, even though the bank had informed Mrs. Logan that her employee had forged her name to a $200 cheque. Mrs. Logan covered the cheque, telling the bank it was all an error.

On May 30, 1944, Louise and her husband moved into the Logan home. Arthur, who appeared calm, welcomed them with open arms. Mrs. Logan was nowhere in sight. A few days later Louise advised the authorities that Mr. Logan had become violent with Mrs. Logan. In fact, the old man had bitten his wife about the face so severely that Mrs. Logan couldn't appear to state her case in person. Based on the evidence Arthur Logan was committed to the Patton State Hospital on June 5.

Soon friends and relatives were inquiring about Mrs. Logan. Louise told them that she had been badly disfigured in the attack made on her by her husband. Her right arm had been severely injured as well. Loquacious Louise even presented a cheque at the bank which had a signature affixed to it only remotely resembling Mrs. Logan's signature. Bad arm, you know.

And so it went, month after month. Louise continued to embellish and improvise. Mrs. Logan was in another city, having plastic surgery done to her face. Little by little the Logans' assets came into Louise's possession.

On Dec. 6, Arthur Logan died in the mental institution. It was never really proven that Arthur suffered from anything more than a placid personality. He died, thinking that his wife had had him committed, when all the while Louise was the culprit. To avoid the expense of a funeral, lovable Louise had his body donated to the hospital for research purposes.

On Dec. 20, the police made their first inquiry into the disappearance of Mrs. Logan. Like the rerun of an old movie, Louise lied to cover every eventuality. Again a search was conducted. Lo and behold, buried under an avocado tree in the back yard, police uncovered the body of Mrs. Logan. She had been shot in the neck, but the wound had not been the cause of death. As she regained consciousness, she had been pistol whipped until she was dead.

Louise was arrested and charged with murder. Lee Judson was also arrested, but was immediately exonerated. He too had been completely taken in by Louise. He knew her only as Anna B. Lee, and had no idea he was living with a murderer. The day after his release he hurled himself from the 13th floor of an office building and plunged to his death.

At her trial Louise took the witness stand in her own defence. She claimed that Arthur Logan had killed his wife. When she found herself with the body on her hands she realized her past would be revealed and she would be accused of murder. She decided to bury Mrs. Logan under the avocado tree. No one believed her.

She was found guilty of murder in the first degree, without recommendation for mercy. All appeals failed, and Louise Peete was executed.

MARTHA LOST
HER HEAD

Martha Marek was one of the nastiest ladies who ever lived.

Martha was born Martha Lowenstein in Vienna in 1904. It was her tough luck to be the offspring of extremely poor slum dwellers. While Martha came into this world without any material advantages, she was endowed with handsome features and grew up to be a stunningly beautiful young lady.

In 1923, Martha was gainfully employed in a dress shop when who should saunter in but a rich, sophisticated old codger named Moritz Fritsch. Moritz had gracefully slipped past the three score and ten mark. Nothing else would do; Martha had to move into his large home and become his ward or whatever they called it in those days. In one fell swoop Martha's life of poverty was over. She now had everything she wanted, and it was an easy matter to provide old Moritz with whatever it was he wanted.

Things went along just great for four years, until, at the age of 74, Moritz gave up the ghost. In so doing, he also gave up his house to Martha. Now I must hasten to tell you that Martha had kept a young engineer, Emil Marek, in the wings for the previous four years. He and Martha were now joined in holy matrimony. Everything would have been hunky dory, but Emil was just starting his career as an engineer and the upkeep of the large house kept the young couple broke.

They put their heads together and came up with a scheme which is unparalleled in the history of crime. First they took out an insurance policy on Emil for $30,000 against disablement due to accident.

Now, folks, are you sitting down? This may be hard to take. The ambitious couple decided to cut off Emil's leg. They set it up this way. Emil sharpened an axe until it was razor sharp. Then he went behind his home and partially cut down a tree. Emil closed his eyes, clenched his teeth, while Martha proceeded to chop off his leg. She returned to the house, Emil cried out and Martha, accompanied by her one servant, rushed to the rescue. She did a commendable job of applying tourniquets and rushing Emil to the hospital.

The insurance company did a double take. First it appeared from the condition of what was left of Emil's appendage that it had taken three blows to separate Emil from his leg. Not only that, but just how does one accidentally cut off one's leg? The insurance company denied liability, and Emil was left with one good leg and one prematurely short one.

It never rains but it pours. Emil went into business and failed. The unhappy couple had two children, and Martha was relegated to selling vegetables from a pushcart on a street-corner. Emil contracted tuberculosis and died. A short time later their youngest daughter, Ingeborg, died.

A well-to-do relative, Suzanne Lowenstein took in the unfortunate Martha. She soon became ill, and died a short time later. People just seemed to keel over when Martha was around. Thoughtful Suzanne had willed her home and small savings to her less fortunate relative. Industrious Martha then took in an eldery roomer, one Frau Kittenberger, who no sooner made out a will leaving Martha $1,000 than she developed a severe stomach disorder and died.

Martha appeared to be a one woman epidemic. Eventually someone became suspicious. Frau Kittenberger's son had a hunch that his mother had been poisoned. Being something of a tattletale he went to the police. They were interested enough to start exhuming bodies, to be precise: Emil Marek, Ingeborg Marek, Suzanne Lowenstein, and Frau Kittenberger. All had been poisoned by the use of thallium, the symptoms of which are startlingly similar to tuberculosis.

Luckily when the case against Martha broke, her other child was living in a boarding house in the slums of Vienna. When the police found him he was suffering from thallium poisoning. His mother had generously been bringing him food parcels. Fortunately he was taken to hospital where he received treatment and recovered.

Martha was apprehended and charged with murder. She was adjudged to be sane, and found guilty. On a chilly December day in 1938, Martha was executed by a swordsman, who cut off her head.

MR. HOGG AND
MRS. PEARCEY

According to all that is right and proper, one small indiscretion should not change an entire life. One path can lead to fame and fortune, while another can spell disaster. Naturally, we are going to deal with the one which proved to be disastrous.

Way back in 1890, in a section of London, England known as Kentish Town, there lived a tall attractive lady, who had a desire, if not a craving, for hard drink and masculine company, not necessarily in that order.

Mrs. Pearcey lived alone, but took on lovers quite nonchalantly. While she is always referred to as Mrs. Pearcey, no one remembers Mr. Pearcey. It is evident that that fine gentleman left the rather drab environs of Kentish Town some year previous to the enactment of our little drama.

In 1890, at the age of 24, Mrs. Pearcey was in love with and distributing her not inconsiderable charms to one Mr. Hogg, who was also 24 years old. Both were experienced in affairs of the heart and enjoyed each other's company whenever the mood struck either of them.

Now comes the slight indiscretion. It was indeed unfortunate that one brisk fall evening Mr. Hogg took up with a rather tiny, insignificant woman. In some circles this is referred to as a one night stand. At any rate, the unfortunate result of this singularly demonstrative act on the part of Mr. Hogg was that the meek little lady later informed him that she was heavy laden with child. She further informed him that he was at least 50 per cent responsible for her embarrassing condition. This news did not make Mr. Hogg chuckle with glee. When told by the meek little lady that nothing less than marriage would satisfy her, Mr. Hogg became definitely depressed.

Well, folks, Mr. Hogg reluctantly entered the sacred state of matrimony. Mrs. Hogg, in turn, predictably presented him with a cute, cuddly, brand new baby. In the meantime, Mrs. Pearcey and Mr. Hogg came to a sort of arrangement. It was quite a simple arrangement, really. They would continue to see each other just as they did before Hogg was married. They decided that Mrs. Hogg should meet Mrs. Pearcey and consider her a friend of the family. In due time, this cozy little setup was solidified, and with Hogg having the key to Mrs. Pearcey's premises things could have been worse.

Human nature is sometimes predictable. Mrs. Pearcey became insanely jealous of little Mrs. Hogg. It just didn't seem fair. Sure Hogg would spend half the night with her, but he always had to watch the clock in order to be certain to return to his wife and child. During her idle hours Mrs. Pearcey couldn't forget the thought of Hogg partaking of domestic bliss with his family.

It became a definite obsession and she decided to do something about it. She invited Mrs. Hogg over for tea, and next to the Mad Hatter's famous party, it may have been the strangest tea party ever held.

Mrs. Hogg brought her baby over to Mrs. Pearcey's house in a baby carriage, which she left in an outside hall. Once Mrs. Hogg was comfortably seated in the sitting room, Mrs. Pearcey picked up a fireplace poker and beat Mrs. Hogg and her baby to death. She placed Mrs. Hogg (remember she was a small woman) in the carriage.

It is Mrs. Pearcey who gives us the Hitchcock-like scene of a lady strolling down the street with two bodies in a perambulator. She let Mrs. Hogg off at a vacant lot on Haverstock Hill and farther on deposited the baby on a heap of rubbish. She then abandoned the carriage on a side street and went home.

The bodies and carriage were quickly found and the very next morning news of the unidentified dead woman and child was in all the newspapers. Before she even had a chance to have her morning tea, Mrs. Pearcey received a visit from Mr. Hogg's sister Clara. That busybody had an inquiry. She wanted to know the whereabouts of the missing Mrs. Hogg. The bodies reported in the newspapers had her more than somewhat concerned.

Clara suggested that Mrs. Pearcey and herself go down and view the bodies at the morgue. Mrs. Pearcey quivered at the thought, but pretty well had to go through the ordeal for appearance's sake. She broke down at the sight of the mutilated bodies and started to scream, "It isn't her, it isn't her!", which was odd because it most certainly was the missing Mrs. Hogg and child. Clara thought Mrs. Pearcey's reaction was so suspicious that she fetched a police officer, who accompanied the two ladies back to Mrs. Pearcey's residence in Kentish town.

When the officer entered Mrs. Pearcey's sitting room it was not necessary for him to have the deductive powers of Sherlock Holmes to realize that he had just stepped into the scene of a murder. Blood was splattered all over the floor, walls and even the ceiling. A blood encrusted poker was there for all to see. Mrs. Pearcey was arrested and taken to the police station, where she was searched. Her underwear was saturated with blood.

Mrs. Pearcey stood trial for her crimes. She sat ashen faced throughout her ordeal, and one wonders what thoughts came into her mind. Did it occur to her that the one indiscretion on the part of Mr. Hogg had placed her in her present predicament? Had he not wandered out that night with the woman who was to become his wife, Mrs. Pearcey would most certainly not have been on trial for her life.

It matters not — she didn't have that long to ponder over anything. Mrs. Pearcey was found guilty, and duly hanged for the murder of Mrs. Hogg.

GRETA HAD A RIGHT

A shot rings out, a man is dead; and a woman hands over the murder weapon to the police. On the surface it hardly seems necessary to have a trial at all, but such is not the case. Every minute detail of the act of murder is investigated. Not only the physical details, but also the mental state of all the principals involved.

The Greta Pelz case best illustrates the importance of what the killer and the victim were thinking at the exact instant the murder was committed.

Greta, a New York University graduate, was not what you would call a beauty, but she wasn't plain either. She fell somewhere in between. Greta had a neat little figure, and was considered to be an attractive woman. After graduation, because her parents could well afford it, she travelled extensively in Europe.

One day in 1934, she decided to go on a West Indies cruise. This decision was to change the course of her life. While aboard the *Vulcania*, she met charming, witty, Fritz Gebhardt. You might say Greta changed Fritz's life as well. In fact, to be more accurate, she was instrumental in bringing it to a premature end.

With the everyday cares of the world miles away, the couple became close friends. They danced the night away when the ship docked at Havana on New Year's Eve.

Back in New York, Fritz showered attention on Greta. It was a whirl of theatre, dancing, flowers and candy. Despite approaching her 30th year, Greta was impressed; and more than that, she was thrilled and delighted. She slipped between the sheets with Fritz on occasion and we assume, became more thrilled and delighted than ever.

Things could have gone on indefinitely except for a couple of distressing facts of life. First and foremost was the inescapable fact that charming Fritz had a wife stashed away back in Germany. While he was gentleman enough to inform Greta of this revolting situation, he reassured her that it was a marriage in name only. He really planned on getting a divorce in the very near future. Greta turned over in bed and thought to herself that that would suffice for the time being.

Another factor which made Fritz a little different than your average lover was that he suffered from a rather pedestrian ailment. Fritz had gas. Many an evening he would double over with a tummy ache. It seems the only thing which would relieve the excrutiating pain was for the faithful Greta to apply a heating pad to Fritz's tummy.

To make matters more convenient all around, Greta moved into an apartment on the 19th floor of the Beckman Towers apartment building. By coincidence Fritz had his pad on the 21st floor. In 1935, it was customary to use the back stairs rather than live together. Greta almost wore a path running up and down those stairs.

One day, after returning from a business trip, Fritz made a terrible mistake. He mentioned that he didn't think this marriage business was such a good idea after all. Why not just leave things as they were. Greta didn't quite see it that way. She had always assumed that Fritz would marry her someday. She let Fritz know, in no uncertain terms, that the pleasures they shared in bed would now come to an abrupt stop.

A few nights later Greta received a phone call from Fritz. He claimed his tummy was acting up. Would she dash up to the 21st floor and apply the heating pad? Greta said sure, anything for a friend. She threw her coat over her flimsy nightgown and dashed up those well worn stairs. Throwing the door to the apartment open, she found Fritz standing there. He exclaimed, "Greta!"

Now, let's continue with the sequence of events as related in the actual trial transcript. The defence lawyer is questioning Greta on the stand.

Q: What did you say?
A: I said, 'You shouldn't be up like this. Go lie down.' I went to the bureau where he kept odds and ends and looked for the heating pad.
Q: Did you see various things there?
A: Yes, a collar box and a gun.
Q: Were you aware of Fritz rising from the bed — any movement behind you?
A: Not until he seized me from behind. He grabbed my elbows and pulled them back.
Q: What did you say?

A: I said, 'If you don't need anything, I'm going.' But he said, 'No, you're not going. You're staying here as long as I want you.' I said, 'You won't keep me against my will.' He picked me up and threw me on the bed. He flung himself on me. He had my arms over my head.

Q: Did you ask Fritz to let you go?

A: I begged, 'Please let me go. I hate you. I hate you. Do you hear me? I'll scream and let the hotel people know.' He said, 'Oh, no, you won't; you're a coward. Don't forget you're in my room. I'm not in yours.'

Q: And Gebhardt did overpower you and have intercourse with you?

A: Yes.

The packed courtroom was as silent as a bat's cave. There was more to come. Fritz, the devil, wasn't through. He exposed himself to Greta and told her he was going to make her perform an unnatural sex act. He advanced towards her. She grabbed the gun she had seen in the bureau. Fritz thought she was bluffing. He clutched the gun and the pair struggled. The revolver discharged. A bullet struck Fritz in the chest. He staggered back momentarily, but again advanced towards Greta. She poured three further slugs into Fritz, and he was through advancing.

Greta, supposedly in a state of shock, went down to her apartment and dressed herself. She then went to the lobby of the building and called the police. When they arrived she coolly gave them her gun and said she wanted a lawyer.

The prosecuting attorney said poppycock to her whole story. Did any of the facts outlined in Greta's tale really excuse murder? There always was the distinct possibility that she ventilated Fritz without any convenient struggle. Fritz wasn't around to dispute her story. When Fritz made his advance towards Greta, she was holding the gun. Instead of shooting, why didn't she flee?

It was left up to the jury to decide. After just under three hours deliberation they returned with their verdict. It was not guilty. Greta Peltz walked out of the courtroom a free woman.

ELVIRA DIDN'T MEAN IT

Elvira Mullens was born with more than just a pretty name. Her daddy, Sir John Mullens, was endowed with the unique combination of being both wealthy and respectable. Sir John and Lady Mullens had a home in fashionable Belgrave Square in London, England, and a summer residence in Sussex.

Despite all the advantages of wealthy, titled parents, Elvira was a bit of a free spirit. To say she burned the candle at both ends would be an understatement. Elvira drove fast cars, drank strong booze, and slept around with whomever she fancied.

One night she met an American singer who had been hired to entertain her parents at Belgrave Square. In one of her wild impetuous moods, Elvira married the singer and became Mrs. Elvira Barney. After a short while Mr. Barney returned to America, claiming that he was unable to stand the life Elvira led. The blushing bride claimed that he was a monster, and that she was happy to see the last of her erstwhile husband.

Elvira moved out of her parents' home and took up residence at 21 Williams Mews, near Knightsbridge. To while away those dreary English evenings, Elvira took a lover.

Michael Stephen, the son of a prominent banker and magistrate, decided early in life that he had an aversion to employment of any kind. Because his father had cut off his allowance, he financed his drinking and carousing by borrowing from his mother and brother. When he first met Elvira, he recognized her as a kindred soul.

The pair, both attractive 26 year olds, carried on a torrid affair. They would alternate between heated arguments and making passionate love.

When his mother and brother grew tired of loaning him money, Michael moved into 21 Williams Mews with Elvira. He was not at all averse to accepting money from Elvira. Anyway, it beat working for a living.

All went along famously for a while. Life was a steady round of drinking, quarreling and love making, not necessarily in that order; right up to the early morning hours of May 31, 1932.

Earlier in the evening, Elvira and Michael entertained numerous guests. The liquor flowed, sports cars raced up and down the streets until all the guests had left. At about 3 a.m. neighbors were awakened by the noise of a terrible fight coming from Elvira's house. At about 4 a.m. a loud crack, which could have been the report of a revolver, broke the still night air. Most of the neighbors turned over and went back to sleep.

Here in essence is the statement Elvira gave the police as to the events which took place behind the closed doors of 21 Williams Mews. She claimed that she and Michael had quarrelled about another woman. She had always had a revolver in the house. During the height of their quarrel, Michael was preparing to leave when he decided to take the revolver with him, explaining that he was afraid Elvira would kill herself. Elvira stated that she had disagreed and had tried to take the gun away from Michael. As the pair struggled for the gun, it went off. Michael made his way to the bathroom, telling Elvira to fetch a doctor. Elvira went downstairs to ring the doctor. When she returned, she found Michael sitting on the bathroom floor with blood pouring from a bullet wound in his chest. She claimed he kept saying, "It was not your fault." When she came back from trying the doctor a second time, Michael was quite dead.

After making this statement at the police station, Elvira was released. The authorities began to dig more deeply into the death of Michael Stephen. Three days later Elvira Barney was arrested, and stood trial for murder.

It is sometimes difficult to capture the excitement and publicity surrounding an event which happened so many years ago, but the fervor accompanying Elvira's trial is well documented. Both the Crown and the defence were represented by the most famous trial lawyers in England. The prominence of the parents of the victim and the accused insured blanket coverage of the case by the press. Twenty four hours before the trial began, long queues of spectators had formed outside the Old Bailey.

The Crown had prepared a formidable case. One resident of the Mews testied that she had heard Elvira scream, "Get out! I'll shoot, I'll shoot!", just before she heard the revolver. Others testified to the many quarrels which the couple had engaged in during months past. Another lady testified that Elvira had shot at Michael on a previous occasion. She said that Michael was in the street below a window when this took place. She further stated that she had seen Elvira holding a shiny revolver in her left hand as a puff of smoke rose from the barrel.

A pathologist took the stand and demonstrated by the direction of the entry of the bullet into the body that Michael could not have inflicted the fatal wound himself. The jury was left with the inference that if Michael couldn't have shot himself, the only other person who could have done so was Elvira.

The defence countered some of this evidence with some strong evidence of their own. They claimed that when Elvira shouted, "Get out! I'll shoot, I'll shoot!" she was referring to shooting herself, not Michael.

The woman who had testified to seeing a shot being fired at Michael from the upstairs window testified that she spoke to him immediately after the shot was fired. She claimed that she scolded him, accusing him of bringing trouble to the neighborhood. In her own words, she said, "I told him to clear off." Michael's reply was that he didn't want to leave Mrs. Barney because he was afraid that she might kill herself. This spontaneous reply from the witness box went a long way toward fortifying Elvira's claim that Michael wanted to take the gun with him when he left.

The story of the shiny gun held in Elvira's left hand as a puff of smoke rose from the barrel didn't stand up under questioning. The gun was on exhibit at the trial for all to see. It was dull black, not at all shiny. Elvira was right handed, not left handed. Cartridges used in the murder weapon were made of cordite, and cordite does not produce smoke.

The judge charged the jury, taking care to point out the various courses open to them. These are his exact words:

"If you are satisfied on the evidence as a whole that it is proved that she did intentionally fire the revolver pointing it at the body of the man, and so caused the bullet wound from which he died, then she is guilty of the crime of murder."

The judge also explained manslaughter as it applied to this particular case.

"If the prisoner threatened to commit suicide — suicide, let me remind you, is a crime — and the deceased man removed the revolver in order to prevent it, and she, in order to carry out her intention, struggled with him and so caused the revolver to go off, she would then be guilty of manslaughter."

Of course, there was Elvira's story of accidental death, and if it was to be believed, the only possible verdict would be not guilty.

The jury took only two hours to bring in their verdict. They found Mrs. Barney not guilty of murder and not guilty of manslaughter. The crowd in the Old Bailey cheered wildly at the verdict.

Elvira continued to live the wild life. She moved to Paris, where she died a few years after her trial.

THE CORPSE
TRAVELLED BY TRAIN

Winnie Ruth McKinnell was born on Jan. 29, 1905, in Oxford, Indiana, the daughter of a clergyman. She was an 18-year-old student nurse at Southern Indiana Hospital for the Insane in Evansville, Indiana, when she met Dr. William C. Judd, who was on the staff of the hospital. When the doctor left the hospital to take a position in Lafayette, Indiana, Winnie followed him, obtaining a job as a telephone operator so that she could be close to him. The doctor, who was Winnie's senior by 22 years, had previously been married to a 17-year-old, Lillian Colwell, in 1920, but his young bride had died of natural causes about a month after they were married. Winnie fell hard for the older man, and he seemingly was attracted to younger women. They were married in Lafayette in April, 1924.

In 1925, Mrs. Judd became pregnant. She started to lose strength and her health deteriorated rapidly. She was almost continually nauseous, and as a result she eventually became so weak that Dr. Judd brought in another physician for a second opinion. He felt that Winnie's condition was serious enough to warrant an abortion, and her pregnancy was terminated in her third month.

Although the doctor led a rather nomadic life, practising medicine in several different cities, the constant moving didn't seem to have a detrimental effect on the couple's marriage, which appeared to be a happy one. They ended up living in a duplex at 2929 North 2nd Street in Phoenix, Arizona. Here they made the acquaintance of two neighbors, Agnes Anne LeRoi and Hedvig Samuelson.

In 1925, Anne had been training to become a nurse in Portland, Oregon, when she met and married Walter Monroe. The marriage last only 18 months, ending in an amicable divorce. Anne later married again, this time to LeRoi James, but this marriage also ended in divorce. In 1929, Anne accepted the position of superintendent of a hospital at Wrangler, Alaska, where she met Hedvig Samuelson, who was a schoolteacher. Sammy, as she was called by everyone, was an outgoing personality who was extremely well-liked. Everyone was saddened when she took ill and her condition was diagnosed as tuberculosis.

The two girls had become such close friends that, when it became imperative for Sammy to live in a drier climate, Anne would not hear of her making the move alone. The two good friends moved to Phoenix, Arizona, where Anne worked as an X-ray technician at the Grunow Clinic. In the course of her work, she met Winnie Ruth Judd, now working as secretary and assistant to Dr. William Curtis. Sammy, who was convalescing at home, was unable to work.

The main characters in the drama had wandered the length of North America. Now, assembled in Phoenix, Arizona, they were ready to play their parts.

Winnie became friendly with Anne at the clinic, and often she and her husband would drop over to the girls' duplex and play bridge. On other occasions Anne and Sammy would visit with the Judds. Everyone seemed to get along extremely well.

In August 1931, the itchy-footed doctor left Phoenix to seek a position in Los Angeles, California. When this happened Winnie moved in with Anne and Sammy, and became as close to the two girls as they were to each other. She took care of Sammy, and was particularly kind to her on a few occasions when Anne had to leave Phoenix for a few days at a time.

In early October Winnie suddenly moved out of the girls' duplex and took an apartment at 1130 East Brill Street, telling them that Brill Street was closer to the Grunow Clinic where she worked.

On Saturday morning, October 17, Winnie Ruth Judd called her office at about nine o'clock and told the receptionist that she would be a little late arriving for work. At 9:45 a.m. the office received another call. This time the caller identified herself as Mrs. LeRoi, and advised them that she wouldn't be coming to work that day. The receiver of the call, Beverly Fox, thought that the caller was really Mrs. Judd trying to disguise her voice to sound like that of Mrs. LeRoi. A few minutes after ten o'clock a shaking and nervous Mrs. Judd showed up for work.

That night Winnie called the Lightning Delivery Co., who dispatched driver John W. Pritchett and a helper to 2929 North 2nd St. Winnie Judd wanted to have a trunk moved, and explained to the men that the darkened condition of the house was due to her having the power turned off because she was vacating the premises. To help the men see their way about the darkened house, she lit some matches and explained that she wanted the trunk taken to the station so that she could check it out on a train leaving at 10:40.

Pritchett gave Winnie one portion of a claim check and fastened the other half to one of the handles of the trunk. Then the two men bent down and heaved. It hardly budged, and the men inquired as to its contents. Winnie told them that it held books, which satisfied Pritchett. He voiced the opinion that he thought the trunk weighed over 400 pounds, and felt it was too heavy to be checked on a ticket, but would have to remain overnight and go by express in the morning. If that was the case, Winnie said, she would have the trunk removed to 1130 East Brill St. With the aid of a handcart the men lifted the trunk on its end and placed it on their truck. Winnie joined them in the cab of the truck and all three drove to 1130 East Brill St. The men placed the trunk in the front room and Mrs. Judd waved to them from her doorway as they drove away.

The next morning, Sunday, Oct. 18, Winnie asked her landlord, M.G. Koller, to take some baggage to the Union Depot, as she was leaving for Los Angeles. Koller showed up with his son to gather up the luggage. He noticed Winnie's hand was bandaged, and she mentioned to him that she had burned it on an electric iron. From the bedroom, the father and son took one large trunk and one smaller one, while Mrs. Judd carried an old suitcase, a little leather grip and a large hatbox. The whole kit and caboodle, including Winnie, left the for the station in Koller's car. When they arrived they received some help with the larger trunk from the baggage agent. Then, at 8:05, the baggage messenger placed the two trunks aboard the Golden State Limited bound for Los Angeles. He noticed a dark liquid dripping from the larger trunk.

In the meantime, Mrs. Judd boarded the train and a porter placed her personal luggage by her side. At 7:45 a.m. on Monday the train arrived in Los Angeles. The two trunks were unloaded from the train and placed on a baggage rack. Winnie gave her personal luggage to a porter and left to get her brother, Jason. At noon she returned with Jason and went directly to the baggage rack containing the two trunks. Winnie didn't know that an unpleasant smell had started to emanate from the larger, leaking trunk. The district baggage agent had been notified and he was waiting for the trunks to be claimed. He demanded that Winnie and her brother open the trunk in his presence. Winnie stuttered a bit and finally said she didn't have the key, but would phone her husband, who would bring the key down to the station. She went through the motions of trying to contact him, but claimed she couldn't reach him. Finally, Winnie left the station with her brother, promising to return with the key.

Winnie never returned to the station, and later it was learned that Jason had loaned her $5 and dropped her off at Sixth St. and Broadway. Back at the station the two trunks lay on the baggage rack, waiting for someone to claim them, but the afternoon wore on and no one showed up. The baggage agent grew increasingly suspicious and finally called the Los Angeles Police, who arrived on the scene and opened the larger trunk.

The officer who opened the trunk later testified:

"There was a number of books and papers, also some bloody clothing and a quilt. I pulled the quilt down at the corner where the blood appeared to be coming from until I uncovered a woman's head.

"Then I returned back out to the platform and, using the same key, opened the smaller of the two trunks. There were several sheets of blank paper, some of these bloodstained, and — what you would call a sheet — blanket. This, when I pulled it apart, I discovered was a bundle wrapped up in a piece of woman's clothing. When I unwrapped it, it proved to be a foot and a leg, from the knee down, of a human being. I opened down a little further through the blanket and discovered a woman's head. That was as far as the examination went at that time."

At no time had Winnie made any attempt to conceal her identity, so she was immediately suspected of murder. Detectives took apart her apartment at 1130 East Brill St., finding a set of surgical instruments and men's clothing. They also found a spent shell from a small-calibre weapon. At 2929 North 2nd St. police discovered several bloodstains on the carpet, and they noted that one piece of the carpet had been cut away. From the appearance of the two residences and the apparent physical strength that was required to dissect the bodies and place them in the trunks, the police surmised that more than one individual had been involved.

The police picked up Jason, and he frankly told them that he knew the trunk contained the bodies of Agnes Anne LeRoi and Hedvig Samuelson, because Winnie had confessed to him that she had killed them. He had accompanied his sister to the station hoping to pick up the trunks and dump them in the ocean. He told the authorities he had dropped his sister off at the street corner, and went on to say that she was a bit unstable, liable to go into fits of rage. Winnie's husband was also questioned, and while Dr. Judd readily admitted knowing the two girls, he could shed no light on Winnie's whereabouts. He pointed out that in his opinion his wife was mentally ill.

Where was the elusive Mrs. Judd? With each passing day her absence seemed to make the already strange case even more sensational. She was reported sighted in twelve different states, as well as Canada. Rewards were posted by the major newspapers for information leading to her apprehension. Through the newspapers, Dr.

Judd pleaded with Winnie to give herself up, and on Oct. 23rd, six days after the murders were committed, she responded to this plea by telephoning her husband's lawyer. They agreed that they would meet in, of all places, the Alvarez and Moore Funeral Parlor. Dr. Judd and Jason were present when Winnie showed up. She looked terrible; her clothes were wrinkled and filthy, a stained rag was wrapped around her hand and wrist, and she complained of excruciating pain from her injured hand. The authorities sent her to the George Street Receiving Hospital, and so widespread was the interest in her case that a crowd of over 500 people had gathered, trying to catch a glimpse of the suspect. A twenty-five calibre bullet was removed from between Ruth's middle and index fingers, and she was taken to the Los Angeles County Jail and booked on suspicion of murder.

The day after Winnie gave herself up, a plumber in the Broadway Department Store in Los Angeles came forward with the interesting bit of news that he had found a scrap of paper in the ladies' rest-room of the store with the name Judd on it. The police descended on the ladies' room. In the toilet drain they found ten handwritten telegraph pages directed to Dr. Judd in Mrs. Judd's handwriting. This letter was much the worse for wear, but only small parts were completely illegible. There was little doubt that the letter was genuine. Its contents are tantamount to a confession of murder, but more than that, it gives us some idea of what one human being felt on killing and dissecting another.

Darling:

A confession I've kept from you for life, because I was so happy with you and loved you, so why tell you. I am crazy only when I am very angry or too tired physically my brain goes wrong. One obsession I've always had is wanted or saying I had a baby. 1st when I was seven years old I wanted a baby at our house so bad I told at school that mother had one and for days told the neighbors we had one and such cute anticks it did far beyond an infants ability. Then when I was 16 on my birthday a fellow I was going with and I had a split up. I was furious my girl friend was the cause curiosly I liked her just as well we chummed together, but this boys cousin antagonized me by crowing that some one could take him from me. I had taken her boy friend months before from her. The man's name was Fred Jensen he wished to be friends but liked my chum Laura Walters. It was OK until j-y Burns I hate her always will crowed (I had taken a fellow Ronald Carpenter from her later they married) I told Fred Jensen about it and asked him not to go with Laura. I loved Laura, but I hated Joy her crowing Fred thought I was doing it for meanness etc. and so finally as so many unmarried girls in that part of the woods were having babys I conceived of stating I was and would make Fred marry me if necessary. I was 16. He was 26. Fred Jensen never touched me. I had never had intercourse with him or with any man until I met you. Fred I believe is honest. He cried and cried and told daddy he'd never touch me. He used to tell me I was crazy. I said well quit going with Laura or I'll send you to the Pen. I won't be tormented by Joy Burns. I was going pretty good at school then my teachers loved me. I was good in English class my stories were published in the school paper and in the city paper I made up in my 90 Botany zoology. The teachers all like me and I did splendid in Modern History my class mates like me and I them but I got so worked up I quit school and said I was pregnant and swore out warrants against Fred made darling dresses all kinds of dainty things I later gave for little girls dolls. Fred would walk home from church with me and tell me I was crazy. I said I knew it, but if I started this thing I would finish it. I wanted him to go away until I went back to college then go with Laura, but please not then that I had an insane temper. So finally after about ten months I decided I'd have to confess a lie or do something drastic so I preceeded to hop out of my window one night in cold October in my gown and I grabbed a few gunny sacks and overshoes and run away and say I'd been kidnapped. First I wrote a letter that I had a baby girl (Why I don't know) then I ran away was going to get some clothes at my home sixteen miles from there and be gone awhile and my Fred had had me kidnapped and I got away. I brought suits against him and assumed a (as soon as) Joy moved I dropped charges and that was the end. This is the first time I have ever told this my parents believe Fred wicked. I did it all myself and never have told it to anyone until now. I've always wanted to tell Fred I was sorry He was a good boy He thought it was funny until I had him arrested for rape and kidnapping etc. I'm sorry to tell you this doctor. Here is a confession I should have carried to my death if I had been intimate with any man I would have told you but I didn't tell you anything to hurt you I've wanted your respect confidence and love. There in Mazatlan or rather Tyoltita I was sick a couple of days so as Mrs. Heinz had been so thrilled over being pregnant I decided I'd say I was. I had hoped for three weeks I might be until I came unwell so when you moved I wrote I had had a miscarriage. Then again I told Mrs. ... and Mrs. Aster I was where you saw I was menstruating the very week we left there. I don't know what possessed me to tell that I had a little boy. I even showed pictures of you with a baby and showed Dyers baby pictures as my baby who was with Mama so I'm crazy on that line. And aside from that and occasionally a rage I get into I seem quite bright I was working so hard at Phoenix when you went to Bisbee then something went wrong in my head and I registered under an assumed name and called you up gave a fictitious address just to hear your voice and see you then cried all night for doing it. Got a car next morning to sooth my nerves at the garage below the Hotel and drove to Warren. Then finally wanted you to soothe me and told you I was there. You know how I cried and cried. I was crazy You said I was at the time. I came back and Mr. H. came out the next evening he had been on the coast and he said what's the matter you look terrible you look crazy. My two doctors said I looked terrible. I've written you for a month how my nerves were doing. Then Thursday Mr. H. bought the girls a new radio Mr. Adams had let them have his but they didn't like him so hated to use his radio. Mr. H. wanted me to get some other girl and go with him out to the house I knew a pretty little nurse who is taking Salvarsan but she has nothing contagious now. I certainly am not expecting them to do wrong, anyhow, so saw no harm she's pretty and can be interesting so we went out to the girls house. Dr. Brinckerhoff and a couple Mr. H. friends were there. The girls didn't like to it so Mr. H. asked us to have dinner with them I refused so he got dinner and came over to the house. The first time he has ever done it but it was a nice clean evening I truly didn't even take a drink you can ask. The remains of their drinks are in the ice box. Next day Ann came over and we had lunch together the remains of the dinner the night before. She wanted me to go home with her that night. Denise Reynolds was going. I had some histories to do and couldn't. I said if I get through in time I'll come over and play bridge, but I stayed all night. The next morning all three of us were yet in our pajamas when the quarrel began I was going hunting. Theuy said if I did they would tell Mr. H. I had introduced him to a nurse who had syphillis. I said Ann you've no right to tell things from the office you know that only because you saw me get distilled water and syringes ready and she hasn't it contageoush the doctor lets her work nursing. Well Ann said I asked Denise and she thinks I should tell Mr. H. too. And he certainly won't think much of you for doing such a thing. You've been trying to make him like you and Mr. D. too getting him to move you and when I tell them you associated with and introduce them to girls who have syphillis they won't have a thing to do with you. And when we tell Mr. P. about it he won't take you hunting either. I said Sammy I'll shoot you if tell that we were in the kitchen just starting breakfast she came in with my gun and said she would shoot me if I went hunting with this friend. I threw my hand over the mouth of the gun and grabbed the bread knife she shot I jumped on her with all my weight and knocked her down in the dining room Ann yelled at us I fired twice I think and since Ann was going to blackmail me too if I went hunting by telling them this patient of Dr. Curtis' was syphillitic and would hand me over to the police I fired at her. There was no harm introducing this nurse who is very pretty to the men. One doesn't get it from contact but they were going to kill me for introducing this her initials are D.E. St. Josephs to their men friends Ann said before Sammy got the gun Ruth I could kill you for introducing that girl to . . . and if you go hunting I will tell them and they won't think your so darn nice anymore. I don't want to bring Mr. H. into this he has been kind to me when I was lonesome at the 1st place I worked and has trusted me with many secrets of all he did for the girls such as caring for Ann giving her extra money and the radio and he's been a decent fellow. It would separate he and his wife and he's been too decent. Mr. D. kept Ann in an apartment here in L.A. for several days then got her state room to Ph and she was mad enough to kill me when he helped me move me over. Part of my things are still the girls 3 hats, thermos bottle, black dress cook book, green scarf you got me in Mexico and a number of things. Doctor dear Im so sorry Sammy shot me whether it was the pain or what I got the gun and killed her. It was horrible to pack things as I did. I kept saying I've got to I've got to or I'll be hung I've got to or I'll be hung. I'm wild with cold hunger pain and fear now. Doctor darling if I hadn't got the gun from Sammy she would have shot me again. Forgive me not forget me. Live to take care of ... sick. Doctor, but I'm true to you ... The thots of being away from ... it me crazy. Shall I give up to ... don't think so the police will hang me. It was as much a battle as Germany and the U.S. I killed in defense. Love me yet doctor.

Blonde, blue-eyed Winnie, who at this time weighed only 109 pounds, was extradited to Phoenix, Arizona, and on Nov. 3 she was charged with the murder of Agnes Anne LeRoi. If for any reason she would be acquitted on this charge, the second murder charge awaited her.

The trial of Winnie Ruth Judd began on Jan. 19, 1932. The first four days were taken up with the selection of a jury, then the police who actually removed the contents of Mrs. Judd's luggage commenced to give their gory evidence. The large trunk held the intact body of Mrs. LeRoi, as well as two ladies' purses. Inside the purses were found two empty shells and one lead bullet. The smaller trunk contained the dissected body of Miss Samuelson; the feet and legs up to the knees were wrapped in ladies' clothing, while the head, arms, and upper part of the torso had been tossed in without any protective covering. The torso had been separated, with the lower portion being found in the brown leather suitcase which had accompanied Winnie on the train. Examination of the parts of the body revealed a gaping bullet wound in the head. The hatbox carried by Winnie on her lap for part of her trip to L.A. contained a set of surgical instruments and a .25 Colt automatic pistol.

Ballistics experts stated that the spent shells, the bullet from the victim's head and the one taken from the accused's hand all came from the same weapon; the gun which was found in Winnie's hatbox.

The jury found Winnie guilty of murder in the first degree, and she was sentenced to death by hanging. She was sent to the Arizona State Prison in Florence, where she was placed on death row. Throughout her ordeal, her father, Reverend McKinnell, stood by her side, and was the first person to visit her in the death cell.

Winnie's case captured the imagination of the country, and indeed of the entire world. Every sentence she uttered, every bit of food she consumed, was reported in the press. If she was newsworthy during her trial, she was even more notorious now that she had the added dimension of death hanging over her head. Her slender five-foot, seven-inch frame, together with her pale, pleasant face, belied the enormity of the dreadful deed of which she had been proven guilty. Legal manoeuvres by her lawyers continued to keep her case before the public, and she received hundreds of fan letters every week. Whenever things slackened, Winnie would provide the press with enough to keep them going.

The months dragged by, and she received many reviews and stays of execution. On one occasion, she came within three days of being executed. Through it all, she acted calmly one minute and hysterically the next. Finally, in 1933, Winnie was judged insane and transferred to the Arizona State Hospital for the Insane.

Normally this would mark the end to a remarkable crime committed by a demented woman. But such was not to be the case with Mrs. Judd. She was to make headline news off and on for the next forty years.

Once Winnie acclimatized herself to the less restrictive routine of a hospital, she started to care for the very ill. She had training as a nurse, and now she applied this training to the benefit of her fellow inmates. Soon she won the sympathy and affection of all who met her.

On Oct. 24, 1939, almost eight years after the double murder, Winnie made a model of herself asleep in bed, fooled her attendants and walked away from the institution. Before leaving, she wrote a letter to the governor of Arizona, saying she was going to see her ailing father and then surrender. True to her word, she rapped on the hospital door a few days later and turned herself in. One month later, Winnie again fled the institution. The hospital came under attack for allowing its most illustrious inmate to leave almost at will. It is believed she had assistance in her escapes, for over the next twenty-four years she was to escape a further four times. On each occasion she was apprehended by the authorities, or gave herself up after a few days of freedom.

Then on the night of Oct. 8, 1962, she escaped from the hospital for the seventh time, and completely disappeared for six and a half years. She changed her name to Susan Leigh Clark, studied practical nursing, and then obtained a job as a housekeeper to an elderly lady in a small central California town. She loved children and baby-sat for the wealthy families in the immediate area. When her elderly employer had a heart attack and died, Susan was so well-liked that one of the lady's daughters retained her to run her home.

During the routine investigation of a murder in the suburb where Susan worked, her parked car was dusted for fingerprints, and the prints were discovered to be those of Winnie Ruth Judd. She was quickly traced and identified. Again she was caught up in a series of legal manoeuvres in an attempt to gain her freedom. A few more years dragged by, and the once beautiful Winnie was now a grey-haired, 66-year-old woman. Finally, in December 1971, the governor of the State of Arizona paroled Mrs. Judd. She is now living with the people who knew and loved her for six long years as Susan Leigh Clark.

UPSTAIRS,
DOWNSTAIRS

The bloody history of murder has been sprinkled with cases where the mild, placid butler or maid has turned on his or her employer.

This little gem started in Le Mans, France in 1932. Rene Lancelin was a successful lawyer who lived with his wife and 27-year-old daughter, Genevieve, in a fashionable section of the city. They had recently hired two sisters as domestics — Christine Papin, 28, and Lea, 21. Both girls had become maids after leaving a convent, where they had been brought up by nuns. Their previous employers had given them the best possible references, emphasizing that they were hard-working, polite and honest. The Lancelins paid higher than average wages, and all seemed well, although Mrs. Lancelin was known to berate the girls for seemingly minor mistakes.

On Feb. 2, 1933, Lancelin had a date to meet his wife and daughter at a friend's house for dinner. The ladies didn't show up, nor did they answer the telephone. Lancelin, somewhat apprehensive, returned to his home. He found the entire house in darkness, and the door locked from the outside. He called the police, and they broke into the house. Nothing was found on the first floor and the police proceeded to the first floor landing.

The mutilated corpses of Mrs. Lancelin and Genevieve were on the landing. Genevieve's legs and buttocks were horribly cut, and one eye had been gouged from her head. Mrs. Lancelin had all her teeth knocked out, and she too had been horribly mutilated about the eyes. The walls were splattered with blood, almost to the ceiling.

Beside the grotesque bodies were the blood encased implements of murder. A knife, hammer and pewter pot lay beside the victims. The police proceeded up to the second floor. The maids' room was locked from the inside. Police broke down the door. Inside, huddled together naked in bed, were the two sisters. They confessed to the murders before they were asked.

On Sept. 20, 1933, Christine and Lea Papin stood trial for the murder of Mrs. Lancelin and her daughter Genevieve. Because of the pleasant appearance of the two girls in contrast to the viciousness of the attack, the trial proved to be a sensation. Uppermost in everyone's mind was the motive. What horrendous deed had been done to the two girls to make them strike out in such a ferocious manner?

Christine took the stand and explained. Lea had damaged an electric iron in January, and Mrs. Lancelin was extremely aggravated, feeling that Lea had been negligent in handling the iron. As a result, when Mrs. Lancelin gave Lea her month's wages on Feb. 1, a day before the murder, she deducted five francs to pay for repairing the iron. The next day the two sisters were ironing when a fuse blew. This not only put an end to the ironing, but also put out all the lights in the house. Mrs. Lancelin and Genevieve returned from shopping and started to berate the girls. Christine claimed Mrs. Lancelin attacked her, and it was this attack that provoked her. The two sisters turned on their employer and daughter. Christine screamed to Lea, "Scratch at their eyes", and between them they succeeded in causing their victims great agony. While they were bent over in pain, the girls grabbed objects which were close at hand, and proceeded to club and hack at the two women until they were dead. Christine, the aggressor of the two, stated that they even exchanged weapons as the wild melee took place. Her sister would pass her a hammer and she would swing it, then pass it back. In this way both victims bore signs of being struck by all three weapons. After the victims lay still, the two girls ran to their bedrooms, and removed their blood-soaked clothing.

The courtroom was silent. Was it possible two women lay dead because of something as trivial as an electric iron? The investigators checked other possible motives, but found that the sisters were well paid, ate the same food as their employers, and had good living quarters. The two girls never changed their story. Their close attachment to each other led the authorities to believe that they had a lesbian relationship. Christine, the older sister, appeared to dominate Lea.

While the girls had been separated in prison, Christine had acted like a madwoman. At night she screamed for her sister and even went on a hunger strike. She became so violent she had to be restrained in a straight jacket. Yet by the time of her trial Christine appeared calm and docile.

The jury brought in their verdict after deliberating only an hour and a half. Christine was found guilty and sentenced to death. This sentence was later commuted to life imprisonment at hard labor. She ended up in a psychiatric hospital, where she died in 1937, only four years after she committed murder. Strangely enough, she had not asked for or inquired about her sister Lea during the entire four years. Lea was found guilty and received 10 years in prison. She was released after seven years and faded into obscurity.

BABY FARMING

The term "baby farming" means little to us now, but before the turn of the century in New Zealand, it was in common usage. The New Zealand government was concerned with the practice of unwed mothers turning over their unwanted babies to people who would look after them for a price. Placed mostly on farms, these babies would often receive less than adequate attention. From the moment the unwed mother turned over her baby with a sizeable cash deposit, the child was treated as the product of a very lucrative business.

Some farms had a dozen, or even more, children stashed about the farmhouse in assorted stages of neglect. Occasionally one of these children would die. No one really cared, and no one paid much attention.

Minnie Dean, a farmer's wife, had a profitable business going as a baby farmer. She decided that the expense and trouble of keeping the children was unnecessary. It occurred to her that she could maximize her profits by systematically killing the children.

Minnie was born in 1847 in Edinburgh, Scotland. The daughter of a minister, she had received a fine education before emigrating to New Zealand at the adventurous age of 21. Three years later, she married a hardworking farmer, Charles Dean. For the next 14 years, the couple farmed peacefully enough. In 1886, they purchased a 22-acre estate known as the Larches at Winton, which is close to Invercargill, and is about as far south as you can go in New Zealand.

A short time after the couple had purchased their new farm Minnie advertised for babies to room and board, with no questions asked. In October of 1889, a six-month-old baby girl died three days after being placed in Minnie's loving care. A doctor attributed the child's death to convulsions. Two years later, a six-week-old infant died on Minnie's farm. This time there was an investigation and an inquest. At the time the inquest was held Minnie had 10 children in her care, all apparently in good health. The inquest jury decided that the newborn child had died of inflamed lungs.

In May, 1895, a strange event took place which came to the attention of the police and eventually led to Minnie's downfall. A railway guard noticed a lady on the train feeding her baby. Later down the line, when the same lady got off the train, she was alone. The guard thought the incident unusual enough to notify the police. They, in turn, thought it more than a coincidence that the strange event had occurred only a few miles from Winton.

Because Minnie was so suspect when it came to babies, the authorities launched a full scale investigation. They located a Mrs. Hornsby, who claimed that in answer to an advertisement she had turned over her illegitimate month-old granddaughter to Minnie Dean. She had also turned over a sum of money for the baby's care. Police brought Mrs. Hornsby face to face with Minnie. She immediately identified Minnie as the woman who had taken her granddaughter. Minnie swore Mrs. Hornsby was making a terrible mistake. When asked to produce the baby, she replied that she couldn't come up with a baby who had never been placed in her care.

The police swarmed down on the Larches. Beneath a flower patch they found the bodies of not one, but two, infants. One was a year-old girl, Dorothy Carter, who had been turned over to Minnie by her grandmother, and the other was the Hornsby baby.

Minnie and her husband Charles were placed under arrest and transferred to Invercargill. Meanwhile the police made further startling discoveries back on the farm. They uncovered the body of another child. This infant was later identified as one who had been placed in Minnie's care. The transfer had been made on a moving train.

Charles Dean was exonerated as having no guilty knowledge of his wife's crime. Minnie was tried for murder. It was during her trial that her diabolical plot was exposed. Her husband knew nothing of the murdered children, because Minnie never killed any of them on the farm. Her meetings were held on trains, where the children would be handed over to her. On these missions she always carried a large tin hatbox. She would strangle the child, place it in the hatbox, and return to Winton, where Charles would meet her at the station. He once remarked that her hatbox was extremely heavy. Minnie replied that she had put earth in the box in order to protect some flower bulbs.

Minnie Dean squirmed in the prisoners' dock when the prosecution stated that chloroform had been found in her bedroom. She became downright depressed when relatives of the dead children identified the youngsters' clothing found in her house.

Minnie was found guilty, but her crimes were always considered to be more extensive than the three murders for which she stood trial. After the trial was over, many people came forward with information about other children left in Minnie's care who were never heard of again.

Throughout it all, Minnie maintained her innocence. She always claimed that she would have had plenty of opportunities to dispose of the children's bodies had she been the real killer. What would her purpose have been to lug them all the way back to the farm?

Minnie left a certain infamy in her wake. She was the first and only person ever to commit murder on a train in New Zealand. On Aug. 12, 1895, Minnie was hanged in the Invercargill Prison, the first and last woman to be hanged in New Zealand.

A MOTHER'S LOVE

Juries at murder trials have often been criticized for bringing in verdicts which seem at odds with the evidence they have just heard. In hindsight, we might think that if we had been on the jury our verdict would have been different.

It is true that hindsight leaves much to be desired. When we scan old transcripts we cannot catch the inflections, or, connotations placed on important and sometimes incriminating statements. Above all, we cannot measure the very human reactions of the accused in court.

Today, we will try to place you, the reader, in the juror's box. You will be able to consider the evidence much as it was presented at the time of this most perplexing murder trial. At the conclusion of the trial you will be faced with the dilemma — is the accused innocent or guilty?

Come along with me now to England at the turn of the century. It is Friday, Oct. 27, 1899. A terror filled scream pierces the musty air of London's Dalston Junction Station. A cleaning lady has stumbled upon a gruesome find. Her terror is well founded, for in the ladies waiting room lies the nude body of a little boy. He had been struck a heavy blow to the head, which probably rendered him unconscious. Then the tiny lad had been suffocated. The body was wrapped in a lady's black shawl.

Within a day the victim was identified as four-year-old Manfred Masset. His mother Louise was sought by the police. Within a week she was arrested and charged with the murder of her young son. The trial which followed was puzzling in many ways.

The Crown subjected Louise Masset's life to the microscopic examination of a woman accused of a brutal and cold blooded murder. At the time of her son's murder Louise was 36 years old. She was a plain, quiet woman who had never crossed paths with the law before.

Four years earlier Manfred had been born, as the result of an affair with a Frenchman, whose identity was never revealed during Louise's trial. Louise, who lived with her sister, Mrs. Cadisch, at Stoke Newington, was a governess to several respected families in London. None of her employers knew that she was the mother of a little boy.

Manfred, who was a cheerful, well adjusted child, was living with and being cared for by a Miss Gentle, while Louise went about making a living for herself and her son. There is every indication that Louise loved her son dearly. On occasion she received mail from France, and it is assumed she was the recipient of some financial help from Manfred's father. Each Wednesday Louise visited with Manfred, bringing the child candy and toys.

Louise had a lover. Her next door neighbor was a 19-year-old boy named Lucas. Louise had told the much younger Lucas of the existence of her son. The fact that Louise had an illegitimate child did not seem to bother Lucas. It is quite possible that had external influences not come into play, the pair might have married.

On Oct. 16, 1899, Louise wrote Miss Gentle that she would be taking Manfred out of her care. She explained that the boy's father had requested that he be sent to France to be educated. She was planning on picking up her son on Oct. 27 and continuing on to France with the boy. Louise told her sister, Mrs. Cadisch, the same story. Both women accepted Louise's straightforward explanation at face value.

In preparation for her trip, Louise had purchased a black shawl at a shop in Stoke Newington. Later she was positively identified by the clerk who had made the sale.

Louise told her boyfriend quite a different story from the one she related to the two ladies. On Oct. 25, she made a date with Lucas to meet in Brighton the following Saturday, Oct. 28. She couldn't possibly have intended to be in Brighton and France on the same day. Lucas travelled to Brighton, fully expecting Louise to arrive on Saturday.

On Friday, Oct. 27, Louise picked up her son as previously arranged. She told Miss Gentle that she would make her way to London Bridge Station and catch a boat train to France. She disclosed that she planned on returning in three or four days.

Substantiating witnesses proved that Louise and her son arrived at London Bridge Station at 1:45 p.m. She spoke to an attendant there, and as she lingered, she idly mentioned that she was waiting for someone. At about 3 p.m., after waiting for about an hour, she told the watiing room attendant that her son was getting restless, as he had just been parted from a nurse of whom he was very fond. Louise brought Manfred a piece of cake to settle him down and then left the station with her son. No one knows for sure what happened during the next three and a half hours. At 6:30 p.m. Manfred's body was found at Dalston Junction Station.

At 7:22 that same evening Louise caught the train at London Bridge and went straight to Brighton. She spent the weekend with Lucas as she had told him she would. As far as he was concerned, nothing untoward had taken place. He was completely unaware of Louise's elaborate plans to transport her son to France.

When police identified Manfred's body, Louise went to a friend for advice. Her friend advised her to go to the police. Louise hesitated, and within hours was being hunted. She was eventually picked up by the authorities.

Louise stood trial for the murder of her son. The Crown proved that the shawl found wrapped around Manfred's body was the one purchased by Louise shortly before the murder. Louise and Manfred's movements were well documented right up to 3 p.m. on the day of the murder. There is a gap of three and a half hours during which Louise's actions are unknown. The child's body was discovered at 6:30 p.m., wrapped in Louise's shawl.

The defence presented Louise's story, and quite a story it was. She claimed that each Wednesday when she visited Manfred at Miss Gentle's home, she usually took him out for a walk on Tottenham Green. One day she met two middle aged ladies who were accompanied by a little girl named Millie. Millie and Manfred got along well. Each Wednesday they had great fun playing together on the green. In the meantime, Louise got to know the two ladies rather well. She confided in them and, in fact, told them her life story, including the circumstances surrounding Manfred's birth. She elaborated that while Manfred's present set-up with Miss Gentle was adequate, now that he was approaching school age she wanted something better for him in the way of education.

By coincidence the ladies revealed that they were in the process of starting a kindergarten in King's Road, Chelsea. Louise expressed great interest, but was concerned that the cost would be prohibitive. The ladies, who were known to Louise only as the Misses Browning, quoted a price of £12 a year for Manfred's care.

Louise was thrilled at being able to place her son for such a reasonable amount. One problem did exist. How could she tell Miss Gentle, who had been so good to Manfred and had grown so fond of the child herself? Louise claimed that she made up the story of taking the boy to France to spare Miss Gentle's feelings.

The defence concurred with the Crown's version of Louise's movements right up to the point where Louise and Manfred were seen at London Bridge Station. Louise, you will recall, told the attendant that she was waiting for someone. She claimed that she was waiting for the two ladies, whom she was to accompany to Chelsea to inspect their school.

Unfortunately, the two women were waiting on the wrong platform. According to Louise, when she at last found them, she knew that if she accompanied them to the school she would miss her 7:22 train to Brighton. Remember, Louise had known the two ladies for some time. Influenced by their urging, she turned her son and £12 over to them. Manfred was quite accustomed to the two women and gladly accompanied them, with the expectation that he would soon be playing with his friend Millie. Louise was assured that the ladies would contact her upon her return from Brighton. She would then visit her son's new home.

That was Louise's story. It was a strange tale, but it accounted for all her actions, and certainly brought up the nagging question of reasonable doubt. Three physical facts couldn't be disputed. Louise could not account for her shawl's being wrapped around her son's body, except to state that Manfred had carried a small bag of clothing with him. The shawl may have been included by mistake with his things. The day after the murder, the coat Manfred has been wearing was found in the Brighton Station waiting room. Louise had no idea how it got there. Police could find no house functioning as a kindergarten on King's Road in Chelsea.

Well, what do you think? Could a woman who obviously loved her son strike him down in cold blood and suffocate him for no apparent reason? Or was her story true? Did the two ladies, who never were located, take the life of a small boy for a measly £12?

The jury took only a half hour to return with its verdict. It was guilty. Louise was hanged on Jan. 9, 1900. At the very last minute she confessed to killing her son, but she never said why. Ah, but that's another mystery.

SHE SHOT THE PRINCE

Aficionados of the manly art of mayhem have often been accused of being morbid. We all know nothing could be further from the truth. Pure curiosity as to the causes that trigger the taking of another's life is our motive.

Some people who apparently have every worldly comfort do not stand up well under the revealing glare of a murder trial. It is only then that we are able to glimpse the terrible lives many of them lead.

Prince Ali Kamel Fahmy Bey was an Egyptian prince who first met Madame Marguerite Laurent, a divorcee, in Paris in 1922. The prince fell head over heels in love with Madame. He had good reason, too. Marguerite was a beauty. She not only had striking good looks, but was a sophisticated worldly Parisienne. The prince followed her everywhere until she caught him. A minor chit chat between the two ended with the understanding that she would become his mistress. In this semi-official capacity she travelled with him to Egypt and throughout Europe. You see, folks, money was no object. The prince's family were large landowners back home along the Nile. The rate at which he spent money was of no concern. Apparently the family fortune was of such magnitude that no amount of spending could dissipate it.

By December, all seemed peaches and cream with the attractive young couple. It became so peachy that Madame Laurent became a Moslem. She then married the prince, who was 10 years her junior, in both a civil and a Moslem ceremony. It seems that back home there was some rider on an inheritance that stipulated that the prince had to marry a Moslem.

Once the marriage ceremony was performed the bloom, as it so often does, faded. The newly married couple quarrelled incessantly. Fahmy would humiliate his new bride at every opportunity. She in turn would yell and scream back at him.

Early in July, 1923, they checked into a luxury suite at the Savoy Hotel in London. The handsome couple had an entourage which included a valet, secretary and maid. On the night of July 9, they had an embarrassing battle over dinner. After dinner their bickering and arguing kept pace with the dance music until 1:30 a.m. when they retired to their suite.

As one of the most severe thunderstorms to hit London in years raged outside, Madame Fahmy pumped three slugs into her husband's body. A porter happened by the suite just then and heard the shots. When the manager was summoned he found Marguerite in a state of extreme excitement, which is, I suppose, the customary state when one has just killed one's husband.

"Oh, Sir," said Madame Fahmy. "I have been married six months, which has been torture to me. I have suffered terribly."

Madame Fahmy never once denied that she had shot her husband. She was arrested and stood trial for murder at the Old Bailey in London.

Marguerite, not one to scrimp with her dead husband's money, secured the services of perhaps the greatest defence lawyer in England, Marshall Hall. After interviewing the accused, he decided to go for acquittal. There would be no compromise.

Most criminologists feel that Marshall Hall conducted one of the finest defences ever afforded an accused murderer.

The dead man's secretary, Seid Ernant, admitted on the witness stand that Fahmy was cruel to his wife. He further admitted that the dead man had her watched day and night. Maybe the straw that broke the camel's back was the revelation that the prince wanted to "break his wife." In effect, he wanted her to become his slave. She, on the other hand, insisted on the same treatment that any French wife had a right to expect.

As month after month of ill treatment passed, Madame Fahmy became sullen and despondent. She was no longer the gay divorcee who had married the Egyptian prince.

Marshall Hall next summoned a gun expert to the witness stand. He stated that the murder weapon had an automatic feature that allowed a continuous flow of bullets from the single pressure of one pull. In this way Madame Fahmy didn't actually shoot three times. One slight pull of the trigger discharged the three bullets. The weapon itself was given to her by her husband for protection.

Little by little, the picture of a tortured, mistreated wife being pushed over the brink by an overbearing husband was being presented to the jury. Still, there had to be a better reason for killing him.

Then came the electrifying sentence that is uttered all too infrequently during famous murder trials.

"I call the Accused."

Madame Fahmy went through her troubled marriage for the benefit of the jury. She added the cute little touch that her husband demanded perverse and unnatural sexual satisfaction from her. She stated his sexual habits almost drove her mad. Hall was quick to extract the missing ingredients of self defence. Here are her exact words.

"He crouched to spring on me, saying: 'I will kill you'. I lifted up my arm and without looking, pulled the trigger. The next moment I saw him on the ground. I did not realize what had happened. I do not know how many times the pistol went off. I did not understand anything. I only saw Fahmy on the floor. I ran to him and took his hand and said: 'Sweetheart, it is nothing. Speak, oh speak to me."

Well, folks, we will never know what the dear lady said that night when she killed her husband. We only have her version as evidence.

There wasn't a dry eye in the courtroom when Marshall Hall summed up. The jury was out for a little over an hour. They brought back a verdict of not guilty. The crowd broke out in cheers. Madame Fahmy collapsed and a doctor had to be summoned to bring her around.

She then left the courtroom to be engulfed in the oblivion that is reserved for naughty ladies who shoot their husbands.

AN IRISH MAID

Those individuals fortunate enough to have servants should treat them with a certain degree of respect. Not only does this make for a more harmonious household, but it also serves as a peacekeeping device. You see, throughout criminal history, servants have frequently turned on their employers, using guns, bedpans, teapots, knives, and bare hands. They have even been known to perform nasty indignities to the bodies of their former employers. These bizarre and cruel acts illustrate a definite lack of respect. Kate Webster didn't know the meaning of the word.

Kate was born Catherine Lawlor in the quaint little village of Killane, Co. Wexford, Ireland, in 1849. From the time she was able to think for herself, Catherine decided that a farmer's life was not for her. She jumped at the first opportunity to leave the soil. His name was Webster and his profession was sea captain. While still in her teens, Catherine became Kate Webster. This transformation was closely followed by the arrival of four little Websters.

By now Kate had taken on a hard countenance, with piercing eyes and turned down lips. To pass the time while the good captain was at sea, she amused herself by stealing. Unfortunately, she wasn't very good at it, and was continually being hustled off to jail. It became so annoying to Kate that she left Ireland and made her way to Liverpool, where, in 1867, she found herself in the pokey for no less than three years. Upon her release she gravitated to London, where she found lodgings in Rose Gardens, Hammersmith.

Around this time in the rather nomadic existence of Kate Webster, two important events took place. Kate made friends with her neighbors, Mr. and Mrs. Porter in Hammersmith. She also became extremely close to a man named Strong. In fact, she was so close to Mr. Strong that she gave birth to his offspring on April 19, 1874. Deserted by Strong, she continued to steal to support herself and her new son. No record exists explaining the whereabouts of Kate's four children sired by Captain Webster, but for the next five years she took care of her more recent child, despite interruptions imposed upon her while serving jail setences for theft.

In 1879, Kate heard of an old English lady who was looking for a general servant. Mrs. Thomas was, in the classical English sense, an eccentric. She lived in a rather gloomy two-storey greystone house at 2 Mayfield Cottages, Richmond. It was a typical English house, just waiting for a murder to happen.

Mrs. Thomas had moved about since her second husband had gone to his great reward in 1873. She had a hard time keeping a lone servant, due to the fact that she seemed to enjoy berating them for some slight or imagined negligence of their duties. No doubt about it, Mrs. Thomas was not an easy old doll to get along with.

Kate applied for the servant's position. As fate would have it, Mrs. Thomas was impressed and hired the confirmed thief on the spot. Kate placed her child with friends and moved in with Mrs. Thomas.

Shortly thereafter, Mrs. Thomas directed one of her rages towards Kate. Instead of cowering in a corner, a reaction we can only assume Mrs. Thomas had become accustomed to, Kate answered the mistress of the house back in no uncertain terms. This turn of events upset Mrs. Thomas no end. When she looked into Kate's eyes, she observed an animal-like ferocity combined with naked hatred.

As the days went by Mrs. Thomas knew she had to dismiss Kate. The fact was that she was too terrified of the younger woman to give her notice. Finally, after Kate had been in her employ only a few weeks, she summoned up her courage and told her servant she was no longer required as of the end of the month, Feb. 28th.

Mrs. Thomas lived in fear until, at last, the 28th came. Kate implored her mistress to let her stay three more days until March 3rd. Probably out of fear, Mrs. Thomas acquiesced. In the meantime, she begged friends to move in with her. All believed her request to be nothing more than the ravings of an eccentric old woman.

On Sunday, March 2, Mrs. Thomas attended the Presbyterian services at Lecture Hall in Richmond. Those who spoke to her say she appeared nervous and agitated. She returned to her home and to her doom. What happened behind the closed door of Number 2 Mayfield Cottages that Sunday evening?

Kate and Mrs. Thomas had one of their regular disagreements, with Mrs. Thomas almost apologizing to her servant, as was now her custom. The mistress of the house went upstairs. Kate followed, spewing verbal abuse. In a fit of rage, Kate shoved Mrs. Thomas down the stairs. The elderly woman lay still where she fell.

Her rage still not satisfied, Kate pounced on the prostrate form of Mrs. Thomas. She clasped her hands firmly around her victim's neck and proceeded to choke her. Mrs. Thomas lay still, but was not dead.

Kate, one of the cruelest women who ever lived, carried Mrs. Thomas to the kitchen table and proceeded to cut and hack off parts of her body. Some parts were burned in the stove. Other portions she boiled in a copper, a container encased in a brick structure found in homes in rural England and normally used to boil laundry. A parcel containing one foot was disposed of that same evening. The following day Kate placed most of Mrs. Thomas in a wooden crate and fastened it securely with a strong cord.

Kate, now working to a prearranged plan, outfitted herself in her deceased mistress' best dress and jewelry. She then placed Mrs. Thomas' head in a black bag and walked out of 2 Mayfield Cottages. She went to visit the Porters, the family whom she had not seen for six years.

The Porters were understandably surprised to see their old neighbor, especially since her circumstances had so obviously changed for the better. Cunning Kate told the Porters that she had married Mr. Thomas, who had since passed away. Now an aunt had died as well, leaving her a home full of furniture. She informed the impressed Porters that she was about to move to Scotland to live with her mother, and was going to sell all her newly acquired furniture. The Porters bought the story hook, line and sinker. While Kate explained her situation over tea and crumpets, the black bag containing Mrs. Thomas' head lay unobtrusively at her feet.

About to take her leave, Kate inquired whether Mr. Porter might put her in touch with someone who could assist her in selling off her assets. Mr. Porter said he knew someone who might fit the bill.

Tea time over, Kate asked a further favor of the Porters. Could Mr. Porter and his teenage son Robert help her with a wooden crate she had to move from her home to Hammersmith Station? Not only would they help her with the crate, Robert offered to carry her black bag back to her home. Kate coughed.

The trio started off. All three made an unscheduled stopover at the Oxford and Cambridge Arms at the foot of Hammersmith Bridge. Kate excused herself, explaining that she had to deliver her black bag to a friend in Barnes. As it was not too far away, she would attend to it right then and return in a few minutes. Twenty minutes later Kate did return without the bag. To this day Mrs. Thomas' head has never been found.

Somewhere along the line everyone agreed that three people would not be required to carry the wooden box. As a result Mr. Porter returned home while Kate, and Robert proceeded to 2 Mayfield Cottages.

The night was pitch black. Robert and Kate carried the wooden box containing various parts of Mrs. Thomas. Once in the middle of Richmond bridge, Kate informed Robert that a friend was to meet her right there and take possession of the box. She told Robert to wait at the end of the bridge. Robert wandered only a few yards. Ironically, he was a bit apprehensive about being alone in the dark. Suddenly he heard a splash. A moment later Kate showed up and informed him that her friend had taken delivery of the box.

A few days later Henry Wheatley was driving his coal wagon along the banks of the Thames near Barnes Bridge. Henry spotted an old box on the bank. Making his way down to the box, he opened and peered inside. He gazed at what appeared to be nothing more than pieces of meat, which seemed to be cooked or boiled. Henry thought the best thing to do would be to advise the police. Doctors later identified the parts as having belonged to an elderly woman.

On March 9, John Church, a broker, was introduced to Kate by Mr. Porter. Church agreed to sell Kate's furniture. During the next few days he was seen entering and leaving the murder house several times. Church, the Porters, and of course, Kate, read the horrible news of the gruesome find along the Thames. All agreed it was the work of some monster.

Church gave Kate a deposit toward the proceeds he would receive for selling her furnishings. On March 17, a van pulled up and began loading the furniture. At this point a Mrs. Ives, who lived next door and who happened to own Mrs. Thomas' house, came over to inquire why Mrs. Thomas had not given her any notice that she was moving.

When Kate was informed of the inquiry, she mustered all her strength and called on Mrs. Ives. Now returning to her real identity of Kate the servant, she told Mrs. Ives she didn't know what had happened to Mrs. Thomas. This did not sit well with Mrs. Ives and Kate knew by her reaction that she had to move fast. She gathered up her son and took off directly for her birthplace, Killane, Ireland, where she found refuge with an uncle.

While sorting out Mrs. Thomas' clothes prior to selling them, Church found several letters written by a Mr. Menhennick. After reading the letters, Church felt that Mr. Menhennick was writing to someone other than the Mrs. Thomas he knew. He and Porter decided to pay a visit to Mr. Menhennick that very evening. Both men were quickly convinced that the real Mrs. Thomas was much older than the lady they had been dealing with. They reported the whole matter to the Richmond Police.

It didn't take the police long to question all the principals. They found out about Robert Porter's macabre walk with a black bag and later a wooden box. Now Porter quickly identified the box.

Kate, who had fled to the most conspicuous spot on earth for her, her home town, was quickly traced to her uncle's home. Kate first accused Church of being the real murderer. Then she tried to pin the rap on Porter. But each of these two gentlemen, while having associated with Kate directly after the murder, proved to have airtight alibis and could not have been involved in the crime.

Kate stood trial and was convicted of the murder of Mrs. Thomas. On the evening before she was to be executed, when all hope of evading the scaffold was gone, Kate Webster confessed in detail to the killing and dismemberment of Mrs. Thomas. Next day, Tuesday, July 29, 1879, Kate Webster was hanged for her crime.

HOW DOES YOUR
GARDEN GROW?

Belle Paulsen's father was a magician who travelled the length and breadth of Norway with his magic act. Belle was born in 1859 and grew up to be a slim, well-behaved child who became adept at tightrope walking, delighting her father's audiences with daring stunts on the taut wire. When her father retired from the transient life of a magician and bought a farm, Belle found the change from being a performer to the solitude of rural life unbearably boring. Now an impetuous teenager, she decided to emigrate to the United States.

After she arrived in the U.S., Belle, a shapely 24-year-old, met Mads Sorensen, a Swede, who courted her and won her hand in marriage. The couple settled in Chicago, Illinois, and the marriage commenced to bear fruit in the form of two offspring, Lucy and Myrtle. Two years after the marriage, Mads had a heart attack and died. There was a small group of friends and relatives in the close-knit Scandinavian community who never for a moment thought that it was a heart attack that had put an end to Mads. They whispered that he had been poisoned, and they fingered the widow as the administrator of the deadly potion. But even though Belle collected $8,500 in insurance money and sold Sorensen's home for $5,000, nothing came of the distasteful rumors.

The now well-heeled Belle and her two children moved to Austin, Illinois, where they purchased a new home. One cold night the house mysteriously caught fire, and while the insurance company suspected that the fire wasn't accidental, there was no proof of any monkey business and they paid off.

Belle moved back to Chicago in the grip of an obsession. She had somehow acquired a ravenous appetite, and ate to such an extent that she started to gain weight rapidly. She became fatter and fatter, until the scales tipped 200 pounds. This five-foot, seven-inch dumpling was no longer recognizable as the slender Norwegian girl who had married Mads Sorensen. Her face had been plain to begin with, but now it became bloated and ugly. In Chicago, she purchased a candy store, which soon burned to the ground. Again with some misgivings, the insurance company paid off. We can imagine Belle, relaxing with a box of chocolates, figuring that the greatest prerequisite for success in the world of commerce was to have a quick hand with a match.

With the proceeds of her fires she purchased a 48-acre farm about a mile from La Porte, Indiana, and quite by chance had an unexpected addition to her family. Antone Olson had recently lost his wife, and felt ill-equipped to take care of his daughter Jennie. Belle, who had known the Olsons for years in Chicago, was only too happy to take Jenny in, and as she put it, "treat her like one of my own."

Belle soon ballooned to a substantial 230 pounds. She worked her farm like a man, and gained a sort of local fame by butchering her own farm animals, particularly hogs, and selling the meat in the nearby town of La Porte. In April of 1902, she met Peter Gunness, who, like Belle, was Norwegian. We don't know where Peter came from, but he settled in on the farm and appears to have been well-liked by his neighbors and people who came in contact with him in La Porte. The neighbors had only a short time to make any judgment about Peter, for only seven months after he married Belle, disaster struck. It came in the form of a sausage grinder, and it struck poor Peter square on the head, killing him instantly. The grinder sat on a high shelf and, as luck, or whatever, would have it, Peter picked a spot directly under the grinder to rest his weary bones. Coincidentally enough, the grinder chose this opportune moment to totter and fall, striking Peter a fatal blow to the head.

During his short but noteworthy appearance upon the stage with Belle, the unlucky Norwegian managed to accomplish three things. He changed Belle's name from Belle Brynhilde Paulsetter Sorensen to Belle Gunness, for which he earns our gratitude. He was also thoughtful enough to insure his life for $4,000, which Belle reluctantly allowed to be pressed into her chubby hands. And he wasn't fully acclimatized to his new surroundings in the grave when Belle discovered that she was heavy laden with child, as they used to say. "Son of a bitch," Belle hissed between her teeth when she discovered the dirty trick Peter had pulled on her from the grave. The object of her dilemma popped into the world in 1903, and was named Phillip for no particular reason.

After the birth of her son, Belle settled down to farming, and occasionally hired a transient hand to help her. Most stayed for a short time and moved on. There was something strange and sinister about working for the quiet, puffing butterball, who could not only pitch hay with the best of men, but who also seemed to take a delight in butchering her own hogs. Rough and tough as these men were, Belle's actions didn't appear natural to them.

Belle worked hard, but a chubby nymphomaniac needs a man around the house. Like so many men and women in similar circumstances Belle gravitated to advertising in matrimonial journals. This direct approach had produced many good husbands and wives, so we cannot completely condemn the practice of selecting a partner by mail order. But it would be as well to warn the lovesick advertiser that a certain risk is involved in communicating with a total stranger. Belle reduced the risk factor, but unfortunately her male partners weren't quite as cautious. She refined the ads and eliminated a lot of the riffraff with her no-nonsense approach.

For example — "Comely widow who owns a large farm in one of the finest districts in La Porte County, Indiana, desires to make acquaintance of a gentleman equally well provided, with view of joining fortunes. No replies by letter considered unless sender is willing to follow answer with personal visit. No triflers please."

The number of men attracted to ads of this nature is uncertain. For one thing, we will never know how many men showed up at the widow's doorstep, took one look at Belle's 230 pounds, and said thanks, but no thanks. Conversely, we have no way of knowing how many prospective suitors didn't measure up to Belle's standards. She obviously preferred men of Scandinavian extraction who had accumulated some cold, hard cash.

In answer to one of her ads, a Norwegian named John Moo arrived from Minnesota in 1906. John must be placed in the missing, presumed dead category, for he was seen and met by neighbors as the bridegroom apparent, and just as suddenly as he appeared on the scene, he vanished. During the inquiries that followed, not a trace of him could be found, and Belle claimed she had no idea where he went when he left the farm.

Another native of Norway, George Anderson, travelled from a small village in Missouri to meet Belle. By now she had developed a line that could charm the birds out of the trees. Mr. Anderson had taken the precaution of not bringing his nest-egg with him, but admitted later to being completely captivated by his hostess. She wined and dined him in the grand manner. Visions of the good life on the farm danced before his eyes, giving a rosy tinge to her obvious shortcomings. One night at the farmhouse, Anderson was startled out of a deep sleep. There, towering over him by candlelight, was the huge form of Mrs. Gunness with a strange, wild look in her eyes. As he awoke she ran from the room, and Anderson, scared half out of his wits, made the wisest move of his life. He got out of bed, put on his pants, ran all the way to the station in La Porte, and went back to Missouri on the next train.

Not quite as fortunate was Bud Budsberg, another native of Norway, who arrived at Belle's door in 1907. Mr. Budsberg had travelled from Iola, Wisconsin, with $2,000 in his poke. Despite extensive inquiries conducted by relatives back in Wisconsin, Bud was never heard from again. He simply crossed Belle's threshold and disappeared.

Nothing seemed very permanent on the Gunness farm. But there was one exception; Belle had finally found a hired hand who didn't move on like the rest. He was a French Canadian named Ray Lamphere, who was not only able to tolerate Belle as an employer, but actually fell in love with her. Ray, who had the personality of a born follower, was of average height and had a handlebar moustache and bulging eyes that made him look as if he was always afraid of something, as well he might have been. It is pretty certain that Belle kept Ray around the farm for a variety of reasons, not the least of which was instant sex. Her other gentlemen friends had developed the annoying habit of disappearing, but steady, if not heady, Ray was always available. Jealous though he was of the other men who were continually coming to the farm, Ray was secure in the knowledge that he would outlast them all.

At about this time neighbors noticed that a large eight-foot-high fence had been put up around the farmhouse. The shutters on the windows were closed for weeks on end, and it was well-known that the basement was equipped as a slaughterhouse for Belle's hogs. She had a large table down there, as well as a pulley system for raising the carcasses of slaughtered animals. Along one wall hung a top quality set of butchers' knives and cleavers.

The parade of suitors continued. Andrew K. Helgelein arrived from Aberdeen, South Dakota, with $3,000 in a bulging wallet. This gentleman differed from those who had come before in that he got under Ray Lamphere's skin. For some reason, Ray, who had become accustomed to seeing his beloved being courted by other men, couldn't take it when Helgelein and Belle were together. Ray and Belle argued bitterly about this, and Ray packed up his belongings and left the farm in a tantrum.

He went to La Porte and started gossiping about his former lover and employer. Nothing serious, mind you, but enough so that when word of his loose tongue got back to Belle she had him arrested and tried to have him judged insane and committed to an institution. A sanity hearing actually took place, and Lamphere was declared sane. He made up with Belle, and returned to the farm. He commenced to pick another fight; this time Belle had him arrested for trespassing. Lamphere was found guilty of this offense and paid a fine.

Still in La Porte, the French Canadian continued to badmouth Belle, even mentioning to a farmer, Bill Slater, "Helgelein won't bother me no more. We fixed him for keeps."

By coincidence Helgelein had disappeared the day before this conversation took place. Then something happened that was even more vexing than Ray Lamphere shooting off his mouth in town. For the first time in all her years on the farm, Belle was the recipient of a serious threat, in the form of inquiring letters from Mr. Asle Helgelein of Mansfield, South Dakota, who was the brother of the missing Andrew. Belle met his pointed questions with the claim that Andrew had gone back to Norway, to which Asle replied, "Rubbish."

With the heat definitely on, Belle hitched up the team, drove into La Porte and paid a visit to her lawyer, M.E. Leliter. On April 27, 1908, Belle asked the lawyer to draw up her will, leaving her estate to her three children, with the proviso that should she outlive her children, the money would go to a Norwegian orphanage in Chicago. She said the reason for this sudden urge to put her affairs in order was because Ray Lamphere was threatening to kill her and burn down her farmhouse. She told Leliter that she was in mortal fear of the insanely jealous Lamphere. The whole thing took a matter of minutes, and was drawn up and signed before she left the lawyer's office.

That very night the new hired hand, Joe Maxon, said goodnight to the family and went to bed. In the middle of the night, he was awakened by the loud crackling of a fire. Shaking the cobwebs from his mind, he rose slowly, then realized that the entire house was engulfed in flames. He shouted at the top of his lungs to wake Belle and the children, then staggered toward the window, and jumped from the second storey, wearing only his underwear.

The next morning, as the charred rubble cooled, the remains of Belle's three children, Lucy, Myrtle, and Philips, together with the headless body of a woman, were found in the cellar, having fallen through the floor.

Because of the veiled threats made by Lamphere, and the well-known feud that existed between him and Mrs. Gunness, he immediately came under suspicion. A youngster swore he had not only seem Lamphere near the farmhouse on the night of the fire, but had actually spoken to him. Ray was arrested, and Belle's lawyer came forward and told of her accusations against the accused man. In due course, Lamphere was charged with the murder of Belle Gunness.

Neighbors who had known Belle for years were asked to identify the headless corpse. At the time of the fire Belle was estimated to weigh 280 pounds; not an easy figure to mistake. All her neighbors said the burnt corpse was too short and far too light to be Mrs. Gunness. This rather startling development threw an entirely new light on the macabre affair. For starters, who was the burned, headless corpse? If the corpse wasn't Mrs. Gunness, then where was she? To further confuse an already confusing situation, Mr. Antone Olson heard about the fire and rushed down to the farm to find his Jennie. She too was nowhere to be found, although neighbors said that some time previously Belle had mentioned that she had gone to California to continue her schooling.

The authorities searched everywhere for the missing head, but try as they might, they couldn't find it. Then Mr. Asle Helgelein showed up, looking for his brother. He didn't even know there had been a fire, but he had a deep suspicion that his brother had met with foul play at the hands of the woman he had come to Indiana to marry. Asle noticed that the Gunness' yard was uneven, and that patches of earth in the yard were of different colors. Maxon, the hired hand, volunteered that there had been slight depressions in the ground, and Mrs. Gunness had told him to bring earth from an adjoining field to even it off. Asle wasn't taking any offhanded answers, and urged the police to dig in these areas. The very first hole they dug uncovered the corpse of Andrew Helgelein, whose brother had the unfortunate experience of staring down at it as it was unearthed. He positively identified the body, and the digging started in earnest.

The next hole produced the body of Jennie Olson, who hadn't gone to California at all. Three more bodies were uncovered before darkness fell on the eerie scene and the diggers had to stop for the night. The next day, May 4, 1908, four more bodies were dug out of the farmyard, and on the third day one further body was uncovered. The bodies were in various stages of decomposition, and some were never to be identified. Others were positively identified as Andrew Helgelein, Jennie Olson, John Moo, and Bud Budsberg. Over and above these complete corpses police uncovered bits and pieces of other bodies that had no matching parts, leading them to believe that many more suitors had been put to death on the farm. With the discovery of these parts of human bodies, the police had to consider Belle's private abattoir in the basement. The implication was obvious — had Belle been butchering more than hogs?

Gossip comes a narrow second to farming as the principal occupation in the Hoosier State, and the murder farm was soon on everyone's lips. Crops lay unattended as men gathered to discuss the case, with the more curious driving out to the farm to peer at the now excavated farmyard. All the while they talked, exchanging information, telling stories, until one bit of gossip became so prominent that it took on the status of a distinct possibility.

The night the house burned Belle had been seen heading for her farm in her buggy with a stout lady. Joe Maxon, who was in the house that night, said that he didn't see any stout lady, but added that it would have been possible for a woman to be in the house without his knowledge. The local speculation was that Belle had somehow arranged to bring a strange woman out to the farm, kill and decapitate her, set the house on fire, and take off, thinking that everyone would believe she had perished in the fire. She had come up with a stout lady, but she couldn't quite duplicate her own massive poundage.

By now the weird case was on the front page of every newspaper in the U.S., and because of its doubtful aspects it gave rise to theory and speculation. Everyone had a story to tell about Belle or one of the victims. Dr. Ira P. Norton read about the case and volunteered the information that he had once done dental work for Belle, and could identify his own work if the authorities could produce it. This appeared to be a hopeless task, as the police felt that a fire hot enough to destroy a head would certainly melt gold caps and change porcelain beyond recognition. The doctor explained that this was not so, and that if his dental work could be found, it would be easy to identify. The police looked at the rubble of the burned farmhouse and realized they had a mammoth task before them.

Into a case already loaded down with strange and interesting characters came the most colorful of all, Louis Schultz. He had heard about the missing gold dental work in the rubble of the fire. Louis was an experienced gold miner just back from the Yukon, and told the police that if they would build him a sluice box he would sluice the entire farmhouse and if there was any gold in the rubble he would find it, using the same methods he had used in the Yukon.

The scheme seemed practical enough. In due course the sluice box was set up in the farmyard with running water piped over from the barn, and Louis set to work.

The sluice box manned by Louis in the yard received almost as much publicity as the crimes themselves. Crowds poured out to the farm to take in the spectacle of a sourdough mining gold on an Indiana farm. They cheered Louis on, and rising to the occasion, he waved and joked with the crowd. Christened Klondike Louis by the press, he was always good for a colorful quote, and because of him and the eeriness of the scene, on a good day the crowd surrounding the farm swelled to 5000. You could even place a friendly wager as to whether Louis would strike gold or not.

Then it happened. After four days on the job, and after washing tons of mud and debris through his sluice box, Schultz came up with a bridgework containing two lower bicuspids capped with gold and four porcelain teeth. Louis was proclaimed a hero, and the teeth were rushed to Dr. Norton for examination. He positively identified the work as his own, and the teeth as belonging to Belle Gunness.

This lent considerable weight to the assumption that Belle's head had been completely burned by the fire and only her dental work had survived, and Ray Lamphere stood trial for Belle's murder. The evidence against him was strong; he had argued bitterly with Belle and had been seen near the house on the night of the fire. There was just one thing — the jury didn't believe that Mrs. Gunness was dead. Lamphere was acquitted, but was tried for arson and convicted. After hearing all the evidence, the jurors came to the conclusion that Belle was alive but that Lamphere had burned down the farmhouse. Lamphere was suffering from tuberculosis, and died in Michigan City Prison in December, 1909.

Before he died, he told two different versions of his life with Belle and particularly what happened on the night the house burned down. The first version was told to a friend in prison who came forward after Ray's death. Ray told him that the whole thing was a setup — Belle did not die in the fire. She had advertised for a housekeeper and had culled the applicants, trying to find one as large as herself. With pressure mounting from Andrew Helgelein, she had to settle for the stoutest woman she could find, but one still far short of her massive structure. After drugging her, Belle cut off her head, and Ray and Belle buried it in quicklime in the nearby swamp. Belle had dressed the stranger in some of her own clothing to further aid in the identification; then she had killed her three children, leaving Ray to light the fire. Ray claimed that he never actually killed anyone himself, but had aided Belle in any way she asked in getting rid of her bothersome bodies. She had killed her own children because they knew too much of the strange goings on. He said there had been 28 more murders committed on the farm that were never uncovered. Belle butchered the bodies in her basement, feeding the smaller parts to the hogs and burying the larger pieces in quicklime in the swamp.

Upon hearing the story of the hogs' unorthodox eating habits the man who purchased them in La Porte was reported to have remarked, "They were still the best damn hogs in the county."

Lamphere said that Belle had sneaked up behind Mr. Gunness and split open his had with an axe. She then placed his body under the shelf that held the sausage grinder and dropped it on his head. A little girl in La Porte remembered a conversation she had with Belle's daughter Myrtle who told her, "Mama brained Papa with an axe. Don't tell a soul."

Lamphere died shortly after telling his friend these details about the crime. After he had passed away, Reverend E.A. Schnell, the prison minister, told of Lamphere's confession of his part in the crimes. This version differs in many details from that given to his friend. Lamphere told the minister that on the night of the fire he had chloroformed the three Gunness children and set fire to the house. He said he was completely captivated by Belle and would comply with anything she desired. But whatever the major variations, the two stories were the same in one important detail — he swore that Belle had not died in the fire.

Readers can pick their own version of what took place that last night on the farm, but whichever they choose they must consider Belle's bridgework found in the debris of the burned out farmhouse. Is it within the realm of possibility that Belle, operating in a mad frenzy, with her three children dead beside her, could have taken a pair of pliers and torn the permanent bridgework from her own mouth? Dentists have recorded instances where lumberjacks and others working in isolation have suffered from terrible toothaches and pulled out several of their own teeth. A 280 pound woman who had disposed of a possible 42 human beings might not find the act as appalling as it appears to us.

Belle Gunness has not been seen or heard of since the night of April 27, 1908, when her house burned to the ground.

Lizzie Took an Axe

- Part 6-

ALL IN THE FAMILY

LIZZIE TOOK AN AXE

When Andrew Borden was 40 years old his wife died, leaving him with two young daughters, Emma, 12, and Lizzie, 2. Two years later, Andrew married for the second time. His new bride was a stout, short little spinster in her late thirties named Abby Grey.

The family lived together in apparent harmony for many years at 92 Second Street in Fall River, Massachusetts. As the girls grew up they partook of certain privileges of the well to do. Lizzie had taken a long European vacation in 1890. This was almost unheard of in the New England of that era. The two girls shared a maid, Bridget Sullivan, with their stepmother. Lizzie, the younger of the two daughters, was extremely religious. She was secretary and treasurer of the Christian Endeavor Society, as well as being active in the Women's Temperance Union.

To the casual outsider, all appeared well with the respected Borden clan, living a frugal but pleasant life in their rambling old home on Second Street. But small differences between the two daughters and their stepmother smouldered until they became major personality clashes. Andrew gave a gift of property to his wife. The girls were furious with their father, but for some reason they blamed his generosity on Abby. Sometime later, to keep peace in the family, Andrew gave the two girls a comparable gift. It was too late. Lizzie never forgave her stepmother. She showed her animosity by never calling her "Mother" again. Lizzie in particular never could reconcile family wealth with the lack of amenities that the family seemed to have to put up with.

Then on Aug. 4, 1894, on a sweltering hot day, an event was to occur that was to place the occupants of the Borden home on the front page of every English language newspaper in the world.

An uncle, one John V. Morse (a brother of the first Mrs. Borden, and therefore a true uncle of the two girls) was visiting the Borden house. He arose at 6 o'clock. Bridget Sullivan got up and lit the fire in the stove. At 7 o'clock, Mr. and Mrs. Borden and Mr. Morse ate breakfast. Bridget ate immediately after. At 8:45, Mr. Morse left the house and has never figured seriously in what was to follow. Lizzie came downstairs alone at 9 o'clock, as Emma was visiting friends 15 miles away in Fairhaven. Lizzie, because of the heat, had only a cup of coffee for breakfast. Mrs. Borden busied herself dusting the dining room furniture. Bridget complained of a headache and nausea, and went out in the backyard and vomited.

At about 9:15, Mr. Borden departed to do some business downtown. Bridget returned to the house feeling somewhat better. Mrs. Borden instructed Bridget to start cleaning the downstairs windows on the outside. She proceeded to get pails and brushes and left the house by the side door to start work behind the house. Mrs. Borden went upstairs, and put the guest room, the one occupied by Mr. Morse, in order. She came down for a minute, chatted with Lizzie, and went back upstairs to put fresh pillowslips on the guest room bed.

If you are following this rather meticulous chronology of activity you may notice that one by one members of the family are vacating the house. Finally the house now contains only two people, Lizzie and her stepmother Abby. No one was ever to come forward to place another living soul in the house. In fact, Bridget, moving from window to window from the outside, looked into the kitchen, dining room and sitting room without seeing anything strange or different.

Not more than a minute or two after Abby went upstairs to finish the bedroom, she was savagely bludgeoned to death with a sharp instrument, probably a hatchet or axe.

Meanwhile, Mr. Borden, who had left home at 9:15, was gone for an hour and a half. Every moment of his time spent away during the hour and a half has been accounted for. At 10:45, he arrived home and entered by the front door. Bridget, who had just finished her windows and was now in the house, went to assist him. As she did so she and Mr. Borden heard Lizzie give what some have described as a laugh. They turned and Lizzie stood at the first landing of the stairs leading to the second floor bedrooms. A slight turn of her head and she could plainly have seen Abby Borden's body not more than 15 feet from where she stood. Abby had now been dead for a full hour. Lizzie came down the stairs the rest of the way, and inquired of her father if there was any mail. Then she said, "Mrs. Borden is gone out — she had a note from someone who is sick."

Mr. Borden was tired after his walk in the heat, and went to the sitting room where he sat down on an overstuffed, black horse-hair couch. Bridget went up the back stairs to her bedroom to take a quick nap. As she lay there she heard the clock on the city hall strike eleven. She dozed off.

Suddenly, she woke up. Lizzie was hollering to her — she listened — "Come down here, Father's dead; someone came in and killed him. Go over and get the doctor."

Bridget ran across the street to Dr. Bowen. He was out; she told her story and returned home. When she got back she was the very first to ask the question, "Where were you, Miss Lizzie, when this happened?"

The reply came, "I was out in the yard, and heard a groan and came in."

Mrs. Churchill, an immediate neighbor, was summoned, and she rushed over. After learning of the tragedy to Mr. Borden, she also asked, "Where were you, Lizzie?"

Lizzie answered, "I went to the barn to get a piece of iron. I heard a distressing noise and came back and found the screen door opened."

Mrs. Churchill then summoned the police. The call was recorded at 11:15, no more than a half hour after Mr. Borden entered his home.

In the meantime, Dr. Bowen came home and received Bridget's message. He rushed over to the Borden home. There he looked at Mr. Borden's remains on the sofa. His head was hacked and the tremendous amount of blood made him unrecognizable. Most of the cuts were about four and a half inches long. Dr. Bowen guessed that an axe had been used to inflict the wounds.

Lizzie suggested that maybe they should look for Mrs. Borden. Bridget was too scared to go upstairs alone, and so accompanied by Mrs. Churchill, they discovered poor Abby's body in the bedroom on the floor, between the bed and a dressing table. She too, had been horribly hacked and cut about the head.

Within minutes the peaceful house at 92 Second Street was overrun with neighbors, doctors, and police. Because of the congealed blood and coldness of Mrs. Borden's body compared to the still wet wounds and warm body of Mr. Borden, the police were able to ascertain that Mrs. Borden had been killed 90 minutes before her husband. This meant that the murderer had to get into the house without being seen, kill Mrs. Borden, conceal himself for 90 minutes, kill Mr. Borden, and leave the house without anyone ever seeing him.

Thank God the invisible intruder spared Bridget and Lizzie!

The police had the unpleasant task of questioning Miss Borden concerning the death of her parents. During these interrogations Lizzie stated that she was up in the barn loft for 20 minutes while her father was being hacked to death.

On Aug. 9, five days after the double murder, the official inquest was held into the Borden deaths. At the conclusion of this inquest on Aug. 11, Lizzie Borden was arrested for the murder of her father.

Lizzie's trial and its rather unsatisfactory outcome was widely followed by the public. With the possible exception of the Lindbergh kidnapping and murder, it ranks as the most notorious crime ever committed in the United States. The proceedings were conducted in New Bedford, Mass., only a few miles from the site of the actual slayings. Normal topics of conversation that summer abruptly came to a halt. The name Lizzie Borden was on everyone's lips. The general mood that prevailed during that long ago New England summer was that the police were incompetent. They had to come up with a suspect. They came up with the most illogical one of all, Lizzie Borden.

From the outset Lizzie received preferential treatment. While in jail she really wasn't in a cell. She had a section of the jailer's living quarters outfitted with some of her own furniture, and spent over six months as a persecuted victim of circumstances.

The power of the church rallied to her defence. She was constantly in the company of a Reverend Jubb, whose review of the evidence consisted of continually issuing statements to the effect that no girl with Lizzie's upbringing could cut kindling, let alone axe her parents to death.

During the trial the prosecution maintained, and Lizzie partly verified, the fact that there was ill feeling between stepmother and daughter. Lizzie had called her stepmother "Mrs. Borden" for the previous five years.

The night before the murders, Lizzie visited a friend and neighbor, Alice Russell. Miss Russell swore that Lizzie told her of a strange feeling she had about something terrible about to happen to the family.

Further evidence revealed that Mr. and Mrs. Borden were not feeling well on the day before their death. They had retched and vomited. Remember, it was stiflng hot, and with no refrigeration food was often consumed that we would find unacceptable. Two druggists were produced who swore they knew Lizzie by sight, and that she had tried to buy poison from them for the ostensible reason that she wanted to clean a fur coat with it. The inference was made by the prosecution that Lizzie was trying to poison her parents using something containing poison from around the home. When they only became ill she tried to buy the real thing at the drugstore. All the poison evidence was ruled inadmissible at the trial. Had the evidence of the attempt to buy poison on the day before the murders been admissable, the outcome of the trial may have been much different.

Finally, the time element and layout of the house weighed heavily against Lizzie. At 9:15 a.m., Mr. Borden left the house. Mrs. Borden was immediately axed to death in the guest room. At 10:45 a.m., Mr. Borden returned to his home and at 11:05, Lizzie shouted to Bridget Sullivan that her father had been killed in the sitting room. Bridget at the time was in another section of the house that was not accessible from the front stairs. Only Lizzie was there. The street outside was a semi-residential, commercial street. It was busy, there were people about, neighbors were active outside their homes due to the heat. No one saw anyone enter the house or leave it.

The prosecution made much of the fact that if Lizzie was innocent, the assailant had to be almost invisible and extremely lucky. He had to enter the house unseen and axe Mrs. Borden in the guest room. Then he had to hide in the house for 90 minutes, during which time he had no way of knowing if Lizzie or Bridget or anyone would discover poor Abby's body. Then Mr. Borden had to go into a room and lie down, and be axed to death without making a sound. Then the assailant had to leave the house, again without being seen.

The defence brought out the unquestioned high moral and social position held by Lizzie. She had never committed a distasteful act of any kind in her entire life. Throughout the proceedings she professed to have been out in the barn loft when her father was being murdered. She gave conflicting stories as to why she was in the barn. The one she settled on was that she was looking for some lead to make sinkers for fishing. It was over 90 degrees that day in Fall River. In the barn loft it may have reached 100. Lizzie hadn't gone fishing during the previous five years.

By far the most startling evidence brought forth by the defence was the fact that immediately after her father's death Lizzie was seen by Bridget, Mrs. Churchill, the neighbor who summoned the police, Dr. Bowen, and others; and yet there were no signs of blood on her dress. Experts were called, and all asserted that whoever killed Mr. and Mrs. Borden would most probably have visible bloodstains on their person.

Miss Russell gave evidence that was not challenged, of seeing Lizzie burn a dress in the kitchen stove on the Sunday following the crime. The defence countered by pointing out that Lizzie had ruined a dress by spilling paint on it and that it was this dress that she destroyed.

Still, the inescapable fact remained. Lizzie apparently did not have any blood on her immediately after her father's death.

On June 20th, the jury came in with the verdict of not guilty, and Lizzie Borden was released from custody.

We will never know for certain what took place that morning in the house on Second Street. For years movies have been made, stories written, and even ballets performed, all offering theories of how Lizzie either killed her parents or presenting a set of circumstances that allows for some strange intruder to have killed the Bordens.

The most imaginative theory is that Lizzie killed both parents in the nude. After each killing she washed herself thoroughly and put her clean clothing back on. It is difficult to imagine puritanical Lizzie dashing around the house in the nude, dripping blood, when at any second Bridget or a neighbor could be at the door.

In reviewing these true life cases we are so often faced with the unusual and bizarre, that the obvious is often overlooked. I think Lizzie committed the perfect crime. Her motives were a smouldering hatred of her stepmother, and desire for her father's money. First she tried to poison her parents. When they only took ill, she tried to buy prussic acid at the drugstore. When this failed, she decided to kill them when her sister Emma was visiting out of town. When her father went out on that hot August morning, she followed her stepmother into the guest room, and as Abby bent over to put fresh pillowslips on the bed, Lizzie rained blow after blow on her head. I believe she wore an apron, commonly used in every home at that time. It came up to the neck, and completely covered the front of her dress. She then hid the apron and waited for her father. She could have kept watch on the stairs leading to the guest room, so that she could intercept anyone who might accidentally discover Abby's body. When her father laid down on the couch, she again put on her blood-stained apron and axed her father to death. Before shouting to Bridget she could have tossed the apron in the kitchen stove.

It was only after the murders that Lizzie started to give conflicting statements. Her plans were only thought out to the commission of the murders themselves, because she never thought she would be suspected.

After she was acquitted, Lizzie and Emma moved back into the house at 92 Second Street. The two sisters inherited the bulk of their father's estate, and purchased a much larger, ostentatious home. In 1904, the two spinsters had a falling out, and Emma moved away for good. Lizzie lived in Fall River for the rest of her life. As the years went by she became a lonely figure who was ostracized by the citizens of the community.

On June 1, 1927, at age 67, Lizzie died. Exactly nine days later, Emma died in Newmarket, New Hampshire. Lizzie's estate amounted to $425,000. Emma left $265,000. Both sisters left the bulk of their estates to charity.

Finally the Bordens were all reunited again. In Oak Grove Cemetery in Fall River, Andrew Borden lies between the bodies of his two wives. At his feet, resting forever, are the remains of his daughters, Emma and Lizzie.

CONSTANCE HAD A CONSCIENCE

In Victorian times in England governesses were held in high esteem. They belonged to that efficient class that performs unobtrusively. On occasion circumstances would evolve when a governess would find herself thrust into a situation quite different from that for which she had been retained.

Now, let's go back to the years between 1845 and 1865. Mr. and Mrs. Kent lived happily enough in the tiny village of Road, located on the Wiltshire-Somerset border. Mr. Kent was an inspector of factories. In their rambling home, called Road Hill House, there lived besides the master and mistress, three daughters and a son. The Kents had four other children who died in infancy. Taking care of this substantial brood was their governess, Miss Pratt. Misfortune befell the Kent clan when Mrs. Kent became mentally ill. Her condition deteriorated until it demanded continual attention. Finally she died. The feeling that accompanied her death can best be described in the words of one of the villagers, who was heard to say, "The Lord took the poor dear out of her misery."

A year after her death, the governess, Miss Pratt, became the second Mrs. Kent. She promptly gave birth to a further three children, and by 1860 we find her pregnant for the fourth time. The three children of the second marriage had a full time nurse named Elizabeth Gough.

The entire family appeared to be a happy, prosperous one, until the morning of June 30, 1860. On this particular morning, the nurse glanced at the cot of little four-year-old Francis. It was empty. Francis was the son of the former governess, the second Mrs. Kent. Elizabeth did not think it unusual that the child was missing, as Mrs. Kent was in the habit of taking Francis into her own bedroom. She turned over in her bed and went back to sleep. When she did get up, she attended to her usual early morning tasks before entering Mrs. Kent's room to pick up young Francis. As soon as she entered the room and asked for Francis, Mrs. Kent knew something was wrong. She ran to the cot. Then she noticed that the drawing room windows, which she had locked the night before, were now open. The whole house woke up and the dreaded word kidnapping was on everyone's mind.

The police were summoned, and with the assistance of villagers, they conducted a thorough search of the grounds. In a sort of indentation or cave in the earth, they found Francis' body. His throat had been cut, and another stab wound above the heart had been inflicted after death.

Now, murder investigations in tiny villages are quite a different thing from those conducted in cold impersonal cities. In villages everyone is involved, and everyone has a theory. In Road, the villagers started rumors that the murderer of the little boy had to be a member of the household.

In the house on the night of the murder were four children of the first Mrs. Kent, the oldest being 16, two children by the present Mrs. Kent, and of course, Mr. and Mrs. Kent, and the nurse, Elizabeth Gough.

An inquest was held, and all members of the family came under close scrutiny. The nurse was criticized for the delay of a few hours between the time she noticed the cot empty and the time she went into Mrs. Kent's room. Mr. Kent himself was the brunt of rumors. Was everything on the up and up years earlier when his wife was so ill and he and the former governess were the only adult occupants of the house? The oldest stepchild, Constance, was known to be the only one of the stepchildren to resent her former governess becoming her mother.

The most baffling aspect of the entire case was the complete lack of motive. What stranger or family member would kill a four-year-old child in the middle of the night? What was to be gained by anyone?

Scotland Yard was conducting the investigation and they doggedly searched for bloodstained clothing in the house. The only unusual thing that this investigation turned up was the fact that a nightdress Constance wore the week of the murder was missing. She owned three nightgowns, but only two were found. Constance and the whole Kent family maintained that the laundress was frequently losing various items of clothing. The laundress said that Constance was present when she was sorting the laundry and making out the laundry list. She stated that Constance could have taken the garment without her knowledge. Elizabeth Gough was detained on two different occasions, questioned, and released. Constance was also detained and released. The English press featured the case for weeks as a bona fide mystery. Every amateur and professional sleuth had a crack at solving the case, but no one succeeded.

Five years went by. Constance was now 21 and was living at Brighton in St. Mary's home run by the Anglican Sisterhood. She electrified England by releasing a written confession in 1865 telling how she murdered her four-year-old brother. In substance, she told how she secured her father's razor and waited until the household was asleep. She opened the drawing room windows to simulate kidnapping, not thinking the body would be found the very next morning. She then carried the sleeping child out to the cave, where she cut his throat. Then, to make sure of death, she stabbed the child once more above the heart. She managed to clean the razor and return it so that her father never knew it was missing. She had two bloodstains on her nightdress, which she washed out. While passing the time of day with the laundress, she noticed the faint outlines of the bloodstains on her nightdress. She took it when the laundress wasn't looking, and successfully burned it.

The motive? It is this aspect of the Constance Kent case that gives it a unique place in the infamy of murder investigations. Constance explained that she had nothing against the victim; in fact, she stated that she was very fond of little Francis. She killed him to gain revenge on her stepmother. For years she felt that every slight toward the members of the first Kent family had to be avenged. She stored up this hatred, waiting for the moment when she could get back at her stepmother. She decided to kill her stepmother's favorite child.

Her foul deed was heavy on her conscience for five long years. This remorse, coupled with the religious influence at St. Mary's Home compelled her to cleanse herself of her guilt.

Constance stood trial for her crime, and received the death sentence, which was later commuted to life in prison. She was released in 1885, after serving 20 years. It is believed she spent the rest of her days with a religious order.

HE WASN'T KIND
TO HIS FAMILY

John Donald Merrett lived with his mother in an apartment in Edinburgh, Scotland. Mrs. Merrett had lived in New Zealand, Russia, and England before settling in Edinburgh.

She knew she had a problem child on her hands.

By the time she moved to Scotland, young Donald was a strapping, 18-year-old, six footer, who was forever getting into scrapes. Petty theft was his specialty, but he also couldn't keep his hands off young ladies. Mrs. Merrett, who was financially well fixed, had enrolled her son in Edinburgh University. It happens that that school doesn't have a student residence. With Donald having to live at home she figured she could keep an eye on her wayward son.

In February of 1926, Donald started to deceive his mother by locking himself in his room, ostensibly to study. He would slip out the window and carouse with girls of ill repute until the wee hours of the morning. Each morning he would kiss his mother goodbye and leave the apartment, but he did not attend classes at Edinburgh University. He passed the time of day stealing, womanizing, and drinking ale.

On the morning of March 17, 1926, matters abruptly changed. Donald's mother was sitting at a desk in the apartment, writing a letter. A Mrs. Sutherland, who came in to clean each day, was fetching some coal from a closet. All of a sudden a shot rang out. Mrs. Sutherland heard a body fall and came running into the room. Donald met her, shouting: "My mother has shot herself!"

The police and an ambulance were summoned. Mrs. Merrett was rushed to the hospital where she lay in critical condition with a bullet wound in her head. She had shot directly into the right ear. Mrs. Merrett hovered near death for nearly two weeks, sinking intermittently in and out of consciousness. Donald told the police that he had acquired a small revolver for protection. No doubt his mother had found it and decided to kill herself. She had mentioned something about money trouble to him.

When friends and relatives heard about the supposed money difficulties, they were amazed. Mrs. Merrett was known to be meticulous about her financial affairs and had never been in any difficulty. Once, when she regained consciousness, she murmured to a relative at her bedside that "it was as if Donald had shot me." The relative dismissed the implications as the ramblings of a delirious woman.

On March 27, ten days after she was shot, Mrs. Merrett passed away. While his mother had lingered close to death, dear Donald had not acted like an attentive son. He visited her on and off but still managed to spend every night at a dancehall and seemed to be having a rare old time. Because of Donald's rather unorthodox behavior the police decided to delve a little closer into his mother's financial affairs. They found that 29 cheques totalling £457 had been forged by Donald. The genuine signature of Bertha Merrett had been traced and then inked over. The police were even able to detect carbon on the cheques from the carbon paper Donald had used.

Once they knew they had uncovered a rotten apple, the authorities took another look at the manner in which Mrs. Merrett had supposedly killed herself. Experts were consulted and they gave the opinion that from the angle the bullet entered Mrs. Merrett's ear it was unlikely that the fatal shot was self-inflicted. On this evidence Donald was arrested and charged with murder and forgery.

On Feb. 1, 1927 his trial opened in Edinburgh. It was only the third trial involving matricide ever to be held in Scotland, and it caused a sensation. The defence produced experts who testified that there was no evidence that was inconsistent with Mrs. Merrett firing the fatal shot. Despite the extreme suspicion that Donald had killed his mother, the jury just didn't have enough concrete evidence to convict him. After only 55 minutes they came up with that uniquely Scottish verdict "Not Proven." Loosely translated, not proven means, we all know you did it, but we can't quite convict you on the evidence presented to us.

Merrett was found guilty of forgery and received 12 months in jail. After serving only eight months John Donald Merrett walked out of prison a free man.

Ah, but we have not heard the last of Donald.

Mrs. Mary Bonnar had been a friend of Donald's mother. She thought it her duty to visit Donald while he was serving time in prison. Obviously she thought a terrible mix-up had taken place and the nasty police had simply made a mistake by placing Donald in jail. To prove to him that she didn't believe any of the horrid insinuations about him murdering his mother, Mrs. Bonnar invited Donald to stay with her in Hastings when he was released from prison.

Mrs. Bonnar had an impressionable 17-year-old daughter, Vera. Donald was a tall, good-looking young man. With the lapping of the waves against the shores of Hastings, and the stars twinkling overhead, and all that sort of thing, it didn't take long for Donald and Vera to pair up. They eloped to Scotland. Mrs. Bonnar was fit to be tied. She managed to drag Vera back home. Donald had unfortunately been held up due to a misunderstanding with the Scottish police. It involved something about obtaining merchandise under false pretenses.

Soon he was back in Hastings. Have you ever been to Hastings? I have. It is steeped in fish, and seawater. Let's face it — Hastings is boring.

Before Donald decided to pull up stakes and get out of town, his grandfather died. At the age of 21, Donald inherited £50,000. On a whim he gave his wife £8,400 and promptly spent the rest on booze and women.

Donald changed his name to Ronald Chesney and embarked on a life of crime. Nothing was heard from him until World War II. During this encounter, Donald or Ronnie, whichever you like, served with distinction in the Royal Naval Volunteer Reserve.

Every time he was hard up for cash he couldn't help but think how stupid he had been in giving Vera that £8,400. When the war ended he took up residence in Germany and didn't have anything to do with his wife and dear mother-in-law back home in England. They had managed to open and profitably run an old folks home in London.

One day, who should show up at the old people's home but Donald. He had shaved his substantial beard, and pleaded with Vera to give him back his hastily bestowed gift. She refused and Donald reacted by drowning poor Vera in the bathtub. When he went to leave the house, who should he bump into but his mother-in-law. A fierce struggle ensued, and Donald ended up strangling his mother-in-law. This time Merrett was seen and recognized by a score of people in his flight from England back to Germany. He was actively sought by the police of several countries.

On Feb. 16, 1946, two weeks after the murder of Vera and her mother, Donald was found shot to death in the woods near Cologne, Germany. Knowing that it was just a matter of time before he would be caught, he had killed himself. His body still bore scratches and bruises inflicted upon him by Mrs. Bonnar in her struggle for life. Textile fibres belonging to Mrs. Bonnar's clothing had adhered to Donald's trousers, and positively linked him to the two bodies back in London.

An inquest was held and it officially deemed Donald responsible for the murder of the two women. Donald Merrett is one of the few chaps in all the checkered history of crime to have killed his mother, his wife, and his mother-in-law.

SHE LOVED HER BOY

When Elizabeth Duncan was in her sixties, she could look back on life with a certain amount of satisfaction. She had been married many times, sometimes with the aid of the clergy, but on other occasions she had entered into the holy state without this assistance. There were so many husbands over the years that their names and faces tended to melt into one another. Try as she might, she couldn't remember them all.

Elizabeth remembered Frank Low, who was the father of her son Frank. She remembered how she left him to team up with Frank Duncan, and how she took his name and kept it for her own, even after she went on to seek greener pastures.

Over the years Elizabeth had only one honest sincere interest in her life, and that was her son Frank. She was with him continuously during his formative years, and doted on him. He in turn proved to be a dutiful, studious son, who showed a remarkable degree of independence, considering that his mother smothered him with affection. The pair lived together in Santa Barbara, California. Frank did well throughout school and university, and became a successful lawyer.

In the early 1950s, Frank's mother could be found in court, tagging after her son and causing him a great deal of embarrassment in front of his colleagues. He took his overbearing mother as long as he could, but in 1947, the pair had a bitter argument. The disagreement culminated with Elizabeth taking an overdose of sleeping pills. She almost killed herself, but was rushed to a hospital and survived.

While visiting his mother in the hospital, Frank couldn't help noticing her nurse, beautiful 29-year-old Olga Kupczyk. Olga took a second look at the handsome, successful lawyer.

Elizabeth fought the rage that was building up inside her at the thought of losing her son. She was actually limp when Frank informed her that Olga was pregnant. She made such a fuss that when Frank and Olga got married, they did so secretly.

Such was the hold that Elizabeth had on her son, that late each night he would leave Olga's side and return to his mother's apartment. When Elizabeth found out that her son and her nurse were married, she stormed over to Olga's apartment, causing such a scene that Olga had to call for help to restrain the deranged woman. Mrs. Duncan was beside herself. There had to be some way to separate her son from his wife. The thought kept building in her mind, until finally she hit on the scheme of hiring killers to do the job.

She confided her plan to her best friend, 70-year-old Emma Short. Emma took the news rather calmly. In December of 1958, the two ladies sauntered down State St. to the Tropical Cafe in Santa Barbara. Elizabeth knew the owner of the cafe, Mrs. Esperanza Esquivel. Her son Frank had defended the woman on a charge of possession of stolen property, and Elizabeth also knew that she was an illegal immigrant to the U.S. Armed with this knowledge and dropping subtle threats, she inquiried if Mrs. Esquivel knew of anyone who would be able to dispose of an undesirable woman for a fee. Lo and behold, Mrs. E. thought she could dig up a couple of boys who might be able to do the job. A meeting was set for the following day.

Straight out of *Arsenic and Old Lace*, the two ladies showed up promptly the next afternoon. Waiting for them at the Tropical were Luis Moya, 21, and Gus Baldonado, 26. Both were unemployed, petty crooks. At first there was some slight disagreement regarding the fee to be paid, but finally they all agreed on the contract — $3,000 in advance, and another $3,000 on completion of the job. There was a shaking of hands all around and the ladies left the cafe after Elizabeth gave the men $175 to show her good faith. She knew she had no chance of raising anything like $6,000.

Moya and Baldonado weren't the brightest boys in the world. They went about gathering the accoutrements of murder. They bought a 1948 Chev for $25, and a used .22 pistol from an acquaintance.

On Nov. 17, 1958, they drove to Olga's apartment building and Moya went up and knocked on the door. He told Olga that he had met her husband in a bar. He said Frank was very drunk and he was bringing him home. He needed some help in getting her husband up the steps. Olga, immediately concerned, followed Moya down to his car. Baldonado was posing as a drunk lying on the back floor of the vehicle. As Olga opened the door and looked inside, Moya struck her a blow to the head. The two men drove the car away, continuing to strike Olga until she was dead. They headed for the mountains, south of Santa Barbara, to bury the body. The not-too-bright pair faced a real dilemma when they discovered that each had thought the other had brought a pick and shovel. They managed to dig a shallow grave with their hands.

Frank immediately reported his wife's absence to the police. They figured they were dealing with a missing persons case. Then two days after the murder, Moya phoned Elizabeth and inquired about his money. Elizabeth told Moya that she couldn't draw money out of the bank because police were investigating the disappearance. She said she would meet the men the following day with as much money as she could raise without going to the bank. Next day she and her buddy Emma met with the two men and gave them a sealed envelope. Later, when Moya opened the envelope he found only $120. He knew he had been taken and was furious. In the days that followed, the two men started to put pressure on Elizabeth to pay up. She in turn told the police that two Mexicans, whose names she couldn't reveal, were blackmailing her. Elizabeth figured that when the two partners in crime heard this they would be too scared to bother her, and would probably move out of the area.

Contacting the police was a bad move on Elizabeth's part. They started to check her out and discovered how much she hated the missing Olga. They also questioned her closest friend, Emma Short. No longer playing a game, Emma told of accompanying her friend on her weird errands, and of Elizabeth contracting to have Olga killed. The police picked up Moya and Baldonado. They quickly confessed and led the officers to Olga's grave.

Emma Short was never charged, but the three conspirators were all charged with murder. Mrs. Duncan's son, Frank, defended his mother and fought to the bitter end to save her life, but all appeals failed.

On Aug. 8, 1962, Elizabeth Duncan, Luis Moya and Gus Baldonado were put to death in the gas chamber of San Quentin.

LINC DIDN'T LIKE LINA

Murderers have used some strange and weird means to dispose of their victims' bodies. They have burned, hacked, dissolved, buried, and yes, even eaten their victims; but maybe none was as innovative as Warren Lincoln.

Linc wasn't a dummy. He was a lawyer, who practised in Chicago, Illinois, a city well known for providing followers of the legal profession with a wealth of criminal activity. He was a defence lawyer who wasn't above crossing a jurist's palm with cold hard cash in order to gain favor.

In 1921, Linc had accumulated a tidy little nest egg and, together with his wife Lina, decided to retire. He and Lina bought a house just outside the suburb of Aurora.

Still on the sunny side of 50, Linc, who was a rather small man, apparently had the world by the tail. There were those who whispered that Lina appeared to be her husband's exact opposite in physical appearance. She was a tall, big boned lady, who tipped the Toledos at 250 pounds. Not only was she grossly overweight, she had long since ceased to care about her personal appearance, with the result that she had become a slovenly old bag.

Mr. and Mrs. Lincoln settled into their new home. Linc took up gardening with a vengeance and it wasn't long before the little retirement cottage was surrounded by several beds of fragrant sweet peas. Each Sunday Linc and the wife donned their best bib and tucker and marched off to church. Lina sang in the choir.

Everything changed abruptly when Linc's brother-in-law, Byron Shoup, came for a visit. Lina's baby brother was a big athletic lout who insisted that frail Linc do strenuous, and annoying, exercises. Lincoln hated Byron's guts. Lina seemed to follow her brother's example and added domineering to the list of traits her husband was fast growing to despise. Byron's visit was turning into a permanent arrangement, and the permanent arrangement was turning into a nightmare. Linc was beginning to get the idea that he was in for a long life of misery unless he did something to get out of his predicament.

The first thing he did was to become a secret drinker. His wife and her athletic brother didn't allow liquor to darken their door, so Linc took to guzzling a few with the boys down at the speakeasy everyday. In an attempt to withdraw even further from harrassment in his own home, he built a greenhouse. There he grew sweet peas, spending more and more time at his hobby. Soon he was providing local florists with all kinds of flowers. The hobby had turned into a commercial success. Linc expanded the greenhouse and hired a helper, Frank, to work full time with him.

Lincoln was happy when he was working with Frank and tending his sweet peas, but as soon as he entered his house he would get into a hassle with either Lina or the overbearing Byron. It was probably in the winter of 1923 that he decided to kill them both. Being a former defence lawyer, Linc knew what he was doing. He set up a series of conditions which would enable him to commit the perfect murder.

One day, while drowning his sorrows in one of the local bars, Linc was cunning enough to let an acquaintance read a letter he carried in a dog-eared envelope. The letter was addressed to his wife and expressed undying love. It was signed George. Soon all Linc's drinking cronies knew that Warren Lincoln's wife was unfaithful to her husband. Of course, we know that Linc had really written the letter himself. Someone suggested that the retired lawyer should kick both his wife and brother-in-law out of his home. After a few days had elapsed, Linc let his buddies know that that was exactly what he planned on doing.

Screaming at the top of his lungs, Linc told his wife and Shoup that he had had enough. He wanted them out of the house. He was clearly heard from another room by Frank, the hired hand. In fact, Frank remarked in the speakeasy the following evening that he had heard the pair quietly consent to leave without making a fuss. Clever Linc had imitated their voices for Frank's benefit. They were already dead. He had shot them with a revolver equipped with a silencer. Then the well organized lawyer cut up his victims' bodies and burned the pieces each evening in his large furnace adjoining the greenhouse. Every morning he would collect what was left and grind it into fertilizer. He used the fertilizer for his sweet peas.

The two victims' heads posed quite a problem, but industrious Lincoln had the answer to that one, too. He placed the skulls in a flower box liberally dosed with lime Frank had given him. As the sweet peas blossomed, Lina and Byron's heads were supposedly disintegrating to nothingness. In the meantime, the word spread that Mrs. Lincoln and her brother had left Aurora for good, which was true enough, in a way.

Linc was now living alone, with his assistant Frank working at his side in the flower business. One night while working late, Frank noticed someone glaring at him through the greenhouse glass. He gave chase but the man got away. The next night Linc was alone when he claimed he saw someone spying on him. Well, folks, I can tell you — there was no spy. Linc was up to his old tricks of setting up conditions to suit himself. He reported the phony intruder to the police.

Linc confided in Frank. He told his helper that he was pretty sure the man spying on him was a private detective. He said that he had found a stack of love letters belonging to his wife just before he told her to be on her way. He believed the detective had been hired to retrieve the letters so that they wouldn't come up in a pending divorce action. Linc made Frank swear that if anything ever happened to him Frank was to go to the police with this information.

No sooner said than done, Lincoln disappeared. Here is what the police found on the day in April when Frank reported for work and couldn't find his boss.

There were three sets of footprints leading from under Lincoln's bedroom window through some soft earth to the street. One pair of prints was identified as Lina's and another as Shoup's. The third pair must have been made by a detective. You see, this sloppy private eye had dropped his calling card. Honest. He was Milo Durand, private detective. In the same field where the card was found, the police uncovered Linc's nightcap soaked in blood.

Two months went by. As mysteriously as he had disappeared, our hero reappeared. He told the police he had been abducted by his wife, his brother-in-law, and a private detective. They had placed tape over his eyes and kept him in a bare room, torturing him to tell where he had hidden the incriminating letters. Linc showed the police ugly whipmarks on his back. They grimaced and said they sure would like to get their hands on whoever had done such a thing. Linc had paid a derelict to whip him.

While the police investigated the entire matter, Linc puttered around the house, taking care of his flowers and doing minor repairs. One of the items he repaired was the flower box which contained the heads of his victims. He poured cement over the earth and used the box as a block to reinforce the front porch which had developed a slight sag. Linc left the house in Aurora the day after making the repairs, telling his neighbors that he was taking an extended vacation to forget the events of the past few months.

The police in their plodding way began to make some progress. They traced the detective's card to a printer in Chicago, who remembered the strange order he had received only a month before Linc was supposedly kidnapped. It was an order for one solitary card, and the man placing the order fitted Warren Lincoln's description to a 't'. Even Linc's bloodsoaked cap proved to be a phony. It had been soaked in chicken blood.

The search was on all over the U.S. Lincoln, who always was full of surprises, showed up himself in January of 1924. Faced with insurmountable circumstantial evidence, he confessed to murder, but swore that no trace of a body would ever be found. He proved to be most cooperative. Linc pointed out the support under the porch, commenting that nothing of the two heads would be left by now. He got a surprise. When the cement was broken the police found the heads of his wife and brother-in-law in a remarkable state of preservation. That careless Frank had not given his boss a bag of quicklime when he had asked for it. There had been two open barrels of lime side by side in the doorway of the greenhouse. Frank had given Linc harmless slaked lime by mistake.

Warren Lincoln had come within an ace of setting up the perfect crime, but in the end he was convicted of murder and received a sentence of life imprisonment. He died in prison in 1941.

Errol Flynn Was Always in Trouble

Part 7

FAMOUS NAMES

ERROL FLYNN WAS ALWAYS IN TROUBLE

Those of us who remember Errol Flynn readily identify him with his portrayals of pirates and cavalry officers in the movies. If you are too young to have seen Flynn act on the screen, try to imagine Redford and Newman rolled into one, and you have some idea of his magnetism.

By 1942, Errol Flynn's stature in Hollywood was equalled only by Clark Gable. He was box office gold, and he acted the part on and off the screen. Flynn lived in a mansion in Hollywood. Although he wasn't an art collector, he had an original Gauguin and a Van Gogh hanging on his walls just to be fashionable. His estate boasted a swimming pool, cock-fighting arena, tennis court, and riding ring. When he ventured out for an evening's entertainment, his companions included the most beautiful and desirable women in the world. He had just shed his first wife, beautiful Lily Damita, and was free to womanize to his heart's content. The handsome, sexy Flynn had everything any man could want.

It was quite a shock to him and the world when one fine day the Los Angeles Police arrested him and charged him with statutory rape. Betty Hanson, an attractive 17 year-old, told how she had met Flynn at a party and how the hard-drinking, good-looking actor had taken her into the bedroom and raped her. She admitted that the rape was really with her consent. Well, actually, with her encouragement, but it didn't matter to Flynn.

Statutory rape by definition meant having "carnal knowledge" with any member of the opposite sex under 18, whether they consented or not. To give you an idea of the life Flynn led, he later was to reveal that he had a hard time remembering the girl. He vaguely remembered hustling some blonde floozie up to a bedroom during some party or other.

Anyway, when Betty gave her statement she left nothing to the imagination. Maybe the most embarrassing moment for Flynn was when she said he undressed completely, but kept his shoes and socks on. He had just completed a movie based on General Custer's last stand. It was entitled — *They Died With Their Boot On.* Flynn knew he would have a hard time living that one down.

Then Peggy Satterlee, a nightclub dancer, came forward with the story that Flynn raped her aboard his yacht, *Sirocco.* The actor kind of embarrassed everyone when he couldn't place her. The 15-year-old Peggy had no trouble placing Errol. She claimed she was a guest on the yacht one night, and while strolling on the deck she bumped into Flynn. The suave movie idol invited her to his cabin. Once inside the door, he thrust her on the bed and violently raped her. She described every detail, including the view from the bed. It seems she had a clear view of the moon through a porthole of the cabin.

Both of these girls appeared in court, and you would swear they were both dying to be Shirley Temple's understudy. They looked like children, but Flynn was to state later that they didn't look or act like children on the nights he spent with them.

The whole episode made worldwide headlines. For a few weeks in 1942, the war news took a back seat to the escapades of Errol Flynn and his partners in sex. To Flynn it was no joke. He stood to spend five years in prison if convicted.

Like all the stars who found themselves in trouble, he engaged the famed Hollywood lawyer Jerry Giesler. Now, Giesler could talk a partridge out of a pear tree, and it wasn't long before he had the two girls' inconsistencies before the court. For instance, Peggy couldn't have been lying on her back looking at the moon out the porthole of Flynn's cabin. The moon was over the yacht that night, but Giesler proved that it was on the other side of the boat. Peggy would have to look through sheets of steel to have seen the moon that night. Every adult realized that Flynn was being dragged over the coals. The jury thought so too; they took only four hours to find the actor not guilty. Giesler's fee was $50,000 and Flynn always thought it was a bargain.

Flynn, flamboyant character that he was, later revealed that he dated an 18-year-old girl while his trial was in progress. She was a city employed clerk at the refreshment stand in the lobby of the courthouse where the trial was being held.

The trial branded Errol Flynn as a rascal for the rest of his life. In October, 1959,

Flynn had a fatal heart attack while living it up in Vancouver. He was 50 years old, and had the dissipated body of a man of 70.

A young lady, Beverly Aadland, was with Flynn when he died. She had been living with him since she was 15 years old.

LANA'S LOVER BIT THE DUST

On December 14th, 1930, Virgil Turner was murdered in San Francisco. His little daughter, Judy, was only 10 years old at the time of her father's death. Turner, who was a miner by vocation and a small time gambler by inclination, left his wife Mildred and little girl with nothing in the way of worldly goods. Mildred worked as a hairdresser, and supported Judy and herself throughout the Depression. They moved from town to town, until finally, five years after Turner's death, on the advice of a friend, they moved to Los Angeles, California. Judy was only 15, but she had become a gorgeous girl. She had satin skin, a regal air, as well as good looks. As a teenager she was a cross between sexy and that wholesome girl next door.

One day, while skipping class from Hollywood High School, she was having a Coke at a drugstore when a man named Billy Wilkerson sauntered up to the bar stool and said those classical words, "Kid, how would you like to be in pictures?" There was one catch to this stereotyped phrase. The guy really meant it. Soon she had an interview with the well known director, Mervin LeRoy, who realized her potential the first time he ever laid eyes on her. He signed her up to $50 per week. If this doesn't sound like much money now, keep in mind that her mother was making $10 per week as a hairdresser.

He changed her name to Lana.

LeRoy put her in the film *They Won't Forget*. Lana wore a tight sweater and skirt, and was only on the screen for two minutes. The movie was a hit, and so was Lana. She was dubbed the Sweater Girl. Her pay was raised to $75 per week. She was dated by some of the most glamorous men in the world. When LeRoy went to Metro Goldwyn Mayer in 1938, he took young Lana Turner with him. She received many parts, and as a contract player was in close contact with all the other young talent in Hollywood. The young social set included Mickey Rooney, Jackie Cooper, Linda Darnell, and Judy Garland.

In one movie, *Dancing Coed*, she met Artie Shaw. On Feb. 8th, 1940, on her 20th birthday, she went for a car drive with Shaw and ended up eloping with him. The marriage lasted only four months. Now earning $1,000 a week, Lana dated such well-known celebrities as Tony Martin, Gene Krupa, Robert Stack, and even Howard Hughes.

In July of 1942, she married an unknown unemployed playboy, Stephen Crane. He was supposed to be connected with the tobacco industry. In reality, his father owned a cigar store in Crawfordville, Indiana. Lana in succession got pregnant, divorced Crane, remarried Crane, and on July 25th, 1943, gave birth to a daughter, Cheryl Christine Crane. A year later she divorced Crane again.

By 1946, Lana Turner was earning $226,000, making her one of the 10 highest paid women in the United States. As the years rolled by, Lana made picture after picture. Not all of them were great hits, but most made money. She married and divorced in succession multi-millionaire Bob Topping and actor Lex Barker.

In 1957, Lana Turner was 37 years old, and her daughter Cheryl was in her teens. Lana had, like so many movie queens before her, a tremendous fear of growing old. At this most vulnerable point in her action-packed career, she met small time racketeer Johnny Stompanato. Stompanato made a meagre living operating a gift shop. His dark good looks brought him substantially more income as a gigolo. He had no trouble ingratiating himself with Lana and her circle of show business acquaintances. To all outside appearances, they seemed to be madly in love. Lana showered expensive gifts on her new lover. In the meantime Cheryl, who had been brought up by nurses, nannies, and in private schools, turned out to be a troubled teenager. In the spring of 1957, she ran away and was found on skid row by the police.

Constantly at Lana's side during the troubled times with her daughter was the ominous figure of Johnny Stompanato. When Lana went to Europe to make a movie, Johnny followed. He was extremely jealous. In a fit of rage, he once almost strangled Lana. While in Europe he threatened to scar her face with a razor. He swore he would never allow her to leave him. She went to the police and Scotland Yard, and had Stompanato kicked out of England. Despite all this, a short time later Lana and Johnny vacationed together for eight weeks in Acapulco. Back home Lana Turner was nominated for the best actress award for playing the mother in *Peyton Place*. She didn't win an Academy Award, but the nomination made her a hot property again.

On April 4th, 1957, Lana, her daughter Cheryl, and Johnny Stompanato were spending the evening at home in Lana's rented mansion in Beverly Hills. Johnny and Lana were arguing as usual. She confided to her daughter that she was deathly scared of Stompanato. The argument turned into a shouting match. Stompanato began shaking Lana. He threatened to scar her with a razor. Cheryl, taking all this in for the first time, was terrified for her mother's safety. She grabbed a knife from the kitchen and in one motion, before anyone could move, she plunged the eight-inch knife into Stompanato's stomach. Johnny died before the ambulance arrived. Newspapers all over the world featured the killing. The adventures of Lana Turner and her family were still of interest to millions of people. The girl's father, Stephen Crane hired famed Hollywood lawyer Jerry Giesler. An inquest into the death was held on April 11th, 1958. It was a sensation, with every breath covered by the press. When fact was separated from scandal, the inquest jury brought in a verdict of justifiable homicide. As a result of the disclosures brought out about Lana's private life and its influence on her daughter, Cheryl was made a ward of the court and placed in the custody of her grandmother.

The never ending saga of Lana Turner and her daughter continues to this day. Cheryl requires the help of a psychiatrist from time to time, and as recently as 1970 was charged with possession of marijuana. As for Lana, she just keeps getting married every so often.

THE OSCAR WILDE CASE

The Marquess of Queensberry will always be remembered as the man whose name is closely associated with the rules that govern the sport of boxing. The manly art of self defence needed a nobleman to lend his name to the boxing game. In doing this, he gave the sport a degree of respectability.

The Marquess achieved another sort of fame. He was the trigger that ignited the spark which was to rock England to its very foundations in 1895. Seldom has the ancient island been witness to a juicier scandal. It seems the Marquess' son, Alfred Douglas, was always in the company of Oscar Wilde, and the old Marquess didn't like it a bit. He felt that it just wasn't natural for two men to be so close, and as things turned out, he was right.

Now Oscar was not your average lad about town. His parents were, as they used to say in Merrie England, of literary genteel stock. Oscar outdid his parents. Born on Oct. 16, 1854, he had an uneventful childhood. He attended a boarding school in Ireland with the grandiose name of Portora Royal School.

In his final year, he won a gold medal in Classics and led the school in Greek, which isn't bad for starters. He also won a scholarship to Trinity College in Dublin.

In 1871, when he entered Trinity, he wasn't yet 17 years of age. Three years later he graduated first in his class, again achieving awards for excellence in Greek and the Classics. He won another scholarship, this time to Magdalen College in Oxford University. Here he excelled in everything, and was considered one of the brightest young intellectuals on the campus. After Oxford he migrated to London, and in 1880 he wrote his first play, *Vera* and a book of poetry appropriately entitled *Poems.*

In January of 1882, Oscar accepted an invitation to give a lecture tour in the United States. From the time the immigration officer asked him, "What have you to declare?" and he answered in all humility, "Nothing except my genius," Oscar was a huge success.

Oscar made a quick £1,200 on the tour and returned home in triumph. He took a vacation in Paris where he became closely associated with such notables as Victor Hugo, Zola, Degas, and Pissaro.

On May 9, 1884, Oscar married Constance Lloyd in St. James Church, Paddington. After a brief honeymoon they returned and set up housekeeping in London. Constance had an income of a few pounds a year and this, added to what Oscar picked up as a critic, was the couple's total income for the first three years of their marriage. In 1887, he became editor of a well known magazine, *The Woman's World*, and seems to have excelled at this position. He resigned after two years.

He started to write seriously in 1888, and by 1892 had reached the peak of his popularity. His play *Lady Windermere's Fan* was breaking records at St. James Theatre. This success was followed by *Salome, A Woman of No Importance*, and *An Ideal Husband*, all hit plays. Then came his greatest success of all — *The Importance of Being Earnest*, which many critics believe to be the best-liked comedy ever written in the English language.

There was one rather startling fact about Wilde that was generally unknown. You see, Oscar was a practising homosexual, and had been for some time. Not only was he a homosexual, but he was a homosexual at the wrong time in history. In the England of the 1890s, this practice was not only illegal but was considered to be so despicable that no one of substance would even speak to a known homosexual.

Wilde was 38, and had had several adventures with young boys, when he met 22-year-old Alfred Douglas. Oscar was a huge unattractive man, while Alfred had the physique of an Adonis. Oscar was on the way up when he met Alfred, but had not reached the pinnacle of his acclaim. The two started a relationship, and in fact one was seldom seen without the other. They became ardent and passionate lovers. Rumors started to get back to Alfred Douglas' father, the Marquess of Queensberry. He continually warned his son to break off with Wilde. He faced Wilde and pleaded with him to leave his son alone. Finally, when nothing else worked, he performed the act that was to start one of the most sensational scandals ever to take place in England.

One fine morning the Marquess walked into Oscar's club and gave the porter a written message for Oscar. The message read, "To Oscar Wilde, posing as a sodomite." When the note was delivered to Oscar, the playwright realized things had gone too far. He decided to get legal advice.

Sir Edward Clarke was one of the best known and most respected lawyers in England. He knew that in Oscar Wilde he had no ordinary client. He considered his client to be a literary genius. Sir Edward asked Oscar one important question, and that was whether he was innocent or guilty. Oscar swore he was innocent and so the decision was made to prosecute the Marquess for libel. In doing this, Sir Edward pointed out to Oscar that the only way to prove libel was to prove that he was not a sodomite. Should they not be successful, then Oscar was liable to be arrested immediately, as indecent behavior was a serious criminal offence. No wonder Sir Edward wanted to make sure his client was innocent before pressing on in prosecuting the Marquess.

The trial started at the Old Bailey to a packed house, with thousands more crowding the street outside. From the very beginning the defence produced all sorts of young boys who testified that they were on intimate terms with Oscar. The jury was digesting this damaging evidence, and it became increasingly clear that they would not convict a father who was trying to save his son from the clutches of a refined, cultured genius with unnatural tendencies.

Sir Edward decided to withdraw. The judge told the jury that the only verdict could be "not guilty".

Oscar Wilde was arrested, and this time went to trial in the Old Bailey as the defendant. He was unmercifully exposed and held open to ridicule as witness after witness told of illicit relations with him. He was charged with 25 counts of gross indecency and "conspiracy to procure the commission of such acts." Mainly because of the brilliance of Sir Edward, the jury failed to agree and they had to do it all over again. For the few weeks between the second and third trials, while Wilde was free on bail, he was ridiculed wherever he went. It got so bad that no boarding house would take him in, and he ended up living with an alcoholic brother.

The third trial started on May 22, 1895, and it was a disaster for Oscar. A whole ring of what amounted to male prostitutes was uncovered, and corroborating evidence was produced proving beyond a doubt that Oscar was guilty of indecent acts.

When we look back at what happened to Oscar Wilde, we realize that a genius was ruined for an offence that doesn't exist now. Today, Wilde and Douglas would be living together openly. Surely the public was the loser, for we can only guess what literary gems were never written because of the laws that denied Wilde his, now legal, perversions.

Oscar Wilde was sentenced to two years in prison. Even in these surroundings he wrote the much quoted poem, *The Ballad of Reading Gaol.* This beautiful poem did much to expose the cruelties of prison life as Wilde found them.

After his release from jail, Oscar lived in France. It is said that, in his last years, he was a confirmed homosexual. The harshness of prison life had taken its toll. In a few years, he was a dying man.

On November 30, 1900, Oscar Wilde was received into the Catholic Church and died a few hours later.

AIMEE WAS A PREACHER

Every so often the world needs a good juicy scandal. Perhaps the Watergate affair was the granddaddy of them all. It isn't every day that an incident comes along which culminates in the resignation of a president of the United States. Still, there have been some dandies. If you remember Babe Ruth, Jack Dempsey, the Charleston and bathtub gin, you may very well remember the subject of one of the most titillating scandals of all time — Aimee Semple McPherson.

Aimee Elizabeth Kennedy was born in, of all places, Ingersoll, Ont. on Oct. 9, 1890. From the time little Aimee could walk, her mother Minnie introduced her into a religious milieu in which, in one form or another, she was to spend the balance of her life. Mother and daughter spent hours reading the Good Book. For a change of pace they attended the sermons of visiting Evangelists.

Actually Aimee, at 18 years of age, did a bit more than attend meetings. She fell hard for Bible thumping Robert Semple, a fine cut of a man, who stood well over six feet, and who was himself a travelling evangelist. Soon the pair was married and off to China to lead the wretched heathen to the light. Unfortunately, before they could light the way, Semple caught a fever in Hong Kong and died.

In 1909, Aimee gave birth to Semple's daughter. Together with tiny Roberta Starr, she returned to New York where her parents resided. Not one to let grass grow under her feet, Aimee tied the knot with a grocery clerk, Harold McPherson. This new alliance only jelled long enough to usher a son, Rolf, into the world. Harold and Aimee were then divorced.

Aimee was not a beautiful woman. Now, that is not to say that she was not attractive and sexy. Photos taken of her while she was in her twenties reveal a catlike quality, nicely packaged in a trim, neat figure. Above all, Aimee had that intangible something known as charisma.

Together with her mother and two children, Aimee travelled across the United States with a tent, spreading the word wherever she was allowed to set up. During this time Aimee was developing an attractive line, later to be known as her "Four Square Gospel". She also was becoming a forceful, fascinating public speaker.

Probably Aimee's greatest single contribution to the religion business was her realization that the spreading of the word, combined with relieving the suckers of their hard earned dollars, required the glitter of show business. When she set up her permanent headquarters in the Angelus Temple in Los Angeles, Aimee was quite a sight to behold as she spoke from an elevated stage, white flowing robes fluttering in the breeze (hidden fans provided the windpower), her arms outstretched to the heavens. The rotating electric cross on the top of the temple could be seen for miles.

To give you an idea of the success of Aimee's temple, it cost one and a half million dollars to build in 1923. The amount of cool cash which flowed into the coffers has never been revealed, but the place had a payroll of over $8,000 per week. Aimee and her mother personally owned the organization. By 1926, both mother and daughter were millionaires.

That's when the roof caved in.

Aimee fell in love with Kenneth G. Ormiston, a radio operator at the Temple. There were complications. For one, Kenneth was married. Besides, Sister Aimee was supposed to be above frolicking with the hired help. While the romance was in full bloom Aimee went on religious safaris to Europe and the Holy Land, where she was a resounding success. Ken was absent from the Temple during these trips, and there were those snide devils who hinted that he clandestinely accompanied Aimee on her quest to save lost souls.

On May 18, 1926, Aimee went for a swim near Los Angeles with her private secretary Emma Schaeffer. While her secretary ran an errand Aimee simply and totally disappeared. By nightfall the evangelist's disappearance was headline news across the country. Believing she had drowned, thousands took part in searching for her body.

Coincidental with Aimee's disappearance, Ken Ormiston's wife reported her husband missing. Never mind coincidence, Sister Aimee was gone, swept off the face of the earth forever. Her thousands of followers could only do two things; pray and send money. They did both. The Sister Aimee Memorial Fund was a huge success. Sums taken in are unknown in total, but must have been substantial. One meeting alone netted $26,000; another $38,000. That's the kind of cash we are talking about.

While all these lucrative shenanigans were going on, Aimee's mother received a ransom note demanding a half million dollars for her daughter's safe return. The note was signed. 'The Avengers'. Police kept the proposed meeting with the kidnappers, but no one showed up.

Excitement, yes, but more was to come. On June 23, 1926, Aimee showed up alive and well in the Mexican border town of Aqua Prieta. She told quite a story. She and been kidnapped by Rose, Steve, and Jake and held prisoner in a little shack somewhere in the desert. She had escaped and walked through the scorching desert all day until she reached Aqua Prieta after midnight.

The dramatic story made headlines around the world. There was just one thing. Los Angeles District Attorney Asa Keyes didn't believe a word of it. He assigned Deputy D.A. Joseph Ryan to investigate the abduction.

Right from the beginning Ryan smelled a rat. Aimee had shown up clean and refreshed in the Mexican town after walking an entire day through the desert in 120 degree temperature. Much was made of the fact that Aimee wasn't even perspiring.

Ken Ormiston was subpoenaed to appear before the grand jury, but by now was living in Norfolk, Va., and had no intention of crossing the country to appear in court. He claimed to have no knowledge of Aimee's disappearance.

On July 20, the grand jury found that there was not sufficient evidence to prove that Aimee had been kidnapped. You can imagine the Evangelist's embarrassment when, two days later, it was revealed by four witnesses that Ken Ormiston had rented a love-nest in Carmel, Calif., on May 19, the day following Aimee's disappearance. He had rented the cottage under the name Henry Benedict. Aimee, using the name Mrs. MacIntyre, had shared the cottage with her lover.

Aimee was down but not out. An appeal to Ken Ormiston to tell all brought forth an affidavit wherein he confessed to have been shacked up with a lady, but he swore the lady was a Miss "X", not our Aimee.

At the height of the scandal the District Attorney filed a criminal complaint against Ormiston, Mrs. Kennedy, and of course, Aimee. They were charged with conspiracy to obstruct justice and giving false evidence before the grand jury.

Aimee's preliminary hearing began on Monday, Sept. 27, 1926. The public loved every minute of it. Witness after witness gave evidence relating to some juicy tidbit concerning Ormiston and Aimee's torrid love affair. Each Sunday, Aimee reviewed the trial on her own radio program, ridiculing her tormentors and proclaiming her innocence. On Nov. 3, all three defendants were held over for trial.

Right in the middle of proceedings District Attorney Keyes, in a separate action, was charged with conspiracy to defraud. The action against him was delayed until the McPherson affair was finalized.

The final blow to Aimee's reputation came when her love letters to Ormiston were found by some busybody who revealed all. Just as things were warming up to a hot criminal trial where Aimee, her mother, and Ormiston stood a chance of going to prison for up to 14 years, all charges against the three were dropped. When Aimee was told the news, she fainted.

Why was such a circus unceremoniously dropped so quickly? We will never know for sure, but there were those who said the fix was in. Aimee had purportedly bought off District Attorney Keyes for $50,000.

Once the fuss settled down, Aimee went back to the preaching business, but times were changing. She quickly discovered that since she had been big box office, no one could take her seriously as a preacher again. Slowly she faded into obscurity.

Ken Ormiston returned to Los Angeles, where he became the respected chief engineer of a local radio station. He died in 1937, at the age of 41. District Attorney Keyes later spent almost two years in San Quentin Prison for fraud. He had a stroke and died three years after his release in 1934.

Aimee never achieved prominence again. In 1944, in her 54th year, she died, her hectic life and international scandal nothing more than a dim memory.

WAS LABATT BLUE?

The most notorious kidnapping to take place in Canada, with the possible exception of the abduction of British Trade Commissioner James Cross, was that of millionaire John Labatt. The president of John Labatt Ltd., one of Canada's largest breweries, was a likely kidnap victim. His case evolved into one of the most bizarre crimes ever perpetrated here.

The Labatt family owned a summer home at Bright's Cove on Lake Huron. On the morning of Aug. 14, 1934, John Labatt left his summer hideaway for the drive to the Labatt Co. headquarters in London. Labatt knew the route like the back of his hand. This morning, as was his custom, he took a shortcut. He always saved miles by driving through Camlachie Village, toward the Warwick Bridge, leading eventually up the provincial highway into London.

Labatt had just passed Camlachie when another car, travelling much faster in the same direction, overtook him. The car was soon beyond his range of vision. Suddenly, the same car came into sight. This time it was blocking the road. Labatt came to a stop. Three men dashed toward his vehicle, two brandishing revolvers. Then John Labatt heard the dreaded words, "Stick them up, quick, this is a kidnapping."

The men acted swiftly. They inquired if Labatt had any cash. He turned over around $100. Now standing beside his own vehicle, he was given a piece of paper and ordered to write as one of the kidnappers dictated.

August 14, 1934.
"Dear Hugh: Do as these men have instructed you to do, and don't go to the police. They promise not to harm me if you negotiate with them.
Your affectionate brother,
John Labatt."

Two of the men hurriedly placed adhesive tape over Labatt's eyes and hustled him into their car, while the third man drove away in Labatt's car. One of the men sat in the back seat with Labatt while his accomplice drove. Labatt's companion was extremely friendly. He called his victim John, and even inquired if there were any good robbery opportunities around the London area. Labatt later claimed that the adhesive tape covering his eyes left a crack through which he could see his captors.

During the long ride the kidnap car stopped for gas and other supplies. At no time did Labatt seek help. Had he screamed or raised an alarm, there was no way the kidnappers could have avoided apprehension.

Toward nightfall, the car pulled up to a cottage. The kidnappers and their hostage were to remain there for three nights and two days. A long dogchain was fastened to Labatt's wrist, the other end being attached to the bed. The kidnappers seemed very concerned over their hostage's comfort. A substantial meal was provided, which Labatt ate heartily. These were not desperate threatening bullies. Obviously they actually cared about the welfare of their victim.

The lone guard excused himself, went into the other bedroom and went to sleep. The thought of escape never entered Labatt's head. He too went to sleep.

Meanwhile, the Labatt car had been driven to City Hospital in London. Hugh Labatt was anonymously phoned and informed of his brother's kidnapping. He was told to proceed to the car for further instructions. Hugh Labatt found the note from the kidnappers on the car seat:

"Mr. Hugh Labatt we are holding your brother John for $150,000 ransom. Go to Toronto immediately and register in the Royal York Hotel. We will negotiate with you from that point, be prepared when I get in touch with you there to furnish me the names of two or three reliable parties who you can trust to deliver this money to us. We advise you to keep this matter away from the police and newspapers so as we can return your brother safely. You will know me as Three Fingered Abe"

With the blessing of the Toronto Police Force, Hugh Labatt was installed in a suite in the Royal York Hotel. Hugh and John were very close, and Hugh was understandably distraught at the thought of his brother's life being in danger. He managed to have $150,000 with him in the suite as he waited for his instructions.

The Toronto Police were now being assisted by the Ontario Provincial Police, the R.C.M.P., and the F.B.I. By Wednesday all four police forces were scurrying about, running down clues. The Labatt kidnapping was the biggest news in the country.

In their cosy cottage in the Muskokas, John Labatt and his captors ate well, slept at intervals, and above all else were extremely polite and considerate of each other.

On Tuesday morning John Labatt, sitting on the edge of his bed, chatted amicably with his companions while he received a first rate shave. This ritual was to be repeated each morning of his captivity. Meals, cigarettes and good conversation made the time pass pleasantly enough. On Wednesday, as far as Labatt could tell, the two men received word (probably from the third kidnapper, who had driven Labatt's car back to London) that the Royal York was teeming with newspapermen and cops. It would be impossible to pick up the ransom money under those circumstances. Rather than simply calling Hugh Labatt with a change of plans, the kidnappers decided to call the whole thing off.

On Thursday, the polite, considerate kidnappers took the unreasonable risk of driving their victim into the heart of Toronto. They let Labatt out at the corner of Bathurst Street and St. Clair Avenue. Considerate to the end, they gave the millionaire a dollar for cab fare to the Royal York. The kidnappers expressed concern about having Hugh worry about his brother even a half hour longer than was necessary.

Once at the hotel, Labatt had a hard time proving he was the missing John Labatt. After a few embarrassing moments for everyone, he was reunited with his brother, Hugh.

The John Labatt kidnapping was over. The victim was safe. Now the hunt was on for his abductors.

Labatt was shown photographs of hundreds of suspects. Finally he pointed a finger at one picture and declared that it was his travelling companion and guard. The picture was of David Meisner. The photograph was distributed throughot the U.S. and Canada. A couple of days later David Meisner walked into a Detroit police station and advised a clerk that he had heard the police were looking for him.

Meisner had wandered from the Goderich, Ont. area to the U.S., where he had drifted from one clerical job to another. At the time of the kidnapping he was living in Covington, Kentucky, making a precarious living as a racetrack follower and gambler. At the age of 55, he had never been convicted of a serious crime.

Meisner was a shy, lean man. His most outstanding feature was a serious growth in his left eye, which gave his eye the appearance of a white lump. Meisner was extradited to London, where John Labatt took one look at him and stated. "That's the man! Marvellous!"

David Meisner was in big trouble.

On Jan. 27, 1935, at the London Assizes, Meisner stood trial for kidnapping. John Labatt took the witness stand and told of his ordeal. He positively identified David Meisner as his kidnapper. Labatt had a few embarrassing moments. He had previously estimated the kidnapper's weight at around 175 pounds. Meisner weighed in at 118 pounds. Labatt's only explanation for the discrepancy was that he simply was a poor judge of weight. He swore that he never noticed the white growth over Meisner's eye, which everyone agreed was pretty hard to miss.

Several other witnesses also positively identified Meisner as the kidnapper. The man who sold the dog chain and the lady who rented the Muskoka cottage were devastating in their effect on the jury. As a result of the many eye witnesses, Meisner was convicted and received a sentence of 15 years in prison.

While Meisner languished in Kingston Penitentiary, one John Basil Bannon of Detroit, a sometimes criminal turned stool pigeon, contacted the Toronto police. He was after the reward money for the apprehension of the rest of the Labatt kidnappers. Bannon led the police to Crown Point, Ind., where a small-time hood was incarcerated, having just concluded a gunfight with the local cops. The man's name was Michael McCardell. After being confronted with the facts, he admitted to being "Three Fingered Abe".

John Labatt was summoned He stood face to face with McCardell, who greeted Labatt like a long lost friend. McCardell reeled off all the subject matter of their four days of conversation. There was no doubt about it. Labatt had made a terrible mistake. McCardell was the kidnapper. David Meisner was an innocent man.

Upon being brought back to London, McCardell told all. He turned on Bannon, and informed the police that while Bannon hadn't taken part in the actual kidnapping, he had planned the whole thing and had rented the cottage in the Muskokas. McCardell named the other kidnappers — Albert Pegram and Russell Knowles. He gave a detailed account of the whole thing from beginning to end. David Meisner had taken no part in the crime.

All the guilty men were brought to trial and received long prison sentences. David Meisner was granted a second trial. In March, 1936, after deliberating over seven hours, a jury found him not guilty of kidnapping John Labatt. He had spent a year and a half in Kingston Penitentiary for a crime he had not committed.

John Labatt died of natural causes on July 8, 1952.

WHO DONE IN
SIR HARRY?

I is always disillusioning to find out that someone who should be from some-where was really born somewhere else. Everyone knows John Diefenbaker was a Westerner through and through. When I think of him, I picture him in the middle of a wheat field in Saskatchewan.

He was born in Ontario.

So it is with Sir Harry Oakes. Everyone knows he was a rough tough Canadian.

He was born and educated in Maine.

Harry was born on Dec. 23, 1874, in Sangerville, Maine. He received his early education at Bowdoin College in Brunswick, Maine. After graduation, he attended Syracuse Medical School for two years.

Thus the first legend of Sir Harry hits the dust, for he was not an uneducated oaf as he is depicted in tales and stories of his life. Although in later years he acted the part, it does not detract from the fact that Harry had a pretty fair basic education. Harry hated medicine, and was happy to quit after the two years at Syracuse.

He heard that gold had been discovered in the Klondike. Gold fever spread through-out the world, and even in those days was well advertised. Harry decided to go, and strangely enough his entire family backed him up. In fact, one brother, Louis, sent him $75 a month for years.

Harry reached the Klondike and there he learned his trade — gold prospecting. In Dawson City there were 30,000 souls, almost all with the same idea as Harry — finding gold. He remained there to take it away from the finders.

Dawson City was remarkable in every way. It was a dirty drunken place, yet it was larger than Winnipeg or Vancouver. Indeed, it was a city of legends. Men walked the streets as gold barons one day, only to sell out an unknown fortune for a few hundred dollars the next day. We talk of inflation now. In Dawson City in 1896, meat sold for $2.50 a pound, bread was a dollar a loaf.

Harry worked day and night in the bitter cold, seven days a week. At no time did he consider giving up, and at no time did he deviate from his goal of finding gold. It was his one and only driving force. He didn't frequent the brothels of Dawson; he neither smoked nor drank. He worked until his hands bled. Harry had various partners when he needed them, but always jettisoned them as soon as he could. Basically, he was a loner and was to remain that way for the rest of his life.

Harry tired of the Klondike and sought gold in Australia, then on to California, then even the Belgian Congo, and finally back to Alaska. There seemed no place else to go.

Rumors were spreading around the north that there might be gold in Ontario. Harry headed for the supposed gold country around Swastika. His lack of money made it almost impossible for him to live, let alone work his claims. His clothing in tatters, and down to exactly $2.65, Harry, with two partners, Tom and George Tough, found gold. They called it the Tough Oakes Mine.

If any point in Harry Oakes' life could be set aside and said to be different, it is this point in time. For Harry realized that here he was with a gold mine with no conceivable way to exploit it. It is one thing to discover gold and quite another to bring in a mine. To my knowledge no prospector up to this point had ever developed his own mine. Harry headed south to Toronto to get some capital. He didn't meet with too much success. They laughed at him on Bay Street.

In the meantime, in 1912, Harry kept right on prospecting the general area on his own and an employee of his, one Ernie Martin, found gold. Not just gold, but in the final analysis a gold mine that was second only to the Homestead Mine in Dakota, the largest in the Western Hemisphere. Meanwhile Harry sold out his interest in Tough Oakes for $200,000, which isn't hay now. In 1916, it was clover. In 1914, Harry incorporated the Lakeshore Mines Ltd. He had two million shares issued at one dollar par value. Still no one rose to the bait; no one figured a real bona fide bonanza could be found in Ontario. Many famous people refused to invest. Sir Henry Pellatt turned him down (he went broke building the Casa Loma). Harry tried to buy groceries with his shares at 30¢ a share in Swastika, Ontario, and was turned down.

A legend in his own right, one Charlie Chow, a Chinese gentleman who ran a rough, tough restaurant in Kirkland Lake accepted shares at 50¢ each for food and drink. Harry paid his help in shares as he had no money. Each one of Mr. Chow's shares would one day be worth $64. And so it went, until one day Harry's mine in vein number two assayed out at $60 a ton. The ballgame was over.

Businessmen in special trains came to Lakeshore. Even at that, thousands of the shares went at 32¢, but when you sell around a half million a day, it does mount up.

By 1921, Harry had a producing mine and an office in Kirkland Lake. Eight years before he had $2.65. Harry still owned 50%, and the mine was shooting out 2,500 tons of ore a day.

Harry Oakes was a multi-millionaire.

It would be pleasant if our story could end here. Unfortunately it can't. Harry Oakes decided to seek revenge on every person who ever refused him credit or friendship. This he did to his dying day. An obscure storekeeper who refused him credit soon found himself with no customers. All Harry's enemies fell one by one.

His only weakness was a young, shy girl everyone loved named Eunice MacIntyre. Harry married her, and a strange couple they made, rough tough Harry and gentle Eunice. In the intervening years, Harry broke many a man who had crossed him earlier. By 1928, Harry was considered to be the richest man in Canada. The depression that followed didn't hurt him at all — gold is still gold.

Like all rich men he took part in certain philanthropies. He liked Niagara Falls and built a home there which still stands. He improved the falls and provided milk for children. He even built a golf course that he could par.

In reminiscing about rich men, it is hard to like Harry Oakes. He lost his temper frequently. Although educated, he had spent too much time in the bush, and was an ignorant tyrant to those who worked for him. In short, Harry was not beloved by all, if any.

In 1930, when the Bennett Conservatives came to power in Canada, they taxed Harry $250,000 on the gifts he had given the country. They also upped his tax at Lakeshore into the 85% category, and Harry was furious. He found out that there were no taxes at all in the Bahamas and he and his family moved there lock, stock and barrel. In Nassau, Harry immediately bought one of the largest homes on the island, and began to mix with the millionaire set who were there for primarily the same reasons as Harry.

At this time one of the most important men in Nassau was Harold Christie. He was a native who realized the tourist potential of the Bahamas. Of course, he was delighted to have Oakes as an inhabitant, and for some reason he became one of the few men who got along with Harry.

The years flew by, and when 1939 rolled around Harry and Eunice had five children, Nancy, Sidney, Pitt, Harry and Shirley. Naturally the war did not affect them in any way. Harry had the bright idea that if he gave enough money to British charities, and as the Bahamas was a British colony, he could conceivably be rewarded with a knighthood. The scheme worked. We now have Sir Harry Oakes, owner of about a third of his island, sitting out a war with his family.

Another illustrious couple was being forced to do the same thing. Winston Churchill decided that a good place to stash the Duke and Duchess of Windsor was the Bahamas. The former King of England was made governor of the Islands. So with Harry insulting everyone, and everyone trying to entertain the Duke and his wife, it was all in all not a bad war.

As in most ideal situations, something was bound to happen. In May, 1942, Nancy Oakes ran away to New York and married one Alfred de Marigny. Sir Harry flipped. Alfred was known around the Islands as something of a playboy. He was a expert yachtsman and mixed with the proper social set, but was never really accepted as one of them. He was 32, Nancy was 18. What's more, he had been married twice before.

Well, Sir Harry and Alfred agreed on almost nothing. It even bugged Sir Harry that apparently de Marigny didn't want any money or advantages, just his daughter. Life proceeded along these wealthy disagreeable lines until July 7, 1943. Harold Christie and Sir Harry played a game of tennis around five that afternoon, had a few guests in for cocktails, all of whom left by eleven. Because it looked as if a storm was coming up, Harold Christie decided to spend the night with Sir Harry. Sir Harry went to his room, Christie went to another.

That night, de Marigny gave a dinner party for eleven guests. Nancy was not at home. By midnight a storm was brewing and only two ladies remained. De Marigny offered to drive them home, and this he did. They lived on the other side of the Oakes estate. He dropped them off and returned home himself past the estate.

Rain poured down, thunder roared, and someone, with a strange instrument that was never found, struck Sir Harry Oakes three times, crushing his skull. Gasoline was then poured over the bed and Sir Harry was placed on top. The intruder lit the gasoline and flames leaped upward as the killer disappeared into the stormy night. The wind howled through the open window, extinguishing the flames. During the investigation that followed it became obvious that the murderer intended to burn down the estate with Sir Harry's body at the centre. However, this was not to happen and, although horribly burned, his body was found the next morning on the bed by Harold Christie, who had slept two rooms away during the whole night.

The Duke of Windsor, who really had nothing to do for so long, did exactly the wrong things. He didn't bother with Scotland Yard or even the F.B.I. Instead he called Miami and two ordinary detectives were sent over. The errors they committed in investigating the crime were so numerous they are difficult to relate. Suffice to say they completely botched the murder scene, making proper identification of finger prints, and other clues, impossible.

The detectives' names were Melchen and Barker, and as soon as they found out about the relationship between Sir Harry and de Marigny they concentrated their investigation on him. It wasn't long before they learned that Alfred had driven the two girls home that night and drove back past the Oakes estate at the time the murder could have been committed.

Before you could say "for the woman I love", they arrested Alfred de Marigny for the murder of Sir Harry Oakes.

Indeed, everyone believed at the time that it had to be Alfred. Only his wife Nancy stood by him during the trial. The Duke, Christie, the detectives and the natives of Nassau all thought it to be an open and shut case.

The trial was a sensation. The press of the world attended. As it progressed a strange thing became obvious. You cannot convict a man because he drove by a house at a time when a murder may have been committed. There was no concrete evidence against Alfred de Marigny.

He was acquitted.

Later, for the benefit of his wife, he took a lie detector test under the strictest of conditions and this too proved him innocent.

Even today the citizens of Nassau talk in whispers about the case to each other. Rarely will they discuss it with a stranger.

For you see, nobody knows who done in Sir Harry.

SCANDAL AT CHAPPAQUIDDICK

How does a married U.S. Senator find himself with the corpse of a beautiful young girl on a lonely road in the middle of the night? One summer evening in 1969, the question was on everyone's lips. The man on the lonely road that night was Senator Ted Kennedy. The then junior senator from Massachusetts was a prime prospect for the presidency of the United States.

Joe Kennedy and his wife Rose had a remarkable family. Money and politics were topics dear to all the Kennedy children. Rose's father, John (Honey Fitz) Fitzgerald, had been mayor of Boston. The Kennedys' oldest son, Joe, Jr., had been killed in action as a fighter pilot during the war. John became president of the U.S. while still a young man. The tragedy of his assassination is still vivid. Youthful looking Bobby became Attorney General and was a serious challenger for the presidency, when he, too, was killed by an assassin's bullet in Los Angeles.

The saga of the youngest brother, Edward Moore Kennedy, really begins back in 1960. His brother, John, had just given up his senate seat to successfully run for the presidency. Ted, then 28 years old, was newly graduated from Harvard Law School.

In 1951, he had been expelled from Harvard for having another student write an exam for him. He then joined the army. When his father, who was Ambassador to England, heard that his son had signed up for four years, he was furious. A few discreet telephone calls set the matter straight. The term of enlistment was halved. Conveniently, Ted missed the entire Korean War, having spent most of his two years serving in England. He was discharged in 1953 as a Private First Class.

In 1960, with Ted out of law school, the Kennedy family had a problem. Joe, Sr., made no bones about it. He wanted his son John's senatorial seat for his youngest boy, Ted. The constitution of the United States was clear. It was necessary to be 30 years of age in order to become a senator. Ted was 28.

John Kennedy solved the problem. He appointed unknown Ben Smith, the mayor of the fishing town of Gloucester, Mass., to serve the remaining two years in his old senate seat. Ben was highly qualified. He had been John Kennedy's roommate in college.

Ben Smith kept the seat warm for Ted. In 1962, Ted Kennedy, aided by his father's money and his brother's influence, easily won his first primary election against highly qualified State Attorney General, Edward J. McCormack, Jr. Later, he demolished Republican George Lodge by close to 300,000 votes to capture the senate seat for the Democrats. As Joe, Sr., once remarked, "I paid plenty for that seat for John; it belongs in the family." And that's how Ted Kennedy became a senator.

After John's assassination in 1963, Ted was flying to Springfield, Mass., to attend the Democratic convention, when his twin engine Aero Commander went out of control and crashed at Southampton. Senator Kennedy suffered a broken back, a collapsed lung, and three broken ribs. Without ever appearing at the convention, Ted was nominated by acclamation. Such was his popularity, that he was re-elected to his senate seat by over a million votes.

Now in the summer of 1969, one of the most recognizable men in the United States was planning on joining friends for a few days of fun at Cape Cod.

To fully comprehend the events which were to take place, one must first understand the popularity and charisma of the Kennedy name in Massachusetts. In Hyannisport, where for years the Kennedy family have spent their summers, the mere mention of the Kennedy name brings inquisitive stares. The natives wonder if you really know a Kennedy, or if you are just another nosy tourist. When I was there, the street leading to their compound in Hyannisport was roped off and guarded. On Sunday morning a crowd gathered outside the church to see if the could catch a glimpse of a Kennedy.

Senator Kennedy flew to Martha's Vineyard, an island off the coat of Massachusetts. He was scheduled to take part in the Edgartown Regatta. Members of the Kennedy clan had taken part in this regatta for years. This July 18, Ted was met by his chauffeur, Jack Crimmins. They made their way to Chappaquiddick Island. About 120 yards of open water separated Chappaquiddick from Martha's Vineyard.

The trip on the two-car ferry, the *On Time*, took only a few minutes. Kennedy had some time before he had to compete in the regatta. He changed into a pair of swimming trunks at a cottage, which had been rented for a cookout to be held later that evening. Crimmins drove him down to the beach and back to the cottage. Their 1967 Oldsmobile crossed the narrow, ten foot, six inch Dike Bridge twice, once going for the swim and once returning.

If you drive from the cottage to the beach, you of necessity come to a fork in the road. If you turn left you head directly back to the site of the two-car ferry landing. If you turn right, you cross the Dike Bridge to the beach. Beyond the beach there is nothing except the Atlantic Ocean.

At 2:50 p.m. Senator Kennedy took part in the Wianno senior heat of the regatta. His yacht, the *Victura*, finished ninth. Ted boarded the *Bettawan*, the winning yacht, congratulated the winner, and left. He returned to the Shiretown Inn, where he was registered in Edgartown, had a few beers with some friends, and left for the barbecue on Chappaquiddick.

Jared Grant, the owner of the *On Time*, ferried Senator Kennedy over to Chappaquiddick at about 6:30 p.m. Grant thought it a bit strange that the senator never returned. At 12:30 a.m. he closed down the ferry, and at 1:20 a.m. he went home.

The barbecue held that evening was a sort of reunion of girls who had worked for Robert Kennedy in Washington before his assassination. They had often held reunions previous to this gathering on Chappaquiddick. Sometimes Kennedy aides attended these parties. Indeed, some of the Kennedy wives had also attended in the past.

On this July 18, Mary Jo Kopechne, Esther Newberg, Rosemary Keough, Susan Tannenbaum, Maryellen Lyons, and her sister, Nance, had come to the remote cottage to partake of the barbecue. All the girls had been associated with the Kennedys as political workers in one way or another. All were well educated, level headed career girls, away for a few days' fun. Also at the cookout were Paul Markham, 38, former U.S. Attorney for Massachusetts; Joseph F. Gargan, 39, lawyer and bank president; Raymond S. La Rosa, 41, an employee of the Massachusetts Civil Defense, Charles C. Tretter, 30, lawyer with the New England Regional Commission in Boston; and of course, chauffeur Crimmins and Senator Kennedy.

The thick frozen steaks sizzled on the small barbecue. Everyone ate heartily, and by about 10:30 the party turned into joke telling and singsongs. Almost everyone had a few drinks, but no one drank heavily. Sometime between 11 and 12 o'clock (the time varies according to whose recollection is believed) Mary Jo Kopechne and Ted Kennedy disappeared. Both had earlier complained of being tired, and if anyone thought of it at all, they felt Ted had given Mary Jo a lift back to her hotel. Crimmins, the chauffeur, remembers the Senator asking for the keys to the car before leaving. Later, the remaining guests realized they had missed the ferry back to Martha's Vineyard, and went to sleep wherever they could find a comfortable spot.

Next morning, July 19, some boys out on an early morning fishing expedition spotted the Oldsmobile upside down in the channel running under Dike Bridge. They went to the nearest house and informed the occupant, Mrs. Malm, of their discovery. She called the police. Edgartown Police Chief, Dominick Arena, was the first law officer on the scene. He borrowed a pair of swimming trunks and dove into the cold water. Arena saw the eerie sight of Mary Jo Kopechne's body in the overturned Olds.

While still at the scene, Arena was advised that Senator Ted Kennedy had walked into the police station and wanted to make a statement. He had been the driver of the ill fated car. Arena rushed back to Edgartown, where he met with Senator Kennedy and Paul Markham. It was decided that the best thing would be for Kennedy to write out a statement of just what took place the night before. It was written out in longhand, then typed by Arena. Here is that statement.

On July 19, 1969, at approximately 11:15 p.m., on Chappaquiddick Island, Martha's Vineyard, I was driving my car on Main Street on my way to get the ferry back to Edgartown. I was unfamiliar with the road and turned onto Dike Road instead of bearing left on Main Street. After proceeding for approximately a half mile on Dike Road I descended a hill and came upon a narrow bridge. The car went off the side of the bridge. There was one passenger in the car with me, Miss Kopechne, a former secretary of my brother Robert Kennedy. The car turned over and sank into the water and landed with the roof resting on the bottom. I attempted to open the door and window of the car but have no recollection of how I got out of the car. I came to the surface and then repeatedly dove down to the car in an attempt to see if the passenger was still in the car. I was unsuccessful in the attempt.

I was exhausted and in a state of shock. I recall walking back to where my friends were eating. There was a car parked in front of the cottage and I climbed into the back seat. I then asked for someone to bring me back to Edgartown. I remember walking around for a period of time and then going back to my hotel room. When I fully realized what happened this morning, I immediately contacted the police.

★ ★ ★

Ted Kennedy retreated to the family compound at Hyannisport for the next three days. On the following Tuesday a twin engine aircraft landed at Wilkes-Barre, Pa. Senator Kennedy had arrived to attend Mary Jo Kopechne's funeral in nearby Plymouth.

Police Chief Arena realized he had a hot potato on his hands. How could the Senator try to open the windows of the car when they had blown out upon impact with the water? How had the Senator, a six foot, two inch, 220 pounder, managed to get out of the car, when Mary Jo, not half his weight and about a foot shorter, got trapped inside? How did the Senator get back to Edgartown when the little ferry had already stopped running? Why didn't the Senator report the accident right after it happened instead of waiting over nine hours? That was against the law.

Rumors of immoral conduct by married men spread like wildfire. Kennedy's friends poured into the compound at Hyannisport from all over the country to offer their advice. Some even flew in from abroad.

Senator Kennedy was charged with leaving the scene of an accident. He pleaded guilty and was sentenced to be incarcerated for two months in the House of Correction at Barnstable. The sentence was suspended.

Despite walking out of court a free man, speculation concerning misconduct by the Senator was so great that his political advisers strongly suggested he appear on television and address the nation. On Friday, July 25, one week after the accident, Kennedy made his T.V. appearance. He cleared up some matters and left others unanswered.

His wife was ill, which was the reason she couldn't attend the cookout. When the car plunged over the bridge, "... the cold water rushed in around my head and I was sure I was drowning. But somehow I struggled to the surface alive. I made immediate and repeated efforts to save Mary Jo by diving into the strong and murky current, but succeeded only in increasing my state of utter exhaustion and alarm."

The Senator went on to tell how he returned to the cottage and drove back to the scene with Gargan and Markham, who immediately stripped and, at great risk to their own lives, made repeated attempts to get down to Mary Jo. Kennedy explained away how he returned to Edgartown after the ferry had closed down by saying that he had jumped into the water and swam across to Martha's Vineyard.

Senator Kennedy's address to the nation received initial acceptance and sympathy. Later, doubts were expressed. He had been a busy boy that night. The Senator stated that he had left the party at 11:15, and took a wrong turn on a road he had traversed and a bridge he had crossed twice before that same day. He plunged the car over the bridge, managed to save his own life, and had made repeated dives to try to save his companion. Then he half walked or ran back to the cottage, summoned two friends, and together they drove back to the bridge. He claimed his friends made repeated dives to the submerged car. Finally, giving up the whole idea, he swam from Chappaquiddick to Martha's Vineyard and made his way to the Shiretown Inn by 1:30 a.m. He had spent a very busy two hours and fifteen minutes.

Kennedy may have been out of the woods as far as the public was concerned, but he still had a few technicalities to overcome for the State of Massachusetts. Massachusetts law decrees that a manslaughter charge is mandatory if someone leaves the scene of an accident, if that accident produces a fatality, and that fatality is caused by negligence.

In January, 1970, a secret inquest was conducted in Edgartown. In April of the same year, the Duke's County Grand Jury convened to hear the details of the Kopechne accident. The entire procedure lasted two days, and only 22 minutes of evidence was heard. The jurors were told that it was not legal for them to see the inquest information. The Grand Jury was disbanded without coming to any conclusion.

Why was Kennedy never charged with any kind of criminal conduct? Kennedy testified that he was travelling at 20 miles per hour when he approached the bridge. In his report, the judge who presided at the inquest agreed that 20 m.p.h. could be construed as reckless driving on that particular bridge. The judge, who failed to act on his inquest findings, retired one week before his report was released.

What about the girls who had attended the ill-fated cookout? Within 24 hours of the discovery of Mary Jo's body, all the girls had left Chappaquiddick. Not one was ever questioned by Chief of Police Arena. Not one has ever testified at any of the hearings or inquests. Despite offers of large sums of money, not one has ever volunteered any statement to anyone about what went on at the cookout on July 19, 1963. Strange, isn't it?

WHO KILLED THE
DIRECTOR?

William Desmond Taylor dealt in make believe. As chief director for Famous Players-Lasky Studios, none of his associates ever dreamed that Taylor's own past was as exciting and strange as any of those portrayed on the Hollywood screen of the 1920s.

Born in Ireland in 1877, Taylor's real name was William Cunningham Deane Tanner. His father, a British Army colonel, had a military future in mind for his son. However, after young Willie graduated from Clifton College, he joined a theatrical company. He then travelled to Canada and gravitated to the Klondike as a prospector.

Tanner's most outstanding feature was his extraordinary good looks. Tall, straight as a ramrod, with finely chiselled features, he was quite a hit with the ladies when he arrived in New York from the Klondike.

In 1901, he married Ethel Harrison, then a leading name on the musical comedy stage. The couple had a daughter and settled down, presumably, to a life of marital bliss. For many years all went well. Then, in 1912, Tanner walked out of the house, went directly to his bank, where he withdrew a sizeable amount of cash, and effectively disappeared.

For two years, Mrs. Tanner tried to trace her husband. Being unable to do so, she divorced him. Later, she was to marry a millionaire.

No one knows how Tanner spent the next few years. In 1915, he joined the Canadian army, using his new name, William Desmond Taylor. At the conclusion of World War I he was discharged from the army as a captain, and made his way to Hollywood.

Because of his good looks and English theatrical training, Taylor had no trouble landing bit parts in the movies. Quickly he graduated to leading roles. He then became a successful director. In 1920, before income tax and inflation, Taylor was pulling down $40,000 per year. Not bad today, but in those days a real fortune.

A series of unrelated events were to take place in 1920, which alone seem innocent enough, but which together went to make up the intrigue which was to follow. While Taylor was on a trip to England, his manservant and secretary, Edward Sands, suddenly disappeared. With him went several suits and forged cheques. Taylor replaced him with another man-in-waiting, Henry Peavey.

During the same year, Taylor became engaged to Mabel Normand. The name doesn't mean much to us today, but in 1920 Mabel was the leading comedienne in the country. She was rolling in dough from playing in Mack Sennett slapstick comedies. Later she was to be Charlie Chaplin's leading lady in several of his films. Mabel had everything except brain power. There were those who said that she and Taylor had nothing in common. Whatever she had was enough for our boy, the director. Their affair continued unabated for months.

Boys will be boys. While Taylor was wooing Miss Normand he was carrying on a torrid romance with Mary Miles Minter, one of the most famous female stars in Hollywood at that time. Taylor also liked to frequent the heroin dens of Los Angeles. Whenever he wasn't treated right, he would run to the police and squeal on the illegal operation. Nothing was ever done with the information he provided the police.

On Wednesday, Feb. 1, 1922, Taylor was served his dinner by Peavey at precisely 6:30 p.m. Mabel Normand arrived in her chauffeur-driven limousine, but stayed only 45 minutes to have a cocktail with her lover. Peavey, who didn't live in, went home. Around nine o'clock that evening, neighbors thought they heard a car backfiring.

At eight o'clock the next morning, Peavey reported for work. He found his boss lying on the floor with a .38 calibre bullet through his heart.

During the murder investigation which followed, Taylor's house was thoroughly searched by the police. They found two stacks of love letters, one from Mabel Normand, and one from Mary Miles Minter. Both sets of letters were intimate love letters. All the juicy details were reported in the press, and for months the movie colony and much of America discussed little else but the Taylor murder.

Investigation into Taylor's past revealed all the information already presented here. Everything was uncovered, except the murderer's identity. There were many theories. Did the disappearing servant, Edward Sands, hold some grudge against his former boss and return to kill him? Did a jealous lover of Miss Normand or Miss Minter decide to kill their competitor? Did one of the heroin operators have Taylor murdered?

Then, of course, in true Hollywood fashion, could it have been the butler, Peavey? We will never know. The murder remains unsolved to this day.

FATTY AND MISS RAPPE

Roscoe Arbuckle started out in silent movies making $3 a day as a Keystone
Cop. He ended up signing a $3 million contract covering his services for three years.
This kind of money is a fortune today. Then it was a King's ransom. With the exception
of Charlie Chaplin, Fatty Arbuckle was the world's leading funny man. He weighed 280
pounds, and had a way of manipulating his enormous bulk and expressive face that was
truly funny.

To depict Fatty and the times in their proper light, it is only fair to point out that
Hollywood's morals at that time were suspect. The players were bigger than life. They
could do no wrong, and sometimes they went too far. Big cars, wild parties, and loose
women were the order of the day. The stars lived it up, and their fans ate it up.

On Sunday, Sept. 4, 1921 Fatty Arbuckle drove into San Francisco in his big Rolls
Royce. He parked it in front of the St. Francis Hotel. Fatty took the manager aside
and told him to take care of his car and the booze. Fatty said he would take care of the
broads personally. He was going to have a party to end all parties.

A continuous parade of chorus girls, bit players, champagne and gin by the case were
delivered to Fatty's room. Laughter and music blared from the Hollywood style party.
Fatty's lady companion knew that to be friendly to a star meant small parts in the
movies, and small parts exposed them to stardom. They would literally do anything for
a grab at the golden ring. The party raged on.

Unknown to the rest of the merry makers, a bit player named Virginia Rappe was staying at the Palace Hotel with her agent and a Mrs. Delamont, a personal friend. The funny man had been making advances to Virginia for years, and for years she had been repulsed by his appearance. For some reason that was never established, she knew Arbuckle would be in San Francisco that Sunday and had given him her telephone number. She waited for his call. No doubt she expected some sort of break in the film industry in exchange for certain favors.

In the meantime, Arbuckle started to tire of his co-operative guests. Suddenly he picked up the telephone and called the Palace. Virginia didn't waste any time in getting over to the St. Francis. She brought her girlfriend and her agent. They all had a few drinks with the comedian. The conversation centred around what he would do to help Virginia's career.

Then, without a word, Fatty got up, and taking Virginia by the arm, led her into a private bedroom. Later some people who witnessed the scene said Fatty pushed Virginia into the room. Others said she entered not only voluntarily, but eagerly. Her girlfriend and agent thought nothing of this and continued eating and talking.

Suddenly the party atmosphere was shattered by bloodcurdling screams emanating from the bedroom. They were the type of screams that indicated to anyone within earshot that something was drastically wrong. They contained that element of desperation which distinguishes them from any other meaning. Virginia's girlfriend rushed to the door. It was locked from the inside. The screams continued. She picked up the telephone and called the reception desk. Just as the assistant manager entered the room, Fatty opened the door. Everyone agreed as to what he said.

"Go in and get her dressed. Take her back to where she came from. She makes too much noise."

Beyond the comedian's huge bulk, on the floor, lay Virginia Rappe. Her pale nude form moaned heavily. She sobbed to Mrs. Delamont, "I'm dying, I'm dying. Roscoe did it."

Arbuckle shouted, "Shut up, you phony. Shut your mouth or I'll throw you out the window."

Someone had called the doctor. Virginia lingered between life and death for a few days. She died on Thursday. An autopsy was performed, and the coroner discovered that she had not died of natural causes. She had a ruptured bladder. He called in the police.

A preliminary hearing was held, and the entire affair was a sensation. Millions of children, and adults as well, revered the robust comedian. He received hundreds of fan letters each week. Was it true? Could he be mixed up in such a sordid affair?

The details of the hearing were considered to be so appalling at the time that the statements as to what actually went on in the hotel room that afternoon were written out on bits of paper and passed around the court.

Now, in every well publicized murder case, some statement or piece of evidence turns the case one way or the other. When death does not occur immediately, people say and do things that return to haunt them. In this case, Arbuckle never felt for a minute that Virginia would die. In the days while she was in hospital, he joked about her.

Then one witness testified that Fatty had told him he didn't rape Virginia at all. In his own words the witness said, "He simply took a piece of ice from an ice bucket and thrust it into her genitals."

This one revolting statement turned the public of the United States away from Arbuckle. They would forgive him almost anything, but not this. The statement was never proven to be true, but it didn't matter. The damage was done.

Fatty was tried three times for murder. The first two trials ended in a hung jury. The third trial returned a verdict of not guilty.

During the years in which his case dragged through the courts, Fatty dissipated his fortune in his successful effort to stay out of jail. Hollywood would have nothing to do with him. He tried touring the smaller centres, but even here he was sometimes booed off the stage. Later he tried directing under an assumed name. Nothing worked for him.

One hot day in 1933, Fatty Arbuckle returned to his hotel in New York after a party. He suffered a heart attack, and died alone in the middle of the night.

LATIN LOVER FOUND DEAD

Scaramouche, Prisoner of Zenda, Ben Hur — all great old movies, first produced during Hollywood's silent era. Later, there would be the *Student Prince* and *The Pagan*. What did all these old movies have in common? The star of every one, and certainly one of the great Latin lovers of all time, was Ramon Novarro.

During the twenties the name Novarro ranked second only to Rudolph Valentino as the screen's greatest lover. When talkies were introduced Novarro's thick accent drastically limited the scope of the roles he could play. Gradually he faded from view and lived off investments made during his heyday, which assured him of a substantial income for the rest of his life.

The handsome Novarro never married, and so wasn't encumbered with alimony payments, as were many of his colleagues of that era. He lived alone on his luxurious estate in isolated Laurel Canyon. When talkies came upon the scene, Novarro hit the bottle hard. His drinking bouts were legendary in Hollywood. The fading star was a confirmed alcoholic. Novarro's bout with the bottle was to continue until the day he died.

Novarro lived alone, but maintained a secretary, Edward Weber, who came in to work each day at 8:30 a.m. When Weber showed up on the morning of Nov. 1, 1968, he found the aging movie star sprawled nude across his bed. He had taken a terrible beating and obviously was dead.

Police were notified and were on the scene in a matter of minutes. It was ascertained that no one had forced their way into the house. Because of this, it was believed that Novarro had known his killer or killers. The entire house had been ransacked, and there was evidence that heavy drinking had taken place in the house before the murder.

A post mortem revealed that one of the blows to the victim's head had broken his nose, causing a hemmorhage which resulted in Novarro drowning in his own blood. Evidence found in the bedroom indicated that he was a homosexual, but did not reveal the identity of any of his acquaintances.

Routinely police reviewed the record of Novarro's telephone calls in an attempt to question individuals who knew him. They were surprised to find that a long distance phone call had been placed from Novarro's home on the night of the murder. Someone had placed a call to Brenda Lee Metcalf in Chicago at 8:15 p.m. and had spoken for 48 minutes.

When questioned Brenda, who turned out to be a pretty 21-year-old brunette, told investigating officers all about her call that night. She had never met Ramon Novarro. Her caller had been 17-year-old Tom Ferguson. He had explained to her that he and his 22-year-old brother, Paul, were in Novarro's home. During the call Tom told Brenda that they believed Novarro had $5,000 hanging around the house, and he and his brother meant to get their hands on it. As they talked Brenda advised Tom not to do anything foolish. Tom assured her that it was Paul who was roughing up Ramon. Occasionally Brenda could hear a blood curdling scream over the phone.

Tom and Paul Ferguson were located in Illinois and brought back to California for questioning. Paul, who had lived in L.A. for several months prior to the murder, had become acquainted with Novarro and had been invited to his home on the night of the killing. He was asked to bring his brother along. In return for sexual favors, Novarro had promised to use his influence to get the two brothers into the movies. The Fergusons planned to con the old actor out of his cash. Both brothers swore that the other had actually killed Novarro when he wouldn't reveal where he kept his money.

Both men were charged with murder. At their trial it appeared that the younger brother Tom was attempting to take the blame for the actual killing. He was informed that because he was only 17 at the time of the murder, he would receive a maximum sentence of life imprisonment rather than the death penalty. If Paul assumed the role of killer, he stood in fear of receiving the death penalty.

The elaborate planning was academic. At the conclusion of the seven-week trial both men were found guilty of murder in the first degree. They received sentences of life imprisonment.

Ramon Novarro, the former heart throb of millions of women all over the world, had been tortured and beaten to death with an ivory handled black cane, an old prop from one of his movies. His killers had robbed him of $45.

Jack the Ripper

– Part 8 –

MONSTERS

JACK THE RIPPER

Jack the Ripper holds a fascination for criminologists and the general public that has not diminished for almost 100 years.

He appeared in the East end of a turbulent London, England in 1888. The Whitechapel District of London was the last stop on the road down for the derelicts of the nation, and indeed a great portion of Europe. It is estimated that 15,000 men, women and children did not have a roof over their heads. Workhouses held over 128,000 souls. There were 80,000 prostitutes plying the oldest profession throughout London. Large ethnic groups from the continent who could neither read nor write English tried to eke out a living.

Gin was the cheapest alcoholic beverage, and it was consumed in great quantities in the pubs that dotted the area. Beds were sold several times in one night. Crime in general and murder in particular ran wild in Whitechapel.

Jack the Ripper was the tip of the iceberg. The horror, audacity and method of his killings were so terrible that they brought the plight of the general population of the worst slums in the world to the attention of the authorities.

Mary Ann Nicholls was a 42-year-old prostitute. She had five front teeth missing. Dental care did not rank high on Mary Nicholls' list of priorities. On the night of Aug. 31, 1888, she could not raise four pennies needed for a bed. As she staggered down Bucks Row, she passed her old friend Nelly Holland. Nelly was later to say that Mary was so drunk she could hardly walk.

In the darkness of Bucks Row just off Whitechapel, a hand clamped over Mary's mouth from behind. A razor sharp knife held in Jack's other hand made a wide arc, starting under the left ear and ending across the throat under the right ear. The rip was so vicious it nearly decapitated the victim. His work not finished, the Ripper plunged his knife into the lower part of the abdomen and cut upward and to the right. Again the knife was plunged into the body, and from the lower abdomen the cut proceeded up the centre of the body to the breastbone. The two slashes just described became the trademark of Jack the Ripper.

Eight days later, Annie Chapman was walking the streets at two o'clock in the morning. She couldn't raise the two pennies for a bed for the rest of the night. Annie was 47, and suffered from consumption. Her body was found next morning behind a house on Hanbury Street. The throat cut, the body laid open were plainly in evidence, but there was much more. The body was disembowelled and the womb had been removed. The intestines had been lifted out of the body and placed on the shoulder of the corpse. The doctors examining the body suggested that some of the incisions showed knowledge of formal medical training.

On Sept. 30, the Ripper struck again, twice on the same night. Louis Diemschultz drove his horse into a yard at 40 Berners Street. The horse shied and Diemschultz noticed what he thought was a bag of something lying against a wall. What he found was the remains of Elizabeth Stride. Only the throat had been cut. There was no mutilation. The Ripper had been interrupted in his work. It is believed that he may have still been at the scene, and was the cause of the horse shying as it did. Certainly he made a hurried exit out the back yard. A few minutes later Catherine Eddowes fell into his grasp. He mutilated her in the style of Annie Chapman. Poor Catherine Eddowes was like her fellow victims, a middle-aged alcoholic prostitute. A man she was currently living with identified the body.

A German immigrant came forward and said he had seen Eddowes with a man shortly before she was killed. He described her escort as a man of about 30, well-dressed, fair complexion, moustache, medium build and about five feet, eight inches tall. The description fit thousands of men in London. Then the police released this letter they had received just before the double killing:

Dear Boss,

I keep on hearing the police have caught me, but they won't fix me just yet. I have laughed when they looked so clever and talk about being on the right track. The joke about Leather Apron gave me real fits.

I am down on whores and I shan't quit ripping them till I do get buckled. Grand work, the last job was. I gave the lady no time to squeal. How can they catch me now? I love my work and want to start again. You will soon hear of me and my funny little games.

I saved some of the proper red stuff in a ginger beer bottle over the last job, to write with, but it went thick like glue and I can't use it. Red ink is fit enough I hope. Ha! Ha!

The next job I do I shall clip the lady's ears off. Keep this letter back till I do a bit more work, then give it out straight. My knife is nice and sharp. I want to get to work right away if I get a chance. Good luck.

Yours truly,
Jack the Ripper.

Don't mind me giving the trade name, wasn't good enough to post this before I got all the red ink off my hands curse it. No luck yet they say I am a doctor now. ha ha.

A few hours after the double murder the police received this postcard:

I was not cidding dear old Boss when I gave you the tip. You'll hear about Saucy Jack's work tomorrow. Double event this time. Number one squealed a bit. Couldn't finish straight off. Had no time to get ears for police. Thanks for keeping last letter back till I got to work again.

Jack the Ripper.

The police considered both the letter and card to be genuine.

A Whitechapel Viglante Committee was formed and was now actively engaged patrolling the streets late at night. The chairman of the committee, a Mr. George Lusk, received a letter enclosed in a box.

It read:

Mr. Lusk

Sir I send you half the Kidney I took from one woman presarved it for you, other piece I fried and ate it was very nice. I may send you the bloody knif that took it out if you only wate a while longer

Signed Catch me when you can
Mister Lusk

This letter too is considered to be genuine. The kidney that had been enclosed with the letter had been removed from a human body not more than two weeks previously. It was in an advanced state of Bright's Disease. Eddowes was suffering from Bright's Disease, and her kidney had been removed by her killer.

Mary Kelly was the last to die at the hands of Jack the Ripper. She was a heavy drinker and a prostitute. Unlike the previous victims she was attractive, and only 25 years old. She even had her own room at 13 Miller's Court. Mary was on the skids but had not made the complete trip. On Thursday night, Nov. 8, she picked up a customer and took him to her room. For the first time Jack the Ripper had no fear of discovery or interruption. He had reached the pinnacle of wanton mutilation and savagery in his treatment of Mary Kelly. Her body was hacked beyond recognition. The police officers who witnessed the scene at 13 Miller's Court were never to forget the sight that greeted them on Nov. 9 when the body was discovered. Mary Kelly had been three months pregnant.

On Wednesday Nov. 21, the police received this letter:

> Dear Boss. It is no use for you to look for me in London because I'm not there. Don't trouble yourself about me until I return, which will not be very long. I like the work too well to leave it alone. Oh, it was a jolly job the last one. I had plenty of time to do it properly in. Ha, ha, ha! The next lot I mean to do with Vengeance, cut of their head and arms. You think it is a man with a black moustache. Ha, ha, ha! When I have done another one you can try and catch me again. So goodbye dear Boss, till I return.

Yours,
Jack the Ripper.

Jack the Ripper was never heard from again. It was generally agreed by the police in 1888, that while there were murders before the outbreak and some after it that were similar in nature, it is only those described here that are attributed to the one person. There were five in all, starting on the night of Aug. 31, and abruptly ending 70 days later in the early morning hours of Nov. 9.

Who committed these horrible crimes? There have been many theories.

Dr. Neill Cream is erroneously believed to be Jack the Ripper by many students of the case. He was born in 1850 in Glasgow, Scotland and immigrated to Canada in 1863. At the age of 26, he received his medical degree from McGill University in Montreal. In 1881, he was found guilty of poisoning a friend in Chicago and was sentenced to life imprisonment in Joliet, Illinois, but was out in 10 years. He appears on the London scene in October of 1891, where he started killing prostitutes by poisoning them. He would write letters to newspapers keeping the unsolved cases alive. In this way he brought suspicion to himself, and was finally tried and found guilty. He was hung on Nov. 15, 1892. On the scaffold Dr. Cream's last words were "I am Jack the ......".

It is unfortunate that positive documentation exists proving beyond a doubt that Dr. Cream was confined to Joliet Prison in Illinois during the 10 weeks Jack was committing his murders in London.

The Duke of Clarence was Queen Victoria's grandson, and was in a direct line to the throne of England. In 1970, Dr. Thomas Stowell wrote an article claiming that the Duke was Jack the Ripper. It seems the Duke was quite a ladies' man. The story goes that he contracted syphillis in his early twenties. As a result he was under the care of a doctor, Sir William Gull. The good doctor tried to restrain the Duke, but after the Kelly murder he knew he had to have him confined to a mental home. Queen Victoria was accustomed to consulting a spiritualist named Lees. It is said that Lees saw the face of the murderer in his dreams. One day while travelling on a bus he saw the man who had appeared in his dreams sitting beside him. He followed this man off the bus to the home of Sir William Gull. Dr. Stowell's theory received wide publicity, and it is disheartening to report that there is documentary proof that Clarence was at Sandringham from Nov. 3 to Nov. 12, 1888, and could not have killed Mary Kelly in London.

And so the theories go, from a Jewish butcher, to a medical student, to a secret agent of the Russian Czar.

There is only one theory and one man who fits all the known facts.

During the course of research for a television program in 1959, Lady Aberconway was interviewed. She was the elderly daughter of Sir Melville Macnaghten, who was Assistant Chief Constable of Scotland Yard in 1889, only a few months after the killings. Surprisingly, after all these years, Lady Aberconway produced her father's notes. Here was a direct link to the man who had actually hunted Jack the Ripper. From these notes we learn what the police believed at the time of the hunt.

Montague J. Druitt was born on Aug. 15, 1857. His father was a doctor and the entire family highly respected. Young Druitt whizzed through school and ended up with a B.A. degree from Oxford University in 1880. On March 30, 1885 he received his law degree. It seems that he was unsuccessful in his practice of law, and in 1888 he was teaching at a private school and living in rooms at Kings Bench Walk. On Dec. 31, 1888, M.J. Druitt's body was recovered from the Thames, his pocket full of stones. He had leaped to his death on Dec. 4, twenty five days after the last Ripper murder.

Shortly before the first Ripper murder, Druitt's mother became insane, and Druitt thought he was going mad. He left a suicide note expressing this fear. The Macnaghten notes reveal the fact that all police agencies as well as vigilante committees were given the word to stop looking for the Ripper after Druitt's body was found. The police kept all information from the general public in order to save the respected Druitt family from unnecessary embarrassment. The eye witness reports fit Druitt. The idea that he was a gentleman fit Druitt's station in life. The Ripper's letters have been analysed by experts, and they believe they were written by an educated man disguising his handwriting and using poor grammar to throw the police off the track. Would a real illiterate write the word "knif" or would "nife" be more natural?

It has always been believed that the Ripper had medical knowledge, or at least medical instruments. Druitt's father, uncle and cousin were all doctors, so he had ready access to medical instruments and could easily have picked up some knowledge from attending post mortems with his father. Druitt also lived in the centre of the area where the killings took place. This would give him the knowledge that the killer obviously had of the general area. It also gave him a place to go immediately after each killing.

Dr. Peter Druitt lives in Christchurch, New Zealand. He is the great grandson of Robert Druitt, Montague's uncle. He says that having Jack the Ripper as a possible ancestor is most enjoyable, and really livens up his otherwise dull family tree.

THE STUDENT WAS
A KILLER

The city of Chicago has long been familiar with violent death. The citizens of that community take a gangland killing as casually as we take our morning coffee. It takes a bizarre and baffling case to arouse public interest. Here is such a case.

On June 3, 1945 Mrs. Josephine Alice Ross was found dead in her apartment. Her body had horrible knife wounds about the head and neck. The jugular vein had been cut, allowing her to bleed to death. A nylon stocking and skirt were wrapped around her neck. The bed she lay on was completely soaked in blood. The investigating officers knew immediately that this was no ordinary crime when they discovered that the body had been washed clean of blood and adhesive tape had been applied to the cuts and abrasions. Mrs. Ross had not been sexually attacked, but her murderer had lingered in the apartment and had meticulously wiped the entire apartment clean of fingerprints.

For the next five months, police investigated several attacks on women in the general area of the University of Chicago. Some were shootings and some were beatings, and all could have ended in tragedy but for the fact that the attacker was either interrupted or was successfully fought off by the women.

Then on Dec. 10, the murderer struck again. Frances Brown's nude body was found draped in a kneeling position over the bathtub of her apartment. She had been stabbed repeatedly in the head and neck, and had been shot as well. Again the murderer had taken great care in washing the body. He had also stayed in the apartment long enough to wash every piece of furniture free of fingerprints. This time he missed one lone print — the right index finger. An attempt to trace him through this print failed.

Overshadowing all other evidence in the Brown case was an actual message left by the killer. On a wall in the living room, written in lipstick, were the words:

For heavens
sake catch me
Before I kill more
I cannot control myself

The similarity of the two murders as well as the several other attacks on women convinced the police that they were looking for one sick man. On the morning of Jan. 7 they were to find out just how sick.

A little six-year-old girl, Suzanne Degnan, had been abducted from the first floor bedroom of her two-storey home. Her father found a ransom note on her bed.

Get $20,000
Reddy &
Waite
For word
do not notify
FBI or
police
Bills in 5's & 10's

One fingerprint was found on the note. It was the print of the left little finger. A check of police files again proved fruitless, as no match could be found.

A search was started for Suzanne in the immediate vicinity of her home. An officer noticed that a sewer lid looked as if it had been recently pried loose. He lifted the lid up and peered into the sewer. There floating on the surface was a human head. A search of other sewers revealed the rest of pathetic little Suzanne's body. She had been abducted and dismembered on the same night. In scouring the neighborhood for any clues to the killer's identity the police found an apartment building close by where Suzanne had been dismembered. The basement like many of the buildings in that area was equipped with washbasins for the tenants. Here the police found bloody rags, and not a great deal more. It was estimated that the killer had spent over two hours cleaning the washroom. Again despite an all out effort by the police, there was a vacuum of concrete clues to the wave of wanton killings. Months dragged by, and then in a completely unrelated incident, the police found their killer.

A young man was interrupted as he was ransacking an apartment. He dashed out of the building, and into an adjoining building at 1320 Farell Ave. He stopped at the back door of an apartment occupied by Mrs. Frances Willett, and asked for a drink of water. He picked the wrong door. Mrs. Willett was the wife of a policeman. She sensed something wrong and told him to sit down on her porch. She then hooked the door from the inside and pretended to get the water. Instead she called the police.

In the meantime, an off duty policeman, Abner Cunningham, was coming home from the beach wearing swimming trunks and a t-shirt. He saw the youth dash out of one building and into another. Cunningham started a door to door search of the second building.

The police, responding to Mrs. Willett's call, arrived at the back of her building. She called out, "He's up here on the back porch."

Det. Tiffin P. Constant started up after him. As he looked up the stairs he saw a young man pointing a gun at him. He was pulling the trigger but the gun failed to fire. The detective caught up with the youth and they started to fight and roll on the porch. Officer Cunningham heard the noise and started up the stairs. As he did so he picked up three flower pots. When he reached the pair, he hesitated for a minute, not knowing which was the fugitive. Det. Constant sensed the hesitation. He screamed, "That's him." Cunningham brought the flower pots down on the young man's head with all his might. The fight was over.

The young man was William Heirens, a 17-year-old University of Chicago student. William was a clean cut, good looking boy, weighing 155 pounds and standing 5 ft., 10 ins. In a routine check of the boy's room at the university, police found two suitcases. They contained several pistols, $1,800 in War Bonds, and a surgical kit. Upon checking Heirens' fingerprints, it was found that the print of his left little finger matched the print found on the Degnan ransom note.

In one fell swoop, the William Heirens case was transformed from that of a prowler to one receiving world-wide publicity as a mass killer.

At first the young student would say nothing, and for a while there was some question as to whether the flower pot had resulted in permanent damage to his brain. A thorough examination proved these suspicions to be unfounded, and gradually young Heirens started to talk. He claimed he was dominated by another person, whom he referred to as George. George, he said, did the bad things, while he, William tried to stop him.

In the end though, William Heirens took the responsibility for his crimes. He confessed in detail to the three killings, and to an estimated 300 robberies. He led police to various caches of loot throughout Chicago. Thousands of dollars in bonds and cash were recovered. Heirens never spent more than five dollars a week on himself. He went to the three murder locations, and while the officers watched, he renacted every horrible detail of his crimes.

The authorities were baffled on one point — what was his motive?

Heirens revealed that while ordinary people received sexual satisfaction from a relationship with a member of the opposite sex, he received this same satisfaction only by breaking into and robbing a house or apartment. He would get this sexual urge that had to be satisfied. He never molested or interfered in any way with the three women he killed. In each case, he panicked when they made too much noise.

Heirens stood trial and pleaded guilty to three indictments of murder, and 26 of assault with intent to kill, burglary, and robbery. He received three life sentences to run consecutively, and a one year to life sentence for the 26 non-murder charges to follow the three life sentences.

He was committed to Statesville Penitentiary at Joliet, Ill., where he is to this day.

A UNIQUE LITTLE PRESENT

Some murderers achieve a place in the murky history of crime because of the sheer number of victims, some because of the unusual method of killing. There are a few really unique cases that are remembered down through the years only because of a couple of extra special sentences uttered by the killer that sets him or her apart from all others.

And so it was with Grete Beier. In 1901, Grete was 16. She had the looks of an angel, the body of a goddess, and the disposition of a devil. Her father was the Burgomaster of the tiny town of Brand in Saxony, and as the daughter of such a man Grete was considered real class. She had attended private schools up until the time she committed a slight indiscretion, that resulted in her dismissal. Actually Grete skipped out for a week to shack up with one of the locals.

Momma and Papa Beier didn't know what to do with their daughter. One fine day Frau Beier met a handsome, distinguished gentleman at a friend's house. She was delighted at the attention he was showing her and asked him home for dinner.

It was the worst mistake she ever made.

Grete took one look and figured — that's for me. His name was Herr Merkur, and he was a real rogue from the very beginning. He knew the old lady had a sweet young thing at home, and had set himself up for the invite.

Within a week Merkur and Grete were frolicking in the hay. In a few months, Grete was expecting a little visitor. Merkur didn't seem to mind. He told Grete to tell mother the awkward news, knowing that the reaction would be negative in every way. He was right. Mother suggested different medicines to terminate the pregnancy. Grete's tummy just got bigger and bigger. Nothing seemed to work. Finally a child was born.

Within hours of the birth Grete calmly smothered the baby and buried it in the middle of the night.

At the age of 17 she had been thrown out of school, given birth to an illegitimate child, and committed murder. Not bad for a start, but there was more to come.

Merkur informed Grete that he had committed forgery, and the only reason he had come to the tiny town in the first place was to escape the authorities. He needed money fast. Merkur, the troublemaker, suggested prostitution. Grete thought it a great idea. Soon she was well established in the oldest profession in an adjoining town. With Merkur acting as pimp, the money started to roll in. He treated her with some degree of kindness, and in return took every penny she earned. It wasn't enough. Now completely under the domineering personality of her lover, Grete was talked into robbing her own family. She went home and managed to gain access to her father's safe. She took the family jewels as well as Papa Beier's cheque book. Merkur had among his many talents an extraordinary ability as a forger. Within a couple of hours he had cleaned out the old man's bank account.

Unfortunately for young Grete, the maid had seen her extract the jewels from the safe. She was arrested immediately. This final disgrace was too much for her staid old father. Upon hearing the news he collapsed and was confined to a hospital.

Grete didn't care for prison life. While awaiting trial she had a great idea. She would smuggle out a note to Merkur telling him to chloroform the maid and strangle her. In this way they would eliminate the only witness against her. The note was discovered, and for her trouble Grete got charged with an additional offence; that of incitement to murder.

She got five years, but with good behavior and apparent remorse for her ways, she was out in two. The family had moved to Chemnitz, and upon release from jail, she joined them. Her father, now fully recovered, welcomed his reformed daughter with open arms.

Grete even met a respectable engineer named Pressler. Soon they were engaged to be married, when who should show up but her old friend the pimp. Soon she and Merkur were doing what comes naturally again. He started making demands of money upon her almost immediately.

Grete decided to raise some cash in her own unique way. First she became an expert at duplicating her fiance's handwriting. One day when the time was ripe, she visited Pressler in his apartment and shared his bed in the usual manner. She then uttered the few lines that are extra special in the annals of mayhem.

"I brought you a present dear. Close your eyes. Say something, darling."

Pressler opened his mouth to speak, and Grete stuck a pistol in his mouth and blew a hole right through the back of his head. She placed a suicide note beside the body. It left everything he had to her. She had another letter written in a different hand, purportedly from Pressler's wife in Italy saying she had heard he was getting married and if he did, she would charge him with bigamy. Thus a phony motive for the suicide was established.

Pressler's body was found and no one suspected anything other than suicide. Grete inherited the equivalent of several hundred pounds, which naturally ended up with Merkur.

But Pressler had a brother who was very close to the dead man, and he started to question the will. He brought in handwriting experts, and before you could say forgery, that's exactly what was proven.

Our heroine was arrested again, and this time charged with murder. Papa Beier collapsed again, and the shock of his daughter's errant ways killed him. Grete confessed to murdering Pressler, and told of having two further children with Merkur. She said she killed them soon after they were born.

So, if you are keeping score, that's three children, one lover, one attempt on the maid, and an indirect victim in her father.

She was convicted of murder and sentenced to be beheaded, as was the custom in Saxony. In 1908, at the age of 23, she kneeled on a cushion, placed her head on a block and, on the stroke of midnight a swordsman cut off her angelic head.

TRULY A DEVIL

Ronald True was a tall gregarious man who was always the life of the party. Casual acquaintances thought he was a real sport, a great guy to have around. Those who knew him better were more cautious. True sometimes went beyond good fun. Sometimes he acted so irrationally it appeared he might not have all his faculties.

When Ronnie was born in 1891, his mother was only 16 and unmarried. Later she wed a wealthy businessman, and she and her son appear to have fitted in nicely in upper middle class British life. Ronnie grew up with a penchant for wandering the globe. As a young man he travelled to New Zealand, Canada, Mexico, and Shanghai, until, in 1914, he returned home to join the Royal Flying Corps.

Despite his idiosyncrasies, one of which was firing a loaded gun at parties just for fun, he became a pilot, but not a very good one. Ronnie simply kept on crashing his aircraft, often sustaining serious injuries. Finally, after one such crash, the Royal Flying Corps gave him a medical discharge. It was around this time that Ronnie confided to friends that another Ronald True was posing as him and acting strangely. He claimed it was becoming an embarrassment. Not only was it an embarrassment to Mr. True, but a downright hint that Ronnie was losing his mind.

In February, 1922 True met attractive Olive Young in the west end of London. The pair struck up a conversation, and Ronnie was somewhat taken aback when he discovered that Olive was a businesswoman of sorts. That is to say she was a member of that old profession of street walker.

But she wasn't your average street walker. Olive was choosy in picking her clients. She had a respectable flat in the respectable neighborhood of Fulham. She even had money in the bank.

Ronnie, who was calling himself Major True that week, seemed to qualify as a customer. The new acquaintances made a date for later in the week.

On Feb. 18, Major True knocked on Olive's door. With a grin on his face and a jaunty bounce to his gait he entered her apartment. Olive began to have a few misgivings about the Major, especially when he started to wave his revolver hither and yon. To add insult to injury, upon leaving Ronnie stole the exact amount of money he had paid Olive for her favors.

Olive made a mental note to scratch True off her list of customers. Ronnie kept calling at her flat, but each time Olive managed to hide. Ronnie would grow discouraged and leave.

Then, on March 5 she forgot to lock the door, and who should show up but the Major, looking for Olive and her particular product. Ronnie stayed the night. Sometime between 7 and 8 a.m., Ronald True killed Olive Young.

They were seated at the dining room table when True volunteered to get cups from the kitchen. He found a rolling pin, sneaked up behind Olive and struck her five vicious blows to the head. To assure her death, he tightly wrapped a dressing gown belt around her neck.

Then Ronnie True did a strange thing. Instead of leaving the scene of the crime he stayed in the flat. At 9:15 the cleaning lady, Emily Steel, arrived and let herself in with her own key. Due to Olive's usual work hours she often was asleep when Emily arrived. Emily was not unduly concerned that the bedroom door was closed. She started cleaning up the sitting room and was somewhat startled when a man approached her from the direction of the bedroom. Emily reconized Ronnie True, whom she had met when he had previously visited the flat.

True said, "Don't wake Miss Young, we were late last night and she is in a deep sleep. I'll send a car around for her at 12 o'clock." Emily helped the major on with his coat. She then decided to peer into the bedroom. The room was in complete disarray. It had been searched and Olive's jewelry was missing. Emily advanced to the bathroom. On the floor she found Olive's body, almost nude and horribly battered around the head.

Scotland Yard was searching for True within a matter of minutes. In the meantime, True wasn't trying to leave the country, nor was he in hiding. No, Ronnie was off in Piccadilly Circus buying a new outfit. He purchased a new suit, tie and hat. A large blood stain on his own trousers was a bit embarrassing, but he explained it away by telling the clerk that he had met with an accident. Then he was off to the barbershop for a shave and a haircut. Next, busy Ronnie stopped off at a pawnshop and hocked Olive's jewelry.

With no thought of escaping detection, Ronnie called up some friends and had a few drinks with them. Finally, Scotland Yard caught up with the carefree murderer in a pub.

Ronnie True was arrested and tried for murder in London's Old Bailey on March 1, 1922. He was found guilty and sentenced to hang. Later he was adjudged to be insane, and was confined to Broadmoor, an institution for the criminally insane.

The rest of True's life was spent in Broadmoor. He was the happiest, best liked inmate in the institution; always gregarious and in good humor. After spending 29 years confined there, he died in 1951.

THE GIANT WAS
A KILLER

Sometime ago I travelled to the tiny village of Bovingdon, England, to research the unbelievable case of Graham Young. Young poisoned his own family in 1963, when he was only 14 years old. Released from Broadmoor nine years later he proceeded to poison his colleagues at his place of employment in Bovingdon. After causing two deaths and many bouts of illness, he was taken into custody. In 1972 he was tried for murder, convicted, and is presently in prison.

The Young case received worldwide publicity, as it went to the very heart of major social questions the western world had been grappling with for years. Should our judicial system emphasize rehabilitation or punishment? Does capital punishment ultimately save lives?

At the time, I believed that the bizarre case of the obsessive child poisoner who had fooled psychiatrists and lawyers into releasing him to kill again was an isolated incident. I was wrong.

At approximately the same time another young man, age 15, was following the same path as Graham Young. The methods of killing were different, but the dates, the motives, and even the mental ability of the two murderers are so similar they stretch coincidence to the limit.

The other boy's name is Edmund Kemper. This is his story.

Edmund was born on Dec. 19, 1948 in Burbank, California. His father was a huge man, towering 6 ft., 8 ins., while his mother, Clarnell, stood an even 6 ft. The Kempers had three children, Susan, the oldest; Edmund, and Allyn. Edmund's parents argued incessantly. The more heated of these arguments usually culminated with Mr. Kemper leaving home for long periods of time.

There is no evidence that either parent ever physically abused their son. Edmund, as the only boy in the house, may have felt some rejection by his mother, who probably identified him with her husband. Eventually, in 1957, Mr. Kemper left his wife and never returned. Clarnell was to go to work to support her three children. She would marry twice again in a futile attempt to find companionship and a father for her children.

In the meantime, Clarnell moved to Helena, Montana, where she obtained employment as a secretary with the First National Bank. She made a new home for her three children, but Edmund was miserable. He longed for his father, and visited him at every opportunity at his new home in Los Angeles. Mr. Kemper had remarried. Edmund may not have been the most welcome of guests with the new Mrs. Kemper.

At the age of 10, Edmund, who was a tall, big boned boy, began exhibiting some strange traits. He enjoyed taking the arms, legs and heads off his younger sister's dolls. When he was only 13 years old, Edmund shot a dog belonging to another boy who lived nearby. Young Kemper had been well schooled in the use of firearms by his father, who prided himself in having been a member of the Special Service during World War II. After the incident with the dog, neighboring children mocked and made fun of Edmund. From then on Edmund Kemper had no close contact with anyone other than his mother. Their relationship was strange in many ways. Edmund always brought his troubles to his mother, who seemed concerned, but their discussions usually ended in shouting matches, with one or the other storming out of the house.

Shortly after Edmund killed the dog, he cut the head off the family pet, a Siamese cat. This time he was terrified at what he had done, and quickly buried the cat in his backyard.

In Sept., 1962, Edmund went to live with his father in Los Angeles. He was ecstatic. For a few months he led a happy, normal existence. At Christmas, Mr. Kemper visited his parents on their farm at North Fork, Calif.

Most 15-year-old boys would look forward to a visit with grandparents down on the farm. Not Edmund. He suspected his family of subterfuge. For the first time in his life Edmund's instincts were correct. His father left him on the farm and returned to Los Angeles. Edmund felt rejected, cast aside, and, above all, bored. His grandparents meant well, but they were old and set in their ways.

Grandfather Edmund Kemper was 72 and retired. He still did some farming on his eight-acre spread. Maude Kemper, at 66, spent her spare time writing juvenile stories. Being something of an artist, she illustrated her own work. All of this was an idyllic situation for the elderly couple, but was utterly boring for 15-year-old Edmund. His grandfather detected the unrest in the young lad and tried to help. He presented Edmund with a rifle to shoot gophers and rabbits. At school in the nearby town of Tollhouse, Edmund did well, making from C plus to B minus in all his subjects.

The school term ended and Edmund went to Helena to visit with his mother and her third husband. In two weeks he was back on the farm with his grandparents. There was a marked change in Edmund's behavior. He now appeared even more withdrawn and sullen. The change was so evident that his grandfather wrote to Edmund's father especially to tell him that the visit with his mother had not done the boy any good.

Later, Edmund was to reveal that his feelings towards his grandparents vacillated from gratefulness for what they were doing for him to resentment. Edmund resented the fact that his grandparents often mentioned how much it was costing them for his room and board. Sometimes his grandmother reminded him of his mother who Edmund felt was the most domineering woman in the world.

Occasionally, deep in thought, Edmund would stare off into space. The weird habit bothered his grandmother. She always shouted at him to bring him out of his reverie. Maude Kemper had no way of knowing that her grandson was fantasizing about murdering her.

On Aug. 27, 1963, Edmund was sitting at the kitchen table proofreading one of his grandmother's stories. Slowly he began to stare off into space. As usual his grandmother shouted at him, bringing him back to reality. Edmund then nonchalantly mentioned that he was going out to shoot some rabbits. He picked up his .22 rifle and went out on the porch. Edmund raised his .22 and took careful aim at the back of his grandmother's head. The bullet travelled through the screen door and into his grandmother's skull. Did Edmund Kemper feel remorse at what he had done? Was he terrified at the consequences? Edmund raised the gun and twice more shot his grandmother in the back. He then dragged the body into the elderly couple's bedroom. Just then a car chugged up the driveway. It was his grandfather. Edmund raised the rifle until the back of the old man's head was in his sight. He squeezed the trigger ever so gently just as his father had taught him. His grandfather fell to the ground never knowing what had killed him.

Edmund went to the telephone and called his mother. His first words to her were "Grandma's dead and so is Grandpa." His mother, understandably shaken, composed herself enough to get the story of the killing from her son. She pleaded with him to call the police. Edmund put down the phone and minding his mother like a good boy should, he called the sheriff's office.

When questioned by police Edmund had a hard time explaining his motive. He had often thought of killing his grandmother, because at times she had annoyed him. His grandfather was another story. Edmund had performed a mercy killing. You see, had the old man discovered his wife's body, it was quite possible he would have had a fatal heart attack. Edmund had mercifully spared his grandfather a great deal of grief.

Psychiatrists who examined Edmund discovered two things. Their subject had an I.Q. of 136, indicating superior intelligence; and they felt he was a paranoid schizophrenic. Still only 15 years old, Edmund was declared insane. On Dec. 6, 1964, the ominous doors of Atascadero State Hospital closed behind him. Ironically, half way around the world in England, 15-year-old Graham Young had already been in Broadmoor for over a year. Both boys would gain their freedom to kill again.

Once in the huge hospital which specialized in sex offenders, Edmund appeared to make a complete adjustment. He responded to treatment exceptionally well. So well, in fact, that eventually Edmund worked in a psychology lab testing other patients. Even in the confines of the institution he led something of a double life. To all outward appearances he was the well adjusted mental patient making an extraordinary recovery. His other life consisted of delving into every detail of sexual perversion garnered from fellow inmates. Edmund's curiosity knew no limits. He wanted to know it all.

After five years at Atascadero, Edmund was enrolled in a community college, where he earned straight As. In the meantime his mother, now Clarnell Strandberg, had moved to Santa Cruz, where she worked at the University of California as a secretary. Clarnell made one close friend, Sara Hallett, while employed at the university. The previous five years had been most pleasant for Clarnell. She didn't have to worry about or argue with her son Edmund.

Now the lumbering 6 ft. 9 in., 280 lb. giant was paroled to his mother. Edmund worked at menial tasks, saved his money and bought a car. He coerced his mother into getting him a University of California sticker for his vehicle, ostensibly so he could park on the campus.

Edmund had a plan. California law had a unique loophole, which Edmund proposed to use to his advantage. On his lawyer's advice he was examined by two different psychiatrists. Both doctors gave him glowing positive reports. Their recommendations were interspersed with such words such as "normal", "adjusted" and "no danger to society". These two reports were placed before a Superior Court judge, who then ruled that Edmund's juvenile record be sealed forever. This meant that Edmund could apply for any job without having to reveal his previous record. He could serve on a jury, or join the army. Why, Edmund could even legally purchase guns.

Edmund Kemper had killed both his grandparents at 15. Now the slate was clean. He had fooled all the experts. Edmund had what amounted to a license to kill again.

It wasn't long before Edmund and Clarnell were taking part in their monumental shouting matches. Edmund drifted from job to job, never approaching a task which would tax his intellectual abilities. He drank some beer at local hangouts and cruised around in his Ford. For no apparent reason, he purchased a few knives and guns and stashed them in the trunk of his car.

The university campus was located a little way from Santa Cruz.

Most students lived in the town and hitch-hiked to the campus. During the day and early evening it was customary to see both male and female students catching lifts to class. One day Edmund got up enough nerve to stop for a girl hitch-hiker. He noticed that the girl glanced at the University of California sticker on his car before jumping in. It was easy.

After that initial triumph, Edmund not only picked up girls near the campus, but roamed all over the state picking up female hitch-hikers. He didn't do anything to the girls, just talked. For two years the young giant spent his every spare moment giving lifts to young girls.

Edmund fantasized about possessing a girl. Later he was to state that possession to him meant not only sexual possession, but a type of total ownership that only death could bring.

On Sunday, May 7, 1972, Edmund Kemper was hunting — hunting for a human victim. He found two. Near Berkeley he picked up two Fresno State College coeds. The two friends, Anita and Mary Ann, were hitching a ride to Stanford University. From the time they stepped into Edmund's car they were never seen again.

Edmund pulled a 9 mm Browning automatic from under the seat of the Ford Galaxie. Anita and Mary Ann were terrified. Edmund found a deserted rural road. Both girls knew they were about to be raped. Mary Ann tried to talk Edmund out of it, but without success. Edmund sized up the two girls, who didn't seem to be overly impressed with what he thought were his daring actions.

Finally Edmund told them he would drive them to his mother's house, but in the meantime Anita would have to be placed in the trunk. All the while Edmund had made up his mind to kill both his captives. With no choice in the matter, Mary Ann allowed herself to be handcuffed. Anita, looking into the barrel of the Browning automatic, was led to the trunk. She got in. In the front seat of the car the insane giant stabbed the 105 pound girl repeatedly until she was dead. He then opened the trunk and proceeded to stab Anita until she lay still in death.

Edmund drove home with the two bodies in his car. First he washed up, then returned to his vehicle and carried Mary Ann's body to his room. Fully aware of his actions, and without panic or remorse, Edmund dissected his victim. He returned to the car for the second bond and repeated his insane ritual. Wrapping the sections of human remains in plastic bags, Edmund drove into the Santa Cruz mountains and buried the two girls. Their heads were thrown over a ravine. Edmund drove home and fondled the girls' wallets.

Four months later, on Sept. 14, a 15-year-old dance student named Aiko disappeared. Edmund had raped, suffocated and decapitated his victim.

In the months which followed three more girls, Cynthia, Alice and Rosalind, were murdered by Edmund Kemper. Parts of the various bodies were found. Some were identified, others were not. Investigating officials knew they were dealing with one killer, but had no idea who he was or why the mad killer struck in such a vicious manner. They also knew they were dealing with a necrophiliac and cannibal.

On Easter weekend, 1973, Edmund decided to kill his mother. The idea so excited him that he couldn't sleep. He tossed and turned in bed until he gave into the uncontrollable urge which boiled within. At a little after 5 a.m., armed with a knife and claw hammer, he entered his mother's bedroom and, without saying a word, bludgeoned her to death. He then decapitated his mother. Later Edmund was to tell police that the whole thing took less than a minute. Edmund placed his mother's body in a closet, cleaned up the bedroom and left to have a few beers at a local hangout.

Somewhere in the dark recesses of his mind Edmund felt that he had to create a reason for his mother's disappearance. She was not the type of woman to leave her job and home without good reason. Edmund thought about the problem all day. As he drove home the solution came to him. If his mother's best friend, Sara Hallett, dropped out of sight at the same time, it would be logical to assume that the two women had gone away together.

At around five that evening Edmund returned home and opened a can of beer. The phone rang. Edmund picked up the receiver. It was Sara Hallett asking for his mother. Edmund explained that his mother was out, but had asked him to invite Sara to dinner that evening. Sara was delighted to accept. A few hours later the unsuspecting woman walked into hell. Edmund throttled her to death, breaking her neck in the process. He placed her body in the closet with that of his mother.

On Easter Sunday, Edmund awoke and decided to flee. He drove his car east to Reno, Nevada, where he rented another vehicle from Hertz. Carefully he transferred what amounted to an arsenal to the rented car. He drove for 18 hours without stopping.

When he arrived in Pueblo, Colorado, Edmund made up his mind to call Lieutenant Charles Scherer, who he knew was in charge of the investigation of the missing girls. When the long distance call was received in Santa Cruz, Lt. Scherer was not on duty. Edmund had a hard time explaining just who he was and that this was no crank call. He was told to call back. When one of the most despicable monsters who ever lived called back at 1 a.m., he was told that Lt. Scherer would not be on duty until 9 a.m. Anyway he was informed that the police were not supposed to accept collect calls. The officer hung up. At 5 in the morning Edmund tried for the third time. This time he contacted a policeman who was familiar with his case. He kept Edmund on the line until the Pueblo police took him into custody while he was still speaking on the phone. Edmund hardly had time to tell the police to go to his home where they would find the bodies of his mother and Sara Hallett.

When taken into custody, big Edmund Kemper directed police to gravesites which had not yet been uncovered. Police were astounded to learn that the monster they were seeking was this intelligent, lucid giant. Edmund resorted to his photographic memory to recount every detail of the eight lives he had snuffed out. He claimed that his reason for surrendering was to get the whole thing off his chest. To psychiatrists he suggested that possible repressed fears and anxieties had driven him to kill. None of this was new to Edmund. He had been though it all before when he had killed his grandparents.

Edmund Kemper stood trial for murder. He was found to be sane and guilty of eight counts of murder in the first degree. Edmund Kemper is now confined to a maximum security prison at Folsom.

GRAVE ROBBER

Ed Gein lived with his brother Henry and his mother on a sixty-acre farm near Plainfield, Wisconsin. Ed's father passed away in 1940, and the two brothers fell under the sole influence of their mother, who completely dominated them. This bible-thumping matriarch seemed to dote on Ed more than she did on his brother Henry. Ed was deeply affected when Henry died while fighting a forest fire, just two years after the death of his father. That same year his mother, Augusta, suffered a crippling stroke. Now alone on the farm with his mother, Ed nursed her and took care of her every wish, but despite his sincere efforts to comfort her, her health deteriorated and she died within a year.

In the space of three years, Ed had lost his entire family. In spite of this, people who knew him described him as being a cheerful, pleasant man of 38, with a winning smile and an even disposition. Left alone in the big farmhouse, he boarded off the upstairs, his mother's bedroom and the parlor. For his living quarters he used only a bedroom, the kitchen and a small shed.

Ed received a small soil conservation subsidy, and as a result stopped farming his land. Instead he became a handy-man around Plainfield, and was sometimes called upon to baby-sit for people he had known all his life. He always brought the children bubble gum, and they all loved him.

From 1947 to 1957, Ed Gein came and went among the 700 citizens of Plainfield. He lived alone, and while he may have been considered a bit odd, he was certainly thought of as a harmless, soft-spoken guy who wouldn't hurt a fly.

Then one blustery November day in 1957, Ed walked into a hardware store in Plainfield, took a .22 rifle out of a display case, loaded it, then shot and killed the owner, Mrs. Bernice Worden. He loaded the body and the cash register into the store's pickup truck. Then he locked up and drove home.

When Mrs. Worden's son Frank returned from deer hunting that Saturday afternoon, he found his mother missing. Nothing like this had ever happened to Worden before. His mother had always been reliable, and he knew she would never leave the store without notifying someone of her whereabouts. Then he noticed a small pool of blood on the floor. Now beside himself with worry, he had the presence of mind to check the last sales slip of the morning, and found it was for half a gallon of antifreeze. He remembered that on the previous night Ed Gein had said that he would be around to pick up some antifreeze the next morning. Frank called the police and told them of his mother's disappearance and his suspicions of Gein.

Sheriff Art Schley and Captain Lloyd Schoephoester drove over to Ed's farmhouse and knocked on the front door. After repeated knocking it became apparent that Ed was not at home. The Sheriff and the Captain entered the unlocked house, and moved about the musty neglected rooms by the light of an oil lamp and a flashlight.

As they groped in the semi-darkness the beam of their flashlight fell upon a bloodcurdling sight. There, mounted upon the wall, was a woman's death mask made of human skin. The Sheriff's hand shook as he played the shaft of light along the wall, revealing three more grisly masks. Lying in the debris of the rooms were ten female skulls cut off at the eyebrow; these had obviously been used as pots and pans. An adult pair of leotards made of human skin was found, and even some of the chairs in the house had been repaired with skin. A human heart sat gently simmering in a pot on the stove; and in the shed the butchered body of a headless woman was hanging by the heels. The officers felt as if the earth had swallowed them up and they were probing the depths of hell.

While the Sheriff and the Captain were being revolted by their discoveries, other officers went to a grocery store in West Plainfield where Ed sometimes shopped. Sure enough, he was leisurely eating supper with the couple who owned the store. Ed was taken into custody and immediately started to talk.

It appeared that Ed Gein operated on two levels; one was the little 51-year-old handyman who bought bubble gum for children, while the other was a cannibal, necrophile, ghoul, murderer and transvestite. Seldom, if ever, has the world had the misfortune to have several of the most revolting characteristics known to man wrapped up in one individual.

Ed started out relatively normal, and it wasn't until he was alone on the farm that he began to fantasize about sex. His late mother's influence made him suspicious of all women, and shy and afraid in their presence. His sexual drive had no healthy outlet, so when he read in the newspaper of a woman who had just been buried, his tortured mind hit upon the idea of robbing the grave. That night he went to the cemetery and carefully removed the fresh corpse from the grave, meticulously replacing everything at the gravesite so that his theft would not be discovered. He placed the corpse in his truck and returned to the farm. The perverted mind of Ed Gein now reasoned that he had his own private woman, as indeed he did. Ed's perversions grew in intensity, driving him to eat parts of the bodies and to make garments of their skin.

When the officers searched the house of horror they carried away the grisly artifacts of murder and perversion. One of the items they removed was the head of Mary Hogan, who had been a tavern keeper in the small town of Bancroft, and had disappeared in 1953. In all, eleven heads were taken from the Gein farm. Only two, Mrs. Worden and Mary Hogan, had actually been killed by Gein. The other nine heads belonged to bodies which had been stolen from the local graveyard.

Ballistics experts proved that the .22 calibre bullets which had killed Mrs. Worden were fired from the gun Ed had taken from the hardware store. When Ed was confronted with this evidence, he readily admitted killing Mrs. Worden. He claimed that when the urge for a woman came over him, he operated like someone in a trance and had no control over his own actions. Each time, he suffered from enormous guilt feelings, swearing he would never do it again.

Ed Gein was judged insane, and in 1957 he was committed to the Waupan State Hospital for life. He is confined there to this day.

THE MONSTER OF DUSSELDORF

Henri Landru burned his lady friends. Reg Christie liked to plant bodies in the walls of his flat. George Haigh disposed of his victims in sulphuric acid. All of them either had a certain type of victim or a definite pattern of perpetrating their murders.

Peter Kurten did it all. He didn't care who the victim was and he used any means he saw fit to dispose of his victims. If one man can be held up to the light of criminal history and be described as the worst monster who ever lived, it is Peter Kurten who must be given this rather macabre honor.

Kurten was one of 13 children whose father was a hopeless drunk. They lived in Dusseldorf, Germany, and each night the father would beat up the whole family just for fun. The father once spent three years in prison for having an incestuous relationship with Kurten's 13-year-old sister.

Kurten became inquisitive and aroused at the open sex taking place in the confined quarters at home. At the age of nine he achieved some perverted thrill from torturing dogs. He became fascinated with the sight of blood, and as a teenager received complete sexual gratification from killing animals.

With this training-ground Peter graduated from experimenting with animals to humans. He took to living with prostitutes who let him inflict beatings upon them. In order to feed his sexual habits, he engaged in petty robbery. He was caught and received two years in prison. Rather than suppressing his sexual urges he found that solitary confinement gave him the peace and quiet he required to take part in sadistic daydreaming.

Once released from prison, he made his first attack on a woman. He raped and stabbed her, but she didn't die and probably never reported the incident to the authorities. We only have Kurten's word that this was his first offence against another human being.

After this original attack, Kurten attacked women, girls, and even men. He received sexual satisfaction from the sight of blood, and had no remorse or feelings of any kind for his victims. Because he devoted himself so completely to his sexual gratification, of necessity he had to steal to live. He was continually being caught and sent to prison. In all, he was to spend 20 years behind bars.

On May 25, 1913, when he was 30 years old, he was robbing an inn at Mulheim where the owners lodged above the drinking area. While rummaging through the rooms he discovered 13-year-old Christine Klein asleep in her bed. He strangled her and cut her throat. He returned to Dusseldorf, but came back the next day to Mulheim and lingered in a cafe opposite the Klein's Inn. In this way, he was able to savor the horror and excitement his crime had caused the people in the immediate vicinity.

For the next 17 years, Kurten kept killing and raping. He would have killed more, but he was continually being put in prison for robbery. He got progressively worse until finally the people of Dusseldorf realized a living monster was in their midst.

On the night of Aug. 23, 1929, a suburb of Dusseldorf named Flene was holding its annual fair. At around 10:30, two foster sisters, Gertrude Hamacher, aged five, and 14-year-old Louise Lenzen were on their way home from the fair. A pleasant man stopped them and asked the older girl to run back and get him a package of cigarettes. The Dusseldorf monster strangled Gertrude and cut her throat. When Louise returned with the cigarettes he did the same thing to her.

Only 12 hours later a servant, Gertrude Schulte, aged 36, was wondering what to do on her night off. A mild mannered, pleasant man stopped her and suggested they take in the fair. While walking through a wooded area the man turned on her. He became furious when she resisted his advances. As he had done so often before, he brought out his knife and with quick sure arcs plunged it into the poor woman's body. Finally the monster literally threw her away. Gertrude Schulte did not die. Her screams caught the attention of a passerby, and she was rushed to a hospital.

It became apparent that the Dusseldorf monster had lost all control of his desires. He was a mad dog stalking victims on a full time basis. In short order two servant girls, Ida Reuter and Elisabeth Dorrier, were raped and stabbed to death.

As summer turned to winter, Kurten attacked and wounded a girl of 18, a woman of 37, and a man of 30, all in a half hour. One child, Gertrude Albermann, was found dead with 36 stab wounds.

On the night of May 14, 1930, Maria Budlick arrived in Dusseldorf looking for work. A young man engaged her in conversation at the railway station. He offered to show her the way to a hotel that catered to young women. As they strolled through the well lit streets all went well, but as they entered the dimly lit area the girl, who had heard all about the Dusseldorf monster, became apprehensive. She tried to get rid of her escort and they started to argue. Just as the argument was becoming more heated, a mild mannered man appeared and inquired if everything was alright. The young escort left and Maria accepted the invitation of something to eat at her new friend's apartment. He took her to a one-room flat in Mettmannerstrasse, where she had a ham sandwich and a glass of milk. Her new friend offered to take her to the women's hotel. Once in an isolated district, Kurten tried to rape her. Maria fought her attacker. As she was about to lose consciousness Kurten asked her if she knew his address, so that if she ever needed help she would be able to find his flat. Maria said no and in so doing saved her life. He let her go.

Next day, accompanied by the police, Maria identified the flat. While she was pointing out the flat to the police, Kurten strolled up the stairs, walked by the police and Maria, went in his flat and closed the door.

The police arrested their cool suspect. Remember, at this point in time he was suspected of attacking Maria only. Almost immediately, as if to get a great load off his shoulders, Kurten confessed, "I am the Monster of Dusseldorf."

Kurten's trial was the most sensational ever held in Germany up to the time of the Nuremberg War Crimes Trial. To ensure his security he was placed in a cage. Kurten was exactly the opposite of what one might envision a monster to look like. He was a slight, pleasant appearing, middle-aged man. He had a remarkable memory, and could give names and dates of his crimes going back years. He liked to describe them all in detail.

He admitted to 68 major crimes, not including those of theft and assault. Offically he was charged with a total of nine murders and seven attempted murders.

Several top psychiatrists declared Kurten to be sane. All agreed he was the most perverted human being they had ever examined.

The jury deliberated only an hour and a half in finding Kurten guilty.

On July 21, 1932, Peter Kurten, the Monster of Dusseldorf, was executed.

MURDER AT THE "Y"

Probably the safest place for a young girl to stay in a large city is the Y.W.C.A. Every precaution is taken to guard against unwelcome strangers.

On Dec. 23, 1959 tragedy came to the Y in Birmingham, England. Many of the rooms were vacant as most of the young girls were visiting at home over the Christmas season. It was late at night.

Stephanie Baird was planning on leaving the following day for home. She had carefully wrapped presents for her family. Stephanie had no way of knowing that someone had gained entrance to the building through the hall window. As she tidied up her room the intruder watched her every move through the transom windows. Standing on a chair, he could observe her without being seen.

Stephanie thought she heard a noise outside the door. She inquisitively went to investigate. It was the worst decision she ever made in her life. The strange man gave some lame excuse for being there. While the nervous girl admonished him, he appeared to sheepishly turn away.

All of a sudden, without warning, the stranger sprang upon the helpless girl. He smothered her face and neck with kisses. When Stephanie tried to pull away, he locked his fingers around her throat and didn't let go until her unconscious form went limp in his hands.

Had the killer left the scene at this time, the tragic murder of Stephanie Baird would have been another big city killing to be dealt with by the police. But the killer didn't leave. Reminiscent of Jack the Ripper, he went about sexually abusing and mutilating Stephanie's body to such an extent that policemen, hardened to scenes of violence, could not look in the room where the tragedy had occurred. The unfortunate girl had been decapitated.

Then the attacker performed his only cunning deed; he remembered the chair outside the door. He reached out, grabbed the chair and flung it into the room. The sounds of other girls in the building made the stranger nervous. He washed the blood from his hands and body, found a ball point pen and wrote on a piece of paper: "This was the thing I thought would never come." As if he had a change of heart about the message, he scratched through the words several times.

The madman made his way to the hostel laundry. Here he studied Margaret Brown, who was ironing some clothing in preparation for the Christmas holidays. The stranger sneaked up behind her and struck her a vicious blow to the head. Margaret staggered, but didn't lose consciousness. Instead, she screamed at the top of her voice. Suspecting that her wild outcry would bring assistance, the stranger turned tail and ran out of the building.

Nearly hysterical, Margaret poured out her terrifying story. In the course of their investigation the police thought it would be a good idea to question all the girls staying at the hostel. The police had no idea that Margaret was the second and by far the more fortunate victim that night. The sight which greeted them when they broke down the door to Stephanie's room turned the investigation into one of murder.

The police did not lack clues. There was the note left by the killer on the dresser, and well-defined footprints under the window where he had gained access to the building. No fingerprints other than those of the dead girl were found in the room, but this information was kept from the press.

Despite every effort the origin of the paper on which the note had been written could not be traced. Photographs of casts of the killer's footprints were widely distributed, and over 100,000 people who lived near the hostel were interrogated. No clue to the killer's identity was uncovered.

At the end of January, the police decided to recheck the area around the hostel in order to question all those people who had not been at home during the first investigation. This list comprised several thousands, as many lodgers and residents were away visiting relatives over the Christmas season.

One of the men on the list was the killer. On the morning after the murder he had given his shoes and clothing to his landlady to throw away. She put them out for garbage collection. The garbage man didn't destroy them; they looked too good to let slip through his hands. He tucked the clothing and shoes away for his own use.

In the meantime, Patrick Joseph Byrne had spent Christmas with his mother in Warrington. Back at his roominghouse after the holidays, he got the scare of his life when he saw a description and photograph of his shoes on the front pages of the newspapers. The garbageman had plucked the shoes out of tons of garbage. After seeing photographs of the footprint casts he recognized that the distinctive pattern on the soles of his shoes matched the pattern in the photographs. He turned them over to the police, who positively identified them as the killer's.

Byrne knew that his name was on the list of persons missing during the first round of questioning. He decided to show up at the police station rather than wait for the police to call on him.

The policeman who was doing the interviewing was instructed to ask everyone one pertinent question. He asked it of Byrne — "Would you have any objection to being fingerprinted?" In that split second the guilty man lost his composure. He was wrongly convinced that his fingerprints were all over the murder room. He confessed to the murder, giving exact details only the killer would know.

Patrick Byrne, one of the most vicious psychopaths who ever lived, was sentenced to life imprisonment.

SON OF SAM

Seldom has an individual criminal managed to hold an entire city in a grip of terror. Jack the Ripper did it by killing and mutilating five prostitutes in London, England, in the autumn of 1888. In more recent times the Boston Strangler assaulted and murdered 13 women. In so doing, he kept the entire city of Boston in a state of fear.

It takes a series of unusual criminal acts to make the good citizens of New York City sit up and take notice. Almost every bizarre occurrence perpetrated by man has taken place in Gotham. The natives are accustomed to the unusual.

When Bette and Tony Falco gave birth to little David Richard on June 1, 1953, they had already decided to put their newborn son up for adoption. The details had all been arranged.

Pearl Berkowitz was an active woman who, at 38, had been informed by her doctors that she could never conceive. Her husband Nathan, a hardware store owner, had often discussed adopting a child with his wife. It was Pearl and Nathan who drove David Richard home from the hospital. They didn't know the soft, cuddly bundle Pearl held so gently was a potential monster. Eighteen months later David Richard Falco legally became David Richard Berkowitz.

David grew up to be a quiet introverted little boy. In hindsight, many friends and neighbors who knew him during his formative years later came forward with some anecdote or other illustrating a streak of meanness or cruelty in David as a child. In actuality there was probably nothing to distinguish David from thousands of other children being brought up in like circumstances.

When David was 14 his mother died of cancer, after a long and painful bout with the dreaded disease. Pearl had been a kind and loving mother, and we have every reason to believe that her son was truly affected by her death. In 1971, when Nathan remarried, David displayed open resentment toward his stepmother.

His father's marriage coincided with David's joining the army. David, who had always expressed patriotic sentiments towards his country, was shipped off to Fort Dix, New Jersey. During rugged basic training he showed some skill with a rifle. Pursuing this natural aptitude, he soon qualified as a sharpshooter.

From Fort Dix, David was sent to Fort Polk, Louisiana, for advanced training. On Dec. 13, 1971, he was shipped to Korea, where he served with the 17th Infantry, 1st Battalion. After his tour of duty, David was posted to Fort Knox, Kentucky. On June 24, 1974, he was discharged from the U.S. Army after serving three years.

David returned to his parents' apartment in the Bronx. He was mildly surprised to find out that they were trying to sell their apartment in order to retire to Florida. By the end of the year David had found a one-bedroom apartment for himself at 2161 Barnes Ave. in the Bronx. He registered at the Bronx Community College in February, 1975, and did well there, attaining a high C average. During the summer he worked for his uncle as a sheet metal worker. To all outward appearances, David Berkowitz was going to make something of himself.

Donna Lauria was an attractive, 18-year-old with shoulder length brown hair. Donna and her friend Jody Valente were sitting outside Donna's apartment building double parked in Jody's car. It was 1:10 a.m. on a hot July morning in 1976. Donna's parents walked by and entered the apartment building. Without warning, a man appeared beside the automobile occupied by the two girls. He pointed a long barrelled revolver at Donna's head and fired. Donna Lauria was dead without ever knowing what had happened. A .44 calibre slug slammed into Jody's left thigh. Despite bleeding profusely, her wound was not serious. No one knew it at the time, but the killer later to be known and feared as the Son of Sam had claimed his first victim.

A short time later David Berkowitz left his sheet metal job.

Rosemary Keenan and Carl Denaro, a pair of 20 year olds, had promised to meet friends at a tavern in Flushing. It was about two in the morning when they drove into the tavern parking lot. Carl was about to open the car door when a bullet crashed through the car window and lodged in his head. Fortunately the slug missed Carl's brain. His friends from the tavern rushed him to the nearest hospial, where an emergency operation, lasting over two hours, saved his life. The senseless attack on

Carl Denaro and his girlfriend was not connected at the time with the Lauria-Valente shooting.

On a cool November night, two teenagers, Joanne Lomino and Donna DeMasi, sat on Joanne's front steps talking about boyfriends and job opportunities. The two girls had taken in a movie and had finished off their night out with hamburgers. Now they were preparing to part. Out of the darkness a man approached the two girls. He appeared to be of average height, about 30 years old, and wore a green army-type three quarter length coat. The man extracted a revolver from his belt and began shooting.

The first slug entered Donna's neck and shattered her collarbone. She fell to the sidewalk. Joanne took a slug directly into her back. Of the five shots fired at the girls, three went astray. Donna DeMasi recovered from the attack, but Joanne Lomino will forever remain paralyzed from the waist down. The mad killer who used a .44 calibre revolver had struck again.

John Diel was a 30-year-old bartender. He and his girlfriend, Christine Freund, had a lot to talk over. They were planning to get engaged in two weeks time. Now, as they sat talking well past midnight on the morning of Jan. 30, they had no way of knowing there would be no engagement party. Christine would be dead in a matter of hours. Two explosions interrupted their conversation, sending a shower of windshield glass cascading into the interior of the car. Diel lifted his girlfriend's limp form out of the car and gently placed her on the ground. At 4:30 a.m. Christine died in hospital from bullet wounds to the head.

The wanton attacks had all been treated as individual cases. Now the cases were cross checked, and police attributed the attacks to the frenzy of one man. Lauria, Valente, Denaro, Lomino, DeMasi, and Freund. A monster with a .44 calibre revolver was loose on the streets of New York. No wonder the police could find no motive for the individual attacks. The madman didn't even know the victims. He killed at random.

David Berkowitz applied for a job at the Bronx General Post Office. He scored an exceptional 85.5% on the post office test. David got the job on a part time basis at $7 an hour.

Virginia Voskerichian was a 5 ft., 6 in., 19-year-old student at Columbia University. She lived in fashionable Forest Hills Garden with her parents. One evening in March, as she walked home, the crazed killer shot her dead with his .44 calibre revolver.

Back at the Bronx Post Office David Berkowitz often talked of the .44 calibre killer to fellow employees. It seemed to be one of the few topics pleasant, quiet David liked to talk about.

Valentina Suriani lived at 1950 Hutchinson St., only a few streets from the killer's first victim, Donna Lauria. Valentina attended Lehman College, where she was majoring in acting. Her fiance, Alexander Esau, parked his car early on the morning of April 19. Both fell under the rage that burned within the .44 calibre killer. This time he left a sealed envelope beside the bodies of his victims. The contents of the letter were not revealed by the police at the time. From it police knew that the killer had no intention of curtailing his murderous rampage.

The killer then wrote to *Daily News* columnist Jimmy Breslin, signing his letter Son of Sam. The letter was authentic, having been written by the same crazed mind which had composed the letter found beside Valentina Suriani's body.

In April, 1977, within days of the Suriani-Esau murders, a man not connected with any victim, Sam Carr, received an anonymous letter at his home at 316 Warbuton Ave. in Yonkers. It contained gibberish about his Labrador retriever being a menace, saying that the dog should be removed from his home. Carr mentioned the crazy letter to members of his family and then dismissed the incident from his mind. He then received another more threatening letter, but still did nothing about it.

On April 27, someone shot Sam Carr's Labrador retriever. The dog, Harvey, had been severely wounded in the thigh. Carr was to spend over $1,000 to save his dog, but the bullet remained lodged in Harvey's thigh. After this incident, Carr took the letters to the Yonkers police. They attributed the letters and the shooting as the work of a schizophrenic, but did not connect the incident to the mass killings which were now under the jurisdiction of a task force formed exclusively to capture the .44 calibre killer.

David Berkowitz had moved. He now lived at 35 Pine St. in Yonkers. His apartment building backed on to Sam Carr's back yard.

Sal Lupo and Judy Placido frequented the same discotheque in Queens. They had never dated, but knew each other rather well and often danced together. Judy was in a good mood. She had just graduated from St. Catherines Academy that day. Now, it was after 3 a.m. Sunday morning, June 26th. One of the main topics of conversation that evening was the crazed murderer who killed without reason.

Sal asked Judy if he could drive her home. Judy, still wearing her special graduation dress, was thrilled to accept the ride. Before Sal could turn the ignition key in his car four slugs poured into the interior of the car. The wound inflicted to Sal's arm was not serious. Judy had taken one bullet behind the right ear. One lodged close to her spinal cord, and the third pierced her right shoulder. All three bullets were removed from Judy's body, and miraculously she recovered. The bullets were .44 calibre and had been fired from the same weapon which had felled the other victims.

David Berkowitz did commendable work at the post office. He often told fellow employees that he sure hoped the police would catch that Son of Sam fellow. A year had passed since the first Son of Sam murder.

Sixteen-year-old Stacy Moskowitz of Brooklyn had been asked out by the best looking boy she had ever dated. Robert Violante, a recent graduate of Brooklyn's New Utrecht High, was by any standards a handsome young man. Before seeing a play, Stacy brought Robert home to meet her family.

After the play and a bite to eat, the young people parked alongside the Shore Parkway at Bay 14th St. Several other cars were parked there. Four successive explosions roared into the open car window. Robert received a bullet in the temple which exited at the bridge of his nose. He recovered, but will only have partial sight for the rest of his life. Stacy Moskowitz died later in hospital.

David Berkowitz left his job at the post office a few days later and never returned.

On the night of Stacy Moskowitz' murder, Mrs. Cacalia Davis took her dog Snowball for a walk. As she walked she fixed her gaze on a young man approaching from the opposite direction. They passed within touching distance of each other. Mrs. Davis noticed that the young man's right arm was stiff. Later she found out it was because Son of Sam carried his .44 calibre revolver up his sleeve.

Next day, when Mrs. Davis became aware of the murder which had taken place close to her home, she was positive that it was Son of Sam whom she passed on the sidewalk. She informed the police of her suspicions. When she told her story she mentioned that during her walk with Snowball she had noticed a cop writing out a traffic ticket for a car parked too near a hydrant.

Police checked on all traffic tickets issued in the early morning hours in that area. There were only three. Two had been issued to respectable citizens in their late sixties. The third was issued to David R. Berkowitz.

Son of Sam, who had terrorized an entire city for over a year was to be taken into custody because he had parked too close to a hydrant. When picked up, Berkowitz' car yielded a sub-machine gun, a rifle with several boxes of ammunition, and a .44 Charter Arms Bulldog small revolver. Later it was proven that the .44 was the weapon which Son of Sam had used for over a year.

Why had David Berkowitz killed six innocent individuals and wounded seven others? He had no choice. You see, the devil who lived in Sam Carr's Labrador retriever Harvey commanded him to kill.

David Berkowitz was adjudged unfit to stand trial by reason of insanity. No doubt he will spend the rest of his life in custody.

NICE OLD MAN

Cannibalism! The word itself screams out from the page as no other word in the English language. Incidents of human flesh being consumed by fellow humans to sustain life are well recorded. Marooned sailors, bush pilots, and surviving victims of plane crashes have all forced themselves to eat human flesh in order to survive. North American Indians and some African tribes ate portions of their fallen enemies as an act of respect, in the belief that they would acquire some of the admirable qualities of their former foes.

Those cases where cannibalism is practised for the sheer perverted pleasure of the act are much rarer. In the 20th century, the case most often referred to as an example of pure cannibalism is the bizarre saga of Albert Fish.

"Young man, 18 years old, wishes position in the country for the summer." The ad appeared in the Situations Wanted column of a New York City newspaper on Monday, May 21, 1928. Edward Budd was to regret placing the ad for the rest of his life.

The Budd family lived in a West 15th St. apartment house in what was then the edge of New York City. Edward Budd, Sr., and his wife, Delia, had four children, the oldest being Edward, Jr., and the youngest Grace, 12. Ed Budd had made up his mind. This summer he would escape from the city heat and the city noise. He placed the ad for summer employment in the newspaper.

Two days after the advertisement appeared an elderly, respectable looking man arrived at the Budd's door. He explained to Mrs. Budd that he had a large vegetable garden operation near Farmingdale, Long Island, and could use help over the summer months. Edward was enthusiastic. A deal was struck then and there. The elderly gentleman, who had introduced himself as Frank Howard, would pick Edward up the following Thursday or Sunday. The Budds invited Howard to come early on Sunday and have dinner with them. The old man promised to try. Later in the week, the Budd family received a telegram advising them that Howard couldn't make it on Thursday, but would arrive early on Sunday.

Sure enough, Mr. Howard arrived the following Sunday and broke bread with the Budds. He said grace and proved to be a charming conversationalist. At the conclusion of the meal he informed his hosts that he had a surprise. His sister, who lived in New York, was having a birthday party for her daughter, who just happened to be Grace Budd's age. He was planning on attending and would take Grace along if it was alright with her mother. When they returned he and Albert could then leave for the country. Mrs. Budd was at first apprehensive, but with exuberant coaxing by her daughter, she finally consented. Hand-in-hand, little Grace and one of the worst monsters who ever lived strolled out of the apartment and, in Grace's case, into oblivion.

By subway, Frank Howard led Grace to Westchester County near Irvington. There, in a ram-shackle house called Wisteria Cottage, the old man choked the life from the little girl. He then dissected his victim and wrapped a portion of the body in his bandanna. Frank Howard left the house of death and proceeded to his rented room. Next day he ate the portion of meat that had once been Grace Budd. Every few days the old man would return to Wisteria Cottage. Each time he left with a parcel, which he later consumed. Nine days after the murder he made his final trip. What remained of Grace Budd was thrown out of a window into a weed infested back yard.

Grace was reported missing. The case, considered to be a kidnapping perpetrated by an old man, presented only one clue. The missing person's bureau of the New York City Police Force was able to trace the telegram sent to the Budd family. This provided them with a sample of the kidnapper's handwriting, but nothing further turned up.

Years went by, and the little girl's disappearance was all but forgotten. From time to time the Budd family received crank notes and letters, which they routinely turned over to the police.

Six years after the kidnapping, one of these letters, thought to be from a crank, proved to have been written by the same hand which had written the old telegram to the Budds. The contents of the unsigned letter described Grace Budd's fate in detail.

Police were able to trace the writing paper to a type used by an organization known as The Private Chauffeurs Benevolent Association. A janitor for this organization admitted taking some of the stationery to his rooming house for his personal use. He told police that he had left some in his room at 200 East 52nd St. when he had moved out.

The police proceeded to Room 11 at the janitor's former address. The landlady gave the police a description of the occupant of Room 11. There was no question about it — the occupant was Frank Howard, who had abducted Grace Budd almost six years previously.

The landlady informed police that Number 11 was often vacant for most of the month, but her tenant, known to her as Albert Fish, always returned to pick up a cheque sent to him by a son in North Carolina. This time when Fish returned to his room, police were waiting for him.

The mild-mannered old man readily confessed to the abduction. His story was one of perversion, which had begun at the age of five, when he discovered that he enjoyed pain after being spanked by a teacher. Brought up in an orphanage, he later married and had several children. His wife always considered him strange, but lived with him for 20 years before leaving him. His grown children later testified that their father often thought he was Christ, and from time to time would disappear without explanation.

Police uncovered the skull and some bones of Grace Budd, which had lain where they had been thrown so many years before. In the same weeds, they found a rusty knife and cleaver.

Fish was examined extensively by both psychiatrists and police. It was discovered that he had visited various communities in the north eastern U.S. at the exact time when young children had been murdered. Fish denied any knowledge of these crimes, but admitted to leading a life of molesting children, while he wandered from one job to another, usually as a house painter.

In a case as weird as any ever recorded, there was still more to come. While X-raying Fish, doctors found 29 metal needles in various parts of his body. Some were as large as those used to repair canvas. All had been inserted by Fish to cause pain. Doctors stated that some of the needles had been in his body for as long as seven years.

When Fish related his life story to doctors he revealed that over the years he had been in several mental institutions for short periods of time. On each occasion he had been released as harmless.

Albert Fish stood trial for the murder of Grace Budd on March 11, 1935 in White Plains, N.Y. Despite the efforts put forward by his defence counsel, pleading that his client was insane, the jury deliberated only a few hours before finding Fish guilty of murder.

Just before being transferred to Sing Sing, Fish confessed to four additional murders of small children.

As the end drew near, Fish told the guards that he was delighted at the chance of experiencing the ultimate thrill of being put to death. Albert Fish was electrocuted on Jan. 16, 1936.

THE SAVAGE CLAN

Back in the seventeenth century rumors drifted back to Edinburgh that travellers in the southwest part of Scotland were disappearing. People would start out from one town and drop out of sight before reaching their destination. Not a trace of a violent act was ever uncovered. Alarmed by the frequency of the disappearances, King James took a personal interest in the strange happenings, finally sending his own officers to investigate. They picked up a few tramps in the Galloway area and hanged them, but the mystery still wasn't solved.

Then one fine day, a man and his wife were returning from a fair in a neighboring village, both riding the same horse. Suddenly, without warning, a group of sub-human savages surrounded the terrified pair. The woman was pulled from the horse to the ground, where one of the savages cut her throat from ear to ear and disembowelled her. Her husband fought with all the strength he could muster, slashing at the frenzied tribe with his sword, to little avail. Meanwhile, some of the savages were tearing at the dead woman's body, ripping off pieces of flesh and eating it raw.

A group of about thirty citizens, returning from the same fair as the man and woman, came upon this gruesome scene. As quickly as they had appeared, the cannibals vanished into the surrounding countryside, and the newly-widowed traveller was rescued.

Now all the disappearances that had taken place over the past 25 years took on a new aspect. Could this band of savages have been practising cannibalism for a quarter of a century without anyone surviving their attacks? Even in those distant times the horror of the possibility brought King James himself and 400 men from Edinburgh to investigate.

They started off where the most recent attack had taken place. The posse proceeded across the moors to the sea, where dark tunnels cut into the steep, rocky shore. They were not going to bother searching these narrow openings, thinking they were too small for any appreciable number of fugitives to hide, when suddenly one of their dogs started barking at the entrance to one of the cracks in the rocks, and finally several dogs entered the tunnel. Lighting torches, the men squeezed into the narrow openings one by one. The odor emanating from the warren almost sent them back. Abruptly the hole in the rocks opened into a huge cave.

There, lurking on shelves and in corners, crouching and shielding their eyes from the light, were the figures of human beings. Though they put up a fierce struggle they were outnumbered and quickly overpowered by the King's men. In all, 48 people were taken from the cave. Inside their lair, the soldiers found assorted arms, legs, heads, and torsos of victims, some hanging from the ceiling and others preserved in pickle. The soldiers buried the human remains and took their prisoners to Edinburgh.

Who were these wild, inhuman savages, and who was their leader? Little by little, the King's men pieced the story together. Sawney Beane was born in East Lothian, a few miles from Edinburgh, and was, as they used to say, a ne'er-do-well. His parents were hardworking ditchdiggers, but Sawney was lazy and tried to get out of performing any manual labor that was thrust upon him. He played around with loose women and eventually took up with a permanent mate without benefit of clergy. They ran away and lived together in a big cave near the sea, which not only provided them with shelter, but also gave them a headquarters from which to strike out at travellers and rob them of their money and goods. Soon they began to fear detection, and commenced to murder their victims, dragging the bodies into their cave.

We can imagine Sawney and his mate during one of the frequent famines which swept the country in those days. He now had several offspring; food was scarce and there were few travellers to rob. The family attacks and kills one lone stranger, dragging the body to their lair only to find that the victim has no money or food. The thought occurs to Sawney that to eat the human flesh means life to him and his family. At the beginning, the meat was probably cooked over a flame, and from there it was only a small step to eating it raw.

The children born to Sawney and his mate, and other offspring born incestuously later, were brought up eating human flesh, and to them this practice was most natural. In all, Sawney is reported to have had eight sons and six daughters. Various other combinations went to make up the total of 48 tribe members.

As the family grew, their ability to make successful attacks on groups of five or six foot-travellers increased, and they became a still bigger terror in the countryside. They always avoided molesting more than two men on horseback, for the cunning Sawney knew that he could ill afford to let one victim get away. For 25 years no one did escape, until that day when the traveller and his wife were returning from the fair.

There was some speculation as to how many innocent souls fell victim to Sawney and his family during the 25 years they terrorized southwest Scotland. Estimates range from a minimum of 100 up to 1000, making them one of the highest-scoring families of mass murderers in recorded history.

The whole family was immured in the Tolbooth Prison in Edinburgh. It was thought that a trial was unnecessary, and every last one of them was executed. The men had their hands and legs cut off and were allowed to bleed to death. The women were made to watch this gruesome sight and were then burned alive in three large fires. It is reported that not one showed any remorse, and all cursed their tormentors until the end.

PERVERTED KILLER

Arnold and Mary Corll were both 23 years old when their first son, Dean, was born on Christmas Eve, 1939. The Corlls almost immediately started to disagree on the way the child should be brought up. Arnold was a strict disciplinarian who thought that young Dean should be taught to obey his parents, almost before he learned to walk. This proved to be a bone of contention, and when Arnold was drafted in the Air Force and stationed in Memphis, Tennessee, it became apparent that the marriage had a limited lifespan. Sure enough an amicable divorce took place and the couple separated, but not before another child, Stephen, was born.

Mary, who still loved Arnold, sold her comfortable little home, bought a trailer and headed for Memphis, where she put Dean in school. She and Arnold took up where they had left off, fighting and arguing, and eventually, despite bickering, they decided to give marriage another try. When Arnold received his discharge from the Air Force, Mary, Arnold and the two children headed for Houston, Texas. At first they lived in a trailer, but later they bought a house. Their attempts to salvage their marriage proved futile, and they agreed to their second amicable divorce. Mary and her two sons moved again, this time to an apartment.

Dean and Stephen were again enrolled in a strange school, and it was here that doctors discovered that Dean suffered from a congenital heart defect. Dean had his first taste of being different from other boys; while they played energetic games he watched from the sidelines; while they ran, he walked.

In 1953, when Dean was an impressionable fourteen years old, his mother married a salesman named West. The entire family moved to Vidor, Texas, where Dean attended Vidor High School. Because of his heart trouble, he took up music, and played the trombone as a member of the school band. Dean was an average trombone player, an average student, and was so inconspicuous that many of his teachers don't remember him.

In his spare time he helped his mother sell pecans from her garage. When he graduated from high school in 1958, he saved his money and bought a car. His mother started to manufacture pecan candies and he worked for her for two years, delivering candies to stores which had placed orders.

In 1962, Mary West had a flourishing little candy business going at 721 East 6½ Street. She had set up a kitchen and turned the garage into a candy store, and Dean's workload grew steadily as the family business prospered.

In 1964, Dean was drafted into the army and sent to Fort Polk, Louisiana. He was later transferred to Fort Hood in Texas, but received a hardship discharge on July 11, 1965, as he was needed at home to keep the candy factory going. By this time the factory was relocated at 505 West 22nd Street, and the West family moved to an apartment at 1845 Airport Blvd., with the exception of Dean, who lived by himself in an apartment a block away at 444 West 21st St.

Across the street from the Corll Candy Company was the Helms Elementary School, and quite naturally the children were constantly dropping into the store section of the candy factory. Dean built a games room at the back of the factory and installed a pool table for the use of his customers. At the time the family thought the room was an astute business move, but in hindsight Dean's motives appear more sinister. The nature of his mother's business was enough to attract young boys, and the poolroom made the bait doubly alluring. If Dean had homosexual tendencies at this period in his life, he had managed, by accident or design, to place himself in an ideal position to indulge his sexual appetite.

Dean's mother went through another divorce, and then met and married a seaman, who took an immediate dislike to Dean and his habit of entertaining young boys in the candy factory. The marriage only lasted a matter of months, ending in divorce in 1968. Then the Corll family started to break up. Mrs. Corll dissolved the business and moved to Manitou Springs, where she set up another thriving candy factory, Stephen took a job as a machinist in Houston, and Dean went to work for the Houston Lighting and Power Company as an electrician.

By 1969, it is certain that Dean Corll was a confirmed homosexual who regularly enticed young boys to his residence at 2020 Lamar St. No physical harm was done to the youngsters, and either fear or shame prevented them from ever talking about their experience. One youngster, fourteen-year-old David Brooks, came under Corll's spell so completely that he dropped out of high school in order to spend all his time with his older friend. Brooks was to state that their relationship started with Corll paying him for sexual favors. Brooks was a tall, slender, good-looking boy, with long hair falling to his shoulders. His parents were divorced, and he spent time with each parent, travelling from Houston to Beaumont.

In 1970, David Brooks introduced Dean to Wayne Henley. A relationship grew between Wayne and Dean, until gradually the boy fell completely under the spell of the older man's dominant personality. Wayne was a carbon copy of Brooks in appearance — lean, good-looking, with long hair. The three of them, all the products of broken home, were inseparable. The two younger boys were so subservient to Corll that they would carry out his every desire without question.

The world heard for the first time of Dean Corll, David Brooks and Wayne Henley on Wednesday, August 8, 1973. The police received a telephone call reporting a shooting at 2020 Lamar St. When they arrived at the scene they were stopped by three youths, two boys and a girl, standing in front of a white frame house. Wayne Henley gave his name to the police, and handed them a .22 calibre pistol. The gun held six spent shells. Then Henley introduced five-foot-two-inch Rhonda Louise Williams, a fifteen-year-old with the knowing look of someone twice her age. She hung on Henley's arm while he told the officers that the other youth's name was Tim Kerley.

The three teenagers told of shooting a man named Corll, and were hustled into a patrol car. As the officers entered the hall of 2020 Lamar St. they could see the naked body of Dean Corll spread out on the floor. Tiny holes dotted the deadman's back, and his legs were entangled in telephone wire. The police went on to a bedroom, where they carfully opened the door and stood amazed at the strange paraphernalia which lay before them. The floor was covered with beige carpeting, which in turn was covered by a sheet of clear plastic. The room contained a long pine board with holes in each corner. These holes had chains running through them, and at each corner of the board was fastened a pair of handcuffs. On the floor the police also spotted a long knife.

Detective Sergeant Dave Mullican, a huge, 220-pound, six-foot-two career cop, had investigated many homicides, and he knew instinctively that he was now involved in something beyond a routine killing.

An examination of the body showed that Corll had been shot six times, the full capacity of the .22 calibre revolver which Henley had turned over to the police. He had been shot once in the shoulder, once in the head, and four times in the back. The board found in the bedroom measured two and a half feet wide by eight feet long, obviously designed to accommodate a human being. A total of eight sets of handcuffs were found in the house, as well as a gas mask. In the garage attached to the house, the police found traces of dehydrated lime on the floor.

Henley told the story of what went on at 2020 Lamar on the night Dean Corll met his death. It all started when Corll asked Henley to a party in his house. Henley had brought Kerley, and the three men sat around smoking pot and drinking beer, when Henley thought it would be a good idea to bring his girlfriend Rhonda Williams over to the party. He called Rhonda, who managed to sneak out of her home to meet them. The two boys picked her up in Kerley's Volkswagen and drove back to the house. Corll was furious that they had brought a girl to the party, but was soon pacified. The three youngsters started inhaling the fumes from acrylic paint sprayed in a bag. All the while Corll smoked pot and drank beer, the three youngsters "bagged" the fumes. Eventually, they passed out.

When Henley came round, he found that Corll had handcuffed him. He looked about the room and saw that Rhonda and Kerley were both handcuffed and had masking tape over their mouths. Corll was acting like a madman, waving a knife and brandishing a pistol. When Kerley and Rhonda regained consciousness he threatened to torture them all and then kill them. Henley realized that somehow he had to reason with Dean, for he was the only one who could talk. He started to get on Corll's good side by promising him that he would assist him in torturing Kerley. Slowly he gained Corll's confidence, convincing him that he would help him to kill his two friends. Corll and he devised a further plan; Corll would assault Kerley and Henley would rape Rhonda, after which they would kill them both. On this understanding, Corll unlocked Henley's handcuffs.

With a great deal of difficulty Corll proceeded to handcuff his two captives to the board. He then undressed the pair and started to assault Kerley, who despite being handcuffed, tried to fight him off. In the meantime, Henley tried to have intercourse with Rhonda, but found that he couldn't.

While all this was going on Henley noticed a pistol on a small table, the one piece of furniture in the room. On the pretence of going to the bathroom, he managed to leave the room. When he returned he picked up the pistol and pointed it at Corll, who was still fighting with the desperate Kerley. The moment Corll saw the gun, he rushed Henley, who started pressing the trigger and didn't stop until all six bullets were discharged. Corll fell to the floor and died instantly. Henley unlocked Kerley's and Rhonda's handcuffs. The three got dressed and called the police; and not wanting to stay with the dead man, they waited outside for the police to arrive.

Had Henley stopped talking it is in the realm of possibility that the police would have wound up the case. It was a weird sex dope killing, but Henley's story had a ring of truth to it, and was corroborated by all the physical evidence.

But Henley didn't stop. For some reason he thought the police didn't believe him and he figured the only way out of his dilemma was to paint Corll as a sex-crazed monster. He requested another interview with the police, and this time he added that Corll had once boasted that he had killed some boys. He remembered the names Cobble and Jones, and thought Dean had mentioned that he had buried them in a boathouse. Detectives checked the names, and sure enough, Charles Cobble, 17, and Marty Jones, 18, who had lived together, had disappeared on July 27, about two weeks prior to the shooting of Corll. The backgrounds of these two boys had already been checked, and had been found to be normal in every way. They were achieving good marks at school and both got along well with their parents. They had disappeared without any warning and no trace of them had been found since they were reported missing.

Henley told the police he thought he could direct them to the boathouse. The police took him up on his offer, and equipped with shovels and ropes, they proceded out of the city. The handcuffed Henley directed them to a field adjoining Silver Bell Street, where there stood a long corrugated steel structure. "That's the boathouse," said Henley. Inside were 20 stalls, measuring 12-feet wide and 30-feet deep. Each stall had six-foot-wide double doors, which were securely locked. Henley pointed out Stall 11 as Dean's, and volunteered that the owner of the boathouse lived just a minute or so away.

The police explained their mission to Mrs. Mayme Meynier, the owner of Southwest Boat Storage. She confirmed that Stall 11 had been rented to Dean Corll, but stated that only he had the key. The police broke the lock and entered. The first thing that came into sight was a bicycle leaning against the righthand wall. As their eyes became accustomed to the semi-darkness they discovered two bags of dehydrated lime and a plastic bag containing a pair of new red shoes and other clothing. The police cleaned out the stall and commenced digging. Only six inches below the surface their shovels struck something harder than earth. The heat inside the corrugated boathouse was intense, and the men soon became soaked in perspiration, except Henley, who sat handcuffed on the ground beside the patrol car.

The men were now being hampered by the fading early evening light, but they carried on, gently parting the earth with their hands. Finally the object of their efforts became all too visible; the body of a young boy wrapped in a clear plastic sheet. The body was removed from the hole with great care and placed outside the boathouse. The men returned to their distasteful task. A second corpse, which had been buried for a longer period of time, was uncovered and removed from the boathouse.

By this time, the unmistakable stench of death was permeating the entire area surrounding the boathouse. The police installed fans and lights to aid the diggers, who were now reinforced by eight trusties from a nearby jail. The entire floor of the stall was being excavated in six-inch levels. As the night wore on, the fans whirred and the lights cast strange shadows on the eerie scene; and the diggers found a third body, then a fourth, then a fifth and a sixth. Some were recent victims, wrapped in clear plastic, while others had been in the earth longer and were decomposed beyond recognition. By the time the diggers stopped at 1 a.m., two further bodies had been dragged from the boathouse.

By now the case was receiving nationwide and even worldwide attention. On Thursday morning, August 9, 1973, newspapers, radio broadcasts and early morning television news carried the sensational story of the eight bodies found in the boathouse. One ghostly presence held sway over the eerie events, and that presence belonged to Dean Corll. His name was on everyone's lips, but he was dead and it was left to others to explain his strange impulses and passions.

Wayne Henley told of an association with Corll which went back several years. It all started when Dean offered him $200 to procure young boys. Henley said he did nothing about the offer for a full year, but then, when he badly needed money, he took Corll up on the proposition. And so it began; sometimes he would just pick up a lad who was hitchhiking, and on one pretense or another delivered him to Corll. Dean was a sadistic homosexual, and often he would use the boys, then kill them in front of Henley. Henley claimed that although he had been present, he had never taken part in torturing or killing anyone.

Typical of the many stories Henley told of picking up boys for Dean, was the one about the youngster who was reported missing only six days before Dean himself was killed. Fourteen-year-old James Stanton Dreymala was riding his bike when Henley and Corll, who were parked in Corll's van, called him over. Dean told the boy he could have some empty Coke bottles he had found in his van and take them in the store to get the deposit, which he could keep for himself. When James came out of the store he strolled over to the van and thanked Dean. Corll then told the boy to throw his bicycle into the van, explaining that he had more bottles at home. James jumped at the chance to earn some extra money, and after putting his bike in the van, he clambered in beside Henley and Corll. They drove out to 2020 Lamar St. where Corll assaulted the boy, tortured him, and then strangled him to death. It was his bicycle which was found in the boathouse. Henley kept up his nonstop stories of horror, but the strange case was to take another bizarre twist.

A Mr. Brooks arrived at the Houston police station with his son, David, who gave the police a statement about his relationship with Henley and Corll. He implicated Henley far more than Henley had admitted, but predictably stated emphatically that he himself was only a witness to all the unnatural sex acts and murders. When Henley was told that David Brooks was making a formal statement he immediately said, "That's good, now I can tell the whole story."

Henley told of meeting Brooks, who in turn had lured him to Corll. He now described in detail how he had actively participated in killing some of the boys and he offered the startling information that there were a lot more bodies than those found at the boathouse. Henley was blossoming in the glare of publicity, and once started he didn't want to stop. He said one burial site was near Lake Sam Rayburn in San Augustine County and another was on High Island Beach in Jefferson County.

Hardened detectives winced; they believed the boy had believed they would find more bodies at these locations. How was it possible for a man and two youngsters to kill in wholesale lots and remain undetected? Henley explained that Corll moved a lot so that any suspicious action would be an isolated case and not one of a series of incidents that might be reported to the police. His van was ideal for transporting bodies. It could be backed up to a door, so that no one could see what was being put in or taken out. There were a lot of hitchhikers who didn't hesitate to accept a ride, and were susceptible to being invited to a party. Dean had developed these parties to a fine art, and always had some beer and grass available for the youngsters. Nothing untoward happened at many of the parties; sometimes they were over early and the boys left with a promise that they would be asked to the next one. Some of them felt secure because they knew either Henley or Brooks personally.

Brooks and Henley both felt that Corll was growing more demanding in his desire for young boys, and was in fact going mad. As matters now stood, Henley admitted to active participation in the murders, but Brooks claimed he was only a bystander.

Digging at the boathouse continued the next day, and more bodies were uncovered. Four further bodies were lifted from Stall 11 before the diggers broke for lunch. In the afternoon and early evening five more bodies were brought to the surface, making an unbelievable total of seventeen excavated from the boathouse in two days. The diggers then hit solid rock, and the authorities knew that here at least their work was done.

The ever co-operative Henley led police to where he and Dean had buried more boys on the shores of Lake Sam Rayburn. He even gave the police the name of one of the youngsters before they started digging. Sure enough, only a few minutes later the body of a young boy was uncovered. He pointed to another site, where he said Corll and Brooks had buried another boy. In a matter of minutes another body was uncovered. In all, four bodies were removed from the shores of the lake, making a total of twenty-one victims.

Brooks and Henley then directed the police to High Island where six additional bodies were found, bringing the final total to twenty-seven. The two boys couldn't remember any more names or grave sites, so the search was stopped. At the outset they had estimated that there had been between twenty and thirty victims. No one will ever know for sure if twenty-seven is the correct total.

Tim Kerley and Rhonda Louise Williams, the two youngsters who witnessed the shooting of Dean Corll, were released. Wayne Henley was charged with the murder of eight boys, and David Brooks was charged with two. Both received lengthy prison sentences designed to keep them behind bars for the rest of their lives. The authorities ruled that Henley's killing of Corll was an act of self-defense, and Henley was not charged with Corll's murder.

* * *

At the height of the investigation, a small fifteen-minute service was held at Pasadena's Grand View Memorial Park. About 35 friends and the immediate family of the deceased wept as the Reverend Robert D. Joiner of the Sunset United Methodist Church said a few kind words. The flag of the United States draped the casket. Just before it was lowered into the ground forever, the flag was presented to Dean Corll's father.

CASTLE OF DEATH

Herman Webster Mudgett was born in 1860 to a respected family in the tiny New England community where his father had been postmaster for over twenty-five years. Though young Herman early showed a vicious streak — neighbors of the Mudgetts were to recall seeing him setting a cat on fire — he had many redeeming features, not the least of which was his keen intelligence. His teachers remembered him as a bright, alert scholar. After his graduation with honors from Gilmanton Academy, he eloped with a farmer's daughter from the nearby village of Loudon, and paid his tuition at the University of Vermont, at Burlington, from a small inheritance his wife had just received. He transferred to the University of Michigan at Ann Arbor, where his wife gave birth to a son.

Mudgett started his criminal activities while still at university. He and another student concocted a scheme whereby Mudgett took out an insurance policy on his friend's life in the amount of $12,500. The friend promptly disappeared, leaving the way clear for Mudgett to steal a corpse from the dissecting room of the university, positively identify it as his missing friend, and collect the insurance. Shortly after the successful completion of this scheme, he qualified as a Doctor of Medicine and abandoned his wife and infant son. Mrs. Mudgett returned to Gilmanton, never to lay eyes on her husband again.

The doctor, now a tall, good-looking twenty-four-year-old with all the qualifications to be a legitimate success, struck out on his own. With his fashionable walrus moustache and his luminous brown eyes, he was altogether a distinguished-looking gentleman. And when he was decked out in his bowler hat, tweed suit and shiny shoes, Herman held more than a little attention for the opposite sex.

For six years he wandered through Minnesota and New York, making a dishonest dollar wherever he could. The fact that he could have made a fine living at his own profession apparently didn't enter his mind. Records show that in St. Paul he was appointed receiver of a bankrupt store. He filled the store with merchandise purchased on credit, sold off the stock at cost price or less, and took off with the proceeds.

In 1885, he reappeared in Wilmette, a suburb of Chicago, as an inventor, using the name Henry H. Holmes for the first time. He met a dark-haired beauty named Myrtle Z. Belknap, who was not only a stunning looker, but also had a father who was one of the wealthiest residents of Wilmette. Holmes married her without going through the annoying formalities of a divorce from his first wife. He succeeded in getting enough money out of Myrtle's daddy to build a house, and then started forging Mr. Belknap's name on cheques. Though the family was furious, they decided to sidestep a scandal and not to prosecute the scoundrel, for he still held a fascination for his wife, who stood beside him no matter what sort of scrapes he managed to get into.

Next, Holmes answered an advertisement in the local newspaper requiring a chemist for a store owned by a Mrs. Holden on the corner of 63rd Street and Wallace, in Englewood, another suburb of Chicago. Mrs. Holden, who had been recently widowed, was thrilled to have such a highly qualified and handsome man apply for the position, and gave him the job without any qualms whatsoever. Almost at once she became disillusioned with her new employee and confided to close friends that she suspected him of theft from her store. Early in 1890, Mrs. Holden suddenly disappeared without mentioning anything to friends, except to Holmes, who claimed she had told him she was taking a long holiday in California. Then he soothed nervous acquaintances by telling them that she had sold the store to him and was staying on the West Coast. It seems that no one was interested enough in Mrs. Holden to delve deeper into her disappearance, and she was never seen again.

In the meantime, with his knowledge of medicine, Holmes was making the business prosper. He had a few sidelines, such as his own patent medicines which he sold at enormous profits, and things were going so well that by 1892 he figured there was nothing further to be gained from the Belknap family, so he left his wife and moved into rooms above his store. Then he commenced the construction of a monstrous building directly across the street. It was three storeys high, measured 50 by 162 feet and contained more than 90 rooms. On the main floor Holmes opened a jewelry store, restaurant and drugstore. The false turrets gave the whole structure a somewhat mediaeval appearance, and the ugly pile soon came to be known as Holmes' Castle. Ostensibly Holmes built the structure to accommodate the huge crowds which were expected for the Chicago World's Fair in 1893, and the third floor of the castle was divided into apartments for this purpose; but the second floor had winding staircases, connecting hallways, trapdoors, and asbestos-lined rooms, some of them equipped with gas jets. Holmes had his own comfortable quarters on the second floor, inside his closet were valves that controlled the flow of gas to the various rooms. From his bedroom Holmes could gas a victim, turn a switch that controlled a trapdoor and plunge the body down a chute to the basement. The basement was equipped with a dissecting table, medical instruments, a crematorium, a huge vat of corrosive acid and two further vats of quicklime.

Into this veritable murder castle came Mr. Icilius Conner, his wife Julia, his sister Gertie, and his eight-year-old daughter Pearl. Conner was a jeweller by trade and was looking for ways to get into business. Holmes obliged by making a part of his drugstore available to him for the sale of jewelry, and by hiring Julia as his personal bookkeeper. The Conners were an extremely handsome family, particularly Julia, and it wasn't long before the cunning doctor had alienated her from her husband, and she had in effect become his mistress. Holmes let it leak to Conner that his wife had been sharing his bed, and Conner left Chicago in disgust. Mrs. Conner and her daughter Pearl were to live with Holmes for the next two years. During these two years, Holmes took a trip to Texas, where he stayed for over six months, engaging in his usual activities of thieving and swindling before returning to Chicago.

In 1893, the doctor received a visit from an acquaintance he had met during his stay down South. Her name was Minnie Williams, and her greatest claim to fame was the fact that she and her sister Nannie jointly owned property valued at $50,000 in Fort Worth, Texas. She was a welcome guest to the castle, and it wasn't long before she was Holmes' mistress. Coinciding with her coronation as queen of the castle, Julia Conner and her daughter disappeared. Holmes and his new flame lived together for a full year, and it was during this year that more visitors started to enter the death castle than were seen to leave it. It is difficult to believe that Minnie could have lived there at this time without having some guilty knowledge of what was going on. Holmes was easier to figure; if ever there was a born criminal it was Henry H. Holmes. He was motivated by lust and greed, not necessarily in that order, and seems never to have even considered leading an honest life.

The list of his known victims is a long one. A young girl, Emily Van Tassell, worked as a clerk in Holmes' drugstore for a month and then disappeared. Years earlier, while serving a three-month jail sentence in St. Louis, Holmes had met fellow inmates

Benjamin F. Pietzel, a small time con artist, and a rather well-known train robber, Marion Hedgepeth. Pietzel was soon to be released to join his wife and five children, but Hedgepeth was awaiting transfer to a penitentiary and a lengthy sentence. Pietzel now showed up in Chicago and looked up his friend Holmes. He kept telling Holmes about a beautiful young girl he had met in Dwight, Illinois. Her name was Emeline Cigrand, and she had made a lasting impression on Pietzel, who told Holmes she was the most beautiful girl he had ever seen. Finally, at Pietzel's urging, Holmes corresponded with the girl and offered her a job at a salary far above the average. She couldn't resist the temptation, came to Chicago, entered the castle, and was never seen again. Her boyfriend, Robert E. Phelps, inquired about her at the castle, was invited in, and never left. Holmes was later to confess to Emeline's death, describing in detail how he kept her in a soundproof room for the sole purpose of having sexual relations with her. He claimed he didn't want to kill her, but Minnie got jealous and he had to do it. The boyfriend, Holmes said, was just too nosy to live.

Nannie Williams, Minnie's sister, came to visit. Holmes made love to her, got her to sign over half the property in Fort Worth, and killed her, in that order. He told friends of Minnie's that her sister had returned to Texas.

Now we enter the even stranger period in the saga of Henry H. Holmes. In the fall of 1893, he left his friend Ben Pietzel in charge of his various businesses and took a trip with Minnie to Denver. Using the alias of Howard, he married a Georgianna Yoke of Richmond, Indiana, without Minnie's knowledge. He spent many weeks in Denver, living alternately with the two women, neither of whom knew of the other's existence. Even after Georgianna returned to Indiana, Holmes visited her on many occasions during the next two years and seemed to have become quite attached to her. She lived to testify at his trial and was the only person to speak highly of him.

Before Christmas, 1893, Minnie made the same mistake as her sister Nannie; she signed away her half of the Fort Worth property and promptly disappeared. Later Holmes was to show the police where to find her skeleton and her sister's, in the cellar of the castle.

How was Holmes able to build a structure that was obviously custom-designed for murder? Firstly, he personally supervised the entire construction, from the cellar to the top floor. Then he only kept the same crew of workmen for a few days before he discharged them. A new crew would start, often entirely unaware of what had transpired before they appeared on the job. In this way, no one saw the master plan or knew that the cumulative effect of their labors was a bona fide murder castle.

When he had been in jail with Pietzel and Hedgepeth years earlier, Holmes told them that he had figured out a foolproof way of defrauding an insurance company. He said he needed a really smart lawyer to pull it off. Hedgepeth gave Holmes the name of his lawyer, Jeptha D. Howe of St. Louis, and received in return a promise of $500 after the scheme was successfully completed. Holmes kept this plan under wraps for a few years, and then took it out of mothballs in the early summer of 1894. The scheme was the same one that Holmes had used so successfully in university. Pietzel was to have his wife take out insurance on his life, and then he was to drop out of sight, while Holmes was to come up with a corpse which would be identified as that of Pietzel. Mrs. Pietzel would collect the insurance and the partners would divide the spoils. Everyone agreed that the plan had some merit. Pietzel took out a policy amounting to $10,000. Then he went to Philadelphia and set up a shop as a patent attorney, using the name B.F. Perry. Within a month his body was found on the floor of his office, badly burned, particularly around the face. The police investigating the accident found a broken bottle of benzine on the office floor. The preliminary assumption was that an explosion had taken place, causing the accident. Then an autopsy was performed and the death was found to have been caused by chloroform. Jeptha D. Howe appeared on the scene and informed the authorities that the dead man was Ben Pietzel, and as Mrs. Pietzel's attorney, he was representing her in asking for any insurance money that was due his client. Pietzel's good friend Holmes arrived and also identified the body. The insurance money was paid off to Mrs. Pietzel; it was later divided up, with Howe getting $2,500, Mrs. Pietzel $500, and Holmes receiving the balance.

Holmes, the arch-criminal, had really murdered his friend Pietzel. The corpse was no stranger to him, but he managed to deceive Howe and Mrs. Pietzel, who throughout the con thought that Pietzel was in hiding. Howe returned to St. Louis assuming that the scheme was a complete success and that Mrs. Pietzel would be joining Mr. Pietzel in a few months and that everyone would be happy. He visited his client Hedgepeth in prison and mentioned how well the scheme had worked. Hedgepeth was furious, as he had been promised $500 by Holmes and never received a cent. Hedgepeth called the warden and told the whole story. The warden called the insurance company, who in turn called in the Pinkerton Detective Agency to investigate the case. When Hedgepeth told the story he naturally repeated it as he had heard it from Howe; that it was a stranger's body that was found on the office floor, not Pietzel's. It didn't take long for the Pinkertons to realize that there was more than simple fraud involved, and they called in the police.

By this time Holmes had fled, and he proved to be an elusive quarry. He had talked Mrs. Pietzel into meeting him in Detroit. She took two of her children with her, while Holmes took the other three, Alice, Nellie and Howard. He told her they would all meet with Mr. Pietzel in Detroit in two weeks' time. Holmes arrived before the allotted time and placed the three Pietzel children in a boarding house while he scampered to Richmond, Indiana, returning with the lady who really thought she was his wife, Georgianna Yoke. Holmes set up three different groups while in Detroit. One consisted of the three Pietzel children, another consisted of Mrs. Pietzel and the other two children, while a third contingent was made up solely of Georgianna. Holmes would join any of the three groups, who at no time knew of the others' presence in the city. Finally he took all three households on the road, and it is a measure of his cunning that he managed to stay ahead of the police for two months. They finally caught up with Holmes in Boston on Nov. 17, 1894. The other two detachments were accounted for when gullible Georgianna, who was innocent of any wrongdoing, was located by the police in Indiana where Holmes had stashed her, and Mrs. Pietzel and her two children were discovered living in Burlington, Vermont, waiting for the reunion with her husband that was never to come.

Only Nellie, Howard, and Alice Pietzel, the three children who were travelling with Holmes, could not be found by the police, and Holmes steadfastly refused to give them any information concerning the three children.

The interior of Holmes' murder castle was now exposed, and the police realized they were dealing with one of the most hideous monsters who ever lived. The search was on for the three children; the trail led from Detroit to Toronto to Cincinnati to Indianapolis, throughout the midwest and back into Canada. Finally, at 16 Vincent Street in Toronto, the authorities found a house that had been rented to a man with two little girls. The police found out that the man had borrowed a spade to dig a hole, supposedly to store potatoes. They were able to find the neighbor whose spade had been used, and he loaned the same spade to the police. The police dug up the same hole, and in it they found the pathetic bodies of Nellie and Alice Pietzel. In an upstairs bedroom of the house they found a trunk with a rubber tube leading from it to a gas outlet. Diabolical Holmes had enticed the girls to enter the trunk and had asphyxiated them. This discovery now accounted for all the family, except Howard. While questioning neighbors in the area of 16 Vincent Street, the police found one who had talked to the two girls. This neighbor remembered that the girls had mentioned their little brother lived in Indianapolis. The investigation moved to Indianapolis, where 900 houses were searched, and finally, in the suburb of Irvington, police found the house in which Holmes had lived for a week. It had been vacant since Holmes left, and the charred remains of Howard Pietzel's body were found in a stove in the kitchen.

Holmes made a full confession while in jail, but as it is sprinkled with proven lies it does not give an accurate account of his atrocities. While it seems that he operated basically for gain, when his castle was dismantled it was discovered that he had a rack which he used to try to stretch people, believing that he could make them permanently taller.

Holmes' trial for the murder of Ben Pietzel began on Oct. 28, 1895. It was one of the most widely publicized trials of the last century. Every detail was reported in the press, for nothing quite like it had ever been perpetrated in the U.S. before. The jury was out for two and a half hours, but later a member of the jury was to state that the verdict was decided in one minute with a show of hands. They stayed out because it was a capital case, but no one wavered from their unanimous one-minute verdict.

While his appeals were being heard, Holmes embraced the Roman Catholic Church. All of his appeals failed, and on May 7, 1896, accompanied by two priests, Holmes mounted the scaffold at Moyanensing Prison. He made a short speech to the assembled onlookers, but saved his last words for the gentleman who adjusted the noose around his neck.

"Make it quick," he said.

H.H. Holmes, one of the most notorious murderers who ever lived, would have been thirty-six had he lived nine more days.

St. Valentine's Day Massacre

- Part 9-

AMERICANA

STARKWEATHER'S MURDEROUS SPREE

Wanton murder is impossible to anticipate. There is very little defence against it. The difference between a traffic light turning red or green can place an innocent victim in the sight of a deranged sniper. You can cross the paths of desperate men during the commission of a robbery through no fault of your own.

When innocent people become the victims of such a murderer, the public has a natural abhorrence to the crime. We can all relate to being in the wrong place at the wrong time.

On Tuesday, Jan. 27, 1958, Charlie Starkweather, 19, visited the home of his 14-year-old girlfriend, Caril Fugate. It was a blustery gray day in Lincoln, Nebraska. Charlie had brought along his .22 rifle. He and Caril's stepfather, Marion Bartlett, had a date to go hunting. As soon as Charlie entered the house, Caril's mother, Velda, started telling Charlie that she didn't want him around the house any more. A heated argument erupted and Velda slapped Charlie in the face. Charlie retaliated by slapping his girlfriend's mother. Finally, Mr. Bartlett couldn't take any more. He came at Charlie. Without any more provocation than that, Charlie Starkweather raised his .22 and calmly shot Marion Bartlett in the head. Mrs. Bartlett grabbed a knife and advanced towards Charlie. The rifle was raised a second time and Charlie shot her, again with a bullet to the head. Two-and-a-half-year-old Betty Jean Bartlett started to cry. Starkweather beat her to death with the butt of his rifle.

The house became silent. Everyone but Caril and Charlie was dead.

Charlie carried Mr. Bartlett's body out to a chicken coop at the rear of the house. He dragged Mrs. Bartlett's body to an outhouse. Little Betty Jean was placed in a cardboard box and put beside her mother. Charlie cleaned the blood off the floor, and unbelievably, he and Caril settled down to watching television for a few hours. Then Charlie went out to use a phone. He called Mr. Bartlett's employer and told him that Bartlett had the flu and wouldn't be in to work for a few days. Upon returning to the house he had intercourse with Caril. Later, he was to state that he had sex with Caril every day and twice on Sunday.

The young couple stayed on in the house. In the normal course of events, people started to arrive at the front door. Caril didn't answer some callers and they went away. The more persistent were told through the door that everyone had the flu and the doctor had ordered the house placed under quarantine. For six days the two teenagers stayed in the house after the killings. Finally Caril's elderly grandmother, sensing that something was wrong, went to the police, who investigated and discovered the three bodies. Caril and Charlie had left just before the police arrived. Starkweather took Bartlett's .410 shotgun with him.

They hadn't travelled far when Charlie's car got stuck near August Meyer's farm. Charlie, who knew Meyers, walked up to the house and asked for help in getting his car out of a ditch. The farmer went into the house for his overcoat. When he came back out, according to Charlie, he had a gun. Without hesitation, Starkweather shot him in the head. They got the car out of the ditch and drove away, but it wasn't long before they were stuck again. This time young Robert Jensen and his girlfriend, Carol King, stopped to see if they could help in any way. Charlie and Caril pulled their guns on the surprised pair. They had the terrified couple drive to a deserted school a few miles from Bennet, Nebraska. Starkweather led the pair to a storm cellar. He shot young Jensen in the head, raped and stabbed Carol King, and shot her in the head as well.

That night Starkweather and Fugate spent the night in the Jensen car. The next day they walked into the home of wealthy Laver Ward in Lincoln, Nebraska. A maid opened the door to the young couple. It was to be her last day of life. Mrs. Ward came downstairs in her nightclothes. Later, on some pretext, she got permission from Starkweather to go upstairs to dress. Charlie waited for her for 40 minutes, and then went upstairs to investigate. He claimed later that Mrs. Ward was waiting for him with a rifle. He overpowered her and stabbed her to death in minutes. At 6:30 in the evening Mr. Ward arrived home. He immediately sized up the situation and instinctively knew his only chance was to attack Starkweather. He lunged at Charlie with an electric iron. Starkweather shot him in the head, and as he spun around, he was again shot in the back. The maid was then taken upstairs, tied and gagged. She was found dead of suffocation.

Charlie and Caril left the house and headed for Wyoming. They decided to change cars about 10 miles outside of Douglas, Wyoming. They hailed a passing motorist, salesman Merle Collison. In order to gain possession of his car Charlie shot him nine times.

Then Charlie's luck ran out.

As soon as he killed Collison, another motorist stopped, thinking the two vehicles were having difficulties. The driver, Joe Sprinkle, got out of his car. Charlie levelled a revolver at him and said, "Raise your hands, help me release the emergency brake or I'll kill you."

Out of the corner of his eye Sprinkle saw the body of Merle Collison lying on the floor of the car. He lunged for the rifle and wrestled it away from Charlie. Later he was to state that he knew instinctively that to lose this tug of war meant death. Unarmed, Charlie dashed for his car. Strictly by coincidence, Deputy Sheriff Bill Romer drove up. Caril, who had been in the dead man's car, ran to the deputy. Starkweather roared away in Collison's vehicle. The sheriff used his radio and a car driven by Douglas Police Chief Robert Ainslie took up the chase. He fired some shots at the fleeing vehicle. One bullet went through the rear window of Starkweather's car. Charlie pulled up and dashed out of the car screaming that he was bleeding. A sliver of glass from the broken window had nicked his ear.

Immediately after his capture, Charlie Starkweather started to talk. He confessed to one other murder that had taken place seven weeks before his murderous spree began. It involved a gas station robbery where the owner was taken into the woods and shot to death. In all, 11 people fell to the deadly impulses of Starkweather, the last 10 in the space of two weeks.

From the beginning Charlie insisted that Caril was a hostage and had nothing to do with the actual killings. Caril also professed to be terrified of Charlie, and thought she would become a victim at any time during the killing orgy. Later Charlie, who made seven different confessions, changed his story and implicated his girlfriend stating that she was a willing lover and accomplice.

When they placed Charlie in the electric chair on June 25, 1959, his last request was to ask the guards to tighten the leather straps holding his chest and arms.

Caril's main defence was based on the fact that she was a hostage. The prosecution attorney pointed out the many times she was armed or alone and could have run away during the deadly two weeks.

In the end, she received a sentence of life imprisonment. Imprisoned at the age of 14, Caril spent more than half her life in prison. She was twice denied parole. However, she had her sentence of life imprisonment commuted. Caril has since been granted parole.

THE BRILLIANT KILLER

Edgar Smith holds a dubious record. He spent over 14 years in the death house in New Jersey State Prison at Trenton, the longest period of time any prisoner has ever spent on Death Row in the U.S. Not only did Smith eventually save his life, he managed to gain his freedom as well. This is his remarkable story.

* * *

Ed Smith first saw daylight in Hasbrouk Heights, N.J. on Feb. 8, 1934. The town, then a suburb of New York City, had a population of 5,000. When Ed was only five, his parents were divorced. His mother went to work and managed to make a living to support herself, Ed, and his older brother.

In 1948, Ed's mother remarried while her youngest son completed grammar school and entered Don Bosco Preparatory School in Ramsay, N.J., a few miles from his home. Ed, who was a good student, completed his sophomore year and then transferred to Ramsey High School. The Smith family moved to Ramsey, but Ed had had enough of school. He tried to join the Marines, but couldn't enlist until he became 18 without his mother's permission. He quit school, took odd jobs, and a few days after turning 18, joined the Marines.

While in the service, Ed underwent training in California and Hawaii before being shipped out to Korea. In 1954, he was discharged due to a hearing defect in his left ear.

Returning to Ramsey, Ed went through a few jobs before settling down to a responsible position as a machinist. In 1955, he met an attractive 18-year-old girl, Patricia, who soon became his wife. The young couple bought a modern house trailer for their first home. On Dec. 23, 1956, Patricia gave birth to a baby girl. The new edition to the family was her father's pride and joy.

The above facts of Ed Smith's life fit millions of young men — small town upbringing, school, service, back home to a job, a marriage, and parenthood.

On Monday evening, March 4, 1967, all the routine aspects of Ed Smith's life were to change abruptly and forever.

At precisely 7:30 p.m. Victoria Zielinski, 15, and her 13-year-old sister, Myrna, prepared to walk to Barbara Nixon's house. Vicki was planning on studying with Barbara. Mrs. Zielinski always made Myrna walk partway with Vicki. It wasn't that far. Both homes were located on Wyckoff Ave., but the seven or eight homes between the two residences were well off the road, which can best be described as lonesome. The two sisters parted and made a deal that Myrna would leave her house at 8:30, the same time as Vicki. They would meet at the halfway point for the return walk home.

Vicki and Barbara did some homework and listened to the radio. Before Vicki realized it the time was 8:40. She hurriedly put on her coat and dashed out into the chill March air to meet her sister. Meanwhile Myrna had left home at 8:30 as arranged and was puzzled that she didn't meet Vicki. She kept walking to the Nixon residence. Barbara was surprised to see Myrna. How come she hadn't met Vicki? There was one possibility. In the few moments before the two sisters should have met on the darkened street, Vicki may have accepted a ride from a friend. Myrna returned home, but Vicki wasn't there. Mrs. Zielinski came up with a logical solution to what was fast becoming a minor mystery. The Zielinski's eldest daughter, Mary, had gone out with her steady boyfriend, George Self. Perhaps they had picked Vicki up and taken her along to one of the several teenage hangouts in town.

Myrna persisted. The only car she had seen on her walk was Don Hommell's, speeding down the road. In the meantime, feeling that Vicki would show up at any moment, Mrs. Zielinski was hesitant to wake her husband from his evening nap. When Mary and George returned without Vicki she quickly changed her mind. Mr. Zielinski was furious that his wife had not told him of their daughter's absence sooner. Three and a half hours had elapsed.

Mr. Zielinski and Mary got in their car and proceeded to look for the missing girl. During the course of the evening they met a patrol car and reported Vicki missing to the police. Throughout the wee hours of the morning the anxious father drove up and down the deserted streets. Finally he went home to try to catch some sleep.

Early the next morning, Mr. and Mrs. Zielinski continued their search. A few streets removed from Wycoff Ave., in the adjoining township of Mahwah, they entered a sandpit which ran off Chapel Rd. As they peered down the road, Mr. Zielinski spotted a shoe, which he immediately recognized as belonging to his daughter. Seven yards further down the road leading to the sandpit he found a bloodstained kerchief. Still further on he came across a pair of red gloves. Mrs. Zielinski ran to the nearest house and called the police. She returned to her husband. Not daring to proceed further, the Zielinskis waited in the car for the police to arrive.

Capt. Edmund Wickham of the Mahwah police arrived on the scene a few minutes after receiving the call. Accompanied by Mr. Zielinski they proceeded further into the sandpit area. It was Mr. Zielinski who found his daughter's body. A portion of the girl's head was nothing but a large cavity. Her brains were splattered over some nearby rocks. Vicki's brassiere was hanging loose around her waist. A post mortem later indicated that Vicki had died a virgin.

The day following the murder Ed Smith's best friend, Joseph Gilroy, was getting out of his car when he noticed a small but distinctive spot of blood on the front seat. Joe went to the police. He had loaned the car to Ed Smith the night before. Joe explained to the police that Ed's car was in the garage for repairs. Ed had needed some kerosene in order to fix the heater in his house trailer. Ed drove Joe home and took his car at about 7 p.m. He was supposed to get together with Joe later that night but called at 9:30 to say that he had been sick. He also asked if Joe would drive him and his family to his mother-in-law's house. Joe agreed. During the course of the drive Ed mentioned that he had vomited on his pants earlier that night and had thrown them away. Joe had been with Ed, his wife and baby at 9:45 p.m. and had dropped them off at his mother-in-law's at about 10 o'clock.

Next day when Joe picked up Ed at his mother-in-law's, Ed was carrying an old pair of shoes. Later during the day he no longer had them.

After hearing Joe Gilroy's story, detectives picked up Ed Smith and took him to the Mahwah police headquarters for questioning, Ed told a straightforward story of borrowing the car to pick up kerosene for his broken heater. He said that at one point he got sick and drove onto the road leading to the sandpit to vomit. Ed claimed that he returned home, but couldn't repair the heater. He then picked up Joe Gilroy for the trip to his mother-in-law's at about 9:30 p.m.

Ed explained away the old pair of shoes by stating that since the shoemaker thought they weren't worth repairing he threw them in some garbage cans in Ramsey. Police took Ed for a ride. They couldn't find his pants where he said he had thrown them, nor could they find the location where he supposedly had been sick. They did find his shoes exactly where he said they would be. One shoe had a tiny spot of blood on its side.

The interrogation continued. A physical examination revealed that Smith had abrasion on both knees. Now a prime suspect in the murder of Vicki Zielinski, police had established the following facts: 1. Ed was driving a car on the night of the murder which was later found to have a bloodstain on the front seat. 2. He lived one mile from the murder scene. 3. He was at the murder scene on the night of the murder. 4. He threw away the pants he was wearing on the night of the murder and couldn't explain where he had thrown them. 5. He threw away his shoes, which were later found with a bloodstain on one of them.

One glaring inconsistency shone through this maze of circumstantial evidence. The doctor who had examined the dead girl estimated the time of death to be not much before 11 p.m. Ed was with Joe Gilroy, his wife, baby and, later, his mother-in-law from about 9:45 p.m. on.

Although Ed repeatedly requested a lawyer he was refused one. At no time was he warned that he could remain silent should he choose to do so.

Detectives continued to question Ed Smith hour after weary hour. Finally, bone tired, he agreed to tell the officers exacty what happened on the night Vicki Zielinski met her death.

After picking up a five-gallon tin of kerosene and starting for home, Ed claimed that he had seen a girl walking on the crowded street. He recognized her as Vicki Zielinski, whom he knew well. Ed pulled over to the side of the road and Vicki asked him for a lift to her home. The time was 8:40 p.m.

As Ed approached her home Vicki said that her sister was supposed to meet her, and that he had better drive around the block. The family didn't like her acceptng lifts. Ed pulled into the sandpit road. Vicki was chatting about schoolwork and how strict her father was with her.

Suddenly Vicki turned on Ed, saying he was just like the rest of the boys she knew. She quickly informed him that she was getting out of the car and walking home. As she stepped out of the car, Ed grabbed her by the shoulder. At the same time Vicki slapped him. He swung at the girl with his right hand. Vicki managed to get out of the car while Ed grappled with her. One of his shoes came off in the soft mud. He then climbed back into the car and drove home alone.

When he arrived at his trailer home he told his wife that he had been sick and threw his soiled pants on the patio. She fetched him a clean pair. Noticing that he was only wearing one shoe, he changed into a pair of loafers. Ed claimed that he then tried to repair his heater, but found that it wouldn't work.

In order to pour kerosene into a retaining tank, it was necessary for Ed to climb up on a plank superstructure and balance himself while he poured. While doing this he lost his balance and fell, skinning both his knees. This conveniently accounted for his badly skinned knees which the police were so delighted to photograph.

As Ed still had Joe Gilroy's car, he called Joe on the telephone and asked Joe to give him and his wife a lift to his mother-in-law's home in Ridgewood. Gilroy agreed. Ed gathered up his old soiled pants and drove over to pick up Giloy. On the way he threw away his pants and then returned to the sandpit to retrieve the shoe he had left there earlier in the evening. As luck would have it, he had no trouble finding the shoe. He and Gilroy returned to the trailer, picked up Smith's wife and baby and proceeded to his mother-in-law's, were the family spent the night.

Next morning, Vicki Zielinski's body was found. The murder was big news in New Jersey. Radio stations issued special reports detailing the progress of the investigation. As soon as Smith was picked up he became a prime suspect. As the questioning continued the details of his interrogation appeared almost simultaneously in the newspapers. Smith's pants were found. They were splattered with blood on the lower right leg. Ed Smith alternately claimed that he couldn't remember how they became bloodstained, or that he didn't think they were his pants. Ed claimed that he threw the pants away on Pulis Ave. They were found some distance away on Oak St. No one, including the police, could figure out how the incriminating trousers got to where they were found.

Ed's entire statement made to the police was full of evasive and unsatisfactory answers. Many questions were answered by, "I don't know" or "I can't remember". Later he was to claim that the statement was squeezed out of him in return for a promise that he would be permitted a visit from his wife.

Throughout the questioning, no lawyer was made available to Ed, despite his repeated requests for one. His statement was typed up and presented to him for his signature. He refused to sign, insisting that the police had told him beforehand that it would not be necessary for him to sign the statement. He was then asked to read the statement and initial each page. Again he refused.

After 19 straight hours of questoning Ed was permitted a visit from his wife. As once can well imagine young Patricia Smith was distraught. Newspapers carried front page stories of the heinous crime perpetrated in the small town. All the reports said that her husband had confessed to the murder. Ed assured his wife that the newspapers were wrong. He was in a jam, but the whole thing would be straightened out. They would soon be together again, just like old times. She left the police station not knowing that she would never see her husband as a free man again.

On March 6, at 7:15 p.m., Ed Smith was charged with the murder of Victoria

Zielinski. He was then allowed to sleep.

Ed's first contact with the legal profession did not go off well. His lawyer met with the state attorney and elicited an agreement that his client would be allowed to plead guilty to second degree murder. The condition of the deal would be a confession given by the defendant in court from the witness stand. In this way his lawyer assured Ed that he would be a free man in eight to 10 years. Smith refused to consider the deal, and as a result his lawyer removed himself from the case.

A month after the murder, Ed Smith met veteran lawyer John E. Selser, who had been retained by Smith's family to represent him. Selser was amazed to learn just how ignorant his client claimed to be concerning the murder of Vicki Zielinski. Ed inquired about the exact cause of death. While he had heard that the victim had been killed as a result of a fractured skull, he hadn't had access to a radio or newspapers, and now he wanted information about the actual murder.

For the first time Ed Smith let a fellow human being in on a secret, something he hadn't told police despite their hours of questioning. He hadn't even told his wife. Smith told his lawyer that he didn't murder Vicki Zielinski. There was more, much more. Ed knew who had killed Vicki. He had been in the sandpit at the time and had left the girl with her killer.

Ed had initially lied to the police to remove himself from the murder scene. As the questioning continued and fatigue set in he decided to lie about any detail which appeared to be advantageous to him. He didn't realize it, but with every word he was incriminating himself further.

Neither John Selser nor Ed Smith knew it at the time, but it would take over 14 years to undo the damage caused by these lies.

Edgar Smith changed his story. He now claimed to be telling the truth. It is a story he was to stick to for more than 14 years.

Smith claimed that on the night of the murder he was driving home with a five gallon can of kerosene when he picked up Vicki, who asked him for a lift to her home down the road. Once in the car Vicki, whom he knew quite well, said she had something to tell him. He pulled into the sandpit road and turned off the ignition. Vicki then informed him that his wife Patricia was seeing one of his friends on the sly. Initially Ed shrugged off the inference as being ridiculous, but as Vicki insisted on pressing the matter he became angry. In a blind rage he slapped the girl. Vicki opened the car door and ran toward the street. Ed decided to back the car down the road, at the same time trying to make up his mind whether or not he should catch up to Vicki, apologize for losing his temper and take her home.

As this thought was going through his mind he heard two voices, one male and one female, coming from further down the road. Ed applied the brakes. Not knowing what to expect in the darkened sandpit Ed took with him a baseball bat which had been lying on the back seat of Gilroy's car. In getting out of the car he slipped in soft mud and lost his shoe. As he approached the two agitated figures, he noticed a car parked on the street at the intersection to the sandpit. He recognized the car as belonging to an acquaintance of his, Ed Hommell.

Vicki was crying. She had a nasty head wound which was bleeding profusely. Hommell, who was somewhat of a regular boyfriend of Vicki's, was berating her for having parked with Ed Smith. Vicki was obviously afraid of Hommell and asked Ed to take her home. Hommell explained to Smith that Vicki had fallen and cut her head.

Smith claimed that he offered to take the girl to a doctor. With this suggestion Vicki jumped into his car. Hommell then flew into a rage and grabbed Vicki by the arm, pulling her out of the car. Vicki grabbed Smith's legs as the upper portion of her body fell out of the car. She held tight to his legs as he stood beside the car. In this way Smith's pants, particularly the right leg, became bloodstained. During the commotion Smith had discarded the baseball bat. Hommell and Smith began shoving each other, but in a moment it was all over. Vicki got to her feet. Hommell said he would take care of the bad cut on his girfriend's head. Everyone seemed to make up after a fashion. Edgar Smith departed, leaving Vicki and Hommell alone on the sandpit road. The baseball bat was forgotten.

After arriving home Smith discarded the bloody pants and tried to repair his space heater. He fell down while pouring kerosene into a retaining tank and skinned his knees. Later, he threw away his bloody pants and returned to the sandpit to retrieve his shoe. He found the shoe without any trouble and observed no one on the sandpit road. He did notice Joe Gilroy's baseball bat. It was split beyond repair. Ed gave this little mystery some thought and came to the conclusion that the bat was worthless, and that Hommell had broken it on purpose in a fit of rage or in an act of spite. Hommell did have a local reputation for being a bad actor when antagonized.

Why didn't Edgar Smith tell this supposedly truthful tale to the police instead of fabricating a confession punctuated with evasive answers? Ed had good reason. The next day after Vicki's body was found, Hommell supposedly had threatened to kill Smith's wife and child if he ever told the true story of meeting him and leaving him alone with Vicki in the sandpit on the night of her murder. Besides, once the doctor announced that Vicki couldn't have met her death much before 11 p.m., he knew he would be cleared. He had several witnesses, including Joe Gilroy, who would swear that he was with them from 9 p.m. on.

What happened to the split baseball bat, which Smith claimed to have left in full view in the sandpit? It was later found a short distance away in some woods. How did it get there? Did the real killer return after Smith's trip to pick up his shoe? Did the real killer attempt to hide the murder weapon? It hardly seems plausible that if Smith were guilty he would return to the sandpit to pick up a shoe.

On May 13, 1957 Edgar Smith stood trial for the murder of Vicki Zielinski. At the conclusion of the trial the jury took only two hours and 20 minutes to find Smith guilty. A week later he was sentenced to death in the electric chair.

Whatever else Edgar Smith may be, he has never been accused of being dull. Once in the death house he began his struggle to stay alive. Appeal followed appeal over the next 14 years. In all, 19 appeals were filed proclaiming his innocence.

Smith accomplished more during his 14 years on death row than he ever did on the outside. To facilitate his struggle he studied law. Many of his legal efforts have been lauded as the equal of anything produced by experienced lawyers. To help finance his legal endeavors, he wrote three books while on death row, all of which sold briskly. Tested by Mensa, an organization which only accepts individuals with extraordinary intelligence quotients, it was discovered that Smith had outstanding mental capacities. He became a member of Mensa.

Smith's gallant struggle to prove his innocence captured the imagination of journalist William F. Buckley. He believed implicitly in Smith's innocence. Buckley was instrumental in raising funds to further help Smith's continual legal moves to stay alive and eventually prove his innocence.

As the years passed, and appeal after appeal was turned down, it became increasingly evident that pursuing a new trial on technical grounds was impractical. Smith had now been on death row for 14 years, longer than anyone in U.S. history. Caryl Chessman had held this dubious record before being put to death in San Quentin's gas chamber after spending over 11 years in the death house.

A deal was struck. Smith went through the charade of admitting his guilt in return for a sentence of from 25 to 30 years in prison. Because of his complete and outstanding rehabilitation, the sentence was reduced to time already spent in prison. Smith was released. The battle was over. The victory wasn't sweet, but the electric chair had been cheated. Edgar Smith was free.

News conferences and television talk show interviews followed. Alert, bright, mature, and obviously a man imprisoned by overzealous law enforcement officers, Smith had at last gained his liberty.

*   *   *

Five years after Edgar Smith's release from the death house, Mrs. Lefteriya Ozbun was kidnapped from a San Diego, California parking lot. Her kidnapper forced her into a car at knifepoint. The terrified woman struggled with the man and was stabbed during a wild ride on the freeway. Mrs. Ozbun managed to get away and her attacker escaped.

Later, the now 43-year-old Edgar Smith returned to San Diego and surrendered to authorities. He confessed to kidnapping Mrs. Ozbun. In his own words he intended to "tape her up and rob her." Why had he turned himself in? Smith explained that after the kidnapping of Mrs. Ozbun he had visited the grave of Vicki Zielinski in Honesdale, Pa. It was then he decided to turn himself in. "I recognized the devil I had been looking at in the mirror for 43 years was me, and I admitted what I was. I never admitted the truth to anyone, not even myself. I didn't want to believe I am what I am."

Charged with kidnapping with attempt to rob and attempted murder, Smith testified about the 25-year-old Zielinski murder. "I knew her for a year. She dated my friends and she led me to believe she would not mind seeing me." . . . "I gave her a ride and we had some preliminary sexual activity, and there came a point when she resisted. I struck her a couple of times in the car. She got out."

Smith said he chased the girl with the baseball bat, caught up to her and clubbed her to death. He described his celebrated 14-year struggle to gain his freedom as nothing more than "judicial theatrics".

In 1977, Edgar Smith was found guilty of the charges pertaining to the Ozbun crimes. He was sentenced to life imprisonment without possibility of parole.

THE MAN WHO KILLED MARTIN LUTHER KING

James Earl Ray was born in Quincy, Ill., on March 10, 1928 to James and Lucille Ray. He was one of four children to be born to the dirt-poor family in the first seven years of their marriage. James, Sr., had been to prison for theft before his marriage, and now, with four children to feed during the worst depression the world has ever known, he took to drinking heavily. The family moved to Ewing, Missouri. Things were no better, but like everyone in the tiny hamlet of 350 souls, they did survive.

Young James started school at the Ewing Consolidated School, and is remembered as a shy, retiring youngster.

By 1943, the head of the family abandoned the farm and moved his household to Galesburg, Ill., where he got a job on the railroad. Just before they pulled up stakes, young Jimmy graduated from the eighth grade. Jimmy didn't accompany the rest of the family. Instead he struck out on his own, getting a job with a shoe manufacturing firm in Alton, Ill. In 1945, Jimmy joined the army. After serving a stint overseas, he received a discharge in 1948. Upon returning home, he found his mother had given birth to two additional children. Lucille was now a confirmed alcoholic who hung around bars with strange men.

James Earl Ray left home, and from the age of 21 became a small time thief who wasn't very smart. In 1949, he was caught stealing a typewriter in Chicago, and received 90 days in jail. A few years later he was apprehended by a passing citizen as he held up a cabdriver for $11.90. He received a sentence of from one to two years in the State Penitentiary at Joliet, and was released after serving 22 months. When he got out of prison Ray went home to Alton and got a job in a gas station. A short time later, a cop making nightly routine calls along the main street of the tiny town saw a window open. As he went to investigate, a burglar rushed out the door and outdistanced the policeman. Returning to the scene the policeman found a pair of shoes stuck in the mud beside the sidewalk. Next day, James Earl Ray was picked up walking along railroad tracks on the outskirts of town. His feet were horribly swollen and bleeding. The total take from the robbery was $23. A relative posted bond, and Ray promptly skipped.

Next, Ray was picked up passing forged postal orders. This time he received three years in Leavenworth, gaining his release on April 15, 1958. A little over a year later, Ray received his most severe sentence. Now a four-time loser, he was sentenced to 20 years for armed robbery of a grocery store in St. Louis. After serving approximately eight years in prison, Ray escaped. On April 23, 1967 he secreted himself in a truckload of bread that was being sent from the prison proper to a prison farm close by. The truck was routinely searched but Ray had concealed himself in the middle of the load of breadboxes, and cleanly escaped, then promptly disappeared.

* * *

This, then, was James Earl Ray. To this point in his life, he is one of those gray, faceless thousands who start as juvenile delinquents and progress through correctional institutions for the rest of their lives. Ray's criminal activities were planned and executed ineptly. In everything he did, he was totally incompetent.

This man, with this background, was to fire a shot and kill a man. In one split second he may have changed the course of history. In doing so he also triggered the greatest manhunt in the history of crime.

* * *

After his successful escape from prison, Ray called himself John Larry Rayns. He made his way to Chicago and got a job washing dishes at the Indian Trail Restaurant. He stayed eight weeks, got along well with the rest of the kitchen staff, and made a total of $700. On July 16, 1967 he crossed the border at Windsor, Ont. and made his way to Montreal. Two days later he took a six month lease on a room at the Har-K apartments at 2589 Notre Dame St. E. He signed the lease as Eric S. Galt. It is believed that at the time of the signing of this lease, Ray was now actively involved in conjunction with others in a master conspiracy to assassinate Dr. Martin Luther King.

Eric S. Galt's activities in Montreal are well documented. He paid $150 in advance for his room at the Har-K Apartments. On July 18, he bought a suit, pyjamas, gray slacks, two t-shirts, swim trunks, underwear and ties at Tip Top Tailors. Two days later, he had his nails manicured at the Queen Elizabeth Hotel.

On July 31, he went to the Laurentian Mountains where he checked into a luxury resort. He stayed a week. Where did the money come from? Throughout Ray's travel, this question arises again and again. For a man with no income, money seemed to be no object in Ray's date with destiny.

Another mystery is the fact that there appears to be a marked change in Ray's personality at this time. The man who bought drinks at the bar in the Laurentian resort was not a shy hillbilly hood on the lam. Ray-Galt was now a confident, smooth talking, free spender. He even managed to bed down with a cultivated employee of the federal government. This poor lady was to be questioned extensively by the federal police of the two countries because of her connection with the dapper Eric Galt.

Later, Ray-Galt was to claim that he met with a man in Montreal he was to know only as Raoul. Ray says he entered into an agreement with Raoul that he would do anything Raoul asked, but in turn would ask no questions himself. Ray claims that if he was now part of a conspiracy, he knew nothing about it. Under the auspices of the mysterious Raoul, who incidentally has never been identified, Ray-Galt travelled from Montreal to Birmingham, Ala., to Mexico, to New Orleans and Los Angeles. Contact was always made with him and money was provided to finance his travels.

In Birmingham, Ray bought a white 1966 Mustang. He answered an ad in the Birmingham *News*, met William D. Paisley and paid cash for the car.

This was certainly strange behavior for an escaped convict who was on a mission to murder a Nobel Peace Prize winner. Dr. Martin Luther King was a living legend to both white and black. Those who disagreed with his views still admired his courage. Those who agreed with the black leader considered him a god. All agreed that he was the one man who had any chance of unifying the various black groups in the United States. They also agreed that Dr. King had no ulterior motives. He was willing to give his life for his people.

In 1968, Dr. King had already made public his plan for a camp in Washington. The whole operation was to be called Resurrection City. On Feb. 19, in Los Angeles, Ray-Galt had some plastic surgery performed on the tip of his nose and on his left earlobe. These minor but identifiable marks were successfully removed.

Again, receiving mysterious instructions from Raoul, Ray moved from Los Angeles to Atlanta and on to Birmingham. In Birmingham, using the name Harvey Lowmeyer, Ray bought a 30.06 calibre Remington rifle with a telescopic lens. Ray then drove the white Mustang back to Atlanta, then on to Memphis.

Meanwhile, after a bomb scare on his plane, Dr. King arrived in Memphis. He was met at the airport and accompanied to the Lorraine Motel. Dr. King was assigned Room No. 306.

Using the name John Willard, Ray checked into a dilapidated boarding house at 422½ South Main St. The manager of the boarding house, Mrs. Bessie Brewer, thought her new customer too well dressed for her establishment. She showed him the best rooms in the house, but Mr. Willard didn't like the view. He thought Room No. 5B was perfect. It was filthy, had a lumpy mattress and nondescript green spread on the bed. The dirty window gave an unobstructed view of the Lorraine Motel. In his direct line of vision was Room 306.

Down the hall from his room Mr. Willard noticed that the common bathroom gave a still better view of Room 306. He entered the bathroom and locked the door. At 6 o'clock Dr. King came out of his room onto the balcony for a breath of air. John Willard stepped into the bathtub, rested his Remington on the windowsill and squeezed the trigger. Exactly 205 feet, 3 inches away (the distance was later measured) Dr. King was slammed against the wall. The bullet tore into his lower right jaw and hit his spinal cord. At five minutes past 7 Dr. Martin Luther King was officially pronounced dead.

* * *

James Earl Ray, alias John Willard, rushed from the boarding house, and for some reason dropped his rifle in front of a store close by. He entered his white Mustang, and in the confusion got clean away. He made it to Atlanta in the Mustang and then abandoned it. Somehow (no one to this day knows what means he used) Ray headed for Toronto.

In his wake, Ray left a nation in a state of hate. The non-violent advocate King lay dead by an assassin's bullet. Surely, if the white man would kill the leader of the non-violent movement, could non-violence ever achieve the black man's dream of full equality? The answer came in the form of riots and fires. From Memphis, Washington, Chicago, Albany, Youngstown, Baltimore, Kansas City, Newark, and Pittsburgh, the hate, fires and rioting spread. It is estimated that damage amounted to $50 million in the one week following the murder.

The F.B.I. recovered a note left by Galt in Atlanta. On the note they discovered a fingerprint. The authorities started matching it with prints of known fugitives of the same description as Galt. On the 702nd card pulled the print was matched. The name on the card — James Earl Ray. On April 8, James Earl Ray walked up the steps at 102

Ossington Ave., Toronto and rang the bell. There was a room for rent sign in the window. The red brick has been painted many times since the evening Ray introduced himself to Mrs. Szpakowski as Paul Bridgman. The neighborhood is surprisingly the same now as it was then. A few doors away is the Maple Leaf Confectionery. The Portugal Tool Rental Co. had a modern sign over the front window giving evidence of the ethnic mix of the neighborhood. A potpourri of Italians, Portuguese, Spanish, and Chinese live in the area. Typical of Toronto and different from other large cities, these ethnic groups seem to be able to retain their culture and yet mix with the community at large. In this mixture of nationalities, no one noticed Paul Bridgman. Well, almost no one. One day his landlady, Mrs. Szpakowski mentioned to her husband the striking resemblance between their quiet boarder and the fellow the whole world was hunting. Her husband told her not to make a fool of herself — what would such a man be doing in their rooming house? Two days later, the reward for James Earl Ray hit $155,000.

On April 11, Ray-Bridgman got a passport photo taken at the Arcade Photo Studio on Yonge St. Five days later he entered the Kennedy Travel Agency. Ray-Bridgman said he wanted a 21-day excursion ticket to London, England, leaving on May 6 and returning on May 27. The agent, Mrs. Spencer, explained that he needed a passport. The stranger said that he had no birth certificate. Next she suggested that he come up with someone who knew him for the past two years. He replied that he had just returned to Toronto after a long absence, and didn't know anyone. Mrs. Spencer had faced this problem before. There was one further thing to do to get a passport. Her customer had to swear before a notary that he was a Canadian citizen. Henry Moos, the president of the travel agency, was a notary and would do the necessary. The agency would send the application to Ottawa. Bridgman answered some further questions and gave his name as Ramon George Sneyd. It was under this name that the application for a passport was sent to Ottawa.

From Eric S. Galt, John Willard, Paul Bridgman to Ramon George Sneyd. Where did Ray get this assortment of names? How could he feel so safe using them for passports and freely establishing new identities? He was relatively safe because all four men existed and had the same general physical characteristics as Ray. They were all respected citizens of Scarborough, Ont. They never knew each other, and certainly had never met Ray. Somehow they had made an underworld list of safe names to use and were purchased by Ray or someone else, not by chance, because each one generally fit his description.

On April 19, with the newspapers full of the latest news of the most wanted man in the world, James Earl Ray changed rooming houses. He moved eight blocks away to 962 Dundas St. W. His new address was in the same ethnic area. Ray could still remain a faceless nonentity among thousands. Mrs. Sun Fung Loo didn't speak any English. Her new roomer paid his $9 for the week in advance with a crisp $20 bill.

On May 2, Ray picked up his ticket from Mrs. Spencer. He had applied for and received a birth certificate in the name of Sneyd. He paid $345 in cash for the ticket. Four days later he left his rooming house on Dundas St. W. He hailed a cab and the most wanted man in the world drove up Hwy. 27 (now 427) to Toronto International Airport. By 6 p.m. that evening he was on his way to London.

The F.B.I. realized the ease with which a Canadian passport could be obtained. They reasoned that Ray might try to leave the continent via Canada. The R.C.M.P. were asked to check passports issued since Ray escaped from prison. Over 218,000 had been issued. The Mounties set to work.

On May 7, Ray left London for Lisbon, Portugal. Still travelling under the name of Sneyd, he stayed in Lisbon eight days. It is speculated that a rendezvous was not kept by someone who was supposed to meet Ray. He was forced to return to London. Once back in London he checked into the Ekfield House Hotel, and stayed there until May 28, when he moved to the New Earl's Court Motel in Penywern Rd. Meanwhile, the Mounties in Ottawa had been checking passports for 10 days, and finally came up with one in the name of Ramon George Sneyd that had a general description that could have fitted Ray. A phone call to Toronto verified that Ramon George Sneyd did indeed exist, but he had never applied for a passport. The police now had the information supplied by Ray in order to purchase his ticket and passport. They traced his actions and learned of his flight to London.

In London, Ray was starting to panic. Moving to another hotel did nothing to calm his nerves. He made inquiries about becoming a mercenary soldier in Africa.

Had the elaborate plot commenced to deteriorate? Was Ray now alone; the old Ray who left his shoes at the scene of a robbery?

On June 8, he checked out of his hotel and booked a flight to Brussels. By this time Scotland Yard had been alerted to be on the lookout for Ray traveling in Europe under the name of Sneyd. At 11:30 a.m. on the morning of June 8, when Ray rushed to the airport to catch his Brussels flight, Det. Sgt. Phillip F. Birch was checking passports and keeping an eye open for the name Sneyd. Dapper James Earl Ray dashed up to the booth and flashed his passport. Birch saw the wanted name. He said to the most wanted man in the world, "Would you please step into our office, Mr. Sneyd?"

* * *

On Monday, March 10, 1969, in Memphis, Tenn., Percy Foreman, Ray's defense counsel, informed the court that his client had signed a Petition for Waiver of Trial and request for Acceptance of Plea of Guilty. This document was signed with the firm understanding that Ray's life was to be spared. He received a sentence of 99 years in prison. No one has ever been given the opportunity to inquire about a conspiracy. Did James Earl Ray act alone? Perhaps we will never know. Not long ago, his petition for leave to appeal was turned down. He remains confined in prison.

A FAMILY AFFAIR

$\mathbf{T}$here have been some nasty families down through the years. I don't mean yours or mine, but those families who slayed together and stayed together.

One of the vilest little domesticated groups to kill together were the Benders of Kansas. Pop Bender was originally from Germany, and was around 60 years old when he settled in the Sunflower state. Ma Bender was a tough looking doll about 10 years Pop's junior. The hard rock couple had two children. John Jr. was a strapping, dull 27 year old, while daughter Kate was 25. Kate was a looker with an hourglass figure, who attracted members of the opposite sex like honey attracts bees.

In 1871, the Benders moved into a dilapidated house in Labette County, halfway between the small railroad crossroads of Thayer and the tiny town of Cherryvale. Old man Bender divided his 16 by 20 ft. home into two parts. One half was used as living quarters for the Bender clan, while the other half was used as a store and what could charitably be called a restaurant. The two sections were divided by a canvas partition.

Situated on the main road, and with Kate as a build-up attraction, the Bender establishment, despite its humble appearance, did a thriving business. During the daylight hours horsemen stopped for groceries. At dusk travellers stopped for a hotel meal, and were later put up on cots to spend the night.

If one were to believe rumors which circulated through the Kansas prairies, one would be forced to come to the conclusion that Kate did more for the tired strangers than wait on tables. Other than the oldest profession, Kate had another vocation, which to us unsuspecting souls appears to be diametrically opposite to her horizontal activities. Are you ready? She was a spiritualist who claimed to heal the ill. When thusly employed, she billed herself as Professor Miss Kate Bender. When the mood moved her, she also gave lectures on spiritualism.

From 1871 to 1873, using Kate and apparently good food as bait, the Bender family started killing people. Kate would seat the unsuspecting travellers with their backs to the canvas partition. Choosing only those who looked prosperous, Pop Bender and Junior would wait for an opportune moment to bring a sledge hammer down on the unsuspecting victim's head. The only thing left for the Bender family to do was slide the body under the canvas to effectively remove it from the public eating area and into the privacy of their living quarters. Here they would combine their talents to strip and rob the victims. Then the body would be dropped through a trap door in the floor into a pit. Later the family would pick a few quiet moments under the Kansas sky to plant the strangers in an adjoining pasture.

For almost two years this simple, diabolical little drama was enacted time and time again. Like most foolproof schemes something happened to cramp the Benders' style. In the spring of 1873, Dr. William York was returning home from visiting his brother, a colonel in the army. His route took him past the Bender establishment. He had mentioned to his brother that he would be stopping over at the Bender place. When Doc York mounted his trusty steed for the trip, he waved goodbye to his brother. The doctor then rode into the sunset, never to be heard from again.

Well, folks, Col. York went looking for his brother and ended up at — you guessed it — the Benders' friendly inn. The Bender group offered to look for the missing doctor. Remember this all took place in 1873 when travelling was sometimes hindered by outlaws, not the least of whom was that well-known chap Jesse James. Anyway, Col. York was satisfied with the Benders and rode off to continue his search for his brother elsewhere.

The Benders figured that with guys like the colonel showing up, it was time to leave the scene. Neighbors first noticed that the house was deserted on May 5, 1873. Soon after, who should show up but Col. York, still looking for his lost brother. The colonel, accompanied by other men, discovered the murder pit under the trap door. It was encrusted with blood. The colonel stood looking out over the Benders' property and noticed several indentations in the pasture.

The men started to dig and ironically, the very first grave uncovered contained the body of Dr. York. The back of his head was crushed and his throat had been cut. In all, eight bodies were taken from the Benders' pasture, including that of a little girl who was unlucky enough to be travelling with her father. During the 18 months in which they operated, the family killed eight innocent people, averaging a victim every 10 weeks.

Later, men were to come forward with little tales of how angry Kate used to became when they chose not to sit at the table with their backs to the canvas. Their random choice of seating arrangements saved their lives.

Just like in the movies, a posse was formed to find the Benders. When members of the posse returned they were extremely grim and close mouthed. Later one of the Benders' wagons was found riddled with bullet holes which gave rise to the rumor that the posse had lynched the Bender family and decided not to talk about it.

You may choose to believe that the Benders got clean away. For 50 years off and on people believed they spotted members of the family. In 1899, the case again received a measure of notoriety when two women were extradited from Detroit in the belief that they were Kate and her mother. When they arrived in Kansas there was a great deal of difficulty in identifying the pair and they were eventually released.

If you're ever down Kansas way, you can drop into the Bender Museum in Cherry-vale and see first hand relics of the Bender clan and their crimes. You will notice a canvas partition dividing the room. While the gentle folks running the museum are hospitable enough, I might suggest that you don't sit with your back to the canvas.

BURIED ALIVE

Some years ago, young Samuel Bronfman, heir to the Bronfman liquor fortune, was kidnapped. A rumor quickly circulated that he was buried alive in a box that had enough air to sustain life for ten days. Fortunately, the rumor proved to be false, and the Bronfman youth was eventually returned to his father unharmed.

The one case where a kidnap victim was actually buried alive was the diabolic kidnapping of Barbara Jane Mackle.

On Dec. 17, 1968, Mrs. Robert Mackle was in Decatur, a suburb of Atlanta, Georgia, visiting her daughter Barbara, who was a student at Emory University. There was a flu epidemic at the school and Barbara couldn't get a bed in the university infirmary. She had a fever, and took a room at the Roadway Inn with her mother, who had arrived in Decatur to take care of her.

In the evening, they responded to a knock on their door. A man, and what they then thought was a young boy, barged in and carried Barbara away in her nightdress. She was driven by car for what she estimated to be fifteen minutes and then carried through thick woods. Her captors kept assuring her that they wouldn't harm her. She couldn't believe her ears when the man told her, "We are going to put you into an underground room."

Then her abductors explained that her room was really an underground capsule made of fibreglass and plywood. The man told her she would have a ventilation fan and a light operated by a battery. Barbara, shivering in only her nightdress, was given a shot of medication to calm her. Then the kidnappers took several pictures. Finally she was unceremoniously slid into the fibreglass box. Once inside, Barbara could hear the lid being screwed down on top of her. She tried reasoning with the man fastening the top of her tomb, but soon experienced the horror of hearing shovels full of earth being dropped on the box. The noise became fainter and fainter and then — nothing, except the devastating silence of literally being buried alive.

Nothing can describe the intelligence and thoroughness of the kidnappers better than the instructions Barbara read, once she was buried in the capsule.

Do not be alarmed you are safe

You are presently inside a fibreglass reinforced plywood capsule buried beneath the ground near the house in which your kidnappers are staying. Your status will be checked approximately every two hours.

The capsule is quite strong. You will not be able to break it open. Be advised, however, that you are beneath the water table. If you should break open a seam you would drown before we could dig you out. The capsule instrumentation contains a water sensitive switch which will warn us if the water enters the capsule to a dangerous degree.

Your life depends on the air delivered to your chamber via the ventilation fan. This fan is powered by a lead-acid storage battery capable of supplying the fan motor with power for 270 hours. However, the use of the light and other systems for only a few hours coupled with the higher amperage drain will reduce this figure to only one week of safety.

Should the air supplied prove to be too much you can partly block the air outlet with a piece of paper. A muffler has been placed in the passage to prevent any noise you make from reaching the surface: If we detect any commotion which we feel is dangerous, we will introduce ether to the air intake and put you to sleep.

The fan operates on 6 volts. It has a switch with two positions to switch between the two available circuits. Should one circuit fail . . . to the other.

The box has a pump which will evacuate any accidental leakage from the box when you turn the pump switch on to the "On" position. This pump uses 15 times as much power as your ventilation fan (7.5 amps); your life support battery will not allow the use of the pump except for emergency water evacuation.

The light uses 2.5 times the amperage of the air circulation system. Use of the light when not necessary will cut your battery safety margin substantially. If you use the light continuously your life expectancy will be cut to one third of the week we have allotted you before you are released.

Your capsule contains a water jug with three gallons of water and a tube from which to drink it. Be careful to blow the water from the tube when you are finished drinking to avoid siphoning the water onto the floor when the tube end drops below the water level.

Your capsule contains a bucket for refuse and the products of your bowel movements. The bucket has an antibacterial solution in it; don't tip it over. The lid seals tightly to prevent the escape of odors. A roll of wax paper is provided — use it to prevent solid waste from contaminating your bed. Kotex is provided should you need it.

Blankets and a mat are provided. Your warmth depends on body heat so regulate the air to prevent loss of heat from the capsule.

A case of candy is provided to furnish energy to your body.

Tranquilizers are provided to aid you in sleeping — the best way you have to pass the time.

The ventilation system is doubly screened to prevent insects or animals from entering the capsule area. You risk being eaten by ants should you break these protection screens.

The electrical components behind these screens are delicate and they support your life. Don't attempt to touch these circuits.

We're sure your father will pay the ransom we have asked in less than one week. When your father pays the ransom we will tell him where you are and he'll come for you. Should he fail to pay we will release you, so be calm and rest — you'll be home for Christmas one way or the other.

In the meantime, Barbara's father, Robert Mackle had been notified of his daughter's abduction. Mackle was a prime kidnapper's target because of his prominence and wealth. He was the largest housing developer in Florida. His organization, the Deltona Corp., had assets in excess of $100 million dollars.

His chief aide and confidante, Billy Vessels, is well-known to Canadians. As a member of the Edmonton Eskimos football team, Vessels had won the Schenley Award as Canada's most outstanding player in 1953. He was at his boss' side throughout his ordeal.

The kidnapper contacted Mackle, and with his usual thoroughness gave explicit instructions where to drop $500,000 in $20 bills. The location was to be near Miami, Florida, where the Mackles live. The F.B.I. and the local authorities agreed to stay in the background until the ransom was paid and the girl returned. Mackle and Vessels successfully dropped off a briefcase containing the money near the ocean in the middle of the night.

Then two unrelated strange events took place. A man who lived close to the shore heard a boat's engine abruptly stop. He looked out his window and saw a man race across his neighbor's property. He called the police. At the same time, two policemen were checking out a Volvo that was suspiciously parked close by. They saw the same man running, and shouted for him to stop. They ran after the fugitive and several shots were exchanged. The stranger dropped a briefcase he was carrying and got away.

They had, without knowing it, stumbled upon the transfer of the ransom money, and recovered it. The Mackle family thought they had signed their daughter's death warrant.

They pleaded via newspapers, radio and T.V., that the whole thing had been a mistake. They wanted the kidnapper to know they still wanted to deliver the money and get their daughter back alive. The very next day a picture of Barbara that the kidnappers had taken before they buried her, arrived in the mail. The kidnappers made contact again, and once more gave complicated directions about where and when to drop off the money. This time Billy Vessels and an F.B.I. agent made a successful drop.

Meanwhile, the F.B.I. had meticulously examined the boat and Volvo that was believed to be used by the kidnappers during the first unsuccessful transfer of the ransom money. The car and boat were full of clues, such as an actual picture of Barbara as well as underwater marine supplies that were traced to the University of Miami Institute of Marine Sciences. These supplies, as well as other property, were traced to an employee of the Institute named Gary Steven Krist, and his girlfriend, a postgraduate student, Ruth Eisemann-Schier. Their past activities were now being traced by the F.B.I.

At an F.B.I. office in Atlanta, a receptionist, Trisha Poindexter, got a phone call from Krist. He gave her the exact location of where Barbara was buried. The F.B.I. raced to the scene. They were at first able to signal to Barbara, and she signalled back to them indicating she was alive. Then as they dug closer to the box, she confirmed she was alright. At last the lid was pried open and a horrendous ordeal had come to an end for Barbara Mackle. She had been buried alive for three days, eleven hours and thirty three minutes.

Now desperate, and with a half million dollars, Krist purchased a boat but was spotted by police aircraft in the Gulf of Mexico. He ran his boat aground on Hog Island, and he took off into the jungle. With the aid of bloodhounds, the F.B.I. captured Krist, who was still holding on to that half million.

Ruth Eisemann-Schier was discovered through a wanted poster in Norman, Oklahoma, living under the assumed name of Donna Mills. She was working as a carhop in a drive-in restaurant.

On May 19, 1969, Gary Krist stood trial for kidnapping. After deliberating four hours and five minutes, the jury found him guilty. He was sentenced to life imprisonment. A few days later Ruth Eisemann-Schier received seven years imprisonment.

LEOPOLD AND LOEB

Of the thousands of murders which take place throughout the world, only a handful are remembered for any length of time. One of those which has gained a unique place in the annals of crime is the Leopold and Loeb case. Billed as the crime of the century and later the trial of the century, the old Chicago murder received world wide publicity. So keen was interest in the case that minutes after details were revealed they were splashed across the newspapers of the capitol cities of Europe.

To fully comprehend the unusual aspects of the case we must delve into the lives and, indeed, the minds of the two main characters involved in the murder, namely Nathan (Babe) Leopold, and Richard (Dickie) Loeb.

Both boys were born and raised in Chicago. Their parents were multi-millionaires. Loeb's father was a retired manufacturer, while Leopold's was still active as the vice-president of Sears-Roebuck, the giant U.S. catalogue house. The boys had been brought up in the lap of luxury, and were quite accustomed to chauffeur driven cars, butlers, and servants.

Friends practically from birth, both attended Harvard Preparatory School, where they were top students. Loeb, considered something of a genius, graduated from the University of Michigan at the age of seventeen. Leopold was the youngest honors student attending the University of Chicago. At the time, he had studied and spoke Greek, Latin, Russian, German, French, English and Sanskrit.

While specializing in languages, Leopold's real love was ornithology. His knowledge of this subject was so extensive he often took younger students on field trips to study various species of birds in their natural habitat. He also gave lectures on the subject.

While still in their early teens the boys read and were greatly influenced by the philosophy of Nietzsche. His superman theory appealed to the brilliant minds of the wealthy, bored teenagers. Could it be true that man-made laws did not apply to the intellectually superior? If so, then whatever the superior Leopold and Loeb decided to do would be the correct and proper thing. They concluded that they were really supermen, operating outside the laws which govern ordinary men.

To prove their personal theory they decided to perform criminal acts for the sheer pleasure of the exercise. Nothing spectacular, but fulfilling enough to prove their superiority. During their petty criminal spree, Leopold, who was unemotional about most subjects, became fascinated by his belief that his buddy Dickie Loeb was superior to him, and was therefore his master. Leopold relished the idea that he was Dickie's slave.

These two brilliant young men were now operating in a slave-master relationship. When the master Loeb suggested criminal activity, Leopold the slave thought it was an extraordinary idea. Certainly neither cared for any monetary gain derived from their crimes. The idea was to prove that ordinary laws didn't apply to supermen.

In November, 1923, Dickie Loeb, 18, and Nathan Leopold, 19, robbed Leopold's fraternity house. The boys netted $74 in cash, some jewelry, a typewriter, and assorted junk. They had worn masks and carried flashlights. While returning from this successful caper, Loeb had another brilliant idea. Why not kidnap someone and collect ransom money? Only he and Nathan would ever know the real identity of the kidnappers. What a way to prove one's superiority — to get away with kidnapping, murder, and even collecting ransom money. Leopold thought it was a great idea. They would meticulously plan the crime, eliminating all possible chances of detection.

Dickie and Nathan bought a chisel. It would be used to club their victim. They decided to purchase some rope to fasten around their victim's throat, so that each could pull an end. In this way, both of them would be equally responsible for the murder. They worked out an elaborate plan to dispose of the body and collect the ransom money. Little preference was expressed regarding the choice of a victim. Dickie's sister was considered, but rejected. It really didn't matter that much. They would pick their victim at random.

On May 21, 1924, while Chicago was experiencing an unseasonable hot spell, the two boys rented a car, a Willys-Knight. Leopold left his own car parked in his garage at home. The boys cruised around in the Willys-Knight looking for a victim. They parked near their old alma mater, the Harvard Preparatory School. A 14-year-old cousin of Loeb's walked by. The two boys engaged him in conversation. They told the younger boy they were going to look at some tennis rackets and would appreciate some advice. Bobby Franks jumped into the car. In ten minutes he would be dead.

Still within sight of Leopold's home, Bobby was struck a vicious blow to the head with the chisel. He slumped to the floor. Fearing that he was only stunned, the boys rained blow after blow down onto their hapless victim's head until he lay still. The car drove slowly through Chicago's streets. The killers were waiting until nightfall before disposing of their cargo.

On the southern rim of Chicago, there was an old swamp beside some railroad tracks. Leopold had been there many times before on field trips, studying birds with his students. Little Bobby Franks was carried from the car. His body was stripped and liberally sprinkled with acid. Finally, the body was stuffed inside a culvert.

Leopold and Loeb returned to Loeb's house and burned Bobby Franks' clothing in the furnace. Now operating according to a prearranged plan, Leopold called Bobby Franks' father, informing him that his son had been kidnapped. Using the name George Johnson, he told the anxious father that his son was safe and that further instructions would follow.

The next day, Sven Englund, the Leopold family chauffeur observed the two boys cleaning out the back of the Willys-Knight. He offered to give them a hand, but the boys said that they could handle it. It seems they had spilled some red wine on the back seat and floor, but it was coming out nicely. Sven thought it odd that Nathan would rent a car while his own had been sitting in the garage all the day before. Sven never expressed his opinion at the time, as he had long since ceased trying to figure out the idiosyncrasies of the very rich.

The boys had a busy day before them, for this was the day that Jacob Franks was supposed to receive the ransom letter. It arrived at his home promptly that morning. It follows word for word:

Dear Sir,

As you no doubt know by this time, your son has been kidnapped. Allow me to reassure you that he is at present well and safe. You need fear no physical harm for him, providing you live up carefully to the following instructions, and such others as you will receive by future communications. Should you, however, disobey any of our instructions, even slightly, death will be the penalty.

1. For obvious reasons, make absolutely no attempt to communicate with either the police authorities or any private agency. Should you already have communi-

cate with the police, allow them to continue their investigations, but do not mention this letter.

2. Secure, before noon today, $10,000. This money must be composed entirely of old bills of the following denominations:

$2,000 in $20 bills

$8,000 in $50 bills

The money must be old. Any attempt to include new or marked bills will render the entire venture futile.

3. The money should be placed in a large cigar box, or if such is impossible, in a heavy cardboard box, securely closed and wrapped in white paper. The wrapping paper should be sealed at all openings with sealing wax.

4. Have the money thus prepared as directed above, and remain home after one o'clock p.m. See that the telephone is not in use.

You will receive further communications instructing you as to your future course.

As a final word of warning, this is a strictly commercial proposition, and we are prepared to put our threats into execution, should we have reasonable ground to believe that you have committed an infraction of the above instructions. However, should you carefully follow out our instructions to the letter, we can assure you that your son will be safely returned to you within six hours of our receipt of the money.

Yours truly,
George Johnson

Leopold and Loeb planned carefully. They phoned the distraught Jacob Franks, who had by now complied with every demand made of him. He had the money securely wrapped as instructed. The phone rang. A voice told him to take a cab which would shortly arrive at his home. He was to take the cab to a drugstore on 63rd St., where he would receive further instructions.

The plan was to have Franks reach 63rd St., where he would be told to catch the 3:18 p.m. train at Central Station. He would just have time to make the train. Once on the train he was to proceed to the observation car, where he would find a letter in a rack. This letter, already planted there, would instruct Mr. Franks to toss the package off the east side of the train as it passed the Champion Manufacturing Co. factory. There, Dickie Loeb would be waiting in a car to retrieve the package. The boys had rehearsed the entire procedure many times. The plan appeared foolproof.

Mr. Franks was peering out his window looking for the cab when the phone rang. It was the police, informing him that his son was dead.

Meanwhile, Leopold couldn't understand why Franks wasn't answering the phone at the drugstore. As he passed a newspaper stand he spotted the reason. The headlines of one of the dailies stated, "Unidentified Boy Found in Swamp". Nathan picked up Dickie and told him the news. Some laborers had taken a shortcut across the swamp and, by chance, had come across the body of Bobby Franks. They had immediately informed the police.

While news of the chance discovery of the body had shattered their master plan to collect ransom money, it did nothing to connect them with the murder. The boys got rid of the typewriter on which they had typed the ransom note, as well as the chisel used to club Bobby Franks to death.

During the following days Nathan and Dickie derived great pleasure discussing the case with their family and friends. Dickie particularly joined in discussion with detectives investigating the crime. He offered all kinds of theories and seemed to be thoroughly enjoying himself.

The police were doing all right on their own. While searching the terrain where the body was found they came up with a pair of spectacles with unusual rims. They traced the spectacles to an optician who was able to give the police some startling information. He had sold only three pairs of glasses with the identifiable rims. One pair was purchased by a man who was currently in Europe, one pair by an elderly lady who still had possession of them, and the third pair had been purchased by Nathan Leopold.

Police questioned Leopold about his glasses. He swore they were exactly like his, but his were at home. Taken to his home by police, he couldn't find his glasses. However, he explained that he had been in that swamp studying birds on dozens of occasions and his glasses could have dropped out of his pocket. His explanation sounded reasonable enough. Then he was asked the routine question. Could he account for his movements on May 21, the day Bobby Franks was kidnapped?

The two boys had planned the murder for five months and had an answer for every eventuality. Nathan said he had been driving around in his car all day with Dickie Loeb looking for girls. Loeb gave the same answer when he was questioned separately.

Did Leopold own a typewriter? Nathan admitted that he did, but a search of his home failed to produce it. The police were successful in locating classmates of Leopold's who had used his typewriter. They turned over several typewritten pages to the police. Upon examining these pages, experts stated that the same typewriter which had produced the student notes had been used to type the ransom letter to Mr. Franks.

Sven Englund, the Leopold's chauffeur, stated that Nathan couldn't have been driving his car May 21. It was parked in the family garage all that day. He remembered well, because he had offered to help clean red wine stains from the back seat of a Willys-Knight the boys had been driving that day.

The perfect crime had crumbled away to dust. Both boys confessed, outlining in detail the entire plan and its execution.

The Leopold and Loeb families sought out Clarence Darrow, perhaps the most able defense lawyer who ever walked into court. Darrow had a reputation of accepting and winning hopeless and unpopular cases. The distraught families of the two boys pleaded with the famous lawyer to defend their sons. They didn't want the boys to die on the gallows, and felt if anyone could get them a life sentence, Clarence Darrow was that man.

They were right. Darrow accepted the case and from the outset admitted that his clients had taken Bobby Franks' life in just the manner which they had outlined in their confessions. Leopold and Loeb pleaded guilty but, to everyone's surprise, not by reason of insanity. Darrow claimed they were sane under the legal definition of the term. They did know right from wrong, but Darrow stated they could still be mentally ill and that this should be brought to the attention of the court.

Darrow was successful in having his case heard before a judge, and was allowed to present his unusual evidence. The most respected psychiatrists in the country testified as to the mental state of the two boys. Those appearing for the defense all agreed that they were far from normal. Conversely, the state brought forth medical opinions stating that the two defendents were sane and responsible for their actions. The two opposing medical teams took a full month to present their evidence.

Clarence Darrow made his final plea for the lives of Leopold and Loeb. He spoke for three full days. Many consider his mammoth three-day dissertation the finest ever given in a courtroom anywhere. In essence he pointed out that vengeance is not the primary consideration in a murder trial, that at one time in England there were over one thousand offenses punishable by death. He felt his clients had to be mentally diseased to devise such a diabolical plot. Most of all, Darrow attacked capital punishment as a barbaric, vengeful act which, if practised on the defendents would make the state itself an instrument of murder.

On July 21, 1924, Leopold and Loeb were sentenced to life imprisonment with a rider on their sentences that they never be paroled. The gates of Joliet Prison closed behind the two millionaires' sons. Dickie Loeb was stabbed to death in a shower stall by a fellow convict in 1936.

Leopold became active in the prison educational system, and was instrumental in perfecting and improving the system. He also completed an in-depth study of how certain men would behave once they were paroled. During the Second World War he volunteered to be bitten by infected mosquitoes to assist in discovering a cure for malaria.

After serving 25 years in prison, Leopold applied for parole, but the judge's rider to his sentence proved an insurmountable obstacle. Eight years later, in 1958, after serving 33 years, six months and two days in prison, Nathan Leopold was paroled. He went to work for $10 a week as a laboratory technician in a hospital in Puerto Rico. He attended the University of Puerto Rico, where he received his Master's degree. He taught at the university, as well as doing research for Puerto Rico's Department of Health, specializing in leprosy.

In Feb., 1961, Nathan married the middle-aged widow of a San Juan doctor. In 1963, at the age of 58, he was released from his parole. He had served just under 40 years, and at last was a totally free man.

On Aug. 30, 1971, Nathan Leopold suffered a heart attack. He was rushed to Mimya Hospital in San Juan, where he died. Leopold donated his body to the University of Puerto Rico's School of Medicine for research purposes.

THE RED LIGHT BANDIT

Caryl Chessman was probably the most famous prisoner who ever lived. For almost twelve years he was a living symbol for individuals and organizations who believed capital punishment is barbaric and should be abolished. At the same time, the crimes for which he was convicted were heinous. Many felt he deserved to be put to death.

Born in St. Joseph, Mich., on May 27, 1921, the first nine years of Caryl's life were uneventful. His parents, Hallie and Serl Chessman, were lower middle-class, hard working and God fearing. The family fell on hard times in 1930, when Mrs. Chessman was severely injured in an automobile accident. She was left paralyzed from the waist down and was destined never to walk again. The crushing expenses of the accident placed added hardships on the family. They moved to a poorer neighborhood to make ends meet.

By the time Caryl was twelve, he was stealing food. He graduated to car theft at the age of fourteen. Chessman's record reads like the case history of a punk on his way to inflicting pain and misery on his fellow human beings.

In 1937, he was apprehended for auto theft and placed in an industrial school. A few months after his release, he was sent to a reformatory. By 1941, Chessman was a brutal, lawless hoodlum, making his living off crime. He never denied the accusation.

In 1941, he was incarcerated in San Quentin prison on four counts of first degree robbery and one count of assault with a deadly weapon. He escaped from San Quentin, but was quickly recaptured. Late in 1947, he was released on parole. It was within days of his release that the saga of Caryl Chessman really begins.

Coincidental with Chessman's release, a bandit began terrorizing the Los Angeles area. The lone bandit preyed on couples parked in secluded lovers' lanes. His gray Ford coupe was outfitted with a red light, a duplicate of those affixed to police cars. The Red Light Bandit, as he was called, would sneak up on young lovers, flash his red light, and ask the unsuspecting occupants for identification. Thinking that a policeman was conducting a routine check, the young people quickly produced their wallets and purses. He would then level a .45 calibre revolver at them and relieve them of their money.

Sometimes he would do more. At random he would pick a female passenger and take her with him. Three times he raped his victims, and forced them into acts of sexual perversion. One such victim, 17-year-old Mary Alice Meza, was held for over three hours by the Red Light Bandit before being released.

On the night of Jan. 23, 1948, two police officers, James Reardon and Robert May, spotted a vehicle which matched the description of the Red Light Bandit's car. They signalled the wanted car to pull over. The driver of the car, Caryl Chessman, stepped on the gas. A wild chase ensued, with the police officers gradually gaining on the wanted car. Finally the officers rammed the gray Ford. Chessman was taken into custody.

The Ford contained loot from a robbery which had taken place earlier in the evening. The vehicle had been stolen in Pasadena shortly before the Red Light Bandit had started his operations. Besides stolen goods, the police uncovered a .45 calibre revolver and a pen-type flashlight, similar to one used during the kidnapping of the girls from the parked vehicles.

Chessman, who stood six feet, seemed taller than the Red Light Bandit. Despite this discrepancy, many of his victims did not hesitate to identify him.

As a result of the public response to the famous Lindbergh kidnapping case, California had enacted a law which became known as the little Lindbergh law. In essence, it stated that kidnapping with bodily harm, with intent to commit robbery, was a capital offence. Technically the victim could be moved a matter of inches, and the kidnapper would become subject to the death penalty. Chessman was indicted on three counts of kidnapping, and fifteen counts of robbery.

Chessman chose to conduct his own defense. He was found guilty of 15 counts of robbery and two of kidnapping and received two death sentences.

His trial was strange in many ways. Shortly after he was arrested, Chessman confessed to being the Red Light Bandit. By the time he stood trial he repudiated his confession, saying he was a victim of coincidence and mistaken identity. He claimed detectives had beaten him into making the false confession.

During the course of the trial, the presiding judge let it be known that he thought the accused man was guilty. As a result of his animosity toward Chessman he denied the accused access to the transcript of the daily proceedings. Normally the defendant is allowed to see the daily transcript. It is his right.

To further confuse matters, the court appointed shorthand reporter dropped dead of a heart attack two days before the end of the trial. At the time of his sudden demise, the report was only one third complete. The court ordered another reporter to transcribe the balance of the trial with the assistance of the presiding judge and a deputy. The newly appointed reporter was the brother-in-law of the deputy. Eventually, the judge, the deputy and the new reporter officially approved the final transcript. The defendant Chessman never saw it.

Based on the fact that his constitutional rights had been violated, Chessman was granted a reprieve. Instead of languishing on death row in San Quentin, he turned his cell into a study capsule. There, far into the night, he studied law. In the opinion of many, he became a competent lawyer. He gained reprieve after reprieve as the months turned into years.

Chessman was found to have an I.Q. of 138, the highest ever recorded by any inmate of San Quentin. During his sixth year on death row, he wrote a book *Cell 2455 Death Row*, and had it smuggled out of prison. The book was a bestseller and provided Chessman with the funds he needed to carry on the battle to save his own life.

Many of his reprieves did not come through until the execution date. On more than one occasion he was almost on his way to the gas chamber when some legal ploy or other saved him.

Two further books, *Trial by Ordeal* and *The Face of Justice*, followed, making Chessman, the condemned convict, a well known author. News of his plight spread beyond the United States, making his case the battle cry of abolitionists all over the world.

As each new execution date was set, a public outcry would take place. Many thought Chessman had suffered enough. Famous writers and lawyers interviewed him on Death Row. All came away impressed. Others thought he should pay the supreme price for his crime. The mother of Mary Alice Meza thought so. Her daughter became mentally ill, and never fully recovered from her three hours spent with Chessman.

In all, the 38-year-old Chessman had been reprieved a record eight times over a period of just under 12 years. On an average he faced the gas chamber every 18 months for the last 12 years of his life.

On May 2, 1960, time ran out for Caryl Chessman. Despite thousands of appeals from all over the world, the condemned man was led to the gas chamber. At exactly 1:03 p.m. E.D.T. a bag of cyanide pellets was dropped into a small vat of sulphuric acid. Nine minutes passed before Chessman was pronounced dead.

Later it was revealed that Chessman was about to be granted a one hour stay of execution. The telephone call had been received at precisely 1:04 p.m. It was too late. The pellets had already been dropped.

Chessman's last words were uttered to Warden Fred Dickson as he was led into the gas chamber. He told the warden that he was not the Red Light Bandit.

ST. VALENTINE'S DAY MASSACRE

In all the annals of U.S. crime, one man has become synonymous with American gangsterism. That man is Al Capone. The very name brings to mind images of fast cars, fast guns, fast women, and rivers of booze, as well it should, for Al Capone was surrounded by all of these and much more. He was to attain a stranglehold on the rackets of Cook County, Ill., and its major city, Chicago.

Al was a small time robber and killer at the age of 21 when Johnny Torrio picked him from the hundreds of hoods who made Chicago their headquarters. Torrio may have been the first to realize that there was a fortune to be made in illegal beer and liquor during prohibition. He picked big, pudgy Alphonse "Scarface" Capone because of his reputation for being hard as nails and twice as cruel.

In a few short years, the partnership of Torrio and Capone controlled the Chicago suburb of Cicero. The partners were splitting $200,000 per week. They were into everything: beer, liquor, gambling, and prostitution. They were ambitious men who wanted more money and more power, but there were other notorious gangs who controlled other sections of greater Chicago.

Dion O'Banion, a mild mannered little florist, with an estimated 20 killings to his credit, controlled the rackets in certain sections of the city. On Nov. 4, 1924, three men walked into O'Banion's flower shop. One of the men shook hands with Dion as six slugs poured into his body. He was dead before he hit the floor. Al Capone had removed another competitor on his climb up the ladder. The hoods of Chicago sent O'Banion out in style. There were 28 truckloads of flowers valued at over $55,000 at his funeral. One basket of roses contained a card. It said simply, "From Al."

Thousands, including Capone, attended the opulent funeral. Some noticed that Dion's head was lying to one side. There was a reason for the odd angle. You see, one side of his head was blown away.

Retaliation followed O'Banion's death in the form of an attempt on Al's life. By luck and caution, he avoided being killed, but another threat loomed in the shadows of Chicago's underworld. His name was Earl "Little Hymie" Weiss, and a more vicious killer never lived. It is said that Capone feared only one man in his life, and that man was "Little Hymie." Weiss and O'Banion had been friends, and Weiss now took over the O'Banion gang. It was he who had organized the unsuccessful attempt on Capone's life. Al knew that Weiss was the only obstacle standing between him and his taking over as king of Chicago's rackets.

Al's boys took two rooms overlooking Weiss' hangout. One fine day as he got out of his car, they shot him dead. There were ten bullet holes in "Little Hymie's" body.

For a while Capone had his way, and the magnitude of his empire boggles the imagination. Politicians, judges, police, and hoods alike all wanted to be Al's friend. He could make them or break them with a nod of his head. Big Al had an estimated 12,000 speakeasies in Chicago, all being supplied with beer and liquor, which he either made or smuggled into the country. He controlled, either directly or indirectly, an army of over 700 gangsters. Alphonse Capone had come a long way — his income was estimated at over six million dollars a week, or just under a million a day. He patrolled his domain in a bullet proof touring car which had been made for him at a cost of $20,000. He travelled with an entourage which included 18 body guards, and a bevy of beautiful ladies. Al maintained two palatial homes in Chicago, and an estate on Palm Island, just off Miami Beach.

All minor threats to his kingdom were eliminated as they vied for power. Only one enemy returned to haunt Capone. The old O'Banion gang, now under the leadership of Bugs Moran, had managed to infringe on Capone's speakeasy business to the extent of pushing Capone's product out of 29 establishments. Besides, they had hijacked nine truckloads of liquor coming across the border from Canada. Capone was furious — Moran had to go.

Capone called a war council, and the job of annihilating Bugs Moran was entrusted to Jack McGurn. McGurn, who had been given the honor over the notorious Frank Nitti because he knew some of Moran's habits, went about his task with military efficiency. Two professional assassins, Paul Salvanti and Alex "Bobo" Borotto, rented a room on

North Clark St. overlooking the SMC Cartage Co. garage which was used by Moran as one of his many headquarters. When they paid nine dollars for a week's rent in advance, the landlady warned them that they couldn't practise their violas. It was obvious they were musicians, as both men carried viola cases. When the landlady finished showing them the room, Paul and "Bobo" set up their Thompson submachine guns.

After the room was secured and the machine guns successfully hidden, McGurn called a meeting. Besides Salvanti and Borotto, McGurn had recruited six other professional killers. He explained that on the following Friday, Valentine's Day, Feb. 14, 1929, Moran would be visiting the garage. Several other members of his gang would be there as well. Salvanti and Borotto were given a picture of Moran, who would be readily recognizable because he always wore brown. As soon as he entered the garage Salvanti and Borotto would make a telephone call from the payphone in the hall of their rooming house. This call would serve as a signal for McGurn's plan to swing into motion. Awaiting the signal were two of the professional killers dressed as policemen. They would swoop down on the garage in a police car and take control of all the occupants of the garage. Two more companions would enter the garage, and together McGurn's men would annihilate everyone in the building. If by some miracle Moran escaped the fusillade and got out of the building, Salvanti and Borotto had their Thompson submachine guns trained on the door.

McGurn phoned Capone at his Palm Island estate to let him know that everything was set. When informed that it was to happen on Valentine's Day, Capone is reported to have said, "Ain't that a hot one. A Valentine for Bugs. Say, Jack, make sure it's a great big red Valentine."

Valentine's Day rolled around, and Borotto and Salvanti took up their stand in the rooming house overlooking Moran's garage. As the two men peered out the window, men started to wander into the garage, singly and in groups of two. In all, the signalmen watched six men enter the garage. They started to get nervous; no one told them there would be that many — all they wanted was Moran. All of a sudden a man dressed in brown came into view. Borotto and Salvanti had a quick discussion. They couldn't see his face clearly, but the clothing was brown. He had the right build and was the right height, it had to be him. They rushed to the phone down the hall and gave the signal that Moran was now in the trap. Capone's police car swung down Clark St. A short distance away, walking towards the same destination, was Bugs Moran and two henchmen. The lookouts had identified the wrong man. Moran wasn't in the garage. Spotting the police car, Bugs thought it was a raid of some kind and decided to wait out the action in a nearby restaurant.

Inside the garage, the seven members of Moran's gang knew nothing except that all of a sudden their mascot, a German shepherd dog, started to growl. Then two uniformed officers burst into the room. The men, who felt they were above interference with the police, at first thought someone was playing a joke on them.

The two uniformed policemen disarmed the seven captives and lined them up against the wall. Two more gunmen joined the bogus cops, and all opened fire. In five seconds more than one hundred .45 calibre slugs tore into the seven men. One man, Frank Gusenberg, lived through the initial onslaught only to die the same day in hospital. The German shepherd dog was the only living thing to escape without a scratch. All the killers left the garage in an orderly manner, and got away clean.

Back in the restaurant, a passerby ran in and informed the occupants that Bugs Moran had just been killed. Moran's face went white.

Later, when questioned about the killings, which were forever after known as the St. Valentine's Day Massacre, Bugs Moran was quoted as saying, "Only Al Capone kills that way." When Capone was questioned he could only say that at the time of the killings he was attending an amicable meeting with the district attorney in Miami.

No one ever stood trial for the St. Valentine's Day Massacre, but within two years the men who actually fired the fatal shots were all dead. They were either killed by police during the commission of crimes or were assassinated gangland style by other gangsters. The era that gave rise to huge profits and the power it gave men like Al Capone came to an end with the repeal of the National Prohibition Act on Dec. 5, 1933.

Al Capone was finally cornered by the law. He received a prison sentence of 11 years for income tax evasion, and actually served eight. Al lived well in jail, but an earlier case of syphillis began to affect his brain. He retired to his estate on Palm Island and died a syphillitic lunatic in January, 1947, at the age of 52.

Bugs Moran left Chicago after the attempt on his life by Capone. Nearly 20 years later he was convicted on a charge of bank robbery, and received a sentence of 110 years in Leavenworth Penitentiary in Kansas. The man who wasn't in the garage on Valentine's Day outlived them all. He died of lung cancer while serving his prison sentence.

ICE PICKS AND
THE MAFIA

Cosa Nostra — Mafia — Black Hand — the names are synonymous with organized crime. How did it all begin? Where did it all begin? Where did they come from? Who are the men at the top who give the orders? This is the story of one man, whose career parallels the emergence of the Mafia in North America. His name is Umberto Anastasio.

* * *

When France invaded Sicily at the end of the 18th century, a band of guerrilla fighters formed to resist the hated invaders. The word Mafia was used to describe the resistance movement. Some say the word was derived from the first letters of the words "Morte alla Francia Italia anela" — Death to the French is the Cry of Italy.

In order to raise the necessary funds to support the resistance movement, the Mafiosi levied a sort of tax or compulsory contribution on local peasants, most of whom contributed willingly to the men who were attemping to drive the despised French from their land. Merchants and other businessmen were not as willing to support the Mafia, but threats of kidnapping and physical damage to their assets usually brought on a spasm of patriotism in the form of healthy contributions of hard cash.

The French eventually were driven out of Sicily, but the Mafia didn't disband. The gang of former resistance fighters now harrassed Italian law enforcement agencies. Again, they had some support from the peasant population who distrusted soldiers and police, particularly those sent over from mainland Italy.

The gang continued to be an adventurous, glamorous, secretive society to young Italians who sought admission. As the years passed, its popular causes faded, and the very peasants who supported them now fell prey to the scavenger society they had helped create. Robbery, extortion, and murder on a scale never before dreamed of eventually brought the Italian government down hard on the Mafia.

In the 1880s, Italian police launched an all out war against Mafia corruption. They managed to jail scores of Mafiosi, hang some, and shoot many more who resisted capture. It became so hot in Sicily that many Mafiosi migrated to America. Although they brought their ritual initiation ceremonies and secretive code to the new world, it wasn't until 1890 that they made big news. They murdered New Orleans' police chief David Hennessy.

The Mafia at this time was made up of poor peasants who found comfort in belonging to the loosely knit gang. Their code of conduct was strange in many ways. It was acceptable to beat, even kill, fellow immigrants, but Mafia members were looked down upon if they used foul language. A Mafia member could run a string of brothels, but it was unacceptable if he was unfaithful to his wife. Usually he was a good family man and, above all, a regular church goer.

In the tiny Italian town of Tropea, the Anastasio family was celebrating the birth of yet another son, Umberto. For the first 12 years of his life there was little to distinguish Umberto from the rest of the children of Tropea. At the age of 12 he left school to work as a cabin boy on an Italian steamer. It was Umberto's initial introduction to boats, an association which was to last for over forty years.

It wasn't long before Umberto was elevated to the position of deckhand. In 1917, the black haired, good looking young man with the driving ambition landed in New York. Umberto Anastasio changed his name to Albert Anastasia and got a job on the docks.

Young Albert had picked the right time and the right place. The Mafia was taking a long look at the docks as a potential source of income. In 1919, Albert joined the secret society. He was 18. With the Mafia organization at the control, theft on the New York docks skyrocketed, but the big pickings were still to come.

In 1920, Prohibition became law in the U.S. What this actually meant to the Mafia is hard for us to fathom today. The figures are so large they tend to become meaningless. In one year the American public consumed almost one-billion gallons of alcohol in one form or another. Half of the total was smuggled into the country, and the other half was produced illegally. Hundreds of thousands of people were employed in illegal activities associated with liquor. The possibilities were unlimited, and the Mafia took advantage of every possibility.

Within a year, the organization was wealthy. As a Mafia member, Anastasia enjoyed the prosperity. He graduated from dockhand to liquor distributor, pulling down money which a few months previous would have been beyond his wildest dreams.

Anastasia's boss, Salvatore "Lucy" Luciano, kept his eye on Albert. He looked like a comer, a boy with a future in the organization. First, of course, he would have to be tested.

A dockhand, George Turello, needed killing. Anastasia was acquainted with Turello, having worked with him on the docks. What better way to test Albert's loyalty than to appoint him executioner. Young, gentle Albert Anastasia, who had never committed a violent act in his life, didn't waver. Ten days later Turello was dead.

Anastasia and a friend were immediately picked up, tried, and convicted of murder. Albert was dispatched to Sing Sing to await the death sentence. Not once did he plead for mercy nor did he attempt to incriminate others. Now the Mafia, too, was being tested.

For 19-year-old, close mouthed Anastasia, the stakes were his life. The organization didn' let him down. A battery of lawyers was employed by the mobsters. They went to work and managed to obtain a new trial on a technicality. By the time the trial date rolled around the four main prosecution witnesses had disappeared. Vanished into thin air. Not one speck of evidence, nor any trace of the four witnesses has been uncovered to this day. Charges against Anastasia were dropped. Later he was charged with the murder of the four disappearing witnesses, but these charges too were dropped for lack of evidence.

During the course of his career, Anastasia was responsible for over 50 murders. Most were carried out by others, but in the early days it was necessary for him to prove himself to his superiors. Luciano liked Albert's style.

Anastasia's next hit was Carmello Ferraro, an ambitious man, who tried to set up a bootlegging establishment in Mafia territory. He should have known better. Within days he was the late Mr. Ferraro. Again, Albert was arrested and charged with murder, and again the charges were dismissed due to lack of evidence.

Anastasia was now a full time hit man employed by the organization. Police finally were able to put him away in 1923 for two years. Ironically, the charge they nailed the multiple murderer with was carrying an unlicensed gun.

During the two years Albert spent in prison, both he and the Mafia underwent a change. Now highly organized, the Mafia looted the New York waterfront, not only by open stealing, but by having their members elected as union officials. It was neat, clean, and profitable. Anyone who got in their way was killed.

After his release, Anastasia never again carried a gun. From the time he left prison his personal instrument of death was to be a utensil found in almost every home in America — an icepick.

* * *

When Anastasia walked out of prison, his superior, Joe Adonis, had a new position waiting for him. Albert became the superintendent of six union locals. He now had an income from dock pilferage, bootlegging, and a salary from the union. Not bad for a man fresh out of prison. Anastasia knew what he was doing. Soon, as lord of the docks, he was importing labor from Italy. Each man was intensely loyal to the benafactor who had brought him to the new world. That, and a closed mouth was all Albert demanded.

Two personal killings solidified Anastasia's position as an enforcer on the waterfront. John Bazzano and Carmine Cenatiempe were both exterminated. Anastasia used his favorite weapon — an icepick.

As in all large organizations, a changing economy brought about changes in leadership. In 1933, President Roosevelt repealed Prohibition, and in one fell swoop cut off the Mafia's most lucrative source of income. Joe "The Boss" Masseria moved or was firmly shoved aside as leader of the Mafia. Lucky Luciano took over the reins of the American operation.

Times were different. The crazy twenties had run their course and came tumbling down on notorious Black Friday of 1929. The U.S. was enduring its greatest test. The Great Depression hung heavy over the land.

Luciano called a conference in New York. Mafia kingpins Joe Adonis, Willie Moretti, and Frank Costello were in attendance. From all over the nation they came. Some were not Mafia members, but all controlled lucrative territories. "Bugsy" Siegal, "King" Solomon, "Longie" Zwillman, and perhaps the most powerful of them all, Meyer Lansky, sat side by side with their Mafia brothers in crime.

By mutual consent, territories were defined. Monopolies of corruption, theft, prostitution, and anything which could turn a dollar were distributed. Rules and regulations were laid out to cover every eventuality. From this time forward there would be no indiscriminate killings. The new organization, known as The Syndicate or Combination, would set up its own enforcement arm to police its members and anyone who infringed on the members' territories. The enforcement arm could not be used to settle personal disputes or grudges, only to take care of affairs common to the organization.

Who was ruthless enough and still had the organizational ability to run the enforcement arm of the Syndicate? Joe Adonis was the one who picked Albert Anastasia. Unfortunately, Albert was tied up for a month or so. He had just killed Joseph Santori. Naturally he was acquitted. Once again, all the prosecution witnesses had disappeared.

Anastasia took to his new assignment like a duck takes to water. He set up the machinery of what was later to become known as Murder Inc., with himself as its head. He picked as his second in command professional assassin Louis "Lepke" Buchalter, a man who would kill his best friend without question if given the command. Murder Inc. was unique. Nothing like it had ever been tried before. Under Anastasia's leadership it operated like a well-oiled machine.

Syndicate members picked their victims as carefully as a business executive makes a major business decision. The victim may have squealed on a Syndicate member, or infringed on a closed territory. Proof was required, but once the die was cast there was no reprieve. A professional assassin was assigned the contract. He never met the victim, but was given his photograph and habits to study. The hit man was always from a different city. After the killing the assassin would fly back to his home base. Neat, efficient, and above all, there was never any connection between killer and victim.

As the supreme head of such an organization, Anastasia now became known as "Lord High Executioner", which indeed he was. For five years Murder Inc. killed with impunity. It is estimated that 100 murders were committed over that period, more than one every three weeks for five full years.

In 1939, it appeared that a crack had formed in the Syndicate's code of silence. Brooklyn District Attorney William O'Dwyer arrested a Syndicate lieutenant, Abe "Kid Twist" Reles. In return for police protection, Reles was willing to talk. He told of eleven personal killings, and was willing to divulge Syndicate secrets. O'Dwyer stashed him in a hotel on Coney Island, under heavy police protection. With uniformed police supposedly inside the room and outside the door, Reles' body was found on the pavement below his fourth floor window.

From Reles' statements the authorities were able to send five members of Murder Inc., including Buchalter, to the electric chair at Sing Sing. Murder Inc. scattered. Anastasia joined the army. Later, when his record caught up with him, he was unceremoniously mustered out. In the meantime, Lucky Luciano was deported to Italy. Vito Genovese was now chief of the Mafia. Anastasia returned to his old haunts along the New York docks. The law, desperate to nail him for something, finally put him away for one year on income tax evasion.

After his release, things were never the same for Anastasia. A man who always took good personal care of himself, he now had developed a slight paunch. The jet black hair was sprinkled with gray. Maybe Anastasia had lost a little of his former finesse. A bungled assassination attempt on Costello's life was hinted to be Anastasia's responsibility. Undaunted by what should have been a major setback to his career, Anastasia swam toward still more dangerous waters.

One night at a dinner party, Anastasia announced with pride that he was taking over the gambling concession of one of Cuba's most luxurious watering holes. Albert's guests almost choked on their pasta. Everybody knew Meyer Lanksy owned Cuba, lock, stock and barrel. Not only was Lansky an avowed ally of the Mafia, but he counted as his personal friends all the Mafia leaders. If this wasn't enough, the frosting on the cake was Fulgencio Batista, dictator of Cuba, who was the power behind Lansky. In fact, Batista was really Lansky's partner, himself skimming off millions from the gambling industry.

Anastasia had taken on a group of powerful men. Wily old Lansky did all the right things. He let it be known that his friend Batista didn't approve of Mr. Anastasia's plans. Anastasia replied, "I'm coming to Cuba no matter what he says." That sentence was tantamount to a death warrant.

Ten days later, on Oct. 25, 1957, at precisely 10:15 a.m., Anastasia walked into the barber shop of the Park Sheraton Hotel in New York City. While the barber was busy clipping his hair, two men walked in wearing sun glasses and hats pulled down over their eyes. One said to the barber, "Keep your mouth shut, if you don't want your head blown off." With that statement, the two gunsels fired 10 bullets toward the old mobster. Five missed, but five found their target. Anastasia lay still in death on the barbershop floor.

The two killers turned and walked out of the hotel. They dropped their guns at rear exit. One was an ancient 1934 Colt .38 revolver, the other a long nosed Smith and Wesson. Neither had fingerprints. The two men were never seen again. It is believed they were hit men, imported from out of town. They probably took a plane to their home base immediately after the killing.

Umberto Anastasio would have smiled. After all, he perfected the method.

SHE WAS EVER
SO BONNIE

In the early 1930s, the exploits of Bonnie Parker and Clyde Barrow were for
many the only diversion from the grim realities of a crushing Depression. Their
unplanned robberies and daring escapes captured the imagination of the public throughout North America. Almost lost in the folk hero aura surrounding Bonnie and Clyde
was the fact that they were both cold-blooded killers. As John Dillinger once said,
"They are kill crazy punks and clodhoppers, bad news to decent bankrobbers. They give
us a bad name."

Clyde Chestnut Barrow was born on March 24, 1909. His parents, Henry and Cumie
Barrow, barely eked out a living on their Telice, Texas farm. All of the eight Barrow
children were expected to do their share of the chores. Little Clyde had a distinct
dislike for anything rural. By the time he was nine, he was committed to the Harris
County School for Boys as an incorrigible truant, thief and runaway. Later, the Barrow
clan moved to Dallas, where Clyde's father ran a filling station.

While still in his teens, Clyde teamed up with his older brother, Buck. They
sometimes worked with a gang and sometimes operated alone, robbing grocery stores
and filling stations. In 1928, in a shootout with the police, Buck was wounded and
captured. He was sentenced to five years at Eastham Prison Farm. Clyde was by now
a small time hood, wanted in several states for penny ante crimes. At the age of 21, he
was a five foot, six inch, slim, brown-haired little man, with no thought in his head
beyond the present.

Bonnie Parker was 18 months younger than Clyde. Her father, a bricklayer, had died when she was four. When she was 16, she married a childhood sweetheart, Roy Thornton. The marriage didn't have much of a chance. A short time later Roy was convicted of murder and sentenced to the Eastham Prison for 99 years. The 19-year-old Bonnie, who stood five feet and weighed a mere 90 pounds, was restless, bored, and hungry for excitement when she met Clyde Barrow.

They hit it off from the very beginning. Soon they were living together. Then events took a turn for the worse. One fine night the police knocked on their apartment door and arrested Clyde for a series of burglaries he had committed in Waco, Texas. He stood to receive a sentence of 14 years in jail, but because he pleaded guilty to two of the charges, his sentence was reduced to two years.

The Barrow boys were now news. Buck managed to escape from Eastham on March 2, 1930. When Bonnie heard of Buck's success, it gave her ideas. She taped a .38 calibre colt to her thigh and smuggled it in to Clyde. That very night Clyde forced his way out of jail. He managed to get as far as Middleton, Ohio, before he was apprehended jumping off a freight train. Clyde was thrown back into Eastham to serve his complete sentence.

While in prison, an informer, Ed Crowder, squealed on Clyde. He told the prison authorities that Barrow had been gambling. When Clyde found out, he clubbed Crowder to death with a lead pipe.

Conditions were so tough at Eastham that prisoners would often mutilate themselves to avoid the back breaking work in the broiling sun. Clyde had another prisoner chop off two of his toes in order to be excused from the tortuous labor.

In 1932, Clyde's mother made such an impassioned plea to the governor of the state, Ross Sterling, that she was successful in gaining her son's release. In March of the same year, Bonnie and Clyde teamed up. Only death would separate them.

The daring couple would rob any type of establishment when they ran short of money. They stole cars at random, sometimes only because they were running short of gas. The take from their robberies was pitifully small, in many cases only a few dollars. In Hillsboro, Texas, a jewelry store owner, John M. Bucher, was shot dead by Clyde during the commission of a robbery. The take — $10.

In Atoka, Oklahoma, the Barrow gang, which now consisted of a few other hoods, the best known being killer Ray Hamilton, decided on a little relaxation. They went to a dancehall. There, Sheriff C.G. Maxwell, unaware of whom he was dealing with, asked Clyde not to drink in public. Clyde pulled his gun and shot the sheriff. Then he turned on Deputy Sheriff Eugene Moore and fired twice. One bullet struck Moore in the head, while the other entered his heart, killing him instantly. Maxwell died later of his wounds.

The heat was on. The gang took off, robbing as they went. On the spur of the moment, they decided to visit Hamilton's mother in Michigan. Once there Hamilton got drunk and revealed his true identity. He was apprehended and returned to Texas to stand trial for his various crimes. He received a sentence of 263 years in jail for robbery and murder.

With Hamilton behind bars, Bonnie and Clyde not only lost a fellow gunslinger, but it is believed both lost a lover. Clyde had become a homosexual while in prison, while Bonnie enjoyed normal heterosexual relations. Hamilton, busy boy that he was, became her lover as well.

During 1932, the pair of desperados robbed filling stations and banks throughout Michigan, Kansas, Mississippi and Texas. It was probably their most lucrative twelve months. They managed to steal enough money to be well dressed and stay at decent motels and fishing lodges off the beaten path. Bonnie even had her hair done regularly.

In the course of their rampage, a 67-year-old butcher in Sherman, Texas, resisted having his store robbed. Clyde poured six bullets from his .45 into the hapless man. Two hours later he was dead. The ruthless couple walked away with $50.

From the end of 1932 on, there was no rest for Bonnie and Clyde. No motel or lodge was safe. They slept in stolen cars, eating take out food whenever they could. Sometimes they went hungry and were always on the move.

During a sneak visit home to see Bonnie's mother, Bonnie and Clyde picked up a service station attendant, W.D. Jones. The 16-year-old Jones later claimed that he was forced to live and work with the desperate pair for the next 18 months. There are those who doubt that he needed much forcing. Jones was probably picked up for two reasons. He could repair a car, and he could fulfill both Bonnie and Clyde's need for a sex partner.

On Dec. 5, 1932, the trio were stealing a car in Temple, Texas, when the owner's son surprised them in the act. Clyde unhesitatingly shot him dead. The following month Bonnie and Clyde drove into a trap in Dallas, set to catch other robbers. In order to escape, Clyde killed Deputy Sheriff Malcolm Davis.

They continued to rob to remain alive. In the meantime, Blanche Barrow, Buck's wife, pleaded with the Governor of Texas, Mrs. Miriam "Ma" Ferguson, to release her husband. Blanche had three children and no means of support. Mrs. Ferguson, in her wisdom, released Buck.

Blanche and Buck now joined Bonnie and Clyde and W.D. Jones. Five strong, they raided the Federal Armory at Springfield, Missouri, and came away with a regular arsenal. The Barrow gang was now at the height of its notoriety. Their robberies, their escapes, and their wild car chases were duly reported in the pages of the nation's press. The Barrows were camera buffs and loved to pose with their revolvers and rifles. They sent many of these pictures to newspapers.

The public loved to read about Bonnie and Clyde. Bonnie captured their imagination by sending long poems to the newspapers. From these poems emerged another aspect of their continuing melodrama. It became obvious that Bonnie and Clyde knew there was no way out. They accepted the fact that for them the end would be a fusillade of lawmen's bullets. The last stanza of one of Bonnie's poems reads:

Some day they will go down together,
And they will bury them side by side.
To a few it means grief,
To the law it's relief,
But it's death to Bonnie and Clyde.

The gang was again surrounded by armed men in Joplin, Missouri, but still managed to escape by killing two law officers. After the Joplin incident they were pursued relentlessly. Buck was badly wounded in Dexter, Iowa, on July 24, 1933. Six days later he died in hospital from his wounds. At the same time, Blanche was apprehended.

Clyde suffered a slight headwound at Dexter, but he, Bonnie, and W.D. got away. Times were tough. They still had to eat and sleep in their car. W.D. left the gang, but Bonnie and Clyde continued on their merry way, robbing as they went.

In a daring raid, they succeeded in springing their old sidekick, Ray Hamilton, and four other convicts, from prison. They hid their weapons in bushes close to where the men were working. Clyde drove the getaway car.

On April 1, 1934, Clyde, and Henry Methuin, one of the escaped prisoners, killed two highway patrolmen in Grapevine, Texas. The officers had recognized them. Five days later another policeman, Constable Cal Campbell, was killed when he went to help Clyde extradite his car from a muddy ditch.

There are several theories as to just who put the final finger on Bonnie and Clyde. The most probable is that Henry Methuin's father made a deal with the police. In order to guarantee that his son would be free from prosecution, he would deliver the fugitives.

On May 23, 1934, six police officers waited in bushes as a Ford V8 sedan approached Gibsland, Louisiana. Clyde was at the wheel. Bonnie was eating a sandwich. The officers opened fire. One hundred and eighty-seven bullets tore into the car. Fifty found their mark.

ALVIN OUTLIVED
THEM ALL

John Dillinger, Baby Face Nelson, Pretty Boy Floyd, Bonnie and Clyde — the daring deeds of these desperados produced headlines throughout the late '20s and '30s. All were thieves and killers, but their timing was perfect. The entire world was in the throes of the great Depression. Average citizens just didn't care if some hoodlum held up a bank. In fact, many felt it was ironically just that banks had their share of trouble. After all, wasn't it the banks who foreclosed on honest farmers who couldn't meet their mortgage payments?

Books, magazine articles and, maybe more than anything else, movies have kept the well known gangsters' names before the public to this day. All the Dillingers and Nelsons were killed by police bullets or were jailed and died in prison. A few were released, but passed on years ago.

Only one lived on. Through dozens of shootouts, trials, jail sentences, and old age, one former gangster lived into the 1970s. He was a Canadian, Alvin Karpowicz, but you probably know him better as Alvin "Creepy" Karpis, notorious member of the Ma Barker gang.

Alvin was born in Montreal to honest, hard working immigrants from Lithuania. When their only son was four years old, the Karpowiczes made their way to Topeka, Kansas, where Mr. Karpowicz worked at the Santa Fe railroad.

While other children may take to schoolwork or athletics, Alvin walked over that thin line to juvenile delinquency. He ran errands for small time punks and prostitutes. When he was only 10 he burglarized a grocery store and got away clean. It seemed so simple. Work was for other people — stealing was for Alvin Karpis.

For the next eight years of his life Alvin intermittently worked at some cover job and stole everything he could get his hands on. In 1926, when he was 18, police surprised him inside a warehouse. He received a sentence of from five to 10 years in the reformatory in Hutchinson, Kansas.

After serving three years in Hutchinson, Karpis, together with three other convicts, sawed through some iron bars and escaped. Karpis and a prison buddy, Lawrence Devol, stole clothing, guns and cars and made good their escape. They didn't stop until they hit Devol's home state of Oklahoma.

Small robberies kept the two men solvent, but as escaped cons the increased pressure to keep moving was always with them. Leaving Oklahoma they moved on to Chicago, where Devol was spotted and picked up. He was returned to prison. Without his sidekick, Karpis kept a low profile until a year later when Devol was released.

Unbelievably, the first job the two friends pulled was a clothing store robbery. Devol had promised his buddies back in prison that he would treat them all to new clothing as soon as he got out of prison. Keeping his word, he and Karpis sorted the clothing as to size and color. They then mailed individual parcels to Lansing Prison. All the cons received their new duds.

In 1930, Karpis was picked up by the police in Kansas City and returned to Hutchinson to serve the balance of his sentence. On May 2, 1931, Karpis was released from prison. In a manner of speaking Karpis had graduated. While serving the balance of his sentence he had been transferred to Lansing, where he met more mature and hardened men. Among them was Freddie Barker. The two men had become fast friends and had made plans to get together once Freddie was released.

Freddie Barker looked up Alvin Karpis in Tulsa, Oklahoma, as soon as he gained his freedom. Freddie was planning a bank job. This was more like it, thought Alvin. No more penny ante stores and warehouses.

Alvin, Freddie and two accomplices walked into a bank in Mountain View, Missouri, and walked out with $7,000. Creepy Karpis had become a successful bank robber.

Working loosely as a gang, sometimes with Freddie Barker and sometimes with his old buddy Lawrence Devol, Karpis and his friends terrorized the midwest. In 1932, the gang successfully hit the big time when it robbed the Northwestern National Bank in Minneapolis of $81,000 in cash and $185,000 in Liberty Bonds. The gang roared through Kansas, Wisconsin, South Dakota, North Dakota, and Minnesota, robbing banks in broad daylight. Not all the jobs went smoothly. Sometimes local cops would block off escape routes and wild shootouts would result. Many small town cops fell to the bullets of the Karpis-Barker gang.

Around this time Freddie's brother, Doc Barker, joined the gang. Doc would have been in the thick of things earlier, but he had been detained for 13 years at McAlester, Oklahoma for killing a night watchman during a holdup. Years earlier a third brother, Herman, was so badly wounded after killing a policeman that he turned his revolver on himself and ended it all. No question about it, the Barker boys were quite something.

No tale of Alvin Karpis would be complete without the inclusion of Ma Barker, the mother of the infamous Barker boys. Ma was an overweight, short woman, who travelled from state to state as homemaker to her bankrobbing sons and Alvin Karpis. Throughout their relationship Ma Barker always treated, and no doubt loved, Karpis the same as her natural sons. Whatever the reason, there was a deep bond between Ma and Alvin.

The F.B.I. always maintained that Ma was the brains behind the gang, plotting and planning daring robberies behind the scenes. Karpis swore that Ma was a simple woman who accepted her sons' profession, but had no connection with actual bank robberies. In the five wild and woolly years during which the gang robbed at full steam, Ma become a folk heroine.

In April, 1933 the gang decided to branch out into another lucrative activity — kidnapping. Their victim was to be William Hamm Jr., the 38-year-old millionaire president of the Hamm Brewing Co. On June 15, Hamm was picked up off the streets without incident and transported to a secluded location. As soon as he was kidnapped, Hamm made the mental decision to co-operate with his abductors in every way. He signed ransom notes and never gave his captors any trouble. The whole thing went off without a hitch. Hamm was returned safely and the gang received a cool $100,000 ransom.

Throughout the reign of the Karpis-Barker gang, the director of the Federal Bureau of Investigation, J. Edgar Hoover, himself something of a folk hero, was fit to be tied. The gang was actually making the bureau look bad. Hoover named Karpis as the most wanted fugitive in the entire U.S.

The gang returned to robbing banks, but the easy money of the Hamm kidnapping was hard to forget. They decided to pull their second kidnapping. This time the victim was to be Edward Bremer, president of the Commercial State Bank of St. Paul.

On Jan. 19, 1934, the gang snatched Bremer. Things didn't go according to plan. Bremer wasn't the co-operative captive that Hamm had been. He complained constantly and wouldn't sign the typed ransom note until Doc Barker slugged him over the head with a revolver. Negotiations for the ransom money didn't go smoothly. It took a full twenty days until the gang was able to exchange Bremer for $200,000. J. Edgar Hoover lived for the moment when he could put the Karpis-Barker gang behind bars.

Slowly, pressure from Hoover was instrumental in bringing an end to the era of big name robbers and killers. Bonnie and Clyde drove into an ambush and were blown apart by a hail of bullets. John Dillinger was killed on the streets of Chicago. Baby Face Nelson killed two F.B.I. agents before being shot to death himself.

Christmas of 1934 found the gang relaxing in Florida. Freddie and Ma had a cottage at Lake Weir. Karpis, along with another hood, Harry Cambell, and their women joined Ma and Freddie. Everyone had a good time hunting and fishing. Unknown to the gang, Doc Barker had been picked up in Chicago. Perhaps through Doc or because of something found on his person, the F.B.I. learned of the Barker gang's location in Florida. Secretly, they surrounded Ma's cottage and opened fire. A few shots were returned, and then nothing but silence. Ma Barker and her son Freddie were dead. The rest of the gang had not been in the cottage. Karpis, Cambell, and the women had moved out to find better fishing.

Karpis, Cambell, and their lady friends headed for Atlantic City. There would be no rest for them there. Cornered in the hotel, the two men managed to get away but the two women were taken into custody.

Fugitives on the run need money to survive. With the heat on, the two men made their way to the Toledo area. They successfully relieved the Youngstown Sheet and Tube plant in Warren, Ohio of their payroll. The heist netted $72,000.

In 1935, with the F.B.I. doggedly tracking down every clue which could possibly lead to his whereabouts, Alvin Karpis decided to rob a train. On Nov. 7, at Garrettsville, Ohio, Karpis, with a well organized plan and a makeshift gang, robbed the train as it stopped at the station. Everything went well. Karpis had previously arranged for a small airplane and pilot to fly him and his buddy, Freddy Hunter from Port Clinton, Ohio to Hot Springs, Ark. It worked like a well executed military maneuver. The loot was a disappointing $34,000.

Despite his success, the pressure remained on Karpis to avoid detection as the most wanted man in the U.S. Conversely, the heat was on the F.B.I., and particularly J. Edgar Hoover, to apprehend the gang of robbers and killers, who seemed to operate beyond the law's reach.

Where were Karpis and Hunter during the intensive manhunt? Vacationing with lady friends, but the final scenario was drawing to a close. Holed up in New Orleans in 85 degree heat, Karpis left his apartment with Hunter to pick up a box of strawberries. Because of the heat, he didn't wear a jacket and so wasn't carrying his revolver. This time, F.B.I. agents surrounded their car before they had a chance to move. The two fugitives surrendered. Hoover was there in person and always claimed that he was in the forefront of the arrest. Karpis swore that Hoover hid until he was taken into custody and then appeared for publicity photos. Whatever the actual facts, an era had come to an end.

Karpis made a deal and was charged with only one crime in return for pleading guilty. It was the Hamm kidnapping. He received a sentence of life imprisonment.

On Aug. 7, 1936, Karpis was incarcerated in dreaded Alcatraz. Three years later, his old partner Doc Barker was killed while attempting to escape from the same institution. Karpis was to stay in Alcatraz longer than any other prisoner — 25 years. In 1962 he was transferred to McNeil Island, where he remained until January, 1969.

Whatever else the little bank robber was, he was a survivor. Because he never gave up his citizenship, Karpis was still a Canadian. Upon his release he was deported to his place of birth, Montreal, Canada.

After spending 33 years in prison, Karpis became something of a celebrity on the outside. He proved to be a lucid, intelligent guest on T.V. talk shows. Like a ghost from the past, he spoke of shootouts and robberies much as other people relate office scuttlebutt. In 1971 he wrote a book, *Public Enemy Number One*, in which he detailed his most daring exploits. The proceeds from the book, and occasional guest appearances on radio and television, allowed Karpis to live in a certain degree of dignity.

On Sunday, Aug. 26, 1979, Alvin "Creepy" Karpis was found dead in his bed in Toremolinos, Spain. He had outlived them all, even his nemesis, J. Edgar Hoover.

CALL ME LUCKY

Lucky Luciano dominated the criminal scene in the United States like no other individual, with the possible exception of Al Capone during his heyday. Lucky was the Mafia's boss of bosses. A piece of the action always ended up in Lucky's smartly tailored suit pockets. Prostitution, drugs, gambling, protection, and even legitimate business ventures were but a few of his profitable enterprises.

What few people know is that Lucky Luciano worked undercover for the U.S. Navy, with the blessing of the U.S. government. He did it all while serving a sentence of 30 to 50 years at Clinton Prison in Dannemora, N.Y.

Born Salvatore Lucania in Palermo, Sicily, the dark, good looking youngster went to America with his parents when he was only nine. Salvatore learned the facts of life in New York's lower East Side. One night, while returning home from his $7 a week job in a hat plant, Salvatore stumbled across a crap game taking place in an alley. Clutching his hard earned pay in his hand, the 16-year-old Salvatore joined the game. Later that night he walked away with $244. From that moment he was called Lucky, and never saw the inside of a hat plant again.

By 1920, the young punk with the infectious smile and winning manner came to the attention of the Mafia. The loosely-knit crime organization was in the throes of an internal power struggle. Lucky was approached by several factions. He threw in his lot with Joe Masseria. It was a wise decision. In the gang war which followed, Masseria became the boss of bosses. Lucky Luciano was appointed operations chief of Manhattan. The dark, sharply dressed Charlie Lucky was on his way.

Lucky's rise to kingpin of the rackets was not all smooth sailing. There was that annoying incident when big time gambler and sophisticated loan shark, Arnold Rothstein, was murdered in 1928. Lucky was picked up as a main suspect, but was released shortly after. A year later he was taken for a gangland drive, which always ended up as one way trips for compulsory guests. All except one. Lucky was taken for a ride in typical gangster style and, although badly beaten, lived to tell of his experience.

In 1931, while having dinner with his boss Joe Masseria, a scenario took place which was to become the blueprint for fiction writers for the next 40 years. Lucky excused himself to wash his hands. In his absence, two punks poured 20 bullets towards Masseria. Five found their mark. The old loosely knit combine died with him. New alert leadership stepped forward. At the helm was Lucky Luciano.

Together with Louis Buchalter, better known as Lepke, Lucky infiltrated the unions controlling the clothing industry in New York. From clothing alone, Lucky's take home pay was a cool $1 million a year. Lucky's tentacles reached out and extracted union dues or protection money from the shoe manufacturing industry, motion picture theatres, the bakery industry, poultry processors and taxicab drivers. Very few ordinary citizens during that period in New York failed to contribute either directly or indirectly to the mob and Charlie Lucky. Liquor, drugs, prostitution and gambling added greatly to the millions pouring into Lucky's coffers.

Lucky's contribution? He brought a certain amount of peace to mob life. Under his chairmanship, the syndicate discussed their problems rather than shooting it out in gang wars. Territories were split across tables rather than by a show of force. A word from the boss of bosses was all that was required to enforce the law.

When not in Miami or Hot Springs, Lucky oversaw his domain from a swank suite in Manhattan's plush Waldorf Astoria. A nod from Lucky could bring a friend a prostitute for the evening or sudden death to an enemy.

Prostitution brought about Lucky's downfall. The racket was a multi-million dollar enterprise, with everyone making a fistful. Everyone, that is, except the prostitute. The average hooker netted only about $50 out of her earnings of from $400 to $500 per week.

There was already unrest in the ranks when Thomas E. Dewey was appointed District Attorney in 1935. The actual crack in the armor of silence came from a bookkeeper, one Dave Miller, who informed to protect his wife from being incriminated in his illegal work. Lucky, who always remained several times removed from anything as sordid as prostitution, did have a direct hand in supervising the weekly take. He was on a first name basis with bookkeepers in the organization.

It took months, but once Miller talked, other witnesses were found who, although frightened, were willing to testify against Lucky. Finally, Dewey collected enough to gain an indictment and go to trial. Lucky was charged with 90 counts of extortion and organized harlotry. Found guilty, he was sentenced to from 30 to 50 years in the State Prison. The mob was flabbergasted. Was it possible? The boss of boses having the book thrown at him? It was not only possible, it was a fact. Despite using every device money and the law allows, Lucky failed to avoid becoming a permanent resident of Dannemora in upper New Yok State.

That, for all intents and purposes, should have been that, but not so. The strangest and most unlikely incident in Lucky's unusual life was about to unfold.

Year after year Lucky had every conceivable luxury that money could buy in prison. With the '40s came the United States' involvement in World War II. German U-boats patrolled the Eastern seaboard and were so successful in sinking Allied shipping, it was felt the war might never be won as long as the U-boats were free to roam the sea lanes. In the first year after the American entry into the war, 500 Allied ships were sunk in the Atlantic. U.S. Naval Intelligence felt that spies were providing the U-boats with information and supplies. This enabled them to remain at sea far longer than otherwise would have been possible. Strong suspicion fell on those pro-Mussolini Italians who might be willing enough to provide their services to the enemy for a price.

Naval Intelligence decided to approach the underworld and ask for assistance. Many pro-Fascists were employed in the fishing industry and were in a perfect position to offer information and supplies to the German U-boats at sea. It so happened that most of these vessels supplied fish to New York's famed Fulton Fish Market. Fulton's is more than an ordinary fish market. It is the distribution point for almost a quarter of the U.S. fish supply. The huge operation was controlled by several labor unions and management rackets. All of these in turn were tightly controlled by underworld racketeer Joseph Lanza, better known as Joe Socks.

Naval Intelligence approached Joe through his lawyer. They were mildly surprised when he volunteered to co-operate. He did stipulate that he was never to be seen with anyone connected with the government. Joe didn't want to end up at the bottom of the Atlantic with his fish.

Joe saw to it that Naval Intelligence undercover men were accepted into the proper unions. Some were placed on fishing boats, others became truckers hauling fish. Soon, a network of undercover men was well placed and a fresh supply of information flowed into Naval Intelligence. The information was invaluable. Quietly, arrests were made.

Despite his valuable assistance, Joe Socks could only deliver so much. He informed the Navy that throughout other unions and along the docks there were information leaks which went directly to the Germans. Rumor had it that acts of sabotage were about to take place. Joe couldn't help any further afield than the fishing industry. He suggested that there was only one man in the United States who could assist the government along the docks. That man was Lucky Luciano.

The Navy took up the challenge. To avoid suspicion, Lucky and other prisoners as well were transferred to Great Meadow Prison at Comstock, north of Albany. Here the Navy approached Lucky Luciano. They had brought along a friend to plead their cause. His name was Meyer Lansky. Meyer asked Lucky to help. Lucky, who never was one for long winded speeches replied, "Okay, I'll help."

The scheme was called "Operation Underworld." The Navy told Luciano which unions they wanted undercover men to infiltrate, which docks would require special Naval men. Joe Socks took periodic trips to prison. He received his instructions from Lucky. Luciano always reminded him, "Tell them Charlie Lucky told you." As if by magic, labor bosses became patriots. Union cards were issued without question. Sometimes it took a little persuasion. Emil Camardo, vice president of the International Longshoremen's Association, didn't want to co-operate. Lucky told Joe Socks to have a certain friend speak to Camardo. Camardo co-operated. The friend was Frank Costello.

To illustrate the efficiency of the mob's undercover work, and, let's face it, the fear they could instill, not one single case of sabotage was uncovered along New York's waterfront during the entire duration of the war.

As the war progressed and the balance swung to the Allies favor, it became obvious that the invasion of Italy was imminent. Lucky's new assignment was to dig up details about the Sicilian coast which would assist an invading army and find those people in Italy who would help the Allied cause. Soon, reams of valuable information was made available to assist the Allies in the invasion.

The war ended in 1945. While no promises had been made to Lucky, there was no question that he wanted his reward. Under the glare of peacetime conditions, the U.S. Navy was somewhat embarrassed to admit that top Mafia members had assisted them during the war. A discreet inquiry was held, and Lucky was paroled toward the end of 1945. He was immediately deported to Italy.

Exile wasn't all that bad. The old mobster lived in a penthouse in Naples. When the mood struck him, he would hide out in his villas in Capri or on the Tyrrhenian Sea.

On Jan. 26, 1961, a movie producer flew in from Rome to discuss making a movie of Lucky's life. He met the producer's flight and was walking through Capodichino Airport when it happened. Lucky clutched his chest and slumped to the floor.

Salvatore Lucania, at 64, was dead of a heart attack.

THE JIGSAW MURDER

It all started in New York City in 1897, on a sunny Saturday afternoon in June. Two young lads, James McKenna, 13, and John McGuire, 14, were swimming at an unused dock at the foot of East 11th Street, when they saw a brightly-wrapped parcel floating in the water. They swam out and succeeded in pushing the parcel into shore. The bright wrapping proved to be red oilcloth with small golden stars; really quite a joyous-looking prize. The boys eagerly opened the parcel. It contained the joyous trunk of a man, or rather the shoulders, arms and chest of what had once been a man. Mysteriously, a patch of skin had been neatly cut away from the area below the left breast.

The boys called off their swimming for that day, but for the rest of their lives they were able to relate how they found the first piece in what was to become New York's famous Jigsaw Murder.

The next day another pair of boys, picking berries with their father near East 176th Street on the Bronx side of the Harlem River, came across a parcel wrapped in red oilcloth with a pattern of gold stars. When the Bronx cops opened this little treasure, they found the lower part of a torso. While the neck had been cut neatly and professionally, the legs were severed from the trunk in a most haphazard manner, because as anyone in the dismembering business knows, you can cut a head off rather easily but legs are a tiresome task. This lower portion was matched up with the first find, and they fitted perfectly. Not only that, but the cut edges of the oilcloth also matched up.

There was more to come. In the middle of the same week some sailors on the USS *Vermont*, over at the Brooklyn Navy Yard, found some brightly-wrapped legs. They matched up with the previous two pieces. If you are keeping close track of all the parts, we now have everything except the head. Everyone was baffled. Even in little old New York, it's not every day they find pieces of people scattered hither and yon over several boroughs. All the daily newspapers in New York featured the story on Page One. Each time a new fragment turned up, it fostered new theories and kept the story fresh and exciting.

The New York papers were extremely competitive at this time, and some of their ace reporters were as good as top detectives at cracking murder cases. The papers featured pictures of pieces of the corpse, as well as theories by learned medical men. The main dailies ran contests offering cash rewards to the public for furnishing the clues that would crack the case.

What they had to go on was as follows. The man's weight was estimated to be 180 pounds. He had big, powerful arms, a husky, well-developed chest and he was in perfect health. His flesh was white and untanned, but his hands didn't go with the rest of his powerful physique. The hands came under close scrutiny as a means of figuring out his occupation. The fingers were small and uncalloused, indicating that he was not accustomed to hard manual labour. The fingernails were carefully trimmed and cut short; not at all like the long polished nails found on the society dudes of that era. The tip of each finger was slightly shrivelled. It was estimated that the first section of the body to be found had been in the water for less than a day. The best police officers, top reporters, and the public all had a crack at guessing the man's occupation, and none of them came up right. Only one boy, fresh out of his first year at medical school, came up with the correct answer. His name was Ned Brown and he had a summer job as a cub reporter with the New York *World.* By correctly deducing the occupation of the victim, he went on to solve the murder.

If you want to play detective and try to guess the occupation of the corpse, review the facts, no peeking below, and give it a try.

Ned correctly figured out that the well-built corpse had been a masseur or "rubber" in one of the hundreds of Turkish baths that dotted New York at the turn of the century. The heavy, muscular, well-built chest and arms came from massaging twenty to thirty men each day. His work kept him indoors all day, which accounted for the lack of a tan. Carefully trimmed fingernails were necessary in order to avoid scratching his clients. If you go swimming for any length of time or even take a long shower, take a look at your fingertips and you will notice a crinkling effect. This feature of the fingers, coupled with the general condition of the hands, left Ned with the correct occupation.

He started canvassing the Turkish baths to try to find one that had a rubber missing. On his fifth try, an attendant told Ned that one Willie Guldensuppe had taken the previous Friday off and hadn't shown up for work since. Ned got the missing Willie's description and it exactly matched the jigsaw corpse. It seems Willie had a tattoo under his left breast. Remember the piece of skin that was missing? Ned figured it was taken away to remove the tattoo. He went to Willie's address, and found it to be occupied by a fine cut of a woman, standing 5 feet 6 inches tall, and weighing in at 200 pounds, give or take a bulge. Her name was Mrs. Augusta Nack, and she had formerly lived with Willie. Unfortunately, poor William was now missing. Mrs. Nack had a not-so-new lover, one Fred Thorn.

Subsequent investigation proved that the 200 pound Augusta led an active sex life. She had originally been married to Mr. Nack, a baker, whom she had left. He never entered this case except to express relief that his head was on his shoulders, and to imply that this might not still be the case had he remained under the same roof as the ever-loving Augusta. Augusta then took up with Fred Thorn, whom Willie threatened and scared away. Thorn moved out, and Willie moved in. Well, not exactly. You see, Fred became a thorn in Willie's side by dropping in to see Augusta during the day when Willie was busy rubbing down stiffs at the bath.

The reason the overweight Mrs. Nack was able to command so much attention from her suitors was because of her lucrative profession of midwife, supplemented, it is suspected, with the odd abortion. In any event, she was a fine means of support for any man who could stomach her.

Mrs. Nack and Fred Thorn were arrested, but knowing the identity of the victim and the suspicious lives of the accused was not proof of murder.

Enter the duck.

In a sparsely populated area in the suburb of Woodstock, there was a man who owned a beautiful white duck. One day he noticed the duck came home with all its feathers coloured a bright red. He followed the duck the next morning, and beside a house he found a little pond with blood-red water. The duck had stumbled onto the scene of the murder.

Mrs. Nack and Thorn started to talk. She had lured Willie out to the isolated house on the pretence that they would set up a prostitution operation. Thorn was waiting in the house. He shot Willie in the back of the head and placed him in a bathtub, where he cut his throat with a razor. They cut up the rest of Willie right there and then. The reason the head was never found is that it was encased in plaster of Paris, and as a result sank beautifully. The murdering couple, for some reason, thought the other bundles would sink without the plaster.

Thorn had kept the water running in the bathtub all the time in order to get rid of the blood. How was he to know that the pipes were not connected to any sewage system, but ran directly into the little pond beside the house?

During the trial, Mrs. Nack's most embarrassing moment came when a shopkeeper positively identified her as the purchaser of several yards of bright red oilcloth. Mrs. Nack turned state's evidence against her lover, and was allowed to plead guilty to manslaughter in the first degree. She received the relatively light sentence of fifteen years. Fred Thorn was electrocuted in Sing Sing in August of 1898, possibly the first and only murderer to have the dubious distinction of being placed in the electric chair by a duck.

Ned Brown, the first-year medical student who really cracked the case, got a $5 bonus from his paper. He never went back to medical school, and his summer job with the New York *World* lasted thirty-four years.

THE CANDY MOSSLER CASE

It has been said that no millionaire has ever been executed in the United States. Candy Mossler almost became the exception to the rule.

Born Candace Weatherby in Buchanan, Georgia, in 1919, she was the sixth of 10 children. Her father was a not-too-prosperous rancher. At the age of nine, she was crippled with polio. The dread disease left Candy with one leg completely paralysed. For five years her brothers carried her to school on their backs. By diligently exercising the leg, she was able to walk again by the time she was 14. Everyone agrees that Candy was a bright, beautiful child who was soon to blossom into an extremely attractive young lady.

Candy left school in Grade 11 to marry Norman Johnson, a civil engineer. The young couple had two children. Norman Jr., and Rita. Later they had an amicable divorce, and remained good friends. After the split-up, Candy went to New York where she became a successful model. By 1949, she was in business for herself, and profitably ran the Candace Finishing School, Candace Modelling School, and the Candace Model Agency. She was so successful that she had the resources and ability to take part in charitable causes. It was while soliciting funds for worthy causes that she met Jacques Mossler, who had just lost half of his fortune through a divorce. He had four children, and four finance companies. Jacques was down to his last million when he met Candy. He fell hard for the blonde beauty. Despite being over 20 years her senior, he married Candy on May 24, 1949 in Fort Lauderdale, Florida.

The Mosslers were devoted to each other, worked hard at the finance business, and branched out into banking and insurance. The money poured in — they became multi-millionaires.

In 1957, they made national news when they adopted four children at one time. In Chicago, a psychopathic war veteran ran amuck and killed his wife and baby. The remaining four children, Martha, 6; Dan, 5; Chris, 3; and Eddie, 2, were adopted by the Mosslers and became instant millionaires.

The Mosslers and their 10 children lived like kings. Their home in Houston was a 28 room mansion with rolling formal gardens and an Olympic size swimming pool. Candy received $7,500 a month to run the show, except when there was a birthday or party in the family, then she usually received an extra $5,000 for incidentals. At this time the Mossler empire included the American National Bank of South Bend, Indiana; The First National Bank of Coral Gables, Florida; The Mutual Bank of Chicago and The Central Bank and Trust Co. of Miami. A further 35 companies were controlled by a holding company — the Mossler Acceptance Corp. We needn't go into their vast real estate and property holdings. Suffice to say, the Mosslers were loaded.

In 1961, Mossler gave a job to Candy's nephew Mel Powers, the son of one of her older sisters. By 1962, Mel was living with the family in the mansion in Houston. Later evidence was to reveal that it was around this time that the warm relationship which existed between Candy and her husband began to cool. Candy was the first to drop the hint that she thought her husband had acquired homosexual tendencies at this time. Still, to all outward appearances, they had the ideal marriage.

Mossler, who was later suspected of many things, was never accused of being dumb. In June of 1963, he fired Mel Powers and had him removed from his home in Houston. Harsh words were exchanged between Mossler and Powers. Because of the convenience and mounting business interest, Mossler rented an apartment on Key Biscayne, Fla., in May of 1964. Soon the family joined him.

In the early morning hours of June 30 that year, tragedy was to descend on the Mossler clan. Candy was suffering from a migraine headache. She piled her four children into her car and took off for Miami's Jackson Memorial Hospital at about 1:30 in the morning. This may seem like strange behavior, but the family had made many excursions of a like nature in the middle of the night. They lingered, buying stamps and mailing letters on the way to the hospital. Candy received treatment at the hospital and arrived home at about 4:30 a.m. She and the children found Jacques Mossler lying on the living room floor, with a head wound and a further 39 stab wounds over his body.

The police were able to ascertain from people who lived in the apartment building that Mossler's killer had sped away in a white 1960 Chev which had been parked beside the apartment building. Later the car was found in the Miami Airport parking lot, and was traced back to Candy. It seems she was accustomed to borrowing a car any time she wanted from one of her husband's finance companies. Candy had actually taken delivery of the car days before the murder and delivered it to Mel Power at Miami Airport.

As soon as the police got a line on Powers, other revealing tidbits started to come to light. Witnesses were found who told of a torrid affair taking place between Candy and her nephew over the past several years. Then police found out that Powers had flown from Houston to Miami the day before the murder.

Because of the wealth of those involved, the case became a celebrated one and was covered extensively by the press. It wasn't until Jan. 17, 1966 that Candy and Mel stood trial for the murder of Jacques Mossler.

During the trial four different criminals testified that they were offered the contract to kill Mossler by Powers and Candy. All flatly refused, except one who testified that he had accepted $7,500 in advance. He claimed to have spent the money without ever going through with the scheme.

The prosecution came up with Powers' palm print, lifted from the formica counter in the Mossler apartment. A handyman testified that he had washed down the counter on the afternoon preceding the murder. Thus Powers was placed in the apartment at least close to the time of the tragedy.

Perhaps the most damaging evidence of all was that of the witness who told of Powers bragging about his sexual prowess with Candy. This evidence was given in detail from the witness stand and caused the courtroom to hum. The underlying motive of the whole crime was attributed to sex.

The defence, led by famed lawyer Percy Foreman of Texas, tried to establish that there were scores of men who, for business reasons, wanted Mossler out of the way. The defense also made light of the affair between Candy and Powers, proving that in many instances Candy's children accompanied her and Powers on supposedly illicit trips. Foreman pressed home the fact that all the evidence was circumstantial; there were no witnesses to the crime.

An all male jury brought in the surprise verdict of not guilty. Candy and her nephew walked out of court into the Florida sunshine.

Despite her wealth, tragedy continued to stalk the attractive blonde. In 1971, she married again. This time the groom was Barnett Garrison, an electrical contractor. About a year later he fell off the roof of their home in Houston and was seriously injured. Later Candy divorced him, and he remains a semi-invalid to this day. Melvin Powers is a successful building contractor in Houston, Texas.

On Oct. 25, 1976 Candy flew to Florida to attend the monthly board meeting of the Central National Bank, which she controlled. The next day she didn't appear for breakfast. When she didn't respond to phone calls, officials of the Fountainbleu Hotel decided to investigate. They found her dead in her bed. She had apparently passed away peacefully in her sleep.

MRS. SPRINGER SLEPT AROUND

Prominent married ladies should as a rule be extremely discreet when they take a lover. If they decide to have two lovers and a husband all at the same time, they should be downright cautious. This is the story of a lady who didn't know the meaning of discretion, and threw caution to the wind.

John W. Springer never knew what it was like to be poor, for the simple reason that he had always been rich. Born in Illinois on the right side of the tracks to a wealthy and socially prominent family, he had the distinction of being elected to the Illinois House of Representatives at the rather tender age of 22.

They say money goes to money, and John was no exception. He married an extremely wealthy cattleman's daughter from Colorado, and thus ended up with money on both sides so to speak. In order to participate in his father-in-law's many interests, he moved to Denver. John became a power in banking, real estate, and politics. He ran unsuccessfully for mayor of Denver in 1904. But not everything came up roses — John's wife took ill and died of natural causes.

A few years after Mrs. Springer's demise, John met beautiful, vivacious Isabelle Patterson of St. Louis. Isabelle had divorced her first husband. Despite this minor mar on her track record, John married the lady and brought her to Denver.

John had a rambling cattle ranch outside the city for relaxing, yodelling, and whatever. He also had a palatial home in the centre of Denver. Would you believe it, Isabelle didn't like the setup. She craved the action she had grown accustomed to as a gay divorcee in St. Louis. To pacify her, John rented a suite on the sixth floor of the aristocratic staid Brown Palace Hotel in downtown Denver. Here Isabelle could entertain to her heart's content.

Into this comfortable menage came daring Tony von Phul, a nationally known balloonist. In the spring of 1911, Mrs. Springer was bedding down with Tony at every oportunity. With Isabelle firmly ensconced on the sixth floor of the brown Palace and Tony living on the fifth floor, we can only assume that the opportunities were numerous.

On occasion, Tony's enterprises necessitated his taking excursions away from Isabelle's side. During these temporary absences Isabelle would write Tony little letters, the contents of which should have been coated with asbestos. They were very, very warm.

While all these dalliances were taking place on the sixth floor, John continued to invest wisely and make money. One of the new citizens of the community with whom he became friends was none other than Tony von Phul. Trusting John didn't suspect a thing.

Now, folks, we all know that there are more triangles in most hotels than there are in symphony orchestras. Sometimes these cute little arrangements carry on for years. In the celebrated Springer affair, still another actor was destined to walk upon the stage.

Frank Harold Henwood arrived in Denver in the winter of 1911. He was there to help promote a new gas company, but what was far more important, he arrived with a letter of introduction to John Springer. John liked Henwood. The pair became business associates in the gas company and saw a great deal of each other socially. One fine day John Springer introduced his friend Frank Henwood to his wife Isabelle, thereby proving once and for all that lightning certainly can and often does strike twice in the same place. Mrs. Springer promptly fell hard for Henwood.

Throughout the late winter and early spring of 1911, Henwood and the durable Isabelle were using the sixth floor often. During their many months of gallivanting on the sixth floor, the pair had the good fortune not to be concerned with von Phul, who was away in St. Louis on wine business. John Springer, it appears, knew nothing about anything. It must be remembered that both Mrs. Springer's lovers were on a first name basis with hubby John. They would often attend the opera or take business trips with Springer. Sometimes they were even accompanied by Isabelle.

One evening, while warming Henwood's bed, Isabelle revealed her relationship with von Phul. She told Henwood that, try as she might, von Phul would not return some rather revealing, foolish letters she had written to him. Henwood went so far as to dictate a letter to von Phul, which Isabelle copied in her own handwriting. It stated in no uncertain terms that she was finished with von Phul, and that he should do the honorable thing and return the foolish little letters and that was that.

She received a reply from von Phul telling her to get rid of Henwood. If she wouldn't do it, von Phul said he would take matters into his own hands.

On May 23, 1911, von Phul returned to Denver from his business trip. He met Frank Henwood for the first time. Naturally he took his old room on the fifth flor of the Brown Palace Hotel, which gives us the rather unlikely situation of having von Phul on the fifth floor, Henwood on the fourth, and Isabelle in her suite on the sixth. Where John Springer was is uncertain.

The adversaries met in the lobby of the hotel and started to argue. They returned to von Phul's room, where von Phul revealed he was carrying a revolver. Henwood's reaction to this startling revelation was to announce, "Any man who carries a gun is a coward. I never carried one in my life."

Henwood pleaded with von Phul to return the incriminating letters. Von Phul slapped Henwood across the face. Again Henwood pleaded for the return of the letters. This time von Phul picked up a wooden shoe tree and struck Henwood with it across the temple, whereupon Henwood wisely left the room.

Von Phul was furious over the whole situation. He rushed up to Isabelle's suite and told her she was stupid to let Henwood come between them. Isabelle, whose affections could swing either way at the drop of a hat, said it just wasn't so. Then she ran to Henwood and told him to drop the whole matter. She told him he wasn't a match for von Phul, and no good was to come from the two of them arguing and threatening each other. Isabelle was right. She had set in motion a situation where two desperate men wanted her, and would go to any lengths to have her.

That evening John Springer dined with his wife in the Brown Palace Hotel dining room. At separate tables in the same dining room sat Tony von Phul and Frank Henwood. That night rooms were occupied on the fourth, fifth, and sixth floors by all the participants in what was to become the city of Denver's most celebrated case.

Next morning Henwood went to the police and demanded protection. The chief of police informed him that he could do nothing unless specific charges were brought against von Phul. This Henwood refused to do for fear of involving Mrs. Springer. Instead, he went out and purchased a .38 calibre revolver.

That same evening Henwood took Mr. and Mrs. Springer to the opera. After the performance he dropped them off at their suite on the sixth floor, and went down to have a drink in the bar. The room was filled with prominent Denver gentlemen having a nightcap.

At about 11:30 p.m., Tony von Phul walked into the bar. Von Phul joined Henwood. A few words were exchanged. Then von Phul punched Henwood on the chin, sending him sprawling to the floor. Some say Tony made a move toward his pocket, as if to reach for a gun. Others swear von Phul contemptuously turned his back on his fallen adversary. Anyway it was Henwood, the man who only the day before proclaimed that only cowards carry guns, who drew his own gun. Henwood emptied the .38 calibre revolver in von Phul's direction. Three bullets found their mark. One hit von Phul in the shoulder. The second grazed his wrist, and the third brought him to the floor with a bullet to the groin.

Two men, who had never met any of the principals in the case, were unlucky enough to be in the wrong place at the wrong time. J.W. Atkinson, a Colorado Springs contractor, received a bullet wound in his leg; while G.E. Copeland, a businessman from Victor, Colo., took two slugs just below the knee. His revolver spent, Henwood went into the lobby of the hotel and awaited the police.

Strangely enough, no one died in the fusillade. Von Phul never lost consciousness and remained lucid throughout the ordeal. When asked about the reason for the outbreak, he made up a story about the two men becoming jealous over the attentions of a chorus girl. He refused to be taken to the hospital by ambulance. He went by cab. Next morning at 11 a.m. von Phul died from his wounds. He had not mentioned Mrs. Springer's name. Henwood also said the bone of contention between the two men had been a chorus girl.

However chivalrous the two men had tried to be, there was no way they could protect Mrs. Springer. Von Phul's belongings revealed photographs and the incriminating letters. The scandal broke, but even more startling events were just over the horizon.

G.E. Copeland, whose leg wounds were considered minor, contracted gangrene. He was operated on and died a few hours after the operation. Henwood, who was already charged with the murder of von Phul, was now charged with the murder of Copeland. Under Colorado law, if death comes as a result of another murder, the second death, no matter how accidental, becomes murder as well. A few days later, as if to add more turmoil to an already tumultuous affair, John Springer instituted divorce proceedings against his wife.

Henwood's trial was a celebrated one. No one will ever know why the district attorney chose to try Henwood for Copeland's murder rather than von Phul's. This is extremely strange, for in order to get a conviction for the murder of Copeland, the jury had to be presented with proof of the murder of von Phul.

All the dirty linen and all the nocturnal habits of Mrs. Springer were dragged through the courts. Servants and hotel employees told of the visits of the two lovers to the suite on the sixth floor. Who knows how many deaths would have resulted had von Phul remembered to bring his gun down to the bar that fateful night. He had forgotten it under his pillow.

Henwood was found guilty and sentenced to life in prison. His lawyers appealed for a new trial. One of their main arguments was that the presiding judge, in instructing the jury, had noted that, "There is no manslaughter in this case." The Supreme Court ruled that the judge had been in error, and the case was remanded for retrial.

On May 28, 1913, Henwood's second trial for Copeland's murder began. By this time John Springer had divorced Isabelle. He appeared as a broken man at the second trial.

Henwood was found guilty again, and this time he was setnenced to death by hanging. When all legal efforts to save his life failed, his lawyers appealed to the governor of Colorado, the last and only man who could save their client's life. At the last moment the governor commuted Henwood's sentence to life imprisonment. Henwood served 10 years in prison before being paroled. He changed his name and moved to New Mexico.

Within three months of his release a waitress filed a complaint against him for propositioning her. Henwood was returned to prison as a parole violater. He died there of natural causes in 1929.

FAT MARTHA AND RAYMOND

Nineteen-forty-seven was not a good year for Martha Beck. Her husband had just divorced her and to make matters worse, she lost her job as a nurse at a home for crippled children in Pensacola, Florida. Fate had left her with two children; one sired by her former husband and the other the result of a tryst with a bus driver.

Martha had been willing to marry the bus driver, but unfortunately he had an aversion to settling down, particularly with Martha. You might call it an absolute phobia, because the bus driver took a step which assured him that no marriage could take place. Rather than marry Martha, he committed suicide.

You see, Martha was not a raving beauty. She was of average height, but that is about all that was average about her. Tipping the scales at 203 lbs., Martha had an array of chins and extra slabs of blubber that she wasn't even using. She was inclined to wear bright red lipstick, and overindulged her ample face with layers of rouge, which gave her an overstuffed, ghostlike appearance.

Martha had those normal urges which ladies sometimes have and longed for the company of a man. Facing the fact that she was no cutie she joined a Lonely Hearts Club. Before long she received a letter, which read:

Dear Martha,

I hope you will allow me the liberty of addressing you by your Christian name. To tell the truth, I don't quite know how to begin this letter to you, because I must confess, this is the first letter of this sort that I have ever written.

Would you like to know a little about me? I am 31 and I've been told I'm not a bad looking fellow. I am in the importing business from Spain, my mother country. I live alone here in this apartment, which is much too large for a bachelor, but I hope some day to share it with a wife.

Why did I choose you for my debut friendship letter? Because you are a nurse, and therefore I know you have a full heart with a great capacity for comfort and love.

Your friend,
Raymond Fernandez.

Martha didn't know it, but Raymond Fernandez was having a busy year as well. He was a swindler and killer who worked the Lonely Hearts Clubs. Once Raymond met, seduced, and got his hands on a lady's available funds, he disappeared leaving the poor woman dabbling at her bloodshot eyes with the corner of a handkerchief. When absolutely necessary, he killed his victims.

Raymond was a very busy boy. He had just returned from Spain where he had gone vacationing with a Jane Thompson. Jane unfortunately, didn't come back to the U.S. It seems she met with a car accident in La Linea, Spain. Fernandez had all the documentation concerning her death. He even had her last will and testament. Naturally it left the contents of her apartment to none other than Raymond Fernandez.

And so at Raymond's invitation, Martha went to visit him in New York. Raymond, always frugal, had moved right into the late Jane Thompson's apartment. My, my, what a surprise Raymond had when he threw open his front door and there stood the overstuffed, over-rouged, over-lipsticked Martha. Raymond gulped and said, "Come on in."

Fernandez was repulsed at the sight of Martha, but she thought he was an absolute heartbreaker. She fell madly in love with Raymond at that very first meeting. Not one to let grass grow under her bed, she let Raymond have his way with her the very first time they laid eyes on each other. Raymond, in his experienced way, checked out Martha's assets, and all things considered, decided to give Martha what they used to call the cold shoulder. Martha would have none of it. In desperation, Raymond decided to tell her the truth, namely, that she was falling for a con artist and killer. You can imagine his surprise when Martha professed undying love for him in spite of his wayward habits. She even went so far as to suggest that they should become a team. She would pose as his sister, and instill confidence into the ladies he proposed to fleece.

Raymond warmed up to the idea and the partnership was formed. From the very beginning the Spaniard and the fat lady were a perfect combination. Raymond would correspond with lonely ladies, mostly widows, through several Lonely Hearts Clubs. Once contact was established, usually instigated by the ladies themselves, Raymond and Martha would show up at the mark's house. The unsuspecting victim would be impressed with Raymond and appreciate his honorable intentions of lugging his sister along with him. After they got their scheme rolling, the odd couple averaged one fleecing a month.

There was one fly in the ointment. Martha was almost driven crazy with jealousy. She couldn't stand the thought that her Raymond had to caress and make love to other women. Raymond assured her that it was just part of his chosen profession and that it meant nothing personal.

Business is business, as the saying goes, and the partnership continued on its merry way. One incident is worthy of note. Raymond and Martha had made contact with a 66-year-old widow, Janet Fay of Albany, New York. After Raymond had seduced her and gotten his hands on Mrs. Fay's life savings of $6,000, Martha wanted to leave her high and dry. It appeared to Martha that Ray was lingering a little too long after the money was safely in his hands.

In a jealous rage, Martha hit Mrs. Fay over the head with a hammer. Ray finished the job by strangling her with a scarf. Martha was later to state that she and Ray made love on the floor beside the body of their victim.

The following day Fernandez bought a trunk and placed the body of Mrs. Fay inside. He then managed to store the body at a friend's house for a few days. Raymond and Martha located a house for rent at 149th St., Ozone Park, Queen's, and took it on a trial basis for one month. They dug a hole in the basement, placed Mrs. Fay's body inside, and cemented the floor over. They remained in the house for four days until the cement dried. Then the odd couple moved out, informing the real estate agent that the house was unsuitable.

In this way they effectively disposed of Mrs. Fay's body.

Out of sight out of mind — the strange pair went on their merry way. Six weeks later they made contact with a widow from the suburb of Grand Rapids, Mich. Mrs. Delphine Downing had lost her husband two years previously. She was leading a lonely existence, raising her three-year-old daughter Rainelle by herself.

Soon Raymond and Martha visited Mrs. Downing at her invitation. In his usual charming way, Raymond made friends with little Rainelle. Then, following his regular script and drawing on his vast experience, he seduced the lonely Mrs. Downing. She became so enthralled with her lover and his large sister that she invited them both to move in with her and Rainelle. Raymond added to his role of lover and took on the extra responsibility of financial advisor. He and Mrs. Downing soon contemplated wedding bells. Raymond got busy converting her worldly assets to his name in anticipation of their impending marriage.

It appeared that Mrs. Downing could be the source of future concern for Raymond and Martha, so one fine day Raymond shot her in the head. Rainelle kept crying, and as a result made Martha nervous. Martha cured her nervousness by strangling the child. That same night Raymond dug a hole in the cellar. Here he placed the two bodies and poured cement into the hole. To relax after a hard evening's work, Raymond and Martha took in a movie.

The next morning, when neighbors couldn't get a satisfactory answer as to Mrs. Downing's whereabouts, they didn't hesitate to call the police. The authorities just couldn't believe that a woman who had lived in the same house for years would leave with her daughter, and not tell her future husband where she was going. They decided to search the house, and lo and behold they discovered that damp patch of cement in the basement.

Once the bodies of Mrs. Downing and Rainelle were uncovered, both Raymond and Martha poured out the whole horror story. They led police to the exact location in Queen's where the body of Mrs. Fay was buried under cement in the basement. As the house was now rented to new tenants, we can only speculate how they felt when informed that there was a body in their basement.

The authorities decided to extradite the pair from Michigan to New York State and charged them with murder. Michigan had abolished capital punishment while New York still retained the ultimate penalty.

Both were found guilty. On March 9, 1951, in the company of a Roman Catholic priest, Raymond was executed in the electric chair in Sing Sing Prison. Twelve minutes later Martha joined him.

WHOOPS, BOB, I'M PREGNANT!

Remember when it was unfashionable for unmarried ladies to have babies? If the father was known to the lady, it was a source of embarrassment to him as well. In less enlightened times men quaked at the dreaded words, "I am going to have a baby, and you are the father." This provocative little statement elicited a variety of reactions.

In 1934, Freda McKechnie uttered the phrase to her boyfriend, Bob Edwards. Freda was pleasantly surprised when Bob yawned and replied, "You can do one of two things. We can get married, or you can go to a doctor about it. I'll give you your choice." Before you could say birth control Freda blurted out "I'll choose marriage."

Freda thought she knew her Bob inside out. Obviously she knew him well enough to join him between the sheets at every opportunity. There was, however, a lot that Freda didn't know about her boyfriend.

Bob Edwards' family and Freda McKechnie's family were next door neighbors in Edwardsville, Pa. The town was named for ancestors of the Edward's family. The neighbors were close friends. Bob was 21 and was studying to become a minister. He was a quiet, well-behaved, good-looking young man. Freda was 26 and was not good looking. You might charitably describe her as being plain.

Now the plot thickens. You see, up the road a mere 100 miles away in East Aurora, N.Y., lived 23-year-old Margaret Crain. Margaret was not pretty. In fact, she was ugly. Her most prominent feature was a rather large hooked nose, and I hesitate to report that it appeared to be perpetually running. Whatever Margaret lacked in appearance she made up for in the sack. She and Bob saw each other every weekend. So there you have it, folks. That handsome rascal, Bob, was wooing Freda next door all week long, and Margaret every weekend in East Aurora.

We now have a nice little triangle, with Bob enjoying every minute of it all, right up until the moment Freda babbled out the news about being pregnant. In ecstacy over Bob's proposal, she announced her engagement. Her family and friends were thrilled. There was no nicer guy in town than Bob Edwards. We must report that right through his engagement to Freda, nice guy Bob spent every weekend up in East Aurora with Margaret.

On July 30, 1934, a Monday evening, Bob had dinner with Freda, her parents, and her best friend, Rosetta Culver. Later that evening Bob and Freda drove Rosetta to her home. On the way back, Bob was later to claim, Freda suggested a swim in nearby Harvey's Lake. The couple drove to the lake and undressed in Bob's car. Bob thoughtfully had brought along a blackjack in the glove compartment of his car. He slipped it into his swim trunks. Hand in hand the couple walked into the cold waters of the lake. Only Bob walked back out. He threw Freda's clothing under a tree and drove to his home.

Next morning Freda's mother frantically called Rosetta Culver, who told her that Bob and Freda had dropped her off at her home and had driven away. The worried Mrs. McKechnie called Bob. He appeared surprised to receive the call and said he had let Freda out of his car in front of her house the night before.

By mid-afternoon a bather discovered Freda's body. Her head had been horribly crushed. A blackjack was found near her clothing. Later an autopsy disclosed that there was no water in the dead girl's lungs, indicated that she was dead before going under the lake water.

Bob was immediately questioned by the police. At first he denied committing the crime, then he claimed it was all an accident, and finally he confessed. When Freda's back had been turned, he had viciously attacked her with the blackjack. He said he loved Margaret Crain with the running nose more than Freda, and couldn't stand the thought of being married to anyone else.

Later Bob recanted his confession. He claimed that he and Freda went out on the lake in a boat. Bob said that when Freda put one foot in the water she fell back in the boat, dead of shock from the cold water. He said he panicked and decided to hit Freda with the blackjack to simulate murder. Obliging Bob demonstrated the whole thing in court. There was one basic flaw in his story. No one believed him.

To make matters worse, love letters from Bob to Margaret Crain were admitted in evidence. They were almost too hot to handle, and proved without a doubt that Bob wanted to get rid of Freda in order to carry on those hot weekends with Margaret.

If you feel you have heard this story before, it is because of its startling similarity to another case immortalized in Theodore Dreiser's book, *An American Tragedy*. In that case, the setting was Moose Lake, N.Y., the young man was Chester Gillette, and he too killed his pregnant girlfriend in the lake because he wanted another woman.

Bob Edwards came to the same end as Chester. On May 6, 1935, Bob, now 22 years old, was put to death in the electric chair in Rockview Penitentiary in Bellefont, Pa.

Bluebeard's Ladies

– Part 10 –

AROUND THE WORLD

BLUEBEARD'S LADIES
(France)

Henri Landru was born in Paris on April 12, 1869, to honest, hardworking parents. His mother was a dressmaker who ran her business from her home on Rue de Puebla, and his father was a book seller. These occupations did not place the Landru family in the highest income bracket, but it did allow them to lead comfortable, if frugal, lives. Henri attended a school run by Jesuits, and was a good, hardworking, intelligent student.

At the age of fifteen he was initiated into the delights of sex by the neighborhood prostitute, but despite these attractions, he had eyes only for the daughter of a neighbor who lived not far from him on Rue de Puebla. Her name was Marie Catherine Remy, and in his unique fashion Henri loved her. As a result of his affections she became pregnant, at which point Henri, coincidentally enough, left Paris and joined the French Army.

After three years of military service, Henri desperately wanted out. He wrote to Marie's father, who used his influence to get Landru a discharge. Henri came home, married Marie, met his two-year-old daughter, and got a job as an accountant. Within the next two years, the couple was blessed twice more. Now twenty-six years old, Henri found himself in a dead-end job, with three children and a wife to support.

In the years between 1900 and 1910, Henri tried his hand at swindling women, using any ruse to gain possession of their money and furniture. It didn't seem to matter what he did, he always got caught, and received a series of short jail sentences for fraud. In between sentences, Henri never forgot Marie — in fact, he remembered her to the extent of another bouncing baby daughter. The Landru family now totalled four children.

Henri's profession was that of con artist and thief, with no gainful employment other than the courting, wooing and fleecing of members of the opposite sex. He had a magnetic personality, but at this point in his life he had not yet perfected the fine art of escaping detection after the fact. From 1910 to 1914, he corrected this flaw in his operating procedure to a degree that put his frauds in the top professional category. He kept meticulous notes and records on every lady, her likes, dislikes, and habits. He categorized the potential degree of difficulty in fleecing them, and how big a financial reward was waiting to be plucked. Six days a week, Henri left his wife and four children to go to his work.

Only Henri knew that he was busy building up another life and another role, which he entered fully and completely. Sometimes when he left his family, he would have to stay away for a few days. He always told Marie the length of his business trips, and if he was held up for any reason, he was always considerate enough to phone her. She never questioned his absences, nor did she inquire about the cyclical nature of his income. She had a general idea that her husband was in the used furniture business and had several warehouses which he visited. When he made a profitable deal the family shared in the good fortune, but when he had trouble putting together a lucrative transaction, the exchequer suffered. Marie was a perfect wife for Henri Landru; she cared for her brood, but more important, she didn't have an inquisitive bone in her body. The family moved frequently; this too she took in her stride without question. She knew her husband would be home at least one day a week, for on that day Henri opened his huge desk and did his bookwork.

At the age of 45, Henri had grown a long, flowing red beard that was without a doubt his most outstanding feature. He had a rather long body for a small man, which gave him the appearance of being taller than he really was. His pale complexion contrasted sharply with his bright red beard, and he was bald as a billiard ball, with large, powerful hands for a man of his size and build.

In order to guarantee a constant supply of ladies, Henri used the simple but efective method of placing matrimonial ads in the newspapers. He studied the best ads, and by trial and error he developed the wording that brought the best results.

On Bastille Day, July 14, 1914, the Landrus had just moved into another new home in Clichy. Henri had to go to work soon after they arrived in their new home, and this particular job was to be concluded in a most unique way. Using the name Raymond Diard, he had received a reply to one of his ads from Jeanne Cuchet. Jeanne fell into the exact category that rated an A in Henri's book. She had been married to a commercial traveller, who had unfortunately died of naural causes. She lived with her elderly parents and teenaged son, Andre. Best of all, she had a substantial nest-egg of 5000 francs.

A tall, thin, plain woman, she was flattered and thrilled to be singled out, and soon became completely infatuated with Henri. An expert at his chosen profession, he knew the words, the topics and above all the manners that appealed to Jeanne. As Monsieur Diard he dined with her parents, careful to agree with her father's views on the conduct of the war, and careful to have an extra helping of her mother's biscuits a la cuiller. This milieu was Henri's business office, and in it he labored as patiently and efficiently as any accountant. The couple announced their engagement, received congratulations from the family, and another plum of a set-up was ready to be plucked. The 5000 francs would go a long way — wouldn't Marie be pleased at the successful conclusion of this piece of business!

In subsequent meetings with his fiancee, he let it be known that he was a qualified engineer who ran a small business currently making lighter flints. Lovestruck Jeanne's life had changed in three short months. It was too bad that her son Andre didn't take to Raymond; but never mind, he would doubtless grow to love him as much as she did. What a trusting man Henri was, thought Jeanne. He insisted that he put his money and hers together in the bank. The happy couple moved into a little apartment, and as soon as the money was safely placed in the bank, Henri cleaned out the account and took off.

Months later, quite by accident, Henri bumped into Jeanne, who was tossing flowers at the feet of passing soldiers during a military parade. One of the flowers landed at his feet, and when he looked up it was into her eyes. It was a tribute to his ingenuity and her stupidity that he was able to make up a story that placated her. He admitted to her that he had lied — he was really married and had two daughters — his divorce would become final any day now — the day he left her he had received word that his wife had balked at the divorce and was coming to Paris with his two daughters — he had held her money for it — it was safe in a Swiss bank.

Bluebeard was able to pull it off, and the pair took up where they had left off months before. In November, three months after his reunion with Jeanne, Henri rented a house in the country. It was a villa called The Lodge at 46 Rue de Mantes in Vernouillet, a small town just outside Paris. Henri took Jeanne to this villa. He usually only worked for profit, and there was nothing further to be had from Jeanne but her life. While lying in bed with Jeanne, Bluebeard leaned over, placed his large hands firmly on her neck, and strangled her to death. He then left for Paris with her bankbook. He had noticed that she had managed to save a paltry 400 since her last plucking, and it was not difficult for a man of his experience to extract it from the bank. The next day he was back at Vernouillet, with a bothersome body on his hands.

The unheated lodge was cold and damp, and when Henri arrived he was altogether uncomfortable. But repeated trips to the woodhouse soon warmed him up. He piled the logs high in the stove, and the fire caught on his first attempt. Next, operating according to his prearranged plan, Henri cleaned out the bathroom tub, which was in the cellar. Revolted as he was at handling Jeanne's body, he managed to place it into the tub. Ditchdiggers don't necessarily like digging ditches, but it's their job. And this was Henri's. With crude household implements Henri managed to dissect the body in the tub. As he proceeded, he decided he would never be this ill-prepared again, but after all, this was only his apprenticeship. If butchers learned how to dress game, he could learn to become as efficient as a butcher.

Over the next several days, Henri lugged his gruesome cargo piece after piece up the stairs and placed it ever so carefully in the stove. Black smoke billowed out of The Lodge's chimney, and the smoke was accompanied by a repulsive odour. The wind carried it to every nook and cranny of Vernouillet. Later, many villagers stated that they had noticed the smoke, and more particularly the offensive smell. Some even said it smelled like roast beef. One villager complained to an official, who knocked on Henri's front door to question him about the terrible smell emanating from his chimney. Henri told the official that the chimney was defective and promised to have it fixed immediately. This seemed to satisfy the official, and he went away.

Soon afterwards, while walking on the streets of Paris with the signs of war all about him, Henri was accosted by Jeanne's son Andre, in one of those chance meetings which plague murderers.

"Monsieur Diard, where is my mother?"

Henri had to shift into high gear in a hurry. Again it is a tribute to his guile that he convinced the lad that his mother and he were living together in Vernouillet, happy and contented. He placated Andre by telling him that his mother was planning to send for him, and now that they had met in this way he wanted Andre to accompany him to Vernouillet. Henri always liked to put a bit of frosting on the cake. "She is pregnant," he told her anxious son.

They arrived at Vernouillet; Jeanne, it seemed, was not in. Henri offered Andre something to eat. While the young man sat at the table Henri's strong hands firmly clapsed his neck and squeezed the life from his body. This time the operation went more smoothly. Henri had bought a hacksaw, meat cleaver and mallet, so it was not long before the black smoke and offensive odor billowed forth from the chimney once again.

In December of 1916, Monsieur Diard closed The Lodge at Vernouillet and left it forever.

It is one thing to swindle women one at a time, but it is quite another to be playing many roles simultaneously. Henri always kept extensive notes to remember which lady knew him under which name. He couldn't afford a mistake, because sometimes he had to deal with bank officials, using his many aliases without the slightest hesitation. He even got into the habit of talking to himself, using the alias of the moment in order to implant the proper name in his mind. On many occasions he would rush from one apartment to another, consulting his notebook to refresh his memory as to which name and personality he had to assume.

In the summer of 1917, Henri rented a house in Gambais, not far from Paris. He picked it carefully. The house adjoined a cemetery; there were no inhabitants for miles around. Using the name of Paul Fremyet, he purchased a good stove and connected it to the existing smokestack. Then he set about enticing more women, making sure that they turned over their worldly belongs to him before they turned over their lives. In all, Henri Landru strangled and burned eleven people — young Andre Cuchet and ten gullible women.

One of his victims, Anna Collomb, had invited her sister, Madame Pillot, to Gambais to visit the man she was soon to marry. After returning to Paris, Madame Pillot never heard from her sister again, though she wrote to her at Gambais. In desperation, she wrote to the mayor of Gambais, who answered that he believed he had located the house mentioned in her letter, but that no one had ever heard of her sister's fiance, Monsieur Fremyet. The mayor stated that the tenant of record of the house in question was a Monsieur Dupont. He volunteered that he had received another inquiry about the house from the sister of one Madame Celestine Buisson. The writer of the letter was Mademoiselle Lacoste, and the mayor suggested that Mme Pillot might find it useful to contact Mlle Lacoste.

The two ladies did indeed meet and compare notes. No one could mistake that red beard. Diard, Fremyet, Dupont, Cuchet, the names went on and on. Landru was readily traced and arrested. The police found him trying to destroy a notebook in which he had the names and addresses of all his victims.

One woman, Fernande Segret, visited the house in Gambais and lived to tell about it from the witness stand. For some unknown reason the mass murderer put the pretty Fernande in the same class as his wife, Marie Catherine. They lived as man and wife, and she claimed he was normal sexually and in every other way. There was nothing perverted or sadistic about Landru, nor did he ever cheat or swindle her, as she had no worldly goods. But relatives and swindled ladies kept coming forward, and from these women and the detailed files Henri kept in his desk at Clichy it was estimated that he had had intimate relations with close to 300 women in the five years before his trial.

On Feb. 24, 1922, Henri Landru, now known throughout the world as Bluebeard, admonished his keepers for offering him a mug of rum and a cigarette. "You know I neither drink nor smoke," he said. The tired old man of 52 was still receiving over a 100 letters a day from women offering everything from a lock of their hair to proposals of marriage. His loyal and faithful wife visited him in jail, and it was only when he refused to see her that his ties with her were finally severed.

His keepers tied his hands behind his back as was the custom, and Henri walked steadily to the guillotine, taking his brief instructions from the executioner. Then his head tumbled into a basket of bran that had been placed in position for that purpose.

THE PERFECT
HIDING PLACE
(Hungary)

The tiny village of Czinkota, Hungary, is one of the most beautiful spots in the world. Before the First World War it could have appeared on a postcard, representing all the quaint villages of Central Europe. It had a few commercial establishments — a general store, post office, and blacksmith shop were as near as you got to big business in Czinkota — and nothing exciting ever happened in the village.

Then Bela Kiss and his wife arrived and immediately bought the only imposing house in the area, a huge greystone structure on the outskirts of the village. Bela was about 40 years old, and his wife was fifteen years his junior when they took up residence. Mr. Kiss immediately impressed the locals with his acts of kindness towards the less fortunate in the village. He made it his business to find out who was ill and who needed assistance; nothing seemed too insignificant for the unselfish Bela to lend a hand. He owned a dashing red roadster, and many a night it would be seen roaring up the main drag, sometimes to deliver a food basket to a needy citizen, sometimes to bring some much-needed medicine to a sick friend. Everyone agreed that Bela was the greatest thing that ever happened to Czinkota. He seemed not to worry about money at all, though he had no visible means of support. But the villagers must have felt that it was not for them to look a gift horse in the mouth.

Despite his magnanimous gestures, Bela was a shy, introverted man, short of stature but with considerable presence. He sported a black handlebar moustache, which accentuated his oval face, and made him appear somewhat chubby. His wife, Marie, was a real knockout in the looks department, with a voluptuous figure to match. She and Bela hired two girls from the village to act as servants, but they only stayed during the day, returning to their own homes each night. As for Bela, he sometimes left in his red car for a few days, but generally could be found at home, in his great greystone house, living the life of a country gentleman.

It is too bad that such scenes of marital bliss and tranquillity should have to come to an end. In Bela's case, the whole thing came to an abrupt stop when he learned that Marie was seeing an artist, Paul Bihari, on the side. Actually, she was doing more than seeing him; she was sharing his bed. Imagine Bela's disappointment when he found out that the one woman he ever cared about was being unfaithful to him, particularly since it coincided with his purchase of their new home and their good life in Czinkota.

At about the time that this revolting development came to Bela's attention, the village constable paid a social visit to the Kiss residence. Constable Adolph Trauber, who didn't have that much to do in the village anyway, occasionally did a little public relations work to pass the time of day. He wanted to know if there was any way he could be of service to the village's most illustrious resident. Bela said that he would appreciate it if Trauber would keep an eye on the property on those nights when he was away and Marie was left alone in the house, and the constable said that he would be delighted to do so. Trauber, a big, friendly man, immediately liked and admired Bela, and a warm friendship grew between the two men.

In the meantime, every time that red roadster disappeared over the hill, who would show up but Marie's lover, Paul. In a village the size of Czinkota it was impossible to keep tongues from wagging, and the townspeople passed the days wondering about the outcome of the triangle. All agreed that the shabby artist couldn't be half the man kind Mr. Kiss was, but there were a couple of things — the artist was tall, slender, and above all, the same age as Marie.

One day just before Christmas, when the two servants reported for work in the morning, they were surprised to find Bela in his study with his head buried in his arms. They gingerly asked him what was wrong. Bela passed them a letter written to him by his wife to the effect that she had left him for the artist Paul Bihari. Bela, beside himself with grief, informed the two servants that he wouldn't be needing them any more now that he was alone in the big house, and that anyway he wanted to be alone in his sadness.

As the weather grew colder and the grey house remained dark and quiet, the only break in the monotony of village life came when one evening a wagon pulled up at Bela's door and deposited two large metal drums. Then the cold winter descended like a blanket, leaving the villagers with only one piece of gossip to discuss during the long dark evenings — poor Bela's beautiful wife running off with an artist.

Weeks passed into months, and one day it dawned on Constable Trauber that he had not seen his friend Bela since his wife ran away. He decided to pay him a visit. When he knocked at the door, though he pounded long and hard nobody answered. He broke the lock and entered the dark interior. In the study he found Bela, looking half-starved, his clothes in rags and the house a shambles. It was obvious to Trauber that his friend had not taken care of himself or the house since his wife left him.

"I have nothing to live for, Adolph," said the downhearted Bela.

"Nonsense," said the constable. "First we will get someone to look after you and the house. You are both a mess."

The very next day an old woman knocked on Bela's front door, announcing that she was the widow Kalman and that Constable Trauber had sent her to take care of him and the house, and that was that. Under the widow's supervision Bela once more began to look like his old self. He started to gain weight, and with the improvement in his health, his old cheerful but reserved disposition returned. By spring he appeared to be back to normal.

One fine day, when the snow had melted and flowers were beginning to show their buds, Bela had a little tete-a-tete with the widow. He thanked her profusely for being such a great help to him, but felt that he was sufficiently recovered so that he no longer needed her at night. She could return to her home each evening and come back each morning. The widow didn't know whether to take this new arrangement as an insult or a compliment, but eventually she found out that when Mrs. Kiss lived in the house the two servants had returned to their homes each night, so all things considered she decided not to take offence. At least nice Mr. Kiss was well enough to take care of himself. Anyway, Mr. Kiss had some strange ideas, thought Mrs. Kalman. Take the upstairs closet which he always kept locked — she had once asked about cleaning in there, but was told that it wasn't necessary. It was none of her business, mind you, but a body couldn't help but be curious.

Shortly after Bela's little meeting with the widow, he left the village in his smart red car and returned with a lady. The widow Kalman was given to understand that the visit would be a more or less permanent one. The Madame, as Bela called her, was an overweight blonde in her late fifties. She was just getting settled in when a wagon pulled up to the Kiss residence and deposited another metal drum. Bela had the delivery man carry it to the upstairs closet which already held the other two drums.

Kiss, who never ceased to amaze the widow Kalman, then offered to send her on a week's vacation with full pay. The widow took her boss up on the offer, and was on her way the same day the proposition was put to her. When she came back from her unexpected vacation, she noticed that the madame was nowhere to be seen. Bela nonchalantly told her that the madame had left. This puzzled Mrs. Kalman, because when she had set off on her travels a few days earlier it had appeared that the madame would be a permanent resident.

Maybe Bela realized the widow was having some misgivings about her boss, because he came to her and invited her into his study. The widow, who was becoming accustomed to their little chats, nevertheless shifted uneasily in an overstuffed chair. Bela coughed one or twice, and then confessed to Mrs. Kalman that he liked women and he intended to indulge himself with them. He was sorry if he shocked her, but out of respect for her he thought it best to let her know that he planned to invite several ladies to the house in the future. She could, of course, leave his employ if she wished, but Bela would rather — indeed positively insisted — that she stay. To sweeten the pie, Kiss let it drop that there would be quite a few paid vacations during the coming months. The widow Kalman made up her mind. Women or no, she would be happy to remain in his employ.

Next day Bela took off in the red roadster and returned with a six-foot, 300-pound Amazon. He winked knowingly at the widow Kalman. "Madame will be with us for some time," he said. Mrs. Kalman nodded understandingly and started to unpack madame's bags. She then went on one of her periodic vacations, so she didn't see the wagon when it delivered the fourth steel drum. Upon her return she inquired after the new madame, and was told she had left. The widow Kalman nodded her head and went about her dusting.

One day Constable Trauber, who by now was justifiably proud of butting into Bela's life and bringing him out of the doldrums, paid his friend a semi-official visit. Two Budapest widows had mysteriously disappeared of late, and as Bela had recently entertained two ladies, would he mind answering a few questions? Evidently a man named Hofmann had enticed the ladies to his flat, and they were never heard of again. The Budapest police had found the flat, but Hofmann had long since gone. The police felt that the women had been murdered, because both had withdrawn their life savings immediately before their disappearance. Trauber and his friend had a good laugh. Such gullible women almost deserved whatever fate befell them. The two men had a glass of wine, a good cigar out of Bela's humidor, and spent a pleasant few hours, as good friends will. Bela told Trauber that he had something he had been wanting to show him. He took the constable upstairs and unlocked the closet door. Inside were four metal drums which Bela started to bang on with a stick. They all gave off a dull thud as if they were full of liquid. Bela took the cover off one of the drums and told his friend to look in.

"Petrol," Trauber said.

"Yes," replied Bela. He had a friend who could only pay off his debts in petrol, which was just fine with him. With the sabre-rattling that was going on throughout Europe, Bela explained, it was only a matter of time before the world would be at war and petrol would be better than hard cash. Trauber agreed, as Bela replaced the lid. Bela tapped the other three. "See," he said, "they contain petrol, too. Here, take the keys to this room. If anything ever happens to me, you take the petrol. I wouldn't want my wife and her artist friend to have any claim to it."

The two friends returned to the study to have a few more glasses of wine, Trauber protesting that nothing was about to happen to Bela.

In 1914, the war broke out. Time and again Bela was seen with middle-aged ladies by his side as he roared from Budapest to Czinkota in his red roadster. Mrs. Kalman was taking more and more paid vacations, and the man with the drums kept reappearing at Bela's door. Bela, always an impressive figure around the village, distinguished himself by acting as a voluntary recruiting officer. The young, able-bodied men had to be on their guard if they shirked their duty, because Bela didn't take his job lightly.

Then one day it actually happened to him. He was taken without notice from his house to Budapest to join the army. He never even got a chance to return to his home to tidy up his affairs, and nothing further was heard from him. Often on a cold winter evening the very old, for they and the very young were the only people left in Czinkota in 1914 and '15, wondered how their distinguished little neighbor was making out at the front.

In May 1916, Adolph Trauber received word that Bela Kiss had been killed in action at the front. Constable Trauber had lost a friend, the village its most illustrious citizen, and Hungary a true patriot, in one fell swoop. Having spent many an afternoon in his cups with Bela, Adolph felt that he had suffered a personal loss. He went down to the village square and inscribed Bela's name on the roll of honor. Grief-stricken villagers joined the constable, and with bowed heads they mourned the passing of Bela Kiss.

Not long after the touching scene in the village square, representatives of the government entered Czinkota looking for the most precious of all commodities — petrol. They looked up Constable Trauber and made their mission known to him. It was only then that the constable remembered the hoard of petrol which Bela had shown him so many months before. He took the soldiers to the austere gray house, and up the stairs to the closet where the petrol was stored. The soldiers tilted the first drum and one peered inside. He said, "My God," and started to stammer, pointing into the drum. The second soldier took a look, and he too became incoherent. Finally the constable looked into the drum and saw the well-preserved body of a woman, submerged in alcohol.

In all there were seven drums in the closet. All but two contained the bodies of middle-aged ladies; in the sixth was the body of Paul Bihari, and the seventh contained petrol — the same petrol that Adolph had peered into when Bela showed him his secret.

A top detective was dispatched from Budapest to take over the strange case of Bela Kiss. Detective Nagy pasted together the baffling pieces of the case. He searched Bela's house, and found his desk full of letters from women all over Europe. The mass killer had used the simplest of schemes, that of placing matrimonial advertisements in newspapers and luring rich widows to his home in Czinkota, where he had strangled each of his victims with a rope and pickled them in alcohol. Detective Nagy traced the supplier of the drums and found out that he had delivered many more than the seven that were found. As a result a thorough search of the entire area was conducted, and several more drums were uncovered. Each of them contained the well-preserved body of a strangled lady.

When news of Detective Nagy's gruesome find spread, several farms came forward and told of turning up skeletons when they were ploughing fields adjoining Bela's property. In all it seemed that Bela Kiss had murdered 23 women, including his wife, and one man, the artist Paul Bihari.

Then, in 1919, people who knew his face reported seeing him in Budapest. The reports were so positive that Detective Nagy went to the hospital in Belgrade where Kiss had died of his wounds during the war. He was shocked to find out tha Bela was a tall, blond, blue-eyed Nordic type. It was obvious that Bela had managed to switch papers with a critically wounded soldier. When the soldier died, Kiss had assumed the dead man's identity, and had been discharged at the war's end.

Cunning little Bela Kiss had made good his escape. Years passed without word of the mass killer, until in 1952, a deserter from the French Foreign Legion told of a companion named Hofmann, who used to amuse his fellows in the desert with stories of how he had loved and strangled women in Hungary. When Detective Nagy heard these stories he recognized details that had never been made public, and he knew that the teller was in reality Bela Kiss. But by the time Nagy got in touch with officials of the French Foreign Legion, Bela had deserted.

Though some criminologists who have studied the Bela Kiss case believe he emigrated to the United States, he has never been apprehended.

THE WHITE WITCH OF ROSEHALL
(Jamaica)

Over the years we have travelled some strange paths together, searching out authentic new crimes. From the fogbound streets of London, England, to the art museums of Holland, and deep into the Canadian bush, the dastardly acts of abnormal characters have led us a merry chase.

Come along with me now to Jamaica. It sounds far away and, in fact, is over 2,000 miles from Toronto; but with today's jets you can land in Montego Bay three hours and 50 minutes after takeoff from Toronto.

When Christopher Columbus landed in Jamaica in 1494, in one of those boats whose name you had to memorize in school, he stated that he thought Jamaica was the fairest land in all the world. Nearly 500 years later, no one has ever argued with Mr. Columbus' opinion. Jamaica is beautiful.

As I write this the temperature is hovering between 83 degrees F. The Jamaicans, who are amongst the friendliest people I have ever met, are quick to point out that it is now winter. In summer it is between 7 and 10 degrees warmer, and it simply never gets cold.

* * *

A few miles from Montego Bay, off the main road up a slight rise, stands a restored house called Rose Hall, which was once a stately home on a flourishing plantation. The owner's house on a plantation is by far the most impressive, and is always referred to as the Great House.

In 1964, John Rollins, an American industrialist, purchased the plantation, which was in a state of ruin, and commenced to restore Rose Hall to its 18th and 19th century elegance. His wife, Linda, has travelled the world to furnish the Great House with antiques which duplicate those contained in the old home when it was the centre of a turbulent plantation consisting of thousands of acres of land and worked by hundreds of slaves.

In 1746, Henry Fanning purchased the plantation, which was comprised of 290 acres of sugar cane land. Fanning took a wife, Rosa Kelly, and then promptly died of natural causes. Rosa proved to be hard on husbands. In the next 20 years she went through three more, each of whom left her better off financially when they died. Her fourth and last husband was the Hon. John Palmer, who owned the adjoining plantation, Palmyra. It was he who built Rose Hall between 1770 and 1780, the finest home in all Jamaica.

In 1821, the plantation passed by inheritance to Palmer's great-nephew, John. In this way he became owner of the now huge 6,600 acre plantation. John took as his bride a rare beauty, Annie Patterson. Annie had been raised by a voodoo priestess in Haiti, and married John shortly after arriving in Kingston, Jamaica. A petite young girl of 18, all the old records describing her appearance emphasize her chalk white skin and her contrasting black hair. Friend and enemy alike recognized her as an extremely beautiful woman.

And now to fully comprehend the story of Annie Palmer, we must almost shut out everything we think of today as being normal social behavior. In Annie's day, planta- tion life was dominated by its labor supply, and that labor was supplied by slaves.

The social order of all plantation life was vertical. At the apex was the Great House. The next most imposing structure at Rose Hall was the residence of Mr. John Ashman, the overseer. Everyone, other than the owner, was answerable to the overseer, including the handful of whites who acted as accountants, foremen, and other skilled labor. At the bottom of the social ladder, and the most numerous by far, were the slaves. All were black, and all had nothing except what was doled out to them to keep them alive. With the temperature ranging between 80 and 100 degrees, cutting sugar cane and distilling rum was hot, backbreaking work.

Annie Palmer immediately asserted herself as the real master of Rose Hall. She accomplished this by poisoning her husband, John Palmer. He died in his upstairs bedroom. As my charming Jamaican guide, Deleta Kemble said, "It was right in this very room that she fed him deadly African beans, crushed and mixed in milk."

The woman who was to become known as the White Witch of Rose Hall was now the owner of one of the great plantations in Jamaica. Annie ruled her domain like a dictator. Each day she left the house only once when the sun was up, and that was to supervise the whipping of her slaves in her back yard. Men and women alike were stripped naked and flogged in front of Annie. Many times she wouldn't give the order to stop and the slaves died tied to the whipping post. The slaves came to believe that she could cast voodoo spells. Some old records hint that using the power of suggestion she conjured up apparitions.

To add to the slaves' fear, she kept a torture chamber under the house. Of course, here in Jamaica, there are those who, even today, say that Annie Palmer was a bona fide witch of the devil.

At night she would don men's clothing, and dressed in black, astride a galloping horse, she would roam her vast estate. What horror must have filled the mind of a slave who Annie stumbled upon during her nocturnal wanderings. Annie was above all a passionate female, who sometimes took a slave as a lover. Her erratic and eventful life at Rose Hall continued. It is reported that when she tired of one lover, she did away with him by pouring boiling oil in his ear as he slept. Another was pushed through the upstairs sitting room window of the Great House.

Annie was to take two additional husbands, both of whom fared no better than John Palmer. One she strangled to death with the aid of a slave, and the third was stabbed to death in his bedroom. During the restoration of this bedroom, bloodstains were found on the wall under a layer of wallpaper.

Robert Rutherford arrived at Rose Hall from England to take up his duties as bookkeeper on the plantation. Known only to himself, he had another purpose for being in Jamaica. His father had inherited a plantation in Barbados. Young Robert was to observe and learn how a plantation was run, and later take over his father's operation. Thus Robert did not have the innate fear of being left without a job in a strange land, if he incurred the displeasure of the overseer, Mr. Ashman.

Within a few hours of his arrival at Rose Hall, Robert was told that it was quite normal for him to be issued a slave as housekeeper, who would cook his food and wash his clothing. She would also act as his lover. In the subculture that was slavery, if you had a kind and attractive master, this type of position was considered to be very desirable. Also vying for these preferred positions were a handful of free women who lived off the estate, but were allowed to move in under certain conditions. In this way Robert met Millicent, a perfectly proportioned, statuesque black girl. Millicent liked

Robert, but he was still not wise in the ways of the tropics and accepted her for her household duties only. He refused her offers of intimacy.

Within a matter of days Robert met the mistress of Rose Hall — Annie Palmer. He couldn't believe that this beautiful, petite woman was the feared witch of Rose Hall. Annie was at once attracted to Robert, and almost immediately the pair became lovers. Their torrid romance had to resist a multitude of external influences. The overseer Ashman had been Annie's lover before Robert came on the scene. He seethed with jealousy when Robert took his place in Annie's bed. Robert was enthralled with the beauty and passion of his lover, but was unable to reconcile her treatment of him with the harsh treatment of the slaves, and the rumors about her three deceased husbands. Both Millicent and Annie, in her way, dearly loved Robert. He could resist Millicent no longer and succumbed to her charms, so that we now find him with two lovers, one white and one black.

In the society in which slavery flourished, this situation could not exist for long, for Millicent was not an ordinary member of plantation life. To fully comprehend her rather unique position one must realize that the slaves brought many of their tribal beliefs with them from Africa. The practice of Obeah or witchcraft was the most powerful of their beliefs. An Obeah man had unlimited power. By using blood, bones, feathers, and other symbols, the Obeah man could inflict a curse which could cause sickness and even death. The slaves believed in witchcraft to such an extent that if a curse was inflicted they actually became ill. There are recorded cases where deaths have been attributed to these curses.

Millicent was very special indeed, for she was the granddaughter of Takoo, an Obeah man. Annie Palmer, who had been raised by a voodoo priestess in Haiti, was also said to have Obeah powers. Robert Rutherford was sleeping with two very influential women.

One night Annie, who suspected that Millicent was more than just a housekeeper to Robert, surprised her lover and Millicent in bed in Robert's quarters. A quarrel ensued, and Millicent told Annie in no uncertain terms that Robert was her man. She insinuated that she was a better woman than Annie. No one had ever spoken to the mistress of Rose Hall in that manner before. Millicent was ordered off the plantation. She fled to the home of her grandfather, Takoo.

That night Annie Palmer went to Takoo's home and hung the small bloodsmeared skull of a child on the door of the house. A deadly curse had been placed on Millicent. Next day, after the discovery of the skull Millicent grew lethargic. Soon she became ill and her breath came in gasps. Despite the incantations of he grandfather, her condition deteriorated. When Robert heard of the curse placed on Millicent he fetched a medical doctor from Montego Bay. The doctor examined the semi-conscious girl but could find nothing that contributed to her condition. He could do nothing for her, and Millicent died.

Takoo and several slaves armed with machetes, stormed the Great House in search of Annie Palmer. Upstairs in her spacious bedroom they found Annie. The room is the same now as it was then. A hand embroidered red and white canopy covers the oversize bed. Large windows where Annie had gazed over her domain now overlook the rolling grounds and the sea. Annie's eyes filled with terror as Takoo's hands choked the life from her body. The White Witch of Rose Hall was dead.

Takoo and his men fled to the hills. John Ashman, who truly loved Annie, formed a posse and tracked them down. Takoo was strangled to death by Ashman.

Robert Rutherford, the young accountant, left Jamaica shortly after Annie's death and never returned. Annie's grave lies a few hundred yards from the Great House. Her headstone is there to this day. In a field across the road from the present estate, five tall palm trees mark the graves of Annie's three husbands, one of her lovers, and her rival, Millicent.

Strange things are still rumored to occur in the Great House. There are those who think that Annie Palmer still stalks the halls and rooms. In 1905, one of the girls sent to clean the interior of the house fell down the stairwell, broke her neck, and died on the spot. Some Jamaicans feel the ghost of Annie may have assisted with a slight push.

The sun shone brightly as I left Rose Hall. As I went to the parking lot I glanced over my shoulder for one last look at the impressive structure. My eyes gravitated to Annie's bedroom window. I stopped short — just for an instant, was a flashing white form staring down at me? Nonsense, I thought, it might have been the reflection of the sun on a mirror in her room that caught my eye. Next day I mentioned the rather strange occurrence to a Jamaican friend. "There is no mirror in Annie's room at Rose Hall," he told me.

MAD MADAME
WEBER
(France)

In all the annals of crime, perhaps no case has been as baffling as the Jeanne Weber case. Not because Madame Weber was a master criminal, but because her crimes were so horrible that medical doctors did not want to believe the truth.

Jeanne was born in 1875, in the fishing village of Cotes-du-Nord, France. She left home at the age of 14, and wandered throughout the country. Jeanne existed by taking odd jobs before moving on to another village or town.

By 1893, she was a not too attractive slum dweller in Paris. But all was not doom and gloom for Jeanne, for around this time in her life she met Marcel Weber. Soon the pair married, and Jeanne moved in with her husband and a host of in-laws.

The young couple produced three children, and while any marriage that is confined to the slums of Paris cannot be described as delightful, the Webers seemed to be relatively happy. Their happiness was shortlived. Tragedy struck the household when their two youngest daughters died of natural causes. Jeanne took their deaths hard. She began to join her husband in drinking bouts, and it wasn't long before her consumption exceeded his ample capacity. When not into the sauce, Jeanne kept to herself, and suffered from long spells of depression.

Thrown together with her in-laws, she was often given the task of taking care of her nieces and nephews. One fine day in March, one of her sisters-in-law asked Jeanne to babysit her two daughters, Georgette and Suzanne, while she took her laundry to the local wash house. Jeanne obliged and went to her sister-in-law's apartment in Rue Pre-Maudit.

A neighbor, Madame Pouche, was walking by the open door of the apartment and saw Georgette on Jeanne's lap. It appeared to her that the child's face was turning blue. She ran and fetched Jeanne's sister-in-law from the washhouse. When they arrived back at the apartment they found Jeanne massaging the child's chest. Georgette recovered from what seemed to be a convulsion. The mother thanked Jeanne for her quick reaction to the emergency, and went back to the washhouse.

Within an hour Pierre Weber, the child's father, arrived home to find his daughter dead. Her face was blue, and it was obvious that she had gone into convulsions a second time. Apparently, this time Jeanne was unable to save her. Madame Pouche, who was again at the scene, mentioned the strange discoloration on the child's neck, but no one paid any attention to her. When a doctor arrived she mentioned the markings to him, but he too dismissed her probing inquiries.

Nine days later, the unsuspecting mother left her other daughter, Suzanne, with Jeanne while the family went shopping. When they returned, Suzanne was dead. Again, Madame Pouche pointed out the strange markings on the child's throat. To appease the talkative woman, the doctor informed the police. A gendarme arrived and did a cursory investigation. He believed that the child could have received the marks while convulsing, and stated that he found no evidence that Suzanne had died of anything but natural causes. He further stated that it was apparent convulsions ran in the family — hadn't they recently lost another daughter in exactly the same way? "A tragedy," he exclaimed, and probed no further.

Two weeks later, another sister-in-law, left her seven-month-old daughter, Germaine, with Jeanne. When she returned from a shopping trip she found Jeanne massaging little Germaine's chest. It seems she had convulsed while her mother was out. Luckily the child recovered. Much relieved, the mother again went shopping — this time when she returned her daughter was dead. That same night Jeanne's one remaining child, Marcel, died of suffocation in his sleep.

Up to this point no serious suspicion was cast upon Jeanne. It boggles the imagination to fathom how this could be so, but one must remember that our pleasant little narrative took place in the slums of Paris at the turn of the century. There was a high mortality rate among children. Diptheria often raged through the slums leaving hundreds of children dead. Diagnoses were casual and often ambiguous.

Yet another sister-in-law left her one year old son, Maurice, in Jeanne's care. She returned unexpectedly a few minutes later to find Maurice blue in the face and gasping for breath. She accused Jeanne of choking the child. Then she gathered up her son and rushed him to the emergency ward of the Bretonneau Hospital. In the course of treatment, the doctor discovered tell-tale red marks on the child's throat. He stated that the marks were caused by attempted asphyxiation. Jeanne's sister-in-law was justifiably furious. She went to the police and related the history of death that seemed to follow Jeanne.

On this information, Jeanne was later arrested. Doctors examined young Maurice's throat, but there were no visible marks left by the time the examination was performed. Some of the bodies of the young victims were exhumed. No distinct conclusion could be reached which pointed to manual strangulation as the cause of death. Despite this, the authorities were so convinced of Jeanne's guilt that they proceeded to commit her to trial for murder. No matter what else she may have been, Jeanne was no fool. She kept her mouth shut, hired a good lawyer, and was acquitted.

Nothing was heard of Jeanne (who was now being referred to in the press as L'Ogresse) for over a year. Then, in a small village in central France, a nine-year-old youngster, Auguste Bavouzet, was found dead under mysterious circumstances. There was discoloration about the throat, but after examination by the family doctor, it was decided that the child had died of natural causes. Auguste's older sister didn't believe the doctor. In fact, she was extremely suspicious of the family's new housekeeper, Madame Moulenet. She was so suspicious that she secretly searched the housekeeper's belongings. She found newspaper clippings and photographs revealing that Madame Moulenet was none other than Jeanne Weber.

The sister rushed to the police with this startling information and an expert pathologist was brought in to examine Auguste's body. He stated the cause of death was strangulation. Jeanne was arrested again and caused some embarrassment to the doctors who had examined her other victims. Despite the overwhelming series of coincidences that put one woman at the scene of so many similar deaths, these doctors continued to maintain that they had been right in their original diagnoses as to the cause of death of the earlier victims.

At Jeanne's trial these same doctors were called upon to testify. Auguste's body was exhumed, and the doctors claimed that the cause of death was typhoid fever. The press and the public alike declared that Jeanne was a mass murderer. Unbelievably, once more, she walked out of court a free woman.

In May, 1908, Jeanne was up to her old tricks. She was now living in a rented room as the wife of a man named Bouchery. One night Bouchery's employment necessitated his staying out all night. Madame Bouchery asked her landlord, Monsieur Poirot, if his seven-year-old son Marcel, could stay overnight with her for company. You guessed it — that night the whole house was awakened by the child's screams. When they rushed into the room they actually found Madame Bouchery in the act of strangling the boy. A doctor was summoned to the scene and readily identified thumb and finger imprints on the child's neck. A check by the police revealed that Madame Bouchery was our friend Jeanne.

In October, 1908, Jeanne was declared insane and was confined to a home for the mentally ill. She was a violent patient and was kept in close confinement for two years. Then Jeanne once more did what she had so much practice doing — she firmly clamped both her hands against her throat and succeeded in choking herself to death.

MATE BRAM
(U.S.)

oday when we think of a sailboat, we are inclined to picture a small boat out on a lake. At the turn of the century large, graceful sailing ships carried cargo all over the world. They were working vessels manned by tough men. Most of the proud sailing ships of yesteryear either ended up rotting in drydock or at the bottom of the sea in some watery grave. Very few are remembered today.

One such vessel that tragedy plucked out of the depths of oblivion is the *Herbert Fuller*.

The *Fuller* was built in Harrington, Maine in 1890, and had an uneventful sailing life for the first six years of her existence.

On July 8th, 1896, she set sail for Argentina with a cargo of lumber. There were eleven men and one woman on board. She was under the command of Captain Charles Nash, 42, a native of Harrington. The Captain owned shares in the *Fuller*, as did his wife, Laura, who was also aboard. The Captain and his wife were childhood sweethearts in Harrington. Being without children, the couple often sailed together.

Strangely enough, only one man of the entire ship's complement was known to the Captain for any length of time before sailing. He was Jonathan Spencer, 24, from St. Vincent in the British West Indies. He had been on one previous voyage to Martinique with Captain Nash. The rest of the crew met each other for the first time just before sailing. They were Hendrik Perdock of Holland, Francis Loheach, a Frenchman; Charley

Brown from Sweden, who was obviously using an assumed name; Henry Slice, a German; Oscar Anderson and Folke Wassen, both of Sweden, completed the ordinary crew.

The Second Mate was a Russian named August Blomberg. The First Mate was Thomas Bram from St. Kitts, British West Indies. The *Fuller* carried one lone passenger, Lester Monks, who was a little over 20 and a student of Harvard University. He was on board because of a bronchial condition that he thought might be cleared up by an ocean voyage.

Nothing unusual happened for the first six days of the voyage. The Captain, his wife, the first and second mate, and the passenger had their meals together in the cabin, served by the steward. These six of the eleven aboard got to know each other rather well during the first uneventful week.

On Monday night, July 15, Monks, the passenger, locked the door to his room at a little after eight o'clock and went to sleep. In the middle of the night a scream startled Monks. Up on his elbows, and listening intently now, he heard a loud gurgling sound. He reached under his pillow for his revolver and cautiously opened his door. He peered into the Captain's quarters. The Captain was lying beside his cot covered with blood. A loud gurgling noise came from his throat.

Monks realized he was alone with a dying man in the confined quarters of a cabin in the middle of the Atlantic Ocean surrounded by men he didn't even know. He decided the best thing to do was to get up on deck. He approached the forward companionway. Looking up he saw the first mate, Mr. Bram, on deck. He pointed his revolver at Bram and called out to him. The first mate threw a plank at him, but it did not come close to striking Monks. Monks shouted, "Come below. The Captain has been murdered." The first mate cautiously joined Monks and after viewing the dying captain they again went on deck. The two men curiously enough made no move to comfort the poor Captain. They discussed their predicament, and decided to wait right there on deck until morning. With the coming of daybreak the two men woke up Spencer, the steward. They took him down to view the now dead Captain Nash. Spencer noticed that the second mate's door was ajar. He peered into his cabin. He found the second mate in his bunk with his feet crossed and his head cut open. The men went to question Loheach, the Frenchman, who was at the wheel. While doing this they discovered a bloody axe on deck. Bram made the off-hand remark that no one was going to use it on him, and in one motion threw the axe overboard.

The murder weapon was thus lost forever.

The whole crew, except for the man at the wheel, were now gathered together and proceeded to the Captain's quarters. Here, in her own room, the corpse of Mrs. Nash was found. Her head had been split open. Although the Captain and second mate had obviously been killed in their sleep, Mrs. Nash had realized she was being attacked. Her hands and arms were badly cut where she had tried to ward off the blows delivered by her attacker.

Now the drama and tension aboard the *Herbert Fuller* reached its peak. Twelve people started out from Maine. Six days later, three were murdered, leaving nine alive. None of them knew each other more than a week. Eight of them were living in a nightmare, knowing full well that they didn't kill anyone, and wondering if the killer would strike again. Of course, the ninth was the killer of three people. Did he plan on killing more? Was the tension starting to tell on him as well? Surrounded by innocent men, was he acting out his part well enough?

Murder in the confines of a small ship is not like murder on land. There can be no allowance for a deranged strangler to have committed the crime. The nine survivors must have eyed each other. Talk, as well as action, was strained as they decided to place the three bodies in a row boat and tow its macabre cargo.

The crew then agreed to make for the nearest port. Because of a favorable wind, they decided to make for Halifax. Bram assumed command and appointed Charley Brown and Frank Loheach as first and second mate respectively. Everyone now slept on deck. Later they were to testify that no one had more than one hour of sleep per night. The truth is, they were all plain scared. A rumor spread among the survivors that Charley Brown had changed his clothes on the night of the murder. This seemed highly suspicious. Brown had also become moody and withdrawn since the night of the murder. On Thursday, everyone was so suspicious of him that the rest of the crew overpowered him and put him in irons.

For the next few days several of the survivors had an opportunity to talk to Brown. They estimated that he had been tending the wheel at the time the murders took place. He told his fellow sailors that he had seen Bram strike at someone in the cot as he had a clear view through the window in the after house. He convinced them that he feared for his life since only he knew who was in reality, the murderer. The rest of the crew overpowered Bram and placed him in irons.

On Tuesday, July 21, a pilot came aboard, and taking command, guided the *Herbert Fuller* into Halifax. The next day, just about every paper in North America featured the story on the front page.

A grand jury found an indictment against Bram, but not Brown. He joined his shipmates in jail. Monks and the steward, Spencer, were released on bail. Finally the whole thing was transferred to Boston, and Bram's trial started on Dec. 14, 1896. The trial attracted world wide attention for the simple reason that the term "murder on the high seas" held as much attraction then as it does now. There was also the fact that there was no doubt the murderer, whoever he was, was in the courtroom.

As the evidence and statements of all the survivors were correlated and compared, it became obvious that only three people were in close proximity to the scene of the crime, and had the opportunity to perpetrate the murders. These three were the passenger Mr. Monks, Charley Brown, who was tending the wheel at the time of the crime; and the first mate Bram.

Monks, in his locked room, was never really suspected. Brown fell under great suspicion, but an array of old sea captains swore that you couldn't lash the wheel of the *Fuller* for more than a minute. If the wheel was lashed any longer, the sails would commence to flap, making a noise loud enough to wake the crew. Everyone agreed it would take more than a minute to kill three people.

That left first mate Bram, who was actually standing trial for the triple slaying. By elimination he appeared to be the guilty party. The prosecution introduced a witness who had sailed previously with mate Bram. This witness, one Mr. Nicklas, told the story of how Bram had approached him to kill their Captain, seize and sell the ship and cargo. When Nicklas refused, Bram suggested another ship that had fewer men to contend with. Over and above this witness, the steward's and the passenger's evidence placed Bram in a position to have easily killed the three victims.

The jury is said to have cast 50 ballots before coming in with a "guilty" verdict. Bram was sentenced to hang. The Supreme Court of the United States set aside this verdict and a second trial took place on March 16, 1898. This time the jury was out for over 10 hours before bringing in a verdict of "Guilty without capital punishment".

On July 12th, 1898, Bram was sentenced to imprisonment for life, and taken to serve his time at the U.S. Penitentiary at Atlanta. He was paroled on August 27, 1913, after serving 15 years. For the next five years and seven months on parole his record was perfect. As a result, on April 22, 1919, President Wilson granted him a full pardon. When last heard of in the 1920s, Mr. Bram was a prosperous peanut wholesaler in Atlanta.

Because of her notoriety the *Herbert Fuller* had her name changed to the *Margaret B. Rouss,* and under this name she sailed the seas for a further 20 years. On April 27, 1917, a German torpedo struck the old *Fuller* and filled her hold with the sea. Because of her cargo of lumber she didn't sink immediately.

The Germans boarded her and looted the very cabin where so much tragedy had occurred many years before. Then they placed bombs in the hold and rowed away, pausing only long enough to see the proud old *Fuller's* hull sink below the surface forever.

A BROTHER'S DEADLY DREAM (England)

Sometimes an incident associated with a murder case becomes more celebrated than the murder itself. The untimely departure of Neville Norway from these worldly confines precipitated such a phenomenon. Today the unusual happening is the only reason the murder is remembered.

It all took place in 1840, in Wadebridge, County Cornwall, where Neville pursued the occupation of selling lumber and general goods. The 39-year-old entrepreneur did most of his business at markets in the scores of villages which dotted the countryside.

On Feb. 8, 1840, Neville conducted business at the market in the neighboring town of Bodmin. As usual, all transactions were for cash. During the course of a purchase Neville emptied his purse into his palm, revealing several gold and silver coins. He picked the pieces necessary to complete the transaction and thought little more about it.

Later, witnesses standing close by recalled the incident. They also recalled noticing William Lightfoot taking in the scene. Lightfoot was a local lad who knew Norway by sight.

That evening Neville Norway transacted business right up till 10 p.m. At that time he saddled up his horse for the rather lonesome nine-mile trip from Bodmin to his home in Wadebridge. Neville never made it.

For the first three miles he was accompanied by a friend. Then his friend branched off, following another road. Neville continued on alone.

When Neville's horse showed up riderless at his home, his family was justifiably apprehensive. The discovery of blood on the saddle turned their apprehension to fear. Servants and neighboring farmers combed the road for some sign of the missing man. The night was pitch black. It wasn't until daylight broke over Pencarrow Woods that someone spotted a piece of white shirt sticking out of a brook which meandered along the roadside. They had found the body of Neville Norway.

He had been savagely beaten about the head. These blows had caused death. Some mystery developed when an examining physician reported that he had discovered gunpowder on Neville's neck. There were no bullet wounds about the body.

Local police searched the scene. They found a pool of blood on the road, and a smoothed out path to the stream, where the body had obviously been dragged. They also found a tramped down area behind a nearby hedge with two sets of scuffed footprints, indicating that Neville had been ambushed. His turned out pockets left no doubt as to the motive for the crime. When the police found the broken off hammer of a pistol close by, they realized that Neville probably had gunpowder spilled on his neck while being pistol-whipped.

The citizenry of the area were incensed at the cold blooded murder. Travelling the deserted dark roads of rural England over 100 years ago was a necessity to many occupations. If one couldn't travel in safety, the selling of farm produce would be greatly hampered. The murderer must be brought to justice as speedily as possible.

A reward was posted, and a constable sent down from Cornwall to conduct the murder investigation. The constable went about tracing Norway's activities on the day of his death. During the course of these inquiries he was informed that William Lightfoot had been seen drooling over the late Mr. Norway's gold coins. Moreover, William and his brother James had not left the Bodwin market until shortly before 10 p.m. on the night of the murder. This was a late hour for men whose business didn't require that they be up and about.

A neighbor of James Lightfoot informed the constable that James had arrived home very late that night, and that he had heard Mrs. Lightfoot crying shortly after his return.

The homes of the Lightfoot brothers were searched. In a hollowed out ceiling beam in James' home, the constable found a revolver with a broken off hammer. The hammer found at the scene of the crime fit the revolver perfectly.

Two days later William was in his cups at the local grog shop. While being offered sympathy over his brother's predicament by a fellow imbiber, he let slip that he too was involved in the murder. This bit of information was passed along to the police and soon after William was arrested.

At first each man tried to cast the full blame on the other. Then they decided tell the truth. It was a simple story of murder for gain. The brothers had lain in wait for Norway. They knocked him off his horse, and when their pistol wouldn't fire, they beat their victim to death.

The two men were tried for murder on March 30, 1840. Thirteen days later they were hanged before 10,000 cheering spectators, and so ended the lives of the two killers.

The case, so similar to hundreds of others, should have long since passed from memory. But this was not to happen, for a psychic phenomenon, much more unusual than the murder itself, was to unfold.

Neville Norway's brother, Edmund, was a sea captain. On the very night of Neville's murder Edmund was at sea, somewhere between Manilla and Cadiz.

Edmund went to bed early on the evening of Feb. 8, 1840. He dreamed that his brother was riding his horse between Bodwin and his home in Wadebridge. Two men dragged his brother off the horse. One drew a pistol and fired twice. In the dream Captain Norway heard no sound from the pistol. The two assailants dragged his brother across the road and dumped his body in a brook. In his dream, Captain Norway observed a house on the left hand side of the road.

At 5 a.m., Norway awoke and took command of the ship. When he relieved the Second Officer, Henry Wren, he told him about his strange dream. Captain Norway expressed the opinion that his brother had been murdered. He told Wren that he was very familiar with the road leading to Wadebridge, and was puzzled by one discrepancy in the dream. He had dreamt that there was a house on the left hand side of the road. In reality, he distinctly recalled that there was a house there, but it was located on the right hand side of the road. Captain Norway comforted him with the thought that since there was one glaring error in his dream, it was possible that the entire dream had no relation to actual events.

Still, Captain Norway was so affected by his realistic dream that he wrote it all out in the ship's log.

Upon his return to England, Captain Norway found out that his brother had indeed been murdered. It all happened in precisely the way he had dreamed about it at sea. Moreover, the murder had taken place at exactly the same time as the dream.

As for the house being on the wrong side of the road: In Captain Norway's absence the road to Wadebridge had been diverted to the right of the house, so that the house now stood on the left hand side of the road, just as the Captain had so clearly seen in his dream.

ONE WAY VOYAGE
(South Africa)

Eileen Isabella Ronnie Gibson was born in India, but was educated and lived most of her life in England. The daughter of a well-to-do businessman, she had always been drawn to the theatre. The attractive, shapely brunette had served with a theatrical touring company during the war.

After the war, she and her mother travelled to South Africa to join her father, who was employed near Durban. Taking the stage name of Gay Gibson, the 21-year-old beauty gravitated to Johannesburg. Gay met with moderate success on the stage and had a long run in a hit play.

London's west end offered the ultimate in fame and fortune. The young girl, who had everything to live for, booked passage on the *Durban Castle* out of Capetown bound for Southampton, on Oct. 10, 1947. Gay Gibson never reached home.

Assigned to Cabin 126 on B deck, the beautiful Gay didn't take long to make friends. She took her meals in the salon with Mr. Hopwood, who was an official of the shipping line, and a Wing Commander Bray. Each evening, well before midnight, Mr. Hopwood would accompany Gay to the door of her cabin. She always locked the door behind her when she retired for the night.

On Oct. 17, seven days out at sea, the evening began much as usual. The ship was travelling through tropical shark infested waters, and the night was a scorcher. At about 7 p.m. someone suggested that they all take a dip in the ship's swimming pool. Gay thought it was a great idea. She went to her cabin to put on her swimsuit. She returned in approximately a half hour and explained that she couldn't find her suit. The rest of the evening was spent in idle chatter with the two men, until around 12:40 a.m. when Hopwood escorted Gay to her cabin. The couple said goodnight. Gay walked inside. She was never to walk out.

At about 3 a.m. Fred Steer, a night watchman, heard a cabin bell ring. He was in charge of answering all rings. An indicator showed him that the call had come from B deck, Cabin 126. As Steer approached the cabin he saw that the door was slightly ajar, and the lights in the cabin were on. As he reached the door it was quickly closed in his face. Steer was amazed to catch a glimpse of the deck steward, James Camb, inside a female passenger's cabin at 3 in the morning. Through the door Steer heard the gruff, "It's all right," and then nothing.

Steer reported the incident to his superior who told him that the best thing to do would be to keep quiet about the entire matter. The sex life of the passengers was not their business, and since no harm was done, they should forget the whole thing.

At around 7:30 in the morning the stewardess, Miss Field, knocked on the door of Cabin 126. She didn't receive any answer. The door was unlocked. Miss Field entered the cabin and found it to be empty. There were a few dark stains on a sheet on the bed, but nothing else of a suspicious nature caught her glance. Miss Field reported the missing girl to her captain, who immediately instituted a ship-wide search. No trace of Gay was found and the Captain had to presume that she had gone overboard by some method or other.

It wasn't long before Steer approached the Captain and told him of finding Camb in the cabin of the missing girl at 3 a.m. Camb denied ever being in Cabin 126, but during the inquiry he had a hard time explaining away scratches on his wrist and back.

The Captain of the *Durban Castle* wired Southampton. By the time the ship docked, the police were waiting to question Camb. After completing their interrogation they arrested Camb and charged him with murder. His trial began in Winchester on March 18, 1948.

By the time the trial began, he had changed his story. He admitted being with Miss Gibson on that fateful morning. They were engaging in sexual intercourse with Miss Gibson's consent, when all of a sudden the girl started to foam at the mouth. Her body went completely limp. Camb figured that no one would ever believe that she had consented. In a frenzy he tried to bring the girl around by applying artificial respiration. She did not respond. Then he panicked and pushed her body through the porthole.

Once Camb was rolling he told in detail how Gay had invited him to her cabin. When he arrived she was wearing only a dressing gown and nothing else. In fact, the way

Camb described the whole episode, it was Gay who had seduced him.

One irrevocable fact which shed some light on the victim's morals was a contraceptive appliance found in her luggage. Much was made of this fact by the defence in trying to prove Gay was of loose moral character.

It was a great story, but it didn't explain the scratches found on Camb's back and wrist. Nor did it explain who rang for assistance in the early morning hours when Gay's death occurred.

The jury chose to believe that Gay Gibson was frantically trying to summon help to the cabin when she was being raped and murdered. It took them only three quarters of an hour to find Camb guilty.

He was sentenced to hang, but escaped the gallows when the parliament of England suspended the death penalty for five years. His sentence was changed to one of life imprisonment.

In Sept. 1959 Camb was paroled. Soon after he sexually attacked a 13-year-old girl. He received a further sentence of two years probation. Still later he moved to Scotland, where he was charged with indecent exposure on the complaint of three young schoolgirls. This time he was sent back to prison to continue his original life sentence.

THE SHARK ARM CASE
(Australia)

Bodies have the nasty habit of turning up in the most embarrassing locales. Over the years we have followed the trials and tribulations of those enterprising individuals who have shipped their victims by air, land and sea. They have tied up the bodies or parts thereof in suitcases, gaily decorated oilcloth, and a vast array of other receptacles.

Coincidence often plays a large role in the discovery of the victim. Children playing on the side of Hamilton Mountain uncovered various parts of the former John Dick's torso. A duck, stained red, led to the solution of the Fred Thorne case in New York City.

To say that coincidence played a large part in Australia's famous shark arm case would be an understatement. The series of coincidences surrounding this case baffles the imagination.

It all began innocently enough in 1935. Albert Hobson and a companion were fishing at sea out of Sydney, Australia. Hobson hooked a small shark. While he was doing his best to land his catch, a 14-foot tiger shark appeared on the scene. In an instant the larger shark became entangled in Hobson's line. With assistance Hobson managed to land the monster.

Coincidentally, Hobson's brother owned the Coogee Beach Aquarium. The enterprising fisherman realized that he had caught a prize exhibit for his brother's aquarium. In a few days the huge tiger shark was on display. The shark refused food and swam incessantly back and forth in its pool, obviously not taking kindly to life in captivity.

On April 24, 1935, a week after its capture, the shark went berserk. It turned and thrashed in the water as if in great distress. Finally the shark regurgitated the contents of its stomach. Among the contents was a human arm.

Think of the odds. For this weird event to take place Hobson had to be fishing on a certain day in a certain spot. The shark had to get tangled in his fishing line. Hobson's brother had to own an aquarium and the shark had to suffer indigestion. Above all, this particular shark had to somehow, somewhere, out of an entire ocean, manage to swallow a human arm.

Police, accompanied by experts in various fields, examined the limb. Fishery experts volunteered the information that a shark's digestive system would normally completely digest flesh in 36 hours. They felt that the reason the arm was in such good shape after a week was due to the fact that the shark's digestive system may well have been disrupted because of its capture and confinement in the pool.

Tattooed on the mysterious arm were two tiny boxers in a fighting stance. Part of a rope was still tied around the wrist. Police went about investigating missing men with distinctive tatoos. They immediately came up with James Smith, a 40-year-old former boxer, who was listed as missing. Smith's wife and brother positively identified the arm as belonging to Smith. A fingerprint check established the identity beyond a doubt.

On April 8, nine days before Hobson captured his celebrated shark, Smith had left home. He had told his wife that he was going on a fishing trip with a friend, but did not reveal the friend's identity. Two weeks went by before Mrs. Smith reported her husband missing to the police.

At this point in the police investigation there was some speculation that Smith may have committed suicide. People have been known to tie down their arms and legs with weights before tossing themselves into the sea. Then, of course, there were those optimistic individuals who suggested that Smith may have lost his arm to the tiger shark, but could very well still be alive. Perhaps the shark held the secret.

As if anticipating officialdom's next move, the shark conveniently died. Upon being dissected it was found to contain no further portions of James Smith.

Investigating officers then turned to tracing Smith's actions from the time he had left his home. His employer, Reg Holmes, a boat builder, could shed no light on the movements of the missing man. However, police were successful in tracing Smith to a rented cottage at Cronulla on the coast. A friend of his, 42-year-old Patrick Brady, had accompanied Smith to the cottage. Brady had a police record and, at the time of the Smith investigation, was awaiting trial for forging cheques. The cottage at Cronulla was searched by police, but no bloodstains or other pieces of direct incriminating evidence against Brady were uncovered.

It was learned that a large mattress and a tin trunk normally in the cottage were now missing. Police felt that Smith could have been murdered and dismembered on the mattress, stuffed into the tin trunk, and the whole works tossed into the sea. On this supposition Brady was arrested and charged with murder. During questioning he incriminated Reg Holmes in a forgery ring, but Holmes steadfastly denied ever knowing Brady.

A few days after Holmes denied knowing Brady, Sydney Harbor police noted a speedboat being driven erratically in the harbor. They discovered Holmes drunk at the wheel of the boat. Holmes had a superficial gunshot wound on the side of his head. Investigating officers felt the wound was self inflicted and believed that Holmes had attempted suicide. He told a different story. He swore that Brady had confessed to him that he had killed Smith. Holmes was certain that someone was trying to kill him. They had just missed killing him on the boat, and he was sure they would try again. The police didn't believe him. They should have.

On the evening before the inquest into Smith's death, Holmes' body was found in his parked car under Sydney bridge. He had been shot three times with a .32 revolver. Someone, no doubt a passenger in the car, had timed the killing to coincide with the passing of the train overhead. No one had heard the fatal shots.

At Brady's murder trial the prosecution was hampered by not being permitted to present the deceased Holmes' statement incriminating Brady. Obviously the accused could not have been personally involved in the Holmes killing as he had been in jail at the time of the murder. Lurking over the entire proceedings was the slight doubt as to whether Smith was actually dead. After studying the arm, medical experts agreed that it had not been bitten off by the shark, but had been surgically, if crudely, removed by a cutting instrument. Brady, although strongly suspected by one and all of being the real culprit, was found not guilty.

While the shark arm case was occupying the front pages of Australia's newspaper, Sir Sidney Smith, the illustrious British forensic expert, was in Australia attending a meeting of the British Medical Association. He was invited into the case by the Sydney Criminal Investigation Branch.

After studying the arm and all circumstances surrounding the case, Sir Sidney came up with what is probably close to the truth. He concluded that Smith and whoever shared the cottage with him argued over something which led to Smith's murder. The body was then dismembered on the mattress. The parts were placed in the tin trunk, but the arm wouldn't fit in. The murderer then attached the arm to the outside of the trunk by means of a rope. Everything was dumped at sea. The arm worked loose and was swallowed by our friend, the shark.

Two men were later tried for the Holmes murder, but they too were acquitted. No one has ever been convicted for the Smith murder.

LAW OF NECESSITY
(U.S.)

Pay attention now. We are about to walk a thin and precarious line known in legal circles as the law of necessity. When does the very necessity of taking a human life deem the act to be excusable? The case which best illustrates the law of necessity is the United States vs. Holmes.

On March 13, 1841, the U.S. vessel *William Brown* left Liverpool bound for Philadelphia. Over a month later, on April 19, the ship struck an iceberg about 250 miles off Cape Race, Nfld., and commenced to sink rapidly. The ship's complement consisted of 17 seamen. She also carried 65 passengers, mostly Scottish and Irish immigrants. A longboat was lowered and was immediately overcrowded with the first mate, eight sailors, and 32 passengers — in all 41 persons. A jolly boat was also lowered and cleared. It held the Captain, eight crew members, and one passenger. An hour and a half after the ship struck the iceberg, she sank with 31 passengers aboard.

As soon as the longboat was launched it began to leak badly. By bailing furiously the passengers and crew were able to hold their own against the Atlantic, which was becoming increasingly rough.

Next morning, a Tuesday, the jolly boat containing the Captain, and the overcrowded longboat parted company, but not before the Captain informed the First Mate that he was to take command of the longboat. The First Mate voiced the opinion that he didn't have a chance with the overcrowded boat. It might even become necessary for him to cast lots and throw some people overboard. The Captain agreed, advising, "Let it be the last resort."

As they parted, the Captain and crew members agreed that the longboat could not possibly survive more than a few hours. The boat was still leaking badly. Ice floes crashed about in the heavy seas. Even a sudden shift by the passengers would have been enough to lower the side and bring the sea roaring in on the freezing passengers.

Six days later the Captain and all the other occupants of the jolly boat were picked up by a french fishing vessel. Still later, in Philadelphia, the Captain made a deposition describing the grim plight of the seamen and passengers aboard the longboat, which must by now be at the bottom of the Atlantic.

Meanwhile the overcrowded longboat had survived all that Tuesday by frantic bailing on the part of the passengers and the crew members. By 10 p.m., the 24 hours of hard work and freezing cold were beginning to weaken the occupants of the ill-fated boat.

Little was said, but the crew knew what they intended to do. The boat had to be lightened if any of them were to survive. Finally, the First Mate gave the guarded order, "Men, you must go to work or we will all perish." The crew pounced on one man and threw him overboard.

Soon crude rules developed. A man was not to be thrown overboard if his wife was on board. No woman or children were to be cast over the side. No other guidelines were expressed, and by this selection system 14 individuals were cast into the sea. Many dramatic moments took place on the longboat that stormy Tuesday night.

We need only concern ourselves here with one seaman named Holmes, for it was against this man that the law of necessity was to be tested. Holmes was one of the seamen actively tossing passengers overboard. When Holmes selected Francis Askin, the hapless Askin offered Holmes five sovereigns to let him live till morning. Askin explained, "If God don't send us some help, we'll draw lots and if the lot falls on me, I'll go over like a man." Holmes replied, "I don't want your money, Frank." Over the side went Askin.

As daylight came on Wednesday morning, the weather cleared. Miraculously the good ship *Crescent* picked up all who were left on the longboat.

Later, Holmes was charged with manslaughter in the case of Askin. Holmes' defence lawyer pleaded that the act of throwing Askin overboard was performed under orders. Moreover, it was a necessary act, performed as a last resort in order to save others.

In charging the jury, the judge explained the complicated law of necessity and its application. To stringently apply the law of necessity, the peril to one's life must be instant and leave no alternative but to take another life. A sailor is obliged to withstand the perils of a voyage even if he is removed from his ship to a smaller and more dangerous vessel. When it comes to sacrificing human life because of necessity, a sailor should receive no more consideration than a passenger, except when a sailor must be spared in order to command or man the vessel. That number of sailors required to man the vessel are exceptions and should not be placed in a position where they could be thrown overboard. All sailors over the number required to man the vessel would then become equal to the passengers.

In charging the jury, the judge pointed out that there is no selection in law as to who should live and who should die, but the fairest way is by drawing lots, the very method the First Mate of the *William Brown* suggested to his Captain before they parted company on the high seas. The judge further stated that Holmes was not compelled to obey an unlawful order.

The Holmes jury deliberated for more than 16 hours before returning a verdict of guilty with a recommendation of mercy. The press of the day was extremely sympathetic to Holmes. Everyone agreed that had lots been drawn resulting in 14 men being thrown overboard, no trial for manslaughter would have taken place.

Holmes received the relatively light sentence of six months imprisonment at hard labor in Eastern Penitentiary of Pennsylvania.

A Look Alike

- Part 11 -

QUESTIONABLE CASES

A LOOK ALIKE

It must be terrible to be accused and convicted of a crime if you are innocent. Many men have gone through this experience. Perhaps the strangest case of all is that of Adolf Beck.

It all began in London, England in 1877 with a gentleman by the name of William Augustus Meyer. Willie was a short, stocky charmer of German extraction.

His occupation can only be described as falling into that dubious category of con man. Willie would case a likely looking mark of the opposite sex. His practiced eye would pick out those ladies who were over the hill, but whose appearance showed signs of affluence. He flattered them with his well chosen and rehearsed line. Devil that he was, he always succeeded in escorting his chosen lady home and gaining entrance to her flat. Once inside he told the unsuspecting, about-to-be-fleeced victim that he was despondent. Even worse, he was depressed. Tell me more, the lady would undoubtedly exclaim, completely entranced with the genteel aristocratic language that was well calculated to lower her guard. Willie, who by the way used the alias of Lord Wilton of Willoughby, would sob out the story of how, during a heated argument, his mistress left him. It had become unbearably lonesome in his apartment alone. Willie always mentioned one of the wealthiest neighborhoods in London when he dropped the address. Just about now the member of the over the hill gang was under his spell.

Then he would venture, in his best possible manner, that he wouldn't dare ask his new friend if she would try out his flat, the better to quell his attack of lonesomeness.

Of course, he would see that her wardrobe was refurbished in keeping with her new station in life.

Would she be willing? You're damn right she would. With exclamations of undying love, the pact was sealed. Willie would get out pen and paper immediately and write an open letter of credit to a top ladies' store in London. He professed to be no good at picking ladies' clothing. Jewelry, however, was quite another matter. He told his new friend he was a connoisseur and would like to pick out some rings and watches for her personally. Of course, this was impossible as he did not know the ladies' wrist or finger size. Not to worry, the lady would say, take this watch and a ring or two for samples.

Lord Wilton of Willoughby would leave the lady full of anticipation, never, he hoped, to see her again.

Willie Meyer had made a pretty fair living off this scheme for several years, but like all good things, it came to an end. One day he ran flush into one of his victims on the street. This led directly to the inconvenience of a five-year jail sentence. Upon being released from jail in 1885, Willie left for New York City. While he was in New York a Norwegian named Adolf Beck arrived in London from Peru. He had lived there since 1868. In London, he bought and sold merchandise of any kind. When he pulled a profitable deal he used to seek out the company of prostitutes. Adolf was not a saint, but the one fact that was to affect him for the rest of his life was that he had a slight resemblance to our old friend, Willie Meyer. Not a great resemblance, but enough. To make matters worse, Willie came back from New York and was working the same old scheme with the single ladies.

One day a woman grabbed Adolf by the frock coat. She wouldn't let go. Finally Adolf summoned a cop. Much to his surprise the constable believed the lady. She said he had conned her out of some rings and watches. Adolf was detained. The next day more women came forward and unhesitatingly identified him as the elusive Lord Wilton. Then a constable positively identified him as none other than Willie Meyer who had served five years in jail for this very scheme in 1877. Beck had the unfortunate experience of sitting in the famous Old Bailey and hearing all sorts of untrue stories about himself.

His lawyer thought he could get him off by proving that the frauds committed in 1877 and the current ones were perpetrated by the same man. Beck, of course, could prove that he was in Peru in 1877. However, British justice being completely fair, wouldn't allow any reference to the crimes committed in 1877. In so doing, they inadvertently took away poor Beck's only defence.

Adolf Beck received five years in jail. In 1901, friendless and penniless he was released from prison. He struggled along as best he could until April of 1904, when there was an outbreak of frauds perpetrated against women. Having already served time in prison for exactly the same crime, Beck became a logical suspect. The authorities still believed Beck and Meyer to be one and the same man. Unbelievably, a lady victim identified Beck as Lord Wilton once more. This time four more women came forward and positively identified poor Beck.

On April 27, 1904 Adolf Beck was convicted of crimes he didn't commit. Between the time he was convicted and the time he was to be sentenced the real Willie Meyer was caught in the act and arrested. He received a sentence of five years, but more importantly all the facts came out at his trial and everyone involved realized a great injustice had been done to innocent Adolf Beck. He was immediately released from custody and completely exonerated of all guilt. There was a great public outcry at the injustice done Adolf. He became something of a folk hero. A committee was appointed by the government to delve into the strange circumstances that convicted an innocent man. In the end the committee didn't blame anyone, but claimed it was just an unfortunate incident that couldn't have been avoided.

It seems the committee overlooked one fact. When Adolf Beck was picked up and identified as Willie Meyer by a constable, Willie's prison records were routinely checked. The descriptions on the documents matched Adolf in every detail but one. Willie Meyer was circumcised. Adolf Beck was not. If the authorities had noticed this anatomical discrepancy, Adolf would never have been convicted.

Released a broken and disillusioned man, Adolf Beck received £5,000 by way of restitution. He died in Marylebone Infirmary in 1909.

THE SCOTTSBORO BOYS

During the great depression one of the main means of transportation was stealing a ride on a train. Men moved from place to place seeking work. Some just moved for the sake of moving. There was little else to do.

On the afternoon of March 25, 1931, four black youngsters hopped a freight train that was leaving Chattanooga, Tennessee. As the Alabama Great Southern chugged its way toward Alabama, a group of white boys who were also hoboing a lift on the same train were walking from car to car, when they came across the black boys. A few angry words were exchanged for no apparent reason. This was the deep south of 1931, and no reason was needed. The train was moving so slowly that the youngsters were able to jump off and throw rocks at the black youths. They then got back on the train below the car occupied by the four boys from Chattanooga. The train pulled into Stevenson, Alabama for water. The four Chattanooga lads got off the train and discovered another group of black boys on another car. They decided to join forces for their mutual protection. More rocks were thrown. Finally an open fight broke out between black and white. The 10 or 12 black boys succeeded in kicking their white tormentors off the train.

The boys who were thrown off the train were so angry that they returned to Stevenson and complained to the stationmaster. He in turn called ahead to Paint Rock.

One must realize the racial prejudice that existed in the deep south to fully comprehend what soon followed. Whites of any strata of society were not accustomed to being set upon by blacks in Alabama.

An armed mob was waiting for the train at Paint Rock. Some of the blacks simply ran away before the mob met the train and were never heard of again. The original four from Chattanooga, Andy Wright, 19; his brother Roy Wright, 14; Eugene Williams, 13; and Heywood Patterson, 18; were joined by five others they had just met on the train for the first time. They were Olen Montgomery, Willie Robinson, Clarence Norris, Charlie Weems, and Ozie Powell, ranging in age from 14 to 20.

Among the whites who lodged the complaint were two girls dressed in overalls.

To avoid a lynching right then and there the nine youths were hustled off to Scottsboro, and were forever after to be known as the "Scottsboro boys." Here, too, a mob quickly formed outside the jail. By nightfall it is estimated that there were 500 people milling around outside their window. Some of the younger boys started to cry.

A guard brought two women into the jail. He asked the boys, "Do you know these girls?"

"No", they all replied.

"You damn liar niggers! You raped these girls."

The National Guard was brought into the town, and the next morning the Scottsboro boys were transferred to Gadsden, Alabama, which was supposed to be safer.

The law moved fast for blacks in 1931.

On March 31, an all-white jury indicted all nine boys for rape. The trial started on April 6. The two girls, Victoria Price and Ruby Bates insisted that they were held down while all the boys took turns raping them. The boys insisted they only noticed the girls after the train got into Paint Rock and was met by the mob. On April 9, all but Roy Wright were sentenced to die in the electric chair on July 10. One juror held out for life imprisonment for Roy, and as a result a mistrial was declared in his case. The sentences were greeted with cheers and clapping. Outside a brass brand played *There'll be a Hot Time in the Old Town Tonight.*

Over the years, the Scottsboro boys were to face many trials, both individually and collectively. The case received world wide attention. The International Labor Defence sent lawyers to Alabama to get a stay of execution for the prisoners, and conduct their defence in future litigation. In Europe, organizations were formed to raise money for the defence. On May Day of 1931, over 300,000 citizens in more than 100 cities of the U.S. demonstrated for the release of the Scottsboro Boys. On the very day set for the execution, July 10, a stay was granted. In France, Germany, England, and even Latvia organizations were formed to help the defendants.

The months slipped into years, and on March 13, 1933, almost two years after the alleged crime, Samuel Liebowitz took charge of the defence. In the many legal battles that Liebowitz fought regarding the case, he always attacked the fact that no black person sat on an Alabama jury. One of the girls, Ruby Bates, finally admitted that she was never raped by any of the nine boys. All were framed because they had thrown the white boys off the train.

It is difficult to relate to the Depression years in the deep south, and the excitement and clamor that this case held for the general public in the early thirties. Even President Roosevelt was continually besieged by delegations pleading with him to intervene. Heading one of the delegations was Ruby Bates who had now become a defence witness. The State of Alabama would not give up these poor boys caught in a net they hardly understood. It appears that from the outset their innocence was really never in question.

Whatever happened to the Scottsboro boys?

Roy Wright, who was the only one not sentenced to be executed was released with Olen Montgomery, Eugene Williams and Willie Robinson on July 24, 1937, after spending over six years in various jails and prisons.

Ozie Powell slashed a guard with a knife, and while the rape charge against him was dropped, he received 20 years for assault. He was paroled on June 16, 1946. He had spent almost 15 years in prison.

Clarence Norris had his death sentence commuted and was paroled in 1947, after 16 years imprisonment.

Charlie Weems received a 75-year sentence and was paroled in 1944, after 13 years in prison.

Andrew Wright received 99 years, and was paroled in 1950, after 19 years in prison.

Haywood Patterson escaped from prison in 1948, and has never been apprehended.

The nine lads spent a total of 104 years in prison for the crime of fighting back when white boys threw rocks at them.

A LYNCHING IN
ATLANTA

On April 26, 1913, Atlanta, Georgia was celebrating Confederate Memorial Day. The old veterans marched down Peach Street in their grey uniforms proud to have served their beloved southland. General Stonewall Jackson's widow took the salute. All business establishments were officially closed for the holiday.

Across town at the National Pencil Factory, Newt Lee, watchman, was making his rounds. He had to go to the basement to use the "colored" toilet. In the basement he found the body of 14-year-old Mary Phagan. She had been strangled with a piece of cord that was tied so tightly around her neck that it was barely visible. Within four hours, Newt was in jail on suspicion. He was terrified. A black man who found a white woman dead was bait for a lynch mob in 1913. In fact, the very next week, three Negroes were lynched in Georgia. Their crimes were staring at a white Sunday school teacher, shooting off a gun while drunk, and talking back to a white man.

The manager of the pencil factory was Leo Frank. In the political and social climate of Atlanta during this time, Leo Frank had an unbelievable number of things against him. He was not an impressive appearing man. He was five feet, six inches tall, wore thick glasses, and was slight of build. He had protruding eyeballs, and could not be described as a man's man. Frank was born in Texas, but his family moved to Brooklyn before he was a year old. He was a graduate of Cornell University, and was the President of the Atlanta Lodge of B'nai B'rith. In brief, he was thought of as a

Yankee capitalist Jew. His uncle, Moses Frank, was the main shareholder of the factory, and it was through his uncle that he was offered and accepted the position of manager of the business.

From the moment he was asked to identify the body he was the main suspect in the case.

Poor little Mary Phagan was an employee of the pencil factory. On the day of the murder, Mary took a streetcar to the factory to pick up her pay envelope. This was not unusual. Other girls had stopped by the factory earlier for the same reason. Leo Frank was just finishing up his weekly report when he heard a tap at his office window. It was Mary Phagan. She gave her payroll number to Frank. He went to the safe and got her pay packet. It contained $1.20 for 10 hours work. She took her pay and walked out of his office to her death. This was Leo Frank's story. It was his story only hours after the murder, and it was his story when he was sentenced to death. No concrete piece of evidence has ever been produced to contradict his version of what took place between him and Mary Phagan that morning.

Three days after the murder took place, Leo Frank was arrested and charged with murder. On the day of his arrest the *Georgian*, one of the leading newspapers in Atlanta, ran a picture of Frank under the caption "Monster." The next rumor about Frank that was given by the press was that he was a pervert. In fact, some papers went so far as to say the pencil factory was really a house of prostitution.

Witnesses gave conflicting evidence as to Frank's activities that Saturday morning. There was maintenance staff around the four-storey building, as well as people coming back and forth for their pay. As soon as Frank's lawyers came up with a witness proving that Frank couldn't have been the murderer, the prosecution would produce a witness that would place Frank at the murder scene at the time the murder took place.

During the search for witnesses, the prosecution dug up Jim Conley, a sweeper at the factory. Now it seems some handwritten notes were found near the body. They were written in such a way to make it appear that little Mary wrote them after rape had been attempted upon her. They were illiterate. When all the employees of the factory were questioned about these notes, Jim Conley swore that he couldn't write. When Frank was told this he knew Conley was lying, because he had seen Conley write and in fact had a sample of his writing at the factory. Conley was confronted with the sample and he confessed he was a liar. The notes found near the body had been written by him, he said. He claimed they had been dictated before the murder by Frank. The notes proclaimed that the attacker was a tall, slim, black man.

This evidence was in the end to convict Leo Frank of the murder of Mary Phagan.

In the meantime, Conley kept changing his story for the obvious reason that he now found himself in the role of accomplice. In order to exonerate himself, he gave a total of four statements, all naming Frank as the actual murderer. The last of these four statements was a detailed study of how Conley helped Frank hide the body in the basement of the factory.

Under Georgia law Frank was given the opportunity to give a statement on his own behalf. He had written it out well in advance and it took him over four hours to read it in court. He told his life story from birth to the moment he found himself in court. It was obvious to anyone with an open mind that Leo Frank was innocent. He probably had not committed a violent act in his life. It was equally obvious that he really didn't think that an innocent man could be found guilty.

He was wrong.

An ominous crowd of more than 2,000 waited outside the courthouse. Hundreds flocked to the jail each day trying to catch a glimpse of the monster. The jury brought in a verdict of guilty. The prosecution attorney was carried through the streets on the crowd's shoulders. A large crowd danced in front of the factory where the crime took place. At the ballgame in Atlanta that day, the guilty verdict was flashed on the scoreboard and the game was held up while the fans held a happy demonstratiion.

After the verdict was announced, the discoverer of the body, Newt Lee was released after four months in jail.

Because of his co-operation with the authorities Jim Conley was given one year on the chain gang as an accessory after the fact of murder.

Two years were to drag by during which all stays and appeals were exhausted. Finally, on June 21, 1915 Governor John M. Slaton, in a long statement reviewing all the evidence, showed proof that there was really no clear evidence of guilt. He commuted Frank's sentence from the death penalty to imprisonment for life.

To protect his life, Frank was spirited away to Milledgeville Prison farm 200 miles from Atlanta. The public mood in Atlanta was such that leading Jewish families were warned that the authorities could not provide them with protection. Some moved into hotels. Others left Atlanta, fearful of mob rule. A mob of 5,000 marched on the Governor's mansion, and only the Horse Guards that had been called earlier by an assistant, saved the governor himself from being lynched.

Back in the prison, a convicted murderer named William Creen slashed Frank's throat so viciously that his life was only saved by a doctor inmate who was on the scene at the time of the attack.

To further emphasize the mood that permeated the state of Georgia, it is important to note that a petition was circulated asking for Creen's release as a reward for attacking Frank.

On Aug. 16, 1915, eight cars arrived at Milledgeville. They contained a total of 25 men. These men cut all the telephone wires leading out of the prison, and within ten minutes had placed Frank in one of the vehicles. They drove him all the way back to Mary Phagan's hometown of Marietta. They tied his hands behind his back, and tied his feet together. Then they threw a rope over a tree and lynched Leo Frank.

A reward of $5,000 dollars was offered for information about any one of the 25 men. Not one clue or lead was turned up by the offer. A photo of the lynching was a best selling novelty item throughout the state for years after the event took place.

Up to the time of his death in 1962, Jim Conley had told several people that it was he who had killed Mary Phagan.

WAS HANRATTY GUILTY?

All executions are revolting. The execution of an innocent man does not happen very often, but it does happen. The thought of a man or a woman becoming entwined in a series of circumstances that inadvertently makes them appear guilty, yet knowing of their own innocence, boggles the imagination.

They sit in the witness stand and listen to eye witnesses positively identify them. They are placed at the scene of a murder, when in reality they were miles away at the time the crime was committed. Sometimes realizing the futility of their dilemma, they change their story to a more plausible one.

In some cases, after an execution takes place, new evidence comes to light that casts a shadow of doubt on the guilt of the person just executed. The doubt itself is enough to conjure up the thought of the convicted prisoner going through the horror of the final days on death row until a noose is placed over his head.

Typical of all such doubtful cases is the one of James Hanratty.

It started one evening on a country road not far from Taplow, near London, England. Dusk was enveloping the countryside as a little Morris Minor pulled off the road into a deserted cornfield. It was Aug. 22, 1961, and the occupants of the little car were to spend the next six hours in abject terror.

Michael Gregsten was a married man, and maybe he shouldn't have been parked in a cornfield with Valerie Storie, but he was. Michael and Valerie were lovers. Gregsten had not been getting along with his wife for some time. They were both startled when someone knocked on their window. A stranger pointed a revolver at them, forcing his way into the car. The intruder got into the back seat and warned them not to turn around. He took three pounds from Gregsten's wallet, and some coins from Valerie's purse. The stranger started to talk, and he continued talking for almost two hours. Then he got Gregsten to back the car out of the cornfield, and proceeded to drive aimlessly through country roads. They even stopped for petrol and food, but the two terrified passengers could not attract attention.

Finally, the little car came to a stop just off a deserted stretch of road, A6, between London and Bedford. Gregsten was ordered to squeeze the car behind a hedge at the side of the road. The stranger with the gun asked Gregsten to pass a small duffle bag from the front seat to the back. As Gregsten went to comply with this command, the stranger fired two shots at him. They entered his left ear and went directly through his head, killing him instantly.

Miss Storie shouted, "You bastard, you shot him." The stranger said, "He frightened me. He moved too quick."

Storie, with the bleeding body of her boyfriend beside her, collapsed. She has never been able to account for the fifteen minutes that elapsed following the killing.

When she did come to her senses, the stranger ordered her into the back seat and raped her. He then made her give him a short course on how to run the car. Next she was ordered to drag Gregsten's body out of the car, and she was told to sit down beside the body of her friend. He then proceeded to pump four shots into her before the gun ran out of bullets. The now murderer and rapist reloaded the gun and casually shot a further six times. This time one additional bullet entered Miss Storie's body. In all she had taken five slugs. The killer bent over her bleeding body and left her for dead. He was wrong. Incredibly Miss Storie was alive. She lay unconscious for some three hours before she was discovered. Rushed to the hospital, this remarkable woman was able to give the police a description of the killer. She told the police her attacker was about 30 years old, five feet, six inches tall, with brown hair and eyes, and spoke with an East London accent. She confidentially told police of a phrase the killer kept mispronouncing. It was "I am finking" instead of "I am thinking." She was sure she would recognize this phrase if she ever heard it again.

James Hanratty was a small time housebreaker. Two days after the murder he was taking a suit to the drycleaners when, in an unbelievable coincidence, he was spotted by Michael Gregsten's widow. She claimed it was a supernatural hunch, that she instinctively knew that the man passing on the street was the killer of her husband. She made such a fuss that she talked a relative into going into the cleaning establishment and getting the name and address of the man who had just dropped off his suit. It had been deposited under the name J. Ryan. The police hesitated to act on such information.

On Sept. 11, something happened to make them change their minds. William Nudds worked in the Vienna Hotel. While routinely checking a room, he found two .38 cartridge cases. When police checked the cartridge cases it was found that they had been fired by the gun that killed Gregsten. On the night before the murder, the room had been rented to J. Ryan.

On checking further, the police found that the day after the murder the room was rented to one Peter Louis Alphon. On Sept. 22, Alphon surrendered to the police. Valerie Storie failed to pick him out of a lineup. The police started to concentrate on the man who had the room the day before the murder. He was now identified as James Hanratty, using the name of J. Ryan. This was the same man Mrs. Gregsten had pointed out as her husband's killer.

With a flair for the dramatic that is so typically British, Hanratty kept calling the police on the telephone proclaiming his innocence. Finally he was picked up in Blackpool on Oct. 9, and Valerie quickly identified him as her attacker. They asked him to repeat the phase "I am thinking." He replied, "I am finking."

Hanratty was arrested and charged with murder. There were some inconsistencies brought out at his trial. He had blue eyes rather than brown. Valerie volunteered that she may have been mistaken with her earlier description. Hanratty, throughout his trial, said that he was in Liverpool on Aug. 22, the day of the murder, and had been with three friends. They were all small time crooks wanted by the police, and he wouldn't have them picked up to testify for him. His lawyers pleaded with him, but it was no use. Then in the middle of the trial things were going so badly for Hanratty that he informed everyone that his whole story of the three men was a lie. He really had spent the night at Rhyl, in a rooming house. The rooming house was located. There was no record of J. Ryan or Hanratty having stayed there on Aug. 22. No lodgers who had spent that particular night there, remembered Hanratty.

If this were a fictional account of a murder, the case would be marked closed. However, as is so often the case, the truth that unfolded became stranger than fiction.

Remember Peter Louis Alphon, the man who had rented the hotel room where the fatal cartridges were found? He confessed that he was the murderer. He said he was hired to scare the couple into breaking up, but he wouldn't divulge who had hired him.

Since his initial confession, Alphon has retracted and reinstated it many times. However, new evidence has come to light since the execution. Several witnesses have come forth stating that they saw Hanratty at Rhyl on the evening of Aug. 22, 1961. If these people are to be believed, certainly Hanratty is innocent. There are those who still wonder what a housebreaker was doing in a cornfield. Hanratty had no record of ever being involved in a sex crime. Is a woman who has seen her boyfriend shot twice in the head, subjected to a violent rape and then herself shot five times, in any shape to identify anyone?

As Alphon said, "The reason she couldn't identify me is because she never saw me."

It all doesn't matter that much to Hanratty any more. Like I said before, he was executed on April 4, 1962.

THEY PLACED A NOOSE AROUND HIS NECK

Not many men have had the bone chilling experience of having a noose placed around their neck and live to tell about it. J.B. Brown found himself one second from being executed. This is his story.

On Oct. 17, 1901 in Palatka, Florida, at 5:30 a.m., H.W. Gordon rose at the crack of dawn to go to work. He always took a short-cut through the Florida Southern Railway yard. On this particular morning, with the sun just rising, Gordon stumbled and almost fell. When he looked down at what had blocked his path, he was horror stricken. There at his feet was the body of a man. Gordon immediately summoned the police.

The body was identified as that of Harry Wesson, an engineer on one of the freight trains operating out of the yard. Harry had been shot in the head. A few feet from the body the police found a .38 calibre pistol. The victim's pockets were turned inside out, indicating robbery had been the motive, but Harry had fooled his killer. He had tucked a roll of bills totalling $130 inside his overalls. His killer had missed the main loot.

The killing was a cold callous one, performed during the commission of a robbery. The police immediately deduced that Harry had been killed by a co-worker in the yard. They began their investigation by tracing Harry's last known movements. Luckily enough, this proved to be an easy task, for Harry had signed his name to a register in his foreman's office at precisely 4:19 a.m.

A night watchman named Scott claimed he and Harry had left the foreman's office together. Once outside, they had gone their separate ways. Sometime within the next hour and eleven minutes, someone had shot Harry in the head.

Feeling ran high among the railroad fraternity, and action was demanded of the authorities. The police reacted by questioning and detaining anyone even remotely connected with the murder.

Harry Landon, a switchman, who was around the yard during the critical time period was questioned extensively. J.J. Johnson, a night watchman who actually lived at the railway yard, was also pulled in. While both men were being detained in the jailyard, a minor incident took place, which materially changed the course of the investigation.

J.B. Brown, a former brakeman on the railroad, was well known to all the principals in the case. One of the jail guards had seen him talking through a fence to prisoner Johnson. The guard reported that he had recognized Brown, and had heard him say to Johnson, "Keep your mouth shut and say nothing." Acting on his information, the sheriff in charge of the case pulled Brown in for questioning.

The sheriff discovered that Brown had been in a fistfight with a conductor. Wesson had broken up the fight and kicked Brown out of the railway yard. Brown swore to get even with Wesson, and never reported back to work after the scuffle.

In his defence, Brown swore that he had been playing poker the evening before the murder. The game continued, but he left at 11:30 p.m. and went to his rooming house. He swore he never left the room until the following morning shortly after Wesson's body was found. After the excitement had died down, he rejoined the poker game, which was still in progress.

Now that a semblance of a motive was available to the authorities, they concentrated on Brown. They discovered that he left the poker game without a quarter, but returned the next morning with three or four dollars. The other suspects were released after questioning, but Brown, now the prime suspect in the case, was placed in jail.

While confined to jail, Brown shared a cell with two other inmates. After a few days these two men came forward and stated that Brown had confessed to the murder of Wesson. They claimed he said that he lay in wait for Wesson, shot him in the head, and robbed him of the princely sum of $4.75. Despite denying the confession, Brown was arrested and charged with murder.

His trial began on Nov. 19, 1901. Brown's landlord explained that Brown's room was located beside his own. In order for Brown to leave the rooming house, he would have to pass through his landlord's room. The landlord swore that Brown never left the house until after the body was discovered. It may be noted that Brown's landlord was not the most savory character in the world. His testimony did not hold the weight it might have if it had come from a more reliable witness.

The landlord even said that he had loaned Brown a few dollars when he came home the night before the murder. This conveniently accounted for the money Brown had in his possession when he rejoined the poker game.

In his own defence Brown swore that he had never said anything to any inmates of the jail. He also claimed that the guard had made a mistake in identifying him.

No one believed J.B. Brown and no one believed his landlord. He was found guilty and sentenced to hang. An appeal was carried to the Florida supreme court but the conviction and the sentence were affirmed.

The gallows was built in the jailyard. As Brown's hanging date approached, he was resigned to the fact that nothing could save him. When the day came, he walked straight to the gallows, muttering prayers which were barely audible to the crowd gathered below. The noose was placed over his head, and the death warrant was read. To everyone's amazement, the name mentioned in the warrant was not Brown's. Someone had made a mistake. Brown, now near collapse, was rushed from the gallows and placed back in his cell. His lawyers went to work again, and this time were successful in obtaining a commutation of his sentence of life imprisonment.

J.B. Brown languished in prison for a full 11 years. The bizarre events of his life were yet to take another strange turn. Remember the night watchman, J.J. Johnson? Well, in 1913, J.J. made a deathbed confession that he alone had killed Harry Wesson, and that Brown had nothing to do with the crime.

Despite the dubious nature of such confessions, this one was so detailed and revealed so many facts that only the killer could know, that it was taken seriously. All the details in the confession were checked. It was uncovered that Brown's two cellmates had tried to elicit a confession from him on a promise of favors from the authorities. When Brown refused to confess, they lied and said he had anyway, in order to ingratiate themselves with their jailer. This perjured evidence, plus circumstantial evidence given at the trial, had placed a noose around Brown's neck and very nearly claimed his life.

On Oct. 1, 1913, Brown received a full pardon from Gov. Park Trammell of Florida. Sixteen years after his release, in 1929, he was allotted the sum of $2,492 compensation for his years in prison. It was to be paid to him at the rate of $25 per month.

J.B. Brown outlived many of the witnesses at the trial, his lawyers, and even the presiding judge. He died years later, of old age.

WYLIE-HOFFERT CASE

On Aug. 28, 1963, in New York City, three career girls, Janice Wylie, Emily Hoffert, and Patricia Tolles awoke bright and cheerful. By mid-day two of the girls would be dead.

The three girls shared an apartment on fashionable 88th St. in Manhattan. All three came from socially prominent upper middle class families. Janice's uncle was the well known writer, Philip Wylie. Her parents lived only a few blocks from the apartment.

Emily Hoffert gulped down her orange juice, said a hurried goodbye to her two roommates, and by 9:20 was out of the apartment. Ten minutes later Pat Tolles was on her way to the subway and work. Janice Wylie didn't have to report to her job at *Newsweek* magazine until 11 o'clock. She decided to sleep an extra hour. In the meantime Emily had completed some errands and returned to the apartment on 88th St.

Eleven o'clock came and went and Janice failed to arrive for work at *Newsweek*. By 2:30 her superiors and fellow employees became concerned about her absence. They called the apartment, but the telephone went unanswered. Finally, they phoned Janice's parents, who could shed no light on their daughter's absence. They then spoke to Pat Tolles at her place of employment. Pat assured everyone that something must have come up, and no doubt there would be a note of explanation at the apartment. She promised to contact everyone concerned when she got home from work.

At 6:25, Pat Tolles entered the apartment. Her bedroom was in a state of complete disarray. Her clothing was scattered all over the room. Stunned, she retreated to the bathroom where she saw a large blood splattered kitchen knife. Patricia fled the apartment in horror and called both Janice's parents and the police. Janice's father was the first to arrive on the scene. He found the nude body of his daughter, stabbed through the heart and Emily Hoffert's clothed body horribly slashed about the neck. The entire room was saturated with blood.

An intensive police investigation began almost at once. The two victims' lives were examined with microscopic attention to detail. No motive for the atrocious crime was apparent. Months passed with no concrete clues as to the identity of the attacker.

On April 23rd, at 1:15 a.m., in Brownsville, the notorious New York slum area, an isolated incident took place which was to have far reaching effects on the Wylie-Hoffert murders. Mrs. Elba Borrero, a 20-year-old practical nurse, left Long Island College Hospital after her shift was completed at midnight. About a block from her home she heard the ominous sound of footsteps following her. As she approached her home a hand closed across her mouth and strong arms dragged her into an alley. Just then patrolman Frank Isola thought he saw suspicious actions coming from the alley. He ran over and shone his light on a man holding Mrs. Borrero against the wall. The attacker said, "Oh, my God!", and took off with Isola after him. The policeman fired three shots but the man got away. Mrs. Borrero, badly shaken, had managed to rip a button from her attacker's coat.

That same day patrolman Isola casually met George Whitman, a teenage youth, loitering near the scene of the previous night's chase. Isola asked him if he had seen anything suspicious the night before. George said he sure had. First he heard shots, then a man raced past him, half scaring him to death. Patrolman Isola could get nothing further from George and let him go on his way. Still later, Isola mentioned his conversation with the boy to Det. Richard Aidala, who was investigating the murder of one Minnie Edmonds. Her body had been found in the general area of Mrs. Borrero's home. Det. Aidala thought that this George Whitman may have had some connection with the attack on Mrs. Borrero as well as the murder of Mrs. Edmonds. He brought George in for questioning.

Mrs. Borrero was rushed from her home and asked to identify George. Upon seeing him and hearing him talk, she positively identified him as the man who had attacked her. George was arrested on the spot for attempted rape.

He was questioned extensively that night and finally gave a detailed confession to the attempted rape of Mrs. Borrero. When the police showed him the button she had ripped from the attacker's coat, George volunteered that it was his button. When questioned about the murder of Mrs. Edmonds, George was quick and almost happy to confess to her murder as well. George Whitman, a slum kid who never had anything in his life, was being doted on. The cops even brought him coffee and cakes. He had arrived. George was really somebody.

Now that George had confessed to attempted rape and murder, the detectives in charge of the Wylie-Hoffert case took an interest in him. When Whitman had been arrested he was carrying pictures of some girls in his wallet, one of whom bore a slight resemblance to Janice Wylie. On this slim connecting link, George was questioned about the girls' murders.

After hours of questioning Whitman admitted stealing the incriminating pictures from an apartment on 88th St. in Manhattan. Once the link between George and the murdered girls had been established, he poured forth a confession to the double homicide. George was now a bona fide celebrity. In 22 hours of questioning he had managed to confess to one attempted rape and three murders.

Eventually, George stood trial for the attempted rape of Mrs. Borrero. From the witness stand she positively identified George as her attacker. The jury returned a verdict of guilty. Months later Whitman stood trial for the murder of Minnie Edmonds. He repudiated his confession, and after 34 hours the jury couldn't agree on a verdict and the trial ended in a deadlock.

While languishing in jail, waiting to be tried for the Wylie-Hoffert killings, an incident took place which had a direct bearing on the charges against Whitman.

Jimmy Delaney was a 37-year-old dope addict and trafficker in drugs. He had stabbed a man to death for selling him inferior drugs. Delaney told the police he had crucial information concerning the Wylie-Hoffert murders. He would trade the information if the authorities would offer him immunity from prosecution on the murder charge. A deal was struck, and Delaney told the police that a young "junkie", Ricky Robles, had met him on the afternoon of the double murder. Robles had told him, "I just iced two dames." Later, with Robles and Delaney present, a session of dope taking was set up by the police. The authorities had bugged the room, and based on Robles incriminating statements, he was arrested and charged with the murder of the two girls. Robles professed his innocence throughout his trial, but was found guilty, and on Dec. 1, 1965, he was sentence to life imprisonment with eligibility for parole in 26 years. What ever happened to George Whitman? A public hearing was held to investigate George's conviction in the attempted rape of Mrs. Borrero. The hearing uncovered that an F.B.I. report proved that the button ripped from the attacker's coat by Mrs. Borrero did not come from George's coat. This report had been suppressed at George's trial. It was also uncovered that all the jurors knew and openly discussed George's involvement in the Wylie-Hoffert murders. Their minds were prejudiced against him because they felt that they were trying a double murderer. Based on these facts, the judge set aside the guilty verdict. George was completely exonerated of all complicity in the Wylie-Hoffert murder. In June, 1966, the U.S. Supreme Court ruled that in order for a confession to be valid it must be proven that the suspect was informed of his constitutional rights. None of these rights had been afforded George, and all charges pending against him were dropped.

Referring to the Edmonds case, the district attorney of New York said, "It is conceded that other than his confession there was not a shred of legal evidence to connect the defendant with this crime."

It took over two years to finally prove that George Whitman was guilty of nothing more than loitering on a street corner in broad daylight.

SACCO AND VANZETTI

The case of Sacco and Vanzetti was one of the most widely discussed murder cases ever to come before the public's attention. From 1919 to 1927 the two men, their political beliefs, and their many appeals provided the world with its most interesting news.

There were never two more unlikely actors to occupy centre stage than these two Italian immigrants to the U.S. Both Nicola Sacco and Bartolomeo Vanzetti arrived in the United States in 1908 and settled in New England. Each held a variety of menial jobs, but the driving force that each man carried in his heart was an overpowering hatred of the capitalist system. These beliefs, naturally, did not sit well in America.

Sacco and Vanzetti were confirmed pacifists and anarchists. They met for the first time in 1916, and together fled to Mexico in order to avoid being called up for military service. When the war was over they returned to Massachusetts, where Sacco became a shoemaker and Vanzetti made his living as fish peddler. It was a difficult time for immigrants who held unpopular political beliefs. Anarchists, pacifists and communists were being arrested and deported throughout the United States. Sacco and Vanzetti were activists. Both distributed anarchist pamphlets and gave public speeches bemoaning the conditions of the working man and his sad lot under the capitalist system.

On the day before Christmas, 1919, events were to unfold which would change the course of both men's lives. In Bridgewater, a town about 25 miles from Boston, a truck was delivering the payroll for the White Shoe Co. Suddenly a car pulled up beside the truck. The occupants of the car started shooting at the truck driver. Armed with a revolver for just such an occasion, he returned their fire. Discouraged in their hold up attempt, the robbers drove away.

Later, in the course of their investigation into the attempted robbery, the police uncovered an Overland car in a garage operated by a Mr. and Mrs. Johnson. The car had been left there by an immigrant named Boda. The police believed that the Overland was the car used in the attempted robbery, and left instructions with the Johnsons to let them know when Boda turned up for the car.

Four months later, in April, in nearby South Braintree, another robbery was attempted. This time two men were on foot delivering the payroll of the Slater and Morrill Shoe Co. Just as they were about to enter the company offices two men who had been loitering nearby opened fire, killing them both instantly. A car pulled up and picked up the two gunmen. They got clean away with $16,000.

After a few days the police found a deserted Buick, which had previously been stolen. They felt the car had been used in the hold-up. About two weeks after the murder of the two men, Boda walked into the Johnsons' garage to pick up his Overland. He was accompanied by Sacco and Vanzetti. Mrs. Johnson slipped away and called the police. All three men left the garage before the police arrived.

That night the three men were picked up and questioned. Boda was released because he had a ready alibi for the two days when the attempted robbery and the murders had taken place. Both Sacco and Vanzetti had loaded revolvers on them when they were apprehended. They were charged with possession of a firearm without a permit.

Witnesses to the attempted robbery were brought to the jail to view the two men. Five identified Vanzetti as having taken part in the hold-up attempt. On June 22, 1920 he stood trial and was found guilty. Vanzetti received a sentence of from 10 to 16 years in prison.

It is only after this first trial had been concluded that the real saga of Sacco and Vanzetti begins. On May 31, 1921, they stood trial for the murder of the two men in South Braintree. From the beginning it was obvious that Vanzetti would have difficulty receiving a fair trial due to his previous conviction on the attempted robbery charge. While no mention was made of it at the second trial, it was apparent that the feeling was if Vanzetti was guilty of the attempted robbery, he must also be guilty of the murder.

Throughout the United States there was a great deal of sympathy for the defendants. The stern and repressive measures the government was taking against radicals were beginning to receive some criticism. A defence fund had no trouble raising

$50,000 to be used for legal fees to defend the two men. This fund was later to swell to a quarter of a million dollars. Their case was no longer an obscure shootout, but was now gaining national prominence because of the underlying principles involved. Top notch lawyers were employed by the defence and prosecution.

Sacco and Vanzetti swore they were innocent, and the entire case rested on eye witness identification of them as the killers. All other evidence was circumstantial. To illustrate the meticulous preparation which went into the case, it is noteworthy to point out that on the identification aspect alone the prosecution presented 59 witnesses, and the defence countered with 99. The entire trial was a study in conflicting stories. An expert prosecution witness stated that bullets fired from Sacco's gun had killed the two men delivering the payroll. The defence had its own expert who stated that Sacco's gun had not fired the fatal bullets. Both men took the stand in their own defence and admitted telling lies to the police at the time of their arrest. They lied because they were afraid they would get into trouble for delivering anarchist literature.

The trial lasted a full 37 days and every detail was reported around the world. On July 14, 1921, the jury found Sacco and Vanzetti guilty of murder in the first degree. When the verdict was read Sacco screamed, "They kill an innocent man. They kill an innocent man."

For six long years every legal means was employed in an effort to save the two men. At one point a young gunman, Celestino Madeiros, confessed to being the killer and swore that neither Sacco nor Vanzetti were at the scene of the crime. The story was closely investigated, but found to be untrue. Governor Fuller of Massachusetts appointed an independent committee to look into the entire affair. Its findings agreed with the verdict of the court.

Ironically Celestino Madeiros, the man who confessed to the murders for which Sacco and Vanzetti were about to pay with their lives, now found himself convicted or another murder. He was scheduled to be executed with Sacco and Vanzetti.

On Aug. 22, 1927, Madeiros, Sacco, and Vanzetti were electrocuted in Charlestown Prison. Sacco and Vanzetti maintained their innocence to the end. Vanzetti's last words were, "I am innocent of all crime, not only of this, but all. I am an innocent man. I wish to forgive some people for what they are now doing to me."

Fifty years later there are many who believe he may have been telling the truth.

MISTAKEN IDENTITY

In the early morning hours of Jan. 7, 1929, Virgil Romine staggered to the telephone. He managed to get the police on the other end of the line and blurted out a cry for help.

Virgil was well known in Herculaneum, Missouri, as the attendant of the Artesian Park filling station and restaurant. Moments after receiving the call the police arrived on the scene. They found Virgil bleeding profusely from bullet wounds in the abdomen. Although still conscious, the wounded man realized that he was badly hurt. He spoke coherently to the authorities about seeing that his mother was provided for should he not survive. The investigating officer, Sheriff J.W. Dugan, asked the distressed man who had shot him.

Virgil told the sheriff that two or three men and one woman had come into the restaurant and ordered hamburgers. When he went into the kitchen to prepare the order a tall, skinny youth followed him and, without any warning, shot him. Virgil swung wildly at his assailant, and in the ensuing scuffle managed to tear the gun away from his antagonist. Fighting desperately for his life, and in great pain, the wounded man could not describe the battle any further except to state that he must have fought off the men so that they turned tail and ran away.

Virgil stated that he knew the men by sight, although he did not know their names. He had caught them using slugs in the slot machine. When he confronted them, they ran out, leaving their automobile behind. A few days later, he made them pay up 75 cents before he released their car. He told the sheriff that some of the men stayed with a family up the road named Vinyard.

Two hours later Virgil Romine lapsed into a coma and died from his wounds.

That same morning Sheriff Dugan called at the Vinyard residence. Mrs. Vinyard told the Sheriff that her two roomers, Alvin Craig and Walter Hess, both 19 years old, were asleep in the same room with her son Jimmy. The boys had played cards with her son and herself and then gone to bed. They had remained in the room since that time and couldn't be involved in any crime which had taken place after six o'clock the previous evening.

Alvin Craig and Walter Hess both readily admitted having an argument with Virgil about the slugs. They had paid back the 75 cents and considered the whole matter closed. Sheriff Dugan felt the Vinyard woman was not telling the truth. Besides, Virgil had identified his killers before he died. The two boys were taken to jail for further questioning.

The next morning some employees of the State Highway department found a colored shirt with a hole in it. The area around the hole was saturated with blood. The police believe that one of the men may have been wounded by Virgil during the struggle with the gun.

In the meantime, two reputable citizens came forward with the information that, as they were leaving the Artesian Park restaurant, two lads accompanied by a girl, were entering. The men heard the new arrivals order hamburgers as they left the restaurant. While they couldn't positively identify Craig and Hess, they did say that the two suspects did fit the general description of the two boys they had seen.

A week after the murder, Craig and Hess were formally charged with first degree murder. Their trial began on April 19th. The dying man's declaration held sway over the jury. The defense had gone to great pains to prove that no other shooting had taken place in the area of Herculaneum around the time of Virgil's murder. They claimed that the shirt with the bullet hole must have belonged to the wounded killer. Quite obviously, neither Craig nor Hess had been wounded. Despite this theory, both boys were convicted of second degree murder and sentenced to ten years in Missouri State Penitentiary.

A year later, Mamie Woolen walked into a police station in St. Louis. She told quite a story. Mamie, with her old boyfriend Louis Taylor, and two buddies, Radford Browning and Joe Muehlman, had attempted to rob the Artesian Park filling station back on the morning of Jan. 7, 1929. She described the killing in detail, naming Taylor as the one who actually fired the shots. The three men were rounded up and questioned. The old colored shirt was placed on Taylor and sure enough, right where the bullet hole appeared on the shirt was a corresponding healed scar in Taylor's side. Faced with this incriminating evidence Taylor confessed to killing Virgil. Once they heard that Taylor had admitted firing the fatal shots, Browning and Muehlman also confessed.

At the time of the investigation into the murder, the authorities were on the lookout for a wounded man. How had Taylor managed to avoid detection? To begin with, his wound was a flesh wound, which Mamie Woolen had cleaned and bandaged. Taylor, who was in the army at the time of the murder, reported back to his post then applied for a few days leave. He lived with Mamie during his leave. She tended the wound and cared for Taylor. At the expiration of his leave he was well enough to carry on with his regular duties. No medical authority was ever approached to care for Taylor's bullet wound.

How had Virgil made such an error in pointing the finger of suspicion at the wrong men? He was mortally wounded at the time and we can assume that his judgment may have been impaired. He associated his current predicament with the lads who had given him trouble over the slot machine. Taylor did not physically resemble Craig or Hess in any way. The resemblance was in Virgil's mind.

Why did Mamie Woolen walk into that St. Louis police station a year after she and her friends had gotten away with murder? It seems Taylor's affection for Mamie had begun to wane. He had taken to running around with other women. Mamie decided to fix his wagon by going to the police. She did a good job. Taylor received life in prison and his two buddies each received 10 years. Mamie didn't fare so well herself. She always claimed that while she was at the scene of the crime, she had no idea that the men intended to rob the filling station. Her three companions turned state's evidence against her, claiming that she was the mastermind behind the whole thing and had actually planned the robbery. Mamie ended up receiving a life sentence.

Alvin Craig and Walter Hess were released from prison. They had no connection whatever with the murder of Virgil Romine.

A NIGHT OF TERROR

Bob Patience had worked long and hard to develop and promote his sprawling night club. Located near the tiny village of Braintree, England, it was the largest and most successful operation of its kind in the area. Most nights The Barn Restaurant was a bustling concern, with band playing and clients eating and drinking. The Patience family lived in a large home beside the nightclub.

Bob Patience was a jolly, aggressive, plump middle-aged man who had it made and knew it. His wife, Muriel, assisted him in operating The Barn, as did his daughter Beverly and son David.

In the space of a few hours, in the early morning of Monday, Nov. 6, 1972, all of their lives were to change forever. At approximately 1:30 a.m., Bob Patience drove several members of his staff home in his shiny new Mercedes. In his absence his wife and daughter decided to call it a night. Muriel and Beverly made their way home at 2 a.m. Entering the house Beverly turned on the kitchen light and immediately let out a scream. Standing before the startled women were two men, one holding a revolver. Muriel and Beverly were ordered to sit down. One of the men wanted to know where the keys of the safe were kept. Beverly told him they were kept in the restaurant.

Just then the Mercedes drove up. Bob Patience entered his home and stared directly into the barrel of a .32 calibre revolver. He too was made to sit down and was asked to reveal the location of the keys to the safe. Patience decided to outsmart the gunmen. He told them that the keys were in the restaurant, and that anyway the safe didn't contain any money.

The gunman placed a pillow over his revolver. Pointing the gun first at Muriel's head, then at Beverley's head, he said, "What will it be, your wife or your daughter?" When he did not receive an immediate reply he pointed the gun at Muriel's head and pulled the trigger. Muriel slumped to the floor moaning, with a bullet in her right temple. Patience immediately turned over the keys of his safe to the intruder. Keeping his revolver trained on the back of Bob Patience's head, the intruder herded the terrified man to the safe, forcing him to open it. Patience, still using a certain amount of cunning, threw a bag of currency and coins at the robber's feet. Over £7000 in cash and some jewelry were left untouched in the safe. Patience begged the robbers to call an ambulance for his wife. They ignored his pleading.

One of the men tied and gagged Beverly and her father. As the two helpless victims lay face down on the floor, the armed bandits bent over Beverley. Again, using a pillow to muffle the sound, he shot directly into the girl's back. Moving over to Bob Patience, the gunman placed the pillow against the side of his victim's head and fired.

Both men then sped away in David Patience's Volkswagen, which was parked outside the house. The bandits had no way of knowing that a million to one chance had taken place. When the gunman had fired directly at Patience's head, the bound and gagged man had shuddered, moving his head at the precise moment the shot was fired. The bullet ricocheted off his skull, causing nothing more than a superficial wound to his ear. Patience crawled to an intercom and was able to raise the alarm in the restaurant, where he was heard by his son David.

Muriel Patience died from her head wounds two days after the attack. Beverly miraculously survived. The bullet fired directly into her back had plowed through her body and was found in the sheets of a hospital stretcher. Bob Patience had not been seriously injured.

The hunt for the vicious killers swung into action. David Patience's Volkswagen was found abandoned a few miles from the scene of the crime. Beverly and Bob Patience gave detailed descriptions of the two men. Rewards were offered and tips poured into the police. One of these tips led to George Ince, a small time hoodlum. The description given by Beverly matched Ince in most major details. Beverly was shown Ince's picture amongst several others. Unhesitatingly, she picked Ince's photo out of the group. There was no doubt whatever in her mind. Ince was the gun-wielding killer.

About two weeks had elapsed since the murder when George Ince called his mother and happened to find out that the police were looking for him. He thought about his predicament for a day or so and decided to turn himelf in. In hindsight, this action may appear to have been foolhardy, but Ince knew something the police didn't know. He had had nothing whatever to do with the Patience killing.

Ince figured it was all a mistake, which he would clear up. In fact, he recalled that at the very time the murder was taking place he was sleeping with a married woman whose husband was serving time in prison. Ince contacted the woman, who told him she would swear she was with him at the time of the killing. George Ince turned himself in. Ten hours later he was charged with the murder of Muriel Patience.

Police proceeded to concentrate on Ince's friends in their search for the second robber. They came up with several acquaintances, but none could be positively identified as the second man. George Ince stood trial alone for the brutal killing of Muriel Patience, as well as the attempted murder of Bob and Beverly Patience. In addition, he was charged with theft.

Ince had the frustrating experience of attending his own trial for murder knowing full well that he was innocent. He sat in disbelief as the most damaging witness against him, Beverly Patience, positively identified him as the killer. Despite this evidence, several members of the jury could not find Ince guilty. They returned from their deliberations hopelessly deadlocked, and were dismissed by the presiding judge, who immediately ordered a retrial.

At his second trial for murder, the testimony of Ince's lady friend was believed by the jury. Ince was found to be not guilty on all counts.

Who were the real killers of Muriel Patience?

John Brook was a smalltime punk who had been released from prison five weeks before the Patience murder. Brook and a former cellmate, one Nicholas de Clare Johnson, had teamed up to pull off the Patience caper. Johnson was officially in prison when the murder took place. He was out on a weekend pass and had returned at his scheduled time.

On Nov. 27, when George Ince gave himself up, Brook read about it in the newspapers, and realized he was in the clear. That winter, as Ince's two trials dragged on, Brook moved north, where he obtained employment as a kitchen porter at the Salutation Hotel in Ambleside.

While employed at the hotel, Brook became friendly with a smalltime thief named Peter Hanson. On several occasions Brook brandished his .32 Beretta, bragging that he wouldn't hesitate to use it if necessary. Other employees heard the bragging and saw the gun as well. The Beretta was the weapon which had taken the life of Muriel Patience. Once, during an outburst of temper, Hanson was flabbergasted when Brook admitted being the Patience killer.

Three weeks after Ince was acquitted at his second trial, Hanson was being sought by police for robbery. Thinking that the authorities might be more lenient with him for voluntarily surrendering, he walked into a police station and gave himself up. While being questioned, Hanson informed police of Brook's confession.

Detectives swooped down on the Sutherland restaurant in Bowness, where Brook was then employed, and took him into custody. The Beretta was found in his room. Ballistics tests proved that the Beretta was the murder weapon, but Brook insisted he was not the killer. A check of Brook's former cellmates uncovered his accomplice, Johnson. By this time Johnson had been released from prison, but was back in court for stealing a wallet.

When questioned, Johnson at first denied any knowledge of the killing, but finally broke down and confessed. He had been the passive intruder. Brook had been the killer.

Both men eventually stood trial. Brook was found guilty of the murder of Muriel Patience and two charges of attempted murder. He received three life sentences. Johnson was found guilty of manslaughter and was sentenced to 10 years in prison.

MRS. PARSONS WAS WRONG

We have all been conditioned by movies and television to the sight of someone alone being threatened by a man with a gun. The simple scene is so commonplace as to be boring. Usually the victim exchanges smart remarks with the armed man. Is this the way it really happens? How does it actually feel to know that the slightest pressure of an index finger can hold your life in the balance?

The night of Oct. 18, 1924 was cool and clear in Los Angeles, California. Mrs. Dick R. Parsons found herself alone in her spacious home and decided to spend an hour or so practising on her piano. As soon as she sat down she sensed that there was someone else in the room. Before her thought processes could produce words, she heard the terrifying command, "Stick 'em up. I want your diamonds." The voice had a distinct cackling quality which chilled Mrs. Parsons down to her toes. She whirled and faced the menacing sight of a masked man with a wavering revolver.

The intruder again shouted at her to produce her jewelry. Mrs. Parsons passed him the ring she was wearing. The robber harshly instructed her to gather up the rest of her valuables. Mrs. Parsons nervously searched for the jewelry, but was so utterly terrified that she couldn't remember where she had put her valuable pieces. She wasn't bluffing, she really couldn't think straight.

The robber, of course, didn't know this, and with each of her fumbling attempts to find the diamonds, he became more agitated and threatening towards her. Finally she could stand it no longer. She panicked and raced for the front door of the house. The masked man ran after her, firing his gun as he went. Mrs. Parsons fell to the floor with a bullet in her back, while the robber ran from the house.

The wound wasn't fatal, and Mrs. Parsons made a slow recovery in the hospital. She described the abject horror she felt when the armed man became agitated. She said she simply was so terrified she couldn't think straight. Despite this, while still confined to bed, she gave the police a full description of her attacker. She said he was about 5 feet, 6 inches tall, weighing 130 pounds. She described his distinctive cackling voice and piercing blue eyes. Even though he wore a mask, Mrs. Parsons said his eyes narrowed to slits when he was angry.

The police found out that the robber had entered through a first floor window. A clear fingerprint was lifted from the edge of the screen.

Within a week, from the time of the shooting, James W. Preston was arrested for illegally wearing a naval uniform. As a matter of course his fingerprints were checked against those found on Mrs. Parson's screen. They were not the same.

Preston did have a distinctive cackling voice, and because of this he was brought before Mrs. Parsons to see if she could identify him. She heard the unmistakable voice, and positively identified Preston as her assailant. She said his eyes formed narrow slits exactly as she had seen on that terrifying night in her home.

Preston was charged with burglary, robbery, and assault with intent to murder. Before the trial started, the prosecuting attorney suggested that if Preston would plead guilty to simple assault which carried a maximum sentence of six months, all other charges would be dropped. This was quite a proposition, because the three crimes which Preston was charged with each carried a minimum sentence of 11 years imprisonment to a maximum of life. Preston was adamant; he claimed he was completely innocent and refused to plead guilty to anything.

The trial began. Mrs. Parsons took the stand and identified Preston as the robber. Preston claimed he was at Long Beach, twenty-two miles from the Parsons' home, at the time of the shooting. He even produced a girlfriend who swore she was with him at the time. Under cross examination she proved to be something less than truthful. Her story wasn't believed by the jury. The prosecution produced Preston's previous record. He had been convicted of vagrancy, desertion from the army, and had been dishonorably discharged from the navy. Not a very good record, but still nothing that could be used to pinpoint an armed robber. He explained away the arrest for wearing the naval uniform by informing the court that he had been recently discharged from the navy and hadn't had the money to buy civilian clothing before he was picked up.

Somewhere along the line the judge had been erroneously told that Preston's fingerprints matched the prints taken from the Parsons' screen. The fingerprint evidence was never introduced in court, but the fact that throughout the trial the judge firmly believed Preston to be guilty influenced his conduct throughout the proceedings.

Preston was found guilty of burglary and robbery. The charge of assault with intent to kill was reduced to assault with a deadly weapon. He was found guilty of this as well. Preston had gambled a maximum of six months imprisonment and ended up with three sentences of eleven years to life to be served consecutively. On March 21, 1925, the doors of San Quentin Prison closed behind John W. Preston.

The Parsons-Preston case should have been closed forever. Nothing could be further from the truth.

Preston's conviction didn't sit well with Sergeant H.L. Barlow, who was a fingerprint expert with the Los Angeles Police Dept. Despite the eye witness identification of Preston, Barlow knew that the intruder who had left a fingerprint on the screen had to be the real culprit. He made it something of a hobby to check the fingerprints of anyone arrested with the fingerprints lifted from the Parsons' screen.

Over a year went by, with Preston languishing in San Quentin, before Barlow had any luck. In May, 1926, Earl M. Carroll was arrested and charged with several break-ins in the Los Angeles area. His prints were checked against the prints found on the screen, and they matched perfectly. Barlow approached Carroll and told him about Preston being imprisoned in San Quentin. He wanted a confession. After some thought Carroll replied, "I will neither admit nor deny I was on the Parsons' job. It's up to you guys to convict me if you can prove I was there. That's what you're paid for."

Even with the positive fingerprint identification, Barlow needed another piece of corroborating evidence. Mrs. Parsons was summoned, and for a moment thought that Carroll was Preston, so stunning was the similarity of their physical appearance. Carroll was made to say, "Stick 'em up. I want your diamonds." The same cackling voice Mrs. Parsons had heard in her home over a year before made her shudder.

Could two men have the same odd, distinctive voice and be so similar in appearance? The answer was a positive yes. In time, with Barlow's urging, the judical system started the process of reversing Preston's conviction. On Sept. 2, 1926, after serving a year and a half for another man's crime, Preston was released from San Quentin.

Sometime later he was arrested for vagrancy in Oakland, Calif. When the judge who was hearing his case learned of his previous unjust conviction, he released Preston into the custody of his wife and wished him good luck. Preston walked out of the courtroom, and has never been heard of since that day.

In hindsight, the Preston conviction has come under close scrutiny. The prosecutor knew that Preston's prints did not match the prints on the screen. It was later discovered that Mrs. Parsons was told that Preston's prints matched those on the screen before she positively identified Preston. Even the judge had this same false information.

While there was no fingerprint evidence of any kind brought out at the trial, it is obvious that a mistaken impression was imparted so that everyone connected with the case believed a positive fingerprint identification had been made.

By suppressing the fingerprint evidence, the prosecuting attorney sent an innocent man to prison for a year and a half.

OSCAR DIDN'T DO IT

Glasgow, Scotland is not the most glamorous city in the world. However, in the annals of the art of mayhem, it has given us some prime murders.

Unfortunately for Glasgow, but more unfortunate still for Oscar Slater, its most famous case involved the conviction of an innocent man.

Poor Oscar was no saint. He was born in Germany in the early 1870s. When he became old enough to be inducted into the army, he did what many young boys have done before and after him. He skipped the draft. He ended up in England, where, under various aliases, he had the rather dubious occupation of managing social clubs. He pursued this occupation both in England and America, where he spent a year.

In November, 1908, we find Oscar living under the name of George Anderson in Glasgow with his mistress, Junio Antoine. She even had her German maid, Catherine Schmaltz, living with them. Oscar was turning the odd dollar selling jewelry, and in general was living by his wits.

The event that was to change his life forever happened on the evening of Monday, Dec. 21, 1908.

An old lady, Marion Gilchrist, lived in an upper flat at 15 Queen's Terrace in Glasgow. She was kind of a weird old thing and kept jewelry valued at over £3,000 around the house. She had double locks on the doors and had let the Adams family, who lived in the flat downstairs, know that if she ever needed them she would knock on the floor. She also had a maid named Helen Lambie.

Now, on the fateful night, Helen was out of the flat picking up a newspaper for her mistress. All of a sudden the Adams family heard strange and repeated noises from the upper flat. Mr. Adams went upstairs to investigate. As he did, he met Helen in the hall. She had keys to the flat and she proceeded, with Mr. Adams, to enter the flat. As they did so a man walked out of the bedroom past them, then ran down the stairs.

Marion Gilchrist was found on the dining room floor with her head horribly smashed. Her jewels and papers were scattered over the flat. Surprisingly enough, only one piece of jewelry — a crescent brooch — was missing.

As the killer left the house, a 14-year-old messenger girl, Mary Barrowman, was passing the flat. The killer, rushing from the house, brushed up against Mary as he ran down the street.

Four days later the police got word that a man named Oscar was trying to peddle a crescent shaped brooch. Upon investigating they found that Oscar had sailed for New York on the *Lusitania.*

In order for the Scottish authorities to extradite Oscar, they had to have a damn good case. Slater's counsel thought the case so weak that he advised his client to resist the application for extradition. However, Slater wanted to return and clear his name.

On Monday, May 3, 1909, the trial began and the two girls positively identified him as the man they saw leaving the scene of the crime. His "flight to America", as the prosecution put it, did him no good. He was sentenced to hang. Two days before he was to be executed, his sentence was commuted to life imprisonment.

The years slipped by and every so often Slater's case would come up in the public press. People of some considerable influence started to question the verdict. Sir Arthur Conan Doyle, the creator of Sherlock Holmes, was one of those who claimed Slater was innocent. Newspaper articles were written and new facts uncovered. Finally, after nineteen years in prison, Slater was paroled.

By this time so much new evidence had been uncovered that, even though technically free, Sir Arthur Conan Doyle and others persuaded Slater to appeal his conviction. The entire matter was thus revived and caused a sensation not only in Scotland, but throughout the press of the world.

It is indeed seldom that a man who has spent nineteen years in prison has the opportunity to sit as a spectator in court, and hear the very witnesses who convicted him so long ago. We will never know what feelings Oscar had as he sat there listening to it all over again.

Strange and contradictory facts started to unfold. The brooch Oscar was trying to sell did not match the missing brooch. Besides, Oscar was trying to sell it before the date of the Gilchrist murder.

Remember the little messenger girl? She was now a middle-aged married woman. She gave evidence that while she thought at the time Slater resembled the man who brushed up beside her, she was told to change her story to say, "he was the man." A simple change for a 14-year-old girl. As evidence the difference in implication is poles apart.

Helen Lambie never appeared, and there was no way that she could be forced to do so. However, an affidavit was admitted in evidence stating that it was quite possible that it was not Slater who walked past her on that fateful night so long ago.

It turned out that the reason Slater was so easily traced to the *Lusitania* in what was termed his "flight from justice" was because he did nothing to cover his tracks. In hindsight he had completely no reason to do so, as he had done nothing wrong. Indeed, he had no idea that anyone was looking for him.

On July 20th, 1928, Oscar Slater's conviction was set aside. He received £6,000 as compensation for his years in jail.

He later married and lived out his remaining days as a respected citizen of Ayr, Scotland. He died in his home in 1948 at the age of 76.

Miss Gilchrist's murder remains unsolved to this day.

THE BLACK DAHLIA

Thousands of young girls living in small towns throughout Canada and the United States long for the excitement of the big city. They dream of bright lights, big time entertainment, and the action. Each year droves of teenage girls arrive in large cities convinced that they will make it big. Some dream of a glamorous career, others of a handsome millionaire husband. A few manage to pull it off. Some fail and return to their home towns. Then there are those who manage to find a routine but rewarding city life.

Elizabeth Short was the exception, for she fell into none of these categories. She was one of the very few who just couldn't seem to cope with the change from small town life to that of the big city. Ironically, Elizabeth wanted nothing more than to leave her hometown of Medford, Mass. Maybe she had good reason. You see, her parents separated in 1931, when she was only six years old, and her mother Phoebe found herself alone with four children to raise. Because she had to seek employment to provide for her brood, little Elizabeth was often neglected.

By 1942, Elizabeth was a beautiful young girl of 16. The United States, as well as the rest of the world, was at war. With the economy of the country booming, Elizabeth decided that this would be the best time to leave Medford.

She picked the most distant and most glamorous place she could think of — Miami. She had no trouble finding work as a waitress, and for a while was very popular with airmen stationed close to the city. It was not as glamorous as Elizabeth had dreamed it would be, but it was a start. She was soon going steady with a handsome airman. Was it possible that her dreams would come true? The hope was short lived. Her boyfriend was shipped overseas, and a short time later Elizabeth was notified that he had been killed in action.

The young and beautiful Elizabeth Short didn't take her loss well. She started to drink heavily, and soon gained a reputation among the servicemen who frequented Miami bars as a promiscuous woman who would bed down with anyone.

Elizabeth was picked up by the police in a bar, and as a juvenile delinquent, she was placed aboard a train for Medford. She got off the train in Santa Barbara. Here Elizabeth met an Air Force major and fell madly in love. The pair planned to get married when the major concluded his tour of duty in the Far East. Elizabeth returned to her mother in Medford to wait out the major's absence.

On Aug. 22, 1946, Elizabeth received a wire informing her of her fiance's death. Could fate play this horrible trick on her not once, but twice? Was happiness to be denied Elizabeth Short forever? The answer to both questions was yes.

Elizabeth proceeded to get drunk and hopped a train for Hollywood. Because of her stunning looks, she had no trouble getting work as an "extra" in the movies. She also wasn't above passing out sexual favors to anyone who could put in a good word for her in the right places.

While mixing with the Hollywood set, Elizabeth heard that it was smart to have an identifying feature or trademark. She came up with the rather novel idea of dressing completely in black from her head to her toes. She carried her penchant for black to the point of wearing black underwear and even wearing a black ring. Someone christened her the "Black Dahlia", and the name stuck.

Elizabeth dressed entirely in black, became a regular in the bars around Hollywood. She drank heavily and took on lovers whenever the mood struck her.

Later, men were traced who admitted going on drinking bouts with Elizabeth and having sexual relations with her. They all stated that it was as if she were propelling herself towards doom.

One man who had been drinking with her let her out of his car on Jan. 12, 1947 in front of the Biltmore Hotel in Los Angeles. The "Black Dahlia" had told him that she was going to meet her sister at the hotel. She was never seen alive again.

Three days later, on Jan. 15, Elizabeth Short's body was found on a vacant lot. Her nude body had been horribly mutilated. From its condition the police were able to ascertain that Elizabeth had been hung upside down with ropes and tortured. Deeply engraved into a thigh were the initials B.D., obviously standing for Black Dahlia. Her body was found in two pieces, having been completely severed at the waist. Police also believed that her murderer was only known to her on the last three days of her life.

The man who dropped her off in front of the hotel proved beyond a doubt that his story was true in every detail. He was exonerated of any guilty knowledge. Elizabeth's sister was not registered at the Biltmore, and it is believed that Eizabeth herself never entered the front door. Probably she met her killer shortly after she was dropped off in front of the hotel.

The police were baffled. Who could grow to hate this girl so much in such a short time to do these horrible things to her? The police managed to trace Elizabeth's life right up until Jan. 12, 1947, when she was last seen in front of the Biltmore Hotel.

For some strange reason, the murder seemed to elicit confessions from a variety of men. All proved to be cranks or mental cases, and none became bona fide suspects.

At the height of the investigation a Los Angeles newspaper received a letter which read: "Here are Dahlia's belongings. Letter will follow." Attached to the note were Elizabeth's social security card, her address book, and birth certificate. All were genuine and obviously had been sent by the killer. One page had been torn out of the address book, and the police believed it was possible that this page contained the name and address of the killer. No letter ever followed the note.

It is now over 34 years since Elizabeth Short's brutual murder. The case remains unsolved to this day. Somewhere there is someone who has guilty knowledge of how and why he killed the "Black Dahlia."

The Chicken Farmer

Vince Desai

– Part 12 –

MERRIE ENGLAND

MAN'S BEST FRIEND

Merrie England has contributed more than her share of ladies and gentlemen who have been faced with bothersome bodies. I don't know why this is so; maybe the neatness lies in the innate English urge for neatness and secrecy. Whatever the reason, perhaps the man who best exemplifies these qualities is Donald Hume.

Donald Hume was born at Swanage, England, in 1919, the illegitimate son of a schoolteacher, who had no use for him. As a result of this lack of motherly love, he spent most of his formative years in assorted orphanages. By the time he was 14, Donald was a lone, brooding youngster, deeply aware of the stigma of not knowing the identity of his father. Many lads of his age might have accepted the cruel blow that fate had dealt them, but not Donald. He resolved to strike back at life, to claw his way into a station in society where he would be the dealer, not the receiver, of cruel blows.

All his early luck was not bad. While seeking his first job in London he met a Mr. Fox, a builder, who took a liking to him and hired him at 25 shillings a week. Taking a sincere interest in Hume's welfare, Mr. Fox went as far as getting him a place to stay with his foreman's wife. This woman was also fond of Donald, and he was immediately received as "one of the family."

At the age of 15, Hume had friends, was learning a trade, and was living in good surroundings. But this was not enough for him. In an effort to make more money he took a second part-time job in a chemist's shop. To augment his earnings still further, he started to steal small items from the shop and sell them to his friends. Then he began to take cars for joyrides, and his circle of friends widened to include youngsters who felt that roaming the streets at night, mugging and robbing, was a normal pastime. As a result, his work suffered.

The ever-concerned Mr. Fox had a heart-to-heart talk with his protege, but the grateful lad he had hired a few short years before had turned into a sullen, bitter young man who didn't take kindly to moral lectures. Inevitably, Mr. Fox's talk did no good, and he was forced to fire Donald in November, 1937. To make the break complete, Hume moved out of his pleasant lodgings.

For the next two years he drifted from one menial job to another. When he was 20, World War II broke out, and he joined the RAF. Almost immediately he contracted cerebrospinal meningitis and was discharged twenty months later, bitter and disheartened at being forced to give up his glamorous uniform. Rather than seek normal employment in the many arms factories that were crying out for workers, he decided to try his luck outside the law.

His first scheme turned out quite well. He made contact with a firm of manufacturing chemists and purchased quantities of surgical spirits. He laced this potent brew with some legitimate gin, put fancy labels on the bottles, and sold the stuff at an enormous profit to any nightclub which would pay his price, averaging over sixty pounds a week, which wasn't bad in 1941. The scheme lasted a year, but then his supply of surgical spirits was cut off and he found himself out of business.

When this happened Hume dressed up in an RAF officer's uniform, and started passing bad cheques at Air Force bases all over England. He was caught, arrested, and committed for trial at London's famous Old Bailey. The young man who stood before Sir Gerald Dodson that day was now 23-years-old. For Sir Gerald's benefit, Hume played the repentant orphan. Good-looking, immaculately dressed, he made an excellent impression in the dock. His full crop of black hair squared off a not unpleasant face, though his expressive mouth turned down disturbingly at the corners. The full lips twitched into a smirk as Sir Gerald gave him a two-year suspended sentence.

After this harrowing experience, Hume took a job as an electrician's helper and soon progressed to doing electrical and plumbing work on his own, swindling his customers by using inferior products and overcharging for his services. These methods didn't help his reputation, but they did make him money. An interesting insight into Hume's unscrupulous intelligence may be found in the fact that while he was cheating his customers and using every trick in the trade to line his pockets at their expense, he picked up all the practical knowledge he could about electricity. He made so much out of his customers that by 1943 he opened his own electrical and radio store. The Hume

Electrical Company was located at 620 Finchley Road, and business was so good that within one year he was expanding his premises and employing 45 people, making money hand over fist.

When the war ended in 1945, Donald Hume, at the age of 25, was a successful legitimate businessman. In the same year, the British government relaxed its ban on the production of domestic appliances. Hume saw an opportunity and grabbed it. He designed a toaster that proved to be a winner. He called it the Little Atom, worked like a dog, and marketed 50,000 of them.

He was now a rich man, but despite his wealth and obvious success, he couldn't resist the thrills of the criminal life. For kicks, he associated with known criminals and joined them in the odd robbery and hijacking. His deep-rooted compulsion to hold "straight" society up to ridicule was coming to the surface again. Every time he met with legitimate success, his craving for the thrill and excitement of illegal activites seemed to become more intense. Basically a loner, he only came in contact with his criminal friends when a caper was being planned; he had no intention of making a career out of petty crime. It was only the thrill that compelled him to duck behind the veil. He always came back.

Then he acquired a dog. If Donald Hume ever had sincere feelings about any living thing, they were for his dog Tony. As other men might enjoy a quiet evening at home with a female companion, Hume was content to sit before a fireplace with his Tony. He would actually confide his innermost thoughts to his canine friend. Tony, looking up at his master with understanding eyes, always seemed to sympathize. The dog was an intelligent animal, and whatever chemistry exists to bring dog and man to an understanding of each other existed in full measure between Tony and Hume.

In 1947, Hume met, fell in love with, and married a well-bred, beautiful young divorcee named Cynthia. Shortly after his marriage, he took up flying as a hobby, and got his civilian flying license. His business started to suffer. He had lived high off the hog for his few good years, and didn't have much to show when the situation started to deteriorate. When in 1949 he met a wealthy car dealer named Stanley Setty, he was impressed. Here was a living example of what he himself wanted to be. Setty oozed success. He carried a huge roll of banknotes, and diamonds twinkled on his chubby fingers when he reached for his wad. His large frame was draped in an expensive suit, obviously the product of one of the better London tailors. At 46, Setty carried his 200 pounds well enough, although his dark face was running to fat. He ran a large legitimate operation, but he also dealt in forged petrol coupons and ran guns to countries that would pay the price. Both men realized they were kindred spirits from their very first meeting.

Setty, who had been born in Baghdad and whose real name was Sulman Seti, took Hume into his confidence about his illegal operations. At the time they first met, Setty was selling war surplus trucks to Iraq. This fact stuck in Hume's craw. He was aware that he himself was no angel, but that Setty, a Jew, should be selling war materials to Israel's enemies appalled him. It was as if he had aided Germany during the war. Still, reasoned Hume, money and expediency make strange bedfellows.

Setty, on the other hand, figured he had met a rather intelligent small-time crook whom he could probably use in his operations. Soon the pair started dealing in forged coupons and stolen cars. When Setty heard that Hume could fly a plane he immediately set him up smuggling contraband and illegal passengers to and from the continent. Setty was the contact man, lining up any deal that would make them money. Hume took most of the chances, but the money was good, and the life it enabled him and Cynthia to lead was worth the risk.

Sometimes their deals were no more complicated than picking up an illegal immigrant on the continent and flying him back to a secret landing field in England. No nosy customs inspectors, no passports to be checked — neat, smooth, and profitable. At other times, the deals were more complicated. Once, Hume arranged to have two Dakotas flown with full crews from the U.S. zone in Germany to Palestine. Accompanying one of the planes himself, he pulled off the mission without a hitch. He was also instrumental in supplying Palestine with other war materials. A cargo of guns would take off from England in Halifax freighter planes and land in Spain, where it would be transferred to fishing boats and eventually find its way to Palestine.

And so it went — anything for a price. While they didn't love each other, Setty and Hume were compatible partners. Then one fine day, while visiting Setty at his garage, Hume, accompanied by his dog, Tony, was admiring a freshly-painted car. The dog brushed against the vehicle, leaving a noticeable scratch on the fresh paint. Setty became furious. He gave Hume a tongue-lashing, but worst of all he gave Tony a vicious kick. Hume took his dog and left the garage. From that time on the relationship between the two men was never the same. Hume, whose fondness for his dog bordered on the obsessive, never forgave Setty. His hatred for his associate smouldered within, ready to explode into murder at the first provocation.

On the evening of Oct. 4th, 1949, Setty paid a visit to Hume's maisonette. The two men began to quarrel bittery. Hume grabbed a German SS dagger off the wall and stabbed Setty repeatedly until he was dead. The struggle only took a few minutes, but it left Hume physically and emotionally drained. He looked down at what a few moments before had been a living human being. The dead eyes stared back, seeming to say, "What now, chum; what do you plan to do with me, a body in your living room?"

Hume's answer was makeshift at best. He carried the body to the coal cupboard, which was located on the same floor at the rear of the flat. He then straightened out the furniture and washed the blood from the floor, took Setty's car keys, drove the car to Setty's home, parked it, and got away without being seen. Once a safe distance away, he hailed a cab and returned to the maisonette.

Sleep didn't come easily. He tossed and turned, trying to figure out what he would do with the corpse in the coal cupboard. He knew he would never be able to lift the big, heavyset body out of the apartment by himself.

Next morning he got up and wiped the apartment clean of any fingerprints that Setty might have left. Then he noticed that despite his washing, his carpet was bloodstained. He rolled it up and took it out to be cleaned and dyed a deep green. At the same time he bought some varnish and applied it to his floor. Busy boy that he was, he checked Setty's pockets and found £1000 in five-pound notes. Most of them were bloodsoaked and shredded by his dagger thrusts, and he managed to salvage only ninety pounds. Revenge was the obvious motive for Hume's crime, but if he could make a few quid on the side, so much the better.

While Hume was scurrying about getting rid of incriminating evidence, Cynthia was upstairs in the flat, oblivious of her husband's activities and the weird events that were taking place in her home. Finally she prepared lunch, and Donald had to sit there making small-talk. His grey eyes darted round the maisonette. It seemed to him that evidence of murder was everywhere. A stain here, a splash of varnish there, and of course Mr. Setty, not so very far away in the closet. But Cynthia, blissfully unaware of what had happened, saw nothing amiss.

Hume waited until early in the afternoon, when she went out of the house, once more to confront the annoying Mr. Setty. By now that gentleman was stiff as a board with rigor mortis, and it was no small task to lug the body out of the coal closet and into the area the Humes called the breakfast room. Then Tony, his faithful companion, watched as he coolly cut off Setty's legs with a linoleum knife and a hacksaw. Neatly wrapping the legs in felt, he tied the large parcel with cord. Next he cut off Setty's head, and put it in a cardboard box. He weighted the packages with bricks, then wrapped the torso in a blanket and shoved it back into the coal cupboard to be dealt with later.

Hume cleaned the place thoroughly and drove away from the flat with his two grisly parcels. He went straight to Elstree Airport. Leaving Tony in his parked car, he hired a little Auster aircraft that he had often rented before. Once over the English Channel he dropped his parcels over the side and watched as they disappeared under the water. They sank like rocks. Then he tossed the dagger, knife and hacksaw that he had used on Setty overboard, returned the plane to the airport and drove home.

A murderer's work is never done. The following day he was faced with the task of getting rid of the torso. Not being completely pleased with the coat of varnish he had applied to the floor, Hume brought in a painter to do a more professional job. With a boldness born of desperation, Hume asked the decorator to give him a hand, as he had a heavy parcel to carry down to his car. As the unsuspecting painter and the murderer heaved and puffed with their awkward cargo, Hume noticed that the underside of the blanket wrapping was becoming bloodsoaked. The painter held firmly to the ropes that bound the parcel. Hume's eyes watched his every move, but not once did his hands change position. Had he groped for a better hold and inadvertently touched the bloodsoaked blanket, we can only guess what Hume's reaction might have been ...

In the end, the two men carried the torso down to the waiting car without incident. With Tony by his side, Hume made his second trip to the airport. He managed to heave his bulky parcel into the front seat of the plane, and Tony jumped into the back seat.

It is possible that in all the annals of crime no stranger threesome ever took off in an aircraft. There they were — a torso, a dog, and a murderer, flying over the English Channel. This time all did not go smoothly. When Hume tossed the torso overboard the lead-weighted blanket blew away, and the torso didn't sink. There was nothing Hume could do about it but return to the airport.

Meanwhile Setty was missed, and it was assumed that he had met with foul play because of the large amount of money he was carrying when last seen.

On Oct. 21, the torso of Stanley Setty was found by Sidney Tiffin, out in his boat after geese, on a mudflat near the Essex village of Tilingham. Six days later, the police investigation turned up Donald Hume. They had meticulously checked every airfield for men with flying licenses who had police records. Upon checking further, they uncovered the connection between the dead man and Hume.

It has never been suggested that Donald Hume was not an intelligent man. As evidence of this, he decided upon a remarkable plan of action. He told the police a story which fitted all the facts that could be proved, and later repeated it to the jury at his trial for the murder of Stanley Setty.

Three men named Mac, Greeny, and The Boy, he claimed, had offered him £100 in five-pound notes to fly over the Channel with two parcels and drop them overboard. The next day they offered him a further £50, again in fivers, to do the same thing with a third parcel. Hume agreed that all the evidence of renting a plane, dropping the parcels, and coming back to his flat, was true. His story explained his actions just as well as the Crown's assertion that he was a murderer. There were none of the murdered man's fingerprints to be found in his flat, no murder weapon, no knives or saws for cutting up the body. Hume claimed that the larger parcel had dripped blood on his carpet and stained his floor. He admitted that he knew he was being used to dispose of the much-publicized missing Setty. And faced with the painter, he admitted that the man helped him carry the larger parcel to his car. In fact, Hume confessed to everything except murder. He gave a detailed description of Mac, Greeny, and The Boy, but they were never found. In one fell swoop, Hume had accounted for all his actions and all the evidence.

The jury couldn't agree as to his guilt or innocence. They were immediately dismissed by the judge, and a new jury was sworn in. The judge in his wisdom ordered them to return a verdict of not guilty of murder. Then he read the charge indicting Hume as an accessory after the fact of murder. Hume pleaded guilty to this lesser charge and received a sentence of twelve years in jail.

Eight years later, Donald Hume was released from Dartmoor Prison. He was now 38 years old. His wife Cynthia had divorced him. Even his dog Tony had been put to sleep. Only Donald Hume's irrepressible lust for life and the pleasures money could bring was alive and well. The sensational aspects of his crime were still remembered by the public at large, and Hume received several offers for the full and true story of his part in the murder of Stanley Setty.

One fine day he walked into the office of the *Sunday Pictorial* in London, England, and told them that he was willing to sell his confession. The exact amount paid has never been made public, but we do know he struck a hard bargain. The sum he received was enough to convince him that he could start a comfortable new life under an assumed name in another country. A reporter lived with Hume for three weeks at a hotel, recording his every thought concerning the killing of Stanley Setty. Hume demanded, and got, ten days' lead time to get out of the country before the newspaper broke the story. In his confession, he outlined and had corroborated every detail of the murder he had committed. He revealed that his very vivid descriptions of Mac, Greeny, and The Boy were the true descriptions of three of the investigating officers. Here, too, Hume's basic intelligence showed through. Had he made up fictitious descriptions and had to repeat them at a later date, he could quite easily have tripped himself up. By picking three men who actually existed, his memory was constantly being refreshed when he actually came in contact with them.

With the money from the sale of his confession, he left the country. He changed his name, forged new identity papers and lived for some time in Switzerlnd as a Canadian named John Stephen Bird. When he had sold his confession in England he had sported a moustache and eyeglasses. Now he looked completely different. Dapper Johnny Bird was clean-shaven and wore no glasses. He passed himself off as a test pilot, and in this glamorous guise he frequented Zurich night spots and went the wine, women and song route until the cash from the sale of his story started to dwindle. Along the way he met a real beauty, Trudi Sommer. She had auburn hair, an open smile that showed off her even white teeth, and an hour-glass figure that drew appreciate glances from every man who came in contact with her. Never one to do things by half measures, Hume promptly fell for her and moved into her apartment.

He now needed money and needed it fast. And what could be quicker than robbing banks? But he would have to operate without Trudi's knowledge. His fertile mind wasn't stymied by this one either. He decided to tell her he was a spy working for the United States against the Russians, which would account for his absences from Zurich. Trudi was actually thrilled by her boyfriend's glamorous occupation.

Hume decided to go into his new profession right away. His plan called for him to go to another country, using yet another alias, rob a bank and head back to Switzerland. He returned to London and cased the Midland Bank on Boston Manor Road in Brentford. A short time later, armed with a pistol, he managed to rob the bank, but ran into trouble, shooting and wounding an employee. Still, he made good his escape, and the next day was back, safely bedded down with Trudi in Switzerland. The take from his first venture into the robbery business was £1500.

Then Trudi started to pressure Hume, alias Bird, toward the altar. Donald, alias Johnny, put her off as long as possible. Finally he was forced to become engaged to the girl, and really planned to get married. First, though, he figured he needed more cash. Another bank robbery was planned, and again he headed for London. This time, when he entered the bank an employee grappled with him as he scooped up some bills. His pistol went off and the man fell wounded to the floor. Hume made it safely back to Zurich, only £300 richer for his trouble. Such a paltry amount didn't last him long.

On Friday, Jan. 30, 1959, he walked into the Gewerbe Bank in Zurich. Located on the Ramistrasse, the austere stone structure was designed to give the impression of stability, but for all its Swiss solidity it was not built to prevent a robbery. It was exactly 11:30 a.m. when Hume marched through the massive doors carrying a small cardboard box in one hand and a gun in the other. For no apparent reason, he shot and wounded an employee named Walter Schenkel. The wounded man managed to set off the burglar alarm. Hume, nervous and desperate, grabbed at some bills and ran from the bank with employees hot on his trail. A taxi driver, Arthur Maag, saw what was happening and joined the chase. Hume turned, pointed his pistol and shot Maag dead. A group of men overpowered the fugitive, and he was immediately taken away to the police station, where his real identity was quickly uncovered.

Hume stood trial in Zurich for the murder of Maag. Since Switzerland does not have capital punishment, he received the maximum sentence of life imprisonment at hard labor. In the fall of 1976, he was transferred to the famous Hospital for the Criminally Insane at Broadmoor, England.

By the age of 39, Donald Hume had led quite a life. He had wounded three people, murdered two, and robbed three banks. We mustn't forget he also had the rather unique experience of dissecting one of his victims. Who knows, we may yet hear more from that well-known Canadian playboy and test pilot, John Stephen Bird.

MURDER ON
THE MOORS

T he story you are about to read involves two of the most reprehensible criminals who ever lived. The depths to which their depraved acts plummeted have not been equalled in modern times. If the retelling of this grisly true tale cautions just one parent to the dangers of allowing their children to accompany not only strange men, but strange women, then this effort will have been worthwhile.

At 12:40 p.m. on Jan. 2, 1938, unwed Margaret Stewart gave birth to a son in Rotten Row Maternity Hospital, Glasgow, Scotland. For the first 12 years of his life foster parents brought up the lad as if he were their own child. Margaret, a waitress, visited her son Ian at every opportunity and contributed financially to his upbringing. In 1950, Margaret met Patrick Brady of Manchester. Recognizing her chance for happiness and escape from the slums of Glasgow, she married Patrick and moved to Manchester. Ian remained with his foster parents.

Ian was not your average child. There is evidence of his cruelty to animals while still in his preteens. He threw cats off five-storey buildings to prove that they didn't have nine lives. Once he crucified a frog and relished the sheer agony he caused the helpless creature. Between the ages of 12 and 15 he broke into several shops and houses, getting caught more often than not. Judges were lenient with the pale, lean lad who stood before them. Each time he was apprehended he was put on probation so that he could continue his schooling.

When Ian was 15, he left school and was promptly charged with nine counts of housebreaking. His foster parents gave up. They would have nothing more to do with the problem child. He was given one more chance by another lenient magistrate, and left Glasgow to live with his mother and stepfather in Manchester. He took his stepfather's last name, becoming Ian Brady.

Ian drank, couldn't keep a job and continued to break into houses. Apprehended again in the act, he finally met a magistrate who sentenced him to two years in Borstal. On June 9, 1958 Ian was released from prison, but nothing had changed. He sometimes worked in a Manchester fruit market, but still couldn't hold a steady job. In February, 1959, Ian answered a newspaper ad for a clerical position. He got the job at Millwards Merchandise Ltd., a chemical supply company in West Gorton, Manchester. The job paid £12 a week. Ian kept to himself, opened the firm's mail and filed orders. At night he read about Adolph Hitler and the Marquis de Sade.

* * *

Myra Hindley was born in 1942 on Eaton St., Gorton, in the slums of Manchester. When she was four, her mother gave birth to a second daughter, Maureen. As the result of the overcrowding at Eaton St. Myra moved in with her grandmother a block down the street. She seldom saw her paratrooper father. Although her IQ was slightly above average, she was not a particularly good student. Myra left school while in her teens and drifted from job to job. Finally she managed to secure a position as a shorthand typist. The job paid £8.10s a week. It was with Millwards in West Gorton. Much of her typing was for a lean, pale, rather eccentric young man who fascinated Myra. His name was Ian Brady.

We will never know what catalyst was at work in the offices of Millwards which allowed two children of the slums to meet, become infatuated with each other and ultimately to become monsters living in the guise of human beings. Make no mistake about it; monsters they were to become.

Ian introduced Myra to his library of witchcraft, sadism, and genocide. Myra was a quick learner. What Ian said was law; Myra never argued. The pair became inseparable. Myra purchased a mini-van, and since Ian didn't drive, it was she who chauffeured the pair to and from work.

Throughout the years Myra remained friendly with her younger sister Maureen, who joined Millwards in 1963. Now that the sisters were employed under the same roof, Myra confided to Maureen that she was having an affair with Ian Brady. When Myra and her grandmother moved to Wardle Brook Ave. in Hattesley, Ian moved in with them. The elderly grandmother kept to herself and never interfered with the machinations of Myra and her live-in boyfriend.

Slowly Ian's fascination with Nazi Germany began to rub off on Myra. She became enthralled with Irma Grese, the Beast of Belsen, and tried to emulate her heroine. Evenings were spent experimenting with sexual perversions, drinking cheap wine, and wandering the countryside outside Manchester in the mini-van. On their days off, Ian would indulge in his hobby, photography. Myra was a willing model, posing in the nude in every conceivable position or stance which Ian suggested.

* * *

Mrs. Sheila Kilbride gave her 12-year-old son John a peck on the cheek before he scampered off with a friend to attend the movies. The two lads left the movie theatre at 5 p.m. and wandered over to Ashton Market to see if they could perform some odd jobs for the tradesmen. It was getting late. John's friend caught a bus home. He last saw John talking to a friendly blonde lady. The lady was Myra Hindley.

Little John Kilbride never returned home. Police were notified and a comprehensive search followed. Months were to pass without the police uncovering anything approaching a clue as to what happened to the missing boy.

Ten-year-old Lesley Downey was excited this Boxing Day of 1964. Her mother had reluctantly given her permission to attend a fair being held only 200 yards from her home. Lesley was stepping out with neighborhood children. It all seemed so harmless. By 5 p.m., Mrs. Jean Downey became apprehensive when little Lesley failed to return home. She called on her neighbors and was startled to find out that the other children had been home for some time.

A mini-van parked ominously beside the fair grounds. Every so often the van circled the fair grounds, its occupants looking for a young girl. There's one! A little girl watched the bobbing painted heads of the wooden ponies on the merry go round. The mini-van came to an abrupt stop. A blonde woman approached the little girl and the pair began talking. It wasn't long before the blonde woman found out that the youngster had spent all her money. The blonde lady volunteered that she would be happy to pay for another ride and another after that. What 10-year-old child could resist such good fortune? Lesley Downey jumped on the wooden pony. Later she mentioned to the young lady that she'd better get home as her mother would begin to worry. The kind lady urged the child not to be concerned. She would personally give her a lift in her mini-van so she needn't be late after all. Lesley knew everything would be all right. Her mother had told her never to accept a ride with a strange man, but she had never said anything about a friendly, kind lady.

Lesley Downey jumped into the mini-van beside her new friend Myra Hindley. In the shadows in the back seat, behind the unsuspecting child lurked Ian Brady.

Lesley Downey was never seen again. A massive search was conducted by police which involved the questioning of 5,000 individuals and the distribution of 6,000 posters. Weeks turned into months, until gradually the investigation into the mystery of Lesley's disappearance wound down. Ten months after her ride in the mini-van her fate was to make headlines around the world.

When Myra's younger sister Maureen married David Smith, it seemed most natural for the two couples to become close friends. Especially so, since the Smiths moved into an apartment within walking distance of Myra and Ian. David Smith was not exactly lily white. He had been in several scrapes with the law and had an assault conviction on his record. David could never hold down a job for any period of time. He welcomed Ian's hospitality.

The two men were accustomed to staying up half the night drinking cheap wine, while Myra and Maureen went to bed. During one of these lengthy drinking bouts, Ian broached David with the idea that they rob a bank. He told David he had been planning such a caper for years. David seemed receptive, but Ian's scheme didn't progress beyond the planning stage.

The strange double life being led by Ian Brady and Myra Hindley erupted into violence and terror on the night of Oct. 6, 1965. On that night, Myra's 77-year-old grandmother took a sleeping pill at 8:30 p.m. and retired for the night. Myra and Ian cruised the streets of Manchester in her mini-van. Myra parked the vehicle near Central Station while Ian took a stroll. He soon returned with 17-year-old Edward Evans. Edward was a homosexual who had gladly accepted an invitation to return to Ian's home for a drink.

Once back at Wardle Brook Ave., Ian and Edward engaged in conversation while Myra called on her brother-in-law, David Smith. She convinced David that Ian had some miniature bottles he wanted to give away. David was delighted to accompny Myra back to her home.

Myra and David lingered in the kitchen admiring the miniature bottles. Suddenly a blood chilling scream ricocheted through the house. Myra screamed, "Dave, Dave, come and help Ian." Smith ran from the kitchen into the living room and into hell.

The only light came from a television set. In its eerie glow David saw Edward Evans, whom he didn't know, lying half on the floor and half on a couch. Blood was cascading from Edward's head onto the floor. Ian Brady stood over the fallen youngster with a bloody hatchet in his hand. As David watched in terror, Ian brought the hatchet down on Edward's head time and time again. Edward tried to crawl away from his tormentor, but with each vicious blow his actions became weaker.

Ian interrupted his murderous frenzy to nonchalantly comment to no-one in particular, "This one's taking a while to go." Then he attached an electric cord around his hapless victim's neck, and pulled until Edward Evans lay still in death.

Ian was soaked in blood. The room looked like a slaughterhouse. Myra's clothing had been splattered with blood as well. David Smith had been an audience of one to a murder which had been orchestrated just for him. Ian commented rather sheepishly, "It's the messiest one yet. Normally one blow is enough."

At Ian's urging Myra went about cleaning up the room. Ian then changed his clothing. Upstairs Myra's grandmother slept through it all. Ian solicited David's help in carrying the body upstairs to a bedroom. Myra then put on a pot of tea and while David inwardly shuddered, she and Ian gloated over their recent victim.

At about 3 o'clock in the morning David suggested that he should head home, and was surprised when his companions bade him goodnight and let him leave. For Smith the whole evening had been unreal. He felt he had lived through a nightmare.

David Smith ran all the way home. He was so terrified of Ian and Myra that he waited three hours before he dared to sneak out of the house in order to call the police.

When detectives arrived at 16 Wardle Brook Ave. they were let in by Myra. They had been told by Smith that the living room would be spotless. A search of the back bedroom revealed the horribly mutilated body of Edward Evans trussed up in a plastic bag. Taken to a police station, Ian confessed to murder and at every opportunity tried to implicate David Smith. Three bloodstained carpets and the murder weapon were carried away by the police from the murder house. Later, a post mortem revealed that Evans had been struck 14 blows to the skull.

As police proceeded to interrogate Ian, and later Myra, it became obvious that neither of them had met Edward Evans before the night of the murder. What was their motive for luring the victim to their home to kill him? Was it possible, as it appeared to be, that the murderous pair had timed the first blow to coincide with David Smith's arrival so that he would be a witness to murder?

The house on Wardle Brook Ave. was practically dismantled in an attempt to discover further clues. The investigating officers were successful in their endeavors. They found Ian Brady's notes. On one page they came across the name John Kilbride, the little boy who had been missing for almost two years. There was more. Police discovered that Ian had checked two suitcases at Manchester's Central Station. They were recovered. They contained pornographic pictures of Myra, but more importantly there were weird photographs of the lonesome moors outside Manchester. Some of the photos showed Myra staring straight down at the moors, as if standing over a grave in mourning.

Police searched for and found the actual sites depicted in the photographs. They dug up the bodies of John Kilbride and little Lesley Downey.

The case was one of the most amazing murder cases ever uncovered anywhere. Christened the Murders on the Moors by the press, it received world wide publicity. The trial took place at historic Chester Castle on April 19, 1966. Due to the nature of the evidence it was felt that the two accused could very well be assassinated in the courtroom. When it came time for them to testify they were protected by four-inch thick bullet proof glass on three sides. The pornographic pictures, the photos of the gravesites of the two children, and Brady's diary left little doubt as to the guilt of the accused pair.

One piece of evidence was so horrifying that hardened homicide detectives left the courtroom when this particular evidence was presented. Myra and Ian had lured little Lesley Downey to their home and recorded on tape her agony as they sexually abused and tortured her to death. The tape, which also had Christmas carols as background music to the horror they were inflicting on a 10-year-old child, had been discovered intact by police.

The Moors jury took only two hours and 22 minutes to find Ian Brady guilty of three separate counts of murder. He received three life sentences, while Myra received two life sentences for the murder of Downey and Evans. She received a further seven years sentence for harboring Brady in the case of Kilbride.

Ironically, Ian Brady and Myra Hindley escaped the hangman's noose. A few months prior to their trial capital punishment had been abolished in England. They both remain in prison to this day.

ONCE TOO OFTEN

Many occupations are inherently dangerous. Miners risk their lives every day in pursuing their chosen profession. Fishermen are susceptible to the whims of nature. Prostitution may be the most dangerous profession of all. Many ladies who ply this oldest of trades end up in all sorts of trouble. Unfortunately, some become murder victims, but few attain the status of celebrated murder cases. The Frederick Field matter is an exception. It is unique in the annals of criminal history.

Fred was a nice guy — tall, good-looking, with black wavy hair. In 1931, he was gainfully employed with a firm of signpainters in London, England. For all intents and purposes, he should have gone through life working at his job, visiting his pub, and settling down with a faithful English wife for the rest of his life.

On Friday, Oct. 2, Fred and his foreman were instructed to inspect an empty shop the firm owned in Shaftesbury Ave., London. As they were performing this task, the foreman saw what he thought was a wax dummy lying on the floor. He poked at the unsightly object, and only then discovered it was the body of a partially clad young lady.

He and Fred notified the police. The victim had a piece of clothing stuffed into her mouth and a jacket belt firmly fastened around her neck. The investigating officers recognized Norah Upchurch, a young neighborhood prostitute. Norah kept a flat on Shaftesbury Ave. to entertain her clients, but lived in Pimlico.

Questioning revealed that Fred had visited the empty shop the previous day to take down a "To Let" sign. Field told the police that while he was doing this, a man showed up who claimed to be the gent who had rented the premises. He requested the keys from Fred. Thinking that this was all quite natural, Fred turned the keys over to the stranger. During the course of their conversation, Fred let it be known that he was somewhat of an electrician. The stranger seemed particularly interested in the lighting of his new shop. This topic was discussed for some time. Fred was led to understand that he would be given the contract to alter the lighting system.

The pair made an appointment to meet later that night at Piccadilly Station. Fred claimed that his new friend showed up, but had forgotten the keys to the shop. He left to get the keys and never returned. Fred waited a while and then went home.

Naturally enough, the police were extremely interested in Fred's story, especially since it provided them with a detailed description of the stranger. Before you could say Robert Peel, the bobbies had picked a prime suspect for Fred's perusal. Quick as a flash, Fred identified the man as the stranger who had taken the keys to the shop where poor Norah was killed.

Everything was falling nicely into place, except for one thing. The man Fred identified could not have been the killer. He had an airtight alibi for the night of the murder.

At the inquest into Norah's death, Fred had difficulty answering some routine questions. Why meet the stranger at Piccadilly Station? Wouldn't the shop have been a more convenient location? Why give a stranger the keys to the shop in the first place? How did Fred so enthusiastically and positively identify the wrong man?

The inquest jury brought in a verdict of "Willful murder against some person unknown." It was clear that Fred was suspected of the crime, and it was just as clear that there was no hard evidence against him.

Two long years went by. On July 25, 1933, Fred Field walked into a newspaper office and gave a detailed confession on how he had lured Norah Upchurch into the empty shop and strangled her to death. Fred said that he had robbed her of the few pounds she carried in her purse.

The wheels of justice turned ever so slowly. Fred was arrested and charged with murder. He was committed for trial at the Old Bailey, but when charged before the magistrate, he almost brought the house down when he stated loud and clear, "I plead not guilty, and reserve my defense."

Once his trial began, Fred explained that for two long years he had been scorned by his friends. They all thought he was a murderer. He couldn't stand it any longer. Now he insisted on being proven innocent or guilty in a court of law. The only way he knew to bring himself to trial was to confess to the murder.

Naturally his confession was a complete fabrication. Fred stated that he didn't want to go through life being known as the man who got away with murdering that poor unfortunate girl.

A man confessing to murder to prove his innocence; the story was fantastic enough to be believed. After some brief consultations everyone agreed that a guilty verdict would be impossible to arrive at with the existing evidence. The judge directed the jury to return a verdict of not guilty.

Fred walked out of the Old Bailey a free man. He joined the R.A.F. as an aircraftman in 1933, and for the next three years the world heard nothing of Mr. Frederick Field.

* * *

In April, 1936, the nude body of Mrs. Beatrice Vilna Sutton was found in her flat at Clapham. She had been strangled to death. At this time our old friend Fred was missing from his R.A.F. unit stationed at Hendon. On the very night Beatrice was murdered, April 4, Fred had shown up at the flat of a lady acquaintance. The girl's mother, who was present at the time, later stated that Fred behaved irrationally and had a wild look in his eyes. She said that Field had told them they would be reading about him in the newspapers. The woman who was aware of Fred's past, called the police and reported Fred as a deserter from the R.A.F. She explained that she had made the call to protect her daughter. At the time, she was unaware that the undiscovered body of Beatrice Sutton lay on a bed in Clapham.

Fred was picked up by the police and gave them a detailed confession of how he had strangled Beatrice. He revealed intimate details of the room where the murder had been committed, which only the killer could know.

Again, Fred stood trial for murder at London's Old Bailey. Only the jury was unaware of Fred's past appearance. It was a shock to all when Fred stated once again that he had only confessed to assure himself of a day in court in order to clear his name. At the time of Beatrice's murder he was on the run as a deserter. Fred knew Beatrice, she let him sleep in a small cupboard off a hall outside her flat. Fred claimed that on the night of April 4, he saw a man running from Beatrice's flat. He walked inside the open door and discovered Beatrice's nude body.

Fred knew that, if he called the police, he would be suspected. Later, when he was picked up, he thought he would kill himself. What better way to do it than to confess to a murder and have the Crown execute him. Now, of course, he had thought better of the whole matter and was repudiating his confession. If the jury would just return a verdict of not guilty, he would be on his way.

This time Fred's confession was too detailed for his own good. He had gone to the well once too often. The jury deliberated only 20 minutes before finding him guilty.

Fred, who had thought up one of the most unique defenses ever conceived, was hanged for his crimes.

DOWN THE DRAIN

John George Haigh was born in Stanford, Lincolnshire, on July 24, 1909. It was a difficult time for the family. John, Sr., was an electrical engineer and had been out of work for several months. Being deeply religious (the family belonged to an austere sect known as the Plymouth Brethren) they were too proud to ask for help from friend or neighbor.

Their affairs took a turn for the better when Haigh Sr. obtained employment at the Lofthouse Colliery. He was to stay in their employ for the next 25 years, but the new job necessitated a move to Outwood, a small village near the city of Wakefield. Here they moved into a comfortable house that came with the job.

The Haighs have come under close scrutiny in hindsight, but nothing detrimental can be conjured up about them. John and Emily were a deeply religious couple, and no doubt the severity of their beliefs sometimes spilled over into the upbringing of their only son. Young George was brought up to respect authority in the puritanical atmosphere of their home. His parents were kind and loving to a point, but at the same time they were harsh and stern when it came to the qualities they and the Brethren deemed sacred. Qualities such as punctuality and obedience were deeply instilled in the young lad, and no doubt he chafed at the bit under the strict rules.

When he became a teenager he mastered the organ and piano. His voice was better than average, and soon he was singing in the choir in Wakefield cathedral. The proud and pious Haighs delighted in listening to their John sing — a bizarre picture of domestic bliss in view of the grim events that were to befall the family in later years.

But for the moment, time passed pleasantly enough for the respectable Haighs and their respectable son. In his last year at school, John won a prize for studies in divinity. He became very interested in automobiles and at the age of eighteen got his first job as junior salesman at Appleyards, a car dealership in Wakefield. This position lasted about a year.

Something of a loner, Haigh had no close friends or social life. He was a strange fellow, but no worse than many blokes struggling to make a living. He was of average height, had a full crop of black hair, was always neatly dressed, and generally made a good impression on those he met.

For the next two years John moved from job to job and showed a distinct lack of interest in bettering himself. Then, when he was twenty-one, he and a partner started a business in Leeds, a combination advertising agency and real estate firm. For a short while it prospered, but then the tiny company fell on hard times. In order to keep the business going, John tried to obtain funds by false pretenses. He glibly misrepresented some buildings he was trying to sell, and obtained advances based on his misleading claims. The police picked him up, but because it was a first offense the charges were dismissed.

He then joined a combination car rental and insurance company, again based in Leeds, and again did very well at the outset. In fact, he was remembered as the ace of the staff. Then the bombshell fell. John was making up and signing fraudulent contracts, and had been doing so since joining the company. He had actually started up a dealership to perpetrate his frauds. He would sell a non-existent vehicle from his garage, and send the hire purchase contract to the company he represented. They in turn would send Haigh's garage a cheque, and of course Haigh would receive his commission from the company for bringing in the business. He had to keep meticulous records in order to make sure that all his fraudulant contracts were being paid each month, as it obviously wouldn't do to have someone trying to contact one of the false names and addresss which appeared on the contracts. One wonders if Haigh's penchant for forgery wasn't practice for bigger and better things that were to follow.

When his frauds were uncovered, his father made arrangements to pay the company the money that was missing and keep his son out of jail.

Haigh moved to Leeds, where he met, wooed and married Beatrice Hamer. He hadn't known the twenty-one-year-old Beatrice very long and the marriage was not a gala affair, as John's parents didn't approve of the union and the bride's parents were not thrilled with John. The young couple exchanged vows without benefit of parents at a registry office on July 6, 1934.

Fifteen months later John was again charged with fraud. Unbelievably, he had managed to secure employment with a branch of the same company from which he had previously been fired. He even used the fraudulent contract scheme again. This time he received 15 months in prison. While he was serving this sentence his wife gave birth to their baby. John was never to live with his wife again, nor was he ever to lay eyes on his child; he abandoned them without a thought for their welfare. He received three months off for good behavior, and was out after serving one year. His parents, who by now were feeling the disgrace of their son's petty crimes, still stood behind their only offspring. He swore that he was turning over a new leaf, and like parents everywhere, they believed him.

Haigh's father introduced him to a man who owned a drycleaning plant in Leeds. John told the truth about his past, and because of his sincerity, got the job. As always, things went well at first and John soon became assistant manager. Then, following his previous pattern, he was found to be promising people jobs for small cash considerations. He was fired on the spot, and moved on to bigger and better things in London.

He got a job as manager of an amusement park in Tooting. For twelve months he worked diligently for the owner, William McSwan, and his son, Donald. Then Haigh got that old urge to take another short cut. He left the McSwans and somehow or other hit upon a novel get-rich-quick scheme.

He would find the name of a legitimate lawyer in one town, and set up a law office in another, using the legitimate lawyer's name. He would then write to a selected list of clients that he was winding up an estate. This fictional estate would have some stocks that would be offered at slightly less than the current market price. For a small deposit Haigh would hold the stock for the proposed buyer. After he had accumulated enough cheques, and just before his clients started to demand delivery of the stocks, Haigh would close shop and set up in another town under another name.

On Nov. 24, 1937, the authorities caught up with him. This time he got four years in Dartmoor. He received time off for good behavior and was released in 1940. In the summer of '41, he sold some furniture that didn't belong to him, for which indiscretion he received 21 months in Lincoln Prison. Upon being released in 1943, John moved to Crawley, where, with the help of forged references and educational documents, he got a job with a light engineering firm owned by a Mr. Stevens.

Stevens was so taken with Haigh that he invited him to stay with his family, and John was quick to accept his offer. The Stevenses had two daughters. The younger of the two was usually underfoot, but Barbara was another story. She was an attractive young girl, and she and John became good friends. Barbara, like Haigh, loved good music, and the two of them spent many pleasant evenings discussing various compositions and composers. Sometimes Haigh played the piano while the entire family sat around and listened attentively.

John left the Stevens home and employ after six months, had some personal cards printed that read "J.G. Haigh, B.Sc., Technical Liaison Officer, Union Group Engineering," and started a light engineering firm on his own in London. At first he did rather well, and in 1944 he moved to the Onslow Court Hotel in South Kensington. He had devised another get-rich-quick scheme, and this time it included murder.

One day, John bumped into young Donald McSwan on the street, and the two men struck up a conversation about the good old days when they had worked together in the amusement park in Tooting. Donald was a pleasant enough lad, somewhat taller and more extroverted than Haigh. In the course of making small talk with Haigh, he mentioned that he had sold his share of the amusement park and had invested his money in some property. No doubt Haigh's interest in his old friend blossomed with this information, and they got along so well that Donald invited John over to his home to have a meal with his elderly parents. Haigh accepted this invitation, and the McSwans were genuinely happy to see him again.

Donald and Haigh became chums. They would meet every so often for a meal or just to pass the time of day. There is no doubt that the friendship was being cultivated by Haigh for his own devious purposes, and on Sept. 9, 1944, these purposes became clear enough. Haigh invited Donald over to his workshop at 79 Gloucester Road, sneaked up behind his chum and hit him over the head with a piece of pipe. He later claimed that it was only then that he thought of the perplexing problem of getting rid of the body. The idea of submerging it in sulphuric acid came to him the next morning He had been using the acid to scale metal, and it was "mere coincidence" that two carboys of acid were at hand.

The next morning Haigh placed the body in a drum. He then had the rather difficult task of taking sulphuric acid out of a carboy and transferring it, with the aid of a pail, into the drum containing the body. It was a tough job, and several times the burning fumes were too much for him and he had to go out to get fresh air. But slowly and surely the drum filled with sulphuric acid, completely immersing the body. Haigh was sure that he was removing both the body and all traces of the murder. What he didn't know is that certain parts of the human body, as well as foreign materials, take varying lengths of time to disintegrate. Gallstones may take a very long time to disappear completely, and human fat will remain for years. Haigh was later to refer to this fat as sludge, and it was this that proved beyond a doubt that a human being had been disintegrated in his workshop.

Haigh left his gruesome deposit and travelled to Scotland. Here he forged letter to the elder McSwans in their son's handwriting, saying that he had skipped to Scotland in order to avoid being called into the service. Donald had mentioned his reluctance to enter the armed services before, so the old couple had no reason to be suspicious.

Then Haigh came back to his workshop in Crawley and poured the now dissolved Donald down the drain. With commendable patience, he waited 20 months before he invited the elderly McSwans to 79 Gloucester Road, on a warm July day, and killed them both with vicious blows to the head.

Conscientious monster that he was, he had now outfitted himself with the tools of murder. He wore a mackintosh when he struck the fatal blows, in order to keep the blood off his clothes. He had also outfitted the workshop with a stirrup pump to transfer the sulphuric acid from the carboy into the drum. With two bodies on his hands, he now had two drums to fill, and had taken the precaution of wearing a gas mask to protect himself against the fumes.

Having disposed of their mortal remains, he equipped himself with forged power of attorney documents and ingeniously went about liquidating and transferring all the McSwans' assets to himself. They had two properties, a bank account, and some stocks.

When questioned about the missing couple, he would quickly produce personal letters in the McSwans' handwriting. These letters gave plausible excuses for their absence and assured anyone who inquired that they were fine. In order to make legal contracts, Haigh would produce the necessary forged documents demonstrating that his dear friends had empowered him to make transactions in their names. No one became suspicious. The McSwans were an unobtrusive lot who had never harmed anyone. It was just their bad luck that they crossed the path of our friend, John George. Haigh realized about £4000 from the deaths of the three McSwans, and went home for Christmas, satisfied and now prosperous, to visit his mother and father.

Throughout all his activities Haigh was writing and seeing his old girlfriend, Barbara Stevens. He treated her with the utmost respect, and at no time was he anything but a perfect gentleman to her. A deep and lasting friendship developed between them. He confided many of his innermost thoughts to her, and a strong attachment grew between the couple. Dashing John was the greatest thing that had ever happened to Barbara. The well-groomed, mature charmer was very different from the awkward local lads her own age. They took in symphonies and plays, and had intellectual conversations on a variety of topics. This rather weird relationship got to the stage of discussing marriage, but of course we know that Haigh was already legally married.

Not once did Barbara ever suspect that her boyfriend was anything other than he seemed.

At this stage of his career, John had money in his pocket, a pretty girlfriend, and had successfully murdered three innocent people.

At about this time he decided to give up his shop at 79 Gloucester Road, the scene of his three murders, and take up a new location on Leopold Road in Crawley. He told the company he rented the premises from that he planned to conduct several experiments there.

In September, 1947, Haigh answered an advertisement offering a house for sale at 22 Ladbroke Square, London. The home belonged to Dr. Archibald Henderson and his wife, Rose. Haigh didn't buy the house, but soon became a close friend of the handsome and wealthy Hendersons. For six months he cultivated their friendship and stored away all the personal bits and pieces of information he could. When he knew enough about the Hendersons, it would be time to kill them.

Haigh picked his spot. He waited until they were on vacation. Then one day he dropped in on them at the Metropole Hotel in Brighton, and suggested that the doctor might care to visit his "factory" in Crawley. It wasn't much of a drive, so the doctor accepted. As soon as they entered the storeroom, Haigh shot Dr. Henderson in the head from behind. His now familiar, macabre procedure was set into motion. The stirrup pump transferred the sulphuric acid from the carboy into the drum, and Haigh scurried about the small building in his gas mask, much like a busy chef overseeing a gourmet feast.

He then rushed back to Brighton and told Mrs. Henderson that her husband had suddenly been taken ill. On this pretext she accompanied him back to Crawley. Once in the storeroom he shot her in the back of the head and proceeded to dispose of her body in the same manner as that of her husband. Haigh had taken the liberty of stripping both bodies of a substantial amount of jewelry before placing them in the sulphuric acid, and he later sold the jewelry for £300.

A few days after these murders, on Feb. 16, Haigh showed up at the Metropole Hotel in Brighton. He had a letter, apparently signed by Dr. Henderson, instructing the hotel to give him the Henderson's baggage. Haigh had studied the doctor's handwriting and forged the letter.

Mrs. Henderson's brother soon contacted Haigh regarding the whereabouts of his sister and brother-in-law. Haigh told him the couple had had a very serious disagreement in Brighton and had decided to go away by themselves to work out their marital difficulties. To facilitate their rush to privacy, Haigh told Mrs. Henderson's brother, he had loaned the couple £2500. He added that, if they didn't return in sixty days, the

Hendersons were to give him their car and home. He showed the brother a document to this effect, apparently signed by the doctor.

The brother didn't like this story one bit, and insinuated that if he didn't her from his sister soon, he would go to the police. Haigh dashed off a forged letter from Rose to her brother. Cunning devil that he was, he had learned and stored away very personal family matters. He even copied her style of writing. This letter substantiated Haigh's story, and set Rose Henderson's family at ease for the time being at least.

Haigh followed up with postcards and telegrams, and set up a fictitious situation that was extremely believable. Finally, he forged a 15-page letter from Rose to her brother, postmarked Glasgow, Scotland. In the letter, Rose explained that due to personal financial problems, she and the doctor were going to South Africa. The letter carefully stated that the brother should settle the £2500 debt to their friend, John Haigh, and take his advice in clearing up all money matters.

Scotland Yard maintains that this letter, in the exact style and handwriting of Rose Henderson, is one of the most brilliant forgeries they have ever encountered.

Rose Henderson's family now considered Haigh a dear friend who had done many favors for the doctor. It is estimated from Haigh's bank statements that he realized over £7000 from the Henderson murders, but within a year he had blown the money on high living, and was looking around for more people to kill.

The Onslow Court Hotel caters mainly to elderly ladies who have been left considerable incomes. Most of the ladies are there on a more or less permanent basis. They pass the time sitting on wicker chairs, sipping tea and recalling days gone by. John Haigh, a permanent resident himself, was popular with his more senior associates of the opposite sex. In fact, one might say that many of them doted on him.

Mrs. Durand-Deacon was typical of the residents at the Onslow Court. Grey-haired and matronly, she could have been typecast for the part. She and John Haigh sat at adjoining tables at breakfast and often passed the time of day. Sometimes Mrs. Durand-Deacon expressed an interest in Haigh's engineering business. In fact, Mrs. Durand-Deacon had the bright idea that she wanted to manufacture artificial fingernails. Haigh, who had the patience of Job and would wait until his victims almost begged to become entwined in his net, expressed keen interest in this. He thought it might be a good idea if she were to accompany him one day to his factory in Crawley.

On Feb. 18, Haigh was having lunch at the Onslow Court when Mrs. Durand-Deacon suggested that it would be as good a day as any to visit the factory in Crawley. Haigh thought the day was just perfect. Mrs. Durand-Deacon told her good friend Mrs. Lane that she had an appointment with Haigh later that afternoon.

Haigh left the hotel heading for Leopold Road, carrying a hatbox, which, unknown to the occupants of the hotel, contained a revolver. He entered his workshop with Mrs. Durand-Deacon. Two sides of the main room had work-benches running the length of the walls, and three carboys of sulphuric acid took up much of the available space. By five-thirty that same afternoon Haigh had gone through the preliminary portion of his macabre routine. He had donned his mackinosh, shot Mrs. Deacon, and placed her body securely in the empty drum. Then, exhibiting a quirk that most normal people have difficulty comprehending, John Haigh got hungry. He slipped over to Ye Olde Ancient Prior's Restaurant in the square in Crawley and had poached eggs on toast and tea. This brief respite is well documented, as he chatted with the owner of the restaurant.

Then, back to work. He donned rubber gloves and gas mask, started up the stirrup pump, poured in the sulphuric acid, and poor Mrs. Deacon was well on her way to disintegration in the drum.

Haigh was back in London by ten o'clock that night. When Mrs. Durand-Deacon didn't show up for dinner, her friend Mrs. Lane was mildly alarmed. When her friend didn't show up for breakfast, she approached Haigh for an explanation. He had a story ready. He told Mrs. Lane that he had an appointment to meet Mrs. Durand-Deacon in front of a store, but she didn't show up. He waited for her for over an hour, then decided that she must have been delayed or changed her mind, and went on without her.

He left the worried Mrs. Lane and went to Crawley to check on the disintegration of Mrs. Deacon and pay a visit to his girlfriend Barbara Stevens. Both Barbara and her mother were to state later that on this particular visit John looked ill and had a hoarse voice. The hoarseness of the voice we can attribute to too many acid fumes, and the peaked condition could be laid at the doorstep of the inquisitive and annoying Mrs. Lane back at the Onslow Court Hotel.

Haigh should have known better. Surely one of the first rules in the mass murderers' handbook should be never, never mess with little grey-haired ladies. If either the victim or a friend of the victim's falls into this category, the entire operation is invariably ruined. Ladies of this ilk simply tend to spoil everything.

But let's get back to it. For the first time, one of his victims was missed by someone who didn't accept his glib explanations. The next morning was a Sunday, and Haigh knew he would have to face the troublesome Mrs. Lane at breakfast. He decided to be aggressive, and was the first to inquire as to the whereabouts of Mrs. Durand-Deacon. He suggested they go and report the missing woman to the police. Haigh offered a lift in his car, and Mrs. Lane accepted.

The police took a routine report from Mrs. Lane, and a woman sergeant was dispatched to the hotel to question all the guests, including Haigh, who had been one of the last residents to see the missing woman. The policewoman came away from the hotel with a nagging suspicion about this glib Haigh fellow. It bothered her so much she emphasized her suspicions in her report to her superior, Division Detective Inspector Shelley Symes. His first move was to check Haigh's record, and of course, he uncovered his lengthy criminal past. Inspector Symes decided to pay him a visit. On Monday Symes interviewed Haigh and was given substantially the same story as his sergeant had received. He obtained a picture of the missing woman and circulated it to the press.

The next day, Tuesday, Haigh checked the drum in Crawley, and discovered that the body was completely dissolved. He poured the liquid sludge out into the yard. On Wednesday Haigh was again questioned by the police. Again he gave the same story.

By Saturday, the police had located Haigh's landlord and decided to break the lock of the "factory" door. Inside they found a revolver and ammunition. They also found documents belonging to Mr. and Mrs. McSwan and their son, Donald. Further documents were found belonging to a Doctor Henderson and his wife, Rose. They also found a drycleaning receipt for a Persian lamb coat. Mrs. Durand-Deacon was last seen wearing such a coat. When it was retrieved from the cleaners, the detectives found that there was a patch on the sleeve. Inspector Symes searched Mrs. Deacon's room at the Onslow Court Hotel, and inside a sewing basket he found the same material that was used to patch the coat. Because of the publicity the case was now receiving in the press, a jeweller came forward with jewelry sold to him by Haigh. Mrs. Durand-Deacon's sister identified it as belonging to the missing woman.

The police picked up Haigh outside his hotel and took him to Chelsea Police Station. Inspector Symes produced the fur coat and jewelry, and asked Haigh for an explanation. Haigh was starting to give a cock-and-bull story to his adversary when Symes was called out of the office. Left alone with Detective Inspector Webb, for some reason Haigh started to talk. The conversation bears repeating here. Remember, at this point no one actually knew a murder had taken place.

Haigh said, "Well, if I told you the truth, you would not believe me; it sounds too fantastic. Mrs. Durand-Deacond no longer exists. She had disappeared completely and no trace of her can ever be found again."

"What has happened to her?" asked Webb.

"I have destroyed her with acid. You'll find the sludge which remains at Leopold Road. I did the same with the Hendersons and the McSwans. Every trace has gone. How can you prove murder if there is no body?"

Webb got Symes back in the office, and in front of Haigh told him what had transpired. Haigh interjected, "That's perfectly true, and it's a very long story and will take hours to tell."

Haigh spewed forth every detail of how he killed not only Mrs. Durand-Deacon, but the McSwans and the Hendersons. These former murders were unknown to the police. He elaborated on his diabolic behavior by adding the fact that he had made a tiny incision in each victim's throat. From this incision, he claimed, he extracted and drank a glass of blood.

The authorities converged on Haigh's factory once more. Now they knew what they were looking for, and they found all the paraphernalia of murder. On the ground outside the workshop there was a greasy area where the drums of sludge had been emptied. After a minute examination of the yard (it was all actually lifted up and taken to Scotland Yard) some gallstones and a plastic denture were found. The denture was identified as belonging to Mrs. Durand-Deacon by her dentist. She had also suffered from gallstones. Tiny particles of eroded bones were also found.

There was no doubt about it. Haigh was what he claimed to be — a monster. Realizing that his one chance to live was to appear insane, he maintained that he had killed for a glass of blood and not for material gain. Due to the rather large sums of money he diverted to himself, this reason proved hard to swallow. When questioned by psychiatrists he told about dreaming of Christ with open wounds bleeding into his mouth, and claimed that in this way he acquired the uncontrollable urge to drink blood. No one believed the blood theory. It was obvious that Haigh was trying to feign madness.

While awaiting trial he received a letter every day from his mother. Barbara Stevens wrote to him and visited him often. She was the one exception in his life — the only one he had ever treated decently. In his way, Haigh seemed to be genuinely fond of her. She in turn shared his affection, and remained loyal to him until the last.

On July 18, 1949, Haigh stood trial for murder of Mrs. Durand-Deacon. Huge crowds gathered outside the courthouse to catch a glimpse of the mass murderer. He pleaded not guilty. The defense tried to prove him insane, and the prosecution tried to prove him sane. The jurors obviously believed the prosecution. They took exactly 15 minutes to find him guilty.

Facing death by hanging, Haigh took great pains to bequeath his clothing to Madame Tussaud's Chamber of Horrors. There were certain stipulations. Vain to the end, he insisted that his wax image be kept in perfect condition, hair combed and pants pressed.

He was executed on Aug. 10, 1949.

THE CHICKEN FARMER

With the possible exception of the monastic life, I can't think of any occupation more peaceful than that of a chicken farmer. There is something about a man scattering feed about the barnyard, with the cackling chickens scurrying about, that paints a picture of rural tranquility.

Norman Thorne was a chicken farmer. After the First World War was successfully-concluded he purchased his farm not far from aptly named Crowborough, Sussex, England. Things were not going famously for Norman in the chicken business, but he was doing just great with another kind of chick named Elsie Cameron. The trouble was, Elsie was not a raving beauty. She peered out at him through thick glasses, which gave her the appearance of a sad-eyed spaniel. Thin lips etched across her pale face did nothing to enhance her appearance. Let's face it, folks, Elsie was ugly.

It would be only fitting to report that what Elsie lacked in looks she made up for in brains. Darn it all — that's just not true — Elsie was not that bright, either. One thing, though, she really wanted to marry Norm Thorne. From the moment she met Normie she made up her mind to reel him in, chickens and all. For two years she hung on, giving freely of her dubious charms. Norm, on the other hand, accepted any horizontal pleasures that Elsie dispensed. Sharing a bed was one thing, but marriage was quite another. To keep Elsie happy Norm went as far as buying her an engagement ring, but that was as close as he wanted to get to the altar.

Another year dragged by. It was in 1924 that Elsie got an inspiration. She wrote Norm that she was pregnant, which was a terrible idea for two reasons. Firstly, it wasn't true, and secondly, girls can never be sure how boyfriends will react upon receiving news of an impending blessed event.

Norman did the gallant thing. He dashed off a reply informing Elsie that she was counting her chickens before they were hatched, and anyway he was now sleeping around with one Elizabeth Coldicott. This was not true, although he was in fact keeping company with Elizabeth. Norm figured that Elsie would be heartbroken and go away, or whatever.

Elsie replied that she was disappointed, but forgave Norm. She added the startling postscript that she would be arriving shortly from London, and would be staying with him on the chicken farm until their wedding day.

Elsie arrived bag and baggage at the chicken farm on the evening of Dec. 5, 1924. No one ever saw Elsie again. Five days later the father inquired after his daughter. Norm replied that he was expecting her, but that she hadn't arrived. Elsie's daddy informed the police, who in turn, called at the chicken farm. They looked around, questioned Thorne, but left the farm with the old information that Elsie hadn't arrived.

Days dragged by and the one most concerned with Elsie's disappearance was Norm himself. The newspapers of the day featured pictures of him nervously feeding his chickens and seated anxiously beside his primitive radio listening for news of his loved one.

As word of the disappearance spread, two men came forward and volunteered the information that they had seen Elsie approaching the chicken farm on the evening of Dec. 5. Then a lady said she had seen the missing girl walking toward the farm on the same afternoon. The local police called Scotland Yard for assistance. They searched the farm and found Elsie's suitcase.

Thorne was picked up and questioned. He now calmly told the officers that Elsie had arrived all right, but he had gone out that same evening and left her alone. When he returned he found Elsie hanging from a beam in the house. He cut down her body and placed her on the bed. Believing that the police would think he had faked the suicide and had really killed Elsie, he decided on a plan of action. It appeared to him that the best thing for everyone would be for Elsie to disappear. He cut her body up in small pieces, buried Elsie's parts in the middle of the yard where the chickens grazed.

Norm was so broken up about the whole thing that he relaxed by taking Elizabeth Coldicott to the cinema the following afternoon. Norm's story wasn't half bad and only started to crumble when it came under close investigation. After Elsie's pieces were gathered up, pathologists stated that there was no evidence that she had died as a result of hanging. The beam that she had supposedly used to hang herself was covered with dust, and showed no evidence of a rope having been placed over it.

On March 4, 1925, Norman Thorne stood trial for murder. The jury took 30 minutes to bring in a verdict of guilty, and Norm was executed one month later.

I CAN'T REMEMBER

Guenther Podola was one of the most inept criminals who ever lived, yet he managed to fool reputable medical experts and set legal precedents which are still being discussed.

Podola was born in Berlin, and as far as we can ascertain, led a normal childhood. Later his father, a barber, learned that Guenther was carrying on, as they used to say, with a childhood acquaintance, Ruth Quant. In 1951, Guenther came to his father with the distressing information that Ruth was pregnant. Papa almost dropped his shears, but that didn't help. Ruth gave birth to a bouncing baby boy.

The following year Guenther emigrated to Canada, no doubt feeling that discretion was the better part of valor. He found it difficult fitting into the Canadian scene, and turned to housebreaking to make a living. In July, 1958 he was deported back to Germany as an undesirable. The authorities, figuring good riddance to bad rubbish, placed him on a ship, the *Seven Seas,* headed for Bremerhaven.

Ten months later Podola visited London, England, on a three-month visa. He bought a revolver, some ammunition, and let it be known along the fringes of the underworld that he was available whenever a gun was needed. Podola was even a bust at advertising. The boys around Soho wouldn't take a chance on anyone who mouthed off so blatantly about their chosen profession.

Podola thought he would try his hand at blackmail. The venture proved to be a disaster. While ransacking flats in South Kensington, he stumbled into one rented by an

American lady, Mrs. Verne Schiffman and her daughter. Podola made quite a haul. He picked up some valuable jewelry, a mink coat, and three passports. Had he left well enough alone, he would have been out of the woods, but he clumsily tried to blackmail Mrs. Schiffman.

It should be pointed out that if you are going to blackmail someone, make sure there is something in that person's past which they don't want revealed. Podola neglected to take this factor into account. He wrote a letter to Mrs. Schiffman a few days after the robbery: "I was hired five years ago to check on your behavior. I have a complete file with pictures and tape recordings. For $500 I will hand it over and report to my client that you are leading a blameless life."

The letter was signed by a Mr. Levine, who was supposedly an American private detective. Mrs. Schiffman was above reproach. She went straight to the police with the letter.

Figuring the blackmailer would make a further attempt to contact Mrs. Schiffman, the police had her phone tapped. Sure enough, the bumbling Podola called Mrs. Schiffman, who had instructions to keep the caller on the line as long as possible. Podola, now representing himself as a Mr. Fisher who was calling for Mr. Levine, managed to call from a phone booth exactly a half mile from Chelsea Police Station. Because he stayed on the line longer than your teenage daughter, the police were able to isolate the call and dispatch two police officers from the Chelsea Station to the phone booth.

Detective Sergeants Raymond Purdy and John Sandford arrived at the phone booth while Podola was still talking to Mrs. Schiffman. He was taken into custody quietly enough by the two men.

From this point in the saga of Guenther Podola, every detail of what happened was to come under the microscopic glare of a much publicized unusual murder trial. On the street, walking toward the police car with the two policemen, Podola broke away and made a desperate attempt to escape. The two officers cornered him in the hallway of a building in Onslow Gardens. They had Podola sit on a marble windowsill. Sandford was to get the car while Purdy stood guard over the prisoner. As Sanford made a step to leave, Purdy turned his head. At that exact moment Sandford noticed Podola slip his right hand into his jacket. He shouted to his colleague, "Look out, he may have a gun." A shot rang out and Purdy slumped to the hall floor, dead, with a bullet in his head.

Again, Podola fled. He stayed in his room at the Claremont House Hotel in South Kensington for three days. In the meantime, with the help of the Canadian police, the English authorities were able to identify the killer as Guenther Podola. Palm and fingerprints on the windowsill where he sat before the murder took place, positively verified the identification. Podola's picture was splattered over the newspapers, and it wasn't long before the police located his hotel.

On July 16, police burst into Podola's room. The door was unlocked, so that when they put their shoulders to it, it flew open. As it did so, it struck Podola on the forehead with such force he fell backward over a chair, and ended up with his head in the fireplace. Two detectives, thinking the police killer might be armed, jumped on top of him. Rather than the struggle they expected, Podola went limp.

He was taken into custody and examined by a police surgeon. The doctor brought the gunman around, but couldn't get him to speak. He appeared to be in a daze. Later that evening he was transferred to St. Stephens Hospital. In the days which followed, all the doctors who examined Podola were of the opinion that he was not totally conscious of his surroundings.

On July 20, Podola was the subject of a lumbar puncture. This is a procedure whereby cerebral fluid in the spine is withdrawn. From a study of this fluid it can be established whether the patient had suffered brain damage. In Podola's case there were traces of blood in the fluid, which indicated that there may have been an intercranial hemorrhage or bruising of the brain.

From the moment the lumbar puncture was performed, Podola began to talk and remember small periods of time in his past life. Up to then he had behaved like a man without any past at all. As the days went by, he began to communicate with doctors and jailers, but claimed to have no recollection of killing the policeman. In fact he claimed to remember only short windows of time, and that was all.

While in custody Podola played cards and chess with his jailers, skills which he remembered from the past. Then he received a letter from an acquaintance, Ron Starkey. Podola wrote a familiar letter back to his friend, indicating that he knew Starkey and remembered him well. In other conversations he discussed his girlfriend Ruth Quant and their son Mickey back in Germany. He also remembered the name of the ship, the *Seven Seas*, which delivered him from Canada to Germany.

In all, six doctors examined Podola. Four thought he had truly lost his memory, while two thought he was acting. Podola's lawyers held that loss of memory made a man incapable of standing trial. Crown attorneys claimed that Podola wasn't suffering from amnesia, but was faking the whole thing. They further stated that even if the loss of memory was genuine, it did not make the defendant unfit to plead.

After all the submissions had been studied, a judge decided to hold a trial preceding the murder trial, to decide if Podola had truly lost his memory. The judge charged the defence with the responsibility of proving that the prisoner was not faking. This unusual trial lasted eight days. The most damaging piece of evidence submitted with the letter to Ron Starkey, indicating that Podola certainly remembered large portions of his past life. The jury brought in their verdict — "Podola is not suffering from loss of memory."

The trial of Guenther Podola was anticlimatic. It lasted only a day and a half, and the jury took only 37 minutes to find the accused guilty. There was no doubt whatever. The prosecution presented a trained eyewitness in the person of Det. Sanford, as well as the murder weapon.

Before sentencing, Podola read from a written statement: "Your Honor, Ladies and Gentlemen of the Jury; I stand before you accused of the murder of a man. Throughout the course of this trial I have listened to the various witnesses, and I understand the accusations. The time has now come to defend myself against these accusations, but I cannot put forward any defence. The reason is that I have lost my memory for all these events. All I can say in my defence is that I do not remember having committed the crime for which I stand accused of.

"I do not remember the circumstances leading up to the events in connection with the shooting. I do not know whether it was me, or whether it was an accident, or an act of self defence. I do not know whether at that time, I did realize that the man was, in fact, a detective. I do not know whether I was provoked in any way. For these reasons I am unable either to admit or deny the charge against me. Thank you."

In spite of this plea, he was sentenced to death. Podola was hanged on Nov. 5, 1959 in Wandsworth Prison.

LITTLE MARY BELL

The act of one youngster taking another's life is not common and when it does happen it sometimes is the fault of the parents.

The Mary Flora Bell case is considered to be the classic child killing incident.

Mary was born on May 26, 1957 to 17-year-old unwed Betty Bell. Betty married Mary's father shortly after she gave birth to Mary. Betty had three more children in the years that followed. Life was hard for the young family. They lived in Scotswood, a slum in Newcastle. Mary's mother would disappear for long periods of time and leave her brood unattended. On other occasions she had herself committed as a voluntary patient at mental institutions. Mary's father was often out of work. The house they lived in was dirty and unkempt.

The events which unfolded would have been acted upon at the first sign of danger had they occurred in a middle-class neighborhood. In Scotswood, children received little supervision, and as a result accidents were not uncommon.

On May 11, 1968, pretty 10-year-old Mary and her 13-year-old friend Norma Bell (no relation) found Mary's three-year-old cousin injured beside an air raid shelter. Apparently the child had fallen seven feet from the top of the shelter. The following day the police received a complaint about Mary and Norma. Children had told their mothers that Mary and Norma had struck them and squeezed their throats. The police were summoned and they severely reprimanded the children, but no further action was taken.

Then about two weeks later, on May 25, two boys found the body of little Martin George Brown, aged six years and two months, in an abandoned house in Scotswood. There were no signs on the body, and there was some doubt as to how the child met his death. Finally it was decided that the death was accidental and the matter was not referred to the Criminal Investigation Department of the police force.

The following day a local nursery school was broken into; desks were upset and papers and books strewn over the room. On the blackboard the vandals had left several messages. One message said, "We did murder Martin Brown." The police believed the message to be a sick joke and recommended an improved burglar alarm be installed at the school.

Two days later, Martin Brown's mother was surprised when she answered the door and was confronted by Mary Bell. Mrs. Brown was later to say, "She knocked at the door and asked to see Martin. I said, 'No, pet, Martin is dead.' She said, 'I know he's dead. I want to see him in his coffin.' She was grinning. I slammed the door on her."

Five days later the new alarm at the school went off at the police station, and the police caught Mary and Norma on the premises. They denied having had anything to do with the earlier break-in. This time they were charged in juvenile court and were released into the custody of their parents until their case could be heard.

About two months later, on July 31, Brian Edward Howe, aged three years and four months, was reported missing to the police. Mary Bell took an active part in the search. She suggested to the missing boy's sister that they should look for him among some large cement blocks in a vacant field where children sometimes played. That same evening Brian's body was found exactly where Mary had suggested they look. He had been manually strangled to death. His body had been covered with long grass and purple weeds. Beside the body the police found a small pair of scissors with one blade broken and the other bent back. For some reason the scissors had been used to make small punctures in the child's legs and thighs. The letter "M" had been scratched on his stomach.

A pathologist stated that, in his opinion, the murder was the work of a child. One hundred C.I.D. officers distributed questionnaires to homes that contained children in an attempt to find someone who had seen Brian. When questioned by the officers, Mary and Norma gave conflicting stories. Twice they changed their stories. Mary told of seeing another child playing with a pair of scissors and described them in detail. The description of the scissors found beside the body had not been made public by the police. The youngster Mary accused had spent the day of the killing miles away from Scotswood.

Norma was the first to implicate herself and Mary in the murder, but she claimed Mary did the actual killing. She described the strangulation and the slight mutilations to the body in detail. The interrogating officers began to realize that although Norma was two years older than her friend, Mary was the intelligent, dominant personality, while Norma was the slow thinking follower.

The day after Norma gave her statement, Mary admitted to being present while Norma strangled Brian. The officers were amazed at the attention to detail and lucidity of her narrative. All agreed that she was an extremely intelligent child.

Both girls were arrested and charged with the murder of Brian Howe. Later they were also charged with the murder of Martin Brown. The story of their weird behavior was uncovered much as we have presented it here.

On Dec. 3, 1968, the trial of Mary and Norma started in Newcastle. It was to continue for 14 days. The two children continued to blame each other for the murder of Brian Howe, but both denied killing Martin Brown.

A detailed drawing, depicting Martin's body exactly in the position in which it as found, was discovered in one of Mary's school exercise books. In court she amazed everyone present by her behavior on the witness stand. Although only eleven, she followed the trial attentively, and when on the stand she had the ability to parry with learned lawyers, turning many of their inquiries to her advantage. Norma didn't have the intelligence or the dominant personality of her friend. Psychologists stated that Mary showed no remorse, and in fact did not have normal feelings about the whole affair, other than being annoyed at her detention.

In the end, the charges against Norma were dropped and she was released. Mary was found guilty of the lesser charges of manslaughter of the two boys. The judge expressed the opinion that he wanted her sent to an institution where she could receive treatment, but was advised that no institution would accept Mary out of deference to other youngsters receiving treatment.

She was eventually placed in a maximum security unit of an approved school. She was often the only girl confined to this special unit. The sentence has often come under criticism because there is no psychiatrist on the staff of the institution.

Mary's mother and father continued to visit her until 1970, when her father was sent to prison for robbery. Her mother was absent for long periods of time. Even while she was in confinement, Mary's parents didn't contribute a great deal to her welfare.

In 1970, Mary brought a complaint against one of the teachers at the school, charging him with indecent assault. A defense lawyer, with a few well directed questions, showed without a doubt that Mary was lying and had made up the entire incident.

Mary Bell remains institutionalized to this day.

DON'T LOOK IN THE CLOSET

The draw of Buckingham Palace was too much even for me, a man with a mission and an obsession all rolled into one. I checked into the Rubens Hotel on Buckingham Palace Road, and was relieved to see that the armchairs in the lobby were slightly frayed where thousands of elbows had rested in years gone by, and that the once-beautiful carpet had faded paths leading to doors, worn down by untold pairs of feet, scurrying to dine, scurrying to enter and scurrying to leave.

The year of my visit to England was 1972. I arose bright and early and briskly walked to the lift. Browning's line "Oh, to be in England now that April's there," came to mind. The lift descended ever so slowly to the lobby, and I dashed over to the hall porter.

I inquired of the young man, "Can you tell me how to get to 10 Rillington Place?"

"I never heard of that address myself, sir. Let me get a map," he replied.

I couldn't believe my ears — never heard of 10 Rillington Place! The lad must be pulling my leg. He returned with a street map of London.

"No sir," he said, "there doesn't seem to be a Rillington Place at all."

"But," I stammered, "everyone knows 10 Rillington Place. It's Reg Christie's place — you know, the murderer."

"The name Christie does seem familiar. Let me get the manager, sir," the young man offered.

A tall balding man with a moustache looked down at me and said, "Yes?" in a manner which seemed to demand an explanation.

"Have you ever heard of 10 Rillington Place?" I asked.

"Certainly, sir," he said.

This was more like it.

He took me aside, and in the confidential manner made famous by movie spies giving the secret password to enemy agents on street corners, he said, to me, "They changed the name, you know. It was so notorious after the murders, it was changed to Ruston Close. Nothing much there now, but I'll tell you how to get there."

One hour later, I was looking at the demolished houses that had once been Rilligton Place. At last I was standing on the same ground as that most classical of all murderers, Reginald Christie.

Reggie was born in Halifax, England, in 1898, to normal parents. There is nothing in his early life that can even vaguely be construed as a hint of what was to follow. He was a Boy Scout and eventually became an Assistant Group Leader. In his teens he was a choirboy, and to many I am sure this activity will seem an admirable one. As I have said, the disproportionate number of choirboys who later in life go around killing people has always made me wonder.

Christie left school at the age of fifteen, and got his first job as a projectionist in a Halifax movie theatre. It was around this time that he induced a young lady to accompany him to a local lovers' lane for what was to be his first try at sex. Later the young lady, who was apparently a blabbermouth, told one of Christie's chums that Reggie couldn't get it up. From across the streets of Halifax came shouts of "Reggie no dick" and "Can't-make-it Christie." It seems that after this incident Reggie always felt inadequate around women, and while this experience may not have actually caused his inhibitions, it serves to illuminate the fact that he was never quite normal when it came to members of the opposite sex.

Christie enlisted in the army in September, 1916, at the age of eighteen. He now stood five feet, eight inches tall, with blue eyes and reddish-blond hair atop a round, full ruddy face. The young soldier was a model rookie to everyone with whom he came in contact. We suspect that he gave an external impression of efficiency to his superiors and cheerfulness to his acquaintances, but inside smouldered a deep resentment for women. When he looked at the painted young girls flaunting themselves at the uniformed soldiers, we wonder if deep down he still heard the taunts of his chums of a few years back.

In April, 1918, Christie was sent to the front, and towards the end of June a German mustard gas shell knocked him unconscious. When he regained consciousness he discovered that he had lost his voice. Though he later claimed that he never said a word for over three years, in reality his muteness lasted only a few months and finally gave way to a low whisper. The army doctor diagnosed his affliction as functional aphonia, which means that the explosion scared the wits out of him and left him speechless.

Christie was discharged by the end of 1919, and returned to civilian life to pick up the pieces in Halifax. On May 10, 1920, he married a neighbor, Ethel Simpson Waddington. The young couple, both twenty-two years old, had known each other for some time. Ethel was a plump, matronly type of individual, who did not stand out in any particularly memorable way.

Reggie, who now had a nondescript job as a clerk, moved into a new house with his bride. He did not have full use of his voice at this time, and it's fascinating to imagine the whispering Reggie explaining to the frigid Ethel that he really wasn't that good at this sex business. We wonder who was more relieved, Reggie or Ethel.

To better his lot Christie changed jobs and became a postman. Almost immediately he started stealing postal orders, and almost immediately he got caught and received three months in jail. When he got out things went along routinely enough, but in Reggie's eyes Halifax held no chance for advancement so he headed for London, leaving the wife with relatives in Sheffield.

Once in London, Reggie held a series of dull clerical positions. He took to breaking the law regularly, and just as regularly he received jail sentences for these indiscretions. In 1924, he received a three-month sentence, followed by six months, for two charges of larceny. In 1927, he was caught stealing and received nine months in jail. Two years later Reggie shacked up with a prostitute. Like many men before him who couldn't hack it with normal women, he seemed to be in his element with prostitutes. No inhibitions here; his sex partners quite simply didn't give a damn one way or the other. One day he had a temper tantrum and hit a prostie over the head with a cricket bat, an indiscretion which earned him six months at hard labor for malicious wounding. In 1933, he got three months for stealing a car; it didn't help him that the owner of the vehicle happened to be a Roman Catholic priest.

After ten years of trying to get ahead of the game and finding nothing for his efforts except jail, Reggie decided to import the wife, who was still staying with those relatives in Sheffield. He wrote to Ethel from prison, and the pair reached a reconciliation during a visit at the jail. Coinciding with the reunion with his wife, Christie was released from prison and became a patient of Dr. Matthew Odess — not that he had any major illness, but he lived in fear of recurring muteness and suffered from such ailments as nervousness and stomach trouble.

In 1938, the sickly Reg and the nondescript Ethel moved their belongings into 10 Rillington Place. Situated in Notting Hill, Rillington Place was a dead end street, coming to an abrupt stop at a factory wall. Number 10 was the last building on the left-hand side. Because of the light traffic, Rillington was an active, alive street. Children could play games and dogs could scamper in relative safety from the vehicles. Number 10 consisted of three flats, of which the Christies occupied the ground level. The whole structure was in a state of visible decay. Over the years everything had been painted many times, and was now sadly chipped and cracked; soot from the factory had rained down over the street, coating everything with a greasy deposit.

The flat above the Christies' was occupied by a partially blind old man named Kitchener, and the top flat was vacant. The three flats were connected by narrow stairs that started in the narrow passageway that led to the ground floor past the open door of Christie's flat. Reggie's front room had a baywindow covered by curtains. In the evenings, he would part these curtains to watch the goings-on out in the street.

The passageway and stairs were common territory to the tenants of all three flats, but you were almost in the Christies' flat when you were coming and going. Their front room and back room were both only accessible through the passageway or hall. Behind these two main rooms, the Christies had a kitchen with an empty alcove that was used to store coal, and sometimes other things. Behind the kitchen was a wash-house that was mainly used as a storeroom, measuring four feet by four feet. Attached to this section of the house was a lavatory for the use of all the tenants. The rest of the lot, measuring about twenty feet square, was to become famous as the garden. To gain a proper perspective of the Christie flat, one must try to realize that everything was undersized. Two people couldn't pass comfortably in the hall or on the stairs; the rooms were cramped and small. There was little in the way of comfort at 10 Rillington Place.

Shortly after moving into his new premises, Reggie joined the War Reserve Police. He was assigned to the Harrow Road Police Station, wore a crisp official uniform, and all in all cut a dashing figure. This was more like it. Reggie was a good, efficient cop, and quickly gained a reputation for being very strict with those who didn't obey the air raid regulations.

It was during this rather happy and contented time in Reggie's life that he met, quite by chance, a young lady named Ruth Fuerst. She was an Austrian student nurse who had found herself in England when the war broke out and decided to stay in England rather than return to Austria. When she met Reggie she was working in a munitions factory and living in a furnished room at 41 Oxford Gardens, in the same neighborhood as the Christies. This lonely twenty-one-year-old, who spoke English with a slight accent, was a tall, pretty girl with brown hair and brown eyes. It wasn't long before she and Christie were seeing a great deal of each other.

In the middle of August, 1943, Ruth visited Reggie at 10 Rillington Place. Though we only have Reggie's word for what took place that fateful afternoon, in this instance his account is probably accurate. Ethel was away visiting her relatives in Sheffield. While he was having intercourse with Ruth in the bedroom, Reggie strangled her with a piece of rope.

Pause and reflect on Reggie's state of mind when, as he lies spent, just having had intercourse (we must assume he enjoyed it) and having just strangled a naked woman (we can only assume that some peverted thrill was attached to his act) there was a knock at the door. The blood pounding in his temples, Reggie made himself presentable and answered. It was a telegraph-boy with a telegram. The message was from Mrs. Christie. She was returning home from Sheffield that evening with her brother.

Bothersome bodies, indeed!

Christie was frank about how he solved the problem: "I took her from the bedroom into the front room and put her under the floorboards. I had to do that because of my wife coming back."

A few hours later, Ethel and her brother, Henry Waddington, arrived. Ethel and Reggie slept in the bedroom and Henry slept in the front room, just a few feet from the remains of Ruth Fuerst. Next morning Henry went back to Sheffield, and in the afternoon Ethel went out visiting. At last! Reggie retrieved the body from under the floorboards and removed it and Ruth's clothing to the wash-house. Then Reggie decided to do a little gardening; he dug a grave. That night, on the pretence of going to the lavatory, he moved Fuerst's body from the wash-house and put it in the hole he had dug. Next morning he tidied up, raking over the grave site and burning Ruth's clothes in a dustbin with some other rubbish.

In September, Ruth was reported missing to the police. No one pressed the matter. She had no relatives, no close friends. The bombs had claimed many victims who were not found for months, even years. Then again, she could be a young girl on the loose. She had probably taken a lover and gone away without telling anyone. No one gave her another thought, except Christie.

Let's let him tell it.

"Months later I was digging in the garden and I probably misjudged where it was or something like that. I found a skull and put it in the dustbin and covered it up. I dug a hole in the corner of the garden, and put the dustbin in the hole about eighteen inches down. The top of the dustbin was open, and I still used it to burn rubbish."

In December, 1943, Christie got word that his application for employment at the

Ultra Radio Works, Park Royal, Acton, had been accepted. He left the War Reserve Police, and early in the new year took up his new job. Ethel had gainful employment with a lightbulb factory, and again the Christies settled into that humdrum way of life so typical of many who have stubbed their toes on the ladder of success.

Reggie ate his lunch in the company canteen, and it was here that he met Muriel Amelia Eady, a respectable, thirty-one-year-old-spinster. Muriel had brown hair and eyes and was rather stout and short. Christie overheard that she had a steady boyfriend, so he asked Muriel to bring him over to 10 Rillington Place to have tea with himself and Ethel. A sort of friendship developed, and Muriel brought her boyfriend over to the Christies on more than one occasion. In the course of idle conversation, Muriel complained of catarrh, and Reggie told her he had an inhaling device that would ease her difficult breathing if she cared to try it.

One fine day in October, 1944, Ethel was away visiting her brother in Sheffield when Muriel knocked on the door of 10 Rillington Place, wondering if the kind Mr. Christie would let her inhale some of his cure.

"Come right in," said Reggie. He had planned the whole thing for just such an occasion. His inhaling device consisted of a glass jar with a metal screw top that had two holes in it. The jar contained Friar's Balsam, and a rubber tube was inserted into one hole so that Muriel could breathe through the other end of the tube and inhale Friar's Balsam. Another tube was attached to the gas stove, and the other end of this tube was inserted into the second hole on top of the glass jar. Reggie sat Muriel in a chair so she wouldn't see what he was doing, and as she relaxed and breathed deeply. Gas rushed into the jar and through the tube to Muriel's lungs, soon rendering her unconscious. Reggie carried her into the bedroom, placed her on the bed, took off her panties, and had intercourse with her and strangled her. When it came to disposing of the body, this time he could afford to work more leisurely since Ethel wasn't rushing home. Muriel's body was taken out to the wash-house, and that night it was buried in the garden.

Miss Eady was reported missing by relatives, but no trace of her could be found. No suspicion was ever cast in Christie's direction.

The war ended and Christie changed jobs again. He obtained a position as a clerk in the Savings Bank at the post office. The years passed, and Reggie kept running to Dr. Odess with his minor ailments. Nothing of a serious nature was ever uncovered by the doctor. Perhaps Reggie used these visits to gain a brief respite from his boring existence at home.

A break in the monotony came when another tenant took up residence at 10 Rillington Place. At Easter, 1948, Timothy Evans and his wife Beryl moved into the upper flat. Beryl was nineteen, three months pregnant, and quite pretty, while Tom was twenty-four and not too bright. He was employed as a van driver and could only read with great difficulty, though he was by no means a simpleton, and had definite ideas on world events as he saw them unfold around him. If his interpretations were erroneous, who are we to criticize? He spent many a night at the pub, and prided himself on his capacity for beer. He was also a congenital liar, as everyone who ever came in contact with him is quick to point out.

Six months later Beryl gave birth to a little girl whom the Evans christened Geraldine. The cramped quarters, the lack of toilet facilities, the dirty diapers and the inadequate wages Tim brought home were all conducive to bickering. The bickering led to arguments, and the arguments led to screaming fights. What had started out for the young Evanses as a happy, carefree life together had deteriorated to the point where Tim was spending more and more time at the pub and Beryl was slaving away to keep some semblance of a home at 10 Rillington Place.

In the late summer of 1949, Beryl found herself pregnant again, and resolved to try to bring on a miscarriage. She tried various pills and home remedies without success, then decided to have an abortion. She told several people about this, including the Christies. By now the Evanses and the Christies were seeing each other quite often. Tim and Beryl liked the Christies, and the Christies seemed to take to the young couple living above them. But seeing an attractive girl like Beryl on a daily basis must have played havoc with Reggie's peverted urges. Every time she entered the house, went up the stairs, or went to the lavatory, she had to pass a doorway leading to Reggie's rooms. Only he knew of the two ladies who had been resting comfortably for years in the garden. Later, Reggie was to say he never thought much about the two bodies. Once, while digging in the garden, a human femur popped to the surface. He nonchalantly used it to prop up the sagging fence bordering his property. The weatherbeaten bone was to remain exposed in this way for years.

In October and November, a series of seemingly common, everyday events started to unfold that were later to come under meticulous study. Mr. Kitchener's sight became so bad that he went to the hospital for an operation. He remained in the hospital for five weeks, and was therefore absent from the scene during the crucial weeks that were to follow.

Toward the end of October, the landlord at 10 Rillington Place hired a firm of builders to carry out some repairs to the building. These men were in and around the house on and off for the next 15 days. During this time Beryl Evans told a friend that considerate Mr. Christie was going to perform an abortion on her, despite her husband's objections. The atmosphere between husband and wife was strained over the operation and over a sum of money that Tim had given her to make a payment on their furniture, but which Beryl had spent on something else.

On Nov. 7, it started to rain early in the morning, so the builders, who were not actively engaged in working on the roof, knocked off for the day. When Evans came home from work his wife told him that Christie would be performing the operation on the following morning. The Evanses argued about the abortion all that evening. Next morning, Tim went to work. The weather had cleared and the workmen were back doing their repairs at eight o'clock. Mrs. Christie went out. Beryl waited upstairs, preparing herself for her operation. Finally, Reggie appeared carrying a rubber tube, which he attached to an outlet on the side of the fireplace. He told Beryl that a few gulps of the gas would make the operation less painful.

We do not know exactly what happened next, but it is very possible that Christie made an unmedical improper move, because at this moment she realized what was happening and started to struggle. Christie struck her several blows to the head and strangled her with his rope. He then turned off the gas and had intercourse with her remains.

There was a knock on the door. God, how scared Christie must have been! Remember the telegraph boy arriving at the exact moment he killed Ruth Fuerst? This time Reg didn't know what to do. A friend of Beryl's, Joan Vincent, was surprised to find the door to the flat closed. Beryl had never kept it closed before. She felt her friend was inside and didn't want to see her. Somewhat annoyed, she expressed her feelings through the closed door and left. Reg Christie breathed a sigh of relief.

All the while workmen were scurrying about on the ground floor, in the wash-house and lavatory. Reggie moved Beryl's body to the bedroom and covered her with a quilt. When Tim came home from work Christie met him at the door and explained that the operation had been a failure, and that Beryl was dead. He showed Tim his wife's body laid out on the bed, explaining that she had poisoned herself by trying to induce a miscarriage and would have died in a few days had he not tried to abort her. Evans, a bit slow-witted, accepted this explanation and went about changing his baby's diapers and giving her something to eat. Christie explained that he was in a jam for trying to do Beryl a favor, and needed Tim's help. He said that they would dispose of the body and this way no one would get in trouble. Evans, stunned, scared, and slow to comprehend, put himself in Christie's hands. The two men carried the body down to Mr. Kitchener's vacant flat. Evans inquired of Christie just what he planned to do with the body.

Christie replied, "I'll dispose of it down one of the drains."

Both men went to bed in their own flats. The next day the sun's rays couldn't break through the overcast, dreary sky as Tim Evans awoke in his flat and Reg Christie got dressed on the ground floor. It was Wednesday, Nov. 8, and there was the important matter of an infant child to contend with. Evans and Christie met in the hall, and Christie told him not to worry, he would look after the baby for the day, maybe even make some inquiries about adoption. Tim went to work a troubled, confused man. At eight o'clock the workmen arrived again and went about their tasks. By four in the afternoon they had finished, and stored their gear in the washroom for the night. When Evans returned, Christie informed him that he had found a couple who would make a good home for Geraldine. Reggie told him to dress and feed the baby before leaving for work the next day, and when the couple came around for the child in the morning, he would let them in and give Geraldine to them. Christie told Evans that if he ever received any inquiries about Beryl and Geraldine he was to say they were away on vacation. On Thursday, Nov. 10, Reggie strangled the child with a necktie and placed it beside its mother in Mr. Kitchener's flat. Evans got fired from his job that same day and arrived home by 5:30. Christie told him everything had gone well, the couple had come and picked up the baby. Christie, good friend that he was, had thought of everything — he had even arranged to sell Evans' furniture, so there would be nothing keeping Evans from leaving London. On Friday, Nov. 11, the work-men finished their repairs and cleaned out all their gear from the wash-house, leaving it bare. That evening Christie, knowing the workmen would not be returing, placed the bodies of Beryl and Geraldine in the wash-house.

By Sunday, Evans had sold the furniture (which he didn't own) and said good-bye to the Christies. He told them he was going to Bristol, but actually he caught a train at Paddington for Cardiff and Merthyr Vale to visit his uncle and aunt, Mr. and Mrs. Lynch. Tim said that he and his boss were touring the area for some vague business reason and had had car trouble in Cardiff. He was wondering if he couldn't stay with them until the car was repaired. In passing, he mentioned that his wife and baby were vacationing in Brighton. Evans stayed with the Lynches for the next six days. He acted perfectly normally, went shopping with Mrs. Lynch and to the pub with Mr. Lynch. Once he talked to his aunt about getting his daughter a Christmas present.

On Nov. 23, Evans showed up on Christie's doorstep inquiring about his daughter. Christie replied that she was well and happy with her new parents, but that it was too early to see her. Disappointed, Evans returned to Merthyr Vale. He had to make up more lies to pacify the Lynches, and told them a not-too-convincing tale to the effect that Beryl had left him and that he had left his daughter with friends. On Nov. 27, Mrs. Lynch wrote to Tim's mother saying that he was staying with them and that they felt something was wrong because they couldn't get a straight answer from him. Tim's mother wrote back that she hadn't seen Beryl or the baby for a month. Mrs. Lynch read this letter to Tim and accused him of lying to them. Evans, beside himself at being caught in his web of lies and childlike in his indecision and lack of planning, decided to go to the police.

He walked into the police station at Merthyr Vale and told the officer on duty, "I want to give myself up. I have disposed of my wife, put her down the drain."

The officer on duty took this statement from Evans:

"About the beginning of October my wife, Beryl Susan Evans, told me that she was expecting a baby. She told me that she was about three months gone. I said, 'If you are having a baby, well, you've had one, another won't make any difference.' She then told me she was going to try to get rid of it. I turned round and told her not to be silly, that she'd make herself ill. Then she bought herself a syringe, and started syringing herself. Then she said that didn't work, and I said, 'I am glad it won't work.' Then she said she was going to buy some tablets. I don't know what tablets she bought, because she was always hiding them from me. She started to look very ill, and I told her to go and see a doctor, and she said she'd go when I was in work, but when I'd come home and ask her if she'd been, she'd always say she hadn't.

"On the Sunday morning, that would be the sixth of November, she told me that if she couldn't get rid of the baby, she'd kill herself and our other baby Geraldine. I told her she was talking silly. She never said no more about it then, but when I got up Monday morning to go to work she said she was going to see some woman to see if she could help her, and that if she wasn't in when I came home, she'd be up at her grandmother's. Who the woman was she didn't tell me.

"Then I went to work. I loaded up my van and went on my journey. About nine o'clock that morning I pulled up at a transport cafe between Ipswich and Colcheser. I can't say exactly where it is, that's the nearest I can give. I went up to the counter and ordered a cup of tea and breakfast, and I sat down by the table with my cup of tea waiting for my breakfast to come up, and there was a man sitting by the table opposite me. He asked me if I had a cigarette I could give him. I gave him one and he started talking about married life. He said to me, 'You are looking pretty worried, is there anything on your mind?' Then I told him all about it. So he said, 'Don't let that worry you. I can give you something that can fix it.' So he said, 'Wait there a minute, I'll be back,' and he went outside. When he came back he handed me a little bottle that was wrapped in a brown paper. He said, 'Tell your wife to take it first thing in the morning before she has any tea, then to lay down on the bed for a couple of hours and that should do the job.' He never asked no money for it. I went up to the counter and paid my bill and carried on with my journey.

"After I finished my work I went home, that would be between seven and eight.

When I got in the house I took off my overcoat and hung it on the peg behind the kitchen door. My wife asked me for a cigarette and I told her that there was one in my pocket, then she found this bottle in my pocket, and I told her all about it . . .

"I got up in the morning as usual at six o'clock to go to work. I made myself a cup of tea and made a feed for the baby. I told her then not to take that stuff when I went in and said 'Good morning' to her, and I went to work, that would be about half past six. I finished work and got home about half past six in the evening. I then noticed that there was no lights in the place. I lit the gas and it started to go out, and I went into the bedroom to get a penny and I noticed my baby in the cot. I put the penny in the gas and went back in the bedroom and lit the gas in the bedroom. Then I saw my wife laying in the bed. I spoke to her but she never answered me, so I went over and shook her, then I could see she wasn't breathing. Then I went and made some food for my baby. I fed my baby and I sat up all night.

"Between about one and two in the morning, I got my wife downstairs through the front door. I opened the drain outside my front door, that is No. 10 Rillington Place, and pushed her body head first into the drain. I closed the drain, then I went back in the house. I sat down by the fire smoking a cigarette. I never went to work the following day. I went and got my baby looked after. Then I went and told my governor where I worked that I was leaving. He asked me the reason, and I told him I had a better job elsewhere. I had my cards and money that afternoon, then I went to see a man about selling my furniture. The man came down and had a look at my furniture and he offered me £40 for it. So I accepted the £40. He told me he wouldn't be able to collect the furniture until Monday morning. In the meantime, I went and told my mother that my wife and baby had gone for a holiday. I stopped in the flat till Monday. The van came Monday afternoon and cleared the stuff out. He paid me the money. Then I caught the five to one train from Paddington and I come down to Merthyr Vale and I've been down her ever since. That's the lot.

(Signed) T.J. Evans"

The Merthyr Vale police put in a call to the Notting Hill police, who in turn sent a car over to 10 Rillington Place. Sure enough, there was a manhole in front of Number 10. It took three men to open the lid, but the drain as empty; there was no body. When the Merthyr Vale police told Evans, poor Tim was flabbergasted — the body must be there. Christie said he was going to put it down the drain. Caught in a lie again, he tried to brazen it out. The detectives asked him who helped him lift the manhole cover. Tim said he lifted the lid himself, which was an impossibility. Six hours later he gave another statement. This time he told substantially what he believed to be true, that his wife had died during an illegal operation. The police were again dispatched to 10 Rillington Place to make a thorough search, and this time they found the body of Beryl Evans behind some boards under the sink in the wash-house. Geraldine's body was found behind the door with the necktie still around her neck.

Evans was brought from Wales to London, and told of the gruesome find at 10 Rillington Place. He made a further statement telling how he had killed his wife and daughter. He gave plausible, exact details of how he tied the necktie around Geraldine's neck. He said he was happy to get the guilty knowledge off his chest. He kept up these pronouncements of guilt until he met with his lawyers, at which point he abruptly changed his story to put the blame on the shoulders of Reg Christie. Did the lawyers tell him to cut out his lying and tell the truth, one wonders? Evans' lies were designed to protect his friend Christie and make it appear as if he, Evans, was confessing to clear up a distasteful, unfortunate death that was unavoidable. Evans didn't start out confessing to murder. Read the words carefully. He only wanted to impart the knowledge that his wife's body was down the drain, not that he killed her. It isn't easy not to have murdered your wife and still to have put her down a drain, but poor Evans managed to confess to both without doing either.

On Jan. 11, 1950, Timothy Evans stood trial for the murder of his daughter in London's Old Bailey. Reg Christie, the respected former policeman and neighbor to the accused murderer, was the chief prosecution witness. Evans, begging to be believed, testified that he had found out about his daughter's death only after he had been told by the police. When he was informed of her death he didn't care what happened to him, and confessed, incriminating himself as a double murderer. He started off trying to protect Christie, but now he had to tell the truth to save his own life. He said time and again, "Christie did it," but no one believed him. He further said that the details of the murders had been given to him little by little by the police. They had mentioned that Beryl had been strangled by a rope and Geraldine by a necktie, so that when time came for him to give his statement, he repeated the details. The police denied these accusations.

Evans made a hesitant, unbelievable witness in the dock. Reg Christie's straightforward aloofness was impressive. Wounded serving his country in the First World War, Reg was treated with deference by the presiding judge, even being given a chair to make him more comfortable in the witness box. No one took Evans' irresponsible accusations against him seriously. The jury took only forty minutes to find Evans guilty. All appeals failed, and on March 9, 1950, Timothy Evans was hanged.

And so the Christies returned to 10 Rillington Place. Month after dreary month, Christie complained of minor ailments that necessitated continual visits to Dr. Odess.

Black Jamaicans had rented the flat above him, and this increased his bad disposition. Mrs. Christie, too, couldn't stand the blacks coming and going all day long in her hall.

Reggie worked for two years as a clerk for British Road Services, and being back at work and away from home seems to have relieved his nervousness and minor ailments. Then in the spring of 1952, he became ill with fibrositis and was confined to hospital for three weeks. When his doctors decided his trouble was psychological rather than physical, he was released.

At this time, another real problem came to a head. He had abandoned sexual relations with his wife since Evans' execution. Not only that, but Ethel, nondescript, frigid Ethel, started to get on his nerves about being impotent. Did Reggie again hear those boys from the streets of Halifax shouting "Reggie no dick?" Did he lie beside Ethel night after night with his hands reaching to his ears as the boys' voiced taunted him — "Can't-make-it Reggie?" He left his job, and was thrown together with his wife day and night.

On the morning of Dec. 14, 1952, Reg took a stocking that was lying on a chair near his bed, leaned over and strangled Ethel. Her body was to lie in the bed for two or three days while Reggie decided what to do with it. Then he remembered — of course, the loose floor boards in the front room. He rolled back the linoleum, and under the floor she went. Christie covered the body with earth, put back the linoleum, and it was as if Ethel had gone away to Sheffield for another of her visits. To neighbors and friends who inquired after her, and there were a few, it being Christmas time, Christie explained that she had gone to Sheffield and he was following her there later, as he had accepted a good job opportunity that had suddenly come up. Her friends thought it strange that Ethel didn't say goodbye, but passed it off as a rush trip and let it go at that.

Christmas and New Year's came and passed. Reggie, who by this time was sprinkling deodorant around the front room, made arrangements to sell all his furniture. He received only £12 for the lot. The used furniture buyer wouldn't even take some of the pieces, they were in such bad shape. Reggie stayed on in the flat a little while after the furniture had been removed.

It was now January, and Christie was alone. His wife lay under the floorboards in the front room, Fuerst and Eady were only skeletal remains resting in the garden, the Evanses, mother and child, were gone, and Timothy had met his end at the hangman's noose. Even the furniture was gone. In Reggie's solitude, his mind turned to the necrophiliac thrills that had almost faded from his memory.

On a night in the middle of January, at about eight o'clock, Christie went into the

Westminster Arms, where he met a prostitute, Kathleen Maloney. He had met the twenty-six-year-old Kathleen before, and within a short time the pair was seen leaving the Westminster Arms together. Kathleen was quite drunk, and Reggie was taking her home. She didn't require the finesse of deception; Reggie merely sat her down on his chair, attached the rubber tube to the gas, and placed the exposed end of the tube close to her mouth so she was bound to breathe in some of the fumes. Soon Kathleen became drowsy and Reggie strangled her with his piece of rope. He removed her undergarments and had intercourse with her right in the chair. Then he brewed himself a pot of tea and went to bed. When he got up in the morning Kathleen was still in the chair.

Christie pondered a moment — what to do with this bothersome body? He pulled away a small cupboard, revealing an alcove he knew was off the kitchen. He bundled the body in a blanket, pulled a pillowslip over the head, then hauled the corpse into the alcove, where he arranged it with the legs in the air against the wall. He then covered it with some ashes and earth, and put the cupboard back in place.

The peverse thrill of long ago was now fresh in Reggie's mind, and he wanted more. A few days later he picked up an Irish girl named Rita Nelson, a twenty-five-year-old prostitute who had convictions for soliciting and drunkenness in Ireland. She ended up in Reggie's death chair inhaling gas, and she, too, was ravished after death and her body placed with Kathleen's in the alcove, resting on its neck and head, with the legs extended in the air, propped up against the wall.

About a month went by. Then, quite by chance, Christie met Hectorina Maclennan and her boy friend, a truck driver named Baker, in a cafe. When Christie found out they were looking for a flat he offered to show them his, which he told them he was about to vacate. It was sheer aggravation for Christie when Hectorina brought Baker with her to inspect the flat. Since they had nowhere else to stay, Christie gave them sleeping privileges and they stayed for three days and nights. On the fourth day Christie had had enough of Baker, and asked the couple to leave. Later the same day Reggie sought out the couple and invited Hectorina to visit him alone. He said he had something to tell her. Hectorina showed up at 10 Rillington Place, and Reggie poured her a drink. In a terrible state of nervousness he was fumbling with his rubber tube, connecting it to the gas, when she became suspicious and got up to leave. Christie caught up with her and strangled her in the hall. He lugged her back to the kitchen, and thinking she was still alive, gave her an application of his infernal inhaling mechanism. He then had intercourse with her and put her body with the other two in the alcove.

Baker grew uneasy when Hectorina had still not returned from 10 Rillington Place at

5:30, and he dropped over to inquire. Christie said that he hadn't seen her, and offered a social cup of tea. Later that evening, when Baker went looking for his girlfriend, Christie accompanied him.

Reggie papered over the entrance to the alcove, and set about subletting his empty flat. On the premises, but not included in the inventory, were the two skeletons still resting peacefully in the garden, Mrs. Christie under the floorboards in the front room, and the three bodies upside down in the alcove. Not on the premises, but certainly the responsibility of Mr. Christie, was the entire Evans family. Nine bodies in all.

While sauntering down Ladbroke Grove on March 13, Christie met a Mrs. Reilly who was looking at advertisements showing flats for rent. Christie, who never had any difficulty striking up a conversation, told Mrs. Reilly that he had a vacant flat. She was delighted, and with her husband went to inspect the flat. On March 16, her husband gave Christie £7.13s for three months' rent in advance. Four days later the Reillys moved in, and after borrowing a suitcase from Mr. Reilly, Christie left 10 Rillington Place forever. That very evening the landlord showed up, and was amazed to find the Reillys living there. He informed them that Christie was several months behind with his rent, and that while they could stay the night, they would have to leave in the morning. The Reillys left the next day, unaware that they had spent the night at close quarters with six assorted corpses.

The landlord gave permission to use the vacant Christie kitchen to Beresford Brown, who was occupying one of the Evans' rooms upstairs. He used the kitchen for the next few days and started to tidy up the place. On March 24, he decided to put up a shelf to hold a radio. He was tapping to find a solid wall, but he kept getting a hollow sound from the alcove that Christie had thoughtfully wallpapered over. He tore off a piece of paper, pointed his flashlight into the alcove, and found himself a place in every book ever written about infamous murders. There, in the alcove, with their legs in the air, were the bodies of Kathleen Maloney, Rita Nelson and Hectorina Maclennan.

Scotland Yard descended on 10 Rillington Place, and the three bodies were meticulously removed from the alcove, being photographed at every stage of their removal. Someone noticed that the boards in the front room were very loose, and in due course a fourth body was removed from under the floor.

Old London Town has provided us with some weird murders, and the men who investigate them tend to become blase with the passage of time. But even for them, four bodies in one house on one night was not a routine evening. The word went out; the police would like to question John Reginald Halliday Christie. The days passed and Christie's description was everywhere. The news reached new heights of sensationalism when Fuerst's and Eady's skeletons were discovered in the garden. Where was the elusive Christie? Not really elusive at all — he was wandering the streets of London. On March 31, Police Constable Thomas Ledger saw a man near Putney Bridge. Constable Ledger asked him a few questions and ascertained that the man was Christie. Reggie was taken into custody.

From the beginning, Reggie confessed to all the murders, except that of little Geraldine Evans. He lied about the details to make himself look better, but he didn't deny killing the women.

Christie was charged with murdering his wife, and appeared, ironically enough, in Number One Court of the Old Bailey, the very court where he had been the chief prosecution witness against Evans nearly four years earlier. Christie's lawyers never for a moment denied his guilt; they pleaded that he was quite mad.

On July 15, 1953, Christie was hanged for his crimes. In January, 1966, Timothy Evans was granted a posthumous free pardon by the Queen of England.

PRINTED IN CANADA